TOWARD THE FUTURE
of
REFORMED THEOLOGY

TOWARD THE FUTURE

of

REFORMED THEOLOGY

Tasks, Topics, Traditions

Edited by

David Willis and Michael Welker

With the Special Collaboration of

Matthias Gockel

WILLIAM B. EERDMANS PUBLISHING COMPANY

GRAND RAPIDS, MICHIGAN / CAMBRIDGE, U.K.

© 1999 Wm. B. Eerdmans Publishing Co.

255 Jefferson Ave. S.E., Grand Rapids, Michigan 49503 /

P.O. Box 163, Cambridge CB3 9PU U.K.

Printed in the United States of America

05 04 03 02 01 00 99   7 6 5 4 3 2 1

Library of Congress Cataloging-in-Publication Data

Toward the future of reformed theology: tasks, topics, traditions /
edited by David Willis and Michael Welker;
with the special collaboration of Matthias Gockel.
p.   cm.
Includes bibliographical references.
ISBN 0-8028-4467-7 (pbk.: alk. paper)
1. Reformed Church — Doctrines. 2. Theology, Doctrinal.
I. Willis-Watkins, David.   II. Welker, Michael.   III. Gockel, Matthias.
BX9422.5.T68   1999
230′.42 — dc21   98-42994
CIP

Contents

PART 2
TOPICS AND TRANSFORMATIONS

Contents

INTRODUCTION

Toward the Future of Reformed Theology

David Willis and Michael Welker

Originally this volume was supposed to bear the title *The Future of Reformed Theology*. It was supposed to contain articles by Reformed theologians from throughout the world. There was no problem getting theologians from the United States and Germany to agree to contribute an article. But in other regions of the world our repeated requests for a text on traditions, topics, or tasks of Reformed theology were often in vain. Finally it became clear that this volume could not represent the entire spectrum of contemporary Reformed theology; it reflects, more strongly than we wish, the predominance of the academic theology of the German- and English-speaking countries in Europe and North America. It is also limited in its conception on systematic-theological and ethical contributions. Thus we ended up with the title *Toward the Future of Reformed Theology*.

The title is meant to express the fact that this volume seeks to document a development that has already begun and to which this volume would like to contribute. This volume seeks to promote, within an ecumenical framework, the development of a Reformed theology to which men and women creatively contribute out of the most diverse cultural, historical, and social contexts. Despite the difficulties in procuring texts from a number of countries, this volume shows that it is already possible for Reformed theology to have an ecumenically responsible community of inquiry, research, exchange, and understanding in which women and men, younger and older theologians from many nations of this earth, take part. To this extent the book is a major step toward this emerging reality. About one-third of the articles contradict, simply by virtue of their authors, the still-common prejudice that Reformed theology is essentially a theology by and for white European and North American men. Above all, though, the themes, the contents, the styles of thought, and the prophetic perspectives gathered here contradict numerous prejudices frequently directed toward Reformed theology. We were astonished and delighted to see that contemporary Reformed theology presents itself with a scope, a richness of theological orientations and styles of thought, and an ecumenical openness that can serve as models for all the churches of this earth. *At the same time, by no means are the distinctive contours and coherence of Reformed theology lost in this scope, in this richness, and in the corresponding differentiation and complexity.* The following introductory reflections seek to draw attention to these distinctive contours and to the coherence of contemporary Reformed theology.

The Theology of the Church Reformed according to God's Word

1. The Illuminating and Liberating Power of God's Word: Against Emptying It of Its Content and Domesticating Its Structure

The contributions to this volume are in agreement that the truly reforming activity in the life of the church cannot simply be the enterprise of a particular generation of theologians and of their theology or theologies. Reformed theology is characterized by the fundamental recognition *that the reforming activity in the church and in its surroundings proceeds from God's word.*

Today it is difficult to articulate and communicate this fundamental recognition without reserve. In many cases "the word of God" is regarded as merely either a vague cliché or a cipher that masks all sorts of claims to control and domination. Theology can work against this view only by resisting the temptation to empty God's word of its content, and by reawakening a delight in the content, fullness, clarity, and specific rationality of God's word. It becomes possible to know the clarity, fullness, and content of God's word, its revelatory and liberating power, only when it is not reduced to a mere principle or displaced to a transcendent "beyond." The ecumenical contribution of Reformed theology lies in its calmly, persistently, critically, and constructively resisting the many attempts to empty God's word of its content and to bring it under the dominion of metaphysics, morality, mysticism, or the dictatorship of a "spirit of the age."

The contributions to this volume document this Reformed theological "service to God's word" in the midst of the contemporary crisis of trust in this word, and in the midst of the various forces interested in domesticating it and emptying it of its content. Several articles demonstrate programmatically that it is a task of Reformed theology to make the trusting, critical, and constructive service to God's word a "theological posture," and to mediate this "theological posture." (In an exemplary way, see Brian Gerrish, "Tradition in the Modern World: The Reformed Habit of Mind.") Other articles spell out in concrete detail that Reformed theology must verify this "theological posture" by relating self-critically and innovatively to its own forms, traditions, and "classic" works. (For an exemplary case, see Daniel Migliore, "Reforming the Theology and Practice of Baptism: The Challenge of Karl Barth.")

2. The Theological Art of Discernment in Biblical and Eschatological Concentration

The articles gathered in this volume do not dissipate themselves in laments and speculations on why many cultures in our day no longer trust that God's word holds any power of revelation and renewal. They work against the widespread confusion between "critique" and discouraging "lament over the state of the world." They attempt to restore theological critique to a place of honor as an "oriented art of discernment." Several of the articles show that today a biblical and an eschatological concentration are again necessary in order to unleash the illuminating and creative reforming power of God's word (Jürgen Moltmann, "*Theologia Reformata et Semper Reformanda*").

Today we need a new biblical-theological orientation in order to recognize interconnections of both contents and forms that make it possible to distinguish clearly the word of God from a mere principle controlling everything or from a numinous entity. After the theologies that directed attention to the "wholly other" word of God that comes to us "straight down from above" or that "always precedes us and always comes to us," we need to be instructed in the biblical-theological recognition that God's word has something clear and definite to say in the realm of our experience of self and world. *We need to recognize that God's word — in the midst of complicated, often even desperate states of the world and of life — possesses power that is really illuminating, liberating, uplifting, and creative.* God's word edifies, comforts, lifts up, enlivens, delights, strengthens, and liberates human beings. God's word mediates orientation, certainty, and new hope to human beings. And for millennia, this word in its revelatory power has over and over become fundamentally and concretely knowable (see Willem Balke, "Revelation and Experience in Calvin's Theology"). Several of the contributions to this volume make clear the way in which Reformed theology justifies and verifies its basic trust in the midst of the contemporary situation. The revelatory power of God's word is brought to light with respect to the biblical traditions in such a way that the christological and pneumatological determinacy of God's word, and its dual form as "law and gospel," becomes clear (Michael Welker,

"Travail and Mission: Theology Reformed according to God's Word at the Beginning of the Third Millennium").

While some contributions to this volume attempt to construct and expand bridges between systematic and exegetical theology, others elaborate more strongly the link between systematic and socio-ethical work. In the knowledge that now, as long ago, God's word announces the coming of God's reign, they take seriously the power of this word for ecclesiastical practice, for ethical orientation, and for real liberation. They show that this efficacy of God's word can be brought to expression theologically in the most diverse realms of life (John de Gruchy, "Toward a Reformed Theology of Liberation: A Retrieval of Reformed Symbols in the Struggle for Justice"; Nancy Duff, "Reformed Theology and Medical Ethics: Death, Vocation, and the Suspension of Life Support").

3. Ecumenically Verified Truth, Biblical Orientation, and Contextuality

Reformed theology and the church it serves give ecumenically responsible testimony in all the processes of their life — from doxology in worship to concrete ethical practice — to the revelatory power and the creative activity of God's word. Both the testimony and the ecumenical responsibility can and must acquire greater clarity (Janos Pasztor, "The Catholicity of Reformed Theology"). This ecumenical responsibility is not exhausted by a contemporary and global-political orientation. Instead it takes up *the question of truth and the readiness to warrant truth-claims in the sphere of the churches of every time and every region of the world* (David Willis, "The Ecumenical Future of Reformed Theology"; Thomas Torrance, "The Substance of Faith").

At the same time, Reformed theology verifies its ecumenical responsibility by orienting itself biblically and eschatologically so as to gain a hearing for the creative and re-creative power of God's word and for its call to continual repentance and reformation (Beatriz Melano, "Potential Contributions of Reformed Theology to Ecumenical Discussion and Praxis").

By exposing itself to the renewing power of this word, and by testifying to that power, the service to God's word in ecumenical responsibility will find its ecumenical breadth expressed in the biblical textuality of this word and in the contextuality of this word's activity. Many of the contributions to this volume demonstrate that this tension, which in the past has certainly generated numerous conflicts — including within Reformed theology — can be constructively sustained (Choan-Seng Song, "Christian Theology: Toward an Asian Reconstruction"; Nobuo Watanabe, "Reformed Theology in East and West"; Wafiq Wahba, "The Ecumenical Responsibility of Reformed Theology:

The Case of Egypt"; Lukas Vischer, "The Church — Mother of the Believers"; Eberhard Busch, "The Closeness of the Distant: Reformed Confessions after 1945").

The relation between the church and Israel remains paradigmatic for the fact that difference in contexts and in those contexts' approach to the biblical tradition is fruitful. This relation remains paradigmatic for differentiated complementarity, and must be continually renewed in its paradigmatic function. On the basis of its pneumatological orientation and its orientation to the whole of the Bible, Reformed theology has been able to address repeatedly and constructively the community of the church and Israel in eschatological hope. Today as well, Reformed theology can draw from the biblical traditions and from shared eschatological orientation to contribute to the renewal and revitalization of that community (Hans-Joachim Kraus, "The Contemporary Relevance of Calvin's Theology").

4. Creative Pluralism instead of Relativism; Discerning the Spirits; Culture of the Offices of Ministry

If God's word is not conceived as a mere principle or *numinosum,* if its rich biblical constitution and its vital christological specificity are taken seriously, if the fact is taken seriously that the word is mediated by the outpoured Spirit and by the gifts of testimony in the many-membered body of Christ, then the "pluriformity" of Reformed theology and of the Reformed church can be newly valued, treasured, and correspondingly shaped (Edmund Za Bik, "The Challenge to Reformed Theology: A Perspective from Myanmar"). We can also come today to a new recognition that, or to what extent, Reformed theology and the Reformed church in their differentiation and multiformity are defined not simply by this or that development of the world, but by God's word and its activity (Amy Plantinga Pauw, "The Future of Reformed Theology: Some Lessons from Jonathan Edwards").

Reformed theology cannot add its voice either to the widespread, clumsy, and powerless polemic against "pluralism," or to a vague enthusiasm for postmodern "diversity." Instead it must contribute to clear distinctions between the creative "pluralism of the Spirit" and a disintegrative relativism. It must contribute to clear distinctions between the creative differentiation of the body of Christ and vague notions of "multiformity." Here the way is indicated by reflections on a new culture of "the offices of ministry" in the church and by efforts to develop a clear and more profound understanding of "the covenant" (Christian Link, "The *Notae Ecclesiae:* A Reformed Perspective"; Walter Herrenbrück, "Presbytery and Leadership in the Church").

5. Reformed Theology as a Power Shaping Modern Societies: The Necessity of Self-Criticism and of Creative Renewal in the Crisis of Abstract Bourgeois Theism

For centuries Reformed theology has over and over again looked back with justifiable pride at its own tradition,[1] which more than any other theological tradition must be counted among the major formative powers of modern democratic societies (Hans-Helmut Esser, "The Contemporary Relevance of Calvin's Social Ethics"; Jan Milič Lochman, "Radical and Reformed: The Ecumenical Contribution of the Czech Reformation"; John Hesselink, "Some Distinctive Contributions of the Dutch-American Reformed Tradition").

Today this pride has to a large extent given way to an often diffuse consciousness of necessary self-criticism and of the longing for renewal. It is only in a new focus on God's word that this nebulous consciousness can attain clarity and lead to the renewal of religious practice. The knowledge of God's living word and of its reforming power has great consequences not only with regard to the constitution and expressions of Christ's church in the ecumenical sphere and in global society. The knowledge of God's word also necessitates exemplary theological self-criticism with regard to God. From K. Barth and E. Brunner to J. Moltmann, B. Melano, and J. de Gruchy, Reformed theologians of this century have called into question the unholy alliance between the classical church bodies and abstract bourgeois theism. Reformed theology must continue to render problematic the religious tendency — including its own! — to seek the help of a dualistic metaphysics in bringing to expression the sovereignty and glory of God, rather than honoring them in concentration on God's word and its revelatory power. Reformed theology must grow more emphatic in rendering this religious tendency problematic, and it must do so in Christology, pneumatology, theology of creation, and biblical theology (William Placher, "The Vulnerability of God"; Sang Hyun Lee, "Jonathan Edwards's Dispositional Conception of the Trinity: A Resource for Contemporary Reformed Theology"; Alexander McKelway, "The Logic of Faith").

One of the ways Reformed theology has taken up this challenge is by taking part in the theological reevaluation of Anselm's theology of satisfaction. With the help of recent exegesis, Reformed theology has called Anselm's doctrine into question. Reformed thought has begun to investigate the biblical

---

1. See also the *Reformed Reader: A Sourcebook in Christian Theology*, vol. 1, *Classical Beginnings, 1519-1799*, ed. William Stacy Johnson and John H. Leith; vol. 2, *Contemporary Trajectories, 1799 to the Present*, ed. George W. Stroup (Louisville: Westminster/John Knox, 1993); Donald K. McKim, ed., *Encyclopedia of the Reformed Faith* (Louisville: Westminster/John Knox, 1992).

foundations of this theology of atonement, which has left a profound but highly problematic "normative trace" in Reformed theology, from Calvin's *Institutes* to the Heidelberg Catechism. Reformed thought has begun to correct this theology, even when this leads to calling familiar "dogmatic resources" deeply into question (Leanne Van Dyk, "Toward a New Typology of Reformed Doctrines of Atonement").

While the critique of abstract bourgeois theism and of the classical doctrine of satisfaction is still an unsettling factor in theology and the church, as a rule the attendant effects on Christology are experienced as liberating. Why? Several contributions to this volume show that in the realm of Reformed theology, Christology — which is well developed relative to the theologies of the first and third articles of the creed — makes possible a fruitful mediation between positions that are initially very different or even in conflict. It is obvious that where a certain degree of theological clarity (not reductionistic clarity, but a realistic clarity that exposes itself to the vitality of God's word and corresponds to the complexity of the object of faith!) has been attained, it is also possible both to understand and to interact calmly with heterogeneous theological traditions and positions (Dawn DeVries, "The Incarnation and the Sacramental Word: Calvin's and Schleiermacher's Sermons on Luke 2"; Bruce McCormack, "The Sum of the Gospel: The Doctrine of Election in the Theologies of Alexander Schweizer and Karl Barth").

All this supports the argument that it pays great dividends in theological content when theology engages God's word in all its richness and vitality. We are led "from clarity to clarity," not by our reductions, abstractions, and constructions — even though they might receive the applause of common sense or of a culture's currently predominant philosophy or "general theory" — but by the inner coherence and illuminating power of God's word. We need to gain access to its often foreign rationalities. If theology and the church expose themselves to the foreignness and intrinsic clarity of God's word, they acquire the capacity for an "eschatological realism" that does not need to shy away from critical engagement with all sorts of distorting, obscuring, self-important, and short-lived rationalities and plausibilities of the "wisdom of this world" (John Leith, "Calvin's Theological Realism and the Lasting Influence of His Theology").

What is to be gained by engaging in this service to God's word? A theological realism that is challenged by its context and instructed by the Bible, a theological realism that is in for the long haul and that adopts a truly ecumenical long-range perspective and tolerance. The vitality and multiformity of Reformed theology is sometimes confusing, and the decidedly ecumenical fundamental orientation of Reformed theology appears risky to some. But where Reformed theology entrusts itself to that theological realism, it can affirm and verify its vitality and multiformity, as well as its ecumenical orientation. Where Reformed theology wishes to be and to remain a theology of God's word, it grows into this eschatological realism.

The printing of this volume, both in the United States and in Germany, would not have been possible without the manifold support and fine collaboration both of many theologians and of theologically aware specialists in the English and German languages. Nor would it have been possible without the financial contributions of churches, ecclesiastical alliances, and academic institutions. We extend our thanks on this side of the Atlantic particularly to Matthias Gockel, Gregory Faulkner, Gregor Etzelmüller, the Reverend Lisa Dahill, the Reverend Ronald de Groot, the Reverend Dr. John Hoffmeyer, Marietjie Odendaal, and Johanna Froehlich-Swartzentrueber for their work on translations, drafts, and coordinations that often were quite complicated. We express our gratitude to the Faculty Research Committee at Princeton Theological Seminary and to President Thomas Gillespie. We are indebted to the Center of Theological Inquiry, Princeton, and to William Eerdmans and the Wm. B. Eerdmans Publishing Company for fine collaboration and patience.

Princeton and Heidelberg, Fall 1998   D. W. and M. W.

PART 1

TASKS AND CONTEXTS

CHAPTER 1

Tradition in the Modern World: The Reformed Habit of Mind

Brian Gerrish

The aim of education should be the same for all . . . (i.e. everywhere and always, in every mode of society, every condition of life, etc.). . . . Education should aim at the formation of good habits.

MORTIMER J. ADLER

The theme of this conference requires me to change hats. I am more often asked these days, not: What can Reformed theology do for the seminaries? but: Does any theology, Reformed or not, belong in a university? Though I did teach for seven years in one of our Presbyterian seminaries, for the last quarter of a century I have worked in a secular, pluralistic, research-oriented university. Perhaps it hasn't made much difference to what I do, but it has made a difference to the way I am expected to justify what I do. The university and the seminary both tend to operate out of values and expectations that are seldom submitted to questioning, and they are not the same values and expectations in each institution. No doubt, it is risky to generalize; seminaries and universities come in several varieties. But my impression, at least, is that the two types of educational institutions have drifted further apart in recent years, and there is a double stereotype at work.

On the one side, the seminaries are suspicious of what they call the "academic theology" of the university. They perceive it as addressed to the wrong

3

audience and the wrong situation; namely, to supposedly enlightened colleagues in other departments of the university for whom theology has become
a quaint anachronism. A vital theology will not trouble itself with apologetics
for the cultured despisers but will rather address the oppression, injustice, racism, discrimination, and exploitation that threaten to tear the human community apart and make our planet uninhabitable. A university theology, by contrast, is remote, philosophical, scholastic, inaccessible, and — from the
church's viewpoint — insular, irrelevant, and uninteresting. It is a theology
that has lost touch with the things that really matter.

On the other side, the universities, when they notice theology at all,
gladly turn it over to the seminaries because it is not a serious intellectual discipline: it lacks rigorous norms of argument and inquiry, is helplessly captive
to passing fads and fashions, and trades critical reflection for mere ideology —
to underwrite whatever cause is currently or locally in vogue. To address the
latest burning issue becomes the whole theological task and the only reason for
the seminary's existence, until the next crisis takes over.

Divinity school theologians, like myself, are caught uncomfortably in the
middle: under fire from either side, depending on which of their friends they
are eating their lunch with. For, while their seminary colleagues chide them for
doing academic theology, their colleagues from other parts of the university
seldom differentiate between academic and church theology. Van Harvey, of
Stanford University, for example, is writing simply about *Protestant* theology
when he says: "It could be argued that, particularly in the past two decades,
Protestant theology has been characterized by narcissism and faddism that
have virtually destroyed it as a serious intellectual discipline and deprived it of
any respect it might thus claim."[1] He goes on to quote the verdict of Gordon
Kaufman, of Harvard Divinity School, on the recent theological scene: "Theology apparently had no integrity of standards or demands of its own; its symbols could be used as a kind of decoration for and legitimation of almost any
partisan position found in the culture."[2] For Van Harvey, this means that theology, even if physically located on a university campus, is "marginalized."

By now, I have probably given offense to just about everyone who has an
interest in theology, whether in the seminary or in the university. I do not
doubt that the opposition between academic and ecclesiastical theology,
though the current stereotype overdoes it, will be one of the issues we have to
face in the twenty-first century, along with the marginalization of theology in

---

1. Van A. Harvey, "On the Intellectual Marginality of American Theology," in *Religion
and Twentieth-Century American Life*, ed. Michael J. Lacey, Woodrow Wilson Center Series
(Cambridge: Cambridge University Press, 1989), pp. 172-92, quotation on p. 173.

2. Harvey, p. 174, quoted from *Christianity and Crisis* 35 (1975): 111.

American intellectual life. But it is not my intention to explore the ramifications of these issues here, although I shall touch on them briefly later on. I want to begin, rather, from the interesting fact that, for all their undoubted differences, the university and the seminary suffer from a common educational malaise. Perhaps they can have recourse to a common, if only partial, remedy. The malaise is disintegration: the loss of a sense of being engaged in a single, coherent enterprise. The remedy is education viewed as imparting not information or skills, but good habits. From this beginning in the first part of my presentation I shall go on, in the second, to ask: What good habits ought theological education in the Reformed tradition to impart? For, as Thomas Aquinas says, a good habit is "one which disposes to an act suitable to the agent's nature."[3] We want to arrive eventually, then, at the habit or habits that will dispose to acts suitable to the nature of a Reformed theologian, whether he or she is a university professor, a seminary professor, a pastor, or a layperson.

I. Good Habits and the Goal of Education

Permit me to return briefly, first of all, to ancient Greece. The notion that education is about good habits has its roots in Aristotle's *Ethics*. Moral virtue or goodness of character, he believed, resembles the health and fitness of the body; it is a condition built up by rigorous training. Those who care for the well-being of the young, like the coach and the team doctor, know what regimen of exercises to prescribe. To begin with, the pupils are directed by the wisdom of their mentor, until they grow up to recognize (ideally) that all the discipline they endured rested on a sound moral principle. So, for instance, generosity is demanded of them, and by repeated acts of compulsory generosity they acquire a disposition to be generous and an ability to see for themselves that generosity is right. They actually come to take pleasure in being generous instead of being either stingy or extravagant (the opposite vices between which generosity is the mean). Generosity has become their second nature; they have been made virtuous by growing accustomed to performing right acts. A moral virtue, in short, is a habit: a disposition, induced by custom, to act in a certain way, much as the hands of a budding musician are conditioned by constant exercises to play the piano.[4]

Now, along with the moral virtues Aristotle recognized certain intellectual virtues.[5] He was pessimistic about the likelihood of communicating them

---

3. Thomas Aquinas, *Summa theologiae* I-II, Q. 54, art. 3, hereafter cited as *ST.*
4. Aristotle, *Nicomachean Ethics* 1103a-1103b, 1119b-1120, hereafter cited as *NE.*
5. Aristotle, *NE* 1138b-1145a.

to very many people. He didn't think that men and women, by and large, are governed by their own reason. But *some* people must have intellectual virtues, otherwise there would be no way of knowing what is in fact the right moral discipline to impose on everyone else, who can only be moral by proxy. And Aristotle suggests that for the most part the intellectual virtues are acquired not by custom but by instruction.[6] He must mean, I take it, that the mind cannot be programmed to intellectual virtue in quite the way the desires can be programmed to moral virtue. The goodness of the mind is always inner-directed: it has to come from within, or it isn't really goodness. And yet Aristotle does call it, too, by the same word (in Greek) that the Romans translated as *habitus* (habit). So virtues in general are habits, dispositions to act in one way rather than another, well rather than badly, since, as Thomas Aquinas says, they are "productive of good works";[7] and *intellectual* virtues are good habits of the *mind,* productive of sound *thoughts,* which are the good works of the mind.

Leaving aside the details of this famous theory, let's borrow from Aristotle just the basic notion that what education imparts are good habits of mind: good ways of thinking that have become second nature to us, not unlike the virtues of decency and honesty drummed into our souls since childhood or the facility with which the pianist's trained fingers run across the keys of the piano. I am not concerned, for now, with Aristotle's own list of intellectual virtues, which would raise more questions than we could hope to answer.[8] Let's just pursue a little further the tradition of educational theory he inspired, and then ask whether it has a place in theological education.

The view that education's goal is to turn out a certain kind of mind, or character, or person, has cropped up again and again in Western thought. But

---

6. Aristotle, *NE* 1103a. Thomas held that habits may be natural, acquired, or infused (*ST* I-II, Q. 51), but I am not concerned with this distinction here. The dependence of moral virtue on intellectual virtue in the Aristotelian scheme arises from the fact that the right reason, or right rule, that determines moral goodness is itself determined and applied by the wise man (*ho phronomos: NE* 1106b-1107a), which means, in effect, by the practical wisdom (*phronesis*) of the lawgiver for whom the study of ethics is chiefly of use. As Burnet puts it, "the lawgiver has in his soul the formula or *logos* of goodness, and it is the efficient cause of goodness in others" (John Burnet, ed., *The Ethics of Aristotle* [London: Methuen, 1900], p. 72; cf. pp. 247-48). Practical wisdom or "prudence" depends in turn on knowledge of the highest human end and is therefore, as Burnet says, "the handmaid of Theoretical Wisdom" (p. 249). See n. 8 below.

7. Aquinas, *ST* I-II, Q. 55, arts. 2-3.

8. Aristotle distinguishes five states of mind by which we attain truth: *reason* and *science* are the theoretical virtues which, when directed to the highest objects, constitute *wisdom,* while *prudence* is the virtue of practical wisdom and is distinguished from *art* in that it is directed to conduct rather than production.

let's jump straight to a fairly recent author, John Henry Newman. In his classic study *The Idea of a University* (1852), he argues that the university must provide a home for every field of human knowledge. But the result cannot be a mere pile of information; there must be organization of what is learned, an ordering of it that assigns things their proper value in relation to one another. Hence the communication of knowledge becomes a matter of the formation of the person: it imparts a virtue, a habit of mind, to be esteemed for its own sake and not as an instrument for getting or doing something else.[9]

It was Cardinal Newman, along with Aristotle and Thomas, who inspired the educational program of Robert Maynard Hutchins and his associates at the University of Chicago. Hutchins's provocative book *The Higher Learning in America* (1936) is particularly important for the way in which he sets the habit view of education against what he takes to be the two destructive alternatives. If the sense of the university as one single community of learning has vanished, the chief culprits are empiricism and vocationalism. By "empiricism" Hutchins means the mere piling up of information; and by "vocationalism" he means the functional subordination of learning to practical and professional goals. Where these two hindrances to education dominate, the university disintegrates into independent centers of research and training. And that is what has happened in the American universities. The burden of remedying the situation, in this view, falls initially on the "general education" offered in high school and the first two years of college. But the ideal of a general education must carry over into the academy as a whole:

> Please do not tell me [Hutchins writes] that the general education I propose should not be adopted because the great majority of those who pass through it will not go on to the university. The scheme that I advance is based on the notion that general education is education for everybody, whether he goes on to the university or not. It will be useful to him in the university; it will be equally useful if he never goes there. I admit that it will not be useful to him outside the university in the popular sense of utility. It may not assist him to make money or to get ahead. It may not in any

9. John Henry Newman, *The Idea of a University Defined and Illustrated . . .* , new impression (Westminster, Md.: Christian Classics, 1973). This edition follows the second main revision (1873). For specific page references, see my essay, "*Ubi Theologia, Ibi Ecclesia?* Schleiermacher, Troeltsch, and the Prospect for an Academic Theology," in *Religious Studies, Theological Studies, and the University Divinity School,* ed. J. M. Kitagawa (Atlanta: Scholars Press, 1992), pp. 69-94. Both the Greek *paideia* and the German *Bildung* often implied that education has to do with the formation of the *person*. My epigraph at the head of this essay is taken from Mortimer J. Adler, "In Defense of the Philosophy of Education," *Forty-First Yearbook of the National Society for the Study of Education,* pt. 1, *Philosophies of Education,* ed. Nelson B. Henry (Chicago: University Press, 1942), pp. 238-39.

obvious fashion adjust him to his environment or fit him for the contemporary scene. It will, however, have a deeper, wider utility: it will cultivate the intellectual virtues. . . . The intellectual virtues are habits resulting from the training of the intellectual powers.[10]

Naturally, I do not pretend that this view of education is self-evidently true or beyond debate. But its applicability to theological education is worth considering. My own first exposure to theological education was as a student at Cambridge, England. "Training for the ministry," as we called it, was divided into four fields: Old Testament, New Testament, church history, and systematic theology. Despite a very interesting introduction to theology, of which I still have very happy memories, I don't believe any of us really began to grasp the unity of the enterprise we were engaged in: there were simply four more or less independent bodies of information to be learned (and corresponding exams to be passed). Even the functional unity of preparation for ministry was largely ignored. There was no "practical field," as Americans call it. And when we protested, the best the faculty could think to do was to invite the local Presbyterian minister once a week to chat with us about the ministry. Perhaps I am being too hard, and perhaps I shouldn't let on that when I was a student I, too, grumbled at the education I was getting, as students always do. But was it perhaps a firsthand experience of "empiricism," as Hutchins understood the word?

When I was invited to join the faculty of an American seminary six years after leaving theological college in Cambridge, I looked — fascinated — through the catalogue that was sent to me (we didn't have such things in Britain). I noted that again there were four fields. This time Old and New Testaments were combined; but something called "the practical field" was added, and I was amazed to see that its course offerings ran to about three times the length of any of the others. And how, exactly, the four fields were related to one another remained even more mysterious than the interrelations of the four Cambridge fields. Just about the best theological curriculum I have ever seen was designed and proposed while I was on the faculty of the seminary (not by me, I hasten to add). As every creative curriculum must, it transcended the barriers between the three so-called academic fields, and at each step it maintained a continual interchange between reflection and practice. But the proposal did not win the support of the faculty; it was emended beyond recognition. Reflection and practice tended to separate, and there simply wasn't much interest in conversation between the fields except when we were off duty. Empiricism won again, only this time side by side with vocationalism. The junior

10. Robert Maynard Hutchins, *The Higher Learning in America*, Storrs Lectures (New Haven: Yale University Press, 1936), pp. 62-63; cf. pp. 118-19.

faculty formed their own discussion group and proved that young professors can be just as rebellious as students.

Hutchins proposed to deal with the evils of empiricism and vocationalism by promoting the establishment of research and technical institutes outside the university; they would be "so planned as to draw off the empiricism and vocationalism that have been strangling the universities and to leave them free to do their intellectual job."[11] But it would be a disaster for theological education, I think, if this counsel of despair were followed. What we should rather learn from the educational theory he so energetically advocated is that there is more to being educated than assimilating information and acquiring skills: we have to set our minds on good habits that don't belong to any one field but rather to them all. We must learn to think more about the person who *has* the information and the skills, more about what it is that integrates the fields of study.

Some good habits of mind are, of course, generic: they cut across disciplines, not just across the field within a discipline. If, as Thomas Aquinas says, the good of the intellect is truth, then only those habits are intellectual virtues by which we tell the truth and never tell a falsehood.[12] Absolute *truthfulness*, however inconvenient, would be my candidate for the first generic virtue of the mind. *Diligence*, perhaps, should be the second. As Lessing wrote: "A man's worth consists not in the truth he possesses, or thinks he possesses, but in the honest trouble he has taken to pursue the truth. His powers are extended by the search for truth, not by the possession of it."[13]

A third generic truth of the mind is *independence*, thinking for yourself; that, according to Kant, is what it means to come of age.[14] And so we might go on, filling out the picture by identifying the opposite intellectual vices: dishonesty, laziness, plagiarism, etc. But my question now, to which I want to move, is whether there are any specific good habits, or intellectual virtues, that a theological education in the Reformed tradition should seek to nurture, coordinating the practical skills and the knowledge of Bible, church history, and systematic theology.

I should perhaps mention in passing, before I turn to part II, that I have

---

11. Hutchins, p. 118.

12. Aquinas, *ST* I-II, Q. 57, art. 2, ad 3.

13. Gotthold Ephraim Lessing, *Eine Duplik* (1778), in *Gotthold Ephraim Lessings sämtliche Schriften*, ed. Karl Lachmann, 3rd ed. by Franz Muncker, 23 vols. (Stuttgart: G. J. Göschen [vols. 12-21 were published by Göschen at Leipzig, vol. 22 at Berlin, and vol. 23 was published by W. de Gruyter], 1886-1924), 13:23-24, translation mine.

14. Immanuel Kant, *What Is Enlightenment?* (1784), trans. in Immanuel Kant, *On History*, ed. Lewis White Beck, Library of Liberal Arts (Indianapolis: Bobbs-Merrill Educational Publishing, 1978), pp. 3-4.

found a great deal to agree with in Edward Farley's influential book, *Theologia: The Fragmentation and Unity of Theological Education* (1983), although my actual debts are to other, older writers. Farley reminds us that the word *theologia* was itself once used to denote a habit, and he advocates a recovery of theology as understanding: "the personal, sapiential knowledge . . . which can occur when faith opens itself to reflection and inquiry." Only theology in this sense, he believes, can remedy the fragmentation of the seminary curriculum, which is presently held together merely by the ends of equipping clergy for clerical jobs. "In the clerical paradigm [as he calls it], 'theology' is not something attendant on Christian existence but something clergy need in order to function as leaders of the church community."[15] I am wholeheartedly in sympathy with the main lines of Farley's argument, and I commend his book to you, but it will become evident that in part II of my presentation I am trying to make a more specific application of the Aristotelian term "habit." I invoke it in order to address the question of theological education in our Reformed tradition.

II. Theological Education and the Reformed Tradition

There are many churches and many ways of doing theology, not all of which are options for myself. If it is not permitted to do constructive theology out of a tradition, I don't know how else I could do it. I remember talking some years ago to a mixed group of students about the way the Lutherans and the Reformed try to theologize out of their respective confessional heritages. One student raised his hand and said: "I don't come from a confessional tradition. How do *I* theologize?" I thought for a moment, then gave him my honest answer: "I haven't the faintest idea."

I shall not ask in part II whether Reformed theology is a good thing, or whether the world would be a worse place if there were no Presbyterians in it (a difficult question). I shall simply try, in the light of part I, to answer the question put to me: How do I see the future of theological education in the Reformed tradition? The question presupposes that there will be a future and that it is possible to characterize the Reformed tradition. Had I been asked whether or not the world really needs Presbyterians, or whether the survival of humanity requires Reformed theology, I would have had to take a different tack. But I dare say it will be plain enough to you that I do believe the Reformed churches have a contribution to make to the many-sided theological

---

15. Edward Farley, *Theologia: The Fragmentation and Unity of Theological Education* (Philadelphia: Fortress, 1983), pp. 35-37, 156, 87, 130; cf. p. 146.

conversation of the present day, and perhaps I shall ask your indulgence in advance in case I preach a little before I'm through.

The usual approach to discussing the Reformed tradition is to catalogue some distinctive beliefs or doctrines. We have, for instance, the so-called Five Points of Calvinism, which we don't like to talk about as much as we used to: total depravity, unconditional election, limited atonement, irresistible grace, and perseverance (TULIP). Or there's a list of five essential doctrines drawn up by the General Assembly in 1910, when the fundamentalist controversy was gaining momentum: (1) the inerrancy of the Bible, (2) the virgin birth, (3) substitutionary atonement, (4) the bodily resurrection of Christ, and (5) Christ's miracles. The alliance of Old School Presbyterians with the dispensationalists usually added heaven and hell and Christ's second coming to the list of "fundamentals." Or, again, there's the list provided in our present *Constitution:* one central theme, the sovereignty of God, and four related themes in the Reformed tradition: election for service as well as for salvation, covenant life marked by a disciplined concern for order, faithful stewardship in the use of God's gifts, and — in recognition of the human tendency to idolatry and tyranny — the call to work for justice.[16]

One recent writer, John Hesselink, presents his account of what it means to be Reformed, somewhat unusually, by first listing a dozen common misunderstandings of the Reformed tradition. A dangerous approach, I should think. His list is very comprehensive, and he admits that where there's smoke, there's fire: each of the criticisms brought against the Reformed rests on a degree of truth. A reader who needs converting may be surprised to find out that there are more objections to being Reformed than she or he had dreamed of. But Hesselink has few equals as an interpreter of the Reformed tradition. His insights are always worth reading, and in the final chapter he reverts to the more common approach of listing distinctive "emphases."[17]

The difficulty with all these checklists, as is only too clear, is that they change. Or perhaps that's the *good* thing about them. Puritan Calvinism was not Calvin's Calvinism, and the Westminster Divines were not fundamentalists. The reason why a separate Reformed church first emerged from the Reformation conflict was because no agreement could be reached between the Lutherans and the Reformed on the Lord's Supper. But there wasn't perfect agreement among the Reformed either. Zwingli's doctrine of the Lord's Supper was not Calvin's, and Calvin's was not reproduced in the Westminster Confession, even though the Westminster Divines were supposed to make the English church more Cal-

---

16. *Constitution of the Presbyterian Church (U.S.A.),* pt. II, *Book of Order* (New York and Atlanta: Office of the General Assembly, 1985), G-2.0500.

17. I. John Hesselink, *On Being Reformed: Distinctive Characteristics and Common Misunderstandings* (Ann Arbor: Servant Books, 1983).

vinist. The Westminster Confession was brought to America and became the hallmark of Presbyterian orthodoxy. Yet not even the strictest of American Presbyterians wanted to keep the Westminster Divines' view of church-state relations ("the civil magistrate"), so the confession was edited. Later, the doctrine of double predestination, which had long been identified as the central dogma of Calvinism, was found embarrassing. The Declaratory Statement was added (1903), which pretends to interpret the doctrine but actually dismantles it.

And so we might go on. The list of Reformed beliefs changes. It would be hard, perhaps impossible, to find a single Presbyterian anywhere these days who wants the same list as the Westminster Divines had, and there probably aren't many Presbyterians who are even aware of how far we have moved from John Calvin. This is all the easier because our *Book of Confessions* still doesn't have a confession that stands close to Calvin himself.

What's the alternative, then, to a list of "Reformed distinctives" (as we sometimes say)? Well, it's interesting that Calvin himself thought it important to acknowledge some articles of faith as necessary but didn't venture to give an exhaustive list of them. He says: *such as* that God is one, that Christ is God and the Son of God, and that our salvation rests on God's mercy.[18] (You will notice that he forgot to mention what is supposed to have been his central dogma: predestination.) Elsewhere, Calvin names but one fundamental doctrine, which it is not possible to break: that we cleave to Christ, the only *foundation* of the church.[19] Now, cleaving to Christ is not strictly a doctrine at all. Might we say that it's the habit of mind on which every Christian doctrine, without exception, rests?

It certainly does not follow that we do not need doctrines, or even lists of fundamental doctrines. It would be mere feeblemindedness to say: "We must cleave to Christ. Let's leave it at that." What follows, rather, is first that we try to write new confessions of faith for every generation, and second that we appeal to something more constant and even more fundamental than fundamental beliefs; namely, good habits of mind, all of which rest finally on the one foundation, which is Jesus Christ.

Here, then, are what I myself would propose, not as the five points of Calvinism, but as five notes of the Reformed habit of mind, out of which we make our confession as the times require of us.

The first is at once the most obvious and perhaps the most difficult to commend. Like the ancient Athenians and their guests, we are conditioned to

---

18. J. Calvin, *Institutes of the Christian Religion*, ed. F. L. Battles and J. T. McNeill (Philadelphia: Westminster, 1960), 4.1.12.

19. Calvin, *Commentary* on 1 Cor. 3:11, in *Ioannis Calvini opera quae supersunt omnia* (hereafter cited as *CO*), ed. W. Baum, E. Cunitz, and E. Reuss, 59 vols. (Brunswick: C. A. Schwetschke and Son, 1863-1900), 49: 353-54.

like novelty: we would gladly spend our time telling or hearing something new (Acts 17:21). In a way, I suppose that Paul obliged the Athenians: he spoke of Christ's resurrection from the dead. That, certainly, was something new. But for us it is the now *old* apostolic message of the crucified and risen Lord, as perceived in our Reformed tradition, that defines our existence and gives our existence whatever justification it may have.

The Reformed habit of mind, then, is first of all *deferential*: a habit of deference to the past. I use the word "deference" in its dictionary sense to mean "respect and esteem due to a superior or an elder." That is not a habit of mind that is very highly prized these days, but, as far as I can see, the very notion of "tradition" — whether Reformed or anything else — presupposes it. If there is to be a Reformed tradition at all, there must be a deference to the apostles and fathers of the church. This is not to suppress the energy and excitement that we must bring to each new cause. It is simply to recognize that even after the triumph of Mount Carmel we are still no better than our fathers (1 Kings 19:4): we draw our strength, in part, from them. We pass the torch on. To stand in a tradition is to hand on a sacred trust that, in the first instance, we have simply received. The fact that the tradition is *there*, in the history books, means nothing. But if we receive it and accept the duty to pass it on, then we permit our existence to be defined by the tradition: it makes us, in large measure, who we are.

"I am not better than my fathers." Let's put it in practical, down-to-earth terms. It's partly a question of which books I reach for first when I want to think as a Reformed theologian. Next to the Scriptures themselves, I reach for the confessions and the testimonies of the fathers, or let's say forebears, of my church. I am not yet being genuinely Reformed even if I manage to keep up with the latest thing in the Reformed church. Many seminarians of my generation thought they needed to know about Karl Barth; very few realized that they ought to know what he knew. Barth knew his Calvin. In the preface to his *Romans*, he advised the twentieth-century reader to go back to the commentaries of Calvin:

> My complaint is that recent commentators confine themselves to an interpretation of the text which seems to me to be no commentary at all, but merely the first step towards a commentary. . . . [H]ow energetically Calvin [by contrast], having first established what stands in the text, sets himself to re-think the whole material and to wrestle with it, till the walls which separate the sixteenth century from the first become transparent! Paul speaks, and the man of the sixteenth century hears. The conversation between the original record and the reader moves round the subject-matter, until a distinction between yesterday and to-day becomes impossible.[20]

20. Karl Barth, *The Epistle to the Romans*, trans. from the 6th German ed. by Edwyn C. Hoskyns (London: Oxford University Press, 1933), pp. 6-7.

And Barth knew the old Reformed "schoolmen," too. When he began his first dogmatics lectures at Göttingen in 1924, it was in Heppe's sourcebook of the old Reformed dogmaticians that he found the help he was looking for.[21] Barth even, after a fashion, knew his Schleiermacher — better, certainly, than most who repeat his criticisms of Schleiermacher. In the same year that he began his career as a professor of theology, Barth recalled the opinion of Alexander Schweizer that it was Schleiermacher who brought about the revival of Reformed theology in the nineteenth century. "Awkward for Brunner and me," Barth wrote, "if it were so! That it is *not* so — I should like to be *fully* persuaded of that! But this is not, for now, raised so far above all doubt one can without further ado build his house on it."[22]

We are not better than our forebears! We owe them deference, and we need a Reformed theological education, first of all, to impart to us this particular habit of mind. It does not come easily to us these days: few seminarians expect to acquire it when they apply, and many resist it sullenly or vehemently in the classroom. But if we once lose that habit of mind, we may as well close up, sell the buildings, and leave them to someone who can put them to good use.

Second, however, the Reformed habit of mind is just as essentially *critical* — even of the fathers. And how difficult it is to be both deferential and critical! We run up against that problem every time we open the pages of Calvin's *Institutes*. I bought my first copy of the *Institutes* in 1949, the year I went up to Cambridge as an undergraduate. I knew immediately that Calvin was to be my theological mentor, and in the forty years that have passed since then I have found no one else who can so overwhelm me with the vision of a world filled — or yet to be filled — with the glory of God, or who can so move me with the reassuring sense of the fatherly goodness (or, as we might say, the parentlike goodness) that always surrounds me. But that's only one side of it. Calvin also disturbs me with his rhetoric of disgust at the human condition, embarrasses me with the meanness of his polemical ardor. Even among friends he could be cool, formal, distant, censorious, to the point of tactlessness (the quintessential Presbyterian?). A French refugee who greeted him enthusiastically on the streets of Geneva as "Brother Calvin" received the chilly rebuff that the correct form of address was *Monsieur Calvin*.[23] A complicated man, to say the least: a deep thinker, a faithful laborer, and a loyal pastor and friend, but flawed and

---

21. See Barth's foreword to Heinrich Heppe, *Reformed Dogmatics Set Out and Illustrated from the Sources,* ed. Ernst Bizer, trans. G. T. Thomson (London: George Allen & Unwin, 1950).

22. Karl Barth, "Brunners Schleiermacherbuch," *Zwischen den Zeiten* 2 (1924): 60, translation mine.

23. T. H. L. Parker, *Portrait of Calvin* (London: SCM Press, 1954), p. 13.

fallible like the rest of us; and even when he was not exactly flawed, we don't necessarily find him attractive.

Our attitude toward tradition, which likewise is a living and human thing, is bound to have in it something of the same oscillation between attraction and aversion, so that we learn by *conversation* with the past: neither going our own separate ways nor merely listening and absorbing passively. A Reformed tradition needs no hagiography, and it needs no set of immutable "points" written in stone like the Ten Commandments. Calvin himself wrote to a Roman Catholic opponent who wanted the Genevans to return to the old ways: "The safety of that man hangs by a thread whose defense turns wholly on this — that he has constantly adhered to the religion handed down to him from his forefathers."[24] And to another Roman Catholic critic who accused the Protestants of disloyalty to tradition, he replied: "Our constant endeavor, day and night, is not just to transmit the tradition faithfully, but also to put it in the form we think will prove best."[25]

Without criticism of tradition, there would have been no reformation of the church. Now there is a Reformed tradition, but it cannot be a *Reformed* tradition without continuing self-criticism. The full original title of the Reformed church was indeed "the church [or churches] reformed according to the Word of God." And yet, in faithfulness to the spirit of the founding fathers, we have learned to say: *ecclesia reformata, semper reformanda.* And we had better make it a habit of mind, not an empty motto. Otherwise, we will reduce living tradition to the narrow limits of our favorite shibboleth or checklist and cancel our pledges whenever someone says something we aren't used to hearing. To be Reformed is to *invite* criticism, not to be forever on the defense. The open invitation of the authors of the old Scots Confession (1560) is that,

> if any man will note in our Confession any chapter or sentence contrary to God's Holy Word . . . it would please him of his gentleness and for Christian charity's sake to inform us of it in writing; and we, upon our honour, do promise him that by God's grace we shall give him satisfaction from the mouth of God, that is, from Holy Scripture, or else we shall alter whatever he can prove to be wrong.[26]

---

24. *Reply by Calvin to Cardinal Sadolet's Letter* (1539), trans. Henry Beveridge, in *Calvin's Tracts and Treatises*, 3 vols. (1844-51; reprint, Grand Rapids: Wm. B. Eerdmans Publishing Co., 1958), 1:64.

25. Calvin, *Defensio contra Pighium* (1543), in *CO*, 6:250, translation mine.

26. Arthur C. Cochrane, ed., *Reformed Confessions of the Sixteenth Century* (Philadelphia: Westminster, 1966), p. 165.

The Reformed habit of mind, to be true to the founders, must be deferential *and* critical. Deference will keep the buildings open. But without criticism they will become not seminaries but cemeteries.

Thirdly, the Reformed habit of mind is open: open to wisdom and insight wherever they can be found, not simply among fellow Presbyterians. The original genius of the Reformed church, I believe, was that it borrowed gratefully from both the Lutherans and the Renaissance humanists, creating a "Christian philosophy" (as Calvin called it) that was at once faithful to the gospel and deeply committed to learning. I have no doubt that dependence on secular learning has sometimes led Reformed theology to make mistakes, but Zwingli and Calvin apparently considered it a worse mistake to isolate the gospel from secular thought. In his great treatise on providence (1530), Zwingli writes:

> Some people do not hesitate to make the truth odious by attributing it to the philosophers, not noting that the truth, wherever found and by whomever it is brought to light, is from the Holy Spirit. . . . All that I have said and all that I am going to say in this book is derived from one source, namely from the nature and character of the Supreme Deity. This source Plato also tasted, and Seneca drank from it.[27]

Calvin was a bit more cautious than Zwingli because he didn't want the *mistakes* of the philosophers overlooked. But he still calls it mere "superstition" not to risk borrowing anything from non-Christian writers. His reason is the same as Zwingli's: because all truth comes from God, whose Spirit is the one fountain of truth.[28] He thinks "there can be no doubt that . . . God *sowed,* by the hand of philosophers and profane writers, the excellent sentiments which are to be found in their writings."[29] We know from recent Calvin scholarship that he not only wrote his first book on a treatise by the Roman philosopher Seneca but was still reading and annotating his classical authors in the turbulent 1540s, when one would have expected him to be too busy reforming Geneva.[30]

There is no need to be shocked, then, that I began my remarks on Re-

27. Ulrich Zwingli, *On Providence and Other Essays,* ed. for Samuel Macauley Jackson by William John Hinke (1922; reprint, Durham, N.C.: Labyrinth Press, 1983), pp. 144 (translation slightly altered), 151.

28. Calvin, *Commentary* on Titus 1:12, in *CO* 52:415.

29. Calvin, *Commentary* on John 4:36, in *CO* 47:96.

30. See Alexandre Ganoczy and Stefan Scheld, *Herrschaft-Tugend-Vorsehung: Hermeneutische Deutung und Veröffentlichung handschriftlicher Annotationen Calvins zu sieben Senecatragödien und der Pharsalia Lucans,* Veröffentlichungen des Instituts für Europäische Geschichte Mainz, vol. 105 (Wiesbaden: Franz Steiner Verlag, 1982).

formed theology by referring to Aristotle's *Ethics*. It may betray the fact that I was a classics major before I became a theology student, but so were Zwingli, Calvin, Schleiermacher, and many others of my Reformed heroes. I am in good company. A part of the precious heritage of the Reformed church is its firm commitment to secular, as well as sacred, learning — to what Schleiermacher called the "eternal covenant" between living Christian faith and completely free scientific inquiry. "It is my firm conviction," he wrote, "that the basis for such a covenant was already established in the Reformation."[31]

Theological education in the Reformed tradition cannot be insular, ingrown, defensive, or (in Van Harvey's word) "narcissistic." This brings me back — all too fleetingly, I'm afraid — to where I began. I cannot conceive of a Reformed theology that is not open to the academy as well as committed to the church. But I suspect that in the foreseeable future two somewhat different types of theology are likely to be nurtured in the university and the seminary respectively. Insofar as they are genuinely Reformed types, the differences between them can only be relative. It will be important for them to keep in touch and to avoid mutual recriminations. Perhaps the special responsibility of those who work in the seminaries will be to ask their university colleagues how the scientific ideal is related to other human values. On the other side, I don't see how the seminaries can responsibly address social, economic, medical, legal, moral, or ecological problems, as the church surely must, without the knowledge that comes chiefly from the academy. And this brings me to my fourth "note."

The Reformed habit of mind has always been unabashedly *practical*. Truth, the old divines used to say, stands in accordance with goodness. I'm not sure I would be willing to admit that of *all* truth, but certainly of *theological* truth: the good works of the theologian's mind are not just true thoughts, but thoughtful actions. In our tradition, this has meant two not unrelated things: knowledge of God is for the sake of both personal and social change.

Calvin made it clear that he had no interest in any knowledge of God that did not have to do with "piety," and this repeatedly led him in his *Institutes* to set a question aside if he judged it to be merely inquisitive or speculative ("academic," as we say). He called his *Institutes* not a *summa theologiae*, but a *pietatis summa* (a "summary of piety" or "godliness"), and he wrote: "Properly speaking, we cannot say that God is known where there is no religion or piety."[32] He determined to do theology within the limits of piety alone, and the

---

31. Friedrich D. E. Schleiermacher, *On the Glaubenslehre: Two Letters to Dr. Lücke*, trans. James Duke and Francis Fiorenza, American Academy of Religion Texts and Translation Series, no. 3 (Chico, Calif.: Scholars Press, 1981), p. 64.

32. Calvin, *Institutes* 1.2.1. The phrase *pietatis summa* appeared in the subtitle of the first edition.

result is that again and again he sets boundaries for the doctrines he discusses. On God, for instance: we do not need to know what God is in Godself (that would be cold speculation), but only that God is the fountain of every good. For the sense that we owe everything good to God is to our benefit and to God's glory.[33] Again, on the angels: we have no need for idle questions about how many angels there are because

> in reading the Scriptures we should constantly direct our inquiries and meditations to those things which tend to edification, not indulge in curiosity, in studying things of no use. . . . The duty of a Theologian . . . is not to tickle the ear, but confirm the conscience, by teaching what is true, certain, and useful.[34]

Similar words of caution mark Calvin's chapters on the Trinity, predestination, and so on.[35] Piety, godliness, is what counts.

But no one is likely to conclude that he was therefore shut up in a narrow world of private devotion! History proves otherwise. For Calvin, the practical knowledge with which theology has to do is directed to nothing less than the transformation of society into a mirror of God's glory. There is an interesting difference of emphasis here between Calvin and Luther. For Luther, reformation meant preaching. As he himself put it in a famous sermon: he preached the Word, drank beer with his friends, and slept; and while he did nothing more, the Word did it all.[36] Calvin thought there was more to be done. As he lay on his deathbed, he reminisced with the ministers about the course of his life and remarked: "When I first came to this church, I found almost nothing in it. There was preaching, and that was all. . . . There was no reformation."[37] What we find in Calvin, at the very source of the Reformed tradition, is a powerful sense of the duty to reform every department of public life, not just to preach — much less (in a phrase of James Luther Adams) just to manicure our own souls. Here, too, it is not so much a doctrine as a fundamental Reformed habit of mind that is at stake: theological education in the Reformed tradition has to nurture it if the tradition is to remain true to itself.

The Reformed have not been willing, of course, to leave the preaching to their Lutheran friends, any more than the Lutherans have left social responsi-

---

33. Calvin, *Institutes* 1.2.1-2.

34. Calvin, *Institutes* 1.14.4, trans. Beveridge.

35. Calvin, *Institutes* 1.13.29; 3.21.1.

36. Luther, "Eight Sermons at Wittenberg" (1522), in *Luther's Works*, 55 vols. (St. Louis: Concordia; Philadelphia: Fortress, 1955-86), 51:77.

37. Quoted in John Dillenberger, ed., *John Calvin: Selections from His Writings* (Garden City, N.Y.: Doubleday, 1971), p. 41.

bility to the Presbyterians. For my fifth and last note of the Reformed habit of mind, I come back to the full historic title: *"the churches reformed according to the Word of God"* (which, actually, the Lutherans sometimes claimed for themselves).[38] There surely is the foremost note of all, and even if it sounds terribly self-satisfied, and may even *be* self-satisfied, it has to have the final say. From the very first the Reformed consciousness was dominated by the overwhelming prophetic sense of standing, as Jeremiah was, under a Word of the Lord that we dare not tamper with, and which does not let us remain silent (cf. Jer. 1:1-9; 23:28-36). The Word is not something we discover, or read about, or decide to listen to. It *comes* — comes to us even when we are not listening, would rather not hear it, and would just as soon not have to talk about it. "Then I said, I will not make mention of him, nor speak any more in his name. But his word was in mine heart as a burning fire shut up in my bones . . ." (Jer. 20:9 KJV; cf. Amos 3:8). I admit that (happily) there's nothing uniquely Reformed about that consciousness; but there's no Reformed consciousness without it either.

And what is this Word? For us it is the gospel — the good news that the Word has *come,* come in human flesh (John 1:14). It is not, after all, smugness or self-satisfaction to claim that one preaches this Word. "For if I preach the gospel, that gives me no ground for boasting. For necessity is laid upon me. Woe to me if I do not preach the gospel!" (1 Cor. 9:16 RSV). That is the very heart of the Reformed habit of mind, even if it is not peculiar to the Reformed. Let's call it the *evangelical* habit. And I mean "evangelical" in its good Reformation sense, as distinct from its misappropriation by the fundamentalists. The first Protestants called themselves evangelicals because they put one thing only — the gospel of the Word made flesh — at the center. "The real treasure of the church," as Luther announced in his Ninety-five Theses (1517), "is the sacred Gospel of the glory and grace of God" (thesis 62). To be an evangelical is to think everything is related to the Word of the gospel.

With this, Zwingli's Sixty-seven Articles (1523) were in full agreement. He begins: "All who say that the Gospel is nothing without the approbation of the Church err and slander God. The sum of the Gospel is that our Lord Jesus Christ, the true Son of God, has made known to us the will of His heavenly Father, and by His innocence has redeemed us from death and reconciled us unto God."[39] In the same spirit the Ten Theses of Berne (1528) begin: "the holy, Christian Church, whose only Head is Christ, is born of the Word of God, abides in the same, and does not listen to the voice of a

---

38. In the Formula of Concord (1577), for example, pt. 2, sec. 5, "the reformed churches" means the Lutheran churches.

39. Cochrane, p. 36.

stranger."[40] Allow me just one more example! The preface to the Scots Confession declares: "We call on God to record that . . . with all humility we embrace the purity of Christ's Gospel, which is the one food of our souls and therefore so precious to us that we are determined to suffer the greatest of worldly dangers, rather than let our souls be defrauded to it."[41]

So much has been written about the appropriate image of the Christian minister: priest, pastor, preacher, counselor, pastoral director, reflective practitioner, and (heaven help us!) chief executive officer.[42] But in the Reformed tradition, at any rate, not one of these images — however valid as far as it goes — makes any sense apart from the title by which Reformed clergy once styled themselves: *verbi divini minister*, "servant of the Word of God." It goes with the evangelical habit of mind, and it explains *how* the Reformed habit of mind can be at once deferential and self-critical: because tradition, as Calvin says, is nothing other than a handing down of the Word of God.[43]

Conclusion

The general theme of our conference and of the Moore Lectures has been formulated in more ways than one. The leading question on the brochure is: "Seminary — What shall be taught, and why?" My answer is: Information, of course, skills, of course; but above all the good habit of mind that first created the Reformed tradition, and without which it has no future in the modern world. The end product of a seminary education in the twenty-first century may very well be a *master* of divinity, or a *doctor* of ministry, or even a doctor of divinity *honoris causa*. Let us hope so. But as long as there are Reformed pastors and theologians, they will understand themselves first and foremost, whatever their degree, as *servants* of the Word of God.

40. Cochrane, p. 49.
41. Cochrane, p. 165.
42. "Pastoral director" was the proposal of H. Richard Niebuhr, *The Purpose of the Church and Its Ministry* (New York: Harper & Row, 1956). "Reflective practitioner" has been taken over (and modified) from Donald Schoen by Joseph C. Hough, Jr., and John B. Cobb, Jr., *Christian Identity and Theological Education*, Studies in Religious and Theological Scholarship (Chico, Calif.: Scholars Press, 1985); see pp. 81, 84-94.
43. Calvin, *Defensio contra Pighium*, in *CO* 6:278.

CHAPTER 2

The Catholicity of Reformed Theology

Janos Pasztor

Introduction

0.1. The future vitality and relevance of Reformed theology depends, to a great extent, on its ability and willingness to deepen and extend its ecclesiology, built upon a trinitarian Christology, and give it the rightful place in the living context of the one holy catholic church and the world, both in theory and practice.

0.2. The present writer is a member of the Reformed Church in Hungary, which, along with the other Reformation churches (Reformed, Lutheran, or United), has been influenced, edified, and distorted by the various trends of thought dominating the European theological scene since the Reformation. On the other hand, in spite of, or due to, the unusually difficult political circumstances over 450 years, during which, apart from a short period of 39 years (1881-1920), the powers that were forceful prevented the church from forming a united body under one General Synod (Assembly),[1] there have been no secessions on account of differences in doctrine or polity, as has been the case in the Dutch or Scottish Reformed Churches, with an ample following in America.

0.3. This historical background, along with the theological development

---

1. Even today it is not possible to form one united body. The Reformed churches in Romania, the Czech Republic, Slovakia, and the former Yugoslavia are Hungarian-speaking churches, without the possibility of referring to this fact in their name. There is no reciprocity, since the Serbian Orthodox Diocese of Budapest is under the jurisdiction of the patriarch of Belgrade and the Romanian Orthodox Vicariate is under the metropolitan of Timisoara (Temesvar) in Romania. Cf. the entries in David Barrett, *The World Christian Encyclopedia* (Nairobi and New York: Oxford University Press, 1982).

and renewal of the last 70 years or so and the interaction of these with world events, has made some of us in this church particularly sensitive toward an extremely vital issue, which I would term *the catholicity of Reformed theology,* which is closely related to *the catholicity of the church.* If theology is the function of the church, it is bound to be catholic theology. As Jane Dempsey Douglass puts it: "Reformed theology is catholic reflection on what God does in the world and how God calls us to participate in God's work."[2] In the following, we shall attempt to give some points which seem to be essential and vital elements of a theology which is both catholic and Reformed, and which are considered to be particularly important for the future development of that theology. Before doing so, however, we shall take a short survey of the dynamics of development which produced the situation in which we are today.

The Heritage of the Reformers

1.1.1. For the Reformers, the catholicity of the church was taken for granted and was considered to be fundamental. The theological enterprise they were undertaking was regarded and carried on as the function of the Catholic church. It affected "orthodoxy" as well as "orthopraxis," i.e., the life of the whole church and not only that of a local community. For this reason, it was catholic theology. Later generations seem to have forgotten or, perhaps unintentionally, distorted the conviction and attitude of the Reformers when they acted upon the dubious premises according to which doctrinal or structural differences — however important they may have been — justify leaving their church and setting up a new one. History has shown that the doctrinal differences in churches of the Reformed family were mostly of a secondary nature, such as the Arminian or the lapsarian controversy and the like.

1.1.2. Luther, Calvin, and Martin Bucer, to mention only a few, would not have thought of leaving the church and setting up another one. They tackled the great problem of reforming and revitalizing the one church of which they were members. This view was decisive for Luther. Having written the Ninety-five Theses, he dispatched copies to the most important universities and also to the bishop of the diocese of his area.[3] This was a typical, traditional, "catholic" way of doing things: if there is a problem in the teaching of the church, it is to be analyzed and debated within the competent courts

2. Jane Dempsey Douglass, "What Is 'Reformed Theology'?" *Princeton Seminary Bulletin,* n.s., 11, no. 1 (1990): 3.

3. Joachim Rogge, *Martin Luther: Sein Leben, seine Zeit, seine Wirkungen* (Berlin: Ev. Verlagsanstalt, 1982), pp. 24f.

within the church. In 1520 the papal bull *Exsurge Domine* was made public, which announced Luther's excommunication unless he withdrew the theses deemed to have been heretic. Luther's reaction, in harmony with the catholic tradition, was twofold: (a) He appealed to a council for support, in accordance with the conciliar tradition *(concilium supra papam)* which by that time was already being challenged by the new concept of *papa supra concilium*.[4] (b) He publicly burned the papal bull to express in the customary way that it was a heretic writing. He and others were not willing to accept the view that by rejecting the claim of the papacy in the church they placed themselves outside the church catholic.

1.1.3. For Calvin, the catholicity of his teaching was also fundamental. In the foreword of the *Institutes of the Christian Religion*, addressed to Francis I of France, he emphasizes that his teaching is in full accordance with the fathers of the church. The modern critical editions of this work give the documentation of patristic references and allusions.[5] His intention was to teach "what has been confessed always and everywhere." The most important criterion of catholicity was faithfulness to the teaching of the Holy Scriptures. Even the *sola Scriptura* principle was not an invention of the Reformers. It had been formulated in the Middle Ages.[6] Furthermore, book 4 of the *Institutes*, which might be regarded as the crowning piece of the whole composition, makes it clear that the most important thing to be said about the church is its unity-cum-catholicity which has held together all believers over the ages and geographical distances in union with Christ, which is so real that Christ and the believers together form one body. Thus, the catholicity of the church is derived from and directly related to the "all-inclusive ontological reality" of the body of Christ into which the believers are incorporated by baptism, and in which the believers are in a "mystic sweet communion" and form an ethical as well as ontological union, nurtured by the Eucharist. In other words, "being united with Christ is exactly the same thing as being a member of His Body, the Church."[7] This fact makes it both necessary and possible to do theology only within this body. That is the catholicity of theology in the teaching and practice of Calvin.

1.1.4. The Hungarian Reformers — and I may point to the fact that the Hungarian Reformed Church, in spite of its very turbulent history and mani-

---

4. Hans Barion, "Konzile," in *Die Religion in Geschichte und Gegenwart,* ed. Kurt Galling, 3rd ed. (Tübingen: J. C. B. Mohr, 1957), 3:1801ff., hereafter cited as *RGG*.

5. John Calvin, *Institutes of the Christian Religion,* ed. J. T. McNeill and F. L. Battles, Library of Christian Classics, vols. 20-21 (Philadelphia: Westminster, 1960).

6. Gerhard Gloege, "Schriftprinzip," in *RGG,* 5:1540ff.

7. E. David Willis, "The Eucharist in the Reformed Tradition" (paper delivered at a session of the Orthodox-Reformed Dialogues [Debrecen II], Leningrad, 1976), p. 7.

fold mutilations,[8] is still the largest Reformed body in Europe — were also aware of the same thing, which finds expression in the fact that the title of their important Confession of Egervölgy/Debrecen (1561) is *Confessio Catholica.* Most of the Continental European Reformation church adopted as subordinate standards the Heidelberg Catechism (1563) and the Second Helvetic Confession (1566). Both put great emphasis on catholicity. This can be seen in the fifty-fourth question-answer of the Heidelberg Catechism:

> q: *What do you believe concerning "the holy Catholic Church"?*
>
> a: *I believe that, from the beginning to the end of the world, and from among the whole human race, the Son of God, by His Spirit and His Word, gathers, protects, and preserves for Himself, in the unity of the true faith, a congregation chosen for eternal life. Moreover, I believe that I am and forever will remain a living member of it.*

This is a very comprehensive statement about the catholicity of the church.

1.1.5. In the introduction to the Second Helvetic Confession, it is emphasized that the representatives of churches who signed the confession have nothing to do with schisms or heresies. "We are not seceding from the holy churches of Christ, which are in Germany, France, and England and among other nations of Christianity with evil secession." The introduction is followed by the Imperial Decree of Gratian, Valentinian II, and Theodosius the Great, proclaimed at Thessaloniki on 28 February 380. It describes who is to be regarded catholic or heretical, respectively. Then comes the Confession of Pope Damasius, followed by the Creed of Nicaea, the Nicene-Constantinopolitan Creed, the doctrines of Ephesus (431), the definition of Chalcedon (451), and the *Symbolum Athanasianum.* In the section dealing with the church (chap. XVII), it rejects the notion that only the Roman Church is catholic (XVII.2). Then it continues: "In the Church militant on the earth there have always been several particular churches *(ecclesiae particulares),* which, however, belong to the unity of the Catholic Church *(ad unitatem catholicae ecclesiae)"* (XVII.4). "There have always been serious debates . . . but because of these the Church has never ceased to be what it is" (XVII.9).

1.1.6. The awareness of responsibility for the catholicity of church and theology was very much alive in the Church of Hungary.[9] In the midst of man-

---

8. Cf. J. H. Merle D'Aubigné, *History of the Protestant Church in Hungary from the Beginning of the Reformation to 1850,* ed. and trans. J. Craig (London: J. Nisbet, 1854).

9. The Danube Valley, surrounded by the Carpathian Mountains, has been a meeting place of empires and ideas ever since. The time of the Reformation coincided with the invasion of the middle of the country by the Ottoman Empire, bringing about an encounter between Islam and Christianity in the very heart of Europe. At the same time the Austrian

ifold divisions, when the deplorable process of separation even within the churches of the Reformation was going on, some Hungarian theologians made attempts to keep the unity of the church not based on practical, political, or strategic argument, but on a christological and ecclesiological basis. The much-contested figure of Bishop Janos Samarjai, whose oeuvre would deserve a thorough analysis, is an interesting example of an effort to halt the atomization of the Reformation churches and also of the way the church can be adjusted to its cultural and political environment in a "Catholic way."[10]

1.1.7. We can conclude this section by stating that the Reformation regarded itself as a movement to re-form and renew the Catholic Church, and made all attempts to keep its unity.

1.2.1. There was, however, one crack, hardly visible on the wall of the teaching of the Reformers concerning the church, which would be widening later. This crack is the distinction between the visible and the invisible church taken over from Saint Augustine, which is a typical example of Augustinian dualism. Calvin also uses this expression. But in his ecclesiology it plays only a minor role. Wilhelm Niesel says concerning this matter: Calvin "takes over the ideas of Augustine, not in order to develop a doctrine of two churches, but rather to confront the empirical church which we know with the concept of the invisible church."[11]

1.2.2. In Reformed orthodoxy the *ecclesia visibilis et invisibilis* distinction was to gain more significance.[12] True enough, most of the orthodox theologians emphasized that this distinction is not one between two churches, but between two aspects of the same reality.[13] Nevertheless, due to the silently prevailing Hellenistic understanding of spiritual and material, according to which the former is the real and pure and the latter is lower, less significant, or even evil, the *ecclesia invisibilis* was looked upon as the real one which embraced all

---

Hapsburgs invaded the west of the country, carrying out the toughest line of counterreformation. The east remained Hungarian. Cf. Imre Révész and George A. F. Knight, *History of the Hungarian Reformed Church* (Washington D.C.: Hungarica Americana, 1956), pp. 43-75; D'Aubigné, pp. 214ff.

10. Géza Kathona, "Samarjai János gyakorlati theologiája," *Theologiai Szemle*, special ed., vol. 16 (Budapest, 1940), pp. 1-224.

11. Wilhelm Niesel, *The Theology of Calvin* (Philadelphia: Westminster, 1956), pp. 191-92.

12. Heinrich Heppe and Ernst Bizer, *Die Dogmatik der evangelisch-reformierten Kirche* (Neukirchen: Erziehungsverein, 1958), pp. 527ff.

13. "The distinction between visible and invisible church is therefore not a difference between two *species* of one *genus*, but the definition of one and the same subject, according to different relationships of its existence." Heppe and Bizer, p. 527.

the elect, but not the hypocrites among the dead members and other repro-bates within the *ecclesia visibilis*. As the essential unity, along with holiness, be-longs to the character of the church, this unity is seen through Hellenistic glasses: it means spiritual unity in a dualistic sense. Accordingly, the spiritual is often not comprehended first and foremost as brought about by the Holy Spirit, but as a unity "in spirit," i.e., immaterially. Visible unity and some kind of organization is of secondary significance because it belongs to the world of matter, i.e., the visible world.[14] Consequently, if differences in the doctrine of the church emerge, which are spiritual matters, it is not only permissible, but mandatory, to secede from the organization. Consequently, one can leave a particular organization, e.g., the Church of Scotland at the time of the "Dis-ruption" in 1843, without leaving the invisible church.

1.2.3. This is a long way from Calvin and from the Scriptures: for Calvin, the marks of the church — pure proclamation and right administration of the sacraments — are based upon his sound catholic Christology. As W. Niesel puts it: "there is only one Church which is distinguished from the spurious church by the fact that it exists to serve Jesus Christ."[15] Christ comes to hu-mankind by means of the Word preached and the sacraments celebrated, with the latter being intrinsically related to the former. Both together proclaim the presence of Christ more effectively than the Word preached. In other words, pure proclamation is that of Christ in his full divinity and humanity and in the hypostatic union of the two natures, i.e., God graciously condescending to live, die, and rise again and so to overcome death and sin for our salvation. This full grace is to be received by faith only. Thus, in Calvin's teaching the marks of the church *(notae ecclesiae)* are christologically based. All the other elements of Christian doctrine are derived from trinitarian Christology and are correlated to it. This also means that he takes both creation and incarnation seriously. Consequently, he wants to preserve the unity of the church also in a structural or institutional sense, but he is not willing to identify the latter with the struc-tures of papacy.[16]

1.2.4. The distinction between visible and invisible church, together with a dualistically interpreted spirituality in the teaching of Protestant orthodoxy, contributed much to the atomization of the Reformed church and theology. In this system of thought the right priorities and the right structure of Christian

14. Cf. Fritz Buri, Jan Milič Lochman, and Heinrich Ott, *Dogmatik im Dialog* (Gütersloh: Verlag Gerd Mohn, 1974), 1:27. Calvin said that "the Church can exist without being apparent." *Prefatio ad regem Gallorum*, quoted by E. D. Willis, *Calvin's Catholic Chris-tology* (Leiden: E. J. Brill, 1966), p. 142. Willis rightly points out that this is not a reference to the invisibility of the church, but to the Roman concept of the marks of the church.

15. Niesel, p. 192.

16. Calvin, *Institutes* 4.7.23-26.

doctrine were turned upside down.[17] It was not only the visible church which was seen as of secondary importance. The same was often to be the destiny of the basic Christian doctrine, namely, Christology. The teaching of John McLeod Campbell of the Church of Scotland that Christ died for all, not only for the elect, was condemned, and he was deposed from the ministry.[18] The fact that he professed a catholic Christology was not enough for him to minister in the church because he was in opposition to a particular element of federal theology.

1.2.5. It must be recognized that Hellenistic dualism lurked behind Reformed orthodoxy, which contributed to the distortion of its ecclesiology.[19] Hellenistic influences had been of great significance in the Mediterranean and European culture for a very long time. Since the monumental effort of translating the Old Testament into Greek in the third century B.C.E., we can follow the thrilling intellectual struggle over the centuries to adjust to and make right the relationship with Hellenistic thought and culture on the side of the theology of the church, which was fundamentally based on Hebrew and biblical thinking. Due to the fact that the New Testament was written in Greek in its final form and contains quotations from the Old Testament, the Greek language and culture became an organic part of the revelatory process. Therefore, we must see that the vocabulary of Hellenism, used critically, had a very important positive role in bringing about and developing Christian theology.

1.2.6. As Christianity grew into the Hellenistic world, it became a task of growing importance for theology to reflect upon the faith of the church and express it in and for that culture. The result was a Christian culture crowned by theology as the "queen of sciences." The most significant expression of this kind of theology was that of Saint Thomas Aquinas, an impressive synthesis of Aristotelian philosophy and Hebrew-biblical thinking which was challenged concerning fundamental issues by the Reformation. Protestant orthodoxy, however, resumed applying methods of the logic of Aristotle. Ecclesiology was not its particular concern. The infallibility of the Scriptures was its main issue.[20]

1.2.7. The various revival movements and, above all, German Pietism, which grew out of Lutheran ground, put the emphasis on the personal decision, on conversion experiences and belonging together, over denominational barriers. This view and practice still fit into the pattern of the visible and invis-

17. Franz Lau, "Orthodoxie," in *RGG*, 4:1723.

18. M. Charles Bell, *Calvin and Scottish Theology* (Edinburgh: Handsel Press, 1985), pp. 181ff.

19. For Hellenistic influences, cf. Buri, Lochman, and Ott, 1:26ff.

20. Otto W. Heick, *A History of Christian Thought* (Philadelphia: Fortress, 1964), 1:47ff.

ible church. Some new church bodies came into existence under Pietist influences.[21] There are also analogies with the charismatic movement in the twentieth century, which has groups in most major denominations and has also
established separate denominations. The latter, in certain parts of the world,
particularly in the United States, seem to be in a rapid process of atomization.
They claim to have brought about the "ecumenism of the Holy Spirit."

1.3.1. The reaction to orthodoxy came from two sides. Pietism reacted against
it by putting an emphasis on personal decisions and on subjectivity. The other
reaction came from the intellectual movement climaxing in the Enlightenment. It was fundamentally a *reaction against ecclesiastical domination of European thought,* whether it came from Rome or Dort. This intellectual movement
was a very complex one, as European thinking as part of the culture of Christendom was itself an interesting welding together of Hebrew-biblical and classical Greco-Roman cultural values. Consequently, even intellectual efforts for
liberation from church control could not and very often did not want to get rid
of certain elements and impacts of the Christian heritage. Thus, what was to
come in the development of European thought remained to be colored by the
fifteen hundred years of Christian presence in European culture. That can be
clearly seen in the extreme cases of Feuerbach with his idea of humans creating
gods,[22] and of Marx with his secularized eschatology.

1.3.2. A significant change took place which has been termed by Helmut
Thielicke the "Cartesian turn" in European thinking.[23] Naturally, this turn had
its background and prehistory. In the Renaissance, antique culture was reborn to
be rid of ecclesiastical domination, as is illustrated most spectacularly in painting and sculpture which turned to classical and heathen subjects long forbidden.
It amounted to the secularization of fine arts. With Giordano Bruno, Galileo,
and Copernicus, the same thing happened in the sciences. With Descartes and
the Enlightenment, philosophy took off the yoke of theological domination.

1.3.3. Theology itself was very considerably influenced by this development. It was a 180-degree turn: it began losing its theocentric character and

---

21. The "Brüderunität" of Herrnhut, renewed through Nikolaus L. Zinzendorf, was
meant to be an early "ecumenical enterprise." John Wesley never wanted to leave the Church
of England and considered himself to be Anglican until the end. Ingvar Haddal, *John Wesley:
A Biography* (New York and Nashville: Abingdon, 1961), pp. 149f.; Rupert E. Davis, *Method-
ism* (Harmondsworth: Penguin, 1963), pp. 122-31; Walter J. Hollenweger, *The Pentecostals*
(London: SCM Press, 1969), pp. 244ff.

22. Feuerbach's idea about man creating his gods is quite in line with Isa. 44:9-20. Cf.
Richard Lorenz, "Feuerbach," in *RGG*, 2:928ff.

23. Helmut Thielicke, *The Evangelical Faith* (Grand Rapids: Wm. B. Eerdmans Publishing Co., 1974), 1:18ff.

became more and more anthropocentric. For these kinds of theologies it was not God who would come to man addressing him in his life-giving Word, but man would make attempts to approach God by means of an intellectual enterprise. A late twentieth-century representative of this trend of thought says: "God is the object of my consciousness which I perceive in so far as I perceive *something,* that is I allot him a place within the framework of a sign-system, in order to be able to talk to others about this matter."[24] Consequently, the church is the people, who, by virtue of having accepted the common sign-system, are seeking common answers to the meaning of existence.[25]

1.3.4. These trends of thought, however respectable they might have been otherwise, have rejected most of the things the Reformers stood for. The divine Logos, the eternal Son, "true God from true God, begotten not made, of one Being with the Father," became the Logos of the philosophers, a principle and idea, or a set of thoughts. As Blaise Pascal put it, here one has to deal with the God of philosophers instead of the God of Abraham, Isaac, Jacob, and Jesus Christ.[26] Instead of the listening obedience to the Word of God, one meets the rule of reason in rationalism; instead of the freedom of God's liberated children, one gets the freedom of the individual thinker in liberalism. These ideas had a devastating effect on the field of Christology. They brought about what has been termed by Hungarian theologians, a Unitarian theology in everything but name.

1.3.5. This was bound to affect ecclesiology. In these rationally "clear" sets of thoughts there was no room for a "mystical union with Christ" or a church which was the body of Christ, which were important concepts for Calvin. Everything becomes reasonable and clear; the church is nothing but one of the many human organizations dealing with issues like religion and morals.

1.3.6. No wonder that for some theologians, e.g., Richard Rothe, the church is transitory "help in need" *(Nothilfe)* at a period of process in the progression of humanity. This process will reach the end stage when the church will be superseded by a society in which the "religious and ethical values" of "the Kingdom of God" will be prevailing.[27] For people with that kind of idea, catholicity meant "as opposed to confessional catholicity . . . the universal kingdom of the spirit, but something other than the Holy Spirit,"[28] if it meant anything at all. Thus the very word "catholic" could easily be appropriated by

---

24. Buri, Lochman, and Ott, 2:21.

25. Buri, Lochman, and Ott, 2:142.

26. Wilhelm Weischedel, *Der Gott der Philosophen* (Munich: Nymphenburger Verlag, 1972), 1:xvii.

27. Erdmann Schott, "Rothe, Richard," in *RGG*, 5:1197ff.

28. Buri, Lochman, and Ott, 1:37.

the Roman Church. There was no objection due to the lack of interest and impoverished ecclesiology of the churches of the Reformation.

1.4.1. A dualistic understanding of nature and grace is an important factor behind the withering away of ecclesiology. The Hungarian theologian Ervin Vályi-Nagy has pointed out, in taking up the criticism raised by secular thinkers and Orthodox theologians against certain aspects of Reformed theology, that "grace without nature and body" is bound to lead to the concept of a "merciless nature." According to Vályi-Nagy's diagnosis, Protestant theology has spoken too much about grace and too little about nature, or rather its concept of grace has been reduced and perverted because it was separated from creation. The result was the merciless exploitation of nature, which has often been brought up against Christianity.[29]

    1.4.2. Another consequence of the depreciation of creation along with the separation of nature and grace was a concept of salvation reduced to the forgiveness of sins, which is a dangerous curtailment of the fullness of its biblical meaning. This "reductionist" concept of salvation is a residue of the teaching of Marcion and other Gnostics with their extreme forms of dualism. Where grace and nature are separated or even set against one another, ecclesiology is bound to be affected by it in reducing the concept of unity and catholicity to a nonmaterial and noninstitutional unity of the church, which is invisible. These ideas can be put right only upon the foundation of a trinitarian theology in which creation and redemption, nature and grace belong together.

    1.4.3. The ancient eucharistic liturgies kept the thanksgiving for creation and salvation together. The Hungarian Reformed Church, along with some other European Reformed churches, deprived the eucharistic liturgy of the prayer of thanksgiving altogether and put the prayer of confession in its stead at the very heart of the liturgy.[30] This helped strengthen ideas in the minds of people that salvation is equal with forgiveness of sins and is fundamentally an immaterial thing. Consequently, the Lord's Supper was losing its importance, and the sermon was to occupy the central place within the liturgy, not the crucified and risen Christ, who comes and gives himself to his people as they "follow His example in word and action."[31] If the Logos is not God the Son, but some ideas about God, and the sermon is a rational or free treatise of a free

29. Ervin Vályi-Nagy, "Natur und Gnade — Schöpfung und Erlösung," in *Debrecen V: Theological Dialogue between Orthodox and Reformed Churches*, ed. Karoly Tóth (Budapest: Ráday College, 1989), pp. 115ff.

30. *Agenda a Magyar Református Egyház liturgiás könyve* (Budapest: Bethlen Rt., 1927), pp. 80f.

31. *Book of Common Order of the Church of Scotland* (London: Oxford University Press, 1965), p. 126.

thinker, this development is natural. But it has not much to do with the Jesus Christ proclaimed in the Gospels.

1.5.1. It was not until the coming of the theological renewal of the twentieth century that the basic tenets of this impoverished ecclesiology were challenged in depth. Emil Brunner stated in his *Dogmatics:* "This double concept of the Church is wholly foreign to the New Testament. There is only one Ekklesia, which is at the same time spiritual and invisible and corporeal."[32] There is no room for it in the theology of Karl Barth either. His emphasis on the church being the earthly form of existence *(Existenzform)* of Jesus Christ as his body created by him, being renewed continually by the awakening power of the Holy Spirit, does not give much room for the visible-invisible distinction.[33] By virtue of the case, Jesus Christ, the Word incarnate, is to be seen (John 1:14). It is an essential characteristic of the "Word" in the Old Testament that it not only sounds forth but acts, and that the result is visible, e.g., in creation or in electing a people for salvation. When Saint John's Gospel uses the Greek term *Logos,* it fills it with Old Testament content.[34] Therefore, the church is by the nature of the case to be seen. This does not mean that the church has stain, wrinkle, and blemish (Eph. 5:27), or might not even be hidden from her enemies, like Elijah in the ravine at Kerith (1 Kings 17:1ff.) or the Roman Christians in the catacombs. There is also a sad list of schisms within the one body of Christ. But even in these cases, it is a visible church.

1.5.2. Thus the theological renewal of our days, which this author terms a rediscovery of the Word-Event character of revelation, Reformation, and renewal of church life,[35] has also brought about a renewal of ecclesiology. In terms of catholicity, some progress has also been made. Unfortunately, the latter has so far been limited to theological multilateral and bilateral dialogues, and the results have not yet permeated the congregations. It is a matter of historical truth that Reformed theologians were there at the birth of the modern ecumenical movement and have contributed to the renewal in ecclesiology and

32. Emil Brunner, *Dogmatics,* vol. 3, *The Christian Doctrine of the Church, Faith, and the Consummation* (Philadelphia: Westminster, 1962), p. 30.

33. Karl Barth, *Church Dogmatics* IV/1 (Edinburgh: T. & T. Clark, 1956), p. 653; cf. Buri, Lochman, and Ott, 1:29.

34. John Marsh, *Saint John* (Harmondsworth: Penguin, 1971), p. 96; Siegfried Schulz, *Das Evangelium nach Johannes,* NTD 4 (Göttingen: Vandenhoeck & Ruprecht, 1975), pp. 17ff.; Johannes Schneider, *Das Evangelium nach Johannes* (Berlin: Evangelische Verlagsanstalt, 1978), pp. 51ff.

35. Janos D. Pasztor, "The Heritage of the Reformation: Word-Event for Church and World" (unpublished Warfield Lectures, Princeton, 1992, Lecture One: "The Reformation: Word-Event for the Church").

a deeper understanding of catholicity. Without directly talking about catholicity, both phases of Roman Catholic–Reformed dialogues touched upon this question.[36] In the course of the theological dialogues between the Reformed Church in Hungary and the Russian Orthodox Church (The Debrecen Dialogues I-V, 1972-87), in which the World Alliance of Reformed Churches and also more Orthodox churches participated, David Willis's papers on the Reformed understanding of the Eucharist (Leningrad, 1976) and on tradition in Reformed theology (Odessa, 1983) explored the Reformed conception of catholicity.[37]

1.5.3. Thus the way is open and well prepared, in biblical as well as systematic studies, to go deeper, both in theology and in the life of the church. In the following, some viewpoints and facts will be brought up which seem to be important and which together may present a modest proposal toward deepening the Reformed concept of catholicity, and along with it the catholicity of Reformed theology.

The Catholicity of Reformed Theology

2.1.1. The most important point in relation to the catholicity of theology concerns worship, i.e., the praise and glorification of the triune God, the Father, the Son, and the Holy Spirit. The church is the community of those who have come to the realization of the fact that "man's chief end is to glorify God and enjoy Him for ever." This praiseworthy opening sentence of both Westminster Confessions is not followed up by a detailed explanation. It means that sinful men and women who have responded to Christ's call with their whole existence, offer themselves as living sacrifices, "holy and acceptable to God," which is a worship in the power of the Holy Spirit (Rom. 12:1); which is thanksgiving (eucharistia) in general, and the Lord's Supper in particular. These men and women as worshiping community have been incorporated in the body of Christ by the Spirit through baptism (1 Cor. 12:13). This body is being strengthened when they all share the bread and the wine, which is the sharing of the body and blood of Christ (1 Cor. 10:17; 11:24ff.). By means of participating in Christ, they also participate in his anointment and ministry.[38] This is the content of the expression "to glorify God," which cannot be done without

---

36. *The Presence of Christ in Church and World* (Geneva: WARC, 1977); *Towards a Common Understanding of the Church* (Geneva: WARC, 1991).

37. Willis's papers are available at the WARC offices in mimeographed form.

38. Cf. E. P. Sanders, *Paul and Palestinian Judaism* (Philadelphia: Fortress, 1977), pp. 453-72.

and apart from Jesus Christ. "No worship has ever pleased God except that which looked to Christ."[39]

2.1.2. Traditionally, Reformed theology discussed Christ's ministry as that of the mediator *(mediator reconciliationis inter Deum et homines lapsos)*. When it comes to unfolding the content of mediation, the threefold office is expounded. His office as mediator consists of the prophetic *(prophetia legalis et evangelica)*, priestly *(satisfactio et intercessio)*, and kingly *(regnum universale naturae et gratiae, gubernatio atque defensio ecclaesiae)* functions.[40] According to Heinrich Ott, the three aspects are in "structural unity." In the aspect of prophecy the aspects of both priesthood and kingship are also present. They are mutually reflected in one another.[41]

2.1.3. Thus the threefold office informs us of the content of mediation. From another angle the work of the mediator is a service *(ministerium)*, carried out by a servant. This word sums up the special quality of the work of Christ the mediator. From the very beginning, the church saw in the person and office of Christ the perfect fulfillment of what Deutero-Isaiah said about the "Servant of YHWH." George Knight and Walther Eichrodt point out that there exist elements of the *munus triplex* in the "Servant of YHWH" songs.[42] Due to the fact that the Septuagint uses, with more or less consistency, *pais* for the translation of EBED (servant), a "*pais*-servant theology" developed (Matt. 12:18-21; Acts 4:27; etc.).[43] Christ, the Anointed One, brings full salvation to the world as the Servant of God, who is God.[44] He has not come to be served, but to serve (Mark 10:45). The Servant of the Lord is servant because he carries out the perfect service.

2.1.4. Metropolitan Paulos Mar Gregorios, in his excellent study of *'abodah*,[45] points out that this term refers to the service of God in terms of liturgical ministry. But equally important is that it cannot be restricted within the wall of the sanctuary, but includes serving God in terms of social service

---

39. Calvin, *Institutes* 2.6.1.

40. Heppe and Bizer, pp. 355-63; Heinrich Ott, *Die Antwort des Glaubens*, 3rd ed. (Stuttgart and Berlin: Kreuz Verlag, 1981), pp. 303-12.

41. Ott, p. 274.

42. Walther Eichrodt, *Theologie des Alten Testaments* (Leipzig: J. C. Hinrichs'sche Buchhandlung, 1933), vol. 1. According to p. 262, n. 6, the figure of the EBED JAHWEH is a royal one which took into itself the other characters from elsewhere. George A. F. Knight, *Servant Theology* (Grand Rapids: Wm. B. Eerdmans Publishing Co., 1984), pp. 140-72.

43. Leonard Goppelt, *Theology of the New Testament*, vol. 2 (Grand Rapids: Wm. B. Eerdmans Publishing Co., 1982), pp. 19-22. Moreover, the eucharistic prayer of Hippolytus reflects this servant theology. Hans-Christoph Schmidt-Lauber, "Die Wiederentdeckung des eucharistischen Gebetes in den evangelischen Kirchen," *Pastoral-Theologie* (1984): 134-47.

44. Knight, p. 165.

45. Paulos Mar Gregorios, *The Meaning and Nature of Diakonia* (Geneva: WCC Risk Books, 1988).

(diakonia) and justice. These belong organically together. According to Gregorios, social ministry cannot be comprehended without the service in the sanctuary *('abodah ha-miskan* and *'abodah ohel moed)*. Furthermore, no service is authentic which has no continuation in society.

2.1.5. Christ is the perfect mediator and savior because he is true God and true man. James B. Torrance — following Athanasius and the Cappadocians — tells us about a "God-manward-movement" from the Father through the Son in the Spirit, and about a "man-God-movement" in Christ's vicarious humanity to the Father in the Spirit.[46] These are the dynamics of our salvation as well as of our worship. Thereby, Christ not only brought us forgiveness of our sins, but opened the way for us to participate fully in his life, in its dynamics and in his ministry.

2.2.1. Christian worship reflects God's ways with humankind. It begins with God's gracious condescending to his people, to which they respond. Both movements were perfectly fulfilled by Christ as mediator. He is God in our midst, and he is the true man, the Second Adam performing the perfect human response. In this we participate: our participation is not limited to the "man-God-movement," but also includes the "God-manward-movement." By virtue of having been united with him in the Spirit and sent out to carry on his mission, we have the immense privilege and responsibility in having a share in his coming to humanity. These are the dynamics of the liturgical worship service. The coming of God in his Word, preached and enacted in the sacraments (1 Cor. 11:26b),[47] is not only for the edification of the people present but also for equipping them to turn toward those outside, and so to continue the "God-manward-movement." In the course of the service the sacrifice of thanksgiving is offered on behalf of the whole creation, which includes the whole of humankind.[48] It is also an essential part of the service to offer prayers of intercession for all. Here is the root of the ministry toward those outside. What happens in the service must go on in the "liturgy" *('abodah)* of the weekdays.

2.2.2. Furthermore, Christian worship is to be seen in the light and context of the heavenly worship of the book of Revelation. It should not be taken in a Platonic sense, as if only the heavenly one were the true worship, of which ours is an incomplete copy or shadow. The earthly worship of the church at a

46. James B. Torrance, "The Vicarious Humanity of Christ," in *The Incarnation: Ecumenical Studies in the Nicene-Constantinopolitan Creed,* ed. Thomas F. Torrance (Edinburgh: Handsel Press, 1981), pp. 136ff.

47. Cf. Paul Philippi, *Diakonia. Über die soziale Dimension christlicher Verantwortung* (Neukirchen-Vluyn: Neukirchener Verlag, 1984), p. 62.

48. *Baptism, Eucharist and Ministry,* Faith and Order Paper no. 111 (Geneva: WCC, 1982), pp. 10f.

particular place — however small and seemingly insignificant it may be — is part of that of the one catholic church in heaven and on earth. Local worship is performed in communion with all those who have passed away in Christ, with contemporary human beings. It is an experience of the final consummation as foretaste of the heavenly worship and as such a real experience of the future in the present. In other words, in the worship through Christ the future breaks into the present. Thus, the worshiping community should have an awareness of the unity and catholicity of the church. Naturally the congregation, not to speak of the theologians, has to be told about what has just been explained. This kind of understanding presupposes the pure proclamation of the Word and the right celebration of the sacraments. It would not happen *ex opere operato*.

2.3.1. It has been recognized over the centuries that theology is doxology. However, this clear recognition has not always been carried through in theory and practice, but has often been blurred or forgotten. The most significant reform and revival movements in the church from the early ages onward have grown out of the context of the worshiping community. This was particularly true of the neo-reformation theology of Karl Barth and his circle. Their work is to be continued in terms of teaching and practice alike. Much has to be done to deepen the insights, to correct or extend them where necessary, and to carry them through.

2.3.2. Geoffrey Wainwright has done a great deal along these lines. In his *Doxology* he writes: "My conviction is that the relations between doctrine and worship are deeper rooted and further reaching than many theologians have appeared to recognize."[49] He refers to Anders Jeffner of Sweden, who "considers a systematic theology to be the articulation of a personal vision of faith which includes the insight of worship and carries ethical incidences."[50] It might be useful to add that the "personal faith" of the theologian is the faith of the church over the ages, accepted by him or her personally within the living, worshiping life of the church. The theologian has much to offer to the community in terms of critically reflecting on its life. But he or she is able to do this only as part of a personal involvement in its life.[51] In other words, there is a mutual interaction of the practical church life and the intellectual or theoretical effort of the theologian. The latter has to open up the mind of the church

---

49. Geoffrey Wainwright, *Doxology: The Praise of God in Worship, Doctrine, and Life: A Systematic Theology* (New York: Oxford University Press, 1980), preface.

50. Wainwright, p. 1.

51. John A. Mackay, *A Preface to Christian Theology* (London: Nisbet, 1945), pp. 27-54.

toward the perspectives and obligations of catholicity. At the same time the theologian will have direct experiences of the same, as he or she lives in the congregation.

2.3.3. The theologian is bound to see the necessity of working for the unity of the churches. In our days it has been observed that there is an impasse in the ecumenical movement.[52] The present situation is characterized by two opposing tendencies. On the one hand, there has been a further improvement of relationship among the "historical" denominations, including the relationship between the Reformed church and the Church of Rome. The present pope, who has made some ambiguous steps as if he wanted to reinterpret some decisions reached at Vatican II, seems to be ready to take further steps on the "ecumenical road." Yet, his intention to evangelize Europe is regarded by some with suspicion that it might be intended to "re-Catholicize" the continent with the reintroduction of some elements of the Constantinian era. At the same time, he did make important symbolic gestures toward Reformed Christianity.[53] The common theological work has been going on in the field of biblical research. The denominational walls in this territory have come down.[54] Systematic work within the Faith and Order Commission has also made great progress.[55]

2.4.1. The problem is mostly with those Roman churches that are in an overwhelmingly majority situation, who do not feel any need for ecumenical cooperation with smaller churches. They are to be reminded that catholicity means to be one with all those with a sound Christology (1 John 4:3; 1 Cor. 12:1-3; Matt. 16:16-18). It is not a matter of numbers. To be separated from them means that the body of Christ is wounded, not only that his robe is torn. The same message is to be addressed to those on the Reformed side who still see the

---

52. Konrad Raiser, *Ökumene im Übergang. Paradigmenwechsel in der ökumenischen Bewegung* (Munich: Chr. Kaiser, 1989). Bishop Laszlo Tökés of Nagyvárad-Romania and some other churchmen from what used to be called Eastern Europe criticized the WCC for its lack of insight into their situations.

53. In the course of his visit in Hungary, he participated in an ecumenical worship at the Debrecen Reformed Cathedral, and in August 1991 laid a wreath at the monument of the galley-slave ministers who were victims of the Counter-Reformation. As for reactionary tendencies, cf. Adalbert Krims, *Karol Wojtyla, Papst und Politiker* (Cologne: Pahl-Rugenstein Verlag, 1986).

54. It was under Pius XII that biblical Roman Catholic scholars were given permission to base their studies on the original text.

55. The Roman Catholic Church is participating in the work of the commission as a full member. The moderator of the Apostolic Faith Steering Group and vice president of the commission is Jean-Marie Tillard, O.P. Cf. *Confessing One Faith*, Faith and Order Paper no. 153 (Geneva: WCC, 1991).

pope as the Antichrist and regard the Mass with the later inserted words of the eightieth answer of the Heidelberg Catechism: ". . . Mass is fundamentally a complete denial of the once for all sacrifice and passion of Jesus Christ and as such an idolatry to be condemned."[56] Certain groups in the Reformed church tend to speak about the Reformation as if a new church had then been founded. This is contradictory to the work of the Reformers as well as to the name ECCLESIA REFORMATA, which implies that the church founded by Christ is to be reformed.

2.4.2. The other group of problems is the great number of splits within the Reformed family, with more than one Reformed denomination within a country, due to doctrinal or political issues.[57] There are groups within one organized church which are not willing to accept a positive relationship with one another because of differing views of doctrines that are important yet, in relation to the fundamental Christian doctrines of the Trinity, Christology, and pneumatology, of secondary significance.

2.4.3. I want to mention one sore point in the life of the Reformed churches. This is the rift that exists between "fundamentalists" and "liberals," or "charismatics" and other groups. I am aware that the terms used are inaccurate, which makes things even worse. I also appreciate the concern for the Holy Scriptures as well as the desire to make the gospel understood and relevant for today's generations. It is also of great importance that the church should strengthen its charismatic structure. Yet these camps are far apart. Here again a trinitarian Christology must be the foundation and the guiding principle which could bring these camps together in the spirit of 1 John 3:3.

2.4.4. The other tendency of our days is the growing proliferation of sects, split-away groups from denominations, syncretistic or openly non-Christian religious groups all over the world. Instead of being astonished, we have to be aware of the consequences of the end of the Constantinian era. Today state authorities do not execute decisions of church assemblies, as has happened in the past. The decisions of Nicaea were carried through by the might of the empire. Arians, and later Nestorians and Monophysites, were pushed out of the empire by the power of the state. Today that would be neither possible nor desirable. The Roman Church at Vatican II gave up the claim for oppressing people who have different ideas.[58] We have to live together with these,

---

56. The distinguished Hungarian Reformed theologian István Török, professor emeritus of Debrecen, has recently proposed the abolition of this answer.

57. For instance, the question of Arminianism, Willem Frederik Dankbaar, "Arminianer," in *RGG*, 1:620ff., and the split of the Presbyterian Church in the USA at the time of the Civil War.

58. Cf. *Lumen Gentium* III/34.

in our view, false religions and ideas, just as the apostolic church had to live in the Roman Empire with all religions of the Hellenistic world. We, too, have to wield the only authentic weapons of God's armory (Eph. 6:10-20). So we have to struggle for the visible signs of the one holy catholic church, which would not be a highly centralized organization. It would mean, however, the mutual recognition of churches and ministries and the ability of celebrating full worship together and to establish conciliar fellowship. These are the goals set by the World Council of Churches.[59]

2.5.1. It is a very important element of the worship of the church that the royal priesthood of all believers performs the twofold ministry of representation: it adores the Lord on behalf of the whole creation, offering "spiritual sacrifices" (1 Pet. 2:5); and by proclaiming the wonderful deeds of the Lord (2:9), the congregation is present in creation on behalf of the Lord. That means that the ministry of Christ and his people concerns not only the church, but the whole universe. Christ's saving and mediating activity has cosmic significance (Col. 1:14-20). The realization of the catholicity of the church makes us responsible toward the life of the cosmos, including people and environment, both in prayers of intercession and action in life. For the person and function of the theologian it also means to be in Christ, leading a Christian life, to be a member of this community, and so to exercise the critical function of self-examination and reflection. Without personal involvement on the side of the theologian, this function cannot be undertaken authentically.

2.5.2. The future vitality and relevance of Reformed theology depend on the measure of vitality of the church itself, in which the Word and Spirit of God will bring forth people who commit themselves to praise God in doing theology. The life of the congregation needs academic work. The two must grow together. We need much prayer, much work, and much dedication. The most important contribution toward ecumenical discussion and praxis will occur if we go on reforming ourselves, if the worship will be by the power of the Holy Spirit, which is the worship and praise of the one holy catholic church, in which congregational life and academic work mutually challenge and help one another for more dedication and for more effective witness, in a world facing manifold crises in these days. A theology that is rooted in the life of the local and universal church can be a means of edification for the church, in order to be a sign of God's saving purpose for the whole of humankind.

59. *Nairobi to Vancouver, 1975-1983* (Geneva: WCC, 1983), pp. 77ff.

CHAPTER 3

Reformed Theology in East and West

Nobuo Watanabe

Reformed theology has shaped typical Western thought within the Christian world. Compared to Roman Catholicism, a Western-type Christianity, and the Eastern-type Christianity of the Orthodox Church, Protestantism, which includes Lutheranism and radical Protestantism, is distinctly Western. However, if one compares Lutheran and Reformed theologies, Lutheran theology has preserved Eastern and medieval features and opposed the Western humanism of the sixteenth century, whereas Reformed theology has been characterized more strikingly by Western thought since its inception.

Reformed theology originated in the West and developed together with Western thought. Due to its prominence in the days of Western superiority, Reformed Christianity led the Christian world and was represented outside it. Now that the framework of the world is changing and recognition of the diversity of cultural values beyond a single Western ideal is growing, the superiority of Western Christianity can be reexamined. Accordingly, Reformed theology, too, must be reexamined. This we will do in the following reflections.

I. Learned Ministry

A. In Reformed churches the education of candidates for the ministry has always been regarded as extremely important. This distinguishes Reformed churches from others. Since 1559, when Calvin founded the Geneva Academy, the first model of a theological seminary in the Christian world, theological education in the Reformed churches has been kept at a high intellectual level.

Seminary students study essentials, amongst which is counted the ability to read Scripture in its original languages.

Medieval theological education was not systematized. Priests were usually promoted from the lower ranks and finally installed through the sacrament of ordination according to the principle of *ex opere operato*. The sacrament of ordination was believed to have an objective effect. No education, examination, or public inquiry of the candidate was necessary as preparation for ministry. Most priests were uneducated. Calvin's views on these practices were that "the practice of having an examination of learning has become too old-fashioned"[1] and "it is the same sort of concoction when they are led to the altar for ordination, and someone asks three times, in a language they cannot understand, whether they are worthy of that honor."[2] At universities theology was taught after a four-year course in liberal arts, but this was not education for church ministry.[3] Only a small number of priests were university graduates. The Roman Catholic Church issued its first decree about theological seminaries in 1563 at the twenty-third session of the Tridentine Council.[4] This was four years after the opening of the Geneva Academy.

During the Reformation in Swiss and southern German cities, which originated in Zwingli's Zürich, public lectures in biblical exegesis were offered to ministers, candidates, and citizens who wanted to study the Bible.[5] Although this was the prototypical theological faculty at a university in that city, it was not an institutionalized theological seminary. In Strasbourg the Collegium Praedicatorum was founded in 1534.[6] It was a seminary of sorts, but it also was not yet an institutionalized school.

B. Theological education in Geneva and the Reformed cities in the empire was deeply influenced by the pedagogical thought of sixteenth-century humanism. The theological curriculum, prescribed in the 1561 ordinance for

1. John Calvin, *Institutes of the Christian Religion,* ed. Ford L. Battles and John T. McNeill (Philadelphia: Westminster, 1960), 4.5.1.

2. Calvin, *Institutes* 4.5.5.

3. Hastings Rashdall, *The Universities of Europe in the Middle Ages,* vol. 1 (Oxford: Clarendon Press, 1895), pp. 471ff.

4. "Tridentinum, Session 14: Decretum de reformatione," in *Quellen zur Geschichte des Papsttums und des römische Katholizismus,* ed. Carl Mirbt and Kurt Aland, 6th ed. (Tübingen: J. C. B. Mohr, 1967), p. 634.

5. Cf. Gottfried W. Locher, *Die Zwinglische Reformation im Rahmen der europäischen Kirchengeschichte* (Göttingen: Vandenhoeck & Ruprecht, 1979), pp. 161ff.; Francois Wendel, *L'Église de Strasbourg. sa constitution et son organisation 1532-1535* (Paris: Presses Universitaires de France, 1942), p. 221; Kurt Guggisberg, *Bernische Kirchengeschichte* (Bern: Haupt, 1958), pp. 166ff.

6. Wendel, p. 121.

Geneva schools, shows the textbooks for every course. Theology was studied only after students had done the classics of Greek and Latin literature.[7] At the same time we have to discern that such study, apart from its humanistic ideas, was aimed at fostering in preachers a real understanding of Holy Scripture, the sole foundation of faith, and an aptitude for the true exposition of biblical texts. This relates to the exegetical character of Reformed theology, which we will discuss in another section.

C. In many contemporary churches ministers of the church have different educational backgrounds. Some are highly educated, while others have less training. We see this often, especially in the younger churches in developing countries. Ministers are ranked variously, based mainly on their academic backgrounds. In Reformed churches, however, hierarchical distinctions and other discrimination have no place. The equality of ministers is considered to be essential.[8] In order to maintain such equality, a high level of theological education is required, without exception. The fathers of the Reformed church cautioned against episcopalianism because it runs the risk of denying the rule of the Lord over his church and of replacing it with human rule.

D. It may seem like a weakness in Reformed churches that training candidates for ministry takes such a long time. Sometimes it leads to difficulties in finding gifted ministers for the worldwide mission of the church. Moreover, there is a real danger of theology falling into intellectualism and over-sophistication, thereby losing the vividness of the Christian faith. In fact, in some cases Reformed churches do not appeal to other people at all. In the light of these problems, it should be one task of the Reformed churches to reexamine repeatedly the education in its seminaries.

E. Among people with cultural traditions other than European, Reformed churches usually require a high level of education for the ministry. One has to acknowledge that in non-European countries Protestantism played an important role in social modernization and the development of individual self-awareness. Christian workers in these countries not only proselytized heathen peoples but also taught them a new way of living and thinking. In some cases the flaws in European styles of theological education were brought directly into the new culture. Often students experienced frustration because they lost their cultural identity between two worlds. They understood the conventional articles of the Christian faith and easily imitated a foreign lifestyle, but they could not create new learning. Therefore, they could not become first-class intellectuals among their compatriots. However, were they to study their

7. John Calvin, *Opera Selecta*, ed. P. Barth and W. Niesel, vol. 2 (Munich: Chr. Kaiser, 1926-62), pp. 373ff.

8. Calvin, *Institutes* 4.4.4.

own classical ways of learning where it corresponded with classical biblical teaching, they could make an impression on their own people. They might then be able to become indigenous intellectuals. For instance, amongst the intellectuals of Far Eastern nations there were traditional ways of learning the classical Chinese literature. Christian leaders had to study the classical literature of those countries in order to translate the Bible into the languages of the people with good style and to communicate the Christian message in elegant speech.

F. The humanism of sixteenth-century Europe combined — and confronted — biblical teaching with classical Greek and Latin teaching which differed essentially from biblical traditions. The teaching of biblical literature and that of classical literature began a tense dialogue with each other. Likewise, in countries where the Christian message was brought by Western missionaries, Christian teaching was confronted with the indigenous classical literatures. Inevitably, intellectual conflicts between different traditions were necessary in order to plant Christianity in a new soil. In countries where such intellectual conflicts were absent, Christianization was to be nothing but colonization by Western culture.

II. Exegesis and Theology

A. One of the characteristics of Reformed theology is its dependence on the faithful exegesis of the Bible. Systematic theology in the Reformed church is not so systematic as to be independent of biblical exegesis. By exegesis of biblical texts we do not mean placing particular emphasis on single words, though we should not neglect keen insights into words, but reading the meaning of every word in the context of the history of God's speaking to humanity, especially to the people of God. In other theological systems, theology develops logically from a basic theme or a so-called central dogma. In Lutheran theology, for instance, the whole system centers on the doctrine of justification by faith and grows from this principle. Many people still think the central dogma of Reformed theology is the doctrine of predestination. Since eternal predestination by God seems to precede everything, predestination has been treated before other items of systematic theology from the time of Théodore de Bèze onward.[9]

But this understanding is mistaken. Reformed theology does not assume the construction of a system by piling up theological concepts based on logical

9. Théodore de Bèze, *Summa totius Christianismi, sive descriptio et distributio causarum salutis electorum et exitii reproborum ex sacris literis collecta* (1555).

necessity. Rather, Reformed theology adheres closely and adapts to the biblical text. Of course, the Reformed church has produced a well-ordered systematic theology. Yet this system is not developed deductively from a single principle the way it is done in scholastic theology. It is not even deduced from a biblical principle. The system is arranged for the purpose of catechetical teaching (we will discuss that in the next section), although the system itself is not what is to be taught. The content of true theology is a clear hearing, understanding, and proclaiming of the biblical message through exegesis. Systematic teaching must support that.

Systematic theology is not to be understood as being developed from a single epistemological source, a principle from the Bible. More exactly, theology concerns God's self-communication to humanity when God's word is spoken and humans hear it and respond. Furthermore, the task of systematic theology is not to explain epistemologically the relation between the source of divine knowledge and established doctrinal articles.

B. The exegetical character of theology defines not only the method of investigation and treatment of the church's doctrine but also theology's self-restriction to the revealed and written word of God. A theologian need not inquire into matters concerning God which have not been revealed. All that needs to be known has been revealed, and the revelation is complete in Jesus Christ, although some things still remain sealed. This seal will be broken only by the coming Christ. What has been revealed is sufficient for our salvation. What God has spoken to humanity in the person of the Son is enough and is decisive.

Reformed theology has restricted itself exclusively to the spoken and the written word, defined since 1559 as the canon of Holy Scripture.[10] This does not mean, however, that the theologian is concerned only with the letters of and material from the Bible. Though theology cannot go beyond the written word of God, it is still able to form a worldwide perspective from a standpoint given by the word of God. Since God is the creator, ruler, and redeemer of everything, those busying themselves with the word of God should be able to understand everything. Theology, moreover, does not see things merely in their present shape. It can also imagine them as consummated and renewed at Christ's second coming.

C. Every doctrinal article is restricted to the content of Holy Scripture. It cannot be a speculative product or the result of logical necessity. The doctrinal

---

10. In Article 3 of the "French Confession," the list of canonical books appears for the first time. The draft, supposedly by the hand of Calvin, did not include it. Cf. Calvin, *Opera Selecta* 2:310f. The early Reformers distinguished the canonical books from the deuterocanonical ones, but did not exclude the latter.

article is, so to speak, a fruit of the biblical text and context. This fruit is produced by exegetical inquiry, which is more a matter of obedient listening than of exact conceptualization. Meanwhile the articles have to be tested continually through exegesis. About the relation between Holy Scripture and doctrine, Calvin says that "Holy Scripture contains a perfect doctrine." People, however, who do not have much practice in reading Scripture, need some guidance and direction, lest they get lost.[11] That is why it is necessary to summarize the whole doctrine of Holy Scripture in doctrinal articles or *summae doctrinae.* Such summaries can then serve as maps to guide those who do not know the terrain.

Believers are fed by the word of God. This happens in public preaching and worship, in private pastoral guidance, in family Bible lessons, and in individual Bible study. Of these, preaching is the most important. Reformed preaching is not simply the rhetorical amplification of theological or edifying themes, but the exegetical proclamation of the message of Holy Scripture. Preachers must constantly do exegesis, not only of the text for the next sermon but of the whole Bible in order to perform their duty. Ministers who were not taught that this is their duty or who were not trained to be diligent would find this too difficult to do.

D. Reformed sermons have not always been exegetical, though during the Reformation era they almost always were. The Reformers preached series of exegetical sermons on one book at a time, whereby the biblical word was proclaimed and heard in the context of Scripture. After the advent of commentaries, sermons were arranged according to the catechisms and consisted of exegetical preaching on those texts used as references in the catechisms. Several generations later, in some churches people and preachers became fond of topical sermons. Though doctrines were sometimes the topics of such sermons, the sermons could degenerate into mere encouragement with many illustrations for religious life.

In a next stage, where churches lacked high standards for sermons, preaching became little more than the public expression of opinions to which titles such as "Shall the Fundamentalists Win?" could be given.[12] Hardly any trace of the exegetical preaching of the Reformation era remains in such speeches. Biblical exegesis itself degenerated in the course of modern history. In linguistic and historical investigations, many exegetes overlooked the message of the texts they were studying. Today, recovering the impact of biblical exegesis of the Reformation times is an urgent task of Reformed theology.

11. Calvin, *Institutes,* Argument of the French Edition, *Opera Selecta* 3:7.
12. This is the title of a sermon delivered at the First Presbyterian Church in New York by H. E. Fosdick on 22 May 1922.

E. Many readers of Calvin's *Institutes* think of Calvin as an outstanding systematic theologian and expect his lectures on theology to be equally systematic. In fact, however, his lectures on theology at the Geneva Academy were not systematic at all, but rather the exposition of texts from Holy Scripture. The Order of the schools of Geneva of 1561 stated that "two professors of theology explain the books of the Holy Scripture on Monday, Tuesday, and Wednesday, from the second to the third hour after dinner, each as his weekly duty."[13] For Calvin, who taught theology through the exposition of Holy Scripture, the substance of theology was listening to the word of God, spoken through the written word and mediated to its audience by the Spirit. Theology's listening should be directed by the text and should not extend beyond it. A theology that does not prize hearing above speaking risks affirming only itself. Therefore, hearing must be considered more important than speaking.

F. The ministry entrusted to the preacher is not literal but spiritual. As 2 Corinthians 3:6 says, "The letter kills, but the Spirit gives life" (NRSV). Vivification is a function reserved for the Spirit, not a function of the instrument. Therefore, exegesis is an exposition not of the literal, but of the spiritual, meaning of texts, although exegesis studies the exact letters of texts. This means that exegetes must make themselves instruments of the Spirit. That is why prayer for the Spirit is emphasized as so important in the Reformed church. According to Reformed theology, the Holy Spirit makes us participants in Jesus Christ, sharing all his blessings.[14] In the Spirit the Lord makes himself present to us. Exegetical preaching is not intellectual lecturing, but the application of God's word to all. It is not just an explanation of God's word or only an encouragement to believe. The preacher, as instrument of word and Spirit, performs his or her task in the presence of Christ the Lord.

G. In countries where biblical narratives are less well known, biblical exegesis and its application to relevant situations are not easy. People experience the Bible stories as quite as strange as Greek or Egyptian myths. Those countries usually have their own classical traditions, and often the educated annotate the ancient books as codes of national ethics. Consequently, biblical exegesis is confronted with such traditions. When the Western material civilization still seemed to be superior, those who sought material prosperity took an interest in the Bible as the spiritual basis of Western civilization. But once the non-European countries successfully developed their own material civilizations, many lost interest in the Bible. We see this in present-day Japan, for example. Nations whose self-confidence increased with rising nationalism now regard the Bible as equal or even inferior to their own classics.

13. Calvin, *Opera Selecta* 2:373.
14. Calvin, *Institutes* 3.1.1.

In imperial Japan, for instance, some theologians attempted to read the Bible, especially the Old Testament, alongside classic Japanese myths about the ancestors of Tenno, the emperor. This attempt disappeared promptly after the breakdown of the empire. Even while the imperial oppression of the Christian church lasted, most Japanese Christians were quite doubtful of this theory. Already then it seemed to be a flattery of nationalism and the dictatorial Tenno system, although there was no public criticism from Christians. In present-day Asia similar attempts are made to fix Christian religion in Asian minds by using traditional myths. This could make the approach to Christianity more familiar, but such Christianity, if one can still call it that, has no impact upon people's minds and morality. This kind of Christianity might be understandable, but it does not lead to the birth of any newly created humanity.

The power to make any impact lies in Scripture itself. It is Scripture that will exhibit this power to the people who read and hear it. Yet, as the eunuch said, "How can I [understand], unless someone guides me?" (Acts 8:31 NRSV). Merely offering the Bible profits little, since Holy Scripture has to be preached. Therefore, exposition of biblical passages is needed. It is in such a situation that biblical exegesis, as Calvin did it in sixteenth-century Europe, becomes relevant.

III. The Office of Teaching

A. Almost all mission churches in newly evangelized countries made much of Christian education. They founded many mission schools as a means of evangelizing people ignorant of Western ways of thinking and living. Christian schools were needed to establish the newly converted and their families through education.

Reformers emphasized general education. Luther advised a ruler to found public schools where the catechism was to be taught along with other subjects, although it would not be a church school. Meanwhile, in Reformed cities schools were built and controlled by the church and the church order. Among the four offices regulated by the Geneva Church Order of 1541 and 1561, the office of "doctor," which had its original meaning of teacher, comes second, thus reflecting its comparative importance.[15] Churches related in various ways to school education, though. Some Reformed church orders, such as

---

15. Geneva Church Order (1561), 43-47 (according to the numbering in *Bekenntnisschriften und Kirchenordnungen der nach Gottes Wort reformierten Kirche*, ed. Wilhelm Niesel [Munich: Kaiser Verlag, 1938]).

that of Johannes à Lasco, did not have the office of teacher.[16] The task of the doctor (teacher) was to maintain the church doctrine and to educate young people, especially candidates for the ministry.[17] This ministry was not in charge of teaching church theology only, but was also in charge of the general education of the next generation of the city community. It is not quite clear how the office of teaching in the church was related to education in the city. Yet, on the whole, we see in Reformed churches a distinctive educational character that compared the church to a school.

Reformed churches were not always linked to the educated classes. Although the church was, in several countries, restricted to educated people, in many countries Reformed churches embraced different classes. Sometimes Christian missions had to start among the lower or lowest people because the leading classes adhered to their traditional concepts.

B. In the Reformed tradition the church is likened to a school. The metaphor of the church as mother has been commonly accepted since ancient times. In the Reformed church this mother has to be one who teaches her children who live in this world.[18] This does not mean that the church teaches only doctrine. Yet, teaching the knowledge of God and of salvation is an essential task of the church. The church must give its members a comprehensive and enduring education in living. The church's task is not merely to teach doctrine, but to teach its members how to live as a redeemed people. Such teaching is not covered in the catechisms, but must include some practical training in a life of service and piety. We will deal with the diaconate of the church separately, yet we mention it briefly here in the context of education. The knowledge which must be taught is knowledge that aims at serving God and one's neighbor. Although knowledge can be used to rule over others, true knowledge is attained in serving others.

C. We noticed that the way in which Reformed theology is constructed serves teaching. In the footsteps of Calvin, who led the way, Reformed theology has pursued the proper order in which to teach doctrine. Calvin sometimes discussed the order of teaching which would reflect a distinctively Reformed ordering of doctrinal items.[19] So, for example, Calvin first discusses regenera-

---

16. "Kirchenordnung 1550, Chapter 1: Von den Dienern der christlichen Kirchen," in *Die evangelischen Kirchenordnungen des sechszehnten Jahrhunderts,* ed. Aemilius L. Richter, vol. 2 (Weimar: Landes-Industriecomptoirs, 1846), p. 99.

17. Calvin, *Institutes* 4.3.4.

18. Calvin, *Institutes* 4.1.1: ". . . guided by her motherly care until they mature and at last reach the goal of faith."

19. Calvin, *Institutes* 1.1.3: "Yet however the knowledge of God and of ourselves may be mutually connected, the order of right teaching requires that we discuss the former first, then proceed afterward to treat the latter"; 1.6.1: "I am not yet speaking of the proper doc-

tion[20] and then justification.[21] If the teaching on justification were to precede teaching on sanctification, though it would be easy to develop the teaching on justification by faith, the teaching on sanctification would fade against the brilliant emphasis on justification by faith. Luther's saying, "Sin boldly and believe Christ more boldly," expressed a profound and ironical truth about justification, but it did not explain a life that corresponded with justification.

D. Protestant overseas missions brought a new self-consciousness to the non-European world, where there were no concepts for "person" or "individual," the result of the concept of the equality of all people before God. This new consciousness produced a revolution in societies which had been ruled by convention and superstition. The Western consciousness of the self was nurtured first by the late medieval Renaissance and then affirmed by the Reformation. Modern people discovered their individual selves as different from others and separate from the masses. However, until they found themselves before God, they could not settle their own identities. Renaissance humanity aspired to freedom from all bonds and could only be awed by unlimited human abilities. Yet, when standing before the face of God, it had to be uneasy, because it found itself to be miserable and sinful before a righteous God. Ease would only come when it was informed about a God who accepts and forgives humanity when it recognizes and confesses its sin.

The principle of justification by faith still remains the key to modernity. Outside of God no human freedom is possible. Humanity cannot assert its freedom without having God as creator and redeemer to support it against losing itself and being carried away by the power of the world. Thus the freedom of humans is founded on the principle of justification by faith. Luther showed the way to such freedom and was followed by Reformed theology. From there it developed, in Western society, into social freedom. However, there are few cases that testify to Christian freedom in new mission fields during the early days. Many converts, bearing witness to the truth they believed, were killed without apology. A rare case is the resistance offered by some pastors and elders of the Presbyterian Church in Korea to the forced worship of Shinto

---

trine of faith whereby they had been illumined unto the hope of eternal life. For, that they might pass from death to life, it was necessary to recognize God not only as Creator but also as Redeemer, for undoubtedly they arrived at both from the Word. First in order came that kind of knowledge by which one is permitted to grasp who that God is who founded and governs the universe. Then that other inner knowledge was added, which alone quickens dead souls, whereby God is known not only as the Founder of the universe and the sole Author and Ruler of all that is made, but also in the person of the Mediator as the Redeemer."

20. Calvin, *Institutes* 3.3.

21. Calvin, *Institutes* 3.11ff.

shrines which enshrined the ancestors of the Japanese emperor during the Second World War.

In the process of modernizing society and rationality in the non-Christian world, the most difficult step to achieve is the consciousness of resistance to tyranny. The reasons for its being so difficult are: (1) Authority tends to make itself absolute, without being tempered by the fear of God. (2) People tend to accept tyranny easily. They do this because they do not fear God and, therefore, obey any formidable power unconditionally. (3) A concept of law which subordinates even those who execute power is absent. (4) Christianity is quantitatively and qualitatively weak and lacks persuasion in countries of the non-Christian world. (5) In modern times Christianity has concentrated on the salvation of souls and has forgotten how to live an integrated Christian life, dedicated to the Lord who redeemed humanity. These last two points need to be discussed further.

E. In countries where freedom of religion is not guaranteed, Christian churches and schools have to avoid friction with the government. Once friction is caused, all the activities of churches and schools could be prohibited. It is understandable, then, that churches and schools seek compromises with state powers in order to save their efforts. Very often, unfortunately, they compromise too much and lose the substance of their Christian faith and life.

Foreign missionaries who were sent to countries ruled by nationalist authorities had to avoid conflict with state powers, lest they be rejected by the government or even by indigenous church members with nationalist tendencies. Missionaries therefore kept silent about national and governmental crimes. As a result, the Christians of such countries were left ignorant of national crimes which were openly criticized by the rest of the world and lost solidarity with Christian believers worldwide.

In the sixteenth century, during the persecution of Reformed believers in the Netherlands and France, for instance, the church beyond the national borders assisted the church under the cross. The Reformed church established autonomous national churches in every country, but these churches cooperated with one another across borders. The church knew that the territory of church activity was bigger than the domain of any one nation. We will deal with the issue of the relationship between church and state later.

IV. Church *Diakonia*

A. Throughout the history of Christianity, works of charity have been well known and well attested. The early church established an office for taking care of poor widows, as we see in Acts 6. Churches in other regions gathered and sent alms to Jerusalem during a famine, as we see in Romans 15:26, 1 Corinthians 16:1, 2 Corinthians 8:1, 9:1, etc. During the Middle Ages charity was entrusted mainly to the monasteries. The church acknowledged the work of love as important, but ministries for the poor, the sick, orphans, widows, and the handicapped were not the primary task of the church as an institute of salvation or as holder of the keys of the kingdom. In the Roman Catholic system the diaconate fit into the hierarchy on a lower plane than the priesthood, and the deacon's office was lost in the ecclesial system. The church did not have a variety of ministries, but different categories of a single power, the so-called *magisterium. Ministerium,* the Latin equivalent of the Greek *diakonia,* disappeared from the church hierarchy until the Reformation returned it to the church. In many churches diaconal work was regarded as important, but it was secondary to saving souls. The spiritual and eternal beatitude preceded material and temporal welfare. Generally speaking, *diakonia* was regarded merely as an expression of gratitude in response to love received. In terms of salvation diaconal work counted only as human merit.

B. During the Reformation the church rediscovered the *diakonia* of the church as participation in the ministry of Jesus Christ, who came into the world "not to be served but to serve" (Matt. 20:28 NRSV; Mark 10:45 NRSV). Therefore, the Reformed church instituted the ministry of deacons, mainly as *diakonia* for the needy, although there were two kinds of deacons.[22] In the time since the Geneva Church Order of 1541, four church ministries have been instituted; namely, that of pastor, doctor, elder, and deacon. According to Calvin, the deacon would administer the property of the church in order to help the destitute.[23] The whole church was to give alms, while the deacons were responsible for handing them out. Geneva received very many refugees, fleeing from their own countries where they were persecuted for their faith. The diaconate made their reception possible.[24]

C. *Diakonia* decayed in Reformed churches after the Reformation. In the popular conception of the Presbyterian and Reformed churches, the position of deacon is subordinate and auxiliary to that of elder. So also, in the Reformed tradition *diakonia* was forgotten. In the nineteenth century the diaconate was recovered in the Lutheran church in Germany, but no attention was paid to the

---

22. *Procuratour* and *hopitalier* in the Geneva Church Order.

23. Calvin, *Institutes* 4.3.9.

24. Much research has been done on the Geneva diaconate, for example, Elsie A. McKee, *John Calvin on the Diaconate and Liturgical Almsgiving* (Geneva: Droz, 1984); William C. Innes, *Social Concern in Calvin's Geneva* (Allison Park, Pa.: Pickwick, 1983); and Jeannine E. Olson, *Calvin and Social Welfare, Deacons and the Bourse francaise* (Selinsgrove, Pa.: Susquehanna University Press; London: Associated University Presses, 1989).

Reformed diaconate.[25] One does not know exactly why the diaconate declined in Reformed churches, but one can guess at several causes for it. That the church became self-directed and that the decline of the diaconate reflected Reformed churches' loss of identity cannot be denied.

In Christianized countries welfarism has a Christian basis, even nowadays, but in modernized and non-Christian countries social welfare is controlled by the government. It is no longer care for the needy, but a matter of control over people. Even so, in such countries the church has often transferred its welfare facilities to the government along with its personnel. This creates the problem of the Christian diaconate being subordinated to the ruling powers, so that, in some cases, it can serve governments but not the needy.

V. A Well-Ordered Church

A. The church has to be in good order, because God is a God of order and peace (1 Cor. 14:33). Compared to Lutheran ecclesiology, which counts two marks of the church, namely, the preaching of the gospel and the serving of the sacraments, Reformed theology lists church discipline as a third mark.[26] Church discipline does not mean the control over church members by executives, but is enforced by elders to the glory of the church's Lord and aims at creating an ordered congregation and the final salvation of every member. The ruling elders are elected, called, and installed in their office by Jesus Christ, the Lord of the church, with the approval of the congregation, the people of God, and with due election procedure. The ruling elders' ministry is performed through the collegial council of elders and pastors. In the paternalistic societies of the past, elders were aged men. Though their age made them elders of their families, in the church of Christ natural age or career was not important. Elders of the church had to be appointed because of their calling to the ministry. This calling was accompanied by a promise of the spiritual gifts necessary for the ministry.

B. Christ himself founds, builds, reforms, and consummates the church. He rules his church by the word and the Spirit. Often when upper-class males become church elders, church governments show similarities to conservative governments and seem to be attempts at preserving old social orders. One does

---

25. Cf. Johann H. Wichern, "Diakonen, Diakonissenhaus," in *Realencyklopädie für protestantische Theologie und Kirche*, ed. Johann J. Herzog, 2nd ed., vol. 3 (Leipzig: Hinrichs, 1896-1913).

26. Augsburg Confession, Article 7; Calvin mentioned the third mark only briefly (*Institutes* 4.1.7); the Scots Confession, Article 18, added it as mark of the true church.

not always have to oppose these cases, but one must be careful, lest one confuse the rule of Christ with worldly rule. In Christ's kingdom those who rule are those who serve (Mark 10:43-44; Luke 22:26). Ruling elders must be the servants among church members. Such a serving attitude is not merely humility, but is the fruit of the Spirit.

People from countries outside the West often perceived Western Christianity as behaving with arrogance and self-justification. This might have been due to some misunderstanding, but Western Christianity certainly lacked a searching after true lawfulness, even though Reformed theologians sought a true understanding of the law. They did not neglect the meaning of the law in preference to the gospel, but established the proper usage of the law for newly born people.[27] Accordingly, they made much of the order and constitution of the church. Yet, a continued inquiry into the meaning of the law was absent in the history of the Reformed church.

C. In Reformed churches the presbyterial-synodal system, along with a constitution, was created to avoid false ruling and to ratify true ruling amongst the people of God. This system is reasonable and comparable to the democratic parliamentary systems of modern government. One actually recognizes in this form of church government the model for the civil government in Western countries. Every assembly or council of the church is legitimated by Christ's calling and gathering. Christ promises to be present wherever people gather in his name: "Where two or three are gathered in my name, I am there among them" (Matt. 18:20 NRSV). This passage is the basis for understanding the real presence of Christ in the church's worship,[28] and also legitimates councils: "Since Christ promised that he would be present not in all councils whatsoever but laid down a special mark by which a true and lawful one might be distinguished from the rest, it behooves us never to neglect this distinction."[29] Therefore, every council and synod must be worship of God by God's people. The will of God should emerge in church councils. Hence, delegates must listen to the word of Christ during sessions, through discussion of the word of God.

D. The church can be compared to an organic body. It is not a stiff system but a vital body. We must be careful in using this simile, however, for the church as body is treated by Scripture above all as the body of Christ, whose head is Christ (Eph. 1:22-23; Col. 1:18). We cannot then treat the church as a body without including the lordship of Christ. As a body consists of many members, so the church consists of many and various members with diverse

27. Calvin, *Institutes* 2.7.12.
28. Calvin, *Institutes* 4.1.9.
29. Calvin, *Institutes* 4.9.2.

gifts. Diversity is not all, however. There is also unity in a shared obedience to Christ. The church order is neither a totalitarian dictatorship nor the mere liberal affirmation of variety. Just like a human body has a nervous system, the church has a nervous system. It is the ability of the church to rule and serve for which the session of elders forms the nervous center, as it were. The session is in charge of information and communication. The ruling elders do not rule by power, but must give out information so that church members can find their own missions and judge for themselves what they should do for Christ. A well-ordered church is a church of well-informed members.

VI. Church and State

A. In the early days the Reformed church did not know of any separation between church and state. Soon, however, experiences of discord with the government led the church to a perception of the opposition of church and state. For instance, in 1538 the government of Geneva expelled the ministers of the church who did not obey the regulation forbidding them to preach.

Even after these experiences, Reformed churches who opposed the radical Reformation mostly continued to bond with governments in diverse ways. Different kinds of relationships between church and state existed: (1) One kind of relationship was installed by the National Covenants of Scotland. Aiming at "the full and perfect union of church and state they enter in a covenant and league to realize the confession of faith and reject all the attempts of Antichrist from the state."[30] If the king did not act accordingly, the church, the Covenanters in Scotland, had to offer resistance. (2) Another type of relationship allowed no covenant or any other relations between church and state. The general intention of the church, however, permitted and supported resistance to corrupt authority. The *Monarchomachi* of French Protestantism was such an example.[31] (3) Church and state could also be linked. Then doctrinal assertions became weakened for the sake of religious latitude for people, as happened among the Erastians. Since the time that Bèze raised objections to Thomas Erastus, mainstream Reformed theology has opposed Erastianism. (4) Church and state were sometimes separated completely, as in the First

---

30. From the "Act ordaining, by Ecclesiastical Authority, the Subscription to the Confession of Faith and Covenant, with the Assembly's Declaration" by the Assembly at Edinburgh, 30 August 1639, Session 23 (*The Subordinate Standards and Other Authoritative Documents of the Free Church of Scotland* [Edinburgh, 1933], p. 265).

31. Cf. N. Watanabe, "Calvin's Concept of the Right of Resistance — from the Viewpoint of Asia," in *Calvin, Erbe und Auftrag*, Festschrift für Wilhelm Neuser zu seinem 65. Geburtstag, ed. Willem van 't Spijker (Kampen: Kok Pharos, 1991), pp. 117ff.

Amendment of the U.S. Constitution and in the Japanese Constitution of 1946, Article 20,[32] where it took a stricter form.

Though the essential differences between the two regiments had long been clear, and one can refer to texts such as "We must obey God rather than any human authority," the answer Peter and John gave the Sanhedrin (Acts 5:29 NRSV; cf. 4:19), and Jesus Christ saying "My kingdom is not from this world" (John 18:36 NRSV), it took a longer time for the separation of church and state to become fixed.

B. The mainstream of the Reformed church has moved toward the separation of church and state, because church and state have their own distinctive tasks. This separation results from the church's realization of its identity and the state's consciousness of its autonomy from religious foundations, as during the French Revolution. Besides the separation of church and state, Reformed Christianity is characterized by a notion of the right to offer resistance. Lutheranism introduced the concept of rightful resistance, but after the Magdeburg Confession of 1550 this theory was not developed further in Lutheranism.[33] In France Calvinism took up the idea. When Théodore de Bèze, the successor of Calvin, published his tract on the right to resist under the title *De iure Magistratum,* the first French version of 1574 stated that it was published first in Magdeburg in 1550.[34] As its content was dangerous, the book was published anonymously and its place of origin was camouflaged.

C. The younger churches in the non-Western world did not inherit the Reformed self-consciousness in the face of political powers. In the non-Christian world political powers can easily claim absolute powers, ignoring God's sovereignty. Whereas in the Christian world and especially in the Reformed church people insist on the right to resist, in the non-Christian world people do not know such a fundamental right. In many countries where absolute rule is failing, Christians are remarkably active and the political contribution of Christians is noteworthy. Reformed churches will always have to pursue the right form and relation of church and society, even when the principles of reform are not absolutely clear.

32. The Japanese constitution was fundamentally revised after Japan's defeat in WWII. It is now characterized by Article 9, which rejects war, and Article 20, which regulates the separation of government and religion. This article is necessary, because in the old regime the Tenno is both the high priest of Shintoism and the sovereign ruler.

33. John W. Allen, *A History of Political Thought in the Sixteenth Century* (London: Methuen, 1941), pp. 104ff.

34. *Du droit des Magistrats sur leurs subiets. Traité très-nécessaire en ce temps, pour advertir de leur devoir, tant les Magistrats que les Subiets: publié par ceux de Magdebourg l'an MDL: et maintenant reveu et augmenté de plusieurs raisons et exemples . . . 1574,* ed. Klaus Sturm (Neukirchen-Vluyn: Neukirchener Verlag, 1965), p. 10.

VII. International Church Activity

A. During the Reformation, Reformed churches established national churches in every country. Every church had its own nationality and was self-governing, with its own confession and church order. There was no international code. The Reformed church still has no international confession of faith nor one authorized collection of confessions similar to the Lutheran *Book of Concord.* Against the Rome-centered international church it was not difficult to find justification for defining churches nationally. Reformed theologians cautioned against a concentration of power in a universal church, though they definitely believed in the unity of the church. External uniformity was unnecessary. They sought to realize the unity and catholicity of the church amongst diverse nations in a different way, because they understood the unity of autonomous churches in terms of a federal system.

B. Churches located separately, in many countries, understood themselves as one universal church. As happened in Geneva, Christians of other lands received refugees from persecution who were of the Reformed faith. The church under the cross was helped by churches from other countries, as, in 1571, the Emden church helped the churches of the Netherlands who could not hold a synod in their own territory. The synod of Dort (1618-19) gathered delegates from other countries with delegates from the Netherlands. *The Second Book of Discipline* of the Church of Scotland provided for a fourth assembly "of all and divers nations."[35] So, Reformed theologians in the West kept contact across borders.

C. Yet, if one assesses the international activity of Reformed churches, it seems as though they act internationally only within the West and with Westernized societies. Though Reformed Christians have not neglected the non-Western world or abandoned efforts to understand non-Western minds, it has been difficult for them to understand the non-Western world. This is partially caused by the strictly Western paradigm of Reformed thinking. Even when Western Reformed Christians make an effort in good will, they fail to understand the minds of people from different backgrounds. Probably other Christians could understand the East and the South better than a Western Reformed Christian could, although their understanding of God's word might often be inaccurate.

If Reformed theology were to change its way of thinking, understanding other thought would become easier. However, that could include the risk of losing theological thinking. We therefore have to search for a new way of doing

---

35. *The Second Book of Discipline, 1578,* VII, 2, ed. James Kirk (Edinburgh: Saint Andrew Press, 1980), p. 195.

Reformed theology which would preserve theological properties and make a broad outlook attainable. One suggestion would be for Reformed theologians, who persist with the essentials of Reformed theology, to cross over the barriers between West and East and between North and South. Though there is no objection to Reformed theology's being a theology of the word, the understanding of word has been bound too closely to Western words.

D. In countries outside the West, Christians are not only minorities but also strangers. Since their citizenship is in heaven, they do not belong to their nations. In their native countries they are foreign pilgrims sojourning amongst a majority that belongs. The church is, properly speaking, a *paroikia,* a dwelling place in a strange land. The concept of a national church has weakened the meaning of sojourning. This weakened meaning has been introduced in mission fields, where Christians easily become good citizens of their nations but certify their identity as citizens of heaven only with difficulty.

VIII. Created Nature and Creative Grace

A. With reference to the previous section, we now treat the problem of the natural environment. Historically speaking, the environment was damaged mainly by Western developed countries as the result of industrialization. The industrialized countries of the West are, roughly speaking, Protestant. We must concede the partial responsibility of Reformed theology for the situation. It is like the pattern we see with the colonization by Western countries, which they began without any pangs of conscience. The West, however, became aware of the danger of environmental pollution earlier on and began to take countermeasures so that, in their own industrialized countries, protection of the environment against pollution has advanced further than in other countries. Environmental movements reflect the spiritual backgrounds of Western society.

In comparison, one finds in other countries, such as Japan, very different attitudes, arising from different spiritual backgrounds. In Japan the civil movement against environmental pollution is mainly driven by the claims of those who suffered from it along with those who support them. Although many who are not directly affected also participate in the environmental movement at present, reactions to environmental damage generally come late and slowly. One can thus perceive a different spirit encountering the environment. This encounter concerns the doctrine of creation and, therefore, also Reformed theology.

B. In our times environmental pollution in developing countries is a graver problem than in developed countries. Pollution has met with no strong reactions from citizens, because poverty is a more acute problem than pollution for them. That does not mean, however, that people in developing countries are not eager to prevent environmental pollution. We must accept the fact that pollution in developing countries increases because polluting factories from developed countries are moved to developing countries. Here original sin shows itself. Reformed theology in the sixteenth century treated original sin with an earnestness that should be recovered today. We must point out the sin in ourselves and in humanity more critically with reference to war and pollution.

C. The critics of Reformed theology point out its weak doctrine of nature. We agree that Reformed theology prefers to deal with the relationship between God and humanity, rather than with the relationship between God and nature. For a word-based theology, humanity, created and alienated, its regeneration, consummation, and task, are prior to nature. Yet the work of preserving the natural environment of humankind is the task of a newly created humanity in Jesus Christ.

CHAPTER 4

Christian Theology:
Toward an Asian Reconstruction

Choan-Seng Song

F or Christianity this is a time of soberness and excitement: soberness because it has realized, belatedly, that the religious map of the world has to
be redrawn, and excitement because the new religious map contains real surprises and new possibilities. For the Christian church this is a season of distress
and adjustment: distress because the vision of "evangelizing the world in this
generation" (J. R. Mott) is not fulfilled, and adjustment because its centuries-
old life and worldviews have become obsolete and new ones have to be constructed. As to Christians as a whole, this is an age of expanding our ecumenical horizon that reveals to us God's ways with the nations and peoples with
which we have not reckoned in our faith and theology before. It has become
increasingly evident to thinking Christians that the future of Christianity cannot be separated from the future of other religions, that the welfare of the
Christian church is closely bound with the welfare of the human community,
and that Christians and their neighbors are fellow pilgrims on earth in search
of the meaning of life and the fulfillment of it.

Such a time calls for a self-understanding of the church that is different from the past. Is this not why the Reformation proved to be a revolutionary event in the history of Christianity? A season such as this challenges
Christians to reflect critically on the faith they have inherited from their
forebears. Is this not what the Reformers in the sixteenth century set out to
do? And the era in which we find ourselves demands that Christian theologians be engaged in reshaping and reconstructing Christian theology that is
open to what God is doing in the world, not of yesterday but of today. Is

this not the way *Reformed* theologians should go about their theological task?

Some Christian theologians in Asia, particularly some of us from the Reformed tradition, have taken upon ourselves the arduous task of doing Christian theology in that vast part of the world that is historically and culturally shaped by religions other than Christianity. We find ourselves questioning the ways in which traditional theology has gone about its business for centuries. We are compelled to listen to the voices from the world we share with our fellow Asians. We discover that critical interactions between the message of our Bible and the world of our Asia can deepen our experience of God's saving activity in the human community as well as in the Christian community.

These "theological" experiences of ours are bound to bring about some fundamental changes in the way we do Christian theology, understand the nature and task of the Christian church, and practice our Christian faith in the world around us. We have embarked on a theological course that, though still not clearly charted, promises surprises and fresh insights. What follows is an effort to show how the course of Christian theology is taking place in Asia.

The Marketplace Called the "Circle"

There used to be, on the East Gate Road in T'ai-nan, an old capital city in the south of the island nation of Taiwan, a busy marketplace called the "Circle." The Circle disappeared many years ago, the victim of irresponsible city planning, and has been replaced by hazardous motorways. It used to be a popular market about fifty meters in diameter. It was cluttered with small stalls selling all sorts of food and drink, both hot and cold. There were also shops that sold inexpensive clothes and household goods. It was a noisy place — shop owners soliciting customers at the top of their voices, customers bargaining with shop owners over the price of a broom or a piece of cloth, friends and neighbors greeting one another, engaging one another in loud conversation. There were dogs and cats, too, frightened when chased away by shop owners and customers, barking and mewing when fighting over crumbs of food fallen to the ground. Smells of all sorts emanated from food cooking on the stoves and subsequently served on the tables, from spices liberally used to enhance the aroma of the food, and of course from human beings. Noise and smell together filled the air of the marketplace, defined the atmosphere of the Circle, and created the human community assembled chiefly because of the need for food to delight the palate and nourish the body. It was the place people resorted to, day or night. Particularly, it was a great place at night. People looked forward to it after the day's work was over. There they would enjoy the delicacies not available at home, meet, chat, and exchange gossip with friends and neighbors.

Cities in Asia are rich in marketplaces such as the Circle. It is a "people's marketplace" in every sense of the word. Men, women, and children from all walks of life, young and old, rich and poor, are to be found there. Nothing could stop them from returning to it day after day, night after night, not even the perpetual tropical heat in the case of that island state Singapore. In fact, Singapore has one of the most fabulous night markets in Asia, where people can eat and shop to their heart's content, never minding temperature and humidity. And, of course, Hong Kong is full of them. These markets serve not only the need of the local people but also of travelers from near and far. Once their business is over and shopping done, the adventure they look forward to is a visit to a people's marketplace to taste the local food, glimpse the local customs, and smell the smell of local humanity. And it is the place where the hosts will be proud to take their foreign guests for an evening of "exposure" to the indigenous culture.

Very few Christians, even very pious ones, will have any qualms about taking their visitors there for a brief immersion in the "exotic" ways of life. Why? Surely they know that the world of the people's marketplace has little in common with the world they enjoy in their Christian church and among Christians. Surely their "Christian" sensibility will frown at some of the carryings-on there. But which world is more real: the world of the Christian church or the world of the people's marketplace? In which world would Jesus feel more at home? And in which world would he find more friends and neighbors? If the world of the people's marketplace is a real world, is it not where the faith, the vision, and the dream they have inherited in the Christian church are put to the test? And is it not where they should rethink their faith, redream their dream, and reenvision their vision? The people's marketplace, that world outside the Christian church — is it not the place where Christian theology has to be done all over again? Culinary attractions aside, what make up those marketplaces are people — women, men, and children. A young mother with a sucking baby on her back, a toddler with unsure steps walking close beside her and her husband sauntering nonchalantly and empty-handedly behind her — what is occupying her mind: salvation in heaven or a more understanding husband willing to share her daily cares and burden? A man with the wear and tear of old age all over him from head to toe — what is going through his mind as he casts his glance here and there, trying in vain to recapture in those young beaming faces and jovial voices his own youth long gone? What about an old woman, her face full of wrinkles and her back stooped, knowing that her days of toil and labor are gone — what is utmost in her heart: gratitude for relief from the burden of life, or pain and anxiety that she still has to face for the remainder of her life?

These men, women, and children who frequented the Circle in T'ai-nan, Taiwan, those people who congregate at night markets in cities of Asia such as Singapore and Hong Kong — do they have something in common with the women, men, and children the Hebrew Scripture talks about? Are they preoccupied with concerns similar to those of the people among whom Jesus lived? And these human beings long before us, people in our Bible — are they related to us Christians today in any way? We cannot but answer yes to all these questions. There are of course countless people who have passed across the stage of the world, people with whom we share life on this planet earth, and people who will follow after we have long passed the scene — do they have anything to do with us Christians? Yes, they do in every way. And if they have to do with us, do they also have to do with God? Of course they do. We cannot speak for God, even we Christians, although we are ever so ready to speak for God! But suppose for a moment we can speak for God. Would God be just as concerned about these other people as God is about us Christians, people who are far greater in number than we can imagine? If God be God, God must be concerned about them as much as, if not more than, us Christians.

It follows, then, that God must have been addressing them, just as God has been addressing us Christians. How has God been addressing them? There is no immediate answer. But if God has been addressing them, they must have been responding to God in some way. How have they been responding to God? We cannot but be curious. It makes us ponder who God is, the God who not only addresses us Christians but also people of all sorts. It also prompts us to take a second look at the people who appear to be no less, and sometimes more, devoted and religious than we Christians are. How are we to understand them? How are we to be related to them, not only socially but religiously? And some of us may be tempted to think that they may also have a message for us, a message about life and the world, a message about God, a message about love and hope, a message about the life to come.

People around us are real people. They are women, men, and children with whom we Christians have daily contacts and do business. They are persons with names and faces, hopes and fears. They, like us, are inhabitants of this "global village" with whom we Christians share a common life and history. We eat with them. We work with them. We converse with them and laugh with them. At times we even sigh with them and weep with them. We quarrel with them. From time to time we also stand with them, side by side, bonding together in the struggle for freedom, democracy, and human rights. More and more we find ourselves fellow passengers with them on a bus heading for a destiny not marked on our road map. It is a journey to a great unknown; whether we know it or not, we are bound for a common destination.

According to the Bible?

But there is one thing most of us Christians do not do with our fellow travelers on earth: we do not worship God with them. It is our belief that our God is different from their God. But is it the same God? It is our conviction that the truth of God is revealed to us only. But is it also revealed to others? We do not compromise on the faith that salvation is for those who believe as we do. But suppose there is also salvation for those who do not believe as we do. Suppose that what we believe as salvation is mistakenly conceived, or at least not exactly what Jesus conceived.

This last hypothesis is the most critical. It hits the nail on the head, so to speak. We speak in the name of God; but is it the God of Jesus? We invoke the name of God; but is it the name of the God of Jesus? We pray to our God; but is it to the God of Jesus that we pray? We pronounce blessing on those who believe as we do and judgment on those who do not, by the authority of God; but is that divine authority the authority by which Jesus spoke and taught? We believe God is always on our side and not on the side of others; but is it not possible that the God of Jesus may sometimes be on the side of others rather than on our side?

Most of us Christians do not always think in this way, nor do we raise such questions often. Here is a typical case from India:

> Once a Gandhian leader came to Kohima and we had fellowship with him. As I was sitting by him, he started conversing with me about religious matters: "There are some extreme Christians who say that man can be saved through Christ only and there is no other way. What is your view?" "It is what I believe," I replied. "There are millions and millions of people in other major religions of the world. What will be their fate?," he hastily asked. "According to the Bible those who do not believe in Christ will perish," I replied. He angrily departed. My conviction is that whether we like it or not we cannot compromise the truth.[1]

The story reminds me of a meeting I had with the faculty of the Buddhist Institute in Ho Chi Minh City, Vietnam, in November 1992. We talked about many things, from the role Buddhism played during the Vietnam War to the translation of Buddhist texts from Pali and Sanskrit into Vietnamese to social and political changes in Vietnam. Inevitably we touched on the relationship between Christianity and Buddhism. Quietly and without showing emotions, the head of the institute, a venerable monk more than eighty years old, asked:

---

1. From the monthly *Letter on Evangelism* (August 1992). Quoted by Wesley Ariarajah in *The Bible and People of Other Faiths* (Maryknoll, N.Y.: Orbis, 1985), p. 29.

"Why are Christians so aggressive in their effort to convert Buddhists to Christian faith?" He was in fact making a remark rather than asking a question. How could I respond to him? Quietly but with pain in my heart I replied: "Some Christians are aggressive, but not all Christians are."

The Gandhian leader in the story quoted above must have thought the Christians who received him were a friendly sort. After all, they offered him fellowship. They struck him as open-minded and kindhearted Christians. Still, he did not let down his guard. He struck up a conversation with the Christian who later told the story, and said to the latter: "There are some extreme Christians who say man can be saved through Christ only and there is no other way." He must have said it cautiously. The tone of his voice seemed tentative. He was not seeking a confrontation, a debate, a controversy. Like that venerable monk in Ho Chi Minh City, he was just making an observation. He qualified his remark by saying "some extreme Christians." There are "extreme" believers in each and every religion, believers who refuse to see any good in what other people believe. This Gandhian leader would perhaps be the first to admit that there are "extreme Hindus" in Hinduism. There are of course "extreme Muslims." That is why the feuds and conflicts between Hindus and Muslims in that subcontinent of Asia have often been bloody. But not all Hindus are extreme, just some of them. Nor are all Muslims extreme, also just some of them. It must be the same with Christianity. "There are some extreme Christians," he said, "who say that man can be saved through Christ only and there is no other way."

Some Christians do believe that — most of us, in fact. This often is the cause of Christian intolerance toward people of other faiths and religions. "What is your view?" The Gandhian leader was curious to know where his Christian conversation partner stood on this matter. Perhaps he was looking for an explanation from the latter, an illumination even. Surely there is a lot to explain. For many Christians this is the heart of their faith. They owe an explanation to others whose "salvation" they hold in their hands. But the Christian in this conversation did not seem to see it that way. "It is what I believe," he declared. He seized the occasion to state his conviction, to reaffirm his faith, to "evangelize" the Gandhian leader. The conversation took a different turn. His "missionary" conscience was aroused. He forgot he was one of the hosts at the welcoming party for the Gandhian leader. It did not seem to matter to him even if the party had to end in hostility. This is what happened.

The reply of the Christian did not seem to surprise the Gandhian leader. He must have heard it said more than once. This is how most Christians talked to the men and women outside the church. But is such a view tenable? Is such conviction realistic? Is such faith reasonable? The Gandhian leader wanted to know. "There are millions and millions of people," he said, "in other major religions of the world." He could have been more precise by citing some statistics. According to a 1982 source, "there are 1.4 billion Christians, 724 million Muslims, 583 million Hindus, 278 million Buddhists."[2] If Confucianists, Shintoists, and those who practice ancestor rites, primal religions, and shamanism are counted, then more than two-thirds of the world's population is not Christian. What is going to be their fate? asked the Gandhian leader.

This is not an insignificant question. It is the kind of question that can be described with a Chinese phrase, *yu chung sin ch'ang*, meaning "one's words are serious and one's heart is heavy." It may be your fate to suffer in this life, but you long for a change of fate in the life to come. This is the most elementary desire of most Asians, Buddhists or Confucianists, Hindus or Muslims, even Christians. If there is salvation only for those who believe in Christ, as "extreme Christians" affirm, and salvation for them means eternal life in God, then what will be the fate of the great majority of the people of Asia, or more than two-thirds of the human race? The Gandhian leader wants to know. This is not just a matter of curiosity. Nor is the question raised to rebut the Christian. It is a reasonable question. He must have been genuinely concerned, if not alarmed.

His concern should be addressed. His anxiety must be assuaged. Is it not only right that his question be discussed charitably and with sensitivity? But the Christian in the conversation seemed only interested in getting to the point. "According to the Bible," he declared, "those who do not believe in Christ will perish." This is an ultimatum, a declaration of *fait accompli*, a pronouncement of a verdict. The case is closed. The decision is final. No further discussion is needed. No appeal to a higher authority is permitted. There the matter stands, not only on earth but in heaven. The Gandhian leader must have first been shocked, then furious. He "angrily departed." Who would not in that situation? At least he did the right thing to avoid further confrontation.

"According to the Bible," says the Christian. But which part of the Bible? Whose interpretation of that part of the Bible? Is it "quoted out of context" (*tuan chang chu yi* in Chinese) or not? The fact of the matter is that the Bible is almost always quoted and interpreted out of context by those who insist that there is no salvation outside Christ, meaning outside Christianity. Christians who make such an assertion do not stop to think whether there are other passages in the *same* Bible that speak quite differently. "According to the Bible" is too general a phrase to have any meaning. It is very irresponsible too. How can one be so general and irresponsible when it has to do with serious matters such as salvation and eternal life? Who is this God of theirs who would condemn

2. David Barrett, ed., *The World Christian Encyclopedia* (Nairobi: Oxford University Press, 1982), p. 6.

"those who do not believe in Christ" — billions and billions of them if those before the time of Jesus are also counted — to perish forever? Is that God the God of Jesus? Or are we here dealing with a God who has little to do with the God of Jesus?

But the Christian in the story asked no such questions. Seeing the Gandhian leader leave in anger, he was neither embarrassed nor sobered. He did not show any sense of remorse. On the contrary, he was convinced that he did the right thing. "My conviction," he said, "is that whether we like it or not we cannot compromise the truth." Yes, one should not compromise the truth. But whose truth? God's own truth? The truth Jesus proclaimed? Or the truth of a particular Christian church? The truth of a particular Christian denomination? The truth held by a particular group of Christians? That Christian's own understanding of the truth?

What we see in this Christian is "one who speaks and acts with confidence with the knowledge that one is in the right" (*li chi ch'i chuang*, again to use a Chinese expression). But who told him he was in the right? A particular tradition of Christianity told him so. A particular church to which he belongs taught him so. But what if that tradition, that church, were not entirely in the right? What if Jesus himself would find it offensive? What if God could not agree with it?

A Good Tone for Christians?

Such rigid faith and uncompromising attitude apart, it is clear to more and more Christians and theologians both in the East and in the West that Buddhists, Taoists, and Muslims are here to stay for a long time, to practice their faiths not only in the lands of their birth but also in the Western society in which they have come to live in pursuit of political freedom and personal fortune. Just as Christians are, they are very much members of the human community in the universe created, according to Christian faith, by the God of Abraham, Isaac, Jacob, and Jesus Christ. Some Christians and theologians, open to the world of cultural and religious pluralism, fascinated by it and eager to experiment with alternative ways of practicing their faith, are willing to go a second mile, a third mile, even any number of miles, with their newfound friends and neighbors of other faiths. The world of gods many and lords many, instead of offending their Christian sensibility and repelling their Christian orthodoxy, invites them to experiment with different forms of worship and meditation.

Here is a typical example of a Jesuit priest who directed a meditation center at the Roman Catholic Mercy Center in Burlingame, California, near San Francisco in the United States. He tells us that his "main area of study has been Mahayana Buddhism, especially Zen." He has "also seriously investigated

Vajrayana Buddhism and classical Taoism (Lao Tzu and Chuang Tzu)." This multireligious experience and background of his informs and shapes what he tries to do at his center. In his own words:

> Beginning with the external and bodily, the main place of most of our meditation here at Mercy Center is the Rose Room (so called because the unfolding rose is the symbol of enlightenment in the West just as the lotus is in the East). On the walls are Japanese shikihi (fine paper squares) with Zen sayings in the Sino-Japanese ideographs, two Taoist paintings and a picture of the Miroku Bosatsu (Maitreya Bodhisattva) from Koryuji, Kyoto. These are well received by people and set a good tone to the room. However, the main shrine or centerpiece has, of course, the cross as central. It is hoped that before too long this cross will give way to a statue of Christ seated in meditation, a statue which will include clear influence from Buddhist statuary in its simplicity and feeling.[3]

In this Christian meditation center Buddhist images and symbols provide a setting, an atmosphere. They are said to create "a good tone" for Christians who come to worship and meditate.

The cross, the main Christian symbol, is central, we are told. What we are not told is how those Christians who come to the center meditate on the cross while surrounded by Buddhist images and symbols. How do the cross and the lotus, the principal religious symbols of Christianity and Buddhism respectively, interact with each other in the theology of the Mercy meditation center? Do they inform each other? But *what* do they inform each other of? Do they enrich each other? But *how* do they enrich one the other? Or are they critical of each other? *What* is it, then, that the cross criticizes of the lotus, and the lotus of the cross? Do they find something lacking each in the other? *What* is it that each may find lacking in the other? The cross and the lotus — each represents a vast world of religious culture and a deep universe of spiritual quest for the meaning and purpose of life. A long history is behind each of them. How many hopes are raised and frustrated in each's name! And how much blood has been shed and how many lives have perished all for the sake of them! For the religious mind capable of going deeply into something beyond the sense perception, these symbols — the cross and the lotus — must be telling painful stories as well as edifying ones, crying out in despair as well as in hope.[4] Does not this

---

3. Thomas G. Hand, S.J., "Enlightenment through Zen," in *Spirituality in Interfaith Dialogue*, ed. Toshi Arai and Wesley Ariarajah (Geneva: WCC, 1989), pp. 49-53, here p. 50.

4. For a theological interaction between the cross and the lotus, cf. "Contrast between the Cross and the Lotus," in my *Third Eye Theology*, rev. ed. (Maryknoll, N.Y.: Orbis, 1990), pp. 127-28.

mean that no religious image or symbol is to be just decorative, although all religions, including Christianity, tend to reduce it to being nothing more than a decoration?

We must ask further. In the religious consciousness of the people at worship and meditation, how is the cross perceived in the midst of Buddhist images and symbols? Does the cross appear less startling and painful because of "the unfolding rose," which "is the symbol of enlightenment in the West just as the lotus is in the East"? But if this is true, does not the cross become less than the cross, less than what it was to Jesus, who died a painful death on it? There is in the meditation center also "a picture of the Miroku Bosatsu (Maitreya Bodhisattva)." How do worshipers understand the evident contrast between the Maitreya Bodhisattva with his all-peaceful and compassionate complexion and the haggard Jesus of the crucifix with his contorted body undergoing death spasms? Are they not failing in both directions — failing to come to grips with the pain as well as the compassion the Bodhisattva has toward all sentient beings in the world of suffering on the one hand and, on the other, failing to perceive God's saving love contained in the suffering of Jesus dying on the cross?

In this apparently well-meaning and even innocent effort toward the meeting of the East in the West at this Christian center of meditation, no fundamental theological questions such as these seem to be raised. Perhaps the center is conscious of being inclusive rather than exclusive — a fashionable trend at a time such as ours when religious pluralism has suddenly burst upon us. But if this is all that images and symbols of other religions do for Christians, it is a misuse, even abuse, of them. Uprooted from their Buddhist settings and transplanted to an "exotic" Christian setting, they cease to be what they must be — expressions of struggles of the human spirit for liberation in different social and historical situations. And in this particular case, they are removed from the Asian humanity that has suffered centuries of sufferings and hardships from nature and at human hands. They become disconnected with the women, men, and children of Asia today who continue to seek the meaning and purpose of life in poverty or in affluence. They have lost the history of the people of Asia and their spiritual journey that make those religious images and symbols what they are. They are no longer part of the culture they have helped to create and shape.

"I Have No Image of Christ in My Heart"

Religious faith must be a matter of commitment to the divine on the one hand and, on the other, a matter of human creativity inspired by that commitment. Each and every religious image and symbol comes into being out of the commitment and creativity of the believer and the believing community. No genuine religious image or symbol is conceived as a mere decoration and designed as an ornament. It is not a means that provides "a good tone" for liturgical and meditative purposes. But within Christianity this is what has been done to the cross, that supreme symbol of Jesus' suffering and death. The shining cross on the rooftop of a church building, the glittering cross on the wall of the chancel of a church, or the gold cross of a necklace takes the sting out of the cross and renders it innocuous. It may be the cross of the Christian church, but surely it is not the cross *of Jesus*. It cannot address the deeply troubled souls and hearts of people in fear and confusion.

Some Christian artists in Asia seem to know better. They are attracted by the awesome power of images and symbols that abound in religions of Asia. They know that "Asia remains the heart of the world's great religions. Hinduism, Islam, Buddhism, Shintoism and numerous smaller religions had their beginning on Asian soil and still exert a powerful influence on society. To be a Christian artist in such a setting means coming to terms with the art forms and images of other religions. Artists in Asia struggle with questions which are not even contemplated by Western artists."[5] They set out to explore forms and images of other religions, seeking to express the message of the Christian gospel in ways very different from what is expected of them as *Christian* artists. In the person of Asian Christian artists, the two universes of religious forms and images have come to play one with the other.

Forms and images. But what about the meanings these forms and images of other religions stand for — not just apparent meanings but meanings deeply embedded in the long traditions of those religions and hidden in the hearts of the believers? Looking at artworks of Asian Christian artists, I sometimes wonder whether some of them have reproduced outward forms and images of other religions at the expense of the inner meanings symbolized by these forms and images. It is relatively easy to replace the forms and images of traditional Christian art with those of Asian religions. But my impression is that it is a lot more difficult to create out of the deep and critical encounter of different universes of religious meanings something that is indisputably Asian and yet distinctly Christian. Is this not what those artists who strive to be creative and original have to take into serious account? Asian Christian art has just arrived at the threshold of creative and original Christian artistic expressions. These artists have much homework to do — seeking to penetrate that holy of holies of the human spiritual universe shaping believers' lives, history,

5. Masao Takenaka and Ron O'Grady, *The Bible through Asian Eyes* (Auckland, New Zealand: Pace Publishing in association with the Asian Christian Art Association, 1991), p. 8.

and culture, the universe not visible to the naked eye and not perceptible to the mind not capable of fathoming the complexity of the human heart and spirit.

External forms of a religious devotion may be adapted, but the internal meanings of that devotion may elude the grasp of an artist. This happens to some Asian Christian artists eager to build a bridge between the world of Christianity and the world of other religions. But there are artists outside the Christian church who seem to be aware of this by instinct and experience. Here is a story told by a Dutch missionary about his encounter with a Japanese master wood-carver during his early years in Japan:

> In the east of Japan's northern island of Hokkaido between high mountains and immense primeval forests, lies the Lake Akan. Many fine Ainu[6] and Japanese woodcarvers live and work in the small village of Akan bordering the lake. A few of us missionaries went there in the summer of 1969, hoping to do some evangelism among the woodcarvers and their families. But they were obviously too busy for us so we decided to volunteer ourselves as helpers in their shops. I swept floors, carried boxes to the post office, and so forth in the shop of a Japanese woodcarver, a master craftsman, Mr. Tadao Nishiyama. I was impressed by his work and after some time asked him to carve me a head of Christ. He answered, Yes, I will, but asked me a month later, Do you have a picture of him? Finally, after another month or two he handed me a chisel and said, You carve the head of Christ; I have no image of him in my heart.[7]

A strange and yet a revealing story! It has a lot to tell us, not only Christian artists but Christian theologians, intent on crossing the boundaries separating Christianity and other religions.

Why was Mr. Tadao Nishiyama, master craftsman that he was, not able to carve the head of Christ? He was not a Christian, but why did he agree to do it in the first place? He must have thought it was an easy thing to do — carving out a head of Jesus on a piece of wood. But it did not take him long to realize that he was engaged in a religious project. In the month that followed, his mind must have been very much preoccupied with it. He must have even made a few attempts at it, but was not able to come up with a head of Christ. What was the problem? Why did it turn out to be so difficult? He must have had at least a vague idea of what Jesus looked like to Christians in Japan.

---

6. The Ainus are the white Mongoloid race who were the original inhabitants of Japan. They live isolated on Hokkaido and a few islands in northern Japan.

7. The story is told by Rudy Kuyten. See his "To Be Chosen. . . . In the Shadow of God," in *Image* (Kyoto: Asian Christian Art Association) no. 49 (December 1991): 2.

If his problem was that his idea of Jesus was unreliable, he would ask for a picture of him from the missionary who had requested him to do a head of Christ. This is what he did. Having the picture of Jesus, he thought he could go ahead with his work. But another month had gone, and he was still without a head of Christ. All that time he must have stared at the picture, studied it from various angles, developed ways to execute his project. Finally, he must have mobilized all his artistic sensibility and creative imagination to produce a head of Christ. But still he came back to the missionary empty-handed, saying: "I have no image of [Christ] in my heart."

He said it all in one short sentence. "I have no image of him in my heart." This was not an excuse. Nor was it an explanation. It was a confession. Being a master craftsman devoted to his art, he must have known art is not just a matter of form but a matter of the spirit, not solely a projection of what is in his brain but an embodiment of what is in his heart. For him it was not a problem of forming an image of Christ in his head and transcribing it onto a piece of wood. But since he was not a Christian, he could not image Christ in his heart, however hard he might have tried. Even the picture of Jesus was of little help to him. He was too good an artist to reproduce something that came from another religious world. It would be sacrilegious even to imitate it. He was too honest a believer in the spiritual power of creative arts to carve an image not formed in his heart. And his was too sensitive a heart not to grapple with what Christ might mean to him. In the end the deep meaning of Christ eluded him. He could not grasp it. Without a spiritual communion between him as an artist and Christ, the subject of Christian faith and devotion, he could not carve a head of Christ. He had to hand a chisel to the Christian missionary and say to him: "You carve the head of Christ; I have no image of him in my heart."

Christian Theology in the Midst of Religions

This story of a Japanese wood-carver tells us, Christian artists and theologians in Asia, that we cannot trifle with images and symbols of religions, be they of Christianity, Buddhism, Hinduism, or primal religions. They evoke in us deep respect and awe. They also remind us of the mystery enshrined in them. They let us perceive sparks of light from the depths of human being, and they make us apprehensive about the darkness concealed by those sparks of light. They demonstrate human capacity to transcend the limits of life on the one hand, and, on the other, they remind us of the transitoriness of human existence within the confinement of space and time. They are indicative of human being at its most ecstatic, but also of human being at its most vulnerable.

Religious images and symbols both reveal and conceal truths about human beings in relation to God and the world. You cannot enter the world of religious images and symbols assuming that they will make themselves transparent before your very eyes. The fact of the matter is that they conceal from outside intruders much more than they care to reveal to them. For us Christians in Asia who are awakened to the religious reality of our part of the world, this presents us with an enormous dilemma. How are we to confess Christian faith not as Christians estranged from our own land and people but as part of them? How are we to envision Jesus, God, the Spirit, the church and its task and mission in a society shaped by religious cultures other than that of Christianity? What role, if any, could the historical, social, political, cultural, and religious experiences of our fellow Asians play in our doing of Christian theology? In short, how are we, Christians in Asia, to tell stories of our faith in the world of cultures, religions, and histories which, though unrelated to Christianity in origin and development, cannot be separated from who we are and what we are?

To be aware of this theological dilemma is very much a part of doing Christian theology in Asia. There is no easy way out of it. The dilemma becomes unbearable when you realize that doing Christian theology is an act of confessing Christian faith, an engagement with the life outside the church as well as inside it, and interactions with the people of God not only in the Christian community but in the wider human community as well. And doing Christian theology is a communion with God, who is creator of heaven and earth, lord of the history of nations and peoples, who holds the ultimate meaning of life and the ultimate purpose of the entire creation. The theological dilemma that concerns us cannot be resolved. But it compels us to raise the horizon of our faith beyond ourselves as Christians, to expand our theological frontiers, and to engage ourselves with the life and faith of men, women, and children around us who also have much to tell us about how God has been dealing with them.

Doing Christian theology is, then, the telling of stories of God and humanity known to us Christians as the stories of Jesus' life and mission. The stories we try to tell are *Christian* stories; that is, stories in which Jesus plays a dominant role. These are, first and foremost, Jesus' stories, and then, only then, stories of us Christians. Since they are stories of Jesus in the first place, there is a plenty of room in them for a host of other stories from people of other faiths. Out of the stories of Jesus that contain other stories, we will find ourselves telling Christian stories that are quite different from the stories to which we are used in the church. It is *Christian* stories that we are telling, not stories invented by a sectarian God but stories inspired by Jesus of Nazareth, who has much to tell us about God — the God of Jesus who is quite foreign to the God of the religious leaders of his day and of most Christians, yesterday and today.

71

I cannot, therefore, agree with the statement that "the phrase 'Christian theology,' once one stops to reflect about it, is a contradiction in terms. At the very least, it is un-Christian, in any serious meaning of the word."[8] The view expressed here is puzzling at first, and then misleading. Asian Christians, for example, live in the midst of people of other faiths. They are part of Asian humanity. The awareness of this reality has shaken many of them out of ignorance and arrogance. Not only materially and culturally, but also religiously and spiritually, they have come to realize that they are "soul mates" of their Buddhist, Hindu, or Muslim neighbors. They have no choice but to rethink Christian faith and reformulate their Christian theology in a fundamental way.

But they are not Buddhists. They are not Hindus. Nor are they Muslims. They are Christians. As Christians, their experience and understanding of religions other than Christianity may be very inadequate, inaccurate, and even distorted. They now know that they have much homework to do and have set out on an arduous journey to learn from their neighbors who practice faiths different from theirs. In this way they are trying to fathom the depth, breadth, and height of God's creating and saving activities in the world of Asia. The result is a *Christian* theology with all its limitations and shortcomings, yet a Christian theology deeply involved in the spiritual world of Asia. How can it be anything else when the ways of God with humanity are explored from the perspective of Christian faith?

True, Christians have often insisted that "outside the Church there is and can be no knowledge of God," that faith "occurs in no other form than the Christian."[9] How claims such as these not only fly in the face of facts, but grieve the heart of God! I am quite in sympathy with those Christian theologians who want to take off the theological straitjacket tailor-made according to the specification of traditional theology and put on a more comfortable, one-size-fits-all kind of theological outfit. They strive toward a "universal" theology, a theology that does not carry the trademark of Christianity. It is supposed to be made up of the best and the noblest in human religious endeavors toward the truth of God.

But not all Christians insist that "outside the Church there is and can be no knowledge of God," or that faith "occurs in no other form than the Christian." Surely Jesus himself would not insist on such things. It is not only uncharitable but wrong to insist on them. Such an insistence contradicts what he told us about God and about God's dealings with the world. This, however,

8. The statement is from Wilfred Cantwell Smith, "Theology and the World's Religious History," in *Toward a Universal Theology of Religion,* ed. Leonard Swidler (New York: Orbis, 1967), pp. 51-72, here p. 70.
9. Smith, p. 71.

does not lead to the conclusion that Christian theologians should abstain from Christian theology. The fact of the matter is that Buddhist theologians are engaged in Buddhist theology, Hindu scholars in Hindu theology, Muslim imams in Muslim theology. Why not, then, Christian theologians in Christian theology? Of course, we cannot condone a narrow sectarian kind of Christian theology. Nor, for that matter, can we condone a narrow sectarian Buddhist theology or Muslim theology. But a theological effort, be it Buddhist, Hindu, or Christian, pursued in the spirit of humility and open-mindedness, cannot be narrow and sectarian.

What this age of ours has taught us is that we must, and we can, practice our own faith and reflect about it in the spirit of charity and respect toward people of other faiths, knowing that each and every religion, including our own, carries records that make us both proud and shameful. We are aware, much more deeply now than ever before, that for the survival of our mother earth, mercilessly plundered by us human beings; for the peace of a world torn with division and bigotry; for love and justice to prevail in human community; and for worship of God to be genuinely meaningful, we must learn to be repentant, each of us acknowledging that he or she has fallen short of God's glory. But repentance alone is not enough. We must translate our repentance into action. We must inspire each other, correct each other, and together bear the responsibility of striving toward the world of hope and future.

One thing is certain: the world cannot afford a fanatical faith that treats people of other faiths as enemies to be won over to one's fold or eradicated from the face of the earth. There should be no room either for a sectarian theology, be it Hindu, Muslim, Buddhist, or Christian, a theology that takes its own experience and tradition for nothing less than the very oracles of God. But this does not mean that we must go for a "universal" theology. Theology of whatever brand has to be particular in orientation and specific in context. But if we believe in the God of creation, is it not possible from time to time for people of different faiths to meet that God at the cross sections of our journeys of faith and theology?

The Christian theology that engages us in Asia must have room — yes, plenty of room — for people of different walks of life and of diverse religious traditions and cultural backgrounds. Its stage is the world of Asia — the world blessed with immense human and natural resources and tormented by endless natural disasters and human tragedies. To make sense, as Asian Christians, of this world with all its good and evil, hopes and despairs, joys and anguishes is the main theological task of the Christian church in Asia.

Let us face it. The dream of "Christendom" has, with the demise of Western colonial domination of the Third World, vanished. The Christian church alone cannot deal with the mounting problems that threaten to tear apart the moral texture of human community. As Christians, we have to learn to work together with people of other faiths to be a spiritual force that creates a new vision for humanity. This is a theological experiment fraught with both promises and challenges. Asia, with its diverse cultures and religions, offers a most exciting opportunity for the experiment. Are not Christian theologians from the *Reformed* tradition best equipped to undertake the experiment?

CHAPTER 5

The Challenge to Reformed Theology: A Perspective from Myanmar

Edmund Za Bik

I was walking toward a teahouse near my seminary one day, and I heard people arguing over something with raised voices. As I approached closer and closer to the teahouse, I discovered that the subject of their argument was theology. Those engaged in the argument turned out to be seminary students — some, B.D. students, and others, B.Th. students. Their point of contention was whether theology which keeps on changing is really worth the investment of years of study, especially in view of its tendency to divide people into camps. The students in the teahouse, too, were sharply divided. One of them, picking up an oft-heard phrase, said: "Theology divides, and mission unites," without, it seems, knowing the fact that theology guides mission. In a sense, those not appreciating the value and contribution of theology were right — right because they got confused and did not even know where they were theologically, for example, on the issues of christological debate, eschatological debate (the "realized" versus "not yet realized" debate), and so forth. In another sense they were wrong — wrong because they did not know that theology is never a closed system. As the servant of the Word, theology articulates in the clearest and most coherent human language available how the Word that God spoke through Jesus still speaks and will continue to speak and judge humans, and how it is good news at all times for people of different times, different places, and different situations who have different problems. Unless theology as the servant of the Word is able to read new signs and re-form its articulation of the Word, it becomes fossilized theology and thus loses its ground and purpose.

In this paper I will limit myself to two areas, viz., what is Reformed theology, and what is the future of Reformed theology. In the latter section the strength of a theology that emphasizes pluriformity as its theological approach is stressed.

I. What Is Reformed Theology?

To begin with, it must be said that Reformed theology is that which is primarily rooted in the Reformation of the sixteenth century but branched off in distinction from Lutheranism when attempts to achieve theological and ecclesiastical unity foundered.[1] Reformed theology is also called Calvinism, owing to the towering impact and influence of John Calvin. In fact, terms like "Calvinist" and "Calvinism" were coined in a pejorative manner by the Lutheran opposition during the sixteenth century, while in fact the church groups which accepted the Calvinist confession usually called themselves "Reformed."[2] Calvin took the middle line between Luther and Zwingli in doctrinal matters, an example of which is shown by the three Reformers' positions on the Lord's Supper. Luther viewed the sacrament in the substantial sense of the body of Christ; Zwingli held a commemorative sense; and Calvin maintained a middle-line position in the sense of the spiritual presence of the body of Christ.[3] This open-mindedness and ambivalence on the part of Calvin reflects the spirit of Reformed theology.

Though Calvin considered himself a follower of Luther, his theology bears a stamp different from Luther's, which indicates there were contributions from other sources as well.[4] In spite of the common or central affirmation of the Reformation themes such as "Christ alone" — the once-for-all redemptive work of Christ, through whose incarnation we know God; "by grace alone" — the futility of human reliance on the merits of good works; "by faith alone" — faith and justification as the gift of God, not the achievement of our human efforts; "by Scripture alone" — the unique authority of *the Word of God* as the foundation of theological reflection and the standard by which all our thoughts and actions are to be judged; and "the priesthood of all believers," there were differences which

1. Sinclair B. Ferguson et al., eds., *New Dictionary of Theology* (Downers Grove, Ill.: InterVarsity, 1988), p. 569.
2. Bengt Hagglund, *History of Theology,* trans. Gene J. Lund (St. Louis: Concordia, 1968), p. 267.
3. Hagglund, pp. 264-65.
4. Hagglund, p. 260. Two years after he completed his *Institutes* in 1536, Calvin took residence in Strasbourg from 1538 to 1541, during which time he met Bucer, the Strasbourg reformer who is reported to have had an impact on the later editions (1543, 1559) of the *Institutes.*

ultimately led to the emergence of a so-called Reformed theology. The depth and dimension of the spirit of this theology, which is largely attributed to Calvin, are such that Elton calls it "a revolutionary faith."[5]

The heart of Reformed theology consists of such great motifs as: the trinitarian God — the Creator, Jesus Christ the Son, who through his incarnation revealed the Father and made our redemption possible, and the Holy Spirit, who continues the work of Christ in preserving and re-creating the world; belief in one church and its sacraments of baptism and the Lord's Supper; life after death, which God has promised us through the death and resurrection of Jesus Christ; and Scripture alone as the sole criterion of truth. Out of these recurrent motifs are drawn such principal characteristics of the Reformation theology as the centrality of God, Christocentricity, and theological pluriformity. A brief treatment of each is given below.

A. The Centrality of God

This is the theme that pervades Reformed theology, and it could fairly be called the centerpiece of Calvin's theology. It developed under the compelling demand of God's self-revelation in Christ which is attested by and recorded in the Scripture. The ultimate focus is on the Trinity, with a more immediate focus on Jesus Christ as mediator. For Reformed theology, it means great attempts to bring the whole of reality under the sway of the sovereignty of God. This doctrine is expressed in a number of ways.

1. Our deep-rooted alienation brought about by the fall had rendered us incapable of knowing our true selves and our situation. Authentic human self-knowledge is attainable only in the light of our knowledge of God. But knowing God is impossible for fallen humans because of the barrier erected between God and us humans. It is only possible when we are confronted by the supreme majesty and holiness of God as he makes himself known to us in his Word by the Spirit. Thereby we are enabled to know our sinful wretchedness and the depravity that pervades our entire being.

2. Our salvation is entirely the work of God. Because of our depraved and alienated condition, we stand condemned under God's judgment and are therefore unable to change our status. That is why Reformed theology has consistently testified to the sole and sovereign activity of God in salvation. Its foundation or origin is God's eternal purpose, his sovereign election of his people in Christ before the foundation of the world (Eph. 1:4), a choice made

5. G. R. Elton, *Reformation Europe, 1517-1559* (New York and Cleveland: Meridian Books, 1963), p. 237.

without regard to anything intrinsic in man. The Holy Spirit continues the mission of Christ by drawing us to God. Because we were dead in sin and unwilling to trust Christ, faith is a gift of God.

3. The whole of life — personal as well as corporate — is subjected to the sovereign lordship of God. Reformed theology has, therefore, consistently sought to order the whole of life according to the moral requirements of God as found in the Scripture. That is why Calvin made strong efforts to model civic as well as ecclesiastical life to the rule of God.

B. Christocentricity

This doctrine of "Christ alone" is the logical and consistent follow-up of the centrality of God the sovereign and gracious Father, who revealed himself and his divine scheme of redemption to Israel through the media of prophets and the law, and finally in and through the incarnation of his Son, Jesus Christ. Christ is therefore the sole ground of our knowledge of the benevolent God. Karl Barth, the one modern theological giant of the Reformed tradition, retrieved and restored christocentric trinitarianism back to its original position from what he considered a deviation from its traditional roots it had taken in Reformed theology.

C. Pluriformity

Reformed theology has never been and is not monolithic. Rather, it is open-ended in orientation and is never fixed and final. It has in it creative vitality sufficient to encompass diversity within an overall consensus.[6] To support this claim, it can be pointed out that: (1) Before the Synod of Dort (1618-19), difference existed on the question of limited atonement. Dort worked out a compromise agreement between the powerful British universalizing tendency and the majority's particularizing concern. (2) The development of covenant theology encountered diversity, too. After a long process, starting with Zwingli, this theology was finally formulated in 1669. In spite of its increasing dominance in the seventeenth century, not all were covenant theologians in the sense of commonly using the concept in their theological writings. (3) The covenant of grace was not problem-free either. Such questions as whether grace was a unilateral and unconditional imposition by God or a bilateral pact with conditions to be fulfilled by humans were asked. Most early covenantal

6. Ferguson, p. 570.

theology had to do with just one — i.e., the covenant of grace; it was only at a later time that the idea of the prefall covenant of works emerged. From 1648 a third, pretemporal covenant was proposed. Each position had its adherents. (4) Diversity existed on the question of piety. Puritanism in Old and New England was oriented toward praxis, sanctification, and *pastoralia,* increasingly tending to anthropocentrism. Similar developments took place in the Netherlands and Scotland. This represented a contrast with earlier Reformed theology and with the more scholastically oriented tradition.[7]

In the second section of this paper, under the title "The Future of Reformed Theology," it is my intention to show that in keeping with the spirit of the Reformed tradition, pluriformity is the most viable theological method for preserving and keeping Reformed theology alive and vibrant for the foreseeable future.

II. The Future of Reformed Theology

As the word *"Re*-formed" indicates, Reformed theology is an ongoing and continuous process of theological reflection in obedient service to the Word of God — the Word which is multifaceted in meaning, direction, and purpose. As a theological discipline that reflects on how the Word addresses and judges people of different places and times with different problems and situational contexts, it will not be out of place to say that the main thrust of Reformed theology is to see how God is at work and calls us to participate in his work; and how the Word spoken in and through the Son, Jesus Christ, and recorded in Scripture as the most authoritative revelation of God, which shines like a diamond on a sunny, sandy beach with a variety of colors, has to be deciphered in the context of our changing times and situations. This quite reflects the motto of the Reformed tradition: "The Church reformed, always in need of reform." Jane D. Douglass is right when she says: "Reformed theology is still in the making, still unfinished, and will be till the end of time."[8] There is also wisdom in Daniel Migliore's remark: "preoccupation with a particular theological tradition can of course be more problematic than promising. It could signal a retreat to a romanticized past."[9]

In my opinion, the greatest strength of Reformed theology lies in its

---

7. Ferguson, p. 571.

8. Jane D. Douglass, "What Is 'Reformed Theology'?" *Princeton Seminary Bulletin,* n.s., 11, no. 1 (1990): 8.

9. Daniel L. Migliore, editorial, "Always in Need of Reform," *Princeton Seminary Bulletin,* n.s., 11, no. 1 (1990): 1.

character of pluriformity; that is, its open-mindedness and willingness to let God unveil to us the inexhaustible riches of the meaning of the Word spoken once and for all in and through Jesus Christ and spoken also to us ever anew. Any theological system or tradition that is fixed and final in character and simply rests content with a mechanical repetition of past theological formulations vis-à-vis the multifaceted problems of today's world, is nothing more than moribund theology that is past its usefulness. Even Barth, that towering theological giant of this century, warns vehemently against canonizing his works. In the words of Mackintosh, "he [Barth] offers clear principles, definite assumptions, but never a closed system."[10] What the Reformers did was free theology from the shackles of fixed and one-sided interpretation of the Scripture by the Roman Catholic Church. Understood thus, there is a grain of truth in what G. R. Elton says: "Calvinism became a source of anti-authoritarianism and libertarian thinking. Despite himself, Calvin had founded a revolutionary faith."[11] The open-mindedness and flexibility of Reformed theology is in harmony with Paul's "For now we see in a mirror, dimly, but then we will see face to face. Now I know only in part; then I will know fully" (1 Cor. 13:12 NRSV).

It must be acknowledged, however, that pluriformity as the theological model of the Reformed tradition is not entirely free of problems associated with pluralism and relativism. Diogenes Allen thinks the collapse of the modern mentality (i.e., the Enlightenment's confidence in the power of reason as the epistemological basis for all truth claims) and the accompanying emergence of a plurality of worldviews make many Enlightenment-leaning theologians less confident in their Christian truth claims, thus increasingly finding themselves at the theological crossroads.[12] I think Allen is right when he says these theologians do not know how to avoid relativism.

Relativism ought not to have its negative impact on Christian faith for at least three reasons. Neither do we have to avoid it.

A. Faith in God is above reason because it involves a conscious decision, or an act of will, as Allen puts it.[13] Even in the heyday of the so-called modern mentality, with its obsession with the scientific verification-principle or logical positivism as the epistemological yardstick, faith in God had always held its ground because faith is an act of will. Faith comes before understanding and reason. We do not believe in God because reason has exhausted everything

10. Hugh R. Mackintosh, *Types of Modern Theology*, 9th imp. (London: Nisbet, 1956), p. 264.

11. Elton, p. 237.

12. Diogenes Allen, *Christian Belief in a Postmodern World* (Louisville: Westminster/John Knox, 1989), pp. 134-36.

13. Allen, p. 152.

there is to know about God. Rather, we believe in God because God is God. Though "our various sciences use human sense organs, tools and instruments, words, and socially formed minds to probe the universe,"[14] faith in God lies outside the realm of empirical investigation. Less so after the collapse of modern mentality and its accompanying emergence of relativism.

B. Relativism at most can play a not-too-significant but positive role of being a partner of pluriformity in the search for the light of truths that God is revealing to us through our fresh interpretations of the Scripture in critical relation to the changing contexts and problems of our time. This brings to mind a statement by the Christian Conference of Asia: "Christ has more of his truth to reveal to us as we seek to understand his work among men in their several Asian cultures . . . and their involvement in the contemporary Asian revolution."[15] It is true that faith comes before reason, and when faith seeks understanding, that is, what God is doing in the world and our human parts in it, reason is only one of the many factors employed by theology, the others being revelation, Scripture, tradition, and culture, according to John Macquarrie.[16]

Of course, relativism could be harmful to our faith if, by it, we mean that nothing can be positively established as truth, including our Christian faith in the face of a plurality of worldviews. It can surely lead us to theological crossroads. But relativism, understood as just being "in partnership with pluriformity" in the search for more truths by being more open-minded in order to receive and to learn from whatever sources of truth and wisdom are available, with the express view of enriching and strengthening our understanding of the good news for us today, can surely render inestimable service to our Christian theology. Too often, many Western theologians are too skeptical about receiving or learning anything that does not come through the lens of Western intellectual mentality. In this atmosphere of one-way intellectual mentality, what does Mark 9:40 mean for us when our Lord says: "*Whoever* is not against us is for us" (NRSV, emphasis added)? What does it mean theologically if, for example, we identify this *whoever* with other religions of the world and yet promote, alongside Christian religion, the common values of "justice, morality, peace, and freedom," values that are unmistakably at the heart of the kingdom of God? Shall we throw these away because they do not come through the lens of Western intellectual mentality?

C. Positively taken, relativism in the sense of openness of mind within

---

14. Allen, p. 136.

15. Douglas J. Elwood, ed., *What Asian Christians Are Thinking*, 2nd imp. (Quezon City: New Day Publishers, 1978), p. 43.

16. John Macquarrie, *Principles of Christian Theology*, 2nd ed. (New York: Charles Scribner's Sons, 1977), p. 4.

the framework of pluriformity is not altogether out of step with the spirit of Reformed theology. After all, one can hardly deny the fact that Reformed theology itself is a blended mixture of different strands of theology. So is Reformed tradition Calvin and Calvinism put together. To buttress this claim, let me give three examples: (1) Calvin's theology was not determined and shaped by covenantal theology; yet after his death, covenantal theology became increasingly influential; (2) Calvin's fluid biblicism differs from later resurgent Aristotelian scholasticism, which led to a greater reliance on reason, rigorous deductivism, and greater use of causal analysis; and (3) T. F. Torrance's recent development of a unitary theology interacting with modern science[17] is within the overarching framework of Reformed tradition. These are pointers to a diversity of theological systems that relatively supplement each other and eventually enrich the Reformed tradition.

It must be said that even at the zenith of the so-called modern mentality, basic Christian beliefs in God the Father, the Son, the Holy Spirit; the authority of the Scripture; death and resurrection of life; the providence of God, etc., were able to withstand the brunt of repeated onslaught from the camps of science and rationalism. With the collapse of the modern mentality, there is increasing room for Christian faith to reassert itself more forcefully and vigorously. However, whether we like it or not, with or without relativism, there is bound to be the unfortunate problem of "divergent theological views," as theologians from each geographical region try to decipher new signs of revelation that come out of their reading the Scripture vis-à-vis the religious, social, economic, and political realities. After all, as stated earlier, the greatness and strength of Reformed theology is its particular character of theological pluriformity which is able to absorb pluralism and relativism and thus build itself into a system of "theological unity in diversity."

However, it must be pointed out that the dynamics of pluriformity (relativism and pluralism) have not been vigorously pursued and persistently applied in Reformed theology. If Reformed theology is to be ecumenical and universal in scope and character, it has to take leave of narrow and rigid ways of thinking. The Western theological agendas, for instance, are hardly interested in the problems and concerns of the Third World churches. For example, as recently as the World Council of Churches' General Assembly at Vancouver in 1983, the North Atlantic churches' agenda was dominated by the question of peace and nuclear war, while the concerns of the Third World churches had to do with hunger, poverty, and political repression. Despite honest efforts to accommodate the agenda of the Southern Hemisphere, the agenda of the North Atlantic churches

17. Ferguson, p. 571.

continued to dominate the proceedings.[18] This citation is given here in order to give evidence of how even the scope of Reformed theology has been oftentimes limited to narrow interest, let alone a narrow way of thinking.

It is understandable that the persistent application of logical positivism as the theological epistemological principle in the West was designed, besides other reasons, to prevent syncretism from masquerading itself in the guise of Christian theology. By syncretism we mean, generally and broadly, the blending of Christian theology with valuable insights from other major religions (Buddhism, Hinduism, Islam, Confucianism). If this is the case, any Third World observer is tempted to question the wisdom and logic of readily accepting and justifying many church fathers who had spiritualized and had drawn freely from pagan and secular Greek philosophy for the construction of Christian doctrines while at the same time calling valuable insights of other Asian religions syncretistic. What about T. F. Torrance's putting unitary theology in interacting dialogue with modern science (traditionally considered the enemy of religion)? It is quite evident that the epistemological criterion that had blessed dialogue between Christian faith and pagan (Greek) philosophy, and dialogue between theology and science in the West, is not happy with theology in dialogue with other world religions, apparently for fear of syncretism, within whose pale relativism and pluralism are most busy.

Hence, pluriformity as the theological model of the Reformed tradition will become fully meaningful only when it incorporates relativism and pluralism as a way of theological construction. This need not alarm us, for at least two reasons:

1. This theological approach does not seek the blind and reckless blended mixture of all the religious truths from a wide spectrum of world religions but rather a more comprehensive understanding with a single view to strengthen and help basic Christian beliefs and teachings, because absolutism or an either-or model as the only epistemological principle is now seen to be no longer effective.

2. By lending ears to the spiritual insights and values of the major religions of Asia (Hinduism, Buddhism, Islam, Confucianism), this approach can enrich and strengthen Christian beliefs. There is much wisdom when Jung Young Lee says that the Aristotelian logic of the "either-or" way of thinking, which became the foundation of Western thinking, or its epistemological principle, is opposed to and excludes the middle way of thinking (i.e., a "both-and" category), thus making Christianity a close ally of technology, which rejects the nonrational aspects of human life. According to Lee, this exclusive "either-or"

18. Robert J. Schreiter, *Constructing Local Theologies,* 2nd imp. (Maryknoll, N.Y.: Orbis, 1986), p. 3.

way of thinking is not in a position to solve the problem of theological questions like: whether God is personal or impersonal, or both; whether the historical Jesus was human or God, or both; and whether human nature is material body or spirit, or both.[19]

For Lee, only the yin-yang way of thinking (the "both-and" category) that represents the Oriental way of thinking explains and clarifies the above theological problems.[20] It is true that a narrow and exclusive way of thinking that is trying to bind the universal, transcendental, and unbound Christ will not do justice to the mysterious nature of God in Christ. Buddhism, for example, spread far and wide because of its ability to incorporate different religious insights into its system. So is Hinduism able to absorb spiritual insights other than its own. That is why S. J. Samartha of India claims that the Hindu insight into a larger unity of life can help Christianity to overcome a narrow view of revelation and thus to repel the idea of Christian exclusiveness.[21]

Fortunately or unfortunately, churches in Africa, Asia, and Latin America are no longer satisfied to repeat in rote fashion the traditional theology of an "either-or" mentality as it has come to them, simply because it does not speak relevantly to their cultures, problems, and needs. As is known, the main thrust of existentialism is its dictum that "nothing is real to us unless it speaks to our situation." This existential truth-claim vindicates the position of Third World churches. In the face of this problem, one recurrent question is: how to be faithful both to the contemporary experience of the gospel and to the tradition of Christian life that has been received. As with Rahner, there is the need for a dramatic shift in theological outlook; that is, moving from a predominantly Hellenistic worldview into an era of a world church that is characterized by a pluralism in worldviews and a multiplicity of new pastoral and theological problems that are unprecedented in Christian history.[22] Schreiter, another prominent Catholic theologian teaching in Chicago, voices support for Rahner when he writes: "There was a growing sense that the theologies inherited from the older churches of the North Atlantic community did not fit well into these quite different cultural circumstances."[23]

It is true that unless this theological "either-or" mentality is de-absolutized, following the collapse of the modern mentality, and unless one

---

19. Jung Young Lee, "The Yin-Yang Way of Thinking," in *What Asian Christians Are Thinking*, pp. 60-66.

20. Lee, pp. 66-67.

21. S. J. Samartha, "The Unbound Christ: Toward a Christology in India Today," in *What Asian Christians Are Thinking*, pp. 230-38.

22. Karl Rahner, "Towards a Fundamental Interpretation of Vatican II," *Theological Studies* 40 (1979): 716-27.

23. Schreiter, p. 1.

gives the dynamics that undergird Reformed pluriformity considerable leeway in theological construction, even Reformed theology (still considered to be tamed by the Aristotelian logic of the "either-or" mentality to a certain degree) will not fully meet the issues and concerns of Third World churches.

Having thus far claimed pluriformity as the most viable model of Reformed theology if the latter were to become ecumenical and universal in scope, I would now like to bring this paper to its conclusion by presenting my critique of our theological past, with the sincere hope that I might be a drop in a bucket for the renewal and reshaping of postmodern Reformed theology.

A. In this postmodern period of ours, characterized as it is by pluralism, relativism, and cultural interpenetration, it will be in the interest of churches around the world for Reformed theology to increasingly incorporate into its system not only insights that come through the cultural lens of Western intellectual mentality but also valuable insights from Asian religions as well. Truth, and for that matter the kingdom, is not exclusively restricted to the Christian churches, but is also found where people of different faiths are promoting its values. Buddhism, Hinduism, and Islam are also promoting the common values of justice, morality, peace, and freedom, with a view to build a more humane and just society. All seek to liberate humans from egoism, selfishness, and self-centeredness and to turn them to their neighbors in loving service and to the Absolute as their common end.

B. Any Christian theology, regardless of label, ought to be a theology of reality. This means the primacy of praxis over theory. For us Asian Christians, for example, who are experiencing hunger, grinding poverty, social and economic injustices, and political repression, we are not so much impressed and persuaded by a theology of right belief, right worship, or right theology as by a theology that touches and reflects on our abysmal conditions. There was a time when theology, known as the queen of sciences, was woven in the ivory tower — away from the harsh realities of life of the common people. Unless a theology dirties its hands in the sufferings, struggles, and aspirations of the people it is meant to be serving, that theology becomes unapplied and dead theology.

A living and realistic theology must come to grips with human realities. Spirituality, for instance, is not the practical conclusion of theology, but rather is involvement with the poor, the oppressed, and the exploited, and that is what creates theology. We know Jesus the *Truth* not so much by studying in the seminary the life of the historical Jesus as by following Jesus the *Way*. Hence, if a theology gives more attention to such metaphysical subjects as cosmology, God-talk, right worship, right church ordinance, etc., at the exclusion and callous disregard of the sufferings and struggles of the oppressed poor, that particular theology becomes dead theology. Reformed theology, for that matter, needs to be multidimensional and multifaceted in scope and character by reflecting on the realities of life.

C. One area in which theology, including Reformed theology, needs to voice prophetic criticism more loudly than ever before is the women's liberation movement. The vast majority of people in the Third World are still ignorant of this movement, which has been going on in the West since recent years, and because of discrimination and prejudice against women, which has become built-in and traditional for many centuries, some are simply not moved by it.

In many countries all over the world, including my own, women are still victims of domination and exploitation — an unfortunate hangover of the Jewish culture of the Old Testament period as well as of a system based upon the concept, especially by any agrarian society that uses primitive methods of agriculture, that the muscle (physical strength) is the breadwinner of, as well as the ground of authority in, the family. For men in this kind of society, the fact that woman and man are each a part of the other and that subjugation or exploitation of one is a degradation of both is a philosophy foreign to them. The saddest thing is that in a society where there is an interaction of traditional and modern forces, women are sexually and intellectually vulnerable. They are compelled by this interaction to compromise with consumeristic values of a capitalist society and to engage in prostitution.

Discrimination against women that is traditionally upheld and maintained is opposed not only to the heart of Christ's teaching but also to the teaching of Lord Buddha. Tradition is good, but not all of them are. Lord Buddha is reported to have emphatically rejected authority solely based on tradition. Again, according to one Buddhist scholar, Buddha taught that women have potentialities similar to those of men. So the Buddhist conception of equality of all allows no room for chosen class, race, or creed (cf. Gal. 3:28; Col. 3:11).

In the churches in Burma, nowhere is discrimination against women more evident than in women's ordination. So far, there are two ordained women ministers in the Methodist church, and four or five ordained women ministers in the Baptist church. This discrimination in ordination occurs purely because of sexual difference — an attitude Jesus would condemn harshly if he were physically alive today.

In sum, the core point of my argument in relation to the future of Reformed theology is that, in the age of pluralism and relativism following the collapse of modern mentality, pluriformity as the theological approach of the Reformed tradition is most blessed with the challenge and task of reconstructing and reinterpreting traditional theology in the context of the ever-growing, multifaceted problems of today's world with a view to reorder our lives more meaningfully.

CHAPTER 6

The Ecumenical Responsibility of Reformed Theology: The Case of Egypt

Wafiq Wahba

The fact of the Christian presence in the Middle East, from apostolic times to our own, is hardly known by the average Western Christian. Yet, some 12 million Christians live in the region today as heirs of a rich Christian tradition. By remaining indigenous to the areas where Christianity began, they link the world church historically with its origins.

Through the centuries, the Orthodox churches of the region kept the lamp of faith burning amid much turmoil and difficulty. As early as the middle of the sixteenth century, the Catholic presence in the Middle East started to form an important part in the life of the church. By the middle of the nineteenth century, the Reformed tradition added another rich dimension to the life and witness of the church in the Middle East.

The Emergence of Ecumenism in the Middle East

The formation of the International Missionary Council early in this century is considered one of the early steps toward ecumenism. This step, which was followed up by the World Missionary Conference in Edinburgh in 1910, signifies the degree of awareness of the urgency of ecumenism among the churches originating from the Reformation. One of the most significant consequences of the International Missionary Council was the formation of the Missionary Council in the Middle East, which was created in the Missionary Conference held in Jerusalem in 1927. Membership in this council was confined to mission personnel, although Protestant church leaders were invited to attend as observers. In 1932 in Beirut, Lebanon, further development turned the Missionary Council into the Near East Christian Council, in which churches were invited to accept membership alongside the missionary societies.[1]

In a parallel manner, the Orthodox churches also contributed to the ecumenical movement in the Middle East. In 1902 the ecumenical patriarch of Constantinople addressed an encyclical letter to all the Orthodox churches, calling on them to search for paths of encounter with the other churches. In 1920 he invited "all the churches of Christ" to form "a commission of churches." Such a call from one of the Orthodox churches in the Middle East, along with the Reformed churches' efforts in the West, contributed to the formation of the World Council of Churches (WCC) in 1948.

During the forties and the fifties of this century, and as an indirect result of the presence of Reformed thinking in the Middle East, many Orthodox churches witnessed dramatic renewal from the inside. The Orthodox Youth Movement, born during these years, produced a host of highly educated Christians dedicated to renewing their churches, opening them to the contemporary world, and working for the unity of the churches. During the decades that followed, the Orthodox Youth Movement provided servants and initiatives for the ecumenical movement within the Orthodox Church.[2]

In 1962 the Near East Christian Council, which was formed mainly of Protestant churches, gave way to the Near East Council of Churches, into which the membership of the Syriac Orthodox Church was welcomed. The meetings of the heads of the Oriental Orthodox churches (non-Chalcedonian: Armenian, Coptic, and Syriac) in Addis Ababa in 1965 gave a new impulse to the ecumenical movement in the Middle East.

The formation of the Middle East Council of Churches (MECC) in May 1974 in Cyprus marked an important milestone in the history of the ecumenical movement in the Middle East. The MECC is organized along the lines of families of churches rather than on the basis of individual church membership. Three families of churches — Oriental Orthodox (non-Chalcedonians), Eastern Orthodox (Chalcedonians), and Protestant — were the founding members.[3] At the MECC's Fifth General Assembly meeting in Nicosia, Cyprus, in 1990, the Catholic churches of the Middle East became official members of the MECC. Today, virtually all Middle Eastern Christians are represented in

1. Father Jean Corbon, "Middle Eastern Churches and the Ecumenical Movement," *MECC Perspective,* October 1986, pp. 46-49.

2. Father Jean Corbon, "Ecumenical Movement: An Historical Overview" (paper addressed to the MECC Fifth General Assembly, 22-29 January 1990).

3. Corbon, "Middle Eastern Churches," pp. 46-49.

the MECC. The geographic area covered by the council stretches from Iran to Morocco and from Turkey to the Gulf.

According to its constitution, the MECC aims "to be a point of regional reference in the world-wide fellowship of Christian churches, to establish and maintain churches, to establish and maintain relations with the World Council of Churches, with national and regional councils and with other ecumenical organizations."[4] This already makes clear that most Middle Eastern churches are also active members in the World Council of Churches. The Reformed churches of the Middle East participated in the formation of the WCC and were members as early as its First General Assembly in Amsterdam in 1948. The Eastern Orthodox churches joined the WCC at its Third Assembly in New Delhi in 1961. Later on, the Oriental Orthodox churches joined the WCC as well. Real and enduring ecumenism, however, will only be achieved when the local churches, their people, pastors, and priests, come together to celebrate their unity in worshiping the one God who was manifested to us in the Lord Jesus Christ.

The priorities of the MECC reflect those of the Middle Eastern churches. One of the main concerns of the council is to secure the continuity of Christian presence in the land in which our Lord was born and lived, and which witnessed the formation of the early church. In light of the sociopolitical and religious context of the Middle East, a great effort is needed to insure that Christians and their churches live in freedom in their lands so that they may actively participate in the development of their societies. In the midst of ideological conflicts and suffering, spiritual renewal and education are sought to enable the churches to continue their witness to the resurrected Christ. Another great concern is Christian unity. The current plurality of the Middle Eastern churches has not always been caused by doctrinal difference. The sociopolitical and cultural situation also played a great role in causing such divisions. In a multireligious context where Christians are the minority, the unity of the Middle Eastern churches is essential to the churches' life and witness. The MECC aims to promote communion and ecumenical awareness among the churches to enable each church, through prayer, study, and action, to participate in the riches of the traditional and spiritual experiences of the others.

Certain signs attest the effectiveness of the ecumenical movement on the Middle Eastern churches today. For instance, several theological dialogues between member churches of the MECC have been conducted. The

4. Gabriel Habib (general secretary of the MECC), "The Consensus of the Middle East Council of Churches" (paper addressed to the MECC Third General Assembly, 28 November–4 December 1980).

Oriental and Eastern Orthodox churches met in Lebanon for the first time, after more than fifteen hundred years of separation, in March 1972 to discuss their christological differences. This meeting was followed by others (Greece, November 1978; Cairo, November 1987). Orthodox churches and Catholic churches also have met several times, the result being a willingness to accept each other's sacraments. Protestants also have met with both Orthodox and Catholic churches to discuss their doctrinal differences. In February 1985 nineteen patriarchs and heads of Oriental and Eastern Orthodox, Catholic, and Protestant churches in the Middle East met in an historical meeting in Cairo, Egypt.

Meanwhile, both Oriental and Eastern Orthodox churches have participated in several bilateral theological dialogues with the Roman Catholic Church, the Anglican Communion, the Lutheran World Federation, and the Alliance of Reformed Churches. The most recent meeting between the Oriental Orthodox churches and the Alliance of Reformed Churches took place in the Anba Bishoy Monastery in Egypt in April 1993.

The Ongoing Process of Reformation

Reformed theology has played a very central role in the formation and development of the worldwide ecumenical movement, including in the Middle East. It continues to exert great ecumenical responsibility in shaping the contemporary life and ministry of the church in Egypt.

The Reformed churches in the Middle East did not result from a reformation of the traditional apostolic Orthodox Churches of the region. The Coptic Orthodox Church of Egypt, for example, is proud of being unchanged through the centuries. "The Church (Coptic Orthodox) kept its worship, discipline, and tradition for two thousand years without any changes,"[5] affirms Father Matthew the Poor, a contemporary theologian in the Coptic Orthodox Church.

The presence of the Reformed tradition in Egypt, however, has indirectly contributed to the renewal of the Orthodox Church, its theology and way of worship. The centrality of the Scripture in the Orthodox Church's worship and theological discussions today is a case in point.

Although Reformed theology and tradition was originally formed and developed in the West, and transmitted to some Middle Eastern countries by American missionaries, its core characteristics and transforming power still

---

5. Father Matthew the Poor, *The Christian Tradition* (in Arabic) (Barriyat Shihit: Anba Makar Monastery Press, 1978), p. 2.

represent a meaningful and effective tool for the renewal of the church in the Middle East. Obviously, the context of the original Reformers was quite different from ours, as the East is different from the West, yet the need for reformation continues in every context. The voices of the Reformers in the sixteenth century still echo in many parts of the contemporary world, East and West.

For Calvin, the church under the Word and Spirit only existed in the process of reformation — hence the slogan *ecclesia reformata sed semper reformanda* (the church reformed but always to be reformed). The driving force behind this continuous need for reformation is twofold. On the one hand, the Reformed tradition emphasizes that the church is part of the fallen world, whose members are confessed sinners. It often fails to fulfill its calling. Therefore, there is continuous need for repentance, and for reformation. The center of Reformed theology is the gospel of justification that sets people free from sin, gives new life, and leads to sanctification and righteousness that is not based on people's merit. Since the proclamation of this gospel is the primary task of the church, there must be a constant renewal for the church to be effective in communicating the good news of God's salvation to the world.

On the other hand, the Reformed tradition seriously considers the continual historical changes from one generation to the next and emphasizes the need for rewriting the confessions of faith in the light of historical, social, and political developments. This may be seen historically in the First and Second Helvetic Confessions. When Heinrich Bullinger, Zwingli's successor in Zürich, felt there was a need to stress not only the importance of doctrine and ministry but faithfulness in the life and witness of the church, he wrote the Second Helvetic Confession in 1566, just a few years after the First Helvetic Confession was written. In our contemporary era, when the Confessing Church in the German Third Reich felt responsible to speak out against the Nazi ideology, the powerful Barmen Declaration of 1934 was formulated. The same can be said about the Presbyterian Confession of 1967 in the United States, where socio-ethical concerns were taken seriously as part of the church's confession of faith.

In a predominantly Islamic culture, the Christian communities in Egypt and other parts of the Middle East need to express clearly their faith in the trinitarian God. We need to affirm that our understanding of the triune God is based primarily on the presupposition that God is one. However, the way in which God acted in the person of Jesus Christ led the early Christians to believe that God is triune. The early Christians' understanding of the Trinity was not something they invented. The early church councils never dealt with formulas that simply affirmed God as a Trinity; they rather tried to understand and explain who Jesus Christ is, what his relationship to God is, and how they should relate to him. By the same token, they tried to understand the relationship between God and God's Spirit, and the relationship between God's Spirit and the person Jesus the Christ.

They used certain terms in their context, such as "Son," "Father," "eternal being," "person," "*homoousious*," etc., in order to explain such relationships. By the same token we need to use terms relevant to our contemporary context in order to communicate our faith in the triune God in meaningful language. The fact must remain clear, however, that the concept of the Trinity in Christianity does not mean that Christians worship three Gods. The Trinity expresses the basic Christian understanding of how the one God, the source of all existence, is acting through Jesus Christ. God's Wisdom, God's Logos, or God's Word brings the alienated creation to experience God's love where God's Spirit, who creates and sustains life, is still working on giving life to the world.

Scripture and Tradition

In a country like Egypt, history plays a very powerful role in shaping people's perspectives of who they are and of the world around them. The Christian community carries a deep sense of continuity that goes back, not only to the early Christian era but even to Pharaonic Egypt. The Coptic Orthodox Church is very proud of such a long tradition. The contemporary Coptic Orthodox perspective considers Christian tradition to be the norm of the church's life, faith, and worship. It is a living heritage, handed down from Christ and his apostles to the church. It includes the church's sacraments, liturgy, and Scripture. As non-Chalcedonian, the Coptic Orthodox Church considers the first three ecumenical councils, especially Nicaea, to be the norm of all doctrinal statements and theology. In its handing on and proclamation of Christian tradition, Orthodoxy considers the voice of the church to be infallible. This quality, however, is not localized in a bishop or bishops, but is held to inhere in the life of the church as a whole.[6]

Since the life and theology of the Coptic Orthodox Church revolve around Christian tradition, one of the basic ecumenical responsibilities of contemporary Reformed theology in our context is to clarify and better understand what we mean by Christian tradition. The Reformers' affirmation of *sola Scriptura* did not imply a rejection of all church traditions. To the contrary, they affirmed the value and the validity of the ecumenical councils, the creeds of the early church, and patristic teaching and writings. For the Reformers, agreement with the early church was proof of the true catholicity and legitimacy of the Reformation. The *sola Scriptura* principle implies an adherence to

---

6. Matthew the Poor, pp. 3-13.

the original tradition, unmixed with foreign elements. It meant the primacy of Scripture as a theological norm over all traditions, rather than the total rejection of tradition. Creeds, church councils, and patristic teachings were to be received insofar as they were consistent with Scripture. Since tradition is always in danger of becoming legalistic and falsifying the transmission of the gospel, the correct use of tradition must be guided according to the source and standard of the Christian tradition, viz., Scripture. From that perspective, the gospel message not only liberates us from the false use of tradition, but also liberates us to use it rightly.

The Reformers emphasized that the church had to be always reformed and reforming according to the Word of God. What they meant by the Word of God was primarily Christ, to whom Scripture witnessed. Reformed theology has always emphasized the deep interrelation among the Word of God incarnated in Jesus Christ, Scripture as the written Word that witnesses to Christ, and the Word of God heard in preaching and communicated with in the Lord's Supper.

Furthermore, Reformed theology presupposes the clarity of Scripture and strongly emphasizes that Scripture is its own best interpreter — *Scriptura sua interpretans*. This principle, however, does not minimize the need to study and interpret Scripture in its historical, linguistic, and cultural context. The Reformed theologians thus drew heavily on the history of interpretation in the fathers of the early church. They turned to the ecumenical councils for guiding principles, since the councils' interpretation of Scripture gave the church clear and meaningful interpretations of the basic Christian doctrines.

By the same token, the contemporary responsibility of Reformed theology is to interpret the Word of God in its historical and cultural context, using all the available sources in the Christian tradition — i.e., ecumenical councils, patristic teachings, archaeological findings, etc. At the same time, the Word of God must be interpreted in light of and in relation to our contemporary context. The hermeneutical task here is to let the Word of God speak to us today, addressing our social, economic, and political concerns. Obviously, the preunderstanding of the text, which is usually influenced by one's own tradition, cannot be ignored. However, honesty and openness to new and fresh understandings of the Scripture under the guidance of the Holy Spirit will give us new insights from the Word of God.

Reformed theology is particularly concerned with the right interpretation and the right teaching of Scripture — in other words, with the orthodoxy of teaching and interpretation. In Egypt, where reliance on the past history and civilization is very strong, Reformed theology's responsibility is to transform the past memories and history into a generating power that can motivate new possibilities for a better future. These possibilities must be relevant to the actual situation, and furthermore, they must be able to transform it.

The message of the Reformers stressed continuity with the past — not, of course, with every element of the past, but with those elements of the past that gave expression to the gospel that had brought the church into being. The Reformers felt they were working within and on behalf of the church of Jesus Christ. Their main concern was to call the church back to the gospel that had brought it into being and which it was called to proclaim. In so doing, the Reformers did not neglect other rich sources in the Christian tradition. They took the early church fathers seriously, because the early church fathers had taken Scripture seriously. Calvin's *Institutes* is full of references to the early church fathers. The sequence of his chapters is patterned after the Apostles' Creed. The Reformers' call "to the sources" referred to patristic literature and liturgies. Their fundamental concern was to maintain continuity with all that had been creative in the church's life and witness, and to repudiate only what had been falsely imported into that witness.

Ministry, Baptism, and the Eucharist

Jürgen Moltmann rightly observed that Reformed theology tends to focus "the history of Christ on the justification of the sinners." The church is essentially the community of those who are justified by faith through grace. On the other hand, the Orthodox Church has stressed "the history of the Spirit, his continuing presence since Pentecost."[7] We need to think of the church as a community of those who have been justified by faith through grace and, at the same time, as those guided by the power of the Holy Spirit. Reformed theology needs to emphasize the centrality of the cross of Christ which justified the unrighteous, as well as the breath of the Holy Spirit and the abundance of the Spirit's gifts.

The Reformed churches in Egypt and the Middle East need to experience anew the deep sense of spirituality that is characteristic to the Orthodox tradition. We need to see ourselves as part of the church of Christ that is based on the Word of God and also guided by the power of the Spirit. This dialectical interaction between the Word and the Spirit is the basis of the life and witness of the church. The church continues to live and witness in the Middle East through much turmoil, suffering, and persecution, and has done so from the time of the apostles until now.

The clearest expression of the ethos and life of the Orthodox Church is found in its liturgy, in which those in heaven and on earth are held to be united in their common acts of worship. In such a context, Reformed theology's re-

---

7. Jürgen Moltmann, *The Church in the Power of the Spirit* (New York: Harper & Row, 1977), pp. 35-37.

sponsibility is to remind the church that the focus and goal of worship is to glorify God, who through Christ has called the church to serve and witness in the world. Worship is not service to God or to the self. When Christians gather together for worship, they are nourished in order to grow and witness to the world. Reformed theology emphasizes the role that each and every one has in ministry. Since each one has received a certain gift or gifts, the purpose is to "use it in service to one another, like good stewards dispensing the grace of God in its varied forms" (1 Pet. 4:10 NEB).

Being baptized is the beginning of a process of ministry. The Christian enters into covenant life, is made a sharer in the full benefits of Christ, and accordingly is called to a life of responsible ministry. The Reformers affirmed that ministry in the church is everybody's responsibility, but "the priesthood of all believers" does not negate the fact that certain people are trusted with a special ministry of Word and sacrament. The Reformed tradition regards those chosen for the ministry of Word and sacrament to be in the apostolic succession. According to Calvin, to be a minister of the Word is the "highest calling."

In our Egyptian context, there is a common agreement between the churches that all the people of God are called to ministry. However, there is a great difference in the churches' understanding of how the life of the church is to be ordered. In particular, there are differences concerning the place and forms of the ordained ministry. In order to achieve mutual recognition between the Orthodox, the Catholic, and the Reformed churches in Egypt, we must continue to work from the perspective of the calling of the whole people of God. At the same time, and in light of Reformed theology's understanding of the special ministry of Word and sacrament, we must enable Orthodox and Catholic churches, which are concerned to preserve the apostolic succession, to recognize the apostolic content of the ministry of Word and sacrament that exists in the Reformed church.

Starting from such understanding of ministry, we can come to better understand the sacraments of baptism and Eucharist as essential parts of the life of the church. In the New Testament, the act of baptism is entrusted by the risen Christ to his disciples as a sign of acceptance in the fellowship of the church. Buried with Christ in baptism, the baptized person has died to sin, partakes of the life and resurrection of the Lord (cf. Rom. 6:3-11), and engages in the ongoing ministry of the church. Since acceptance into the life and ministry of the church depends on God's grace that redeems the unrighteous, the baptizer and the baptized have no role except communicating and accepting God's grace through faith. Therefore, there is no legitimate theological reason for the Coptic Orthodox Church not to accept the baptism of other churches. Reformed theology's ecumenical responsibility is to remind the Coptic Orthodox Church that baptism is an unrepeatable act. It is God through Christ who has called us to be what we are. We need to accept God's gift of faith through grace and be faithful to the ministry that God has called us to fulfill. The ecumenical consensus expressed in Faith and Order Paper number 111, *Baptism, Eucharist and Ministry (BEM)*, serves as a guiding principle for us here:

> As the churches come to fuller mutual understanding and acceptance of one another and enter into closer relationships in witness and service, they will want to refrain from any practice which might call into question the sacramental integrity of other churches or might diminish the unrepeatability of the sacrament of baptism.[8]

In this sacramental perspective, Reformed theology also affirms that the church celebrates the real presence of Christ in the Lord's Supper. In our Egyptian context, the common misunderstanding is that the Orthodox and the Catholic hold to the real presence, while the Reformed hold to a spiritual presence of Christ in the Eucharist. It is true that the Reformed emphasize the spiritual presence of Christ. But that means a deep and total participation with Christ. As Calvin put it, "We are made his members and are made one substance with him."[9] Calvin affirmed that we participate not only in Christ's benefits but also in Christ himself:

> I say, therefore, that in the mystery of the Supper, Christ is truly shown to us through the symbols of bread and wine, his very body and blood, in which he has fulfilled all obedience to obtain righteousness for us. Why? First, that we may grow into one body with him; secondly, having been made partakers of his substance, that we may also feel his power in partaking of all his benefits.[10]

Calvin taught that Christ is really and substantially present in the Eucharist by the power of the Spirit, which should not be misinterpreted to say that the Reformed believe only in a "spiritual presence."

Calvin, however, did oppose the concept of the bodily ubiquity of Christ:

> I indeed admit that the breaking of the bread is a symbol; it is not the thing itself. But, having admitted this, we shall nevertheless duly infer that by the showing of the symbol the thing itself is shown. . . . Therefore, if the Lord truly represents the participation in his body through the breaking of the

---

8. *Baptism, Eucharist and Ministry*, Faith and Order Paper no. 111 (Geneva: World Council of Churches, 1982), p. 5.

9. John Calvin, *Institutes of the Christian Religion*, ed. F. L. Battles and J. T. McNeill (Philadelphia: Westminster, 1960), 3.2.24.

10. Calvin, *Institutes* 4.17.11.

bread, there ought not to be the least doubt that he truly represents and shows his body.[11]

Calvin thus taught the apostolic and orthodox concept that the eternal Word of God was and is united to the flesh, but not confined within its bounds. As David Willis put it, "The eternal Word is hypostatically united to the flesh but is (also beyond the flesh) *etiam extra carnem.*"[12]

Reformed theology needs to affirm anew the purpose of the Lord's Supper: to grow into one body with Christ, and to experience his transforming power in order to live a responsible life that witnesses to his salvific act until he comes. In the words of the *BEM* document: "Under the signs of bread and wine, the deepest reality is the total being of Christ who comes to us in order to feed us and transform our entire being."[13]

The Transformation of Society

The Reformation in the sixteenth century was an integral part of a monumental upheaval in the social, cultural, and religious life of western Europe. Motivated by a new experience and understanding of the gospel, the Reformers called for the renewal of the church and the salvation of the individual. This spiritual renewal was also accompanied by a significant transformation of society. Reformed theology emphasized relating the Word of God to the social and political context within which it is proclaimed. It takes responsibility for prophetic witness to transform society. This Reformed emphasis on prophetic witness must be the church's norm for social transformation in the current Egyptian society.

The church should take a clear stand against the current socioeconomic injustices where the rich are getting richer and the poor are getting poorer. There is an urgent need for a democratic and pluralistic system that is not based on favoring one religious group over another. The political system must protect people's freedom, dignity, and basic human rights. In the current Egyptian situation where Christian communities have very limited roles in influencing sociopolitical life, persuasion is their most effective means to cause real change. Nonetheless, the Christian community should be aware that it expresses God's creative power, which is able to transform persuasively.

In our contemporary Egyptian context, the Christian community needs to

11. Calvin, *Institutes* 4.17.10.

12. David Willis, "A Reformed Doctrine of the Eucharist and Ministry and Its Implications for Roman Catholic Dialogues," *Journal of Ecumenical Studies* 21, no. 2 (spring 1984): 302.

13. *Baptism, Eucharist and Ministry,* p. 12.

be reminded that the true church of the poor and the voiceless is able, by the power of the Spirit, to transform the world around it. At the same time, the Christian community needs to be reminded that the incarnated God, who took all human suffering and sin on God's self on the cross, is Immanuel, God with us, who suffers our suffering today and is with us in the time of turmoil and persecution.

As in the past, so in the present, Reformed theology has an ecumenical contribution to make. In the continuous process of change and renewal, Reformed theology proclaims the Word of God as the continuing force for the life and witness of the church. It will maintain the catholicity of the Christian faith and the orthodoxy of its beliefs, while never ceasing to play its prophetic role in transforming society into the kingdom of God.

Jesus Christ Is Our Hope

When the Orthodox and Reformed churches think together about the one authentic Christian tradition, they can come to discover the element of movement in what is permanent and what continues to have essential validity in the reforms — Jesus Christ. In the New Testament there is no conceptually and intellectually developed Christology. For the disciples and the writers of the Gospels, there could not be the least doubt concerning the true humanity of Jesus. At the same time, the disciples were sure that Jesus Christ was not just an ordinary human being. They knew Jesus was also divine. They had known Christ "according to the flesh." They were eyewitnesses of his teaching and life, of his condemnation and his death on the cross. Their faith in the resurrection did not contradict these experiences. To the contrary, they found that God, in resurrecting Jesus Christ from death, was testifying that the one crucified was also the one sent from God. This faith did not result exclusively from experiencing the risen Christ. The earthly Jesus had an authority uniquely different from everything they had experienced before.

The christological two-natures doctrine obviously went through different phases before it was completely developed in the fifth century. Two important factors contributed to this later christological concept. On the one hand, there was the continuous need for the church to express its faith in relation to the context in which it lived. During the second century, for example, the apologists developed their understanding of the concept of the Logos developed in Greek philosophy. They thought of the Logos as a universal mind and cosmic principle.[14] By the third century, Logos Christology had established itself everywhere.

14. Bernhard Lohse, *A Short History of Christian Doctrine* (Philadelphia: Fortress, 1985), p. 76.

On the other hand, the church felt obliged to differentiate the orthodox faith against other false teachings (heresies). In the fourth century Athanasius of Alexandria stood against the arguments of Arius, and the Nicene Creed was formulated as an expression of the church's belief in Jesus Christ, his death and resurrection.

It is beyond the scope of this article to detail the development of christological thinking during the early centuries of Christianity. But we must be concerned that the church's attempt to express its faith in Christ had, by the fifth century, become a heated christological controversy that resulted in the first major division in the church. The council which met in 451 at Chalcedon is known as the Fourth Ecumenical Council. It was decisively influenced by the Christology of the West, emphasizing in its dogmatic decision that the person of God-man who became flesh is identical with the person of the divine Logos. In this one person of the incarnate Logos, the divine and human natures are coordinated but not intermingled.[15]

Prior to the Fourth Ecumenical Council in Chalcedon, a long christological debate between Alexandria and Constantinople had taken place. The council's task, under the influence of the emperor, was to formulate a creed that would be acceptable to all churches in order to maintain peace in the Byzantine Empire. In fact, the council tried to do so by adopting decisive elements from both the Alexandrian and the Antiochene christological conceptions, while carefully avoiding their one-sided features. The creed contains neither the Cyrillic insistence upon "hypostatic union" nor the Antiochene opinion that the Logos dwelt in the man Jesus. Emphasis was rather laid both upon the unity of the person and the individuality of the natures.[16]

Unfortunately, the Chalcedonian creed did not put an end to christological debate, but ended in ecclesial division. The adherents of Alexandrian Christology felt that the Chalcedonian creed did not take sufficient account of their concern. They thought the unity of the natures in the person of Christ should be more strongly emphasized. This rejection of Chalcedon by the Alexandrian church resulted in a controversy which lasted until this century. It is well known that the Alexandrian rejection of Chalcedon was due not only to the christological controversy but also to a political power struggle. In their struggle to maintain peace and control over the Byzantine Empire, the Eastern emperors suppressed the Egyptians and the Syrians. Accordingly, the christological debate turned out to be a political and national conflict.

In the Balamand Monastery, Lebanon, in March 1972, after 1,521 years

---

15. J. N. D. Kelly, *Early Christian Doctrines* (San Francisco: Harper & Row, 1978), pp. 338-43.

16. Kelly, pp. 338-43.

of separation, representatives of the Oriental Orthodox Church (non-Chalcedonian: Armenian, Coptic, and Syriac) met for the first time with the Eastern (Chalcedonian) Orthodox Church's representatives to discuss their christological differences. This first Middle East Consultation on Orthodox Unity expressed its ecumenical consensus in a declaration to the heads of the Orthodox churches:

> We, the undersigned, have met as official representatives delegated by our Patriarchates and religious heads to express the desire of our churches — both clergy and laity — to achieve the ecumenical Christian unity for which we have long prayed ever since the division between us occurred. . . .
>
> After examining the factors which separate us, we are convinced that in addition to the factors of theology and wording, other non-theological factors (historical, cultural, social and political) have had their effect. But fifteen centuries after the schism, after dialogue, study and rapprochement, and after many non-theological elements of division have vanished, we find ourselves this day in a new place with a new understanding, with purer spirits, and a stronger desire to break down the impediments to Christian unity. We have been enabled thereby in the spirit of love and peace to review the doctrinal issues which divided us.
>
> After study and discussion, we as official representatives of our churches agreed that the opinions expressed by the theologians gathered at Aarhus, Bristol, Geneva and Addis Ababa affirm the conclusions reached by the theologians that the traditional Chalcedonian and non-Chalcedonian churches have one faith in the Lord Jesus. . . .
>
> We all believe the Lord Saviour and King of us all, Jesus the Christ, is fully God in His divinity and He is fully man in His humanity; in Him divinity and humanity were truly and fully united without mixing or merger or change or transformation or separation or division; He, the eternal, everlasting, invisible God, became visible in the body, taking on the form of a slave, for He is complete both in His divinity and in His humanity. In His Holy Person were gathered all the attributes of divinity and all the attributes of humanity together in a unity which cannot be expressed, a unity which cannot be differentiated.[17]

The second Middle East Consultation on Orthodox Unity, under the auspices of the MECC, took place at the Pendelli Monastery in Athens, Greece, in November 1978. This second consultation issued an even stronger call for unity:

17. "Middle Eastern Churches' Life and Witness," *MECC Perspective*, October 1986, pp. 34-35.

we endorse the statement and recommendations of the meeting held by our churches at the Monastery of Balamand in Lebanon in 1972. At that historic meeting the conviction was expressed by the delegates that there are no dogmatic differences to hinder the unity of our churches. Therefore, it is our opinion that our understanding of our faith is identical, and thus it is high time for the unofficial negotiations to be given official status, and that a common declaration of the faith become possible and effective in our Holy Churches in the Middle East and in the two Orthodox families in the world at large.[18]

The Oriental and Eastern Orthodox Churches' agreement on Christology is considered to be a great step toward mutual understanding and recognition between churches in the Middle East. The basic ecumenical responsibility of Reformed theology in this emerging ecumenical context is to emphasize anew the centrality of our faith in Jesus Christ's life, death, and resurrection. The church redeemed by the blood of Christ that has experienced the suffering of his death on the cross needs to be recalled to its task of proclaiming the good news to the world. The core message of the church is "Christ is risen!" This is the event that does not pass away, the only one in history that endures and gives life to the church.

Jesus' life, death, and resurrection formed an integral whole for the early church. The Christ-event marked the beginning of a new "aeon," where God's reconciling act in Christ enables people to begin a process of total transformation toward a better life.[19] Such a radical break with the past and entrance into the new order of God's reign is what they termed "justification by faith." For Calvin, human liberation is first and foremost redemption from the bondage of self-worship. Through grace we are restored to our true nature as people made in the image of God, and therefore reconciled to God and to one another. "We now begin," Calvin wrote, "to be formed anew by the Spirit after the image of God, in order that our entire renovation and that of the whole world may afterwards follow in due time."[20]

Recovering and reaffirming this new beginning through justification by faith will enable the church to be a community of transformation in our contemporary world. As Moltmann put it, "The tradition to which the church appeals, and which it proclaims whenever it calls itself Christ's church and speaks in Christ's name, is the tradition of the messianic liberation and eschatological

---

18. "Middle Eastern Churches' Life and Witness," p. 36.

19. James E. Will, *A Christology of Peace* (Louisville: Westminster/John Knox, 1989), pp. 61-79.

20. Quoted by Richard Lucien Joseph, *The Spirituality of John Calvin* (Atlanta: John Knox, 1974), p. 175.

renewal of the world."[21] Though it is important for the church to establish its faith in Jesus the Christ on the basis of the early Christian tradition, on the ecumenical councils and the teaching of the church fathers, the church needs to rediscover the presence of Christ in it today. It needs to experience anew Christ's power that can transform the church and the world around it.

The church also needs to look for the future of God's reign. The church does not only live from the past. Remembrance of Christ's act of salvation, his self-giving and his resurrection, not only gives the church the power to live its present mission and liberating task, but also enables it to look to the future with confidence and hope. It is only when the church experiences Jesus Christ as the living hope that the church can become a sign of hope for the people of the region.

21. Moltmann, p. 3.

CHAPTER 7

Toward a Reformed Theology of Liberation: A Retrieval of Reformed Symbols in the Struggle for Justice[1]

John de Gruchy

Since the sixteenth century, Reformed theology has interpreted its under-standing of Christian faith and praxis in response to a variety of challenges within different historical contexts. Initially the challenge came from Roman Catholic and Lutheran quarters. This led to the formulation of the classic Re-formed confessions and catechisms. While these symbols of faith[2] were not identical, they all showed the same family traits and indicated a common mind against Roman Catholics and Lutherans. While important differences remain, in many respects these early confessional conflicts have been resolved in this century through ecumenical dialogue. Where consensus has *not been

1. For a fuller discussion of the issues in this essay, see John W. de Gruchy, *Liberating Reformed Theology: A South African Contribution to an Ecumenical Debate* (Grand Rapids: Wm. B. Eerdmans Publishing Co., 1991).
2. The term "symbol," as used in this context, refers to what has traditionally been un-derstood as a "confession of faith." While some classic symbols, the Nicene Creed for exam-ple, are affirmed by different Christian traditions, there is often disagreement on their meaning. By Reformed "symbols of faith" we refer not only to those creeds, confessions, and catechisms which are regarded as normative guides to the interpretation of Scripture, but also to the particular ways in which those held in common within the ecumenical church have been interpreted by the tradition. See Wilhelm Niesel, *Reformed Symbolics: A Compari-son of Catholicism, Orthodoxy, and Protestantism* (Edinburgh: Oliver & Boyd, 1962), pp. 1f.

achieved, there is a far better understanding and appreciation of the remaining differences.[3]

The next major challenge to Reformed theology came as a result of the European Enlightenment, and especially the rise of the historical-critical study of the Bible. This challenge confronted all confessions equally, but it was particularly severe on those that, like the Reformed, so strongly affirmed *sola Scriptura*. The acids of modernity drove wedges through Reformed theology which resulted in divergent interpretations of its symbols as well as several schisms. The Reformed tradition was irrevocably divided into more liberal and more conservative streams, with several permutations in between. Ironically the conflicts which have occurred within the Reformed family have often been more bitter and divisive than those historic battles between Rome, Wittenberg, and Geneva.

The major challenge with which Christians of all traditions are confronted today is the struggle for "justice, peace, and the integrity of creation." This does not mean that the divisive confessional issues of the past are no longer of theological consequence and in need of resolution. Nor does it mean that the challenge presented to Christian faith by post-Enlightenment thought has been laid to rest. On the contrary, there is a fundamental connection between the struggle for a just and sustainable world and the need to overcome a significant part of the post-Enlightenment heritage. But doctrinal disputes and philosophical debates can be considered no longer solely within the realm of ideas. They have to be considered in terms of the mission of the church in the world, and therefore in relation to the struggle for a world order which better approximates God's justice and peace for the whole of creation.

In responding to the challenges presented by contemporary struggles for social justice and liberation from oppression, conflicting parties within the churches find themselves in solidarity with like-minded others beyond their particular confessional walls. This could mean that confessional distinctions are now regarded as less important than social and political differences, or that Christians today are confessionally indifferent, or that there is a pragmatic willingness to bracket such differences in the interests of achieving certain immediate social and political goals.

Whatever the reason, the problem posed for doing Reformed theology today is far-reaching. Is there now any point in doing *Reformed* theology? The problem is especially acute for ecumenically and socially progressive theologians and church groups within the Reformed tradition who often feel they

---

3. See Karl Lehmann and Wolfhart Pannenberg, eds., *The Condemnations of the Reformation Era: Do They Still Divide?* (Minneapolis: Fortress, 1990); Alan P. F. Sell, *A Reformed, Evangelical, Catholic Theology: The Contribution of the World Alliance of Reformed Churches, 1875-1982* (Grand Rapids: Wm. B. Eerdmans Publishing Co., 1991), pp. 112ff.

have more in common with non-Reformed Christians, and who find their own tradition captive to bourgeois norms and resistant toward just and liberating social change. Such progressive Reformed theologians often feel far more at home amongst Roman Catholic liberation theologians than they do within their own confessional circle.

This has been particularly problematic in South Africa, where the dominant Dutch Reformed church has, until recently, officially supported the policy of apartheid and given it theological legitimation. In view of this strong connection between social injustice and at least one branch of the Reformed church family, it is pertinent to ask whether it might not be best to put its symbols aside as remnants of a sinful and heretical past and proceed to establish a socially progressive Christian witness on other theological foundations. This is a tempting path to follow, and one which many within the tradition have already taken. An alternative which others have chosen, however, is the creative retrieval of Reformed theology in the interests of social justice.[4]

There are at least three reasons for this latter choice. The first is the fact that theology can never be done in a vacuum; every theologian stands within some tradition, even if his or her stance is highly critical of that heritage. The second is a strategic reason; namely, that social transformation requires the reinterpretation of "the significant symbols that people have inherited" so that these can become "sources for a new social imagination and guides for a new kind of social involvement."[5] This is particularly appropriate in situations such as South Africa where the Reformed tradition is deeply rooted within the culture. Those familiar with the making of modern South Africa will readily recognize that it has "involved a long battle for the possession of salient signs and symbols."[6] Colonial symbols, including those associated with Christianity, have been claimed, refashioned, and used in ways which were unintended by the colonizers, indeed, as means whereby colonialism could be resisted and overthrown. The third, and theologically most important, reason is that there is a strong prophetic and lib-

---

4. The retrieval of Reformed symbols was central to Karl Barth's theological project, and that of many who were influenced by him. See *The Göttingen Dogmatics: Instruction in the Christian Religion,* vol. 1 (Grand Rapids: Wm. B. Eerdmans Publishing Co., 1991), p. 294. More recently, however, others have sought to retrieve Reformed theology in relation to specific contexts of oppression. See, for example, Allan Boesak, *Black and Reformed: Apartheid, Liberation, and the Calvinist Tradition* (Maryknoll, N.Y.: Orbis, 1984); Johanna W. H. van Wijk-Bos, *Reformed and Feminist: A Challenge to the Church* (Louisville: Westminster/John Knox, 1991).

5. Gregory Baum, *Religion and Alienation: A Theological Reading of Sociology* (New York: Paulist Press, 1975), p. 223. Baum's use of "symbol" here is obviously broader than the more specific sense of the word indicated in n. 2 above.

6. Jean and John Comaroff, *Of Revelation and Revolution: Christianity, Colonialism, and Consciousness in South Africa* (Chicago: University of Chicago Press, 1991), p. 4.

erating trajectory within the Reformed heritage which encourages such an attempt. Indeed, there is a remarkable continuity between the Protestant Reformation of the sixteenth century and the renewal which is taking place today, especially amongst Roman Catholics, as a result of liberation theology.[7]

Our contention, then, is that just as it is legitimate and possible to be a Roman Catholic theologian of liberation, so it is legitimate and possible to be a Reformed theologian of liberation. We will argue that much Reformed theology, not least as articulated by John Calvin, is in critical solidarity with contemporary forms of liberation theology, and in some respects is their prototype. Indeed, while Reformed theology must raise some critical questions with regard to aspects of liberation theologies, it shares much in common in terms of method, substance, and goal. We will also argue, however, that Reformed theology needs to be liberated from various captivities, not least that of dominating social groups and ideologies, in order to be a truly liberating theology today. A first step in this direction is to consider the challenge which theologies of liberation present to those engaged in doing Reformed theology.

The Challenge of Liberation Theologies

The real challenge of liberation theologies is not the theologies as such, but the human oppression and suffering to which they have responded. The real challenge is poverty, racism, sexism — indeed, the challenge of all who are victims of social, economic, and political oppression. Nonetheless, the voice of such victims has found expression through liberation theologies in a way which directly addresses and challenges Christians, the churches, and dominant theologies. Liberation theologies have become "the predominant forms of critical consciousness within the Christian church that respond to the dangers of class, racial, and sexual privilege, and project the possibility of class, racial, and sexual equality."[8] Hence their challenge to Reformed theology to become critically conscious of oppression in all its forms and self-critical of the role the Christian church and theology itself have played in that regard.

This challenge differs qualitatively from the challenge presented to Reformed theology by other historic confessional theologies. In the first place liberation theologies arise out of the experience and struggles of the victims of society. In the second place they are theologies which are committed from the

---

7. See de Gruchy; Richard Shaull, *The Reformation and Liberation Theology* (Louisville: Westminster/John Knox, 1991).

8. Cornel West, *Prophetic Fragments* (Grand Rapids: Wm. B. Eerdmans Publishing Co., 1988), p. 197.

outset to the just transformation of society, and therefore to the liberation of victims from their oppression. And in the third place, therefore, liberation theologies demand a more appropriate way of doing theology.

This is at once evident in the opening pages of Juan Luis Segundo's seminal work, *The Liberation of Theology,* where he makes the distinction between a theology of liberation and theologies which deal with liberation.[9] Many traditional theologies, Reformed theology included, deal with justice and liberation as ethical themes which arise from theological reflection. They are items on their social witness agenda. But they do not regard engagement in the struggle for justice and liberation as fundamental to their *dogmatic* concern or theological method. For most it is a consequence rather than a prior commitment. What distinguishes liberation theologies from such theologies is not necessarily the introduction of new dogmatic themes, but the way in which such themes are reinterpreted from within the struggle for justice and liberation. Theology then becomes a socially committed discipline on the side of the victims of social oppression.

Many of the earliest Reformed theologians and pastors, as well as congregations, were the subjects of persecution, and much Reformed theology was conceived in exile and in considerable poverty. Calvin described his fellow refugees as the refuse of the world. In a real sense, then, Reformed theology was born amidst adversity and in the struggle against social and ecclesiastical tyranny. While this has been true of some Reformed communities since then, on the whole the Reformed tradition has become deeply rooted in a relatively comfortable, well-educated, upper-to-middle-class environment which has generally been aligned with the dominant political power. Liberation theologies challenge this alignment fundamentally. This does not necessarily mean that Reformed Christians have to vacate their social location — being middle class is not a sin — but it does mean taking sides with the oppressed in their struggles for justice and liberation.

In effect, this means breaking free from the "Constantinian captivity" which has been part of the legacy of the Reformed tradition since the sixteenth century. But it does not mean adopting a politically neutral stance or eschewing the responsible use of power. Anyone familiar with John Calvin's theology will know that it was "framed by politics."[10] It was essentially a public theology. The question is not whether the church is going to use political influence, but how, on behalf of whom, and from what perspective it is going to do so. Is it going to be used "to preserve the social prestige which comes from its ties to the groups in power or to free itself from the prestige with a break from these

---

9. Juan Luis Segundo, *The Liberation of Theology* (Maryknoll, N.Y.: Orbis, 1976), p. 8.
10. De Gruchy, pp. 236f.

groups and with genuine service to the oppressed"?[11] Thus liberation theologies do not challenge Reformed theology to change its fundamental commitment to the public square, but rather to express that commitment from the perspective and in the interests of those who are the victims of oppressive power. This is the fundamental point of departure for the liberation of Reformed theology, and therefore fundamental to the process whereby the Reformed tradition may be retrieved in the interests of social transformation.

Retrieving the Reformed Tradition

The retrieval of symbols is a major hermeneutical undertaking, but it may be considered in terms of three interrelated tasks. In the first instance it is necessary to identify the symbols and to consider the way in which they have developed within the history of Reformed dogmatics from John Calvin to the present day. Reformed theologians have never felt that they must slavishly follow Calvin in the way some Lutherans follow Luther. But Calvin remains the "decisive generating source"[12] for doing Reformed theology. It is therefore essential to remain in dialogue with Calvin throughout the enterprise.

Calvin's theology was, however, essentially an attempt to interpret Scripture in relation to the life and mission of the church in the world. Hence a truly Reformed approach to theology is essentially that of seeking to interpret the biblical message within the community of faith and within particular historical contexts. Thus by its very nature Reformed theology evokes new theological possibilities in response to contemporary challenges.[13]

Secondly, we have to critically examine the way in which the symbols have functioned within Reformed praxis, particularly in relation to social justice issues. The question has to be faced as to why and in what way these symbols have been used to legitimate oppression. Symbols which have been misappropriated or have lost their potency in the course of history will only regain their transforming power as they are critically examined, redeemed from their ideological captivities, and employed by Christian communities engaged in obedient service in the world. This requires a critical theology which is able to retrieve, clarify, and give fresh substance to the symbols in the midst of the struggle for justice and transformation.

---

11. Gustavo Gutiérrez, *A Theology of Liberation*, rev. ed. (Maryknoll, N.Y.: Orbis, 1988), pp. 266f.

12. James M. Gustafson, *Theology and Ethics* (Chicago: University of Chicago Press, 1981), p. 163.

13. Benjamin Reist, "Dogmatics in Process," *Reformed World* 39 (September 1987): 760f.

In this regard it is vital to recognize that all theologians, including Reformed theologians, are socially located somewhere within the body politic and are inevitably enmeshed with the interests of their particular group or class, be it the privileged or the oppressed. Original sin, which is a cardinal tenet of the tradition, affects theologians as much as anyone else, and perhaps even more so because of the nature of their task. Reformed theology has a "hermeneutic of suspicion" built into its very structure. Hence the urgent need for a Reformed theology which is critical in the sense that it not only prophetically addresses the power structures of the world, but with equal commitment uncovers those elements of alienation and false consciousness at work within the tradition itself.

Thirdly, we have to consider the way in which Reformed symbols have been significant in the cause of social justice, and seek to reclaim them today in such a way that their liberating power can be discerned within the community of faith and released within the world. The original impulse which led to the Reformation and to Calvin's interpretation of it was a rejection of human tyranny of all kinds and the proclamation of the liberating power of the gospel of Jesus Christ. It was this which first led to Calvin's break with Rome, and it was this which motivated his attempt to create a new, just, and equitable if not egalitarian society. Likewise has this been the motivation of all those prophetic Calvinists who have taken the side of the oppressed, whether in the past or the present.

The recalling of this liberating trajectory helps keep alive the "dangerous memory" of the symbols of formative and transforming Calvinism, and so sustains those who seek to embody it today in the interests not only of the Reformed family but of the church as a whole. We need, then, to retell the story so that the symbols of the tradition are not simply reduced to a set of theological principles or cultic acts remote from reality, but are also seen to be embodied in the narrative of the community, the narrative etched in flesh and blood, struggle, suffering, celebration, and hope.

A Paradigm Shift in Reformed Symbolics

The retrieving of Reformed symbols in the interest of justice and liberation today has become possible to a large extent by the pioneering work of several major theologians within the tradition, most notably Karl Barth. Indeed, it has been said that Barth's theology was a "radical liberation theology before all theologies of liberation."[14] As a result, Reformed theology in the twentieth century has undergone a major paradigm shift — a shift which has become apparent in contemporary Reformed symbols of faith.

---

14. Hans Küng, *Theology for the Third Millennium* (New York: Doubleday, 1988), p. 283.

In 1925, in an address given to the World Alliance of Reformed Churches, Karl Barth addressed the question of "The Desirability and Possibility of a Universal Reformed Creed." For Barth, such a creed was neither desirable nor possible for several reasons, one of which was the lack of consensus on the concrete situation which was forcing the church to confess its faith anew. "The Church must have something to say, some pronouncement to make which concerns the concrete life of men." Almost as though he were contradicting himself, Barth then went on to speak of one such concrete situation by way of illustration. "The Church must have the courage to speak today (I mention only one specific problem) upon the fascist, racialist *nationalism* which since the war is appearing in similar forms in all countries."[15] But Barth doubted whether the church really wanted to say anything on such burning and dangerous questions. He reminded his audience, however, that the "old Reformed Creed" was "wholly ethical," and was always addressed to the public sphere.

This Reformed understanding of the integral relationship between Christian confession and ethics was largely lost during the subsequent centuries of doctrinal and philosophical conflict. But it has returned to center stage during the twentieth century, especially since the 1930s. The most significant catalyst was the German church struggle against Nazism, and in particular the drafting of the Barmen Declaration, much of it by Barth himself. The Barmen Declaration profoundly affected more progressive developments within Reformed symbolics during the years which followed the Second World War.[16] In the process two very decisive and complementary shifts have taken place in the way Reformed theology has expressed itself. The first is in relation to social and political ethics, and the second is eschatological.

While Barmen proved to be the catalyst in this confessional development, it was only with the Presbyterian Confession of 1967 in the United States that "a strong social-ethical hermeneutic of faithful obedience is introduced into a Reformed confessional document."[17] In its reflection of the critical sociopolitical issues of its time and in many respects ours, we now find within a Reformed confession reference to the fact that God's revelation in Jesus Christ requires that the church must work for the abolition of racial discrimination, engage in the struggle for justice and peace in society, work to end poverty, and promote a genuinely Christian understanding of human sexuality.[18]

15. Karl Barth, *Theology and Church* (London: SCM Press, 1962), pp. 132f.

16. Niesel, pp. 7ff.

17. Edward A. Dowey, Jr., "Confessional Documents as Reformed Hermeneutic," *Journal of Presbyterian History* 61, no. 1 (spring 1983): 94.

18. The Confession of 1967, Articles 9.43–9.47. *The Book of Confessions*, United Presbyterian Church in the U.S.A., 2nd ed. (1970).

The Confession of 1967 makes it clear that faithfulness to the ethical demands of the gospel is amongst the marks of a true church, while disobedience is among those of a false church. While the Confession of 1967 today is in some respects already dated, it anticipates the challenge of liberation theologies.[19]

Throughout the 1970s Reformed theologians, working in conjunction with the World Alliance of Reformed Churches, gave considerable attention to sociopolitical issues, and especially to human rights.[20] Of primary concern, however, was the struggle against racism and, therefore, apartheid. Thus the significance of the Ottawa meeting of the World Alliance in 1982 when it was challenged to recognize that apartheid is a heresy, contrary to the gospel and inconsistent with the Reformed tradition.[21]

Shortly after Ottawa the Dutch Reformed Mission Church in South Africa drafted its Belhar Confession of Faith, which was formally approved by the church in 1986. This was the first time since the seventeenth century that a member church of the Dutch Reformed family had adopted a new confession as an authoritative standard of faith and practice.[22] Significantly, in terms of our present thesis, the Belhar Confession reinterpreted the confession of Jesus Christ from the liberating perspective of a commitment to the poor. In this we see a creative Reformed response to the challenge of liberation theology. Faithfulness to Jesus Christ made known through Word and Spirit had not only to relate to the struggle against apartheid, but the God revealed in Christ is "in a special way the God of the destitute, the poor and the wronged," who "calls his Church to follow him in this."[23]

The second decisive shift in Reformed confessional documents, especially during the past two decades, has been eschatological. This has been in continuity with the rediscovery of eschatology within twentieth-century theology as a whole. But it was given particular impetus as a result of the influence of Jürgen Moltmann within Reformed theological circles. One commentator on twentieth-century Reformed confessions has noted that political issues are now seen from the eschatological perspective of the kingdom of God rather than from providence and predestination.[24] Their primary consideration is

---

19. See Daniel L. Migliore, "Jesus Christ, the Reconciling Liberator: The Confession of 1967 and Theologies of Liberation," *Journal of Presbyterian History* 61, no. 1 (spring 1983): 38f.

20. Sell, pp. 218f.

21. See Allan Boesak, "He Made Us All, But . . . ," in John W. de Gruchy and Charles Villa-Vicencio, *Apartheid Is a Heresy* (Grand Rapids: Wm. B. Eerdmans Publishing Co., 1983), pp. 1f.

22. On the background to the Belhar Confession and the issues which it raises, see G. D. Cloete and D. J. Smit, eds., *A Moment of Truth: The Confession of the Dutch Reformed Mission Church, 1982* (Grand Rapids: Wm. B. Eerdmans Publishing Co., 1984).

23. Belhar Confession, Article 4.

24. Eugene P. Heideman, "Old Confessions and New Testimony," *Reformed Journal*

not support for those in authority, but concern and commitment to the poor and the oppressed.

These confessional changes reflect both a theological as well as a sociological shift within the Reformed community. The theological shift is not so much a movement away from traditional Reformed doctrines as it is a reworking of those doctrines on a new theological (ethical/eschatological) foundation. The sociological shift is that the Reformed community, with some exceptions, is no longer comprised of those who, having achieved power, wish to maintain it, or those who, while affluent and privileged, have become more aware of and sensitive to the needs and the just cause of those oppressed, but is comprised of many who are black, poor, and oppressed.

What we are proposing in this essay is in direct continuity with this paradigm shift in Reformed symbols of faith. Our proposal is that this needs to be taken further, and that a *constructive* Reformed theology of liberation needs to be developed. This requires that the crucial loci of Reformed symbols of faith need to be restated in such a way that their liberating potential is released. In doing this it may well be that we must go beyond the original intent of such loci, at least insofar as we can determine what that might have been. But such a step is always hermeneutically necessary. Being faithful to the Reformed tradition does not mean repeating past formulae, but discovering their power for today and, in the process, restating them in fresh and evocative terms. In the final two sections of this essay, we make some tentative proposals with this in mind, first by considering key elements in a liberating Reformed hermeneutics, and then by reflecting on the doctrine of *sola gratia* from a liberating Reformed perspective. In the process we will show that a genuinely Reformed theology can be a theology of liberation without losing its identity as Reformed.

Toward a Liberating Reformed Hermeneutic

Reformed theology is essentially an attempt to restate the biblical message within ever-changing historical contexts. Thus its concern is primarily hermeneutical. In this section we shall consider two hermeneutical tenets which are fundamental to all liberation theologies, but we shall do so from a Reformed perspective.

38, no. 8 (August 1988): 7ff. See also Lukas Vischer, ed., *Reformed Witness Today: A Collection of Confessions and Statements of Faith Issued by Reformed Churches* (Bern: Evangelische Arbeitsstelle Oekumene Schweiz, 1982).

The Spectacles of Scripture Require the Eyes of Social Victims

While we must affirm with Calvin that we need "the spectacles of Scripture" in order to know God the creator and redeemer in Christ, we must also affirm that we need "the spectacles of the victims of society" in order to discern the liberating and living Word in Scripture itself. A liberating Reformed hermeneutic must recognize at the outset "the epistemological privilege of the poor." This is because the social location and experience of the poor and other social victims enable them to see how the dynamics of society operate contrary to God's purposes of liberating grace, justice, and life in its fullness.[25] Thus they can discern the liberating Word directly without it being filtered through the various protective devices which the rest of us use to make the Word more acceptable to our situation.

From a Reformed perspective, the idea that the poor have a special insight into the meaning of Scripture should come as no surprise if we are familiar with Calvin's biblical expositions. The Reformer frequently maintained that God prefers to reveal himself to the poor, the simple, and the humble because they more readily recognize their need of God. In asserting this, Calvin was saying no more than what Jesus himself declared in the Beatitudes. God reveals himself only to those who recognize their need of God, the "poor in Spirit" as well as the materially poor (Matt. 5:3; Luke 6:20ff.). Thus the testimony of Scripture corroborates *(Scriptura scripturae interpres)* what we are also able to learn from considering the social location of the poor. Within Scripture itself there is ample evidence that the victims perceive most clearly God's liberating and living Word.

Several qualifications need to be made at this point. The first is the recognition that while we learn from the Scriptures themselves that the poor are victims in a special sense, and that the way in which we relate to the poor is indicative of our understanding of the gospel, not all the victims of society are necessarily poor. The second qualification is the recognition that the liberating Word speaks to all human need, including the desperate need for the conversion of those who oppress others, those who abuse power, those whose wealth prevents them from "entering the kingdom of God."[26]

The third qualification is that the Bible is only truly understood within a community of faith, even though the living Word does speak directly to individual people and their needs. Thus, when we speak of the ability of the poor or other victims to hear God's Word, we imply that they do so as they share a common life together as communities of faith. Neither the poor nor other so-

---

25. José Míguez Bonino, *Toward a Christian Political Ethic* (Philadelphia: Fortress, 1980), p. 43.

26. Calvin's New Testament Commentaries, *The First Epistle of Paul to the Corinthians,* on 1 Cor. 1:27.

cial victims automatically understand the Scriptures simply because of their social location or experience. Like anyone else, they need the opportunity to listen to the Scriptures, and they need the faith that precedes understanding. The Bible must be accessible to the people in a way which enables them to discover its meaning. Hence the importance for the reformers of congregations gathered "around the Word" and, for liberation theologians, of "base communities" reflecting on their situation in the light of Scripture.

The fourth qualification is that, although the God of the prophetic tradition in the Bible takes sides with the oppressed and speaks to their needs, the same tradition indicates that God can also speak against the oppressed. When the Hebrew slaves left Egypt, they continually hankered after the "fleshpots" they had left behind. Hence the constant reprimand of Moses to trust in God and struggle through the wilderness to the Promised Land.[27] In other words, even though the victims may perceive the message of Scripture more clearly, their "epistemological privilege" is not one of determining or controlling what the Word declares.

The Rule of Love Implies the Priority of Praxis

Liberation theologians stress that Scripture cannot be understood except from the perspective of the victims, and that this requires identification with them in their struggle for justice and liberation. Hence their insistence on the priority of praxis, and Gutierrez's definition of theology as "critical reflection on Christian praxis in the light of the Word of God."[28] This definition is highly significant, for it clearly indicates that the Word is not only normative, but that the object of its critical scrutiny is action informed by faith. This was precisely what Calvin himself attempted in his own work as a reformer. His theology was highly critical of the praxis of the church of his day. He placed "the tyranny of tradition" under the spotlight of the Word.

The slogan "orthopraxis not orthodoxy," usually but incorrectly attributed to liberation theology as a whole, is based on a false, unbiblical dichotomy. Right belief and right action need and complement each other.[29] Nonetheless, liberation theology reminds us that we cannot know the truth of the Scriptures by examining them objectively from the outside. We only know the truth as we become engaged in what the living and liberating Word requires of us. We know who Jesus is when we follow him. Without in any way denying the

27. Pablo Richard, "Biblical Theology of Confrontation," in Richard et. al., *The Idols of Death and the God of Life* (Maryknoll, N.Y.: Orbis, 1983), p. 8.

28. Gutiérrez, pp. 5f.

29. See Gutiérrez, p. xxxiv.

important role of critical scholarship in determining the meaning of the biblical text, we always have to affirm, with both the Bible and liberation theology, that "knowing the truth" requires "doing it."

Reformed theology is equally adamant. For Calvin, to know the truth of the Word was to do it: "if we are ready to obey God he will never fail to illuminate us by the light of his Spirit" is his comment on John 7:17.[30] And in his *Institutes* he writes: "Not only faith, perfect and in every way complete, but all right knowledge of God is born of obedience."[31] Likewise, the Scots Confession of 1560 insists that any interpretation of Scripture has to conform "to the rule of love"[32] or, as the Heidelberg Catechism asserts, to "the rule of faith and love."[33] In continuity with this tradition, Barth much later insisted that "we cannot have knowledge in relation to God without action."[34] None of this means that action is placed above truth, nor is it a rejection of theology as rational discourse. It is an affirmation that from a biblical perspective truth is always incarnate truth, truth embodied in action; by the same token, faith is always faith working itself out in love. And insofar as doing justice is the way in which love engages social need and oppression, love working itself out in the struggle for justice becomes the crucial key in discerning God's liberating Word for the world today.

All of this points to a fundamental correspondence between Calvin (and genuinely Reformed theology) and liberation theologians which underlies this emphasis on faith in action — they are practical and pastoral theologians, that is, their work as interpreters of the Bible not only takes place within the context of the community of faith, but it is engaged in the expressed purpose of awakening faith, stirring hope, and enabling love. That is the very reason why they engage in doing theology, why they reflect on praxis in the light of the Word. The motivation for careful biblical exegesis and exposition is precisely to enable the doing of the will of God without which knowledge of God is impossible.

A Liberating Reformed Reading of *Sola Gratia*

In the light of the above, we now turn in conclusion to consider one of the fundamental symbols of Reformed faith, namely, the priority of God's redeeming grace, *sola gratia*, and therefore God's election.

30. Calvin's New Testament Commentaries, *The Gospel according to St. John,* pt. 1.

31. Calvin, *Institutes of the Christian Religion,* ed. F. L. Battles and J. T. McNeill (Philadelphia: Westminster, 1960), 1.6.2.

32. Scots Confession, chap. 18.

33. Heidelberg Catechism, chap. 2.

34. Barth, *The Göttingen Dogmatics,* p. 172.

Liberation through Grace

Largely under the influence of Karl Barth and Karl Rahner, both twentieth-century Reformed and Catholic theology have rediscovered not only the priority of grace, but also its interpersonal, dynamic character as God's love at work in Christ restoring our relationship with God in community. This discovery of the social significance of the doctrine of grace is in continuity with Calvin's own trinitarian understanding of grace which, as Alexandre Ganoczy reminds us, provides the basis for social ethics.[35] More recent developments in Reformed and Catholic theology (Metz and Moltmann) have taken a further step and located the doctrine of grace firmly in the historical arena of the struggle for justice and liberation.

In continuity with this development, liberation theology has posed the question of the doctrine of grace, and therefore the question of human cooperation with God, in a new way by taking as its starting point the reality of social and structural oppression, or human dis-grace.[36] As Leonardo Boff so perceptively argues: "Since classical reflection on grace did not pay sufficient attention to the social aspect of sin, it did not discuss justification in social and structural terms." While Calvin had a profound sense of sin as a social reality, much later Reformed theology along with Catholic theology reduced justification to the private, individual sphere and thereby provided "ideological support for those in power and those responsible for oppression."[37]

Grace, as Boff understands it, is "God's free love and his liberating presence in the world."[38] Reflecting on this concern, Mark Kline Taylor has called for a more immanental understanding of grace within Reformed theology. He proposes that we talk about "the pre-eminence of grace as the power of God that lures us to and meets us in social and historical struggle, above all in the cries of those suffering in our midst."[39] The fear that this undermines the prevenient nature of grace would be misplaced because God's grace still pre-

---

35. Alexandre Ganoczy, "Observations on Calvin's Trinitarian Doctrine of Grace," in *Probing the Reformed Tradition*, ed. Elsie Anne McKee and Brian G. Armstrong (Louisville: Westminster/John Knox, 1989), p. 104.

36. "Dis-grace" refers to those disgraceful actions in history which cause human suffering and oppression, not those actions of redemptive suffering which result from them.

37. Leonardo Boff, *Liberating Grace* (Maryknoll, N.Y.: Orbis, 1981), p. 15. This relates well to the opening theme of Dietrich Bonhoeffer's *Cost of Discipleship;* that is, "costly grace" as distinct from "cheap grace."

38. Boff, p. 40.

39. Mark Kline Taylor, "Immanental and Prophetic: Shaping Reformed Theology for the Late Twentieth Century Struggle" (unpublished paper, Princeton Theological Seminary, 1983), p. 29.

cedes our action and vocation. The choice is not between prevenient and pre-eminent grace, but between a Neoplatonic and an incarnational understanding of grace. The difference is that we as persons are encountered by grace in history rather than in the privatized realm of the soul. We encounter the grace or the saving presence of God not in Word and sacrament isolated from human suffering and the struggle for justice, but "in, with, and under" it. This is precisely where God's grace was encountered by Israel and the early church, according to the biblical record. The Word of grace addressed the people of God in their historical struggle and journey; indeed, the Word gave redemptive, liberating meaning to that history.

If we seek to locate our understanding of grace within history, and the saving power of the gospel as that which not only transforms individuals but remakes humanity, we are in fact in continuity with the Reformed understanding of sanctification as world-affirming and transforming rather than world-denying asceticism.[40] Salvation history, the history of God's gracious election and redemption, rather than being an alternative above the history of the world, is expressed within it, giving it meaning and direction. While the history of salvation and the history of human liberation and social transformation are not to be confused, neither can they be separated. They belong on the same continuum. If this is so, then we must look again at that necessary but awesome doctrine of election which has always been a central symbol of Reformed faith.

Election: God's Preferential Option for the Poor

Apart from the avowals of those who remain tenaciously faithful to its traditional formulation, the most significant affirmation of the doctrine of election, that by Karl Barth, has radically and christologically restated it.[41] Barth was of the opinion that if Calvin had only done the same, Geneva would not have been such a dismal place![42] All of creation and history finds its meaning in Jesus Christ, the beginning and end of God's redemptive purpose.[43] Moreover, the election of the individual, while central to God's redeeming grace and purpose, is firmly located by Barth within the community of God's covenant.[44] In this way Barth was able to maintain the person as the object of

40. Nicholas Wolterstorff, *Until Justice and Peace Embrace* (Grand Rapids: Wm. B. Eerdmans Publishing Co., 1983), p. 66.

41. Karl Barth, *Church Dogmatics* II/2 (Edinburgh: T. & T. Clark, 1957), chaps. 32-35, esp. pp. 325f.

42. Barth, *The Humanity of God* (London: Collins, 1961), p. 49.

43. Barth, *Church Dogmatics* II/2, p. 104.

44. Barth, *Church Dogmatics* II/2, p. 311.

God's grace without falling into either the dangers of individualism or those of collectivism.

In the process of restating the doctrine of election, Barth sought to remain faithful to its original biblical intention, namely, to protect the mystery of God's counsel and assert God's unconditional grace as the ground of our salvation. But Barth did this in a way which affirms that the freedom of God is a gracious, liberating freedom for humanity which seeks to give life to the world as a whole. In other words, God's freedom is the ground of human liberation. God's freedom is a covenanted freedom, not a capricious and arbitrary freedom. God's covenant with humanity and the whole created order, which was renewed in Jesus Christ, is a covenant of liberation and therefore one in which both the community of faith and the believer discover freedom and life.

The question we now wish to pose is whether it is possible to discern an important link between this understanding of the doctrine of election and the claim of liberation theology that God has taken a "preferential option for the poor." Indeed, is it possible that in this controversial formula we may not only discern another important theological link between Reformed and liberation theology, but also be enabled to develop the doctrine in a way which is more profoundly biblical?[45] For, while it is true that we must not confuse God's providence in creation and history with God's election of the community of faith and the believer, it is equally true that we cannot separate them if we, with Calvin, understand God as both creator and redeemer in Christ. The old Calvinists rightly saw the need to relate providence and predestination, to develop doctrines of "common" and "special" grace. Their mistake was not that they made this connection, but that they failed to do so on a trinitarian basis.

Without denying the evangelical truth that personal salvation is grounded in God's gracious and unmerited redemptive action in Jesus Christ, it must also be affirmed that the doctrine of election cannot be confined to individuals any more than it can be confused with doctrines of manifest destiny. From a biblical perspective, the elect in God's schema were a people, and not only a people, but slaves in Egypt. The foundation of the doctrine of God's redemption lies in the exodus event, in which God reveals himself as liberator. Hence, whatever the limitations and problems which this exodus motif may present, it remains fundamental to the Christian understanding of God. God is known through his liberating acts in history through which he calls a people into being who are to become his witnesses. This act of historical providence

---

45. See Zwinglio M. Dias, "Calvinism and Ecumenism," in *Faith Born in the Struggle for Life*, ed. Dow Kirkpatrick (Grand Rapids: Wm. B. Eerdmans Publishing Co., 1988), p. 281.

becomes an essential part of God's redemptive purpose, not least in the election of a people to be witnesses to his gracious liberation.

In the New Testament, election is likewise not only a matter of the individual believer, but of the community; it is related to the covenant that established, in Christ, his people. Like Israel, this people, the church, exists in history and has the historical task of bearing witness to the gospel. That is its reason for existence. The elect people of God is neither an end in itself nor an ethnic group; it is a people gathered in Christ from every nation to serve the world. The coming of the Messiah and the birth of the church are not religious events unrelated to sociopolitical history and therefore to the destiny of nations and classes. God's election of humanity in Christ goes hand in hand with human liberation. Hence Mary's Magnificat, which heralds the coming of the Messiah to redeem the world, sees the significance of that event in relation to worldly reality. It is not surprising to discover, then, that many of those who are called to be the church are, as Paul reminds the Corinthians, not powerful but powerless, not rich but poor, not dominating but the dominated (1 Cor. 1:26ff.).

Paul's comment is first of all sociological — the church at Corinth was made up of people from "the underside of history." Yet there is also a profoundly theological dimension. God's election is seen from the perspective of a *theologia crucis*. God's purposes in history, as revealed in the weakness of the cross, are discerned in his gracious favor to the poor and oppressed, and victims more generally, and thereby the rest of humanity is enabled to know the saving grace and power of God in Christ crucified. This does not mean that only the poor or all the poor will be saved, nor does it mean that the poor are the church, which is sometimes implied or even claimed in liberation theology. It is to assert not only that we do not merit God's grace, but that, like the slaves in Israel, the victims of society have a special place both in the providence and in the redemptive purposes of God. They can become God's special witnesses to liberating grace and the promise of life in Jesus Christ crucified.

What we are here affirming, then, is that without faith in a God who not only acts providentially in human history but also elects people to fulfill his redemptive purposes within that same history, it is impossible to understand the God of the Bible. For that God is the one who, in "liberating slaves from oppression" and "taking a preferential option for the poor," acts both providentially and redemptively. This does not mean that the kingdom of God arrived when the slaves left Egypt and entered the Promised Land, but it does mean that without that act of political liberation, God's redemptive purposes and therefore the coming of the Messiah and the ultimate arrival of the kingdom would not be possible. Seen from this liberating Reformed perspective, the doctrine of election becomes an expression of God's sovereign yet liberating reign in Jesus Christ for the sake of the world.

CHAPTER 8

Theologia Reformata et Semper Reformanda

Jürgen Moltmann

Reformed Theology Is Reforming Theology

Reformed theology is reforming theology. The question, "What is Reformed theology?" is asked again and again by Reformed theologians. This is in a way typical of Reformed theology, for, unlike Lutheran theology with its *Book of Concord*, it is not grounded in confessional statements laid down once and for all, nor is it based on a tradition of infallible and irreformable papal doctrinal decisions, as is Roman Catholic theology. It is grounded in the "reformation" of the church "according to the Word of God" attested in Holy Scripture, which is to be confessed anew in each new situation.

A. Reformed theology is, as its name testifies, nothing other than *reformatory theology (reformatorische Theologie)*, theology of permanent reformation. To be sure, reformatory theology owes its existence to the unique Reformation of the sixteenth century, but it is more than a historical memory and also something other than a historical commitment. Reformed theology lived in community with Zwingli, Calvin, and Bucer, as well as with Luther and Melanchthon. There was no "personality cult" as in Lutheranism with its article of faith *De vocatione M. Lutheri.*

Reformatory theology is theology in the service of reformation; reformation is its historical principle. Therefore, Reformed theology is *reforming theol-*

Translated by Johanna Froehlich-Swartzentrueber.

ogy. Just as the life of a Christian is, according to the first of Martin Luther's Ninety-five Theses of 1517, a "perpetual penance," so reformatory theology is a theology of a constant turning back, the turning back to that future of God's kingdom promised by the Word of God. It is not specifically known who invented this formula, but it accurately describes the principle of the church and theology reformed according to God's Word: *ecclesia reformata et semper reformanda,* and therefore also *theologia reformata et semper reformanda.* Tradition and innovation are one process. According to this principle, "reformation" is not a onetime act to which a confessionalist could appeal and upon whose events a traditionalist could rest. In essence, "reformation according to God's Word" is "permanent reformation"; one might say, adapting Trotsky's call to revolution, it is "an event that keeps church and theology breathless with suspense, an event that infuses church and theology with the breath of life, a story that is constantly making history, an event that cannot be concluded in this world, a process that will come to fulfillment and to rest only in the Parousia of Christ": *theologia reformata et semper reformanda usque ad finem.* As reforming theology, Reformed theology is eschatologically oriented theology.

B. In another respect, too, Reformed theology is nothing other than reformatory theology: it is concerned with the reformation of the whole life. Very soon after the first decades of the historical Reformation in Europe, the call for a "second Reformation" was heard. After the first "Reformation of teaching," a "Reformation of life," which would complete that first Reformation, was demanded. The Reformation of life was to place the life of the church under the guiding principle of God's Word. The ordering of the church and its liturgical regulation, instead of being left to the state, the territorial princes, or the magistrates of the cities, were placed under the mandates of the gospel. Church law is the church's own law, not state law as it applies to the church. This second Reformation, the Reformation of life, spread among the German countries and cities through the Palatinate Church Order and the Heidelberg Catechism of 1563. This combination — the unity of the church's confession and order — is also essentially "reformatory" and therefore typically "Reformed." The church states its faith not only through confessional formulae, as important as they are, but also through the form of its life — as the Huguenots said, its *façon de vivre.* The congregations' form of life was characterized by Reformed "church discipline," which frequently and in many places did acquire "legalistic characteristics." One should not forget, however, that this "church discipline" often kept the congregations in their faith during the persecution and "under the cross," as is evident in the cases of Johannes à Lasco and the refugee congregations. Pastor Paul Schneider, martyr of the Confessing Church in Germany, was Reformed and knew that Reformed church discipline demanded his resistance until he was murdered in the Buchenwald concentration camp in 1939. It made him uncompromising in his personal faith. Confessing Christ and following Christ belong together if the act of faith is really an all-encompassing act of living and not a halfhearted one. During the Reformation, the *Täufer* Hans Denck proclaimed, "No one can truly recognize Christ unless he follows him in his life." This has been the understanding of Reformed Christianity since Zwingli and Calvin.

As Calvin put it, formulating the common denominator of justification and sanctification: true faith and truthful life, live faith and faithful life are two sides of the same coin — the community of Christ.

C. Finally, Reformed theology is reformatory theology in another respect as well: it concerns the *reformation of the world*. As far as I am aware, it was not until Amos Comenius in the seventeenth century that the formula *"reformatio mundi"* was used; but it very aptly describes the goals of Reformed theology with respect to state, society, culture, and nature. Not only the church's proclamation and structure, as well as the life of Christians, but all areas of life are "reformed" according to God's creative, liberating, and redeeming Word, for God is God, unbounded and all-encompassing: "The earth is the Lord's and all that is in it, the world and they that dwell therein" (Ps. 24:1). Reformed theology has always understood the divinity of God as *theocratic* and universal, whether as "the all-determining reality," "the reality which supports all things," the transcendental sovereignty of the God who is totally other, or the spiritual presence of the immanent God, poured out "over all flesh," who sustains everything that is and gives life to everything that lives. Therefore, what is reformed "according to God's Word" cannot be limited to certain areas of life.

Reformed Theology Is Confessional Theology

In a unique way, Reformed churches are *confessing churches*. From their beginnings up to today, the confession of faith in contemporary circumstances has been a virtual hallmark of the Reformed churches. The confessional status of the evangelical Lutheran church was fixed in content and form by the *Book of Concord* of 1580; this is also the reason the Lutheran churches in Germany did not accept the Theological Declaration of the Confessing Church of Barmen in 1934 as a statement of their faith. It is impossible to determine such a confessional status for the evangelical Reformed churches. To be sure, E. F. K. Müller, to his great credit, compiled *Die Bekenntnisschriften der reformierten Kirche* in 1903. But this is only a selection of Reformed confessions whose number — as research shows — is still incalculable. In 1938, therefore, in response to the confessional situation of the Christian church under Hitler's dictatorship in

Germany, Wilhelm Niesel published a smaller selection with the characteristically Reformed title *Bekenntnisschriften und Kirchenordnungen der nach Gottes Wort reformierten Kirche*. The *Collection of Confessions and Statements of Faith Issued by Reformed Churches*, too, published by Lukas Vischer in Bern in 1982, is only a selection from the wealth of the newest Reformed confessions. Several researchers have been working on a new edition of the old E. F. K. Müller for about forty years, but the available material keeps increasing to such an extent that a handy edition of Reformed statements of faith will not be possible. Where does one start, and where does one stop? When a few Huguenots, on the command of Admiral de Coligny, occupied an island in the Bay of Botafogo (the later Rio de Janeiro) in the sixteenth century and lived there for about three years until they were driven out by the Portuguese, they left behind a Reformed confession of faith: the first Christian confession in Brazil. When the Presbyterian Reformed Church of Cuba found itself under a socialist regime, it reacted with a new confession of faith which it ratified and proclaimed at its eleventh national assembly in Matanzas. Other Reformed churches in Taiwan, Korea, Africa, and Latin America continue to respond to their circumstances with new confessions. In the Reformed understanding, confessional writings are meant to be guides for contemporary confessions of faith and of hope. Confessions are not supposed to be rigid formulas, incomprehensible to many. Confessions are meant to express in concrete terms what needs to be said in the name of God concerning matters of faith here and now. The Reformed churches see their confessions, in the present time and context, as answers of faith to challenges of history. The Word of God and the *kairos* of its proclamation are inseparable. Moreover, situations occur again and again in history where political decisions become decisions for or against Christ, for or against the kingdom of God. Whenever such a *status confessionis* exists, the community must search for a common confessional answer to state openly what its responsibility is at that juncture. Three such confessional answers have become personally significant to me:

1. The Barmen Theological Declaration of the Confessing Church of 1934, especially the first thesis: "Jesus Christ, as He is attested for us in Holy Scripture, is the one Word of God which we have to hear and which we have to trust and obey in life and in death."

2. The "Foundations and Perspectives of Confession" of the Hervormde Kerk of the Netherlands of 1949. As the Barmen Theological Declaration points us to Jesus Christ as the center of faith, so the "Fundamenten en Perspectieven" opened our eyes after the war to the free wideness of the reign of Christ and the beauty of the kingdom of God, as Article 1 states: "With our hearts we believe and with our mouths we confess that 'the earth is the Lord's and all that is in it, the world and they who dwell therein.' This world is not at

its own mercy, but belongs to God, the father of Jesus Christ, who is its creator, redeemer and sustainer and thereby its king for all eternity."

3. "The Confession of Jesus Christ and the Church's Responsibility for Peace" of 1981. This is the statement on peace of the Federation of Reformed Churches in Germany in a situation where life is threatened by instruments of mass destruction (atomic, biological, and chemical weapons). It was preceded in 1979 by the "guidelines" of the Hervormde Kerk of the Netherlands concerning "nuclear arming." "The issue of peace is an issue of confession. In it we are faced with the *status confessionis* because in our stance toward the instruments of mass destruction we confess or deny the gospel. . . . The confession of our faith is irreconcilable with the development, deployment and use of instruments of mass destruction. . . ."

I consider such a contemporary articulation of faith the goal of all confessional formulations. Today, we are challenged also to confess God's justice in the face of the increasing misery of the people in the Third World countries, and to confess a reconciliation with the earth in the face of imminent ecological disasters. This does not mean reducing faith to ethical and political decisions; rather, it is the living recognition of Christ, i.e., recognizing Christ through the whole life as it is lived: "Who exactly is Christ for us today?" (D. Bonhoeffer). Such questions are to be answered by confessions. The Reformed churches have always understood the Reformation not as the cessation of the tradition of the church, but rather as a turning back to the wellsprings of tradition. They have therefore accepted and retained the creeds and decrees of the ancient church in matters of Christology and the Trinity. But they have constantly and without prejudice tested the church's confessions against the Word of God as it is attested in Holy Scripture. Instances of confessionalism did occur in the various Reformed churches, it is true; but the forms of "Calvinism" and "neo-Calvinism" were always broken by the authority of Scripture. In contrast, the internal danger of the Reformed churches is "fundamentalism" in the original sense of the word. The verbal inspiration of Scripture was taught in the seventeenth century, e.g., in the Helvetic Consensus Formula of 1675; the eighteenth century saw widespread biblicism, and in the Presbyterian churches of the USA of the nineteenth and twentieth centuries fundamentalism was common. Reformed and Presbyterian missionaries have carried these means of guaranteeing the authority of Scripture into the missionary churches as well, so that today they may also be encountered in Korea, Taiwan, and Africa. These purported guarantees of scriptural authority, which in reality only undermine it, can be overcome not by modernism and criticism but by taking seriously the Word of God. Taking seriously the Word of God attested in Scripture, however, means asking for the binding and liberating Word in one's own contemporary situation. The contextuality of Reformed confessional statements and acts of confessing was always in reference to the textuality of the Word of God in Scripture. The text creates the context, and the context is the *kairos* of the text. In any case, that is the objection of Reformed theologians to newer materialistic, social-historical, and political theories, according to which the political/economic or social/psychological context generates the text merely to create an ideological superstructure for itself.

Reformed theology also reflects the unique character of Reformed confessions just described. In contrast to the Roman Catholic principle of tradition, it is marked by its reference to Scripture, i.e., the necessity of providing a biblical basis for its theological statements. It differs from the Lutheran principle of "pure doctrine" in its contextuality, i.e., the prophetic situational relevance of its statements. Since statements of faith cannot simply be transferred from one situation to another, they must either be ratified again and again, like the *Confessio Gallicana* year after year in the French National Synods of the seventeenth century, or they must be formulated anew. Clearly, Reformed theologians did not rest content with the hermeneutics of their confessions once they were ratified, but much preferred to draft new ones. They put more stock in innovation than tradition. The historical Word of God is the elusive origin of this process; the eschatological kingdom of God, the expected goal.

Reformed Theology on the Epochal Thresholds of History

Reformed theologians were conspicuous participants in the great changes of recent history in Europe and the New World. Most Reformed Christians were in fact living in the developed nations of western Europe. For two centuries Reformed theology, which had its origins in the Netherlands, was the source of new theological movements. In contrast to Lutheran orthodoxy, which passed on its teachings almost unchanged during the one hundred years from Johann Gerhard to Quenstedt and Hollaz, the beginnings of a Reformed orthodoxy in Switzerland and the Netherlands were not able to hold their ground for long. While Heinrich Schmid was able to lay out *Die Dogmatik der evangelisch-lutherischen Kirche* (1869), taking his documentation "from the sources" without much effort at harmonization, Heinrich Heppe in 1861 had great trouble representing *Die Dogmatik der evangelisch-reformierten Kirche* and documenting it "from the sources." Those familiar with the theological history of the seventeenth century know that he harmonized the sources more than he differentiated them. Since Alexander Schweizer, repeated additional attempts to glean the "doctrine on faith" or the "central dogmas" of Reformed theology from the historical variety of the evidence have been made, most recently by Jan Rohls,[1] and have led more to abstractions than to differentiated insights. It is no doubt valid to inquire after the "theological content" of Reformed confessional and dogmatic writings, but to me it seems more enlightening to study the historical figures of this theology: it is more readily accessible through a theological-historical approach. This method also reveals the transformation processes caused by the various theological outlines and movements. This is not the place for a history of Reformed theology, but the following are indications of some epoch-making theological movements of Reformed theology.

The Discovery of the Subject

The roots of modern Pietism are to be found long before Spener and Francke, in the Reformed church of the Netherlands and its theological spokesman Wilhelm Amesius. The way for the discovery of the subject in the European church and culture had been prepared by Gisbert Voet in his *Präzisheit der Lebensführung,* and by Jean de Labadie and his mysticism of the "inner light" of the spirit. The theological background can surely be found in the Reformed doctrine of predestination, which created and strengthened in the individual and in the congregation of the faithful the consciousness of having been elected over and against the institutions of the church, the state, and class society. The vivid example of this is English Puritanism. As Joseph Bohatec has shown, it is no coincidence that the human and civil rights of individuals originated during the first half of the seventeenth century in England and Holland out of the life-forms and demands of this movement and of its theological anthropology.[2] With the discovery of the subject, its dignity and its rights, bourgeois society was born in European culture; it succeeded the old society of guilds and classes and finally asserted itself in the American Declaration of Independence and the French Revolution's Declaration of Human and Civil Rights of 1789: "All people are created free and equal . . ."

Out of this well-known connection of history, Max Weber created his thesis concerning the historical affinity of "Calvinism" and "capitalism."[3] In it

1. Jan Rohls, *Theologie reformierter Bekenntnisschriften von Zürich bis Barmen* (Göttingen: Vandenhoeck & Ruprecht, 1987); Eng. trans. *Reformed Confessions: Theology from Zurich to Barmen* (Louisville: Westminster/John Knox Press, 1998).

2. Joseph Bohatec, *England und die Geschichte der Menschen- und Bürgerrechte,* ed. O. Weber (Graz: H. Böhlaus Nachfolger, 1956).

3. Max Weber, *The Protestant Ethic and the Spirit of Capitalism* (1904), trans. T. Parsons (New York: Scribner; London: G. Allen & Unwin, 1930).

he wanted to counter Karl Marx and prove that the economy could not only influence the spirit, but that the spirit could also influence the economy. According to Weber, the "Calvinist doctrine of predestination" and the "puritanical notion of vocation" engendered a "disinhibiting effect on the capitalistic striving for profit." He claims that the "inner-worldly asceticism" of the Puritans and the Reformed *syllogismus practicus,* according to which a good tree is recognized by its fruit, and consequently one's own economic success as a mark of being chosen, inspired the "spirit of capitalism." Since then, this so-called Max Weber Thesis has been passed on unquestioned, especially by sociologists. As the historian Herbert Lüthy[4] and the theologian Max Geiger[5] have shown, however, this thesis is an imaginary creation for which there is no basis in Calvin, Calvinism, or Puritanism. This is evident to anyone who examines Weber's citations. Weber's actual source turns out to be not Calvin, but Benjamin Franklin, who after all lived not in Europe but in America 250 years later, when capitalism had long been established in the Western world for reasons completely separate from religion. As we know, the great repositories of capital in Reformation times, the Fuggers and Welsers, the Florentines and the Lombard banks, remained Catholic. After the pope's division of the world, exploitation of the newly discovered American territories and the slave trade from Africa to Latin America and the Caribbean rested at first in the hands of the Catholic kings of Spain and Portugal. The "Max Weber Thesis" can be considered disproved; even confessional polemics will not make it true again.

The Idea of the Covenant

The second significant contribution of Reformed theology to the formation of the modern era lies in the unity of covenantal theology and covenantal politics. Reformed covenantal theology is commonly attributed to the great work of Johannes Cocceius (1603-69), but in reality it goes back to Heinrich Bullinger's seminal tractate *De Testamento seu Foedere Dei unico et aeterno* (Zürich, 1534). Bullinger saw God's one and eternal covenant with humankind, established with Abraham and his seed, fulfilled in Christ, foretold by the prophets and proclaimed by the apostles, as the center of Holy Scripture and the union of a biblical theology of the Old and New Testaments. From the beginning of cre-

4. H. Lüthy, *In Gegenwart der Geschichte* (Köln: Kuckelhorn, 1967), pp. 39-100; see H. Löthy, "Variations on a Theme by Max Weber," in *International Calvinism, 1541-1715,* ed. M. Prestwich (Oxford: Clarendon, 1985), pp. 369-90.

5. Max Geiger, "Calvin, Calvinismus, Kapitalismus," in *Gottesreich und Menschenreich, FS für Ernst Staehelin,* ed. M. Geiger (Basel and Stuttgart: Helbing & Lichtenhahn, 1969), pp. 231-86.

ation until the end of the world, this covenant with God is the framework for all human and created life. It includes civil as well as religious life. Reformed covenantal theology originated in Switzerland, the Netherlands, and Scotland and spread, especially to New England, in the seventeenth century. Although Reformed theology, following Théodore de Bèze, had the doctrine of double predestination at its center, covenantal theology became more influential and fruitful because it could be related to the presbyteral-synodal church order as well as to the democratic municipal constitutions of the sovereign free cities, the Hanseatic town leagues, the confederations of Swiss farmers and the covenants of the Scottish clans. Due to the influence of Lutheranism, German Reformed theology began to differentiate between a covenant of works and one of grace (Ursinus); in the seventeenth century, under the influence of early salvation-history thinking, biblical tradition was cast in terms of covenant history (Campegius Vitringa). Cocceius distinguished a whole series of covenants, from Adam to Christ, which succeeded and superseded each other and prepared the way for the arrival of the kingdom of God. His *Summa doctrinae de foedere et testamento Dei* of 1653 can be considered the climax of covenantal theology, which reached from Herborn and Bremen all the way to Hungary and New England. While the doctrine of double predestination emphasized God's absolute sovereignty and his unfathomable will, in covenantal theology his voluntary restraint and loyalty and his reliability attested in the gospel were of supreme importance. The theological and political fruitfulness of this covenantal thought has been demonstrated by Gottlob Schrenk and by Charles McCoy and J. Wayne Baker.[6]

Reformed covenantal theology is first articulated in the *Vindiciae contra tyrannos,* 1579, written by either the Huguenot diplomat Hubert Languet or by his pupil Philippe Duplessis-Mornay in reaction to the horrors of that barbaric Saint Bartholomew's night in Paris in 1572 when all the leading Huguenots that had assembled in Paris, including Admiral de Coligny and the philosopher Petrus Ramus, were murdered by the Catholic authorities, the *"rex christianissimus."* This writing answers the contemporary questions of the Huguenots: Do subjects owe obedience to a ruler whose decrees are contrary to God's law? Is one compelled to offer resistance to a ruler who breaks God's law? Are neighboring rulers, for religious and political reasons, permitted to abet the resistance of subjects not their own? The answer is based on a double covenant: the first covenant is made between God and his people; the second covenant,

---

6. Gottlob Schrenk, *Gottesreich und Bund im älteren Protestantismus vornehmlich bei Johannes Coccejus* (Gütersloh: Gerd Mohn, 1923); Charles McCoy and J. Wayne Baker, *Fountainhead of Federalism: Heinrich Bullinger and the Covenantal Tradition* (Louisville: Westminster/John Knox Press, 1991).

which is a contract, is made before God between the people and their king, transferring their sovereignty to him. If the ruler breaks the covenant between the people and God, then the people are not only permitted but compelled to resist such a lawbreaker. Resistance to tyrants is obedience to God; furthermore, all political sovereignty comes from the people, with whom God has made his covenant. The first principles of the democratic constitutional state are found in this Reformed writing "against tyrants." The term "covenant" was first translated as "constitution" in the American Constitution. These terms form the exact counterpart to the absolutistic doctrine of sovereignty, which was being developed at the same time by Jean Bodin and a little later by Thomas Hobbes in his *Leviathan*. Churches organized in presbyteral-synodal fashion require a democratic political system and a society organized in confederations: no bishop, no king. In Germany, Johannes Althusius published the *Politica methodice digesta* in Herborn, taking the ideas in the *Vindiciae* further: politics is not sovereignty and power, but the *ars consociandi*. It is enacted in the bonding and binding together of people with mutual agreements and commitments, for humans are social creatures *(symbiotes)*, not wild animals . that must be tamed by repression.

The "Feeling of Absolute Dependence"

A new epoch in church history, the modern era in Europe, begins with Friedrich Schleiermacher (1768-1834). Schleiermacher not only founded a theological school which could be called liberal cultural theology, but he determined an entire era in which it was practically impossible for any theologian to escape his influence. This era came to an end only with the horrors of World War I, and was first succeeded by Karl Barth's theology of the Word of God. Schleiermacher's roots are commonly seen to lie in that Moravian piety which, since his upbringing in Gnadenfrei and Niesky, had left so deep a mark that he liked to describe himself as a "Moravian of a higher order." This often leads to neglect of the fact that his father was a Reformed preacher, and that Schleiermacher translated essential elements of Reformed theology and church order into his cultural theology. His brilliant description of religion as a "feeling of absolute dependence"[7] and its localization — "God is given to us in an immediate way in our feeling" — are to be understood as the anthropological counterparts of the theological statements concerning the absolute sovereignty of God on the one hand and his immediate presence in the Holy Spirit on the

---

7. F. Schleiermacher, *The Christian Faith,* ed. H. R. Mackintosh and J. S. Stewart (Edinburgh: T & T Clark, 1928), §4.

other. These theological statements had been at the center of the Reformed doctrine on God since Calvin and Bèze. It is true that, for Calvin, the *testimonium Spiritus Sancti internum* was only an internal witness to the Word of God, but it encouraged the involvement of the believer and the perception of immediate consciousness of self: wherever I am, God is. This still precedes what Schleiermacher called "feeling." His transference, too, of the "being of God in Christ" to Jesus' consciousness of God retains the characteristics of God's nature from the traditional two-natures doctrine. The constancy of God's nature is expressed in the "constant strength" of Jesus' consciousness of God. The redemptive work of Christ is expressed through the depiction of the Savior himself as productive model, and through our admittance to the bliss of his potent consciousness of God, that is, his oneness with God. Schleiermacher thereby invalidated the division of Christology and soteriology — the distinction between the person and the work of Christ, under which the Reformers labored — and once again attained the level of the early church's Christology. The price he paid, however, was replacing God's becoming man in order to make man divine (Athanasius) with the primordial "Man of God" who makes us truly human. The redemptive event lies in the perfect, sinless, and therefore exemplary person of Jesus himself, and not particularly in his reconciling death and resurrection for us.

Measured against Reformed theology, this "Christology from below" is a new phenomenon. One could perhaps think of the emphasis on the active obedience of Christ in the Reformed theology of the first part of the seventeenth century. Measured by the characteristics of reforming theology, however, and by the importance given to contextuality in the theology of the Reformed church, Schleiermacher does belong in this prophetic succession. Under the conditions of the incipient modern era, he represented Christian theology in a way that the "cultured among the despisers of Christianity" could understand and the modern world of that time could believe. In his personal life, too, he retained a characteristic of Reformed professors: the unity of preaching and teaching. He was as enthusiastic about being a preacher as he was about being a teacher of theology. The connection of pulpit and podium is found from Calvin to Karl Barth. That the church is governed by the "office of preaching" rather than by bureaucrats; that the church's constitution is synodal; that the preacher is to stand among the congregation and not at the altar with his back turned; and finally, the congregation's right and the preacher's freedom of conscience — these things Schleiermacher inherited from the Reformed tradition, although he passionately campaigned for the union of the Reformed and Lutheran churches in Prussia. But that, too, is part of the ecumenical breadth of Reformed theology.

The Word of God

World War I, in which the Protestant superpowers Prussia/Germany and Great Britain destroyed each other in turn, led the spirit of the modern era into its deepest crisis. The illusion of a humanly positive cultural theology crumbled in the face of the barbarism of the ruinous battle of Verdun. Religious loss of direction was widespread. In the first years after the war, Germany and Switzerland saw the birth of dialectic theology, crisis theology (Tillich), and the theology of the Word of God (Barth, Brunner, Bultmann), and a renaissance of the reformatory theology of Luther and Calvin. On the brink of this epoch, Reformed theology as reforming theology came to the fore more strongly again. Karl Barth discovered and defended with special vehemence the notion of God as the "wholly other" who shatters all human expectations, shakes up all religious feelings and is himself the crisis of the human world. He was not thereby providing a religious interpretation for the crisis that the world war was for the West, but rather deepening it through the crisis which God himself is for this world. In his second commentary on Romans of 1922 it is the infinite qualitative difference between God and humankind; in the draft of the Christian dogmatics of 1927 it is the absolute sovereignty of God; in the *Church Dogmatics* in outline of 1932 it is God's revelation of himself as the Lord; and in *The Doctrine of Reconciliation, Church Dogmatics* IV, it is the self-abasing Son of God who stands in the center of this theology. Not the religious needs of a pious self-consciousness but solely the divinity of God and the honor due his name provide certainty in an uncertain world and an anchor in a history without moorings.

Barth was not against a cultural theology, but the church which hears God's Word alone is as far removed from culture as it is from barbarism. It can discover parables in culture as well as in creation, but it has broken the bond between throne and altar, between church and art, between faith and religion, and stands on its own feet. To Barth, this meant nothing less than the end of the "Constantinian Age," the *corpus christianorum*, the "Christian world" and so-called Christianity. With theology beginning anew at the "Word of God" and a Christology coming "vertically from above," Barth actively ended those inner-worldly alliances of church and theology. He needed no "borrowed principles" from other disciplines to begin his dogmatics, but began with the God who is grounded in himself, reveals himself, and proves his own existence. Barth was no Calvinist; the Dutch Calvinists criticized him harshly in his beginnings. Barth was a reforming theologian who knew himself to be part of the tradition of Reformed orthodoxy, as many references in his *Church Dogmatics* show. Was Barth just another representative of "modern theology"? At times his critical admiration of Schleiermacher makes it seem as though he is merely revealing the theological side of the former's anthropology. Was Barth's theology a mere "episode" in the Christianity of the modern era? No: Barth neither belongs to the modern era, nor is his theology only an episode. With his theology, Barth stands on the epochal threshold at the end of the modern era. After two world wars, after fascism and communism and especially "after Auschwitz," nothing is as it was in the old Europe. The "Christian world" of the nineteenth century has perished in the human crimes of the twentieth century. Just as Schleiermacher discovered the contextually convincing theology for the developing modern world at the beginning of the modern era, so Barth has given the contextually convincing theology for the survival of the church and the confession of faith at the end of this epoch. The history of the Protestant resistance against Hitler's dictatorship, the Confessing Church, and the Theological Declaration of Barmen in 1934 were all decisively marked by him. With his theology, Barth began a new reformation with which the churches in Europe still have by no means caught up.

Focal Points of Reformed Theology Today

The Kingdom of God

On the one hand, Reformed theologians have always claimed that their theology is a function of "the Christian religion" (Calvin), of "faith" (Schleiermacher), or of the "church" (Barth). But that is too restricted a viewpoint; it diminishes the theological horizon. In truth, reforming theology is a special function of the kingdom of God, of which, according to Reformed understanding, the church is a historical prefiguration and beginning. Christian theology, especially as church theology and as theology of faith, must be theology of the kingdom of God. It then refers to the church, of course, but is not subject to it; it opens up the wide realm of the expected kingdom of God to the church. It refers to faith, of course, but is not dependent upon it — rather, it opens up faith to the hope of God's future. This universal and eschatological orientation has been specific to Reformed theology since Calvin; that is why Thomas Torrance was justified in calling him the "theologian of hope" among the Reformers. Within the horizon of God's kingdom, importance accrues to the relationship of the church to Israel, to the nations, to culture, and to the natural world, since everything must be sanctified in order to be glorified unto the kingdom of God in the new creation. In the church, God's concern is for more than the church. In awakening faith in human beings, God's concern is for more than faith. In the history of this world, God's concern is the perfection of creation in the kingdom of his glory. Every Reformed church theology, every Christian theology of faith, and every fruitful liberation theology must therefore be embedded in the theology of the encompassing kingdom of God. The saying of Jesus, "Seek first the kingdom of God and of his justice . . . ," applies to theology too.

The Unity of Scripture

Because Reformed theology did not begin with the fundamental Lutheran differentiation between "law and gospel," but rather with the kingship of God and his one eternal covenant with humankind (Bullinger), it discovered a positive relationship to the Old Testament which it has retained to the present day. In the Reformed churches, the law of God was not understood as a deadening law, but as the valid form of living before God. The purpose of the law is to be lived and carried out. Therefore, the *tertius usus legis*, the *usus in renatis*, is the true goal of the law, as the Heidelberg Catechism shows. Living within the law is joy, not torture. True, the Reformed Christians did earn the accusation of "legalism," and they probably themselves often misunderstood the law of God as a moral yoke. But if the law of God is not separated from his covenant, then it really is the "form of the gospel" (Barth) and the living form of faith. A positive acceptance of the Old Testament as the history of the promise follows from this positive acknowledgment of the law. The relationship of the Old and New Testaments is like that of promise and gospel. The gospel of Christ confirms the promises to Israel, deepens them into unconditional commitments and disseminates them among the nations. But it is not in itself the fulfillment of the promises. Reformed theology has applied the Old Testament's prophetic history not to Christ, not to the church, and not even to the Christian empire, but to the still-unrealized kingdom of God. With respect to the kingdom, the Old and New Testaments stand not in succession, but side by side with indications and expectations of God's future. For this reason, Reformed theology has searched time and again for a unified "biblical theology." It has seen the "canon within the canon" not in the "center of Scripture," but in the future of Scripture. Scripture, having a center outside itself, points beyond itself toward the future of Christ and the future of the kingdom of God. This eschatological expectation makes it possible to read Scripture historically without burying it as history. It makes it possible to hear it today without idolizing it in fundamentalist fashion.

The Communion with Israel

Its closeness to the Old Testament has also brought the Reformed church into proximity with Judaism. What no other confessional writing had stated before can be read in the Church Order of the Hervormde Kerk of the Netherlands of

1951: "As a community of faith confessing Christ . . . the church, in the expectation of the kingdom of God, fulfills its apostolic task especially in its dialogue with Israel, through its missionary work, through the spread of the gospel and the continuing work in the Christian permeation of the life of the people in the spirit of the Reformation" (Art. VIII). Here, the dialogue with Israel is clearly delineated from the missionizing of the gospel to the nations. As Martin Buber said, one book and one hope connects the church and Israel. This markedly differentiates its relationship to Israel from its relationships with the nations and their religions. Therefore, within the dialogue, solely a witness of faith is possible, but not a "mission to the Jews" as part of the "mission to the heathen." The church of Christ is on a common journey with Israel, to whom Jesus Christ belongs, and in the Parousia of Christ it expects also the redemption of Israel (Rom. 11:26). The "Fundamenten en Perspectieven" of the Hervormde Kerk of the Netherlands of 1949 is the first Christian confession of faith which deals in detail with the "present and future of Israel" (Art. 17). The communion with Israel saves the church from paganization; the communion with Israel makes the church conscious of its temporary nature with respect to the kingdom of God. "After Auschwitz," conscious and even subconscious Christian anti-Judaism must be overcome. On the basis of its tradition, Reformed theology is in a position to lead the way in this matter.

The Divine Mystery of Creation

In the face of the ecological disasters into which the earth has been led by the lordship of humankind over nature, a new and theologically intensive doctrine of creation is on the agenda. With its emphasis on the sovereignty of God, Reformed tradition has, it is true, understood God as one-sidedly transcendent. With its observance of the prohibition against images and its criticism of idolatry, it has also contributed to the modern "demystification" (Max Weber) and secularization of nature: if God alone is the transcendent Lord, then earthly nature loses its divine mystery. There is, however, a Reformed tradition that contradicts this. Calvin taught not only the transcendence of God over his creation, but concurrently also the immanence of God's spirit in his creatures: "For it is the Spirit who, everywhere diffused, sustains all things, causes them to grow, and quickens them in heaven and on earth."[8] As the "source of life," the Holy Spirit is poured out on all things living and is himself the life mystery of his creation. The awe of God includes in itself the "awe of life"

---

8. John Calvin, *Institutes of the Christian Religion*, ed. F. L. Battles and J. T. McNeill (Philadelphia: Westminster, 1960), 1.13.14.

(A. Schweitzer). Love for God includes in itself the love of the earth, for God is present through his spirit in all things and waits for the love of humankind in all things. To the sanctification of human life, so strongly emphasized in Reformed piety, belongs also the acknowledgment of the sanctity of the life of all living things. The modern destruction of nature has its basis in the disturbed relationship of modern human beings to nature. The discovery of God *in* creation and of his spirit *in* all creatures can lead to an altered relationship of human beings to nature and its life processes and become the beginning of an ecological reformation of the world.

What is Reformed theology? To summarize my answer in short: As reforming theology, Reformed theology is:

> biblical theology
> eschatological theology
> ecclesiastical theology
> political theology
> ecological theology
> theology of the kingdom of God.

CHAPTER 9

Travail and Mission: Theology Reformed according to God's Word at the Beginning of the Third Millennium

Michael Welker

A s we move into the third millennium, why are we confronted with "Reformed theology in travail"? Why are many Reformed churches and congregations in this world in sorry shape, characterized by shrinkage, lack of orientation, and theological confusion? For many decades of this century, Reformed theology was to be found on the cutting edge of theological developments in many nations of this world. The names of Karl Barth and Emil Brunner, H. Richard Niebuhr and Reinhold Niebuhr, Thomas Torrance and Jürgen Moltmann make this clear. In the last third of the twentieth century, Reformed theologians — along with Roman Catholics — have developed particularly important contributions to liberation theology and feminist theology. Along with Methodists and Anglicans, they have also been intensively engaged during this period in the conversation between theology and natural sciences. Reformed thought has made its mark on the dialogue with the social sciences and with jurisprudence throughout the twentieth century. And no one will contest the claim that Reformed theology has been one of the most actively committed proponents of the ecumenical movement.

Yet it seems that precisely Reformed theology's delight in innovation and new departures, its interdisciplinary, cultural, and ecumenical openness, has

---

Translated by John Hoffmeyer.

brought it into a profound crisis at the end of the twentieth century. In the last decades of this century, the cultural and social developments in the Western industrialized nations have attained such breathtaking speed and have become so diverse and diffuse, with a complexity eluding explanation by any single overarching model, that precisely Reformed theology with its special openness for contemporary cultural developments has been particularly tested and assaulted by these very developments. Other theologies could recommend themselves as dogmatically or liturgically oriented "brakes," or at least attempted brakes, on these head-over-heels developments. By contrast, the *theologia reformata et semper reformanda* seemed to be at the mercy of the shifting Zeitgeist. At least for many outsiders, the profile of Reformed theology seemed to disintegrate into a plethora of attempts to engage contemporary moral, political, and scientific trends, either strengthening them or fighting them. Reformed theology, exposing itself to continual renewal, seemed to a particular degree — at least in the Western industrialized nations — to fall victim to the cultural stress of innovation. Where it entered into that stress, it seemed to lose its profile. But when it opposed that stress, it seemed to betray its typical mentality and spiritual attitude.

Does this mean that the travail of Reformed theology at the onset of the new millennium is to be attributed to the diverse cultural developments and misdevelopments of the now concluding twentieth century? Is Reformed theology a victim more or less of these developments? Is it condemned to helpless reactivity? Is there nothing for us to do but to repeat — at a higher pitch — the objection of the young Schleiermacher, at the beginning of his famous *Speeches* two centuries ago, "to the cultured among the despisers" of religion: "You have created such a rich universe for yourselves that you have no more room for God and things divine. You have succeeded in making earthly life so rich and variegated, that you no longer need eternity. Having created a universe for yourselves, you are above thinking of that which made you"?

The Travail: The Cultural Calling into Question of the Power of God's Word

The travail of contemporary Reformed theology does not lie in its not having faithfully and honestly exerted itself to be, to remain, and always to become *theologia reformata et semper reformanda*. The travail lies in the profound uncertainty created with regard to the criterion, the motive power, and the orienting foundation of Reformed theology's efforts to remain true to its mission, its definition, and its identity. The blame for this uncertainty is not to be shouldered solely by Reformed theology. As a short review can make clear, this uncertainty is also to be traced back to the diverse and profound cultural, political, scientific, and social developments and crises of this century in general and of the most recent decades in particular. The world wars, the unabating series of military conflicts in many regions of the world, the Holocaust, the systematic destruction of nature, and the plunging of entire peoples or of large parts of the population in many countries of the earth into misery have profoundly and lastingly shaken the credibility of the Christian proclamation and of the ethos shaped by that proclamation. A short phase of repentance, reconsideration, and reconsolidation of ecclesial life in the period after the Second World War later gave way to a whole series of developments that called into question the power of God's word in a more lasting way than human guilt and the powers of public destruction had been able to do.

Recent decades have brought the spread of the television medium across the surface of the entire world. They have brought the electrification of entertainment music and the joining of mass media and competitive sports. This enormous cultural power has captured many human beings to such an extent, and has placed them under such a dominating supply of ongoing stimulation without major demands on their attention or interpretive faculties, that many more refined and more demanding cultural accomplishments have been placed at a severe disadvantage. Without having to leave their houses, without having to enter into a real public sphere, without having to make any special effort, human beings today can let themselves be enveloped in a mist of proffered stimulations. This supply of stimulations has had a druglike effect on a vast number of people. Against the background of the entertainment explosion that we have experienced, the word of God comes across to many people simply as boring. It seems condemned to powerlessness by the permanent stimulation and permanent amusement continually summoned up and offered by television, entertainment music, competitive sports in the mass media, videos, and the Internet.

At the same time, the Western industrialized nations in particular have profited from a huge explosion in education and learning, from the emancipation of women as they entered the full scope of the education system, and from a great surge of tourism putting people on the move. Triumphs of science and technology have become routine, from space travel to computerization and the greatly heightened technological capacities of medical care. On the one hand, this explosion in education and technology has presented human beings with a demanding challenge, even an overwhelming one. On the other hand, it has also offered them countless possibilities for development, tailored to their individuality. Against this background, the educational and formative power emanating from God's word has seemed to grow progressively weaker. Many human beings have discovered that large parts of the Judeo-Christian traditions

138

are shaped by a patriarchal spirit, and that they buttress a hierarchical relation between young and old in which the young get the short end of the stick. Such a relation between young and old cannot be squared with current mentalities in the Western industrialized nations. The explosion in education and the rapid processes of cultural and technological development require not so much the balanced judgment and maturity gained through life experience, as a capacity to pick things up quickly and a type of intelligence that can rapidly accommodate itself to new situations. If the word of God is indeed directed primarily to men and to elders, then it obviously is speaking to a time that has come and gone.

A pluriform, emergent development, in which the dissolution of the ideological conflict between East and West, the rapid change in sexual morals, and the voyeurism inflamed by the mass media all play important roles, has profoundly called into question and supplanted the formative power of God's word. Powers and effectiveness that had once been attributed to God's word have now come to be attributed to other agents, especially the electronic media: liberation and stabilization, edification and consolation, sensitization and empowerment, challenge and calling into question, the creation of certainty and hope and of attentiveness and a feeling of community, etc. At the same time, the structure of values has been displaced. Emptied and distorted, the "word of God" now appears to many people as only an authoritarian principle or a vague cipher, which served as a would-be hiding place for clerical claims to authority as well as for all sorts of religious quandaries.

Yet, taken in itself, this short review yields a one-sided picture — indeed, a picture that is false in its one-sidedness. This review does not make clear that extremely unclear notions and concepts of the "word of God" were and are circulating in our theologies — including Reformed theology. The review does not make clear that these uncertainties have also conditioned the helplessness and defenselessness of theology and piety over against the explosions in cultural development. In order clearly to recognize both the travail of contemporary Reformed theology and this theology's mission, we must come to see that we have great difficulties even in bringing into coherent interrelationships the basic statements and formulations concerning the "word of God" developed by the major theologies since the Reformation. If we cannot attain any clarity in our understanding of the "word of God," it is hardly astonishing if Reformed theology — "theology reformed according to God's word" — and the church which this theology serves fall into an ongoing crisis.

The Mission: Toward the Renewal of the Theology of God's Word

In the midst of a thoroughly corrupt society and church, the Barmen Theological Declaration confessed that "Jesus Christ is the one Word of God."

The great challenge of the Reformation was that Sacred Scripture is the word of God, against which we must continually measure our traditions, norms, and convictions.

"Law and gospel" are the two forms of God's word. The right distinction and correlation between these two "forms" continues to be a subject of reflection and puzzlement in systematic theology to this very day.

"God's word" encounters us in its lively "course" in a threefold form: as revelation, as Scripture, and as proclamation. How is this differentiation to be mediated with the distinction between "law and gospel"? How do both these differentiations relate to the christological specification of God's word?

A successful but deceptive theological oversimplification has rendered the understanding of God's word in our cultures considerably more difficult. This powerful but deceptive oversimplification says God's word always encounters us in the form of "address." On this view, God's word occurs essentially in "address," in a situation of dialogue, in the relation between "I and Thou," in the form of an "encounter." This view has absolutized an aspect which is certainly important, but it represents only one aspect and only one form of God's word and activity among other important forms and aspects. This absolutizing of the dialogical form has obscured and misunderstood the fact that God's word not only is active in a directly received proclamation, but also surrounds us "from all sides." It thus has been difficult to conceive, and easy to completely suppress, the "remaining" or "abiding" of God's word in its many expressions. The recognition has been lacking that God's word also carries us, challenges us, and calls us into question in those places where we are unwilling or unable to perceive it at all directly. The recognition has been lacking that God's word not only can come upon us dramatically, like "a sudden cloudburst" (Luther), but that it also can win the hearts of human beings in unseen ways, in silence and in a gently persuasive manner. The recognition has been lacking that God's word also lives in persistent activity in that which is hidden to us.

Yet how can this manifold power of God's word become clear? And how can we, in our attempts to make it clear, avoid confusing God's word with every possible human form of utterance and every possible human intention of presentation? To be sure, the texts and systems of values of the biblical traditions, and the manifold forms and contents of Christian proclamation, have entered into our cultures, our ethos, our moralities, and our forms of life, all the way to our weekly and yearly rhythms. The effective powers and traces of God's word and its human appropriations undeniably mark the deep levels of our culture, our educational formation, our mentalities, our norms, and many of our visions both large and small. But its distortions and obstructions, the words and powers that oppose the word of God, are also present in these same deep levels of our thought and feeling, of our life worlds and normative forms. Theologies and churches cannot simply trust in a "heritage" that, come what may, will supposedly provide the world on and on with God's good powers. The effort to experience and to recognize the vitality and clarity of God's word is thus an indispensable task of theology in general and of Reformed theology in particular.

In order to attend to this task and to take it seriously, Reformed theology must engage in a variety of ways in the effort to renew a theology of the word of God and, above all, it must make clear that the church of Christ lives in the presence of the risen Christ, mediated by proclamation and celebration of the sacraments. By means of this presence of the "one Word of God," the church, and theology with it, is continually stabilized and strengthened, but also re-formed and renewed. In ecumenical conversations concerning the Lord's Supper, Reformed theology has always attached particular importance to the aspect of "the remembrance" of Christ. It has not always been made sufficiently clear that "remembrance" in the sense of the biblical traditions does not mean merely a cognitive recollection of a past event or nexus of events. For example, the "remembrance" of the Supper is not merely the process of rendering Christ's person and saving action present in the individual or collective consciousness. It is also the creation of a remembrance; that is, it is the public proclamation of Christ. It is the public proclamation of Christ in order that, as the Reformers put it, God's word might be "advanced" and its "course" might be furthered.

Theology of God's Word as "New Biblical-Realistic Theology"

The recognition of the presence of the risen Christ and the proclamation of his presence are dependent on testimonies of the biblical traditions, as those testimonies point to the risen Christ and refer back to the pre-Easter Jesus. Biblical traditions make anticipatory, historical, and eschatological reference, both directly and indirectly, to the pre-Easter, risen and exalted Christ. The *second* task is to open up these traditions in a way that serves the recognition of the vitality of the risen Christ's presence. Over against all "Jesulogical" and "kyriological" reductions, we must take the Bible seriously as an "astonishingly pluralistic library with traditions covering more than 1500 years" (Heinz Schürmann). Reformed theology participates in the cultivation and development of the "new biblical theology," which insists that "the particular must not be lost in the general" (Jon Levenson), and which takes seriously the differences of the diverse biblical traditions with their various "situations in life." Precisely in their differences, they can refer concretely, in a specific regard, to the reality of Christ's presence, which every time and culture seeks to grasp in its own way, yet which cannot be exhaustively summed up by any time and culture. The new "pluralistic" approaches to reflection and research that come under the title "biblical theology" take seriously the fact that the biblical traditions bring to expression experiences of God and expectations of God that are both continuous and discontinuous, that are both compatible with each other and incompatible, at least in any direct way. Precisely so, they correspond to the abundance of human experiences of God's presence, and to the richness and vitality of God's glory.

The pluralistic approach to biblical theology sketched above is accompanied by the insight that important, even central theological concepts often function in our cultures as no more than ciphers. Complex key religious concepts and interrelated clusters of concepts from the biblical traditions (e.g., creation, world, sin, atonement, sacrifice, righteousness, kingdom of God, God's Spirit) — concepts that possessed great orienting power — have, by manifold accommodation to cultural habits of thought and morality, been worn down to the point of being incomprehensible. We must therefore gain new access to the contents and forms that were articulated by these "key theological terms." We must gain new access to them in their "situations in life" and in their complexity and coherence. For a long time theology has engaged in the search for simple, highly integrative abstractions within the forms of power of bourgeois piety (abstract theism, personalism, moralism, existential individualism, metaphysical holism). Now it is time to rediscover the richness of the contents of faith — a richness that does justice to Scripture and to reality. The contents of theology can be retrieved only by way of a new biblical-theological orientation that critically opposes reductionistic and selective "systematizations." Their diverse fruitfulness and inherent vitality will be verified only on the basis of a perception of their differentiated realistic character. This requires theology to be ready to submit its work to the test of interdisciplinary collaboration. This also requires theology to take seriously in a new way the orienting power of God's word.

Church and theology today must learn to rediscover, and to aid others in rediscovering, the word of God in its excellence, its substantiveness, and its rationality, which is often foreign to us. This does not mean that we ought to appeal to a principle, an entity, an agent "beyond immanence and transcendence," a "'yes' beyond 'yes' and 'no.'" It is essential that we regain a substantive concentration on God's word, on its material weight and validity, and on its rationality, if the loss of resonance and reality in both church and theology is not to continue and to grow worse. We will not regain this concentration with the help of a brilliantly exciting idea or a missionary campaign, and certainly not in a rhetorical tour de force. Persistently and in many small steps, Christians must again be made familiar with the pressing nature of the search for God, with active engagement with God and God's word, and with delight in the acquisition of religious and theological knowledge and language. This holds true both for academic theologians and for so-called laypersons. For example, there must at least be renewed access to the experience that the shared search for knowledge of God "is worth it," that this also has positive repercussions for self-knowledge and for orientation in the world.

In this context we must learn how to discover anew that the Bible is not simply "a book," not even a "classic," as David Tracy and other North American theologians have claimed out of the need to make a strong case for the Bible. The Bible is at least an interwoven tapestry of classics. The creation accounts and the exodus story are "classics," as Amos or Micah, First or Second Isaiah, Job, Song of Solomon, and the Psalter are also each classics in themselves. Paul's letters are classics, as are the various Synoptic Gospels, Acts of the Apostles, or Revelation. This biblical tapestry of classics, this "pluralistic library," grew up over one and a half millennia and encompasses a huge amount of human experience in interaction with God. This pluralistic canon offers a great abundance of experiences and expectations of God, arising out of the most diverse exemplary experiences of need and liberation. It also includes expectations on God's part of human beings. This tapestry of classics, this storehouse of one and a half millennia both of human experiences of God and of God's expectations of human beings, has a two-thousand-year history of effects — a history of effects that, in a global perspective, continues in unbroken vitality, albeit with limitations in today's Western industrialized nations.

Theology of God's Word as Theology of Law and Gospel

The christological determinacy and the biblical breadth of God's word become liberating powers and acquire "solid form" as law and gospel. For centuries, Christian theology has had difficulty in clearly distinguishing and relating "law and gospel." Various biblical traditions emphasize the fact that under the power of sin God's good law is enervated and perverted. This fact has repeatedly led to an abstract opposition between law and gospel. The consequences of a merely negative definition of the law, indeed a caricature of the law, were considerable. They were devastating for the relation between the church and Israel. They were also destructive of the relation of theology, churches, and piety to the entire spectrum of normative attitudes and forms. Naive and diffuse forms of legalism moved into the spaces that were supposedly "free from the law." This usually happened in the form of a more or less enthusiastic moralism, and in the form of permanent conflicts between styles of piety. Moreover, this pattern destroyed the most important bridges to understanding with other religions and with serious secular efforts to take account of the faith "from outside."

Reformed theology has seldom allowed itself to be swept along by this type of negative distortion and repression of the law. Reformed theology has sought to understand theologically the differentiation of the *usus politicus legis* and to carry out this differentiation in practice. With the doctrine of the *tertius usus legis,* Reformed theology has also seen to it that the theology of law retained its place in evangelical theology. Admittedly, the specification of this place remained contested. Reformed theology has been unable to bring the theology of law up to the level of differentiation seen in the biblical traditions. One reason for this is unclear terminological moves on the part of Reformed theology. The primary reason, however, is that Reformed theology has been unable to defuse the concern, particularly dominant in Lutheranism, that an insufficient distinction between law and gospel would slough over the power of the law perverted by sin.

In this connection, the *third* major task involved in developing the theology of God's word is a theology of law, developed on a biblical basis, with a clear distinction between law and gospel. God's law is not an abstract "oppressive requirement," like the moral law of the late Kant. Nor is it the Ten Commandments. God's law is a dynamic, normative structural complex. From the earliest bodies of law onward, it contains three structurally different groups of provisions, which reciprocally shape each other. First, there are provisions that are directed toward justice between persons of equal position, and that are supposed to regulate acute conflicts. Second, the law contains provisions for the protection of the weak, the needy, those who are socially disadvantaged and not well-off, the poor and the foreigners. Finally, the law presents provisions concerning worship and the shared knowledge of God; that is, concerning cultic life, the personal and public process of taking up contact with God. This shared knowledge of God also contains knowledge of self and world — specifically, knowledge of self and world that seeks truth: How does our reality look in God's eyes?

Individual provisions of the law change in the course of the Old Testament traditions. The so-called letter changes. But the basic intentions of the law, which are to be grasped in the three pillars of justice, mercy, and knowledge of God, are preserved. Matthew 23:23 states that what is most important about the law is justice, mercy, and faith. "God's law" thus binds together provisions that serve justice, provisions that serve mercy, and provisions that serve faith and the public knowledge of God. This normative structural complex has made a deep mark on those cultures that are shaped by the Judeo-Christian traditions, and on the ethos and morals of those cultures. Indeed, those cultures feed upon that normative structural complex. It is precisely the tensions between justice, mercy, and faith that are important in this law and for the dynamics of the cultural developments shaped by it. Without mercy, without the protection of the weak, there is no justice. Put more precisely, there is at most a so-called justice for a specific social stratum, for a specific class. There are specific groups of human beings who are then no longer included by judicial development. Increasingly large circles of human beings fall out of the network of rights and responsibilities. The society degenerates. The early prophets Amos, Micah, Hosea, and Isaiah gave this diagnosis almost 2,800 years ago.

However, mercy is also out of order when it is not oriented toward justice. When human beings are handled paternalistically as mere recipients of aid, when they are treated solely in a therapeutic mode, then even well-intentioned mercy is inappropriate. Mercy in the sense of the biblical law must always be oriented toward justice and toward the respect and recognition of one's fellow human beings.

The third element of the law — faith, the personal and the public and shared knowledge of God, cultic life — is indispensable to the development of justice and mercy in the sense of the law. For the biblical traditions of law, cultic life and the knowledge of God are not a luxury. Cultic life and the knowledge of God not only cultivate "cultural memory" (Jan Assmann). They also drive us to knowledge of self and world, in the context of a confessional-imbued search for the truth. Here human beings come together in order to come to an understanding about their own history in God's eyes: "You were foreigners in Egypt. Therefore you know how a foreigner feels! Therefore you ought not to oppress foreigners and those who are weak!" In the cult, in the search for God's view of reality, human beings come to an understanding about their common history. But they also come to an understanding about the foundations of their common future, about their norms. Without such acts of specifying a common past and a common future, without shared memories and shared expectations, a human society cannot exist.

We call "ethos" that set of normative evidences which is regarded as the indispensable foundation in a society of human beings. Without a culture and without an ethos, human beings cannot exist together. Without a culture and without an ethos, there is no consciousness of right and no mercy. Conversely, without striving for justice and without continually making the effort to include outsiders and marginalized groups, there is neither a stable culture nor a healthy ethos. The components of the law — the provisions concerning justice, the provisions concerning mercy, and the provisions concerning cultic life, the public relation to God and before God — thus hang together in manifold ways. Even today they shape our culture, although as a rule their workings are hidden. They have entered into our subconscious, our attitudes, our history, our art, our education, and our institutions, and have become their "invisible foundations." A theology of God's word must also clarify and cultivate these foundations of culture within the framework of a theology of law.

On the basis of its dogmatic foundations, Reformed theology is practically unmatched by any other theology in terms of its capacity and responsibility to take up this important third task. Yet the act of taking it up must not lead us to overlook the corruptibility of God's good law and of our best morals shaped by that law. To be sure, Reformed theology must help us understand "the glory" of the law. It must help us understand why the law brings to expression for Israel God's entire will and God's revelation. It must help us understand why Jesus, when asked "What shall I do to enter the kingdom of God?" first points to the law: not only to the Ten Commandments but also to the other legal traditions. It must help us understand that the freedom of the gospel cannot simply be played off *against* the law, that one cannot simply write, at the cost of the law: Here the bad, enslaving law; there the good, liberating gospel. This painting in black and white has not only had devastating consequences for the relation between Christians and Jews. It also has greatly hampered and obscured Christian knowledge of God. It has contributed to the gospel being unclear and nebulous. It has pushed theology out of the position of a competent participant in debates about powers shaping our ethos and allowed theology to become helplessly dependent on moral trends and on the mass media's control of resonance *(Resonanzsteuerung)*.

However, the classically Reformed appreciation of the law must not lead to a failure to recognize that the law can be and is corrupted by the power of sin. It must not lead to slouching over the possibility and reality of that corruption. Reformed theology, in its efforts to renew the theology of the word of God, must resist all frivolous theologies that abstract from human beings' captivity under the power of sin, either because they are too well mannered and proper, or because they are helpless to avoid doing so. Reformed theology must not only join the early prophets in naming the perversion of justice, the misuse of the cult, and the refusal to practice mercy. It must also, as a theology of the crucified Christ, draw attention again and again to the situation in which religion, law, politics, morality, rulers and ruled, natives and foreigners make common cause against God's word and God's presence. Finally, always returning to the theology of the cross as its point of departure, Reformed theology must again and again call attention to the creative power of God's word. It must bear witness to that word's creative power, which overcomes the power of sin, renews and lifts up Christian persons and communities in the church of all times and regions of the world, and radiates a beneficent influence on their environments.

Reformed Theology as Attentiveness to the Creativity of God's Word and to Evangelical Freedom

Without the cross of Christ and the recognition that human beings are threatened by the power of sin, it is impossible to understand that God's word is a creative power that transforms and renews human beings and their life relations. As long as human beings trust only in the powers of education and the media, or in the help of political, judicial, moral, and religious norms and forms, they will remain deaf to God's word. They will turn their attention again to the renewing and restoring power of the divine word only when they recognize that the normative forms that are supposed to serve their education, their entertainment, the ordering of their life together, and the ordering of their relation to God can be completely distorted and perverted. That is, they will turn their attention to the restorative power of God's word only when they become sensitive to the ways in which their norms and forms of life are systematically and systemically endangered.

A new attentiveness, a new sensitivity to the creative power of God's word will not be awakened by threats, by depicting in detail the captivity of human beings under the power of sin and the ways in which this captivity is detrimental to life. Instead theology in general, and Reformed theology in particular, must kindle well-grounded delight in the creativity of God's word, in the word's establishment of strong persons and of lively, exemplary human communities. In doing so, Reformed theology must make clear that the creativity of the word cannot be separated from the activity of God's Spirit or from the presence of the risen Christ. This is the *fourth* task of a renewal of the theology of God's word. Human beings encounter the *viva vox evangelii*, the living voice of the divine word, in its threefold form as revelation, Scripture, and proclamation. It does not sound without its witnesses, just as the risen Christ is "not without his own" (Luther and Barth), and just as the Holy Spirit does not become manifest without those whom the Spirit grasps and upon whom the Spirit comes.

Through the living word, human beings are filled with God's powers with each other and for each other. They become bearers of God's presence. They can participate in God's powers, of which Dietrich Bonhoeffer says: "Wondrously attended and protected by beneficent powers, we await with calm and good courage whatever may come. God is with us: morning and evening and most assuredly every new day." In the evangelical freedom mediated by God's word, each person can become a salutary wellspring of strength, an embodiment of those beneficent powers. Even in our pluralistic and so-called postmodern lives and societies, which elude the grasp of any one analytical perspective, it is possible to rediscover this evangelical freedom. But how? And to what extent is this rediscovery tied to God's word as it is revealed in Jesus Christ, attested in the biblical traditions, and articulated in the forms of law and gospel?

At first glance the crucifixion of Christ presents us with a chaotic situation. The whole world has turned against God: Jews and Gentiles, natives and foreigners, rulers and ruled, the powerful circles of leadership and the so-called general public. They all work together against Christ and against God's presence in him. Even the disciples abandon him and flee. The act of making the cross present and of "proclaiming Christ's death" focuses our attention on blatant injustice, blatant mercilessness, the night of godlessness and of abandonment by God, a situation of chaos in which the only thing left to say is "My God, why have you abandoned me?!" It is into this situation that the gospel, the good news, is proclaimed. It is a strange good news, which initially gives rise not only to enthusiasm but also to doubts and anxieties. The news is that "Christ is risen," and for this reason the gospel is also called the *"gospel of the resurrection."*

This good news does not simply turn the night of the cross into day in one fell stroke. The good news is by no means as triumphalistic or as clear and unshakable as has been repeatedly maintained. "But many doubted," say biblical texts. The good news, the gospel, did not descend from heaven with claps of thunder in such a way that no one could avoid it. Nor does it come in that way today. As God's word, the gospel comes to diverse witnesses in diverse life situations. And it comes to them in strange ways. The story of the disciples traveling to Emmaus is especially instructive. They encounter Jesus. But the text says their eyes are kept from recognizing the risen Christ. Then they sit together at table, and he breaks the bread, thanks God, and gives it to them. At that point their eyes are opened. But then the text does *not* say: and Jesus remained with them, and together they lived happily for such and such a time. Instead it says: "And he vanished from their sight." The good news does not say: Jesus is simply here again! The pre-Easter Jesus of Nazareth is here again! The good news does not say that after Easter things are again as they were before Easter. Jesus is here again, as if nothing had happened. Instead the good news, the gospel, says: here is the risen and exalted Christ, who is present in a wholly new way.

The risen, ascended Christ enters into many and diverse contexts of life. We read in Mark that "he was revealed in another form." He no longer attains presence in his individual, pre-Easter body, but in the body of Christ, in his church, in the community of believers. Modern common sense is quick to respond: therefore the resurrection is an illusion; it was nothing but fantasy. By contrast, the biblical texts say: On the one hand, the appearances are indeed appearances. The encounter with the risen Christ is not like an encounter with a neighbor or with the letter carrier. On the other hand, these appearances of the risen Christ involve a reality that definitely can be perceived by the senses. Here Jesus, the Jesus who had been killed, becomes present for diverse witnesses as a reality that could not arise at all if it consisted only of the encounter with a natural, earthly human being. He is present in a power and vitality vastly superior to the power and vitality of a merely earthly human being. Not only is he grounded in the reality of Jesus of Nazareth, he also creates a reality: *he creates the reality of the church of Christ.*

Through this new reality of the risen Christ and the reality of the body of Christ, God engages evil. With this reality God moves against the misuse of religion, politics, the law, and morality, and against the sin that has perverted the good law into something bad. Human beings are returned to justice, mercy, and the knowledge of God. They are enabled to hope, to love, to believe. Precisely because the gospel grows out of many different experiences of witnesses, it is a message that liberates in continually new ways. In continually new ways, God's word calls people out of compulsion and captivity. This liberating power of the gospel, which grows out of diverse testimonies and diverse encounters with the risen Christ, is a creative power.

This power of the word cannot be separated from the activity of the Holy Spirit, which, according to the promise of the prophet Joel, lays hold of men and women, old and young, bond and free, and enables them to engage in proclamation. The Pentecost account in Acts 2 cites this promise. In addition, the Pentecost account says that human beings have come together out of various lands, out of various regions, out of various traditions, with various languages. Wherever one looks in the story, people are coming together who cannot understand each other. But the outpouring of the Spirit enables these persons to perceive the "mighty acts of God." The Pentecost account highlights more dramatically and in more extreme terms than the resurrection accounts that the testimony of the church, the vitality of God's word in proclamation, is a vitality that grows out of diverse voices and languages, out of diverse environments and traditions, and out of groups of people who do not understand each other. The "good news" is news that enters into diverse directions, traditions, languages, and ears and is passed on by diverse directions, traditions, languages, and voices, yet leads to clarity, to shared understanding.

This says something important about evangelical freedom and about the word of God. The vitality of this word, the power of the gospel, the message of faith, comes to human beings from many sides and from many voices. However, it is a clear message, a message that bears witness to God's mighty acts, to the resurrected Christ and to Christ's action for us. This message is rich and creative, and it self-critically exposes itself to differences and to a corresponding vitality. At least it does so when ecclesial relations are healthy. With each other and for each other, human beings in great number disclose God's reality. The body of Christ not only consists of diverse members, but also has at its disposal diverse gifts. They are called charisms, gifts of the Spirit. God's Spirit endows human beings with diverse gifts, and by their interplay they lead to an increasingly complete knowledge of Christ and to an increasingly rich edification of the community.

Today we call such relations "pluralistic." The early church apparently did not know today's widespread anxiety over "pluralism." It was not yet familiar with the confusion between creative pluralism and relativism. Instead it saw that the vitality of God's word and the freedom of the gospel are tied up with the fact that no single human being and no single hierarchy can define what truth is. Evangelical freedom consists in the good news again and again growing anew out of many voices, out of many testimonies of faith. This does not mean trotting out all sorts of wildly divergent religious opinions. We must clearly distinguish over and over again between the creative pluralism of the Spirit and destructive relativism. Evangelical freedom is not religious arbitrariness. The message of the gospel is the message of liberation from the night of the cross. God did not abandon human beings to their attempts to cut themselves loose from God and to oppose God's presence. God did not hand human beings over to the consequences of the misuse of justice and of the knowledge of God. In the power of the resurrection and through the gift of the good Spirit, God turns again to the world. A new righteousness, God's righteousness, is established on earth. That is what God's word says in the form of the gospel.

Inasmuch as, in God's word, God turns again to the world, human beings are invited and enabled to entrust themselves to the presence of the risen Christ and to the beneficent powers of life, and to oppose the forces of injustice, destruction, delusion, and self-encapsulation. In the community of those who live and bear witness to the freedom of the gospel, human beings are taken on the way of the coming kingdom of God. For this reason the gospel is called not only the gospel of God, the gospel of Christ, and the gospel of the resurrection, but also the *"gospel of God's kingdom."*

What is God's kingdom, and how do I enter it? This question was put to Jesus, and his first answer was to point to God's law. "You have heard what has been said to you," he says, and then points to the Ten Commandments and to the great legal traditions. The kingdom of God most definitely has something to do with the fulfillment of the law — and this means with the perfection of justice, mercy, and the knowledge of God. At the same time, God's kingdom is a powerful reality in which God over and over again engages human distortions of the law, perversions of justice, refusals to show mercy, and roadblocks to the knowledge of God. God does this by making human beings, through God's word and God's Spirit, capable of evangelical freedom.

This means that human beings are placed over and over again in the presence of Christ. Their participation in the "body of Christ" is renewed and confirmed. At the same time, this means that God gives them diverse gifts of the Spirit. God enables them to give diverse and common testimonies of faith, and to live the communion in the body of Christ shared by its members. God enables them to work against religious one-sidedness and distortion. God enables them, on the basis of the richness of their testimonies, to bear witness to the presence of Christ in God's word and in the activity of God's Spirit. God enables them to take other human beings along on God's way. God enables them to be good seed and to bear abundant fruit, as is said in the parable of God's kingdom. In the midst of earthly life relations, a new reality is in the process of becoming. A new power is intervening in the interplay of the powers of this world. The kingdom of God is alive, continually in the process of coming and becoming. In the Lord's Prayer human beings pray over and over for its coming.

The coming kingdom of God, like the activity of the Spirit and the activity of the word, is not something that arrives like a train or a bus, so we could say now it is here or now it is not yet here. Instead the kingdom of God is already at work among us, and *at the same time* is still to come. It is transcendent and comes to us from the future, and *at the same time* it is in our midst, a living presence. It is externally visible inasmuch as proclamation, love, justice, and mercy bear fruit. *At the same time*, it is hidden in human hearts, in memories and expectations. God's kingdom is thus no illusion, but rather the form in which God's rule extends into this reality *by taking human beings into God's service.* God acts in the world by taking human beings into God's service; that is, God acts in the world with a frequently depressing fragility, inconspicuousness, and uncertainty. God acts in the world by selecting persons to spread God's word and God's will, and to bear witness to them. God does this by enabling persons, by means of God's word, to take advantage of evangelical freedom.

Today, too, evangelical freedom can be discovered in the interplay of those who bear witness to the cross of Christ and to the continual jeopardizing and self-jeopardizing of the world, and who proclaim the resurrection and the reality of Christ's presence among human beings. Evangelical freedom and the creativity of God's word can be discovered in the interplay of those who give expression to the outpouring of the Spirit and to the sanctification of human beings by means of the creative collaboration of men and women, old and young, persons of different social strata, cultures, traditions, and languages. Evangelical freedom and the sanctification of human beings can be discovered in the community that announces the coming kingdom of God, and at the same time prays and works for an increasingly clear presence of that kingdom.

In the Reformation, the discovery of evangelical freedom set in motion a great wave of renewal. What occurred was a renewal not only of the church but also of culture and society through the founding of schools, a transformation of education, and a transformation of political relations. Today, too, we need a renewal of culture, a new connection between individualism and communal sense, a new engagement for justice and the protection of the weak, a new seriousness in the search for truth and knowledge of God, a clear distinction between creative pluralism and relativism, a new persistence in the endeavor to spread the good seed of God's word. The knowledge of the form and power of evangelical freedom provides encouragement for this renewal. It is the task of Reformed theology to take part in working for this renewal, which will redound to Reformed theology's own renewal and revitalization.

CHAPTER 10

Potential Contributions of Reformed Theology to Ecumenical Discussion and Praxis

Beatriz Melano

Nobody doubts that the adventure of theology will never come to an end. It forms part of our human responsibility in relation to the grace that has been given to us. If that is quite clear to us as a premise, we will be less exposed to the risk of the kind of dogmatism which throughout the history of the church has led and is still leading to individualistic religious legalism — in the pejorative sense of the term — and to strictly normative ethics in which the law predominates over the freedom and grace of the gospel.

Georges Casalis emphasizes that Calvinist theology

> does not define itself as an academic exercise but as a witness given in a situation. . . . Calvin links theology inseparably to history: there is no *theologia perennis,* there are only provisional attempts with the purpose of nurturing and explaining the actual life of the christian community. That is why all unchangeable fixations of orthodoxy or of scientific pseudo-theology present the risk of the theological creation related to a precise time and place.[1]

For this reason, as we follow one of the basic principles of the Reformation — *ecclesia reformata semper reformanda* — as a *messianic communi-*

---

1. Georges Casalis, *Protestantisme* (Paris: Collection Encyclopédie Larousse, 1976), p. 6.

ty,[2] we cannot avoid the present challenge of the deep and generalized crisis of the church and the "global village" we are inhabiting at the dawn of the third millennium. When writing to the Christians who inhabited the power center of the Roman Empire, the apostle Paul advised them clearly and energetically not to be conformed to the criteria and values of their time and place, but to be transformed so as to be able to do the will of God (cf. Rom. 12:2).

Thus, the motto of *soli Deo gloria* which Calvin used to express his thought and action is at the same time a formula which adequately expresses the adventure of the Protestant Reformation. I believe that, if at that time it was important in order to maintain a clear concept of the mission of theology, it is even more important in our day because we are living in an age in which the lust of power for power's sake predominates.[3] This glorification of human power generates institutionalized violence, and that is why true discipleship can become so costly, as was shown by Dietrich Bonhoeffer, a Christian martyr during the dark age of Germany's Third Reich.

Along the same line, the basic principles of the Reformation — *sola Scriptura, sola fide,* and *sola gratia* — in their dialectical interrelation, constitute a response given by the Reformed theologians of the sixteenth century to the historical predicament of their time, which was marked by social, cultural, political, economic, and ecclesiastical fermentation on the threshold of a new society and a new age.

To the Reformers, and this must also be true for our own time, the hermeneutical key of *sola Scriptura* was Jesus Christ himself, in his liberating and redeeming work for the earth and all humankind. This is the kerygmatic center of interpretation that prevents us from falling prey to biblicism and social absenteeism. Moreover, it gives us the courage, the humility, and the freedom that are necessary for a theological renewal, in our time, at the end of the twen-

---

2. It is precisely in small messianic communities that strive for a responsible participation in history in their search for a more human society, that we perceive this type of social-religious solidarity and concrete ecumenism in their unselfish struggle dedicated to God's glory alone.

3. "God's glory is not the destruction but the liberation, it is not the deification but the true humanization of the human being. And to be able to reach this conviction of heart and mind it is necessary to pass through the deathly experience of St Paul on his way to Damascus, or that of Luther in his tower. This means that the human being is unable to give glory to God on his or her own, that the doors of death and resurrection must open in and for him or her so as to enable him or her to be born again. . . . The *soli Deo gloria* as a response to the dilemma that presents itself to the believer as the dilemma between the grace received and the human response [that is to say, the human responsibility], is the safeguard against all superiority complexes, pride, vanity, search of power, prestige, success, money, not only in our ecclesial life but also in life in general terms and at all its levels." Casalis, p. 18.

tieth century with its dehumanizing dilemmas permanently lying in ambush, as much as it did in the sixteenth century. The life, death, and resurrection of Jesus Christ and the work of the Holy Spirit clearly express God's plan in creation, liberation, and salvation *(soteria)* in their personal, social, and cosmic dimensions. If we lose sight of the dialectics of grace and the works of the kingdom inherent in the gospel message, we stand in danger of idolizing the Bible or our own ideology — our own theology — instead of living and proclaiming the kerygma. That will lead us to lose the relevant and prophetic dimensions of the theological task and of the mission of the church, the messianic community. Thus, centering upon sterile denominationalism, we lose the constitutive element of the church itself: its unity. Apart from that, the church loses its authority — in the eyes of both believers and atheists — as it reproduces the reality of a torn humanity in its own interior.

The assertions of the Reformation and, above all, the question of how we today are to give glory only to God — the only promise of life and power of liberation — have maintained their full relevance. And the question, as it was formulated by the Reformed theologian Georges Casalis, is not so much a matter of making sure we are the successors of the Reformers and their confessing communities as it is of asking ourselves whether or not we are their true heirs.[4]

There are many Protestants in Latin America who believe in the need of a second Reformation, which some of us dare to call the "Reformation of Love" or the "Reformation of Solidarity." We do not understand solidarity simply as Christian charity, but as something far more deep and radical: to render service as disciples of Christ in the defense of the essential rights of all persons of all classes and all nations. In a world in which three-quarters of the population is living in infrahuman conditions, this can never imply political, social, or economic neutrality; it is a world in which the majority simply cannot choose life because they are inevitably destined to die of hunger, of wars, because of omissions due to racism, because of religious fanaticism, because of legitimized ecological disasters, or because of the profits of a small group at the cost of the majority — that is to say, because of sins that form part of the structures and are legitimized by our society. If our lifestyle, priorities, and values are not tuned to the kingdom of God at the personal, communal, and national levels, they are anti-values, or, as Paul says, the values that "conform to this age."

The purpose of this article will be to outline briefly two points which I consider important and which may be able to help us in the ecumenical debate and in praxis. The first priority is the renewal of hermeneutics to help us return to the source *(sola Scriptura)*. To achieve this, it will be necessary to use all

---

4. Casalis, p. 23.

the tools that our time has placed within our reach, that help to liberate the text, that allow it to speak to us with all the power of its urgency. It is a matter of freeing it from false interpretations that have become dogmas in the past and whose burden is still present with us. As we perform this task we will be mindful of our human fallibility, our limitations.

In the second place there is the field of ecclesiology (*ecclesia reformanda*) that constitutes a theological problem whose revision is urgent. This in turn will refer us to Christology with its important implications for pastoral care and ethics. What kind of church, of ministries, of new forms or renewed traditional forms is indispensable to carry out the ministry of Christ in a relevant and prophetic way?

The Renewal of Biblical Hermeneutics

Our first affirmation is, synthetically, the need of a renewal of biblical hermeneutics in order to be faithful to the principles of Reformed theologians and, even more so, to the essence of the mission of the church itself in every moment of history. How do we arrive at a biblical interpretation that is faithful to the text and at the same time relevant to the historical moment in which we are living? This is a fundamental issue which implies the question about the way in which we can be more faithful to the gospel of Jesus Christ today, here and now. I believe this issue of biblical interpretation divides our contemporary theologies across confessional barriers. It divides the Christian church in its theological proceeding and in its historical praxis, and thus adds a new scandal to our society that is already schizophrenically split up in itself under the threat of total annihilation.

The Christian message is not so much a collection of dogmas and doctrines as the interpretation of fundamental events by means of which our God, Yahweh, reveals himself first in the history of the people of Israel and then, supremely, in Jesus Christ. Yahweh is a historical God who acts in history, not in the beyond of trans-history. For that reason, all emphasis on a merely individual and otherworldly salvation is a deformation of the Christian message. God's purpose, as we read in the Scriptures, is that of full redemption of the whole human being within the historical process. Those fundamental events have already been told, interpreted, and reinterpreted orally, and in written form in the Bible itself. They register the communications between God and his people, and even though God may speak through individuals, the overall direction is a global and integrated action which concerns humankind as a whole. That is to say that the hermeneutical task has not been initiated by us; it is present in the Bible itself, describing the historical reality as it was seen and experienced by the people of Israel, by the prophets, by Christ himself, by the early church, and by all whom God has encountered in order to communicate something to us.

In the second place, there is a basic fact to be kept in mind: it has been accepted as a matter of fact that we can approach the Bible in what I would call a state of "original innocence," unencumbered by our own personalities, the culture in which we are immersed, our ideals, our internalized images, our philosophical and ethical assumptions. It has been considered possible to apply the Scriptures directly to the reality of the world, that we can perform an *explicatio-applicatio* of what we read. Theology as well as hermeneutics have been thought of as tasks that can be performed as if we, as scholars of hermeneutics and theology, were working in a laboratory with pure and aseptic recipients. That is erroneous. When we approach Scripture, we must be aware of the fact that we are conditioned by the philosophical, ideological, ethical, social, and political background which is determined by the historical moment in which we are living.

For this reason we start following the Reformed philosopher and theologian Paul Ricoeur, with a *hermeneutics of suspicion.* Ricoeur mentions and points to the need of exposing the false consciousness *(cogito blessé* or *brisé)* which establishes itself as the basis of all meaning. After Nietzsche and Freud, the conscious mind can no longer claim to say the last word or to possess the ultimate truth; the unconscious and the preconscious distort its access to the truth. That is to say, we must be suspicious of our own ideas, our ideology and theology, when we approach the Scriptures.

Apart from that, there is the suspicion of our own methods. In the same way as there is no innocent consciousness, there are no innocent methods. Each method presupposes a theory with its own limitations, with its own purpose and a given epistemology. On these grounds Ricoeur favors a fertile encounter between the diverse rival interpretations in which the hermeneutical task is that of an arbitration of the interpretations in order to be able to obtain greater hermeneutical fidelity. This applies to the field of biblical interpretation as well as to the secular hermeneutics of institutions, rites, myths, dreams, and ideologies.

Ricoeur's proposition has been followed by various Latin American theologians. Juan Luis Segundo suspects that everything that is related to ideas is intimately linked with our present social situation, including theology. That points to the need of combining the disciplines which open up the past with those that explain the present, so that theology is the attempt to interpret God's word "as it is addressed to us here and now."[5] In consequence, Segundo,

---

5. Juan Luis Segundo, *The Liberation of Theology* (Maryknoll, N.Y.: Orbis, 1976), p. 8.

like Ricoeur, sees the *hermeneutical circle* as a "continuing change in our inter-pretation of the Bible which is dictated by the continuing changes in our pres-ent-day reality, both individual and societal."[6] Two conditions must be ful-filled to guarantee the true circularity of the hermeneutical task. In the first place, when we turn to the Bible, the richness and depth of our questions, of our suspicions about reality, must effect a change in our accustomed opinions about the different spheres of human existence. In the second place, the rich-ness and depth of our questions must lead us from our accustomed way of reading to a new interpretation of the Bible. If our interpretation does not change and remains as it was two or three centuries ago, theology will not change either in response to the changes in the world's problems. According to Segundo, in that case "they will receive old, conservative, unserviceable an-swers,"[7] irrelevant to the historical moment of the present.

"Everything depends on the complete reciprocity between biblical intel-ligence and the intelligence of our time."[8] That is one of Ricoeur's central affir-mations. Whereas for Ricoeur, apart from the arbitration between rival inter-pretations it is also necessary to make use of modern semiotics, as Latin American theologians we follow this line of thought, also applying modern so-cial sciences in order to gain a better understanding of reality. This helps us to reformulate theology through a hermeneutical renewal. From this new angle of vision, we might say, theology and the preaching and ministry of the church are applied today to the class struggle, to racial conflicts, to the development of history, to the relationship of men and women and the relationship between the oppressed and the oppressor. Thus the Bible and Christian praxis are re-lated in a continual hermeneutical circle whose heart is the gospel itself: Jesus Christ, whose presence is made perceptible in the ministry of the Christian church that is truly committed to its historical praxis.

We insist that the hermeneutical circle always presupposes a profound human commitment to the historical reality in which we exercise our ministry. It is starting from Scripture and from reality that we establish the guidelines for our theological task and our missiological praxis. This is why, apart from the hermeneutics of suspicion, I would insist on the *hermeneutics of commit-ment and hope,* because commitment gives rise to hope.

This hermeneutical renewal, as we have referred to it, necessarily leads to a conscious or unconscious partiality in the rereading of the text. Precisely, Segundo affirms that such partiality which has been consciously accepted by

6. Segundo, p. 8.
7. Segundo, p. 9.
8. Beatriz Melano, *Hermenéutica metódica. Teoría de la Interpretación según Paul Ricoeur* (Buenos Aires: Docencia, 1983), p. 237.

human criteria is necessary, because there are no hermeneutics which are absolutely unattached (impartial). A theology which is "autonomous, impartial, . . . floating free above the realm of human options and biases"[9] in reality implies a commitment to the psychological, social, or political status quo.

The Renewal of the Church

Faced with the crisis of the church as mentioned in the introduction to this article, I explained that several theologians of the Third World, myself included, see the need of a second Reformation: the "Reformation of Solidarity," a solidarity which implies a concrete commitment of Christians to one another and, above all, to those living in infrahuman conditions. For this reason, although all theological issues are important and stand in need of revision, it is the ecclesiological issue that is fundamental and demands a redefinition of the nature of the church.

Our first affirmation about this issue is that *ecclesiology* and *missiology* can never be separated. The church has defined itself as the place of the proclamation of the Word and the administration of the sacraments. On the other hand, its mission has been conceived of as the sending toward "others," pagans, the poor, as crossing the oceans, carrying the good news of the gospel and the works of Christian charity (schools, hospitals, etc.). It is important to take into account that the Reformers recovered both aspects of the church at the same time. To them the proclamation of the Word, the administration of the sacraments, and the foundation of schools and diaconal works constituted the indivisible task of the body of Christ.

It is therefore necessary to revise our concept of the nature of the church in order to define its ministry in clear and relevant terms. Its essence and its form are intimately linked together. Bonhoeffer defines it as *Christ existing in community*. It is the messianic community, that is to say, the community of Christ, which has manifested the project of the kingdom of God in its life and proclaimed it in its teaching. And if the church by its own nature is the presence, the proclamation, and the foretaste of God's project for the whole of humankind, then it is within its realm that there are neither men nor women, neither exploiters nor exploited, neither Christians nor atheists (cf. Gal. 3:28).

But if this messianic community is not incarnate in historical reality, expressing the values of the kingdom in its own life, then where is the church? Only as the incarnation of the living Christ facing the urgent claims and needs of modern life does the community hold authority and credibility in its rela-

9. Segundo, p. 13.

tion to the world. Only as it lives the life of the gospel does it earn the right to proclaim it in the Word.

In Latin American base communities we have experienced and felt very important things for the renewal of the church. Roman Catholics and Protestants, men and women, laypeople and clerics, committed together in the struggle for human rights, in struggles with the unemployed, together with the landless, with workers and peasants, with abandoned women and homeless children, have in solidarity discovered the living presence and the hope of Christ. The church, which for centuries was the ally of power centers, has found a space in those base communities in which here and now it has been able to be in solidarity with the poor and to acquire a credibility and authority that are unprecedented. As it shares the daily struggle of the marginalized and oppressed in their claim for a decent life, we have been able to sit down to share bread and wine without confessional, racial, cultural, class, or gender distinctions. That is why I am convinced that we will achieve a more visible union of the church of Christ as we start among the bases and not among the hierarchies. It is a movement that starts at the bottom to move upward, not something that is imparted at the top.

As he wrote about Christian discipleship, Dietrich Bonhoeffer expressed very clearly that *cheap grace* is the deadly enemy of our church, grace understood as a mere doctrine, included as an empty concept in the preaching of forgiveness without repentance.[10] Its counterpart, costly grace, is costly precisely because it is the gospel itself, because it is obedience to Jesus with all the consequences this may imply. It was costly to God in the death of Jesus Christ, and that is why it cannot be cheap or easy for us. The words of Jesus Christ are not a doctrine but the creation of a new existence, and "there is no road to faith or discipleship, no other road — only obedience to the call of Jesus."[11]

Nevertheless, and in spite of all that is said in the Bible about Jesus' life and ministry, about the ethics of the kingdom of God and the very nature of the church which is mission, we continue to teach those two aspects as separate fields in seminaries all over the world. On the one hand we teach "Doctrine of the Church," and on the other, "Missiology." And as a corollary of this separation, isn't there, among Protestants as well as Roman Catholics, a separation between what is considered evangelization and what is called diaconal and social service? If we understand that the nature of the church is to be seen in a permanent complementation of its proclamation with solidary action, the message of Jesus Christ must be something that reaches out beyond the word

10. Cf. Dietrich Bonhoeffer, *The Cost of Discipleship*, 2nd rev. ed. (New York: Macmillan, 1959), p. 35.

11. Bonhoeffer, p. 49.

that is preached from the pulpit. It cannot be reduced to the solitary and personal salvation of the human soul. Nor can it be limited to a mere "social gospel." When the proclaimed word is not accompanied by visible solidarity with those who have been relegated by society, it runs the risk of becoming an empty and meaningless word. That is why proclamation and service must be intrinsically related to one another, and the most coherent evangelization is that which is carried out in service next to the poorest.

Yet, that does not mean that the church is called to become something like a miniature United Nations or Red Cross organization. The messianic community must not be on its way to becoming a big institution of charity. The New Testament vision of peace and justice is that of a messianic base community witnessing in word and action in its situation of dispersion. Richard Shaull has affirmed this very appropriately:

> We are . . . in a situation similar to that of the Jews of the Diaspora, scattered among people whose culture, mores and thought patterns are not like ours nor will they become so; our cathedrals and temples are no longer in the center of life nor do they bring the whole community together under God. If we hope to reach modern [women and] men, it will be not so much in terms of gathering [them] into the church as of going to [them] in the midst of our dispersion.[12]

As a corollary to our first affirmation, we would like to make a second one: We cannot separate Christology from soteriology. The saving act of Christ creates community, *koinonia,* and is the reason of its existence: "The Son of Man came not to be served but to serve, and to give his life a ransom for many" (Matt. 20:28 NRSV). Out of a group of fearful and confused disciples the Holy Spirit creates a community of worship, proclamation, and solidary service. Worship and the service of the "others" (without distinction of creed, nationality, or race) must never be separated. Service is an intrinsic part of the reason of the church's existence: it is a form of praise, of true worship, because worship cannot consist of mere individual, spiritual edification. The saving work of Christ, the kerygma, addresses itself to the whole human problem. There is no human affair that is alien to him. Reconciliation among human beings and among nations is related to the reconciliation of humankind with God which has been established by Christ. It manifests the link between God and humanity as a whole. The images of liberation and of exodus in the Old Testament are transferred to a total reconciliation of humankind in Christ, and his work of liberation is closely linked to the whole problematic of peace and justice —

12. Richard Shaull, "The Form of the Church in the Modern Diaspora," *Princeton Seminary Bulletin* 57, no. 3 (1964): 7.

justice, above all, to the oppressed, the needy, and those who are exploited by the powers that be.

The Renewal of Ecclesiology

One of the most alarming facts in our present situation is, therefore, the deep fear of a radical reformation, in the Roman Catholic Church as well as in the churches of the Reformed and Orthodox traditions. We find ourselves in stagnation, in antiquated forms of organization, of liturgy, of pastoral care, and all attempts to conceive new expressions of the true essence of the church frighten us even before we try to put them into practice. The church has started to become a shelter for Christians instead of being the frontier of service and discipleship of Christ. For this reason we would point to what we understand to be three *notae ecclesiae* of a Reformed church *semper reformanda:*

Prophetic Community: A Frontier of Liberation in the Face of the Negation of Basic Human Rights

Two-thirds of humanity is living under infrahuman conditions. What has to be the response of the churches to this situation? We are faced with a tremendous challenge: to become a prophetic community in the frontier of liberation. What would this mean? The churches must become the frontiers of the nations, like the prophets were the conscience of the people of Israel. The prophetic message is focused upon the particular historical situation and points to concrete empirical problems. It is at this point that I see no way ahead but in all earnestness to take the side of the widows, the orphans, the bereaved, the foreigners, and the poor of the biblical times, who today are the dispossessed, the exploited, the prisoners, the oppressed. The churches must be the voice of the voiceless because they have no place and no power. Although we cannot reduce the mission of the church to the sociopolitical dimension of human life, nevertheless we cannot reduce the historical impact of the Christian message. To be a prophetic community means to proclaim the new humanity in Christ and to create the sacred space within which that may take place. The God of Israel, the Father of Jesus Christ, does not merely offer us a religion. He calls a people to follow his purposes. The people of God do not have a message but are a message in themselves.

Ecumenical Community: A Frontier of Unity and Reconciliation

We live in a time of polarization and division in First and Third Worlds (and between them), within the Christian church, and among the world's religions. A few years ago Nelson Mandela made a profound statement to Emilio Castro, former general secretary of the World Council of Churches, expressing this thought: in South Africa we as blacks and whites will be able to sit together at the table of dialogue and agreement before you Christians will be able to surround the same table to partake of the bread and wine together. The scandal of our divisions and subdivisions in Christianity adds one more to the scandal of the cross. What dimension of the Christian message speaks to this situation? The Christian community must take seriously the possibility that the miracle of authentic human communication occurs in her midst. But to become an ecumenical community of reconciliation, needless to say, does not ever just happen, nor does it happen overnight. There is a kind of openness toward "the other," deeply rooted in the openness of the almighty God to us in Jesus Christ. It can become possible to interact with one another as persons, without needing to use those terribly final tags by which people locate and dismiss one another: liberal, conservative, moderate, radical, progressive, capitalist, socialist. It is not at all a matter of calling a moratorium on critical distinctions about ways of looking at things, but rather of discovering that the real raw material of any debate of struggle to achieve something is the people involved, actually or potentially, and that the tags used to dismiss or destroy simply isolate us from that human raw material. As a messianic community, we have to take seriously Jesus' last prayer to the Father for his disciples before he faced the trial and crucifixion: "That they may be one, even as we are one: I in them, and thou in me, that they may be made perfect in one; and that the world may know that thou hast sent me, and hast loved them, as thou hast loved me" (John 17:22-23 KJV).

Community of Incarnated Nonviolence: A Frontier of Shalom

Another symptom which is eloquent of the cruel reality of our current times is the growing rate of violence. Life seems to be "cheap," human life has absolutely no value, there is violence all around the world: in South Africa, Peru, Ireland, former Yugoslavia, the Middle East, some of the former Soviet countries, Mexico, and so on. Added to political violence we have ordinary criminal delinquency, which is the product of the political, social, and economic imbalance. So, in the face of corporal, verbal, and structural violence that mutilates the minimum basic human rights, the messianic community cannot remain in a neutral sphere, in cowardice or in acceptance of this kind of situation. The nonviolent and peaceful community is both called upon and enabled to be the place for an authentic shalom in a world torn asunder, and to announce to women and men everywhere this eternally new divine possibility.

Conclusion

If we are afflicted by the pain of the world, we are not called upon to look for partial and inefficient solutions, but to join in the promotion of drastic changes and significant transformations as messianic communities. The renewal of the church will be achieved through scattered communities which operate as frontiers of liberation, ecumenicity, and nonviolence in a society whose gods are power and money, an idolatrous society which is on its way toward total dehumanization.

After all, why are young people and even adults (of all social classes without distinction) looking for responses to their material and spiritual dilemmas in Oriental religions, in gurus, fortune-tellers, horoscopes, occultism, esoteric rites, and uncountable pseudo-Christian sects? Isn't that so because the Christian churches fail to provide the answers? Isn't it because the church has lost or is losing authenticity and credibility? Isn't it because the church is not present where it is most needed? Isn't it because the church is more deeply committed to the search for power than to the discipleship of the crucified Christ? Isn't it because the church believes it possesses the monopoly of grace within its own boundaries and is blind to the work of grace in "the world"?

PART 2

TOPICS AND
TRANSFORMATIONS

CHAPTER 11

The Substance of Faith

Thomas Torrance

I n determining the meaning of the expression "the substance of the Faith," it
seems right to go back to the act of the Scottish Parliament in 1690 which
ratified the Westminster Confession of Faith (WCF) "as the publick and
avowed Confession of this Church, containing the summe and substance of the
doctrine of the Reformed Churches." There the WCF was regarded as containing the sum and substance of some thirty Reformed confessions, including the
Scots Confession and the First and Second Helvetic Confessions. These confessions expressly acknowledged the ancient catholic creeds and conciliar statements of the church, the Apostles' Creed, the Nicene Creed, the formulations
of Ephesus and Chalcedon, and the so-called Athanasian Creed, and embodied
all their main statements as essential articles of belief. This was true of the
WCF, which, as James Denney once pointed out, "contains everything that is in
the Nicene Creed."[1] That is to say, there was no move away from what the
Athanasian Creed and the Second Helvetic Confession called "the Catholic
Faith," although the basic articles of faith handed down through the creeds
were set within a confessional frame of distinctively Reformed character. It was
inevitable, therefore, that a distinction was made between what Samuel
Rutherford called "a confession *de jure,* what everyman ought to believe, as the
Nicene Creed, and the Creed of Athanasius,"[2] and a wider summation of
teaching common to "true Reformed Protestant religion."

1. James Denney, *Jesus and the Gospel* (1908), pp. 391-92.
2. Samuel Rutherford, *Due Right of Presbyteries* (1644), p. 13.

Originally published as " 'The Substance of the Faith': A Clarification of the Concept
in the Church of Scotland," *Scottish Journal of Theology* 36 (1983): 327-38.

A distinction of this kind was implied in the Acts of the General Assembly in 1696 and 1720, which singled out what were called "the grand mysteries of the Gospel" or "the great and fundamental truths," such as the Trinity, the incarnation, the deity of Christ, propitiation, salvation, regeneration, justification, resurrection, etc., while rejecting any other doctrines inconsistent with the Confession of Faith. In 1711, however, in an act anent the formula of subscription, "the sum and substance of the doctrine of the Reformed Churches" was replaced by "the whole doctrine contained in the Confession of Faith, approved by the General Assemblies of this Church and ratified by law in the year 1690." Did this mean that ministers and office bearers were required to subscribe to the WCF as a whole, i.e., as a unity, without commitment to every proposition it contained, or to the WCF as a system of doctrinal propositions?

The latent ambiguity this involved had not a little to do with the secessions and divisions that afflicted the church in Scotland for the next two centuries, whenever conscientious dissent, relating, for example, to exclusivist notions of predestination or to the doctrine of the magistrate, was registered. Ways of subscribing to the Confession of Faith were sought which would allow reasonable liberty of opinion in assent while leaving the confession as a whole intact. That was not a difficulty confined to Scotland. It was felt very acutely in the American Presbyterian church, which, from its original synod in 1729, demanded reception and adoption of the Confession of Faith "as containing the system of doctrine taught in the Holy Scriptures." Although this was ratified by the union of two Presbyterian synods in 1758 and again in 1788, it gave rise to serious controversy as to how subscription was to be understood, which led to the division of the church in 1838 and continued to the end of the century in the Northern and the Southern Presbyterian Churches. It was in the due course of that debate that a contrast was drawn between "the system of doctrine" and "the substance of doctrine." Charles Hodge of Princeton championed subscription to the system of doctrine contained in the WCF, and wrote a powerful article, "Adoption of the Confession of Faith," in 1858, which had considerable influence in Scotland. He held that "it is impossible in matters of doctrine, to separate the substance from the form. The form is essential to the doctrine, as much as the form of a statue is essential to the statue. In adopting a system of doctrines, therefore, the candidate adopts a series of doctrines in the specific form in which they are presented in that system."[3] Nevertheless, this did not imply, in Hodge's view, that adoption of the system of doctrine contained in the WCF meant the adoption of every proposition contained in it.

Hodge made another significant point, which was to have its due effect

---

3. Charles Hodge, *The Church and Its Policy,* ed. A. A. Hodge (1879), p. 320.

in Scotland. According to him, "the WCF contains three distinct classes of doctrines. First, those common to all Christians, which are summed up in the ancient creeds, the Apostles', the Nicene and the Athanasian, which are adopted by all Churches. Secondly, those which are common to all Protestants, and by which they are distinguished from Romanists. Thirdly, those which are peculiar to the Reformed Churches, by which they are distinguished, on the one hand, from the Lutherans, and on the other from the Remonstrants, or Arminians, and other sects of later historical origin." He went on to add that "any man who receives these several classes of doctrines [the three he mentions above] holds in its integrity the system of doctrine contained in the Westminster Confession."[4] It should be pointed out that while in 1837 and 1892 the Northern Church distinguished those articles of the confession which are more properly creedal from the rest, it was not till 1901 that it decided to deal with the subscription problem either by modification or by declaratory statement. Some changes were made regarding the chapter on the magistrate, for example, and an article was added on the Holy Spirit to make up for a deficiency in the WCF, which eased the question of subscription, but the general approach of Hodge which tended to identify the truth of doctrines with their formulation remained, so that adherence was required to the "system of doctrine" in the WCF rather than to its "substance."

In Scotland the movement was in the other direction. In 1874 the great Robert Rainy drew a distinction between "two strata of confessional matter," those articles which "constitute the solid core, which cannot alter unless the conviction of the whole Church should alter," and those which "may reasonably be regarded as the more variable element, which circumstances might require to extended at one time and contracted at another."[5] Moreover, when Rainy went on to insist that when the confessional formulas of churches diverge "the point of view of the universal Church ought to be accepted as the fundamental one,"[6] he opened the way for an interpretation of the unchanging creedal core or substance of the faith in terms of what the universal or catholic church in all ages must hold central, in distinction from what particular churches may need to affirm in their own conditions of time and place, and so opened up the way for reference to the unchanging core or substance of the faith as a rule or principle in accordance with which other doctrinal determinations may be judged.

The views of Hodge and Rainy were bound to have a significant bearing upon the representatives of the fifty or more Presbyterian churches as they

---

4. Hodge, pp. 333-34.
5. Robert Rainy, *The Delivery and Development of Christian Doctrine* (1874), p. 263.
6. Rainy, p. 271.

came together at the first Pan-Presbyterian Council in Edinburgh in 1877, and the permanent creedal elements in their twenty to thirty different Reformed confessions gravitated to the center. This is certainly evident in the debates that took place in Scotland thereafter, when different views were put forward, for example, by John Cairns in the United Presbyterian Church and Kenneth Moody-Stuart in the Free Church, over the relative merits of "the substance of the faith" and "the system of doctrine" in any formula of subscription to the Westminster Confession of Faith.

It was the United Presbyterian Church under the leadership of John Cairns which took the first decisive step in 1878/79 in passing a Declaratory Act which stated in clause 7: "That, in accordance with the practice hitherto observed in this Church, liberty of opinion is allowed on such points in the Standards, not entering into the substance of the faith, as the interpretation of the 'six days' in the Mosaic account of the creation: the Church guarding against the abuse of this liberty to the injury of its unity and peace."[7] In his *Speech on Subordinate Standards* (1878),[8] Cairns made it clear that no alteration in the substance of what the church had always confessed was intended, but that the formula of subscription proposed was preferable to that of the American church, which required adherence to "the system of doctrine" even though its operation depended on the general sense of brethren in the church.[9]

The Church of Scotland followed this lead ten years later when the General Assembly adopted an Act on Subscription of Office Bearers in the Church, in 1889, which revised and amended the formulas used hitherto. The effective clause was in these terms: "The General Assembly, while desiring by these changes to enlarge rather than curtail any liberty heretofore enjoyed, and to relieve subscribers from unnecessary burdens as to forms of expression and matters which do not enter into the substance of the faith, declares, at the same time, the adherence of the Church to the Confession of Faith, as its public and avowed Confession, and containing the sum and substance of the doctrine of the Reformed Churches."[10] For this to become law in the Church of Scotland a parliamentary act was needed, so that the General Assembly of 1905 called for a bill to amend the law in regard to the Formula of Subscription to the WCF, but this request was made "with the object of securing to the Church the right to regulate her own affairs within and upon the Act of 1690 and the Confes-

---

7. Cf. C. G. M'Crie, *The Confessions of the Church of Scotland* (1907), pp. 283-84.

8. The article is incorrectly dated 1978 (editor's note).

9. *Subordinate Standards of the United Presbyterian Church* (1897), pp. 15ff.

10. *Acts of the General Assembly* (1889), Act 17; see James Cooper, *Confessions of the Faith and Formulas of Subscription* (1907), p. 72; Alexander Stewart, *Creeds and Churches: Studies in Symbolics* (1916), pp. 267-68; and M'Crie, p. 251.

sion of Faith." The Church of Scotland thus claimed "the right as a Church to make our own Formula, and it would then be possible for the Church, while not going outside of the Confession of Faith or derogating from it in essentials, to retain the power of modifying from time to time under its own constitutional procedure the actual terms of subscription."[11] Quite evidently the Church of Scotland was drawing a distinction between the essentials or substance of the faith and detailed formulations of it in a system of doctrinal propositions. This was the line advocated by William Milligan of Aberdeen and by Alexander Stewart of Saint Andrews, the moderator of the General Assembly of 1911.[12]

In 1892 the Free Church of Scotland passed a Declaratory Act which was framed with that of the United Presbyterian Church particularly in view.[13] It was declared "That the Church disclaims intolerant or persecuting principles, and does not consider her office-bearers, in subscribing the Confession, committed to any principles inconsistent with the liberty of conscience and the right of private judgment." And: "That while diversity of opinion is recognised in this Church on such points in the Confession as do not enter into the substance of the Reformed Faith set forth, the Church retains full authority to determine, in any case which may arise, what points fall within this description, and thus to guard against any abuse of this liberty to the detriment of sound doctrine, or to the injury of her unity and peace." As M'Crie pointed out, the Free Church "does not distinguish between what is and what is not *de fide*, between what enters into the substance of the Reformed Faith as exhibited in the Confession and what is outside thereof, although stated in the symbol. It abstains from making any enumeration or giving any illustration of what may be considered matters of lesser importance concerning which diversity of opinion ought to be allowed."[14] But it was nevertheless made clear that the Free Church could not accept any private opinion as to what is of the substance of the Reformed faith — that right of judgment the church retained in its own power. It should be noted that when the union between the United Presbyterian Church and the Free Church took place in 1900 to form the United Free Church, no explicit mention was made of the formulas of subscription, but a happy agreement in regard to doctrine, government, discipline, and worship was recorded. However, this was not a matter that could be set aside when a wider union was

11. *Reports of the General Assembly* (1905), cited by Cooper, p. 81.

12. William Milligan, *The Ascension and Heavenly Priesthood of our Lord* (1891), pp. 320-22; Stewart, pp. 216-17.

13. Act 12, 1892, Anent Confession of Faith; see *Proceedings and Debates* (1892), pp. 145-72; Cooper, pp. 9-10; A. Taylor Innes, *The Law of Creeds in Scotland* (1902), pp. 334ff.; and M'Crie, pp. 287ff.

14. M'Crie, p. 292.

contemplated, embracing the United Free Church and the Church of Scotland. The initiative was taken by the Church of Scotland and pursued in a series of steps from 1907 to 1919 when, in regular consultation with the United Free Church, it sought at the same time to clarify its own position as the national church in respect of its spiritual authority and of its fidelity to the primary and subordinate standards of the faith.[15] In 1911 the Church of Scotland representatives made the following submission: "The Church of Scotland would, it is believed, approve of a fresh declaration of spiritual freedom being embodied in the constitution of a United Church in such comprehensive terms as would include all matters spiritual, always consistently with the word of God and in fidelity to the substance of the Reformed Faith being the fundamental doctrines of the Christian faith contained in the common standards of the conferring Churches."[16] It was with that agreement and understanding that eventually, after the war in 1919, "Draft Articles Declaratory of the Constitution of the Church of Scotland in Matters Spiritual" were submitted, which were turned into an act of the General Assembly in 1926.[17] That was the basis on which the Church of Scotland rested as it went forward to the union between the two churches that was consummated in 1929.

The articles or parts of articles in that act which are relevant to our present inquiry are as follows:

1. The Church of Scotland is part of the Holy Catholic or Universal Church; worshipping one God, Almighty, all-wise, and all-loving, in the Trinity of the Father, the Son, and the Holy Ghost, the same in substance, equal in power and glory; adoring the Father, infinite in Majesty, of whom are all things; confessing our Lord Jesus Christ, the Eternal Son, made very man for our salvation; glorying in His Cross and Resurrection, and owning obedience to Him as the Head over all things to His Church; trusting in the promised renewal and guidance of the Holy Spirit; proclaiming the forgiveness of sins and acceptance with God through faith in Christ, and the gift of Eternal Life; and labouring for the advancement of the Kingdom of God throughout the world. The Church of Scotland adheres to the Scottish Reformation; receives the Word of God which is contained in the Scriptures of the Old and New Testaments as its supreme rule of faith and life; and vows the fundamental doctrines of the Catholic faith founded thereupon.

15. Summarized in the *Reports of the Schemes of the Church of Scotland* (1919), pp. 549-67.

16. *Reports of the Schemes*, p. 554.

17. *Acts of the General Assembly* (1926), pp. 22-23.

2. The principal subordinate standard of the Church of Scotland is the Westminster Confession of Faith approved by the General Assembly of 1647, containing the sum and substance of the Faith of the Reformed Church. . . .

5. This Church has the inherent right, free from interference by civil authority, but under the safeguards for deliberate action and legislation provided by the Church itself, to frame or adapt its subordinate standards, to declare the sense in which it understands the Confession of Faith, to modify the forms of expression therein, or to formulate other doctrinal statements, and to define the relation thereto of its office-bearers and members, but always in agreement with the Word of God and the fundamental doctrines of the Christian Faith contained in the said Confession, of which agreement the Church shall be sole judge, and with due regard to liberty of opinion in points which do not enter into the substance of the Faith.

8. The Church has the right to interpret these Articles, and, subject to the safeguards for deliberate action and legislation provided by the Church itself, to modify or add to them; but always consistently with the provisions of the first Article hereof, adherence to which, as interpreted by the Church, is essential to its continuity and corporate life. . . .

Altogether, these Declaratory Articles constitute a very remarkable document which gathers up, reflects, and interprets salient points in the history of the church in Scotland, which we have briefly traversed, and builds out of them a coherent declaration of the Constitution of the Church of Scotland in Matters Spiritual, in which all articles have to be understood in their interconnection. Several comments may now be offered which may help clarify what is meant by "the substance of the Faith" (spelled in this way, with a capital "F").

1. There is a fundamental difference between the first and the second of the Declaratory Articles, which clearly reflects the distinction Rainy drew between two strata of confessional matter, or even the difference between what Hodge called the first and the other two classes of doctrine, the first being summed up in the ancient creeds, the Apostles' and Nicene and Athanasian. It is only when we come to the second Declaratory Article that we find mentioned the Westminster Confession of Faith, which is referred to as "the principal subordinate standard of the Church of Scotland." While the creeds of "the Holy Catholic or Universal Church," of which the Church of Scotland is "part," are not named, nevertheless definite witness is borne to the essential articles of faith which they enshrine, and in such a way that the first Declaratory Article becomes the equivalent of what Samuel Rutherford had called "a confession *de jure*, what everyman ought to believe, as the Nicene Creed, and the Creed of

Athanasius." Affirmation of these essential articles of faith, however, is made, along with the declaration that "the Church of Scotland adheres to the Scottish Reformation" and a statement about "the Word of God which is contained in the Scriptures of the Old and New Testaments" as the church's supreme rule of faith and life, which is not found, explicitly at any rate, in the ancient creeds.

2. The fact that the eighth Declaratory Article gives the first article a unique place in the Constitution of the Church of Scotland by making it the unchanging point of reference for any change in the future, clearly means that the doctrinal content of the first article has to be regarded as constituting what Rainy had called "the solid core, which cannot alter unless the conviction of the whole Church should alter."[18] The church has no power to alter but can only proclaim and hand on "the faith once and for all delivered to the saints" (Jude 3). That is what the Church of Scotland intended to do through the first Declaratory Article.

3. The first article is brought to a head with the explicit avowal of "the fundamental doctrines of the Catholic faith" founded upon the Word of God. Here the expression "the Catholic faith," as is evident from the discussions of the framing committee, was taken directly from the Athanasian Creed: "This is the Catholic faith, that we worship God in Trinity and Trinity in unity," etc. But it was also taken indirectly from the same source through the Second Helvetic Confession (adopted by the Church of Scotland during the Reformation), which accepted the creedal statements of the Councils of Nicaea, Constantinople, Ephesus, and Chalcedon "together with the blessed Athanasius' Creed": "And thus we retain the Christian, sound, and Catholic faith, whole and inviolable, knowing that nothing is contained in the aforesaid Creeds which is not agreeable to the Word of God, and makes wholly for the uncorrupt declaration of the Faith." When the fifth article, on the other hand, refers to "the fundamental doctrines of the Christian [N.B.: not the 'Reformed'] Faith contained in the said Confession," it is evidently equating these doctrines with those of the catholic faith declared in the first article. Since it is in this connection that reference is made to "liberty of opinion in points which do not enter into the substance of the Faith" [sic], it is clear that the substance of the catholic faith proclaimed in the first article is in view. This is reinforced by the unique constitutional status accorded to the first article in the eighth: "always consistently with the provisions of the first Article hereof."

That all the churches concerned, the United Presbyterian Church, the Church of Scotland, the Free Church, and the reunited Church of Scotland in 1929, explicitly opted for the expression "the substance of the Faith" instead of

18. Cf. Augustus Muir, *John White* (1958), pp. 157-58.

the American expression "the system of doctrine" is very revealing.[19] It shows that they acknowledged that a distinction must be drawn between the substance of the faith and its doctrinal formulation, and that doctrinal propositions about the truth cannot be identified with the truth itself. But it also shows that what they had in view was not some set of definable doctrinal propositions but the unalterable and ultimately indefinable core of the Christian and catholic faith which commands the universal assent of the church in all ages, and to which the church bears testimony in all ages in creedal acknowledgment before the face of God in worship. That is why, in giving expression to the acknowledgment of the Church of Scotland of the Christian and catholic faith, the first Declaratory Article brings together the words "worshipping," "adoring," "confessing," "glorying," "trusting," and "proclaiming," and adds to the expression, "labouring," for what is believed in this doxological way must be acted out in service.

Since the Christian and catholic faith of the universal church was brought to creedal expression in this way supremely in the Nicene-Constantinopolitan Creed, upon which all Christendom rests, it would seem eminently right and reasonable today to appeal to the Nicene-Constantinopolitan Creed in giving operative reference to the "substance of the Faith" as employed in the fifth Declaratory Article. Constitutionally, of course, the reference would have to be made to the first Declaratory Article as an indivisible and unalterable whole, and in terms of "the Catholic Faith" which it avowed, but in the regular life, worship, and discipline of the church, and in all interchurch communion, operative reference to the Nicene-Constantinopolitan Creed as the most succinct and the one universal expression of the catholic faith, which we have constantly used in the Church of Scotland, not least in the Courts of the Church during celebration of the Lord's Supper, would be immensely advantageous.[20] Moreover, it would go far to help the Church of Scotland implement its obligations set out in the seventh Declaratory Article: "The Church of Scotland, believing it to be the will of Christ that His disciples should all be one in the Father and in Him, that the world may believe that the Father has sent Him, recognises the obligation to seek and promote union with other Churches in which it finds the Word to be purely preached, the sacraments administered according to Christ's ordinance, and discipline rightly exercised; and it has the right to unite with any such Church without loss of its identity on terms which this Church finds to be consistent with these Articles."

19. James Taylor Cox, *Practice and Procedure in the Church of Scotland*, ed. D. F. M. MacDonald, 6th ed. (1976), pp. 390ff.

20. *The Ordinal and Service Book for Use in the Courts of the Church* (1931, 1954, 1962).

4. A further comment, of a more epistemological kind, may now be offered about what is indicated by "the substance of the Faith." This has to do with the fact that the substance of the faith is grounded in and ultimately inseparable from the saving acts of God in Jesus Christ. In the NT the gospel refers not merely to the good news about salvation through Jesus Christ but to Jesus Christ, who in his own person, word, and deed is the very core of the gospel — i.e., to what John Calvin called "Christ clothed with his Gospel." Thus the NT *kerygma* refers not merely to proclamation about Christ but to the reality proclaimed, Jesus Christ who is actively and savingly at work in and through the *kerygma*. That is to say, *kerygma* has an essentially objective and concrete sense; the same is true of what the NT calls *baptisma*, which cannot be identified with *baptismos*, the sacramental rite of baptism. Likewise the expressions "the Faith" or "the Deposit," which had been handed on to the church through the apostles[21] and which the church is enjoined to guard intact and hand on again, refer not merely to a body of belief in Christ but to the living substance and foundation of faith in Christ and what he has done for us and our salvation. It is in this sense that we are surely to understand the expression "the substance of the Faith."

It was in just this way that we find the substance or the deposit of faith being understood by Irenaeus. He referred to it as the objective and dynamic core of the kerygma which constantly gives substance to faith and renews the life of the church, the deposit of faith which ever remains the same, identical with itself, and which rejuvenates the faith of the church.[22] Regarded in this light, the distinction between the substance of the faith and dogmatic expressions of it has to do, not merely with the fact that dogmatic expressions of the faith do not encapsulate the truth but refer to it objectively beyond themselves, but with the fact that the truth is embodied in the incarnate person and acts of God the Son in Jesus Christ. That is to say, we have to reckon with the fact which Oscar Cullmann expressed by saying, with respect to Irenaeus's thought, that "the historical kernel is at the same time the dogmatic kernel."[23] It is in this light that we are to understand Irenaeus's many references to the deposit or substance of the faith as "the Canon of Truth" or "the Rule of Faith," and to his insistence that the reception and handing on of the faith require of us acts of living historical obedience to the truth.

Let me use an analogy from modern science to illustrate the basic point that must be grasped here. I refer to Clark Maxwell's emphasis upon "embodied

---

21. 1 Tim. 6:20; 2 Tim. 1:2, 14; Jude 3.
22. Irenaeus, *Adversus haereses* 3.14.1.
23. Oscar Cullmann, *The Earliest Christian Confessions,* trans. J. K. S. Reid (1949), p. 49.

mathematics" or to Einstein's insistence that geometry and experience interpenetrate one another, in view of which both claimed that, taken by themselves, mathematical propositions may be certain but they are not true; they are true only if they are embodied in empirical reality. That is to say, we have to reckon with the fact that empirical and theoretical factors inhere in one another at all levels, in reality and in our knowledge of it. This means that the mathematical formulations of features of reality are true only if they point beyond themselves to structures in which physical and intelligible elements belong inseparably together. The mathematical structures of our scientific theories cannot be identified with ontic structures in nature itself, for they are no more than conceptual means through which we apprehend those structures in nature independent of our theories. We are never able to give a complete and true expression to the objective structures we apprehend, but as we apprehend those structures they confer relativity upon our formalizations or expressions of them. That was of course the immensely important epistemological implication of general relativity.

Mutatis mutandis, that is precisely what we are concerned with in distinguishing the substance of the faith from our explicit formulations of it. Empirical and theoretical, historical and theological elements coinhere inseparably together in the substance of the faith, so that we are unable to reduce it to explicit formulation in doctrinal statements or formulations. The formulations which we are compelled to make in obedience to the self-manifestation of the truth point away from themselves to the truth, and thereby distinguish themselves from it as falling short of it and therefore as in real measure inadequate to it. They would not be true if they claimed to be adequate, far less to substitute themselves in place of the truth, but are true only as they point beyond themselves to the truth which they seek to serve. Thus the very fact that they fall short of the truth is essential to their truth. This means that all the church's formulations of the fundamental doctrines or truths of the faith must be subordinated to the living reality of Jesus Christ, himself the incarnate Word and Truth of God.

As I understand it, that is the epistemological significance of the remarkable blend of *kerygmatic* and *didactic* elements which we find in the apostolic witness to Christ clothed with his gospel as it is embodied in the NT Scriptures. It was, I believe, in intentional subordination to the apostolic witness in the Holy Scriptures and in accordance with the example set by the apostles themselves, that the fathers of the church at the Councils of Nicaea and Constantinople sought to blend kerygmatic and didactic elements in the way they tried to guard and hand on the substance of the faith in the Nicene-Constantinopolitan Creed, and to do so in such a way that reference to that creed could be used in the universal church as indicating the rule of faith in accordance with which it could fulfill its mission to preach and teach the faith that is once and for all handed on to the saints.

CHAPTER 12

The Ecumenical Future of
Reformed Theology

David Willis

R eformed theology is ecumenical in its foundations, scope, and claims because it confesses that the whole universe belongs to the God who is the subject of the church's worship, service, and critically examined faith. There are many senses of the term "ecumenical," and many of them apply to Reformed theology. Without detracting from the other senses, I want here to delineate three principal ways in which Reformed theology's future is ecumenical. Before we consider those, however, we need to clarify the supposition that Reformed theology has any future whatsoever.

The Promised Future of Reformed Theology

During major cultural revolutions such as the present global one, the fundamental presuppositions of the church's life may be so taken for granted that their necessity is not apparent. One such fundamental assumption is the conviction that the church lives according to God's promise. Other confessional traditions have also held to that conviction. It has been an especially prominent feature of the Reformed understanding of the nature of the Word of God and therefore of the church's being continually reformed according to that Word.

The future is a promised creature which belongs to the triune God known to be gracious through Jesus the Christ. This conviction implies an understanding of the future as creature, an understanding of the Word as promise, and an understanding of theology as a practice of the freedom which comes from focusing on the good news.

The Future Is a Creature of God

The language and grammar of this claim is curious but accurate. Augustine's attention to the subject has a strong influence on Reformed theology's understanding of time. The direction of his thought was mostly correct, and it continues to be helpful. As he saw it, when humans create something they are given time as a framework within which they work. They use time and enjoy it, they plan, they take time to do things. With God's creating it is different. Time is not a given framework within which God works; time is the gracious result of God's decision and action to create. It is not the precondition but the gracious result of God's creating. Time is a good creature because it is the work of God, who is good.

The future is one of the ways time is good. There is more of time to come, and that more of time to come is partly what we mean by the future. However, the future already is one of the forms of the creature time which God has made and which belongs to God. In this sense the future, the coming time which belongs to God, is a dimension which breaks into and shapes the present. The present-shaping power of the future transforms the way we remember and our criteria of what is worth remembering. A conversion of delight occurs which is both a liberation and a motivation for new service to all God's creatures — including time. This freeing conversion means that we do not use up time or take it into our own hands, but we delight in time as one of God's good gifts. There is a Sabbath quality to each day in the sense that all our work is also a way of committing all our lives and those of all others into the care of God.

It is not self-evident from the creature itself that time is the result of a benevolent Creator. Alienation from God and each other affects the way we perceive and spend time. Were it not for God's presence and intervention, we could just as well perceive reality as patternless caprice or as cyclical inevitability. As it is, the confession that time is moving from somewhere to somewhere according to God's purpose is the result of the perseverance of God's steadfast love. Those purposes and promises are summed up and fulfilled in the coming, active obedience, death, resurrection, and coming again of Jesus Christ. That is the disclosed mystery of God's purposes, the mystery which the believing community reconfesses in the Lord's Supper: "Christ died, Christ was raised, Christ will come again."

It takes time for us to show forth Christ's death until he comes. It takes measured duration *(chronos)* to show forth Christ's death until he comes

179

again. But taking measured time to live redemptively is living out the prior reality of the purposefulness, the chargedness, the pregnancy of God's timely (kairotic) presence and intervention. Living as witnesses to the presence of eternity in time, living in the specific service of receiving others as Christ has received us, is sharing already here and now in the *kairos* which is the end and fulfillment of *chronos*.

The Word Comes to Us as Promise

When they define themselves most technically, congregations of the Reformed traditions claim that they belong to the one, true, universal church, which is the same as the "church according to the Word of God reformed." There are many forms of the Word of God and many senses of the term "Word of God." The Reformed tradition tends to give priority to the sense that Jesus Christ is the eternal Word by whom all things are made, the same one who became incarnate by the Holy Spirit of the flesh of the Jewish maiden Mary. It has also been the tendency in the Reformed tradition to allow this primary sense of the Word of God to determine how one speaks of the other forms of the Word of God — the Scriptures and proclamation through preaching and sacraments. That is, preaching and sacraments are forms of the Word of God normatively witnessed to in the books of the Old and New Testaments.

What makes the ordinary means of grace the Word of God for us efficaciously, for us as address which convicts and forgives and renews, is God's fidelity. When a forgiven sinner preaches from Scripture and announces the gospel with its demands and comforts, Christ himself is the actively present person speaking through the frail vessel of the preacher. Human communication with human words becomes an event of God's Word — because of Christ's promised presence. When the elements of bread and wine are set apart by the words of institution and prayer, they become instruments through which Christ is actively present — because Christ has so promised.

The Word and Spirit are not separated, and this efficacy of the Word comes about by the power of the Holy Spirit. It is the work of the Holy Spirit that things otherwise separated are joined. It is by the Spirit that the signs and the reality are joined in the sacraments, and it is by the Spirit that believers are united to Christ and to each other as comembers of his body. When it comes to regeneration, the work of the Holy Spirit is to unite us to Christ that we may enjoy him and his benefits, which is the most specific fulfillment of Christ's promise regarding the Holy Spirit in John's Gospel. Christ is really present by the power of the Spirit. Promised presence is real presence, and experiencing the Word as promise is really to experience that Word.

This bears on understanding the future as creature. God creates according to the Word, and it is by abiding by his promises — his Word given in covenanting relationship — that God upholds his creation and moves it forward. The very elements of bread and wine, the very voice of the pastor, the very existence of congregation and pastor and memory, the very environmental and social contests in which all this occurs — all these creatures are and continue to be and have a future because of God's fidelity to his Word. Scriptures in and of themselves (whatever that might possibly mean), the elements in the sacraments in and of themselves (whatever that might possibly mean), the sermon in and of itself (whatever that might possibly mean) have no reality — they are nothing — except as forms through which and in which Christ keeps his promised presence.

There is continuity to grace, and that continuity is reliable, trustworthy, nonarbitrary. God's sovereignty is primarily experienced as God's fidelity to God's freely given covenanting purposes. God's sovereignty is experienced as God's freedom to create and redeem and make holy, God's freedom to give and to keep his Word, God's freedom to become flesh and live among us full of grace and truth. God's sovereignty is simply the opposite of the religiously rationalized capriciousness with which it is often confused. That means that we can know where God is to be met and counted on and responded to in the most focused fashion of which we are, by God's initiative, made capable. It means that we are open to being met by this trustworthy God in ways we could not have fully predicted before. It is precisely because we are assured, through the ordinary means of grace, of the identity and trustworthiness of the triune God we know in Christ, that we are able to be watchful, to be actively caught up in God's new initiatives.

Critically Thinking through the Faith for Proclamation Is an Activity of Christian Freedom

The God who is definitely known through his self-disclosure in the Scriptures of the Old and New Testament as they witness to Jesus Christ draws the believing community forward with the vision of an even fuller experience of the peace they already have. Christian theology is a matter, beginning to end, of the gospel. Theology which is Reformed discovers its vitality and relevance from its focus on the gospel. It is easy to treat "gospel" as a theologoumenon which belongs in tandem with another concept called "law." When that occurs, one has lost the primary impact of what the gospel is: good news, joyful message, blessed communication. Trusting the truth of the good news turns out to be a very difficult thing — because it means relinquishing the numerous ways we escape from God's freedom.

181

This means that there is a need for correction, over and over again, when Reformed theology allows other things than the gospel to become its preoccupation. A correction (repentance) was necessary when this occurred in the past, and is when it occurs now as well. There were long periods, for example, when Reformed theology was in danger of being controlled by a preoccupation with a divine decree considered in general, or by a preoccupation with the symmetry of double predestination, or by a preoccupation with the woes rather than the blessings as motivation for ethics, or by a preoccupation with the fallenness of human nature rather than the goodness of human nature as created and restored.

Those were some of the older preoccupations which threatened the centrality of the good news for Reformed theology. There are, however, newer ones which are no less nefarious. It is quite possible for some contemporary theologians, especially if they suffer loss of memory of the crises the church faced in earlier epochs and are dominated by the "self" (as defined in a consumer economy) and the self's fascination with his or her own narrative, to take the difficulty of "doing theology" far more seriously than the reality and priority and ingenuity of the One who is, after all, the Subject of theology. "Doing theology" (a most infelicitous phrase in any event) which is not the joyful struggle to keep up with the initiative of the living God — such doing is the worst form of works righteousness. It is teaching about grace (and sometimes not even teaching about grace) rather than living theologically by the grace. The result would be an especially perilous form of the godless fetters of the world.

Here a note needs to be sounded which is correct only if it is not exaggerated. It is that one sense — not the only or the most important sense — in which theology is Reformed is that it is done by persons who in their work are simply living out their identity as comembers of the body of forgiven sinners in Christ, freely united to him by the bond of the Holy Spirit. Here we are touching the important and elusive matter of ethos, of ambiance, of style, of élan, yes, of beauty of action which corresponds to the beauty of the Subject being adored, obeyed, served in all our activity — including that very particular métier of theology. It is out of a *sensus ecclesiae* that one engages in this kind of theology — a sense of being nurtured and corrected and guided by other members of the body of Christ — and in one's own responsibility for other members.

Another way of saying that theology is done as an act of Christian freedom is to say that it is doxological in its motivation, sources, and accountability. The whole of the Christian life and theology must be seen and lived as a part of that context, a context of praise-giving in response to God's prior gift of life and redemption. The baptismal formulas, summary hymns of what believers live and die for, are doxologies. We need to remember this when we turn to consider the confessional ecumenism of the future of Reformed theology; the creeds and confessions of the church are themselves acts of joyful and costly service. Here we mainly need to note that the worshiping context, the gathering of God's people to hear and to taste the Word, to confess their sins and receive assurance of pardon and be set walking again in newness of life, to sing praises and to pray for all sorts and conditions of God's creatures, is integral to the *sana doctrina* of the *ecclesia secundum verbum dei reformata*.

Senses of the Ecumenical in the Future of Reformed Theology

Luther comments that the most important word in the Lord's Prayer is "Amen." "Amen" summarizes the sure trust with which faith grasps and holds fast to the benefits of Christ; and closing with "Amen" reminds us that we are not alone but are part of the vast multitude through the ages and in every part of the world whose voice God does not ignore. That same sense of being part of the *communio sanctorum* applies to the context of Reformed theology. The hearing of the Word is a cohearing, transmitting the gospel is a cotransmitting, reinterpreting and reconfessing the apostolic faith is a *koinonia* event. Theology which practices being Reformed is not done *Christo remoto,* nor is it done *ecclesia remota.* At least for Calvin, we cannot look to "Christ alone"; we must look to "Christ only," and that means to Christ joined to his body and clothed with his benefits. The texture and dynamic of this theological procedure move us to consider the senses in which the future of Reformed theology is ecumenical.

The three main senses in which Reformed theology is ecumenical have to do with Reformed theology's confessional nature, with Reformed theology's engagement in dialogue with other traditions, and with Reformed theology's commitment to expanding spheres of the church's mission.

Reformed Theology's Future Is Ecumenical in the Sense That It Promises to Hold On To, Faithfully Transmit, and Interpret the Confessions of the One Holy Catholic Apostolic Church

Reformed theology that has a future will be loyal to the confessions of the church as subordinate standards guiding congregations in interpreting the Scriptures' witness to Jesus Christ, the one Word of God which we have to hear and trust and obey in life and in death. That, of course, is just a paraphrase of the Barmen Declaration. It will not do to make a sharp distinction between the confessing church and the confessional church. For Barmen, at least, the confessing church is truly the confessional church, and those who subvert the congregations with the false doctrine are also unfaithful to the confessions of the church. "Do not be deceived!"

> With gratitude to God they [representatives from all the German confessional Churches] are convinced that they have been given a common word to utter. It was not their intention to found a new Church or to form a union. For nothing was farther from their minds than the abolition of the confessional status of our Churches. Their intention was, rather, to withstand in faith and unanimity the destruction of the Confession of Faith, and thus of the Evangelical Church in Germany. In opposition to attempts to establish the unity of the German Evangelical Church by means of false doctrine, by the use of force and insincere practices, the Confessional synod insists that the unity of the Evangelical Churches in Germany can come only from the Word of God in faith through the Holy Spirit. Thus alone is the Church renewed. Therefore the Confessional Synod calls upon the congregations to range themselves behind it in prayer, and steadfastly to gather around those pastors and teachers who are loyal to the Confessions.[1]

Before we go further, we need to say something about the special place the Augsburg Confession plays in the future ecumenism of Reformed theology. The confessional standards referred to in the Barmen Declaration included the Augsburg Confession; that is one reason it has a special importance for those who include the Barmen Declaration in their books of confessions. Already in the sixteenth century, however, Reformed leaders like Calvin contended they could adopt the Augsburg Confession as their own. For some Reformed congregations, the Augsburg Confession was used alongside the Heidelberg Catechism as the most important of the confessions of the Reformation. In any case, the Reformed congregations of the sixteenth century and subsequent German Reformed immigrant congregations took the Augsburg Confession to be a fair and accurate statement of faith. It is a weakness of recent Reformed books of confessions that the Augsburg Confession is not included (just as it is a drawback that Lutheran books of confessions do not now include the Barmen Declaration).

We now need to get three things straight about this "loyalty to the confessions of the church" to which the Barmen Declaration refers.

---

1. "The Theological Declaration of Barmen," in *The Constitution of the Presbyterian Church (U.S.A.) Part I: Book of Confessions* (Louisville: Office of the General Assembly, 1996), pp. 253-58, here p. 255.

First, the confessions are ways by which the churches are freed to hear the one voice which is to be heard and trusted and obeyed alone in life and in death. That one shepherd is Jesus Christ as he is attested in the Scriptures of the Old and New Testaments. Any so-called confessional loyalty which focuses on the confessions themselves betrays the very nature and intention of those confessions themselves. That is also true for any form of so-called confessionalism which is only an antiquarian interest in what the confessions meant there and back then, without attending to how they help the church here and now respond to God's fresh word to us today out of Scripture.

Secondly, the future of Reformed theology is ecumenical because it embraces the doctrinal decisions of the first four ecumenical councils. Not all the confessions have the same ecumenically binding status for the church. One of the great features of the confessionalism in the Reformed tradition is its responsiveness to the need to speak with particularity, and with the necessary frequency, to numerous crises exposed by the gospel in successive cultural contexts and times. That collection of Reformed confessions began in the sixteenth century and has not abated. Bèze's collection and the collection of Reformed confessions around the world today belong to the same understanding of the timeliness and localness of the church's task to reconfess the one faith over and over again. That strength, however, could easily become a severe weakness if it were not seen that these are timely variations on the ecumenical creeds which the Reformed share with the rest of the one holy catholic apostolic church.

Each of the subsequent confessions aligns itself either explicitly or implicitly with these ecumenical creeds. Such a judgment is not merely descriptive; it entails an evaluation of subsequent confessions which claim to be "Reformed." That means that loyalty to the confessions is really a very dynamic and controversy-laden process; not every self-proclaimed "confession" of every subgroup of Christians is "Reformed" just because it chooses to use that term of itself. One of the criteria of its being both a true confession of faith (Which faith?) and being Reformed (Which church is thus Reformed?) is that it deliberately aligns itself with the ecumenical creeds: not just to repeat what they sing and pray and say, but to sing and pray and say freshly the faith which was there formulated. The formulations of those councils in the face of those threats to the faith function for subsequent confessions as subordinate interpretive guides to the Scriptures — whose authority, in turn, is their witnessing to the living Word who is Jesus Christ. The ecumenical creeds are most important subordinate standards — subordinate to the Scriptures — but they are standards for subsequent confessions of faith.

Each subsequent Reformed confession does not align itself with the ecumenical creeds primarily because of a view of history which said that earlier was closer to the pure fountain of the gospel (though the view is an amazingly strong one among the reforming Christian humanists). Each subsequent Reformed confession does so because it claims that the main doctrinal points on which the church is perennially tested were faced and correctly decided about through the course of the debates and decisions of the first four ecumenical councils. Those councils identified and took a stand on the ways the Nicene interpretation of the apostolic faith was to be formulated so that the gospel was served in successive contexts. Each particular Reformed confession makes the same decision and says that those issues, when raised in different forms, also require those stands. The reconfession of those ecumenical creeds is necessary if the Reformed confessions are not to be the declarations of faith of a new religious movement — which is quite a different thing from declarations of faith necessary to the particularization of the one faith shared by the one holy catholic and apostolic church.

Thirdly, there is no stepping outside the ongoing debate over which confessions or creeds are to have most worth on what matters and how they best function as guides. That debate is one of the ways of taking the confessions seriously — as long as the method of hermeneutics does not itself become a substitute for the moving pilgrimage of obedience even while one is deciding the proper function of the confessions. The hermeneutics of the confessions is now a cross-confessional enterprise. The confessing heritage of the whole church is so rich that even when one accepts the Nicene Creed as foundational, the richness of its meaning is understood only when it is carried out in a context of multiconfessional dialogues. Such a context helps keep before us the many factors that cannot be ignored in the hermeneutics of the confessions.

Those factors obviously include the social, economic, and other cultural factors influencing the positions advanced on the several sides of the debates which lay behind the conciliar decisions. At least of equal importance is to consider the liturgical setting and issues at stake in the confessional formulations. That means not just that one sees the connection between the *lex orandi* and the *lex credendi* in the formation of the creedal decisions. It means also that the very nature of their status is to be grasped only when one understands their doxological nature. They are orthodox because they guide and reflect the doxology of the true God.

Reformed Theology's Future Is Ecumenical in the Sense That It Promises to Continue to Engage in Dialogues with Other Confessional Traditions Which Seek to Make More Manifest the Unity of the Church, More Pure Her Worship, and More Joyfully Obedient Her Worldly Service

To define accurately the Reformed tradition today includes describing the changed emphases and perceptions which have occurred as a result of living ecumenically with other churches. Part of the Reformed heritage has been active in efforts to reconcile differing Christian churches, but there has been a part of the Reformed tradition which has also been divisive. I think it is fair, nonetheless, to say that the preponderant tendency among churches in the Reformed tradition is to be committed to more than cooperation among differing Christian bodies. The tendency has been to be committed also to reconciliation among those bodies at doctrinal and liturgical levels. That was the case with many Reformed leaders in the sixteenth century; surely it is the case with the modern ecumenical movement. The result is a considerable body of theological reflection, an accumulation of shared witness, and a background of common theological education which are now part of the Reformed tradition. With this engagement in the ecumenical movement comes a commitment to be mutually enriched by each other even more in the future than we have already been in the past.

The modern ecumenical movement is at a turning point. One of the features of such large transitions — one of the things that makes them turning points — is that it is not clear what the future holds, even as it is perfectly clear that the future shape of ecumenism will not be just a repetition of any of its past or present forms. The *novum* will be made up of new configurations and transformations of the material of the past and present. That means that two groups alike are discomfited at such a transition: those nostalgic about the supposedly more glorious days of the high-water marks of enthusiasm for the ecumenical movement, and those whose cynicism about the ecumenical movement reinforces their willingness to settle for, as normal, the divisions among Christian churches.

The fact of the matter is that a new configuration of communion among Christians, an emergent future pattern of realignments, is already discernible. I am referring to the fact that the main lines of fellowship, including worship, doctrine, and ethical service, are no longer along denominational lines but are cross-denominational. Some denominations are internally divided more than others, but every denomination in the modern world is experiencing this de facto, if not yet de jure, reconfiguration.

This means that Christians who are serious about their churchpersonship, serious about their unity as being grounded in the order and structure of a particular ecclesiastical discipline, will not exit their present traditions into yet another denomination. They will, however, be encouraged to realize that at the same time they are already part of a larger fellowship that has a specific history and hope for a fuller future. That is the lasting significance of the document *Baptism, Eucharist and Ministry*. It identified the shape of the common theological and ecclesiastical and ethical commitments characteristic of this configuration which increasingly crosses and transcends existing denominations. For the purposes of the present argument, in any case, the Reformed participation in the process resulting in that document indicated some of the trajectories in which we can with confidence discern one of the senses in which the future of Reformed theology is ecumenical.

A great deal of attention has been given by all the churches to the dynamics and problems of reception. Reception is defined differently in different churches, and there are processes for reception in the several traditions. The fact that there was such a document to be received was itself a great step forward. It indicated how far the participating churches had come in their common quest for fuller fellowship. The content of *Baptism, Eucharist and Ministry* — the result of the process and only a step, albeit a highly significant one — is an accurate reflection of the rather remarkable degree of converging understandings and commitments among the churches.

Many items in that document are more programmatically than precisely formulated. That may be appropriate to the stage of the ecumenical movement of which it was a culmination and transition out of. When one studies the responses of the churches to *Baptism, Eucharist and Ministry,* one is struck by the care with which they were usually made. An attitude of gratitude characterized the responses, even over points of serious and sharp disagreement. Over and over again, when an alert was sounded, it was done recognizing that it was a matter of proportion, that such and such an emphasis was good but needed to be taken together with some others. Moreover, there was a remarkably widespread acknowledgment that in the course of the ecumenical movement the particular church responding had already been enriched by other traditions. The responses expressed awareness of things that had to be recovered, which had been neglected in their own traditions or had never been realized before as a part of the fullness of church life.

The balances of attention given to subjects in the document remain subject for subsequent discussion. There was almost unanimous welcome for the attention paid to the Lord's Supper (except in nonsacramental Christian groups). Then the question was often asked in the responses: Does the claim that the Eucharist is the central act of Christian worship suggest a diminution of the importance of the preaching of the Word (as some responding churches apparently felt)? There was almost unanimous welcome for the seriousness with which the ordering of the church's ministry was taken. Then the question was asked: Does the treatment of the ministry under the three forms suggest a diminution of the ministry of the so-called laity and a diminution of the richness of other forms of the ministry (as some responding churches apparently felt)? There was common agreement (in the basis on which churches become members of the World Council of Churches) that there is one baptism and that it is in the name of the Father and the Son and the Holy Spirit. Then the much-debated question was posed: Does the document's acceptance of the practice of infant baptism as common among so many of the participating churches suggest a blunting of the professing sharpness to the act of baptism (as some responding churches apparently felt)?

That these questions remain requires pursuit in two directions. Further refinement is needed on certain matters where what the document apparently intends and how it is heard differ. Further examination is also needed on the part of all the churches on how to distinguish between, on the one hand, responsible restraint which will be helpful to the ecumenical movement in the long run and, on the other hand, paralyzing fears which only serve denominational inertia. The latter danger is real, and overcoming it entails nothing less than a kind of conversion. N. Nissiotis pointed out that each church, drawing on its own theological tradition and understanding of discipleship, had to make a decision in response to the document. The decision would be not primarily about the document itself, but about the churches' own theological resources and discipleship which confronted them through the document:

> What is now required of them is a new spirit of convergence in theology and practice, calling for a change in their way of looking at church divisions, namely, looking at them now from within a church fellowship which is becoming more and more convinced that what unites it is more than what divides it.[2]

The conversion spoken of is not what we primarily expect of others. This particular conversion means that

> each separate confessional family now regards the others with a renewed determination to appreciate them as sharers in the same apostolic tradition. This vision does not mean that conversion occurs first in the outlook of others, a miraculous change in their attitude towards us; it means first

2. "Introduction: The Credible Reception of the Lima Document as the Ecumenical Conversion for the Churches," in *Churches Respond to "BEM,"* ed. M. Thurian, vol. 3, Faith and Order Paper no. 135 (Geneva: World Council of Churches, 1987), p. xi.

and foremost that we ourselves are confronted with the urgent challenge to determined change within ourselves, to accept for ourselves this new era in ecumenical relationships.[3]

Reformed Theology's Future Is Ecumenical in the Sense That It Promises to Attend to the Forms Which the Body of Christ Takes, as the Gospel Is Translated and Heard with Enriching Complementarity in Diverse Cultural and Personal Contexts

Reformed theology's ecumenical future includes its attending to the *sensus fidelium*. This term is occasionally used with a bit of a condescending overtone: the bishops, pastors, and teachers of the church, in order to teach and lead well, have to take account of the experience of the believers. That, however, is not the accurate reading of the importance of the experience of the faithful. True bishops, pastors, and teachers to the body of believers are nurtured, corrected, comforted by that body and reciprocate with others in that body. Hearing the gospel and extending it to others, welcoming others as Christ has welcomed us, caring for and being cared for, constitute life together as the body of Christ. That occurs at all manner of gatherings of believers, not just in the local congregation; but it at least and primarily occurs there. It is in being part of the life of a local congregation of the one holy catholic and apostolic church that a person most immediately shares in the *sensus fidelium*.

What is sensed there, the reality around which the believers gather and what makes that a gathering of believers, is — need it be reiterated? — the one Word which we have to hear, trust, and obey in life and in death, Jesus Christ as attested in the Scriptures of the Old and New Testaments. The *sensus fidelium* is a form of Christ's shaping, by the power of the Spirit, the corporate life of forgiven sinners who seek to be faithful in their own time and place and particular contexts. The idiosyncratic specificity of their response to the gospel within the catholic church itself belongs to the expanding catholicity of the church. Church order, the discipline of polity, studying the peace and unity of the church, social and political witness which is congruent with the justice of the Servant Lord who is the one Mediator — all belong to the right hearing and expressing of the reality of the gospel.

This is the fellowship of those who struggle by grace to exercise the particular gifts of which they are stewards for the health of the body. This is the content of costly discipleship in each particular cultural, personal, economical, linguistic context. There are some forms of togetherness which are not the fu-

---

3. "Introduction," p. xi.

ture of the believing community, forms against which the believing community must take up active resistance. The future of the church's catholicity is shaped by such a confessing tradition of the believing community, which must trust in its present stances that God will shape the future in ways which go far beyond what one can imagine in the present but which will be used by God for this future with his people and his world.

There are many areas of challenge — of *tentatio*, "testing" — in which the believing community is taking new shapes in obedience to the gospel as mediated within the one holy catholic and apostolic church. The areas of testing are so numerous because Christian freedom is active in every area of life, and no one is excluded from the loving care of God to whom the whole belongs. Some areas are especially urgent and are also examples of what is at stake elsewhere. I think especially of the stewardship of the earth's resources, and those of the nearby corner of the universe; the need for greater inclusiveness in all offices of the church's trinitarian ministry; and the renewed need for justice and reconciliation in the face of resurgent racial and ethnic hate and fear. Closely related is the particularity and explicitness of the church's evangelism. There is of course a sense in which all that the church does is evangelism — just as there is a sense in which every act of the believer is a form of prayer. But in both cases, the danger is that they become so generally understood that the specificity of the action is lost. The church today, as throughout the ages, is also called to proclaim, announce, witness to, and teach the gospel to the end, also, that men and women who are not yet — or are no longer — believers in Jesus Christ turn around and become believers in him. There was a time in the not too distant past when such a statement was so obvious as to be slightly embarrassing. Today — of all things, who could possibly have expected such a state of affairs? — that assertion is far from universally accepted. There are some church leaders and some who consider themselves church teachers — not just persons of other religions — who oppose the church's task of evangelism, or who prudently so redefine it that it loses its offensiveness. The primary task of evangelism needs, of course, to continue: for that is the very nature of the church, to be a witnessing body. The contextualization which comes about as the gospel is heard in each successive cultural situation and in each successive generation belongs to the richness of the future of the church of which Reformed theology is a part. To foreclose on continued evangelism, to ignore the joyful service of welcoming others as Christ has welcomed us, would be to decide in advance for others that they should not have the opportunity and freedom and responsibility of taking their own places in the unfolding of God's purposes for the whole of creation.

CHAPTER 13

The Vulnerability of God

William Placher

P erhaps the strangest event in the intellectual history of the West was the identification of the biblical God with Aristotle's unmoved mover or some other picture, derived from Greek philosophy, of God as impassible and unchanging. At least as early as Justin Martyr, Christian theologians were distinguishing the disgraceful, mad passions of pagan deities from the "impassible" God of Christian faith.[1] To be sure, the picture has never been an altogether consistent one. Even Origen, often accused of too much compromise with Greek patterns of thought, insisted that a God who is "long-suffering, merciful, and pitiful . . . is not impassible. He has the passion of love."[2] Mystics and theologians of the Trinity have regularly issued cautionary notes about divine impassibility; but just what it means to be "impassible" and how that might differ from more biblical categories like "steadfast" has often remained ambiguous.

Still, much of the Christian tradition does seem to have portrayed God as unaffected and unaffectable. Jaroslav Pelikan even maintains that "the impassibility of God was a basic presupposition of all Christological doctrine."[3]

1. Justin Martyr, *First Apology* 25.
2. Origen, *Homilies on Ezekiel* 6.6, quoted in Charles Bigg, *The Christian Platonists of Alexandria* (Oxford: Clarendon Press, 1913), p. 197. Note also: "Athanasius unambiguously affirms that we cannot deny in advance God's ability to be incarnate on the grounds of a preconceived notion of divine transcendence. . . . The Athanasian God 'transcends his transcendence' to be encountered in human shape: his hiddenness and unknowability are grasped in and through the weakness of the flesh of Christ" (Rowan Williams, *Christian Spirituality* [Atlanta: John Knox, 1980], p. 50).
3. Jaroslav Pelikan, *The Emergence of the Catholic Tradition* (Chicago: University of Chicago Press, 1971), p. 270.

Aquinas, notoriously, insisted that the nature of God's relations to the world is such that things in the world are affected by God, but "in God there are no real relations to creatures."[4] Protestant Scholasticism picked up much of the same language. The Westminster Confession explicitly affirms that God is "without body, parts, or passions, immutable."[5]

The emphasis on divine impassibility had many philosophical roots, but one of the issues had to do with power. God is powerful, the argument went — all-powerful, in fact. And part of what it means to have power is that one can affect others for good or ill but remain unthreatened by them, invulnerable. Impassibility therefore guarantees omnipotence. The Lord God rules, and a powerful ruler has first of all to be safe and secure from external threat. As Eberhard Jüngel has written, "This is the earthly way of thinking of a lord: first he has all power and then perhaps he can be merciful — but then again, perhaps not."[6]

Love is another matter. Our human experience suggests that to love another is to make oneself vulnerable to suffering, to care enough about the other so that one is in a real, mutual relation, with all the risks involved. Divine love, to be sure, must differ from human love, but a love without vulnerability seems less rather than greater. The Christian commitment to divine power, however, has been such that doctrines of God have often enough been willing to deny any divine passibility, whatever the cost to the resulting image of divine love. In Whitehead's phrase, God came to be pictured as "the ruling Caesar, or the ruthless moralist, or the unmoved mover."[7] If one believed that such a God was revealed in human form in Jesus of Nazareth, who died on the cross, Christology could then only take the form of a radical paradox, for the crucified Jesus seemed hardly the appropriate self-revelation of an impassible, omnipotent Lord.

Given all this long history, it is a fairly remarkable phenomenon that so many theologians of our own century have so emphasized the affectability and suffering of God. Ronald Goetz can even speak with some accuracy of the emergence of a "new orthodoxy" of a suffering God.[8] The theme appears in process and liberation theologians, but also in European theologians of the Reformed tradition like Karl Barth, Jürgen Moltmann, and Eberhard Jüngel. It

---

4. Thomas Aquinas, *Summa theologiae* 1a, Q. 13, art. 7.

5. "The Westminster Confession of Faith," chap. 2 of *The Book of Confessions: Presbyterian Church (U.S.A.)*, 6.011.

6. Eberhard Jüngel, *God as the Mystery of the World*, trans. Darrell L. Guder (Grand Rapids: William B. Eerdmans Publishing Co., 1983), p. 21.

7. Alfred North Whitehead, *Process and Reality* (New York: Free Press, 1969), p. 404.

8. Ronald Goetz, "The Suffering God: The Rise of a New Orthodoxy," *Christian Century* 103 (16 April 1986): 385-89.

could be interesting to speculate on the reasons for this trend — the ways, perhaps, in which a century that has seen the optimism of previous generations so shattered by tragedy finds it harder to accept a God distanced from the sufferings of the world.[9]

The purpose of this essay, however, is not to explore the cultural factors that might be at work in this theological trend but to argue that in writing of a God who is vulnerable in love, a God who freely chooses to suffer, Christian theologians are only reclaiming their own birthright, for it is just such a God that we encounter in the Bible. That is a big argument, and one that could be made in many ways, and what follows will take only one approach, that of attending to the shape of some biblical narratives, especially the Gospel of Mark.[10]

The Bible contains law codes, poems, prophecies, wise and not so wise sayings, and much else besides, as well as stories. The stories themselves are varied, and sometimes even mutually inconsistent; one cannot simply talk about "*the* biblical narrative." Still, stories, some of them interconnected, are surely an important part of Scripture, and one of their functions is to narrate God's identity.[11] Sometimes the details of the stories may not be historically accurate. The Gospels, as Calvin himself said, were not written "in such a manner, as to preserve, on all occasions, the exact order of time."[12] "We know that the Evangelists were not very exact as to the order of dates, or even in detailing minutely everything that Christ said or did."[13] Nevertheless, by attending to biblical stories, we get a picture of the God in whom the Bible calls us to have faith. The stories function as anecdotes which reveal a person's character[14] — in ways that we seem to lose, as is often the case with a good anecdote, if we try to summarize the point of the story in nonnarrative fashion. The Gospel sto-

---

9. One thinks of Elie Wiesel's haunting story of the young Jewish boy killed in a Nazi concentration camp, as the other prisoners are forced to watch: "Behind me, I heard the same man asking: 'Where is God now?' And I heard a voice within me answer him: 'Where is He? Here He is — He is hanging here on this gallows. . . .'" Elie Wiesel, *Night* (New York: Avon Books, 1969), p. 76.

10. For one of the inspirations of this project, see David Tracy, "On Reading the Scriptures Theologically," in *Theology and Dialogue,* ed. Bruce Marshall (Notre Dame: University of Notre Dame Press, 1990), p. 49.

11. Hans W. Frei, *The Identity of Jesus Christ* (Philadelphia: Fortress, 1975), p. 87.

12. John Calvin, *Commentary on a Harmony of the Evangelists,* trans. William Pringle, vol. 1, *Calvin's Commentaries,* vol. 16 (Grand Rapids: Baker, 1989), p. 216.

13. Calvin, *Commentary on a Harmony of the Evangelists,* vol. 2, *Calvin's Commentaries,* vol. 17 (Grand Rapids: Baker, 1989), p. 89.

14. David Kelsey uses this term to describe what Karl Barth does in the "Royal Man" section of the *Church Dogmatics.* See David H. Kelsey, *The Uses of Scripture in Recent Theology* (Philadelphia: Fortress, 1975), p. 43.

ries may do this most clearly, for they show the sort of person Jesus was, and in Jesus God was revealing God's own self in human form.

Individual stories can render a personal identity, but the shape of a whole narrative can do so as well. The way a story presents a character — the first scene in which we meet this person, the way different themes gradually emerge, the dramatic turning point of the story, the feelings with which we are left as the story ends — often provides keys to the identity the character has in the story. Newly popular methods such as rhetorical analysis, reader-response theories, and literary approaches to the Bible, it turns out, can often help in understanding such matters. Looking at the way the Gospel stories identify God's self-revelation in Jesus gives at least some concrete content to the idea of using narrative interpretation for Christian theology, an approach often charged, with some justice, of being advocated in principle more often than it is put into practice.

Consider, for instance, the book of Revelation, hardly anyone's idea of a "realistic narrative." Yet even here there is certainly a kind of story line: On the island of Patmos, the narrator has a vision, first of "one like the Son of Man" (1:13 NRSV), who dictates messages to the seven churches of Asia. Then the narrator passes through a door to see a vision of the heavenly throne (4:1-2). And, in 5:1-4a, the narrator writes:

> Then I saw in the right hand of the one seated on the throne a scroll written on the inside and on the back, sealed with seven seals; and I saw a mighty angel proclaiming with a loud voice, "Who is worthy to open the scroll and break its seals?" And no one in heaven or on earth or under the earth was able to open the scroll or to look into it. And I began to weep bitterly. (NRSV)

The opening of the seven seals generates the rest of the story, so the crisis of whether anyone can be found to open the scroll constitutes the turning point of the whole narrative. But it is resolved in a very odd fashion. As the narrator weeps, one of the elders reassures him, "See, the Lion of the tribe of Judah, the Root of David, has conquered, so that he can open the scroll and its seven seals" (5:5 NRSV). But then, in the very next verse, the narrator sees not a conquering Lion but a Lamb who has been slaughtered, and it is the Lamb who opens the seals — and the rest of the story unfolds. The text offers no explanation, and at least one commentator chalks it all up to confusion, "a quick and somewhat incongruous shift from one type of animal imagery to another," which may confusedly conflate an earlier tradition "in which a lion is the helper of the Messiah, who is a lamb."[15]

---

15. Martin Rist, "Revelation: Introduction and Exegesis," *The Interpreter's Bible*, vol. 12 (New York: Abingdon, 1957), p. 407.

But is this shift of image a confusion or the very point of the story? The imagery earlier in the book consistently presents the language of power. The Son of Man in chapter 1 has feet like burnished bronze, carries a two-edge sword, "and his face was like the sun shining with full force" (1:16 NRSV). The messages to the seven churches speak the language of power and even of threat. And the vision of the throne of God in chapter 4 parades every imperial attribute discoverable by the author's quite considerable imagination. What could be more natural than to expect the arrival of that conquering royal beast, the Lion?

Instead, we get a slaughtered Lamb. Commenting on the passage, G. B. Caird writes that it is "as if John were saying to us. . . . 'Wherever the Old Testament says *Lion*, read *Lamb*'. Wherever the Old Testament speaks of the victory of the Messiah or the overthrow of the enemies of God, we are to remember that the Gospel recognizes no other way of achieving these ends than the way of the Cross."[16] Caird grasps the basic contrast but puts it in a context all too common in the Christian tradition, setting the threatening God of the Hebrew Scriptures off against the gentle deity of the New Testament. Stating the issue in those terms both oversimplifies the two parts of the Christian Bible and misses the more general point of this text. The lesson of this narrative turning point is a more fundamental and general one: to contrast the ideologies of power, *wherever* they are found — in Babylon, Israel, Rome, Beijing, Washington, or the Christian community — with the challenge of the gospel of the crucified One, the crucified One who came to reveal the God already known as the Lord who suffered with the people Israel.

From this moment on, at any rate, the Lamb never long leaves the story. The narrative returns to imagery of power, even of warfare, but the victories are victories of the Lamb who has been slaughtered. As Jacques Ellul puts it, for the book of Revelation,

> The one who . . . unravels the secret of history, who holds it, and allows it to unfold as history is clearly not the All-Powerful Lord: he is the immolated Lamb. In the same way the one who presides at the "Last Judgment," at the separation of good and evil, at the condemnation, at the ultimate combat, is not the powerful athlete, muscular and majestic, of the admirable Sistine. . . . it is not the "chief of the heavenly militia"; it is not the Lord of Lords; it is the Lamb, the crucified, the stripped, the annihilated, the weakest of all . . . the one who has neither beauty, nor honor, nor power.[17]

16. G. B. Caird, *The Revelation of St. John the Divine* (New York: Harper & Row, 1966), p. 75.

17. Jacques Ellul, *Apocalypse,* trans. George W. Schreiner (New York: Seabury Press, 1977), p. 117.

In the cultures in which the New Testament was written, as in our own, such a perspective was radically out of fashion. In the Hellenistic world, it was powerful heroes and mighty emperors who were deified. Indeed, Celsus contrasted the "plainly evident" appearances of the pagan deities with the "stealthy and secretive manner" of "the fellow who deceived the Christians."[18] He knew what a divine epiphany ought to look like, and Jesus hardly fit the requirements. Many among Jesus' Jewish contemporaries understandably hoped for a triumphant Messiah who would defeat the hated Romans, and they, too, could only find this crucified teacher a disappointment if they took him seriously at all.[19] The first century, like the twentieth, expected deity to triumph through power.

But suppose God is not like that. Suppose God is one who loves in freedom, and in that love is willing to be vulnerable and to suffer. Stories, as already suggested, provide a good way of presenting a person's identity, but the task of narrating the identity of a human being who is the self-revelation of such a God poses great problems. On the one hand, one has to make it clear that the story of this human person really is the story of God. After all, as Kierkegaard once remarked, "God did not assume the form of a servant to make a mockery of men; hence it cannot be his intention to pass through the world in such a manner that no single human being becomes aware of his presence."[20] On the other hand, one needs to challenge many of the assumptions readers will bring as to the nature of God. How do you present the story of a human life as the self-revelation of God without falling into the imagery of power and might which shaped thinking about God in Jesus' day and continues to shape it in our own?

The difficulty of the problems posed for narrative strategy may be suggested by the fact that Paul did not attempt to solve them. The story he told was primarily one of the eternal Christ self-emptying into human likeness. In Paul's "Gospel," Jesus of Nazareth is born, shares the bread and cup on the night when he was betrayed, and suffers and dies on a cross. No other stories of Jesus' earthly life, no references, ever, to a single miracle he performed. It has

---

18. Origen, *Contra Celsum* 7.35.

19. The evidence concerning violence and military imagery in messianic expectations is mixed. The Psalms of Solomon and 4 Ezra, for instance, say the Messiah will not use military weapons; 2 Baruch says he will carry a sword. J. H. Charlesworth, "From Messianology to Christology," in Jacob Neusner, William Scott Green, and Ernest Frerichs, *Judaisms and Their Messiahs* (Cambridge: Cambridge University Press, 1987), p. 248. Green's introduction to this helpful volume (pp. 2-3) surveys some of the complexities of first-century references to Messiahs.

20. Søren Kierkegaard, *Philosophical Fragments,* trans. David Swenson (Princeton: Princeton University Press, 1962), p. 69.

become customary to note that, after all, Paul had not known Jesus' life at first hand, and yet I wonder. On one occasion he spent fifteen days with Peter, and he had other contacts with the Jerusalem community. Would he not have known stories about Jesus' life, stories unknown to his readers, stories which might have illustrated points of concern to him with a particular authority? It is dangerous to infer from silence, but at least such questions about what Paul left unsaid provide an entry point for thinking about what the Gospel of Mark does say. It is the earliest instance we have of an extended attempt to present, through narrative, Jesus' identity as God's self-revelation. For all the common condescending remarks about the quality of Mark's Greek and the awkwardness of his prose, considered as a solution to these narrative problems, the text stands as a work of genius.

Theodore Weeden's interesting study of Mark argues that its author wrote with the quite specific purpose of refuting a party within his own community which had developed a divine-man Christology and ecclesiology. Jesus was, for them, the powerful wonder-worker who manifested God, and they, like the Corinthian group Paul attacked in 2 Corinthians, saw themselves as simply continuing the power of Jesus in their own lives, through pneumatic gifts, ecstatic experiences, and miraculous feats.[21] In Weeden's interpretation, Mark wrote, on the other hand, for a community of Palestinian Christians who, "separated from their Lord . . . found themselves in a cruel period of suffering and misery while evil forces still abounded in the world," and who followed a suffering, humble Christ.[22] Therefore, the disciples, who represent the ideology of power, become the villains of the story, with Jesus as the humble, suffering hero.

Weeden's historical conclusions continue to be controversial. While agreeing with Weeden on the centrality of Mark's polemic against the disciples, Werner Kelber has argued that the real issue was historical rather than christological. After the destruction of the Jerusalem church in the Jewish War of 66-70 C.E., Christians needed an explanation of this tragedy, and the author of Mark provided an anti-Jerusalem, anti-twelve-disciples polemic to explain the fall of the Jerusalem church as divine punishment.[23] Many scholars would doubt Weeden's location of the writing of the Gospel in Palestine. Dieter Georgi argues that Mark still presents a divine-man Christology; Jack Dean Kingsbury maintains that *theios aner* was such a rare and variously used term

---

21. Theodore J. Weeden, *Mark: Traditions in Conflict* (Philadelphia: Fortress, 1971), pp. 60-61.

22. Weeden, p. 132.

23. Werner H. Kelber, *Mark's Story of Jesus* (Philadelphia: Fortress, 1979), pp. 88-95.

in classical culture that it does not provide a useful category for thinking about the background of Mark, one way or the other.[24]

Norman Perrin took, he said, Weeden's work as a "catalytic agent" for his own thinking about Mark's Christology.[25] I would like to do the same. Whatever the accuracy of his particular historical claims, his contrast between ideologies of power and of suffering in Mark provides a valuable way of thinking about this Gospel's rhetorical emphases: the consistent undercutting of the language of power and the authority of those who claim it.

The Gospel's title, in most manuscripts, declares that the story before us is "the good news of Jesus Christ, the Son of God," but the narrator's own voice never refers to Jesus as the Son of God again. No sooner does the Spirit descend upon him and a voice from heaven proclaim him "my Son, the Beloved," than "the Spirit immediately drove him out into the wilderness" (1:11-12 NRSV). This will not be a story, we as readers gather, of easy triumphs.

To be sure, this Jesus heals and performs other miracles, but he silences those he has healed, almost as if the act were one of shame (1:44; 5:43; 7:36; 8:26). In the act of healing, moreover, he touches lepers (1:41) and spits and touches the tongue of a deaf man (7:33) — the very forms of his healing would have been, to his contemporaries, both ritually polluting and physically disgusting.[26] When the leader of the synagogue asks for his help in curing his daughter, Jesus makes Jairus wait while he tends to a woman who has been suffering from menstrual hemorrhaging. For the business of wonder working, this gets every priority wrong: he postpones raising a child from the dead for a comparatively trivial cure whose results both their physical character and the cultural taboos of the time would have kept invisible; he turns from the socially important male to heal a nameless woman; he responds to the woman's polluting touch with praise of her faith.[27] Then he turns to the really dramatic miracle and nearly renders it into farce, insisting, in the face of all the evidence, that the child is not dead but merely sleeping, so that onlookers burst into laughter (5:40).

What sort of miracle-worker is this? The wonder-workers of that age, or of ours, know how to milk the dramatic moment. Jesus seems to keep under-

24. Dieter Georgi, *Die Gegner des Paulus im 2. Korintherbrief* (Neukirchen-Vluyn: Neukirchener Verlag, 1964); Jack Dean Kingsbury, "The 'Divine Man' as the Key to Mark's Christology — the End of an Era?" *Interpretation* 35 (July 1981): 248. See also Morton Smith, "Prolegomena to a Discussion of Aretalogies, Divine Men, the Gospels and Jesus," *Journal of Biblical Literature* 90 (June 1971): 174-99.

25. Norman Perrin, *A Modern Pilgrimage in New Testament Christology* (Philadelphia: Fortress, 1974), p. 110.

26. Ched Myers, *Binding the Strong Man* (Maryknoll, N.Y.: Orbis, 1988), pp. 153, 205.

27. Myers, pp. 200-202.

cutting the wonders; Mark, indeed, never uses the usual Greek word for "miracle" in describing these events. Little surprise, perhaps, that such acts seem to do Jesus more harm than good: after healing the leper, he can no longer go into a town openly (1:45); the Gerasenes' reaction to his cure of the demoniac is to beg Jesus to leave their neighborhood (5:17); immediately after the dramatic resuscitation of Jairus's daughter comes the fiasco at Nazareth. Jesus walks on the water of the sea, but the narrator's immediate comment is that the disciples did not understand his miracles for their hearts were hardened (6:51).

This Jesus calls disciples, but the narrative "paints them as obtuse, obdurate, recalcitrant men who at first are unperceptive of Jesus' messiahship, then oppose its style and character, and finally totally reject it."[28] The story ends without their rehabilitation. Yet the blame seems not to rest entirely with them.[29] Jesus speaks to the multitudes in deliberately mysterious parables and explains their meaning only in private to the circle of the disciples (4:34). Yet that very circle consistently misunderstands him. He seems as oddly paradoxical a teacher as he is a wonder-worker.[30]

Who is this Jesus of Nazareth? At a kind of climax in the story, Peter proclaims him the Messiah — and Jesus' response is a sternly delivered command to silence. Then Jesus "began to teach them that the Son of Man must undergo great suffering, and be rejected by the elders, the chief priests, and the scribes, and be killed, and after three days rise again. He said all this quite openly" (8:31-32 NRSV). (Note the pointed contrast between silence and openness.) When Peter protests (no sooner declaring Jesus the Messiah than contradicting him),[31] Jesus thunders, "Get behind me, Satan!" (8:33 NRSV).

Peter expects a Messiah, and thinks he knows what that means, but he has it all wrong, just as anyone with the usual expectations about wandering miracle-workers would have it all wrong. As for us readers, with our expectations set by the opening identification of this text as the gospel of the Son of God, our expectations are also being subverted at every step.

---

28. Weeden, pp. 50-51.

29. Here I would disagree with Weeden, pp. 50-51, who insists that "Mark is assiduously involved in a vendetta against the disciples."

30. This is one of the starting points of Frank Kermode's discussion of Mark, which lies in the background of a good bit of my discussion. See Frank Kermode, *The Genesis of Secrecy* (Cambridge: Harvard University Press, 1979).

31. "Peter's next actions in relation to Jesus are shocking in the extreme. When Jesus starts to teach the disciples about the inevitability of suffering, rejection and death that he faces, Peter rebukes him. (8:31-32) . . . What degree of pride or arrogance must exist to allow one to refute the Messiah?" Mary Ann Tolbert, *Sowing the Gospel* (Minneapolis: Fortress, 1989), p. 201.

Mark uses every strategy to say two things at once: yes, this is the Messiah, the greatest of miracle-workers, the Son of God, but, no, that doesn't mean at all what you thought it meant. Irony is the rhetorical device perhaps best suited for saying "Yes, but no," and the ironies grow as the story progresses.[32] In the transfiguration scene, Jesus appears dazzlingly to Peter, James, and John, with Moses and Elijah beside him. The obvious thing to say would be, "Look!" but the voice from heaven (which speaks only here and at Jesus' baptism) says, "Listen to him" — though Jesus, in the scene at hand, does not speak (9:7). When he does next speak, however, he tells of the suffering the Son of Man must undergo — so that the point of the voice from heaven is to attend not to the dazzling epiphany but to the teaching about suffering. The disciples still fail to understand. Later in the journey they are still arguing about which of them is the greatest; Jesus' message about becoming a servant, becoming like a child, becoming the last of all, does not seem to penetrate (9:34-36).

The ironies continue. Jesus enters Jerusalem on a little colt: it is at once a humble and slightly silly ride and the fulfillment of a messianic prophecy. He is anointed as were the kings of old, as the Messiah ought to be, but by an unnamed woman, and in a context where the act only generates controversy and presages his death. Through most of the Gospel, Mark has presented wonders in ways that undercut our expectations. Now the irony reverses, and he presents tragedy in a way that hints at wonder. Jesus sorrowfully ascends the Mount of Olives, accompanied by three followers who protest their loyalty, only to be betrayed by a trusted follower. It's a story of defeat that exactly parallels the story of David at the time of Absalom's rebellion — David the greatest king, the source of so much messianic imagery.[33]

Peter, the rock, is the first to betray him, but the betrayal fulfills Jesus' prophecy. The soldiers then in ridicule call on Jesus to prophesy; he remains silent, but his prophecy concerning Peter has just been fulfilled.[34] He receives a purple cloak and a crown; the soldiers bow down before him, and it is all intended as humiliating mockery. We, recognizing the irony, see that he really is a king, but his coronation takes the form of a scourging. Only in the midst of his trial does he proclaim himself the Messiah, the Son of the Blessed One. Only as he dies on the cross does a human voice at last recognize him as the Son of God.[35]

32. See Wayne C. Booth, *A Rhetoric of Irony* (Chicago: University of Chicago Press, 1974), pp. 28-29.

33. John R. Donahue, "Temple, Trial, and Royal Christology," in *The Passion in Mark*, ed. Werner Kelber (Philadelphia: Fortress, 1976), p. 76.

34. Robert M. Fowler, *Let the Reader Understand* (Minneapolis: Fortress, 1991), p. 159.

35. Calvin, I fear, got this one wrong. "When Mark says that the centurion spoke thus,

The cross, moreover, does not just represent a painful way to die. It is the humiliating penalty assigned the lowest of criminals, the fate of the rankest of outsiders, full of shame and perhaps — though here I think the historical evidence ambiguous, and Mark does not make the point — subject to curse in Jewish tradition. One might think of those who have AIDS as the equivalents in our culture to one who suffers crucifixion, victims not only of great pain but also of degradation and humiliation from the dominant values of the culture. A few chapters earlier, when Jesus talked most vividly of times of crisis ahead, he said it would be imposters claiming to be messiahs who would work signs and wonders, while disciples would suffer floggings and arrest, betrayal and hatred. In that context, as bystanders call on him to work a miracle and come down from the cross, it is his silent suffering that confirms his identity as the true Messiah.[36]

And then: some women find Jesus' tomb empty, and a young man delivers an enigmatic message that serves only to terrify them, and at that point, notoriously, the Gospel ends, with an abruptness that extends even to the grammar of the last sentence. Jesus proclaimed himself the Messiah in the midst of a criminal trial, and a military officer recognized him as the Son of God as he died on a cross. We do not see a triumphant divine Jesus, pulling away the mask of suffering like a magician at the end of a trick. Mark's Gospel invites us to see Jesus' divinity precisely as he dies on the cross, for, after that, we never see him at all.[37]

"For responsible Christian usage of the word 'God,'" Eberhard Jüngel has written, "the Crucified One is virtually the real definition of what is meant with the word 'God.'"[38] Yet Christian theology keeps losing sight of that point.

---

because Christ, when he had uttered a loud voice, expired, some commentators think that he intends to point out the unwonted strength which remained unimpaired till death; and certainly, as the body of Christ was almost exhausted of blood, it could not happen, in the ordinary course of things, that the sides and the lungs should retain sufficient vigor for uttering so loud a cry. Yet I rather think that the centurion intended to applaud the unshaken perseverance of Christ in calling on the name of God. Nor was it merely the cry of Christ that led the centurion to think so highly of him, but this confession was extorted from him by perceiving that his extraordinary strength harmonized with heavenly miracles." Calvin, *Commentary on a Harmony of the Evangelists*, vol. 3, *Calvin's Commentaries*, vol. 17 (Grand Rapids: Baker, 1989), p. 327. The whole point is precisely that this is not a moment of miraculous or extraordinary strength.

36. Tolbert, p. 261.

37. See Neill Q. Hamilton, *Jesus for a No-God World* (Philadelphia: Westminster, 1969), pp. 62-63; Donald Michie and David Rhoads, *Mark as Story* (Philadelphia: Fortress, 1982), pp. 61-62; John Dominic Crossan, "Empty Tomb and Absent Lord," in *The Passion in Mark*, p. 152.

38. Jüngel, p. 13.

"We need only look at the images of Christ in the great churches from the third century on," Leonardo Boff reminds us. "Jesus of Nazareth, weak in power but strong in love, who renounced the sword and violence, was replaced by a political Christ constituted Lord of the earth by the resurrection."[39]

An orthodox Marxist historian would explain all this as one more instance of political and economic reality shaping ideas and ideology. Of course the powerful shape a Lord in their own image. Push such analyses far enough, and there is little point in mounting theological challenges. Christian theology, however, has not only reflected social attitudes toward power but contributed to them. Too often, theologians have begun with the images of power from one form or another of natural theology — the patriarchs and Caesars of the political theologies of their cultures, the unmoved movers, impervious and imperious in their impassibility, of philosophical speculation. They therefore had to cast Christology in the form of a radical paradox, for only paradoxically could the self-revelation of such a God take the form of the crucified Jesus.

Theological debates have often miscast this issue of the divine nature in terms of intra-trinitarian relations or Christology, and that has muddied the waters. It is easy, for instance, to denounce talk of God's suffering as Patripassianism. But the real issue in the Patripassian debate was the distinction between "Father" and "Son." God the Father did not suffer on the cross. That need not mean, however, that only the second person of the Trinity has experienced suffering. Few pains can be as great as what a parent endures while watching the agony of a beloved child. To say that that suffering is not the same as the child's suffering (for the parent is not the child) is not to deny its reality or its pathos.

Orthodox Christology has often sought to reconcile Christ's suffering with a doctrine of divine impassibility by appeal to the *communicatio idiomatum:* the divine nature and the human nature are so united in the one person of Christ that we can attribute the predicates of the divine nature to the human nature and vice versa. In that sense, we can say that God suffers. But Zwingli merely pushed the logic of this approach one step further when he called it only *alloiosis,* a figure of speech in which we can refer properties of the human nature to the divine nature while in fact "God remains untouched in his sovereignty."[40] The Reformed tradition, indeed, has been particularly insistent on the inability of anything finite fully to manifest the infinite God. Here, too, a valid theological point distracts from an important issue. The

39. Leonardo Boff, *Jesus Christ Liberator,* trans. Patrick Hughes (Maryknoll, N.Y.: Orbis, 1978), p. 27.

40. Jürgen Moltmann, *The Crucified God,* trans. R. A. Wilson and John Bowden (New York: Harper & Row, 1974), p. 232.

communicatio idiomatum may indeed say something about the relation of human and divine in Christ, and no doubt the finite cannot fully contain or manifest the infinite. That said, however, the issue of whether the infinite deity can embrace the vulnerability of love remains a completely different question.

If we take the Gospel of Mark as one trajectory toward understanding the God whose self-revealed identity it narrates, then we encounter a God who, in Karl Barth's phrase, is the one who loves in freedom and who, therefore, living and suffering in humility in Jesus Christ, does not cast "off His Godhead but (as the One who loves in sovereign freedom) activates and proves it" precisely in self-giving.[41] God "does not forfeit anything by doing this. . . . On the contrary," precisely in showing willingness and readiness "for this condescension, this act of extravagance, this far journey," God is marked out from all the false Gods. "What marks out God above all false gods is that they are not capable and ready for this. In their otherworldliness and supernaturalness and otherness, etc., the gods are a reflection of the human pride which will not unbend, which will not stoop to that which is beneath it. God is not proud. In His high majesty He is humble."[42]

If such a God seems at first weak, perhaps that is because we have bought so many of our culture's assumptions about what constitutes strength and success. If we worship power and wealth, then a God who, in the freedom of love, accepts suffering and humiliation may well seem weak to us. Jesus, however, seems, to quote Leonardo Boff again, weak in *power* but strong in *love*. It would be a weak, poor God, Moltmann says, who could not love or suffer.[43] Suffering love has its own kind of strength. It strengthens the suffering with the comfort that they do not suffer alone. It lures the hesitant with the model of the satisfactions and joys it finds in the midst of its pathos. It condemns by example the hating, the bitter, and the merely indifferent.

To mention only such work, however, risks leaving the work of love sounding too subjective. Love's power lies not merely in the action it inspires in others, but in its own doing. If I risk reaching out to you in love, then things are already different, prior to or even in the absence of your response. If I have betrayed you and you forgive me out of love and at the cost of your suffering, then our relationship has changed, even if I fail to accept your forgiveness. If the world is, as Martin Luther King thought, a place where love willing to suffer can triumph over brute force, that's something worth knowing about the world. If a love willing to be vulnerable lies at the core of the origin and sus-

---

41. Karl Barth, *Church Dogmatics* IV/1, trans. G. W. Bromiley and T. F. Torrance (Edinburgh: T. & T. Clark, 1956), p. 134.

42. Barth, p. 159.

43. Moltmann, p. 253.

taining and end of all things, then all things are transformed. Compared with the God implied in such a vision of things, a merely omnipotent deity, isolated in invulnerability, seems oddly enfeebled.

Mark's telling of Jesus' story makes just this point. The story does not begin in the splendor of the heavenly court but in the wilderness. Jesus' own life ends in shameful and agonizing death; he is abandoned by his chosen disciples, with women looking on only from a distance. The story itself ends not with triumph but with fear. Along the way, Jesus seems a teacher whose students never learn, a wonder-worker whose wonders keep backfiring or at least seem to make him consistently uncomfortable. Yet just this story, so its opening declares, is "the good news of Jesus Christ, the Son of God," and of just this Jesus the centurion declares, "Truly this man was God's Son!" We want this story of vulnerable love embedded in some larger, different story of divine glory, but the story as we have it seems to say that precisely such vulnerable love is the image of divine glory. It is a marvel that Jesus of Nazareth should be God's self-revelation, but it need not be a paradox — not unless one has decided in advance, prior to encounter with the crucified Jesus, on the impassibility of a powerful, lordly God.

CHAPTER 14

The Logic of Faith

Alexander McKelway

John Calvin never denied his dependence upon and essential agreement with Luther, and, up to a point, his doctrine of faith was no exception. For both Reformers the meaning of faith involved three assertions: (1) the *origin* of faith is located in the initiating action of God and not in human will; (2) the *content* of faith is primarily divine activity and only secondarily our appropriation of it; and (3) the *effect* of faith is therefore the actualization of saving grace. These assertions present the paradoxical claim that "faith," which by ordinary definition refers to some kind of human activity, is in respect to justification *not* a human activity but an activity initiated and completed by God. In what follows we will briefly review the distinctive features of the Reformers' doctrines of faith and show how their logic was lost in the modern period. Finally, we will consider Karl Barth's attempt to recover that logic.[1]

Faith in Reformation Thought

Martin Luther

In 1545, a year before his death, Martin Luther recalled his discovery of the principle of faith in these words:

---

1. "Logic" is used in this essay in the general sense of a mode of reasoning productive of inferences consistent with the presuppositions belonging to any subject, in this case the Christian faith.

At last, by the mercy of God, meditating day and night, I gave heed to the context of the words, namely, "In the righteousness of God is revealed, as it is written, 'He who through faith is righteous shall live.'" [Rom. 1:17] There I began to understand that the righteousness of God is that by which the righteous lives by a gift of God, namely by faith. . . . Here I felt that I was altogether born again and had entered paradise itself through open gates.[2]

In his preface to Paul's letter to the Romans, Luther defined "faith" in highly dialectical terms:

Faith is not the human notion and dream that some people call faith . . . when they hear the gospel, they get busy and by their own powers create an idea in their heart which says, "I believe"; they take this then to be a true faith. . . . Faith, however, is a divine work which changes us and makes us to be born anew of God, John 1 [:12-13]. It kills the old Adam and makes us altogether different men, in heart and spirit and mind and powers. . . . Faith is a living, daring confidence in God's grace, so sure and certain that the believer would stake his life on it a thousand times. . . . And this is the work which the Holy Spirit performs in faith. . . . Thus it is impossible to separate works from faith, quite as impossible as to separate heat and light from fire. . . . Pray God that he may work faith in you.[3]

While the above quotations link the work of God and human work, it was always Luther's intention to deny that faith was a "work." "Having been justified by grace . . . we then do good works, yes, [but] Christ himself does all in us."[4] Trust in our own work, on *any* basis, "destroys faith and the entire Christ. For it is Christ alone who counts and I must confess this . . . by saying: 'since Christ does it, I must not do it.'"[5] For Luther, the origin of faith is God. "Let no one assume that he has faith by his own powers, as so many do when they hear about faith and then undertake to gain it by their own ability. They thus undertake a task which belongs to God alone, for having true faith is really a divine work."[6]

---

2. *Luther's Works*, ed. Lewis W. Spitz, vol. 34 (Philadelphia: Muhlenberg Press, 1960), p. 337.

3. *Luther's Works*, ed. E. Theodore Bachmann, vol. 35 (Philadelphia: Fortress, 1960), pp. 370-71.

4. *Luther's Works*, 34:111.

5. Paul Althaus, *The Theology of Luther* (Philadelphia: Fortress, 1966), p. 225; D. *Martin Luthers Werke*, Weimar Edition (Weimar: Hermann Böhlaus Nachfolger, 1883ff.), 37:46, hereafter cited as *Luthers Werke*.

6. Althaus, p. 48; *Luthers Werke*, 12:422-23.

Because he considered it to originate with God, Luther could make astonishing claims about faith. "Outside of faith God loses his righteousness, glory, riches, etc." "If you believe that he is your father, your judge, your God, then that is what he is."[7] Read in the simplest way, these statements could be taken as an extravagant form of self-idolatry, or assertions of which only a Ludwig Feuerbach could approve. If, however, we recall Luther's abhorrence of idolatry, his insistence upon the objective reality of God, and his view of faith as an action of God, they make perfect, even tautological, sense. Since faith is God in action, where faith is God is, where faith is not, God, together with his attributes, is absent. Because faith is God in action, it was entirely logical for Luther to assert that "Faith is omnipotent as God himself is."[8]

Concerning the *content* of faith, Luther believed that God addresses a person in such a way that a hearing and believing takes place, but he would not allow doctrinal distinctions to intrude upon the existential encounter of faith.[9] For Luther the doctrinal content of the faith that "saves" is simply that God makes us just through Christ, his cross, and his resurrection, and these are not so much doctrines as immediate and self-evident truths which accompany the operation of God's grace.

In spite of Luther's acceptance of *Anfechtung* (dread/anxiety) as a necessary preparation for faith, he did not believe that religious experience or feeling *(Empfinden)* can produce the trust of faith. The ambiguity that accompanies religious experience is occasioned by the incapacity of human feeling correctly to receive and assess either God's Yes or No. In either case we seem compelled to faithless self-congratulation or an equally faithless self-condemnation. "So now turn from your conscience and its feeling to Christ who is not able to deceive; my heart and Satan, however, who will drive me to sin are liars. . . . You should not believe your conscience and your feelings more than the word which the Lord . . . preaches to you."[10] So great was Luther's distrust of experience as the proper basis for faith that for him "a battle begins in which experience struggles against the Spirit and faith."[11] The "trust" and "confidence" Luther associates with faith obviously do not depend upon the feelings usually associated with those attitudes. Trust is rather an acknowledgment of the power of God which displaces the fear and despair that inevitably result from any dependence upon our own religious or spiritual resources.

---

7. *Luther's Works,* ed. Jaroslav Pelikan, vol. 13 (Philadelphia: Muhlenberg Press, 1958), p. 7.

8. Althaus, p. 48; *Luthers Werke,* vol. 10/III, p. 214.

9. *Luther's Works,* ed. George W. Forell, vol. 32 (Philadelphia: Muhlenberg Press, 1958), p. 244.

10. Althaus, p. 59; *Luthers Werke,* 27:223.

11. Althaus, p. 63; *Luthers Werke,* vol. 17/II, p. 66.

John Calvin

Calvin agreed with Luther that "Men, being subject to the curse of the law, have no means left of attaining salvation but through faith alone."[12] While Calvin laid more stress on the human side of faith, it is nonetheless clear that he, as much as Luther, understood its dialectical nature:

> We shall have a complete definition of faith, if we say that it is a steady and certain knowledge of the divine benevolence toward us, which, being founded on the truth of the gratuitous promises in Christ, is both revealed to our minds and confirmed to our hearts by the Holy Spirit.[13]

Like Luther, Calvin based his definition of faith upon the doctrine of justification, the need and character of which he defined in much the same way as Luther. "He is said to be justified in the sight of God who in the divine judgement is reputed righteous." Justification by works is impossible, for it would require a life of "such purity and holiness as to deserve the character of righteousness before the throne of God." Therefore, to be "made just" does not belong to human capability. "Thus we simply explain justification to be an acceptance, by which God receives us into his favor, and esteems us as righteous persons; and we say that it consists in the remission of sins and the imputation of the righteousness of Christ."[14] Faith, for Calvin, is the means provided by God for our apprehension, acceptance, and conformity to this gift.

So far, there is no difference between Luther and Calvin concerning the necessary logic of faith: it is initiated by God and actualized in an acknowledgment that is at once a work of God and a work of the believer. But while Calvin used the formula of salvation by "faith alone," faith was not as central for him as for Luther. For Luther, faith was the dialectical event of God's grace and our reception. It is God's work and ours, but only ours as a result of God's decision and action. Calvin took the same position, but with this difference: what Luther saw as an immediate and momentary *event*, Calvin saw as a *process*, in which the action of God and the reaction of the believer are more clearly distinguishable. This is why Calvin could say, on the one hand, that, as an extension of God's action, "faith alone" is the means of our salvation, but on the other, that, "with respect to justification, faith is a thing merely passive," and even more bluntly, "faith . . . of itself is of no value. . . ."[15] Here he clearly had in

---

12. John Calvin, *Institutes of the Christian Religion*, ed. Ford L. Battles and John T. McNeill (Philadelphia: Westminster, 1960), 3.11.1.

13. Calvin, *Institutes* 3.2.7.

14. Calvin, *Institutes* 3.11.3.

15. Calvin, *Institutes* 3.14.9 and 3.11.7.

mind the *fides quae creditur,* with its various forms of knowledge and belief, and not the more substantial *fides qua creditur,* the certain confidence and trust in God that undergirds Christian life. However indispensable it may be, faith as only human activity alone can claim no participation in the work of salvation.

Where Luther saw faith as a single phenomenon, an ellipse with two unequal foci, i.e., God's work and our response, Calvin posited two kinds of faith. First, faith is the means of the divine act of justification (and in that sense saves "alone"). In this case the term "faith" often gave way in Calvin's writing to more fundamental terms such as "justification," "grace," or "election." Second, faith could be (and more often was) understood by Calvin to indicate the human response to grace. As such it cannot be said to save. However indispensable, it is merely an "earthen vessel."[16] Because Calvin distinguished in this way the *fides divina* from the *fides actualis,* he could, without intruding upon the priority of God's action, assign to faith definite doctrinal and moral responsibilities necessary for its fulfillment.

In making this distinction between faith as divine act and faith as human response, Calvin was not abandoning the Lutheran logic of faith. On the contrary, he so distinguished faith from faith because he had already made a similar division within the doctrine of justification. Calvin recognized an element of truth in Catholic criticism that the Reformation movement dissolved Christian obedience into a theory of justification. He sought to correct the situation by emphasizing the presence of works in faith, not as a cause, nor as an effect, but as a necessary and inescapable *accompaniment.* Specifically, Calvin signaled the importance of active faith in his system by placing a second and larger exposition of the doctrine of justification after that of regeneration and sanctification.

We may attempt an illustration of Calvin's treatment by an abbreviated comparison of his arrangement of the *ordo salutis* with that of Luther and Rome. For Catholicism the progression roughly was: contrition → regeneration → sanctification → justification → glorification. For Luther the order might be set out thus: [election] → *justification* → (contrition → regeneration → sanctification → glorification). Luther accepted divine election, but he considered it an impenetrable mystery unprofitable for the task of evangelical theology. The whole of Christian life (its sorrow for sin, its rebirth, and its growth in grace) is caught up in the "moment" of faith when the reality of God's justification is applied to the individual's life.

Calvin conceived the order of salvation in this way: election → justification → contrition → regeneration → sanctification → justification → glorifi-

16. Calvin, *Institutes* 3.11.7.

cation. The difference lies in the double entry of justification. The one who is elected receives the benefits of Christ's justifying grace by way of faith. The life of faith involves sorrow for sin, conversion, and rebirth into an existence which struggles to obtain holiness. Naturally, the life of faith cannot do this on its own. The righteousness that belongs to human life is always an imputed righteousness — but nonetheless a *real* righteousness. "Whom therefore the Lord receives into fellowship, him he is said to justify; because he cannot receive anyone into favor or into fellowship with himself, without making him from a sinner to be a righteous person."[17] The person made righteous in God's eyes by a *first* justification is thereafter actually made into a person whose life can be worthy of a *second* justification. The elect are given both the desire and strength to do the good. "Christ therefore justifies no one whom he does not also sanctify. For these benefits are perpetually and indissolubly connected."[18] Sanctification is not only a state; it is a process in which life is rendered, by divine assistance, more and more consistent with the righteousness imputed to it in Christ. Such a life can be judged by God as righteous; it is justified. Therefore, for Calvin,

> [t]here is no objection against . . . calling eternal life a reward. . . . So, likewise, it will occasion no inconvenience, if we consider holiness of life as the way, not which procures our admission into the glory of the heavenly kingdom, but through which the elect are conducted by their God to the manifestation of it.[19]

There is for Calvin a double meaning of faith that accompanies these two views of justification. On the one hand, Calvin insists that faith is a work of God, which "alone" justifies. On the other hand, he dedicates a large portion of his discussion of faith in book 3 of his *Institutes* to faith as human knowledge and action.[20]

Respecting faith as action or a work, Calvin rejects the Catholic distinction between an "unformed faith" (*fides informis* — belief which has not yet the *habitus* of love) and a "formed faith" (*fides formata*, i.e., formed by the practice of love).[21] Yet, for Calvin, "while man is justified by faith alone . . . nevertheless actual holiness of life, so to speak, is not separated from free imputation of righteousness."[22] Sanctification must be actualized in the life of

17. Calvin, *Institutes* 3.11.21.
18. Calvin, *Institutes* 3.16.1.
19. Calvin, *Institutes* 3.18.4.
20. Calvin, *Institutes* 3.6-10.
21. Calvin, *Institutes* 3.2.9-10.
22. Calvin, *Institutes* 3.3.1.

faith by the predestinating and justifying power of God. But both the intellectual certainty and moral steadfastness of faith are possible only insofar as the believer looks to Christ. It is finally the unity of Christ with us that allows Calvin to place such importance upon the actualization of faith in good works. "Not only does [Christ] cling to us by an invisible bond of fellowship, but with a wonderful communion, day by day, he grows more and more into one body with us, until he becomes completely one with us."[23]

Although Calvin's view of faith differs from Luther's to the extent that he places a greater emphasis upon its human side, he does not neglect the polarity of divine and human action in faith. Where Luther sees faith as a single event comprised of the action of God and the reaction of man, Calvin posits justification and faith at two places, before and after conversion and regeneration. While these two placements call attention, respectively, to the divine and human side of faith, in neither case is human activity unaccompanied by a prior divine activity. Just as the believer may be said to be "rewarded" for the life of holiness that belongs to the elect, it is perfectly clear that God merely rewards his own work in the elect. So, too, the faith that grows in sanctification is also the work of God and, in a strictly dependent way, also the work of the believer.

That Calvin's doctrine of faith failed to achieve the desired rapprochement with Catholicism was due to his doctrine of election. In contrast to Luther, Calvin could introduce a strong element of human activity into his conception of justification by faith, because his doctrine of God's eternal election had already and without remainder secured the primacy of grace and the incapacity of human beings.

The Dissolution of the Logic of Faith

Reformed Confessions and Orthodoxy

In the Reformed confessions of the 1550s and early 1560s, the Reformers' logic of faith predominates. The First Helvetic Confession (1536) speaks of faith "as a pure gift and bestowal of God," but also, revealing the Erasmian influence of Ulrich Zwingli, as a human work. It is "the real true service, by means of which we please God."[24] The Scots Confession makes clear that faith is a work of God:

---

23. Calvin, *Institutes* 3.2.24.

24. Reinhold Seeberg, *Text-Book of the History of Doctrines,* trans. Charles E. Hay (Grand Rapids: Baker, 1964), p. 345.

our faith and its assurance do not proceed from flesh and blood, that is to say, from the natural powers within us, but are the inspiration of the Holy Ghost . . . for by ourselves we are not capable of one good thought, but he who has begun the work in us alone continues us in it.[25]

The Heidelberg Catechism reflects the agreement of Luther and Calvin on the divine origin of faith and its biblical content. "True faith . . . is a certain knowledge by which I accept as true all that God has revealed in his word, but also a wholehearted trust which the Holy Spirit creates in me. . . ."[26] The Second Helvetic Confession reflects Luther's denial of faith as doctrine — faith "is not an opinion or human conviction" — but otherwise agrees that faith is a gift "which God alone of his grace gives to his elect."[27]

At the same time there was increasing interest in the human side of faith. Jacob Arminius denied the irresistibility of grace and thereby afforded to human will a cooperative function in the maintenance (but not the origin) of a saving faith. The Synod of Dort (1618) condemned Arminianism in favor of a stricter predestinarianism. God's eternal decree determined before creation for every individual the call of Christ, the bestowal of faith, justification, and sanctification. Thus predestination, and not justification or faith, is the real basis of Christian life.

In collapsing faith and sanctification back into the absolute (and necessarily obscure) decree of God, the Canons of Dort intended to follow the implications of Calvin's doctrine of election. In doing so they may have secured the primacy of God's act in faith from every synergistic tendency, but the question may be asked whether, in making election the theological spring from which must flow every other doctrine (of justification, of faith, of sanctification), the orthodox party at Dort did not in fact reverse Calvin's own procedure. For Calvin, after all, the doctrine of election arose, not from a primary interest in the absolute power of God, but from the mystery of God's justifying grace in Christ. In any case, the troubling obscurity of that "terrible decree" forced the Calvinists to seek assurance elsewhere. The result was that both the intellectual content of faith *(fides quae)* and the moral demands of faith *(fides formata)* became increasingly the real focus of the Reformed doctrine of faith, and to that extent the dialectical logic of the Reformers was lost.

This may be illustrated by the fact that the Reformed dogmaticians of the

25. *The Book of Confessions* (New York: The Office of the General Assembly of the Presbyterian Church U.S.A., 1983), 3.12.

26. *The Book of Confessions* 4.021. Otherwise the catechism shows a decidedly Lutheran influence in avoiding any reference to the requirement of works or to their being, as human works, worthy of justification. Works are here prescribed only in terms of gratitude.

27. *The Book of Confessions* 5.112.

seventeenth and early eighteenth centuries became especially interested in the shape and character of the believing that belongs to faith and undertook to sort out its types, divisions, and functions in a way that closely paralleled that of the medieval Scholastics. Johan Wolleb distinguished five meanings of faith in Scripture: (1) *fides quam credimus,* sincere faith held "in pure conscience"; (2) *fides historica,* the acknowledgment of the fact of God; (3) *fides temporaria,* faith which does not last; (4) *fides miraculorum,* faith that can "move mountains"; and (5) *fides salvifica,* the faith given the apostles to heal the sick and raise the dead. Similar distinctions may be found in Johann Heinrich Heidegger and Gulielmus Bucan. This tendency is well summed up by Peter Mastricht, who defined the essence of faith as "an act of a reasonable soul, which consists in receiving God [by] (1) knowledge . . . , (2) explicit assent, (3) joy, and (4) hatred and detestation of the things which are contrary to [God]."[28]

It is clear from the discussion of the nature of faith carried on by these Reformed dogmaticians that theological interest had turned away from the prior and efficient action of God to focus more and more on faith as an act of the believer. Insofar as seventeenth-century orthodoxy agreed with Mastricht in identifying faith as a function of reason, it unwittingly prepared the way for a rationalist approach to faith in the Enlightenment that would undermine the very faith it wished to preserve.

Protestant Modernism

The fate of faith in Reformed theology was set not only by orthodoxy, but as well by the advent of Pietism, rationalism, and the critical philosophies of the Enlightenment. Pietism's emphasis upon the subjective and emotional aspects of faith may be found in Spener and received further elaboration in Hermann Franke and Nikolaus Ludwig Count von Zinzendorf, who celebrated the ascetic and mystical element of faith. The result was that the Reformers' suspicion of emotional experience was completely forgotten. Against Pietism's emphasis on the emotional side of faith, we find the parallel development of religious rationalism, often called Deism, which reduced faith to a function of reason. John Locke defined faith as "the assent to any proposition . . . upon the credit of the proposer, as coming from God,"[29] and Matthew Tindal subsumed

---

28. Heinrich Heppe, *Reformed Dogmatics,* ed. Ernst Bizer, trans. G. T. Thompson (Grand Rapids: Baker, 1978), p. 533.

29. James C. Livingston, *Modern Christian Thought* (New York: Macmillan, 1971), p. 16.

faith *under* reason. God, he believed, cannot act upon humanity other than by way of the faculties of reason and observation.

It is one of the more astonishing facts of theological history that effective protest against Deism's reduction of faith to reason came, not from theology, but from philosophy. "Our most holy religion," wrote the erstwhile Presbyterian David Hume, "is founded on *faith*, not on reason; and it is a sure method of exposing it to put it to such a trial as it is by no means fitted to endure."[30] One need not imagine that Hume was much concerned to defend or advance "our most holy religion," but he rendered it considerable service by exposing the illogic of Deism's assertion that human reason was capable of the knowledge of faith. Immanuel Kant followed Hume with very much the same intention, but with less salutary results. Kant was able to show in his first *Critique* that when "speculative reason" claims knowledge of God, it must transform deity into an object "of possible experience . . . into an appearance," and on that account he "found it necessary to deny knowledge in order to make room for faith."[31] God cannot be "known" by causal argument, because causality "is applicable only in the sensible world; outside that world it has no meaning whatsoever."[32] Unfortunately, Kant later held that, if faith cannot claim to be "knowledge," it can nonetheless claim the status of a reasonable *postulate*. The universal sense of moral obligation, of "oughtness," implies the existence of a universal moral law, and thus, in turn, a divine Lawgiver. In this way Kant contributed enormously to the dissolution of the Reformers' view, and faith (both *fides quae* and *fides qua*) came in the modern period to be more and more associated with personal and social virtue.

Friedrich Schleiermacher sought in his *Speeches on Religion to Its Cultured Despisers* to formulate a conception of faith that could transcend both emotionalism and rationalism and withstand the assaults of critical philosophy. Schleiermacher argued that "religion has nothing to do with . . . knowledge,"[33] and that "religion by itself does not urge men to activity at all."[34] Faith is a "feeling"; it is not emotion, but a "self-consciousness" which is also a "world-consciousness," and ultimately a "God-consciousness." Here faith is immediate intuition. In his mature work *The Christian Faith*, Schleiermacher also presents faith as the result of the action and presence of God. As "the con-

---

30. *The Philosophical Works of David Hume*, vol. 4, *An Inquiry concerning the Human Understanding* (Edinburgh: Adam Black, 1826), p. 153.

31. Immanuel Kant, *Critique of Pure Reason*, trans. N. K. Smith (London: Macmillan, 1964), p. 29.

32. Kant, p. 511.

33. Friedrich Schleiermacher, *On Religion: Speeches to Its Cultured Despisers*, trans. John Oman (New York: Harper & Brothers, 1958), p. 35.

34. Schleiermacher, *On Religion*, p. 57.

sciousness of absolute dependence,"[35] faith encounters the presence of the absolute upon which one depends. "God-consciousness" is at the same time a "God-presentness." Schleiermacher can even deny that faith, as a human volitional event, is "the *causa instrumentalis* of justification . . . that faith must be our own work."[36] Here, as at other places in his dogmatics, Schleiermacher represents a Reformed interest in the dialectic of faith.

Schleiermacher's theology, however, could not restore the logic of faith, because he gave regulatory power to its subjective side. The forgiveness and adoption that makes man "the object of divine favor and love does not happen until he lays hold believingly on Christ."[37] It is *our* feeling of oneness, of dependence, of grace that defines the attributes of God and the nature of redemption and sin. Rather than the gospel determining the content of faith, faith in this scheme appears to determine the content of the gospel. In this way Schleiermacher neglected the necessary otherness of God, which gave to the Reformation view of faith its dialectical radicality.

Schleiermacher is rightly called "the father of modern theology" because, although many theologians in the nineteenth and twentieth centuries did not subscribe to his definition of religious consciousness, they followed him in viewing faith as a human achievement. Typical of this tendency was Albrecht Ritschl, who found in the concept of value an objective basis for faith. "God is the power which man worships, which upholds his worth."[38]

In his major work, *The Christian Doctrine of Justification and Reconciliation* (1870), Ritschl argued that, since faith depends upon a perception of the actualized value of God, faith cannot be complete without the application of the benefits of grace to the life of the believer. Thus, faith in the Ritschlian scheme is the "act through which the new relation of men to God, realized in justification, is religiously recognized and actually established."[39] In this way faith not only includes works, but may be said to be conditioned by them. Ritschl's influence is nowhere more evident than in his disciple Adolf von Harnack, who dispensed altogether with Luther's teaching of "faith alone," calling it a "convenient misunderstanding."[40] Faith, for Harnack, was a matter of sensibility to the moral

35. Friedrich Schleiermacher, *The Christian Faith*, ed. H. R. Mackintosh (New York: Harper & Row, 1963), p. 12.

36. Schleiermacher, *The Christian Faith*, pp. 504-5.

37. Schleiermacher, *The Christian Faith*, p. 503.

38. Karl Barth, *Protestant Thought from Rousseau to Ritschl* (New York: Harper & Brothers, 1959), p. 362.

39. David L. Mueller, *An Introduction to the Theology of Albrecht Ritschl* (Philadelphia: Westminster, 1969), p. 103.

40. Adolf Harnack, *What Is Christianity?* trans. T. B. Saunders (New York: Harper & Row, 1957), p. 287.

meaning of God, in which we "affirm the forces and the standards which on the summits of our inner life shine out as our highest good."[41]

Recovering the Logic of Faith

Søren Kierkegaard

Liberal Protestantism's reduction of faith to religious self-consciousness and moral striving did not go unchallenged. Søren Kierkegaard denied that faith can be reduced to a theory of moral value, because its object, God, makes an absolute claim of obedience which overrides any universal moral imperative. One who has faith "determines his relation to the universal by his relation to the absolute, not his relation to the absolute by his relation to the universal."[42] Nor does faith possess God as the object of its knowledge, because, "to be known directly is the characteristic mark of an idol."[43] In Kierkegaard's view, faith contradicts knowledge, because the "moment" of faith does not belong to the nexus of cause and effect. Between God and the creature there exists an "infinite qualitative distinction." The truth of faith is therefore paradoxical and "absurd," and is not based upon historical certainty.

For Kierkegaard, faith had the character of an inwardness quite different from Schleiermacher's "feeling," because it corresponds to no perception of our relation to the world. The truth of faith has no objective reference. Only in radical subjectivity does the believer learn that he or she is in error (i.e., can know nothing of God objectively), and then holds this "objective uncertainty" with the most "passionate inwardness." This happens only because God himself is the teacher who brings such "knowledge" to the believer and provides the conditions necessary for its understanding. The movement of faith can, from the human side, only be a "leap" away from all certainty and predictability. In this way Kierkegaard's theology offered a corrective to centuries of Protestant neglect of the dialectic of faith. His protest, however, failed to stem the tide of liberalism's dissolution of faith. This was due, in part, to the fact that, having neglected an exposition of God's action in faith, Kierkegaard's theology could be misunderstood as defining faith as an heroic, if also inexplicable, act of existential courage.

---

41. Harnack, p. 301.

42. Søren Kierkegaard, *Fear and Trembling*, trans. Walter Lowrie (Princeton: Princeton University Press, 1941), p. 80.

43. Karl Barth, *The Epistle to the Romans*, trans. Edwin C. Hoskyns (London: Oxford University Press, 1933), p. 38.

Karl Barth

It remained for Karl Barth to move beyond Kierkegaard's focus on the dialectic of human faith and reestablish the logic of faith as *both* a divine and human act. First, however, he had to reassert Kierkegaard's protest against the presumptions of a Christianity informed by Protestant modernism:

> We suppose that we know what we are saying when we say "God." We assign to him the highest place in our world: and in so doing we place him fundamentally on one line with ourselves and with things. . . . We press ourselves into proximity with him: and so, all unthinking, we make him nigh unto ourselves. . . . In "believing" on him we justify, enjoy, and adore ourselves. . . . We confound time and eternity.[44]

Barth's epoch-making work *The Epistle to the Romans* (1922) may be understood as a recapitulation of the Reformers' conception of faith as the work of God. Where Paul speaks of faith as salvific, Barth followed Rudolf Liechtenhan in rendering *pistis,* usually translated "faith," as "faithfulness."[45] Thus a key passage in Romans is to be read: "For therein is revealed the righteousness of God from *faithfulness* unto faith: as it is written, But the righteous shall live from *my faithfulness*" (Rom. 1:17). In Romans 3:28, where Luther interjected the word "alone," Barth translates: "For we reckon that a man is justified by *the faithfulness of God* apart from works of the law."[46] "Faith is the faithfulness of God, ever secreted and beyond all human ideas and affirmations about him, and beyond every positive religious achievement."[47]

In Barth's *Romans* faith as human activity can only be described in negative terms. The New Testament offers no positive acts of believing, willing, and acting which could constitute some attitude or stance we might call "saving faith." "The activity of the [New Testament] community is related to the Gospel only insofar as it is no more than a crater formed by the explosion of a shell and seeks to be no more than a void in which the Gospel reveals itself."[48] Faith is directed to that which is "most deeply hidden," and "contradicts the obvious experience of the senses." It demands that the person of faith be

---

44. Barth, *The Epistle to the Romans,* p. 44.

45. Barth, *The Epistle to the Romans,* p. 14. See also Lloyd Gaston, *Paul and the Torah* (Vancouver: British Columbia Press, 1987), pp. 56ff. Gaston supports Barth's view that, when Paul speaks of faith as salvific, he means God's or Christ's "faithfulness."

46. Barth, *The Epistle to the Romans,* p. 107.

47. Barth, *The Epistle to the Romans,* p. 98.

48. Barth, *The Epistle to the Romans,* p. 36.

sufficiently mature to accept a contradiction and rest in it. . . . Faith is awe in the presence of the divine incognito . . . a shattering halt in the presence of God. . . . Depth of feeling, strength of conviction, advance in perception and moral behavior are . . . no more than unimportant signs of the occurrence of faith, and moreover, as signs . . . they are not positive factors, but negations . . . stages in the work of clearance by which room is made in this world for that which is beyond it.[49]

In spite of Barth's radical correction, the Reformers' dialectical conception of faith continued to prove elusive for twentieth-century theology. Paul Tillich and Rudolf Bultmann agreed with Barth's attack upon Protestant liberalism's identification of faith with bourgeois values, but they could not agree to his view of faith as God's faithfulness. Tillich embraced what he called "the Protestant principle," by which he meant "the protest against any finite authority that takes upon itself an infinite claim,"[50] and he could say that faith was a condition of "being grasped."[51] He could not, however, recover the Reformation's dialectic of faith, because, for him, faith "is the state of being ultimately concerned."[52] For Tillich, the content of faith is "formed" by the questions raised from an analysis of human existence. Faith is a way of thinking about God; it is "an essential possibility for man."[53]

If Tillich's view of faith tends toward rationalism, that of Rudolf Bultmann recalls the subjective personalism of pietism and evangelicalism. Bultmann, like Barth and Tillich, wished to avoid an interpretation of faith as ratiocination, as mere *fides quae*. "To believe means not to have apprehended but to have been apprehended."[54] And yet, for Bultmann, faith is prefaced by existential self-understanding *(Vorverständnis)*, actualized by existential decision, and represents a self-appropriation of the benefits of God for life. Faith is, therefore, something we do. "This is what I mean by 'faith': to open ourselves freely to the future."[55] For Bultmann truth is true only insofar as it is true *pro me*. Thus, my own disposition defines the content of faith, even to the extent that "the saving efficacy of the cross is not derived from the fact that it is the cross of Christ: it is the cross of Christ because it has this saving efficacy [because it helps me]."[56]

49. Barth, *The Epistle to the Romans*, pp. 39-40.

50. Alexander J. McKelway, *The Systematic Theology of Paul Tillich* (Richmond: John Knox, 1964), p. 33.

51. Paul Tillich, *The Dynamics of Faith* (London: George Allen & Unwin, 1957), pp. 99ff.

52. Tillich, p. 1.

53. Tillich, p. 126.

54. Rudolf Bultmann, *Kerygma and Myth* (New York: Harper & Row, 1961), p. 21.

55. Bultmann, p. 19.

56. Bultmann, p. 41.

The Later Direction of Barth's Doctrine of Faith

The persistence of the modernist interpretation of faith persuaded Barth that the doctrine of faith needed a thorough overhauling. In his *Romans* Barth denied any substantive qualities to human faith, but as his theology developed he recognized a divine activity which makes human knowledge of God possible. Barth argued that when Anselm spoke of "faith seeking understanding" (*fides quaerens intellectum*), he meant by "faith" a knowledge "which God himself compels."[57] Thought about God in theology, in worship, in the Bible, or in any other expression of faith is possible only because God himself empowers thought and language. The epistemological basis of this possibility Barth called the "analogy of faith," because, while all knowledge depends upon analogy, thought and language about God depend upon an analogy made possible by God. It is an analogy of *faith* because, as Luther said, "God does it." God controls the language of faith, "elevating our words to their proper use, giving himself to be their proper object."[58] If the logic of faith for Barth is analogical, the analogy involved is entirely unique. There is no natural correspondence between God's self-disclosure and its human reception, as is the case with all natural theology and the *analogia entis* by which a shared participation in being binds the creator and the creature. Nor is there in Barth's analogy of faith any human "capacity or pre-understanding" which prepares a person for faith. "God's act is the analogue, ours the analogate."[59] The analogy of faith is not based upon a situation in which the human act of faith may rest. "The analogy endures only so long as the revelation-event endures"; God's employment of human language and thought in faith "does not pass over into human control."[60] We will see below that the logic of Barth's conception of the analogy of faith is, itself, informed by (and in a different sense analogous to) the incarnation as the characteristic pattern of God's dealings with his creatures.

When Barth turns in volume IV/1 of his *Church Dogmatics* to faith as human response to the activity of God, he does not mean a human faith that saves "alone." He means a "spontaneous, a free, and active event" which can only respond to grace and can have no role at all in its effectiveness.[61] It is a *human* act, and yet, claims Barth, "justification by faith cannot mean that instead of his cus-

---

57. Karl Barth, *Anselm: Fides Quaerens Intellectum* (London: SCM Press, 1960), p. 167.

58. Karl Barth, *Church Dogmatics* II/1 (Edinburgh: T. & T. Clark, 1957), p. 23.

59. Bruce McCormack, *Karl Barth's Critically Realistic Dialectical Theology: Its Genesis and Development, 1909-1936* (Oxford: Clarendon Press, 1995), p. 17.

60. McCormack, p. 17.

61. Karl Barth, *Church Dogmatics* IV/1 (Edinburgh: T. & T. Clark, 1962), p. 758, hereafter cited as *CD* IV/1.

tomary evil works and in place of all kinds of supposed good works man chooses and accomplishes the work of faith."[62] As a human act, faith must find its establishment elsewhere. Faith has the character of humility, but mere abnegation cannot stand for faith. "If faith in its negative form is indeed an emptying, then it is certainly an emptying of all the results of such practice of self-emptying."[63]

The act of faith by which a person looks to, holds to, and depends upon Jesus Christ is a free human act. *We* turn to Christ. And yet,

> we do not compromise [faith's] character as a free human act if we say that as a free human act — more genuinely free than any other — it has its origin in the very point on which it is orientated. It is also the work of Jesus Christ who is its object. It is the will and decision and achievement of Jesus Christ the Son of God that takes place as a free human act, that man is *of himself* ready and willing and actually begins to believe in Him.[64]

In this way Barth reasserts the Reformers' logic of faith as at once a work of God and humans. The difference between Barth and the Reformers is that he recognizes the logical complexity of that assertion and undertakes an elucidation of it in which this Gordian knot is, if not cut, then at least unraveled in a way sufficient for understanding. The action of God and the action of human being are two different things — yet "The two things are not a contradiction but belong together. If the Son makes us free, we are free indeed (Jn 8:36). The Son makes a man free to believe in Him. Therefore faith in Him is the act of a right freedom, not although, but just because it is the work of the Son."[65] Freedom for Barth is a form of existence disposed toward the actualization of a divine will which, in Paul Lehmann's famous phrase, "makes and keeps human life human." For Barth, then, to speak of faith as a "free human act" requires that the act of faith be neither independent nor autonomous.

If on this account we can understand true freedom as obedience, we still have the question of how the free, obedient human act of faith is at the same time a divine act. Our ability to conceive logically of the duplication of causation in respect to the act of faith may find assistance in what George Hunsinger has called Barth's conception of "double agency," a conception required by the Christology of Chalcedon, in which divine and human agency are united in such a way that the authenticity of both is preserved.[66] Where Western philos-

---

62. Barth, *CD* IV/1, p. 615.

63. Barth, *CD* IV/1, p. 629.

64. Barth, *CD* IV/1, p. 744, emphasis added.

65. Barth, *CD* IV/1, p. 745.

66. George Hunsinger, *How to Read Karl Barth* (New York: Oxford University Press, 1991), pp. 185ff.

ophy since Aristotle insists upon a distinction between various intermediate causes and a single "efficient" cause that is able through them to produce an effect, Barth proposes *two* efficient causes for faith in such a way that the first (divine) cause is superior to the other (human) cause, initiating and controlling it. We have described the Reformers' exposition of faith as a "logic," and we did so on the basis of Barth's exposition. Is it proper, however, to speak of Barth's view as "logical"? If we recall that "logic" in its larger sense is a system of reasoning, an ordering of inferences, which avoids internal contradiction or contradiction of first principles, then the logical coherence of Barth's employment of double agency may be asserted in spite of its counterintuitive nature. This is so because the presupposition of Christian thought is not the "First Cause" of Aristotle and Aquinas, but the God-man Jesus Christ. From this dialectical beginning point the dialectical logic of theology necessarily devolves.

We are now in a better position to grasp the logic of Barth's portrayal of the human act of faith as a free act in which the object of faith initiates and makes possible the subject's belief. If the claim is surprising and appears contradictory to other and more ordinary logic, we must nevertheless admit that it would be *illogical* for a theology which views the Christ-event as normative to say anything else. As a human act, faith is a free decision of the believing subject engaged, encircled, and determined in its freedom by faith's object, Jesus Christ.

The logic of double agency finds further elaboration in Barth's discussion of faith as knowledge. Faith is *some* kind of "knowing," and it has been awkward in the extreme to apply this common definition to "saving faith," to God's act of justifying grace, which is not our act. If it is a knowing, it is not *our* knowing, but our *being known*. On the other hand, from the human side the act of faith is quite obviously a kind of knowing. Even in the more emotive and less cognitive aspects of faith — the trust, or love, or courage belonging to faith — there is still a knowing which accompanies those effects.

Reformed dogmaticians gathered the many types of knowing that belong to faith under *notitia,* immediate knowledge or "recognition"; *assensus,* a knowledge involving acceptance; and *fiducia,* trust and faithfulness toward the object of such knowledge. The traditional ordering of these three kinds of knowledge appears logical enough, insofar as a thing can hardly be understood and accepted before it is apprehended or recognized. If, however, the knowledge under review is the knowledge of faith, and if the object of faith is the one who establishes and enables the subject to have such knowledge, then, Barth insists, there is no possibility of a mere *notitia,* "recognition" or neutral and preliminary apprehension, which does not include an *assensus,* that is, an "acknowledgment" and acceptance of faith's object. The acknowledgment of faith is obedience and subordination. This is so because the encounter is with Jesus

Christ, who initiates and makes possible the free response of the believer. This reaction constitutes a "knowledge," because, as Barth observes, we are not dealing here "with an automatic reflection, a stone lit up by the sun, or wood kindled by fire, or a leaf blown by the wind. We are dealing with man."[67] A cognition is involved.

If we speak here of knowledge in the ordinary sense, then we can only mean a negative knowledge, a not knowing, or no longer knowing, that the presuppositions we bring to that event are true, a knowing that they have been set aside and brought under judgment by the one who claims us. The first movement of faith is not ours; if it is, then the object of faith is not Jesus Christ. As Barth notes, "a self-fabricated faith is the climax of unbelief."[68] We cannot set the stage for faith. A concern for social justice, self-fulfillment, or self-realization in respect to our racial, national, and sexual identity is part of the "religious quest," but it cannot serve as the backdrop for faith. If it does, then the actor acknowledged upon that stage can only play a part already written, but it will not be an encounter with Jesus Christ, who refuses to be cast in a role of our contrivance. Whatever preparations have been made for faith, whatever presuppositions may accompany the first movement of faith, the fact to be acknowledged is that all such preparations and presuppositions are set aside by the one who addresses us and claims us in that encounter.

Conclusion

We have spoken throughout of a "logic" of faith illustrated in the Reformers, abandoned by their successors, and reasserted by Barth. We have seen that the logic involved hinges upon the concept of double agency, the formal necessity of which Barth finds in Chalcedonian Christology. Notwithstanding the fact that his elaboration of faith makes clearer a logic that remained obscure in Luther and Calvin, it has not escaped the charge of incoherence from critics without and within the church. Can its coherence be defended?

Since, for Barth, double agency "has the logical status of a 'divine fact,' the condition for whose possibility can be found only in God, just as . . . its apprehension can only be found in . . . scripture,"[69] we need not imagine that agreement to it will be found in the sciences or other venues of human reason. This is not to say, however, that its "logicality" cannot be recognized. If we take as indisputable the axiom that knowledge can only be achieved by a method

---

67. Barth, *CD* IV/1, p. 758.
68. Barth, *CD* IV/1, p. 745.
69. Hunsinger, p. 197.

consistent with the nature of the object under investigation, then a Christian theology whose object is "God" as revealed in Christ cannot logically proceed in a way inconsistent with the nature of that self-disclosure.

That the logic of faith may be recognized by critics who otherwise hold its content to be fantasy is, however, of little interest to theology. More significant is the charge of incoherence from within the circle of faith. Barth can say: "Faith is altogether the work of God and it is altogether a human work. It is complete enslavement, and it is complete liberation."[70] Against such stark formulations criticism may either hold an absolute determinism (which is purely theoretical) or a human freedom competitive with God (which is all too actual). The latter, objects Barth, "would not be creaturely freedom, but the freedom of a second God."[71] He protests against a common notion of causation which prohibits theological discernment of the operation of God in faith. He declares that

> [w]e must drop the ordinary, but harmful conception of cause, operation and effect. Then, when we know who God is and what he wills and how he works, we have to take it up again, but giving to it a new force and application in which we do not look back to what are at root godless notions of causality.[72]

This "different and higher" form of causation is "defined and therefore pervaded by, the divine love and freedom without which God is never God."[73] The act of the believer in faith, however, is "neither jeopardized nor suppressed" by this higher form of causation, "but . . . is confirmed in all its particularity and variety."[74]

Barth himself was not concerned with the logic of double agency, nor did he defend its coherence. For him it was simple and self-evident:

> Faith is at once the most wonderful and the simplest of things. In it a man opens his eyes and sees and accepts . . . everything as it is: that the night has passed and the day has dawned; that there is peace between God and sinful man. . . . This simple thing, and this mystery, constitute the being of the Christian, his being by the One in whom he believes.[75]

70. Karl Barth, *Church Dogmatics* III/3 (Edinburgh: T. & T. Clark, 1960), p. 247, hereafter cited as *CD* III/3; Hunsinger's translation, p. 201.

71. Karl Barth, *Church Dogmatics* III/2 (Edinburgh: T. & T. Clark, 1960), p. 166; Hunsinger, p. 214.

72. Barth, *CD* III/3, p. 118; Hunsinger, p. 200.

73. Hunsinger, p. 200.

74. Barth, *CD* III/3, p. 146.

75. Barth, *CD* IV/1, pp. 748-49.

CHAPTER 15

Toward a New Typology of Reformed Doctrines of Atonement

Leanne Van Dyk

Early in the morning of 24 May 1831, after a long night of deliberation, the deposition vote against John McLeod Campbell was taken at the General Assembly of the Church of Scotland. By a count of 119 to 6, that Assembly declared Campbell's teachings on the atonement heretical and removed him from the ordained ministry. The principal clerk then solemnly uttered his conclusion but inadvertently reversed his phrases, saying that "these doctrines of Mr. Campbell would remain and flourish long after the Church of Scotland had perished and was forgotten."[1] Happily, the Church of Scotland has not perished nor been forgotten, but the doctrines of Mr. Campbell which evoked the censure of his church, in accord with the clerk's prophetic declaration, have flourished and continue to influence theological reflection on the atonement today.

One of the most influential of Campbell's contributions to atonement theology is his concept of Christ's perfect confession of the sin of humanity to the Father. This essay will consider this important, controversial, and often misunderstood concept in Campbell's atonement theology. It will establish the thesis that the formulation of Christ's atoning work as rendering a perfect confession is a form of a satisfaction account and is a significant and promising alternative to traditional satisfaction accounts using images of penal substitu-

---

1. This anecdote is reported widely in literature about Campbell. It comes from a collection of Thomas Erskine's letters: *Letters of Thomas Erskine of Linlathen*, ed. William Hanna, 2 vols. (New York: G. P. Putnam's Sons, 1977), 1:136-37.

tion. Thus, Campbell's atonement theology exemplifies diversity in atonement images within Reformed theology. In demonstrating the contribution of Campbell's unique concept of Christ's perfect confession, I will first explicate the content of this concept, then establish its continuity with the broader Reformed tradition, identify its several advantages, and finally propose it as a uniquely valuable contribution to ongoing Reformed theological exposition of the atonement.

The Perfect Confession of Christ

An explication of the contours of Campbell's complete atonement theology is first necessary in order to set the particular concept of Christ's perfect confession in context.[2] Campbell's own definition of the atonement displays the scope and balance of his theory as a whole: "[T]he atonement is to be regarded as that by which God has bridged over the gulf which separated between what sin had made us, and what it was the desire of the divine love that we should become."[3] From this expansive definition, Campbell organizes his discussion of the atonement by proposing a pair of words, "retrospective" and "prospective," each of which is then examined from two directions, God-ward and humanity-ward. This pair of words, "retrospective" and "prospective," designates Campbell's central conviction that the atonement not only dealt with our sins and their offense to God but also guarantees our adoption as children of God and heirs to eternal life. The retrospective and prospective aspects of Campbell's atonement theology are captured in the second part of the title of his book: *The Nature of the Atonement and Its Relation to Remission of Sins and Eternal Life*. Remission of sins is the retrospective aspect; eternal life is the prospective aspect.

From this pattern of organization, Campbell has four features of his atonement theory to ponder. The first two belong to the retrospective aspect. They are Christ dealing with humanity on the part of God and Christ dealing with God on behalf of humanity. In other words, Christ, in the work of the atonement, acts as a mediator between God and humanity by performing spe-

2. Citations from John McLeod Campbell's book on the atonement, *The Nature of the Atonement*, or his letters, appear in the text of this paper unaltered. The reader will notice not only the peculiarities of Campbell's style but also his exclusive use of masculine images and pronouns with respect to God and to human persons. I have let these stand as is and trust the reader will be able to profit from Campbell's thoughts in spite of language now perceived to be jarring and insensitive.

3. John McLeod Campbell, *The Nature of the Atonement and Its Relation to Remission of Sins and Eternal Life*, 6th ed. (London: James Clarke & Co., 1959), p. 151.

cific acts appropriate for God or of God as well as for humanity or of humanity, in both life and death, to accomplish the goal of reconciliation.

The prospective aspect of the atonement also indicates the two directions toward God and toward humanity. Christ witnesses for the Father to humanity, and Christ intercedes with the Father on behalf of humanity. In other words, Christ continues to act as a mediator in order to accomplish further goods beyond that of dealing with the remission of sin. Prospectively, Christ assures our status of adopted children and guarantees our hope of eternal life.

The above is a brief explication of the overall structure and scope of Campbell's atonement theology. Although this essay will examine more closely only one part of his complete theory, namely, the God-ward direction of the retrospective aspect, which contains Campbell's controversial concept of the perfect confession of Christ, it is important to remember that any discussion of a small part of Campbell's theory must not neglect recognition of the broader scope and reach of his complete theory.

The motivation of Campbell's formulation of the perfect confession of Christ was his desire to distance himself from traditional atonement theories characterized by images of vicarious punishment, or penal substitution. Such images were dominant in the atonement doctrine taught and preached in the Church of Scotland.[4] Campbell had theological, scriptural, and pastoral reasons for rejecting images of vicarious punishment, but the pastoral reasons were the most pressing for him. He had noticed in his parish ministry believers anxious and insecure about their own salvation. Convinced that the root of this restlessness was a faulty doctrine of the atonement, Campbell sought to formulate an atonement doctrine that was based solely on the love and mercy of God, thus affording comfort and confidence for believers.[5] Highlighting the foundational love and mercy of God is the central focus of all of Campbell's theological reflections on the atonement.

To Campbell, it was inconceivable that God's justice required that Christ bear substituted punishment on behalf of humanity. Such a concept seemed to cancel what must be the primary divine disposition toward humanity, namely, love and forgiveness. So, Campbell proposed an alternate account of how Christ atoned for sin in the sight of God. His idea was prompted by a brief

4. Campbell used both prominent theologians as well as lesser-known thinkers of his own time to illustrate the tendencies in Reformed theology that he wished to repudiate. They include John Owen (1616-83) and Jonathan Edwards (1703-55) as proponents of a penal substitutionary view of the atonement, and near contemporaries of Campbell, John Pye Smith (1774-1851), George Payne (1781-1858), and Ralph Wardlaw (1779-1853), as proponents of a federalist, or rectoral, view of the atonement.

5. Donald Campbell, *Memorials of John McLeod Campbell, D.D.: Being Selected from His Correspondence* (London: Macmillan, 1977), 1:207.

comment of Jonathan Edwards regarding the atonement.[6] Edwards reflected on what he took to be axiomatic: that sin must be accounted for in the sight of God. "Sin must be punished with an infinite punishment . . . unless there could be such a thing as a repentance, humiliation and sorrow for this (sin) proportionate to the greatness of the majesty despised. . . ." In other words, there must be "either an equivalent punishment or an equivalent sorrow and repentance."[7] But Edwards dismissed the second of those options without further deliberation; namely, that an equivalent sorrow and repentance could be the satisfaction for sin.

It was this suggestion, so quickly discarded, that caught Campbell's attention. He, too, was convinced that sin must be accounted for in the sight of God. But he felt Edwards's alternative to an equivalent punishment was promising. Either of Edwards's options could be seen as "equally securing the vindication of the majesty and justice of God in pardoning sin."[8] The possibility of accounting for God's judgment on sin without the accompanying idea of punishment fit well with Campbell's fundamental presupposition that the working of the atonement must primarily display or illuminate the foundational love of God. Therefore, Campbell opted for the alternative that Edwards suggested and developed an atonement account based on an "equivalent sorrow and repentance." He proposed that the way in which Christ expiates humanity's guilt and propitiates God's wrath was by making a perfect confession of humanity's sin.

In the two most quoted sentences from Campbell's book, this theory is expounded: "That oneness of mind with the Father, which towards man took the form of condemnation of sin, would in the Son's dealing with the Father in relation to our sins, take the form of a perfect confession of our sins. This confession, as to its own nature, must have been *a perfect Amen in humanity to the judgment of God on the sins of man*."[9] Although those two highly condensed sentences contain the heart of Campbell's theory, they are far from immediately clear and lucid. Campbell's point here is that Christ offered a perfect response to God's verdict on sin. That response was twofold: Christ's full awareness of the seriousness of sin's affront to God and Christ's perfect acknowledgment of God's judgment of that sin. Christ's response constituted a perfect confession or repentance of human sin, and thus God's judgment on sinners is averted. The confession of Christ was efficacious in that the repen-

---

6. In Jonathan Edwards, *Concerning the Necessity and Reasonableness of the Christian Doctrine of Satisfaction for Sin,* chap. 2.

7. Quoted by J. M. Campbell, p. 127.

8. J. M. Campbell, p. 137.

9. J. M. Campbell, pp. 135-36, emphasis Campbell's.

tance, the contrition, the sorrow were all done in absolute perfection, and thus God's judgment was "absorbed."[10]

What Christ's perfect repentance accomplished and how it effects reconciliation is explained further by Campbell:

> He who so responds to the divine wrath against sin, saying, "Thou art righteous, O Lord, who judgest so," is necessarily receiving the full apprehension and realisation of that wrath, as well as of that sin against which it comes forth into His soul and spirit, into the bosom of the divine humanity, and, so receiving it, He responds to it with a perfect response — a response from the depths of that divine humanity, — and *in that perfect response He absorbs it.* For that response has all the elements of a perfect repentance in humanity for all the sin of man, — a perfect sorrow — a perfect contrition — all the elements of such a repentance, and that in absolute perfection, all — excepting the personal consciousness of sin; — and by that perfect response in Amen to the mind of God in relation to sin is the wrath of God rightly met, and that is accorded to divine justice which is its due, and could alone satisfy it.[11]

This densely packed section contains the key features of Campbell's concept of Christ as Confessor. Because Christ fully realized the sorrow and wrath of God against sin and fully acknowledged and confessed the justice and righteousness of that sorrow and wrath, Christ was able to make a perfect and complete response to both the horror of sin and the holiness of God. That response can only be called a "perfect contrition" or a "perfect sorrow."

What does it actually mean that Christ's repentance or contrition or sorrow "absorbed" the wrath of God? Beyond this crucial and ambiguous word of explication, Campbell does not and cannot go much further. It is the very core of the atonement mystery in Campbell's theology. For Campbell, the central mystery is the absorption of God's wrath in Christ's own perfect response to God's just judgment and his realization of sin in his own spirit.

Campbell used new, unfamiliar terminology to attempt to account for the inner workings of God's salvation in Jesus Christ. Christ as Confessor does not mean that Christ took on a personal consciousness of sin and the weight of guilt and then repented *instead* of us, in a substitutionary sense. Rather, Christ acknowledged fully and perfectly both the scandal of sin and the righteousness of God, and *in that response* sin is conquered, God is satisfied, and we are called to be partakers through Christ in eternal life.[12] This is the whole point: that

---

10. This interesting term is found in J. M. Campbell, p. 137.
11. J. M. Campbell, p. 137, emphasis Campbell's.
12. J. M. Campbell, p. 150.

Christ's perfect response was accomplished *on our behalf* so that we are ourselves irresistibly drawn by its sheer moral and spiritual power to repentance and a full realization of our status as adopted children of God.

Campbell's sense of Christ's representative work is affirmed by one of his interpreters. In reference to Campbell, Vincent Taylor says, "We need a category of representative action, which describes a work of Christ for men so altogether great and inclusive that they cannot accomplish it for themselves, but which, far from being external to themselves, and therefore substitutionary, is a vital factor in their approach to God, because in it they can participate both by personal faith and in corporate worship."[13]

Critical evaluation of this crucial idea of Campbell's theology is not usually as perceptive as Taylor's comment. Theologians who are committed or accustomed to the more traditional doctrine of penal substitution may find Campbell's account curiously soft or undramatic. It seems to them less stirring and climactic than the doctrine that Christ suffered all the wrath of God instead of us and thus set us free from the threat of the punishment properly due us. Campbell's language of the "spiritual and moral" power of Christ's perfect confession strikes others as merely subjective and individualistic. In addition, Campbell's theory seems to receive scant support from Scripture and is thus dismissed by other Campbell interpreters.

Campbell was fully aware of these objections to his atonement theology and tried to meet some of them in his book, especially in an appendix to the second edition, as well as in letters to family and friends. With respect to the objection that scriptural support is dubious for the concept of vicarious confession, he remarks that he wishes he could take the time and space in his book to look at all the Scriptures commonly taken to show the doctrine of penal substitution and demonstrate how they have much more to say of a moral and spiritual atonement.[14]

With respect to the charge that this concept misses the power and drama of the penal substitution view, Campbell most emphatically disagrees. He denies that his theology ignores the scandal of sin and insists that the believer must know "the deep and awful impression of what sin must be in the eyes of God. . . ."[15] It would be a momentous theological mistake to soft-pedal or mute the harsh legacy of sin. Furthermore, Campbell is convinced that the drama of Christ making a full, complete, and perfect response to the holy judgment of

---

13. Vincent Taylor, *The Atonement in New Testament Teaching* (London: Epworth Press, 1954), p. 198.

14. J. M. Campbell, p. 315.

15. J. M. Campbell, p. 312; also Donald Campbell, 2:343.

God and meeting that judgment in his own spirit, contains far more power and drama and truth than all the pains of penal substitution.[16]

As far as the objection that Campbell's theology here tilts dangerously toward subjectivism and individualism, nothing could be further from his intent. A main theme in Campbell's atonement theology is to emphasize quite the opposite. Believers can be confident in their salvation because they need *not* individually examine evidences of their election. Rather, the whole purpose of Christ's salvific work is to bring humanity into the new redeemed community of God's adopted children. The community of believers can be utterly confident in their knowledge and faith of God's unfailing love and mercy.

It is clear in the *Memorials,* a set of Campbell's letters collected and published by his eldest son, that these sorts of objections occupied Campbell's mind for many years and that he continually tried to clarify and specify his thoughts. In a letter recorded in the *Memorials,* Principal Shairp, a friend of Campbell, recalled how Campbell tried to explain the necessity of Christ's suffering and death for our salvation. He remembered that Campbell said salvation "can only enter into us in and through the shedding of the blood of Jesus. 'The wages of sin is death.' This is the Father's eternal and irreversible way of looking at sin. He does not change this will. But Christ meets this will, says, 'Thou art righteous, O Father, in thus judging sin; and I accept Thy judgment of it; and meet it. I in my humanity say Amen to Thy judgement of sin.'"[17]

Here it is clear that Campbell does not espouse a mere "moral and spiritual" atonement. In fact, some of Campbell's language, especially in the *Memorials* account above, is very similar to the traditional language of the Reformed tradition of which Campbell was an heir. Something objective happened, something located in the time and space of Jesus of Nazareth's life on earth. What precisely that "something" is, seems to be beyond the reach of human language and human comprehension. The best Campbell can say is that Christ gave the perfect response to God's wrath against sin and felt that wrath in his own spirit, thus meeting the holiness and justice of God and drawing humanity into a new redeemed community. Because of the life, suffering, death, and resurrection of Jesus Christ, sin is defeated, God is honored, and humanity is called to new life.

Campbell's Continuity with the Reformed Tradition

In spite of Campbell's vigorous rejection of atonement theories of the Reformed tradition that are dominated by images of substituted punishment,

16. J. M. Campbell, pp. 141, 146.
17. Donald Campbell, 2:342.

Campbell's atonement account is in fundamental continuity with those streams of the Reformed tradition which he criticized in at least one important respect: it is a satisfaction account. A satisfaction account of the atonement can be briefly defined as a theory which specifies or implies a change of some kind in God on the basis of Christ's atoning work. The details of satisfaction in the accounts of Campbell and either the federalists or "elder Calvinists"[18] are very different, but the essential point of satisfaction is similar: that the obedient life and sacrificial death of Christ made possible and completed reconciliation between God and humanity.

Campbell himself did not denote his atonement theology as a satisfaction account. Such a framework did not occur to him. After all, Campbell's critique of the standard Calvinist satisfaction atonement accounts, either scholastic or federalist, was very negative. Both the scholastic or Puritan accounts, like that of John Owen, or the federalist accounts, like those of his contemporaries or near contemporaries in Scotland, used the framework of satisfaction in the sense of penalty or punishment. Campbell expended all his critical energies in *The Nature of the Atonement* to refuting these atonement accounts which focus so heavily on penal accounts of satisfaction. Thus he did not consider that perhaps the basic idea of satisfaction might be retained in his atonement exposition with the terms of satisfaction altered.

But, in effect, this is precisely what Campbell accomplishes in his account of the atonement. The retrospective core of Campbell's account, namely, Christ's perfect confession, is an alternate form of a satisfaction account of the atonement. The Reformed tradition of which Campbell was an heir had focused almost exclusively on penal substitution as the means of satisfaction. Campbell presents an option to a penal substitution account in his perfect confession account, thus establishing an important line of continuity in the Reformed tradition.[19] On this theory, Christ makes satisfaction to the Father by offering a perfect confession to God, a confession both of the outrage of sin and the complete righteousness of the Father's condemnation of sin. Through this confession, Christ "absorbed" the wrath of God.

Although Campbell did not claim that his theory was a variant of a basic satisfaction account, he hinted at some awareness of this in his discussion of Christ's confession:

---

18. This is Campbell's term. He designates John Owen and Jonathan Edwards as "elder Calvinists." Campbell intends by this rather loose term to denote the "classic" or "scholastic" form of penal substitution doctrine of which federal theology is a variant.

19. Richard Swinburne makes this point in *Responsibility and Atonement* (Oxford: Clarendon Press, 1989), that there may conceivably be a variety of ways to render satisfaction to the offended party. Cf. esp. pp. 73-92 and 148-62.

> I have endeavoured to present Christ's expiatory confession of our sins to the mind of the reader as much as possible by itself, and as a distinct object of thought, because it most directly corresponds, in the place it occupies, to the penal suffering which has been assumed; and I have desired to place these two ways of meeting the divine wrath against sin, as ascribed to the Mediator, in contrast.[20]

In another place Campbell again alludes to the fact that his theory is a variation of a satisfaction account. He says, "Nor is the idea that satisfaction was due to divine justice a delusion, however far men have wandered from the true conception of what would meet its righteous demand."[21] Here Campbell observes that satisfying the righteous demand of God must not necessarily entail penal substitution. But he does not fully recognize that his own satisfaction account establishes an important connection with the broader Reformed tradition. The continuity between Campbell and previous Reformed thinkers on this issue of satisfaction is routinely missed by Campbell interpreters. Interpretive reaction to Campbell has tended to assume a significant disjunction between Campbell and the tradition of which he was an heir. Such interpretation concludes that Campbell's theory is a rather idiosyncratic version of a subjective, moral influence theory.[22] Here it can be seen that Campbell's atonement theology has stronger affinities with an objective account. The concept of Christ's perfect confession as absorbing God's wrath specifies and identifies the objective nature of his atonement theology.

Advantages of Campbell's Account

Critical response to Campbell's formulation of Christ's perfect confession has been mixed. Some interpreters see this concept as a frivolous innovation.[23] Others greet Campbell's theology as a whole, and this concept in par-

20. J. M. Campbell, p. 147.

21. J. M. Campbell, p. 135.

22. There is a small tradition of Campbell interpretation, represented primarily by T. F. Torrance, James Torrance, and Brian Gerrish, which reads Campbell's theology with much greater accuracy and understanding.

23. For example, Robert S. Franks in *The Atonement* (Oxford: Oxford University Press, 1934), p. 184, says Campbell's theory of vicarious repentance is false because "God *demands* vicarious suffering of some sort from Christ before He can rightly forgive sin." Note that Franks does not actually refute Campbell. He simply, strongly states the theory of penal substitution. John R. W. Stott uses a similar line of approach to Campbell when he concludes that Campbell's atonement theology is an "ingenious attempt to retain language of substitution while rejecting penal aspects" (cf. *The Cross of Christ* [Downers Grove, Ill.:

ticular, as an example of a subjective rendering of the atonement.[24] Yet others see in Campbell's view of Christ's perfect confession an articulation of a Reformed theology of the atonement using innovative metaphors and fresh terminology.[25] This last interpretation is, I believe, the most accurate assessment of Campbell's theology. With such an assessment, several advantages of Campbell's theology emerge.

The first advantage of Campbell's concept of the perfect confession of Christ is its successful and thorough integration of objective and subjective elements in his atonement theology. This integration is frequently missed by theologians who approach Campbell with set patterns of expectation regarding atonement theories. Critical appraisal of Campbell's atonement theology which is offended by his repudiation of penal substitution as well as critical appraisal which perceives Campbell's formulation to be a subjective or moral influence theory both fall into a basic error of classification. Because Campbell does not employ traditional metaphors of penal substitution, there are interpreters who conclude that his theory cannot have objective content. Because Campbell employs metaphors and terminology more typically associated with what is known as a subjective approach, there are interpreters who conclude that his theory is subjective. Neither conclusion is sound. Campbell does, in fact, have an objective view of the atonement, but he deliberately avoids the images that are usually associated with such an account. Fresh, innovative metaphors and terminology, however, do not cancel the objective nature of Campbell's atonement account. Likewise, his frequent use of terminology such as "moral and spiritual atonement" and images of the fatherhood of God and the sonship of redeemed people does not immediately entail a subjective approach.

Campbell understood clearly that an atonement theology can be adequate only if it includes both objective and subjective elements. He said in an

---

InterVarsity, 1986]). A. B. Bruce in *The Humiliation of Christ* (Edinburgh: T. & T. Clark, 1895), p. 318, pronounces Campbell's theory "something very like absurdity."

24. Eugene Garrett Bewkes, *Legacy of a Christian Mind* (Philadelphia: Judson Press, 1937); Thomas H. Hughes, *The Atonement: Modern Theories of the Doctrine* (London: George Allen & Unwin, 1949), p. 140; George Carey, *The Gate of Glory* (London: Hodder & Stoughton, 1986), p. 30, where he says that "Campbell evacuates the atonement of any 'objective' content. . . . We have here, incidentally, a variation of the 'moral influence' theory . . ."; Robert S. Paul, *The Atonement and the Sacraments* (New York: Abingdon, 1960), p. 147, calls Campbell's view a variant of the moral theory.

25. I have identified some of these thinkers above in n. 22. Appreciative accounts of the fundamentally objective character of Campbell's atonement theory can also be found in J. H. Leckie, "John McLeod Campbell's 'The Nature of the Atonement,'" *Expository Times* 40 (1929): 198-204; and Trevor A. Hart, "Anselm of Canterbury and John McLeod Campbell: Where Opposites Meet?" *Evangelical Quarterly* 62 (1990): 211-333.

1853 letter to Thomas Erskine, "[A]ll spiritual occupation with the *objective*, in regard to the sacrifice of Christ, must *imply* the *subjective*, and thus participation in the death of Christ *underlies* the confidence towards God with which that death is contemplated. . . ."[26] Campbell knew from the experiences of his early ministry that it was a truncated, fearful faith which concentrated only on the objective, once-for-all fact of Christ's sacrifice and did not subsequently issue in full confidence and acceptance as well-loved children of God. Thus he, along with the tradition of Reformed theology of which he was a product, placed the primary locus of the salvific event in the life, sacrificial death, and resurrection of Jesus Christ and the sole source of atoning effect in the divine purpose or intent.[27] In this he is an objective atonement theorist. But he also, and emphatically, urged his listeners and readers to participate in the life of Christ, to know with assurance their salvation, to be confident of the love of the Father. In fact, he insists that it is only in the effects of the atonement in the lives of people that the meaning of the atonement can be understood at all. In this he inserts a strong dose of subjective elements in his atonement theology. It is the combination of these two elements which produces the complete and balanced atonement theology of John McLeod Campbell.

The retrospective/prospective scheme by which Campbell unfolds his atonement theology is more effective than the objective/subjective scheme because it highlights the complete interrelatedness of the objective event's impact on the subjective faith experience of the believer. Campbell explicitly says that the prospective aspect of the atonement implies the retrospective aspect and the retrospective aspect reveals the prospective aspect.[28] That is, Christ's confession of our sins (retrospective) implies our participation in that confession (prospective), and Christ's acknowledgment of the full darkness of our sin (retrospective) reveals the light of life desired by God for us (prospective). For Campbell, the response of Christ to the Father in relation to our sins was the heart of the redemptive act. But it is only as we participate in that same response which Christ made that our status as beloved children of God can be realized and actualized. Campbell says "we must partake in it (Christ's response to the Father), and must have its elements reproduced in us. . . ."[29] Ob-

26. Donald Campbell, 1:249, emphasis J. M. Campbell's.
27. How it is that Christ's perfect confession can be considered a sacrifice is another important area of Campbell interpretation. Here it can only be stated that Campbell believed his concept of Christ's perfect confession is a form of sacrifice. Thus Campbell joins those theologians who see the controlling concept or fundamental image of Christ's salvific work in the image of sacrifice. The content of Campbell's concept of sacrifice is representative confession or repentance rather than substituted punishment.
28. J. M. Campbell, p. 152.
29. J. M. Campbell, p. 295.

jective and subjective elements of the atonement cannot be extracted and examined independently of each other. They are completely and irretrievably united.

Each aspect of the retrospective and the prospective has, in Campbell's account, both objective and subjective implications. The retrospective aspect, that is, the focus on the remission of sins, has the objective content of Christ perfectly witnessing the love of the Father and Christ perfectly confessing humanity's sin to the Father. But those two objective events have immediate subjective application. It is only in the believer's full assurance of the Father's love and the believer's participation in the perfect confession of Christ that the retrospective aspect of the atonement is complete and whole. Likewise, the prospective aspect, that is, the focus on the promise of eternal life, has the objective content of Christ displaying the life of sonship and Christ's continual intercession for humanity before the Father. But, again, those objective events have subjective implications that cannot be separated from the objective content. For the believer is a part of the prospective aspect; the believer finds her authentic redeemed identity in the life of sonship, and the believer joins in intercession with Christ through the acts of worship and praise.

Thus it can be seen that Campbell bursts the boundaries of the objective/subjective classification. His concept of the atonement as retrospective and prospective is a suggestive and creative addition to the objective/subjective atonement theory classification. Because Campbell succeeds in thoroughly integrating the objective and subjective, the result is a dynamic atonement account that highlights the connections, relations, and implications of the work of Christ with the response of the believer.

A second advantage of Campbell's concept of the perfect confession of Christ is the nonviolent, noncoercive alternative it presents to penal substitution. Although some theologians are convinced that images of substituted punishment are necessary for a fully objective, fully biblical doctrine of the atonement, many others find these images troubling and problematic. Campbell offers an account of the atonement that not only preserves a vigorous objective content but also makes clear that the sufferings of Christ were not gratuitous but had genuine salvific importance. That is, Christ's sufferings were not evidence of the wrath of God or an equivalent punishment for sin but rather were a response of God's love to the affront of sin. Christ's sufferings were the outward form of the holiness and love of Christ. The sufferings were not punishment. They were a demonstration of, or the visible manifestation of, the primary attribute and motivation of God, namely, love. When the believer looks at the sufferings of Christ, the believer ought not see the punishment of a wrathful God. Rather, the believer ought to see in Christ's sufferings God's love and mercy.

236

Campbell's perspective is in contrast to the Calvinist traditions he is attempting to correct. Instead of construing the sufferings as a punishment for humanity's sin, Campbell wishes to construe them as a perfect and necessary part of Christ's witnessing for the Father to humanity. The core of Campbell's conviction is that the sufferings of Christ, far from a punishment from God, are actually a revelation of the heart of God.

Campbell's belief that the perfect confession of Christ is the heart of the atoning work of Christ casts the atonement in terms that are nonviolent and noncoercive. Yet, because he construes Christ's sufferings as a genuine revelation of the loving heart of God, his atonement theory cannot be accused of ignoring the sufferings of Christ or rendering them superfluous or extraneous. Thus, it can be seen that Campbell's articulation of Christ's saving work is a genuine and promising alternative to standard penal substitution accounts common in the Reformed tradition.

A third advantage of Campbell's concept of Christ's perfect confession is its praxis-oriented direction. Because Christ's confession, although efficacious for satisfying God and rendering atonement in itself, is not made complete until the believer appropriates it in his or her own life in the context of the believing community, Campbell's theology has a practical and ethical pull or direction. This advantage to Campbell's theory was, in fact, noted by Campbell himself. One of the goals of his theology was to make clear the "practical ends of the atonement" as a natural continuation of and connection with the "making of the atonement."[30] Campbell believed that the crucial connection between the work of Christ and the life of the believer-in-community had been missed or muted in traditional atonement accounts. He considered the penal substitutionary view deficient on this score, in that it did not explicitly link the punishment of Christ to the believer's participation in the life of Christ. Thus the atoning work of Christ, on Campbell's view, appears external or remote to the practical life of the believer in the doctrine of substituted punishment. Convinced that his own formulation is a significant improvement, Campbell says, "[T]he pardon of sin is seen in its true harmony with the glory of God, only when the work of Christ, through which we have the 'remission of sins that are past,' is contemplated in its *direct* relation to the 'gift of eternal life.'"[31]

The ethical and practical implications of the concept of Christ as Confessor emerge in Campbell's vision of how the believer takes up Christ's confession personally and reproduces it in faith and faithful action. That is, when the

---

30. J. M. Campbell, p. 153. For Campbell, "eternal life" does not begin at some future time in a perfected heaven and earth but begins now in a full awareness of our status as adopted children of God in the context of the redeemed community.

31. J. M. Campbell, p. 154.

believer accepts God's judgment on sin, he or she then participates in the same mind of Christ which offered confession of sin, and thus, in the righteousness which pleases God.[32] Campbell puts it this way: "In the faith of God's acceptance of that confession on our behalf, we receive strength to say Amen to it — to join in it — and joining in it, we find it a living way to God. . . ."[33]

Campbell does not extrapolate the particular details of that "living way to God." The ethical and practical dimensions of his atonement theology are given a foundation in his concept of the believer's participation in the confession of Christ. The working principles for ethical action and practical faith in community can be a fruitful contribution by the reader of Campbell in his or her own specific context.

Recommendation of Campbell's Atonement Theology

John McLeod Campbell's atonement theology, the heart of which is its view of Christ's perfect confession as effecting satisfaction to God, is a significant contribution to Reformed theological reflection on the doctrine of the atonement. Because it successfully integrates objective and subjective elements, because it emphasizes the divine initiative of the redemptive event, and because it is continuous with other streams of Reformed theology in its character as a basic satisfaction account of Christ's atoning work, this atonement theology clearly stands in the Reformed tradition. But because it employs terminology and images not usually associated with Reformed theology, it demonstrates a diversity and flexibility in the Reformed tradition. This character of Campbell's atonement theology — continuous yet diverse and innovative — is ample recommendation for its inclusion in current discussions of atonement theology in Reformed theology.

---

32. "We are contented and thankful to begin our new life with partaking in the mind of Christ concerning our old life, and feel the confession of our sins to be the side on which the life of holiness is nearest to us, the form in which it naturally becomes ours, and in which it must first be tasted by us: for holiness, truth, righteousness, love must first dawn in us as confessions of sin." J. M. Campbell, p. 178.

33. J. M. Campbell, p. 182.

CHAPTER 16

The Notae Ecclesiae: A Reformed Perspective

Christian Link

> For this is the abiding mark with which our Lord has sealed his own: "Everyone who is of the truth hears my voice" [John 18:37].... Why do we willfully act like madmen in searching out the church when Christ has marked it with an unmistakable sign, which, wherever it is seen, cannot fail to show the true church there; ... the church is Christ's kingdom, and he reigns by his word alone.[1]

With this pregnant response Calvin staked out the lines by which Reformed theology has sought to clarify the question of the *notae ecclesiae,* understood as the question of the being and working of the church. The *fundamental idea* is simple: the church distinguishes the familiar voice from the voice of the world, but also from the voice of the false church, and the church's own name bears this distinction. The church cannot be nameless if its voice is to be more than mere noise. Yet no one bears a name for oneself alone. One's name is for others, who use it to name the as yet unknown person with the already known name, thus by that name identifying and lifting him or her out from the nameless crowd.

---

1. John Calvin, *Institutes of the Christian Religion,* ed. F. L. Battles and J. T. McNeill (Philadelphia: Westminster, 1960), 4.2.4.

Translated by Lisa Dahill.

The church's identity flows from its *name;* the identity of the Christian church derives from its Christian name. If the Christian church with all it is, says, and does is not merely to represent more nameless generality, the only possible way to express its identity will be in binding the content of its preaching, the mission of its diaconate, and the goal of its social and public effectiveness strictly and exclusively to *one* name: the name of Jesus Christ. The church does not control this name; like every child with its own distinctive personal name, the church was given its name by another: "You did not choose me, but I chose you" (John 15:16 RSV). If the church wishes to be recognized by this name, to make itself known by it, so also, like every child, it must grow into its name, be shaped by it, or, as the tradition so pregnantly puts it, confess the familiar name now for itself.

The *confessional writings* of the Reformed churches are the first means by which this fundamental idea is to be developed. Yet, as is well known, these writings are not a self-contained *corpus doctrinae.* It is good Reformed tradition that every church carries the responsibility for its own confession. The formulation of new confessions is still going on today. Thus, instead of speaking of "the" Reformed doctrine or position (which in view of the famous differences between Zwingli and Calvin has in fact never existed), this essay shall speak of bottom lines and content found in practically all of these confessions. We know that, in distinction from the Augsburg Confession, church discipline is considered part of the confession, thus reflecting the witness value of church order,[2] although, as the Lutherans also agree, one cannot push the concept of "marks" too far here. In the Second Helvetic Confession the marks encompass as a matter of course the prayer of Christians, their repentance, their carrying of the cross laid upon them, the *one* Spirit who unites them in genuine love, and therefore finally the bond of peace and "holy" unity.[3] Only in the sense of a clarification of minimal conditions can we isolate two or three constitutive characteristics. Yet Bullinger refused to consider as outcasts from the church those who, "being forced by necessity, unwillingly," are unable to receive the sacrament and thereby do not fulfill an apparently necessary criterion. "For we know that God had some friends in the world outside the commonwealth of Israel."[4] Bullinger obviously understood the marks as sufficient and precisely

---

2. Cf. Scottish Confession, Article 18; Belgian Confession, Article 29. The confessional writings of the Reformed church are cited here in English according to the English edition by Arthur C. Cochrane, *Reformed Confessions of the Sixteenth Century* (Philadelphia: Westminster, 1966), and in German according to the edition by E. F. K. Müller, *Bekenntnisschriften der reformierten Kirche* (Leipzig: A. Deichert, 1903), hereafter referred to as *BSRK.* Calvin himself did *not* elevate church discipline to one of the *notae ecclesiae.*

3. Cochrane, pp. 261ff.

4. Cochrane, p. 266.

not as necessary conditions. They point to a grounding outside themselves (which can therefore never be made "manageable" through doctrine). Is their validity thereby restricted?

To clarify the meaning of this question, I will first attempt to take up what constitutes the church as church. For if the doctrine of the *notae ecclesiae* is a response to the problem of the recognizability of the church (rather than to the problem of its constitution), then the marks are to be measured against what the congregation of Jesus Christ has first received.[5] Only in a second step shall I speak of the marks themselves, whereby the relationship between the foundation and form of the church — thus the problem of its ordering — will stand in the foreground. In a third step I will then attempt to sketch the challenges of the present time.

The Constitution of the Church as Church

The Word

The Reformed tradition has used two complementary and mutually interpreting assertions to describe the foundation of the church. The first thesis of the Berne Reformation Mandate (1528) reads, "The holy, Christian Church, whose only Head is Christ, is born of the Word of God, abides in the same, and does not listen to the voice of a stranger."[6] To this thesis Berthold Haller, one of its compilers, added in the disputation, "This Church is born from the Word of God, from the Word of faith, and this is none other than the proclaimed Word or that found in Scripture (Romans 10). This vocation, enlightenment, and renewal of the heart is what I call the birth of the Church."[7] The Berne Synod (1532) recapitulates the point similarly: "Thus Jesus Christ is the foundation and ground of the spiritual edifice; outside of him there can be no hope of salvation" (*BSRK,* p. 35). This is the fundamental consensus of the Reformation — the church as *creatura verbi* — which derives its particular force from the fact that the Word is identified in all its forms with

---

5. Cf. Otto Weber, *Foundations of Dogmatics,* trans. and annotated by Darrell L. Guder (Grand Rapids: Wm. B. Eerdmans Publishing Co., 1983), 2:547ff.

6. Cochrane, p. 49. This sentence was taken over word for word in the Düsseldorf Theses (1933) and included in the Barmen Theological Declaration (1934); cf. *Bekenntnisschriften und Kirchenordnungen der nach Gottes Wort reformierten Kirche,* ed. Wilhelm Niesel, 3rd ed. (Zollikon-Zurich: Evangelischer Verlag, 1985), 327.3; 335.25-27.

7. Samuel Fischer, *Geschichte der Disputation und Reformation in Bern,* 2nd ed. (Berne: Jenni, 1828), p. 238.

Jesus Christ. The church heeds "not the voice of a stranger"; it heeds alone its Head, Christ.[8]

The birth of the church "from the Word" actually means therefore that it is not the sermon as such which "generates" the church, but exclusively the Word of God. To be sure, this is none other in content than the "external" Word, but it is nevertheless not simply to be identified with it. For God alone by his Holy Spirit is able to effect the decisive step whereby the Word creates faith and thus grounds the church, that it may become, so to speak, the gate through which we enter God's heavenly reign (Geneva Catechism, q. 300; BSRK, p. 145). We must receive it in all reality as a "truth come down from heaven" (Geneva Catechism, q. 300; BSRK, p. 145), so that it may bring fruit for living, in both the individual and the church.

The model for clarifying this appeal to the Word is thus that of verbal assurance going forth in public speech. That which makes faith in Christ possible and legitimate is the Word of promise, of which the Old Testament so vividly says, it "happened," it took place. Such a Word emerges — also theologically — not as a carrier of meaning, not as the conveyer of information, but rather according to its most original intention as *address,* in which a silence is broken, in which God, the speaker, unmistakably reveals God's presence. With Barth we may say: in God's Word God does not communicate something (some content different from God, to be "believed"), but actually communicates God's own self. God becomes present through the *Spirit.* It is the Spirit who effects faith, gathers the congregation around its Head, and makes it church. This does not make the sermon irrelevant. On the contrary, it receives its power and binding force from the presence of the Spirit. This conviction makes possible the bold and otherwise ridiculous assertion, "The preaching of the Word of God *is* Word of God": "Wherefore when this Word of God is now preached in the church by preachers lawfully called, we believe that the very Word of God is proclaimed, and received by the faithful; and that neither any other Word of God is to be invented nor is to be expected from heaven."[9] This puts all "inner enlightenment" clearly in its place. The confession articulates the trust in the wonder of the presence of the Spirit of Christ within human words, i.e., in the capacity of Christ to make himself present "today," as the mystery of the foundation of the Protestant church. Where this wonder takes place, the church is "born from the Word."

---

8. This theological motif goes back to the fundamental principle of Erasmus's reform: "Christus solus audiendus"; Joachim Staedtke, ". . . die ihres Hirten Stimme hört," *Evangelische Theologie* 18 (1958): 65-75.

9. Cochrane, p. 225.

Election

Because the Word, especially when understood as address and promise, seeks its addressees in all freedom, the foundation elucidated here is properly interpreted by an equally important second assertion which places the theme of the church into the broader context of the *doctrine of election*. The connection between the old and new covenants, characteristic of Reformed ecclesiology, as well as the problem of the distinction and relation between the visible and the invisible church, are rooted here. The Geneva Catechism responds to the question, "What is the catholic Church?" with the lapidary assertion, "[It is] the community of the faithful which God has ordained and *elected* to eternal life" (q. 93; *BSRK,* p. 125). The Heidelberg Catechism answers at somewhat greater length: "that, from the beginning to the end of the world, and from among the whole human race, the Son of God, by his Spirit and his Word, gathers, protects, and preserves for himself, in the unity of the true faith, a congregation *chosen* for eternal life . . . [and] that I am and forever will remain a living member of it eternally" (q. 54; *BSRK,* p. 696).

In this tremendously concentrated assertion, the church is envisioned as a work of Jesus Christ's own initiative and as the work of the *preexistent* Son. God's eternal election — the catechism echoes the Abrahamic blessing intended for "all people on earth" (Gen. 26:4) — is directed teleologically at the congregation. While in the *Fidei ratio* (1530) Zwingli refers to the elected *individual* (*BSRK,* p. 84), the main lines of Reformed thought treat the church *as a whole;* the individual's existence is considered here only as a sort of afterthought. As a "congregation chosen" (Heidelberg Catechism), the church stands for all of humanity. It is to reach *all* people with its witness and by its existence call the whole world to faith. It is universal in both space *and* time.

The Church of Jews and Gentiles

The particular consequences of universality conceived in time are considerable. The Reformed confessions made the *perpetuo mansura sit* of the Augsburg Confession to apply without curtailment also for the past, with Romans 9:4 and Ephesians 2:12. The church exists "from the beginning of the world" and, as the Second Helvetic Confession specifies, "since there is always but one God, and there is one mediator between God and men, Jesus the Messiah, . . . [only] one Testament or covenant, it necessarily follows that there is only one Church."[10] If it encompasses the elect of all peoples and times, so it

---

10. Cochrane, p. 262.

encompasses both *Jews and Gentiles* (Scottish Confession).[11] *Israel,* too, belongs to the church as the communion of the elect. This must be stated even more pointedly: if the reality of election — the "sharpest theological statement conceivable"[12] — stands at the outset of ecclesiology, then communion with Israel is, as the logical result, one of the most fundamental marks of the church. It "necessarily includes the unity and reconciliation between Jews and Gentiles which was never accepted by the Jews and never practiced by the Christians."[13] Markus Barth has rightly lifted up this communion with Israel as a *nota* of the New Testament Lord's Supper.[14] For the new people of God stand not in opposition to the old, but rather form with them a unity. Both, as the Helvetic Confession continues, are "*one* fellowship, [with] *one* salvation in the one Messiah, in whom, as members of *one* body under *one* Head, [they are] all united together in the same faith."[15] The Jews, as the Scottish Confession concludes, also "have communion and society with God the Father, and with his Son, Christ Jesus, through the sanctification of His Holy Spirit."[16] Here as well, Calvin set the course: "Who, then, dares to separate the Jews from Christ, since with them, we hear, was made the covenant of the gospel, the sole foundation of which is Christ?"[17] He first emphasizes the material identity of the one covenant before he begins to speak of the differences in its orientation or administration, while never losing sight of this unity.[18]

Visible and Invisible Church

Beginning with election also has consequences for the *structure* of ecclesiology. It grounds the distinction of the "visible" from the "invisible" church. It is of course clear that the "chosen congregation" described by the Heidelberg Cate-

---

11. Cochrane, p. 175.

12. Dietrich Ritschl, *The Logic of Theology: A Brief Account of the Relationship between Basic Concepts in Theology* (Philadelphia: Fortress, 1986), p. 128.

13. Ritschl, p. 126.

14. Markus Barth, *Rediscovering the Lord's Supper: Communion with Israel, with Christ, and among the Guests* (Atlanta: John Knox, 1988), pp. 7ff.

15. Cochrane, p. 262.

16. Cochrane, p. 175.

17. Calvin, *Institutes* 2.10.4.

18. It is thanks to Karl Barth that Reformed churches have been reminded again of these "ecumenical" roots; cf. *Church Dogmatics* II/2 (Edinburgh: T. & T. Clark, 1957), pp. 195-305. Cf. also Hans Joachim Kraus, *Systematische Theologie im Kontext biblischer Eschatologie* (Neukirchen-Vluyn: Neukirchener Verlag, 1983), esp. p. 488; and Friedrich-Wilhelm Marquardt, *Von Elend und Heimsuchung der Theologie: Prolegomena zur Dogmatik* (Munich: Christian Kaiser Verlag, 1988).

chism is not coterminous with a sociologically tangible, empirical church. In addition, if the church has its foundation in the "secret election" and one must therefore "leave to God alone the knowledge of his Church,"[19] then the old concept of the invisible church suggests itself from the outset. Thus Calvin distinguishes with Scripture (he thinks of passages like Eph. 1:13 or 2 Cor. 4:7) between "that which is actually [church] in God's presence" and the "whole multitude of men spread over the earth, who profess to worship one God and Christ."[20] Zwingli's *Fidei ratio* and the First Helvetic Confession (1536) precede him in this matter, while the later confessions, especially the Westminster Confession of 1647, will follow him.

Because on both Reformed *and* Lutheran sides this is a not unproblematic distinction, I would like to point out in a brief historical note its *Augustinian* roots; this approach recommends itself in that Calvin at least can be best understood from these roots. The Augustinian approach to the problem looks initially somewhat different, somewhat more practical, if you will: there are people who participate externally in the church, but in their hearts they do not belong to it. In a corresponding way, Augustine distinguishes in principle the salvific effectiveness of divine grace in the *heart* of a person from the *external* reception of sacraments and hearing of the preached Word. Yet this inner working does not necessarily take effect in all places where the one true church is, so that the true Christians remain "invisible" in the church.[21] Does this imply — so runs the research question ever since Hermann Reuter's *Augustinische Studien* (1887) — the introduction of a *double* conception of the church, on the one side the empirical catholic church, on the other the communion of the predestined?

Misunderstandings of the tradition (up through Protestant doctrinal teaching) are for the most part based on conceiving of the *difference* indicated by the terms "visible" and "invisible" as the contrast between the organized episcopal church and the true church of faith. However, this leads to a misconception of what *ecclesia* signifies for Augustine. So what does it mean? First, Augustine seeks to preserve the *personal* sense of the word: the church is not a sacramental "institution," but it is a congregation, the Christian "we." And second, the word retains for him its *eschatological* meaning: the *ecclesia* is the congregation elected for the last days — a mark that can never recede to such an extent that only the "empirical church" would remain.[22] Its personal nature is

---

19. Calvin, *Institutes* 4.1.2.

20. Calvin, *Institutes* 4.1.7.

21. Cf. Alfred Schindler, "Augustin," *Theologische Realenzyklopädie*, vol. 4 (1979), p. 677.

22. Wilhelm Kamlah, *Christentum und Geschichtlichkeit*, 2nd ed. (Stuttgart: Kohlhammer, 1951), p. 137.

expressed in that the *ecclesia* never signifies merely the congregation of the baptized (a sacramental understanding), but also means the congregation of the elect; its eschatological character is expressed in that the congregation is church only in anticipation of the *ecclesia praedestinata*.

From this eschatological perspective results something like a twin nature of the church. As was customary since Callistus, Augustine distinguishes between the "church that exists now" and the "church that will exist then." Yet this does not result in a differentiation between two subjects or congregations, but rather implies that the congregation has *mali* — bad members — in its midst; it is still a *provisional* representation of the reign of God. It has to bear with the sham Christians in its midst. The "twin nature" of the church is thus to be found *within* the congregation existing in history. For Augustine there is only *one* church, and a person can belong to it truly or merely nominally, i.e., not at all. Augustine detaches the congregation from something (the *mali*) which does not belong to it at all. Thus the very distinction between the congregation of the saints and the sacramental church (permeated with those who are "evil") is as much a sham as is the membership of those "evil" in the *ecclesia* in the first place. The only true distinction, according to Kamlah, is that "eschatological distinction between evil and good, between now and then."[23]

Any speech about the congregation of the elect must be understood in this context. Within time the elect are that historical congregation unshakably defying the most recent persecution. From an eternal perspective the elect congregation manifests itself as the saints' endurance beyond history. Yet none of this affects the congregation in its actual existence — and that fact is what is most important. There are still sham Christians in its midst, but one day it will be freed of them. Appeal to a community of the elect is therefore intended not to devalue the "visible" church over against an "invisible" one; indeed, such an appeal cannot establish any division at all within the realm which we know and make real as temporal congregation. For this reason, the so-called "double" conception of the church is best understood "by means of the contrast between the pilgrim church on earth vs. the coming heavenly church"; yet, in such a way, as A. Schindler points out, "what is 'institutional' belongs *intrinsically* to the true Church despite and *because of* its symbolic nature, despite its misuse by false Christians and regardless of the paucity of true Christians."[24]

Only in the fourteenth and fifteenth centuries, when the reform of the whole church was demanded "in head and members," did exhorters like Wycliff and Hus use the Augustinian *ecclesia praedestinata* as a weapon of criticism. They discovered something far removed from Augustine himself, viz.,

23. Kamlah, p. 147.
24. Schindler, p. 678.

that one can play off the true *ecclesia* of the elect *against* the *ecclesia* as it is. Not merely as an idea among theologians, but as a church-historical event, this is the beginning of the conceptual split between the true church beyond history *(invisibilis)* and the historical church of the Word *(visibilis)* which culminated in the confessional polemic around the Council of Trent.

Luther stands on the front lines of this debate. In the course of his clash with the papacy, the distinction between the church which can be seen and that in which one believes sharpened for him almost to the point of an antithesis between a bodily, external Christendom and a spiritual, inner one: "Therefore, he who says that an external assembly or unity creates Christendom . . . brings divine truth down to the level of his lies. . . . From all this it follows that the first [i.e., the spiritual internal] Christendom, which alone is the true church, may not and cannot have an earthly head. . . . Here only Christ in heaven is the head and he rules alone."[25] The invisible church of faith, the *ecclesia stricte dicta*, ever manifests itself within the *corpus permixtum* as norm of the church. But the intention is clear: the reign of God is not bound to "Rome."

How does the matter stand on the *Reformed side?* The distinction between visible and invisible church remains tied systematically to predestination, which, however, never surfaces as an abstract criterion. Calvin poses the problem by noting that the flock of those who "persevere to the very end"[26] is smaller than the masses of nominal Christians. The invisible church, of which the Geneva Catechism states, "we now treat expressly of the congregation of those, whom God has, in his hidden election adopted for salvation. But this is neither known by signs, nor at any time discerned by the eyes" (q. 100; *BSRK*, p. 126), is therefore no free-floating ideal. It exists not outside of but *within* the visible church. Calvin can refer to it as the church "believed" [not "believed in" — editor's note], and it is not difficult to find also in him the Protestant schema according to which the attributes (unity, catholicity, holiness) are properties of this in the invisible church.[27] Nevertheless, one searches in vain in his writings for Zwingli's statement that the *credo ecclesiam* is applicable only to the invisible church. That is a singular exaggeration. Only someone who has *realized* his or her membership in the body of Christ can also *"believe"* the church; its unity is to be grasped not only in ideas: it presupposes the conviction that we are "truly engrafted" into it. Calvin declares accordingly that the *credo* refers in a certain sense also to the external church.[28] Invisible and

25. *Luther's Works*, ed. E. W. Gritsch, vol. 39 (Philadelphia: Fortress, 1970), pp. 66, 71.
26. Calvin, *Institutes* 4.1.8.
27. Calvin, *Institutes* 4.1.2.
28. Calvin, *Institutes* 4.1.2 and 3.

visible church, "chosen congregation" and "communion of saints" in this world, are so to speak two sides of the same coin, as one recognizes by the sequence of questions 54 and 55 of the Heidelberg Catechism. The attributes outline what God has promised God's church by its election: it shall and will be a holy people (1 Pet. 2:9), encompassing the whole earth by the power of Christ's reconciliation (Eph. 5:25ff.). The marks express the form in which these promises are manifested so that one may in fact recognize the empirical church by means of them (and not by some other means). This visible church is a theme and problem of the Reformed tradition.

Why thus the appeal to an "invisible church"? Because the local congregation must question itself continually regarding its legitimation and identity, yet by this question it is continually being referred beyond itself. It cannot establish itself from within, neither by its numbers nor by its (external or internal) liveliness. Its truth is not wrapped up in its social and legal form. The "invisible" church keeps alive its remembrance of its source, continually effective within it. It stands under the promise of the unity, holiness, catholicity, and apostolicity entrusted to it and is to bring these given attributes to bear as perspectives on its action and ordering; it is to orient its visible form according to them. The church believed in is intended to take shape in the *empirical* congregation.

Thinking further along the same lines as Calvin, Karl Barth wanted to understand the visible church thus as a *parable*, i.e., as a provisional representation of the invisible reign of God. These are not two separate societies standing over against one another, but two realities which relate to one another like a musical score and its performance. There may or may not be a concert hall involved.

> [The] visible and the invisible Church are not two Churches — an earthly-historical fellowship and above and behind this a supra-naturally spiritual fellowship. . . . [T]he one is the form and the other the mystery of one and the self-same Church. The mystery is hidden in the form, but represented and to be sought out in it. The visible lives wholly by the invisible. The invisible is only represented and to be sought out in the visible. But neither can be separated from the other. Both in their unity are the body, the earthly-historical form of existence of the one living Lord Jesus Christ.[29]

The word "invisible" refers to that which is to be embodied *parabolically* in visible form in the empirical church and which therefore cannot be grasped in concepts according to the rules of logic. Why else would parables be necessary? To that extent, the invisible is thus not the opposite of the real-visible. It

29. Karl Barth, *Church Dogmatics* IV/1 (Edinburgh: T. & T. Clark, 1956), p. 669.

is much more truly that which has not yet come into visible form, that which awaits its (present and future) embodiment in the sphere of the visible. Theologically speaking, it is that toward which the visible church is moving, that which is at all times *before* it and which it never has in its back pocket as a conceptually determined reality. The distinction to be made here is consequently not an ontological but an *eschatological* one. The congregation cannot yet be recognized as that which in Jesus Christ it already "is." It is still moving toward its own revealing. "Visible" and "invisible" are separated not in space but in time.

The Form and Mission of the Church

What are the *marks* that distinguish the true church from the false church and at the same time from other religious communities and societies? Since the Augsburg Confession, no Reformed confessional writing has been lacking an emphasis on *Word* and *sacrament*. The Scottish Confession (1560) and the First Helvetic Confession explicitly name *church discipline (disciplina ecclesiastica)* as a third mark of the church;[30] in the Emden Catechism (1554) this follows with a certain logical consistency directly after the article on the Lord's Supper. Modern representations, such as that of H. J. Kraus, propose as the fourth *nota* the principle that the true church is to consecrate to God "all space, all time, and all justice";[31] they consider as a further characteristic the recognition, born of the World War II German church struggle, that the church of God must be a church *"for the world"* and must correspondingly act in "solidarity with the world."[32]

Instrument for God's Action

If one is to avoid misunderstanding the preceding as simply an otherworldly churchly ideal or — even worse — a catalogue of pious wishes, then one must begin with the fact that this is a differently accented understanding of the *notae* from that found in the Augsburg Confession, which limits itself to two marks. The church "pilgriming" on earth proves to be an empirical-historical entity not only by its visibility, but also by its being still "unready." It is not fixed and ordained from eternity but is first gathered and built. That which it already is

---

30. Cochrane, pp. 177, 105.
31. Kraus, p. 509.
32. Karl Barth, *Church Dogmatics* IV/3.2 (Edinburgh: T. & T. Clark, 1962), pp. 772-73.

"vertically" by God's election, it must always still become "horizontally," and the *notae* are given for this purpose, according to the First Helvetic Confession: by them the church is "not only known but also gathered and built up . . . without these marks no one is numbered with this Church."[33]

The new accent or, better, the newly discovered dimension, is that the church is not only the flock of those grasped by God's action. It is at the same time "God's instrument for divine action towards the faithful."[34] Its *notae* name the gifts received so that they can be seen at the same time as corresponding tasks, as a function of and thus finally as fruits of its edification, gathering, and sending. It is for this reason that such a great emphasis falls in the Reformed tradition on the definition ("generally omitted by the ancients") of the church as *communion* of saints: "the saints are gathered into the society of Christ on the principle that whatever benefits God confers upon them, they should in turn share with one another."[35] This requires, however, not so much the certainty of faith as, much more, the "charitable judgment," which, by means of the *notae*, understood as "confession of faith, . . . example of life, and . . . partaking of the sacraments," comes to know what it is to do. "From this," Calvin continues, i.e., from the *notae* understood as "love's doing," "the face of the church comes forth and becomes visible to our eyes."[36]

Representation of the Body of Christ

If one seeks to describe theologically the understanding of the *notae* glimpsed in the Reformed tradition — and thereby also the relationship between the foundation and form of the church — then one must ask, as noted above, "What constitutes the church?" What makes a stranger and spectator into a "citizen and member of the household of God" (Eph. 2:19)? The New Testament, and particularly Paul, answer with the image of the "body of Christ" (1 Cor. 12:12ff.; Rom. 12:5). Calvin employs this image pointedly to characterize the congregation of the Lord's Supper and to ground church discipline.[37] To understand this point, we can safely assume with the newer exegesis "that for the apostle the members do not constitute the body, but the body sets forth its members. Again . . . the body does not just belong to the Messiah but *is* his

33. Cochrane, p. 105.
34. Benno Gassmann, *Ecclesia Reformata. Die Kirche in den reformierten Bekenntnisschriften*, foreword by Max Geiger (Freiburg: Herder, 1968), p. 89.
35. Calvin, *Institutes* 4.1.3.
36. Calvin, *Institutes* 4.1.8 and 9.
37. Calvin, *Institutes* 4.17.9 and 38; cf. 4.12.1.

earthly projection and manifestation on a worldwide scale."[38] For the congregation is called "soma" not because it is a social construction having some of the form of an organism and reminiscent of such, but because it in fact exists from Jesus Christ as *his* body: it is more precisely understood not as a conception of form, but primarily as a conception of function.

Only by perceiving certain functions which correspond to the "reigning" head and bearing fruit does the church attain a clearly contoured, "recognizable" form. The marks define, so to speak, these indispensable functions and fruits; as Jan Weerda formulates it, with an almost disdainful precision, they make the church into a "functional community."[39] Yet, because in this case the functions are derivative actions, because as marks they point back to the "head" who is effective through and in them, this makes clear that the church does not somehow first create this "body" by its faith, its baptism, or its offices by itself, but rather brings it to light "among the people." It is created, "realized," solely through the earthly, lived life of Jesus. The church simply has to embody it, to give it historical dimensions through the power of the Holy Spirit in the congregation, and it does that by placing its own historical existence already, symbolically, under the conditions of the future reign of God which has drawn near in Jesus. For, to be the "Bride of Christ," who awaits its coming Lord and thus strives for its "true fatherland,"[40] is the "conceptual norm" of the Calvinistic congregation. Understood in this way, its marks are the *rules* in accordance with which they embody the reality of the risen Christ and his future, thus "testifying to" (1 John 1:2) the life which appears there, i.e., bringing to light a life marked by a new freedom and community, never before realized in history.

To be sure, no Reformed theologian has ever spoken of the salvific necessity of any particular external form of the church. Yet none would also ever deny that people in fact experience the "treasure" of the promised salvation in precisely these "earthen vessels" (2 Cor. 4:7). Therefore we proceed here from the encompassing presupposition that Christ, the Word become flesh and the "Sun of Righteousness,"[41] created a congregational model that is socially, even legally binding. Like the Old Testament law in its way, Christ is offered to us as a *gift* which can be received in its rich fullness not by individual Christians (let alone merely with respect to the "inner life"), but only by the church itself as a whole, precisely in its visible form. For this reason Calvin emphatically reserves

---

38. Ernst Käsemann, *Commentary on Romans*, trans. and ed. Geoffrey W. Bromiley (Grand Rapids: Wm. B. Eerdmans Publishing Co., 1980), p. 336.

39. Jan Weerda, "Ordnung zur Lehre. Zur Theologie der Kirchenordnung bei Calvin," in *Calvin-Studien*, ed. J. Moltmann (Neukirchen: Neukirchener Verlag, 1959), p. 162.

40. Calvin, *Institutes* 4.20.2.

41. Calvin, *Institutes* 4.8.7.

the special worth of the "representation" of Christ for the (fourfold) *ministerium ecclesiasticum*. He writes of the "servants" of the church, who not only administer Word and sacrament but also are in charge of *diakonia* and church discipline: they "serve as his ambassadors in the world [2 Cor. 5:20], to be interpreters of his secret will, and, in short, to represent his person."[42] And by doing this, they *testify* to his invisible presence.

The *credo ecclesiam* has, therefore, as described in 1 Corinthians 5 and 11:17ff., immediate consequences for the so-called exterior form of the church, including the lifestyle of individual members. It constrains the church not merely to play from its own "score" and thus leave its visible form — "the form of its message and order"[43] — up to either its own whim or the changing moods of the day. For this form determines not least whether Christ as the head of the church "sets forth" (Käsemann) from his own being a historically existing body at all, which, like every historical construct, every corporation and organization, naturally has a visible exterior which "testifies" to the forming principle at work in it. It is thus not possible in principle to exclude these "functions" from the features by which one recognizes the "true" church and reliably distinguishes it from all forms of "false church"; such functions include things like the election of elders, the ordination of pastors, the church's areas of social engagement, and the administration of its finances. To exclude these areas would mean to deny precisely in the church's actual historical existence the *incarnation* of the Word entrusted to it.

The Church as Institution

The basic idea developed here can be expressed, in a somewhat more modern version, as follows: the church is grasped in the Reformed tradition as an *institution*. Institutions combine something given — whether inherited property, an endowment, or a living relationship — with the possibility, even necessity, of its free *configuration* within the framework of a relatively permanent structure. A classic example is that of marriage: it gives the "life force" of partner-shaped community a fixed form not needing to be invented from scratch by each generation; yet it is not such a rigid framework as to stifle the diversity of possibilities for individual configuration. Institutions are "like plants which one can transplant, prune, and care for, but whose resulting forms are given."[44]

---

42. Calvin, *Institutes* 4.3.1.

43. Barmen Declaration (1934), Third Thesis, in Cochrane, p. 335.

44. Hans Dombois, *Recht der Gnade: ökumenisches Kirchenrecht*, vol. 1 (Witten: Luther Verlag, 1961), p. 905.

The point at issue can best be grasped by looking at the process that is being made possible here: a marriage intends to be "lived," a house to be "inhabited," and obviously neither can take place without some minimal amount of external ordering. In and through such ordering, that which is given, the "endowment," is taken up and transformed into a historically livable form. According to Ernst Wolf, the interaction between endowment (given) and taking up (form giving) constitutes the institution.[45]

To apply all this: the church lives from Christ's appointment as Lord over the "powers and principalities" of this world (Col. 2:15; Eph. 4:8). It lives from the opening of a new *kairos* (= given) which both participates in and announces the final future; and it grasps this offer as "God's invitation into ordering and form-giving action" (E. Wolf). What does this mean? At the very least, it means that by its own decision the church must take up this offer; it must allow the "day of salvation" (2 Cor. 6:2) symbolically to become a reality, and that can only occur in that it creates certain forms and orders of life which permit Christ to reach his goal of "filling everything with his presence" (Eph. 4:10) in its midst. For realization is impossible without a concrete *form*. One can speak of an active church living in the context of earthly history only insofar as the church finds its way to the historical configuration of the elements of its life. This unavoidable restriction to a certain form is therefore not something arbitrary, external to the matter itself, but is the (legally binding) necessary expression in which the given "endowment" is ever "taken up." Like the constitution of a nation, it is an essential mark of the church. This does not mean that a church's constitution must regulate every tiny detail of the congregation's life! Yet it does mark the boundaries within which the "day of salvation," the church's foundation in faith, can and is to become visible in history. It is for this reason that it has confessional rank in the church.

If the Berne church constitution in force today states, e.g., that "the Word of God applies to all arenas of public life such as state, society, economy, and culture," it is clearly not the description of a situation presently or ever the actual case; nor is it a text of law which conclusively prescribes how the church must act in every possible case, such as in adopting its budget. Rather it is a self-binding declaration which asserts that in carrying out the life described here, we intend to correspond to the gospel of Christ; the foundation of the church is to find here its visible expression in our communion. As the text itself states, these lines from the constitution can only be "witnessed to," and this citation is perhaps an especially telling example of the fact that church constitutions in general have the character of *witness*. For they describe the structure

---

45. Ernst Wolf, with Frieda Wolf and Uvo A. Wolf, *Sozialethik: Theologische Grundfragen,* ed. Theodor Strohm (Göttingen: Vandenhoeck & Ruprecht, 1975), pp. 171-72.

in which the church is to embody and make real its theological "genius," that which Christ has given it.

Witnessing

This much has become clear: the *notae* primarily describe realms of action of the present Christ, who unites the congregation to his life. They are given into human hands only derivatively, representatively, for parabolic representation in the arena of history. Thus, in place of the teaching church emerges generally the preaching church, for all is centered in *hearing*, in the reception and formation of the gift. Where God's Word is preached and heard purely, Calvin goes on, there is the church of God before us; and equally characteristic is his addition that such churchly hearing is "not without fruit."[46] In the administration of the sacraments as well, the main accent lies on Christians' participation in something which they have received. The Holy Spirit, "who lives in Christ and in us" (Heidelberg Catechism, q. 76; *BSRK*, p. 702), is the actual subject of the holy meal. The Spirit increasingly unites us with the risen body of Christ, and the congregation gives this body historical-visible expression in that "it is necessary that all of us also be made one body by such participation."[47]

This example allows us to explicate the meaning and significance of the *notae ecclesiae* especially well. The church is recognized by that which it is *given*. With the sacrament it is given a visible and effective sign of invisible grace. Calvin speaks of the "seal" *(obsignatio)*[48] of the promise of John 6:48: "I am the bread of life." By means of these signs, God reminds the church of all God's benefits and at the same time renews it. They give external form to that which God internally provides, and the church bears this in mind by the only means possible, by using these signs as a community of the Lord's Supper, i.e., by allowing itself to be made a representational space for the truth intended here, for the "thing signified."[49] By this means it attests that the Christ who is removed from the circumstances of history does not withdraw himself from history: he remains present to the church in its spiritual *and* social expressions — in its prayer, its community, and its societal existence — and leads it along the way. For "the principal thing which God promises (to us) in all sacraments . . . is Christ the Savior" himself.[50] Christ does not disappear into Word and

---

46. Calvin, *Institutes* 4.1.9.
47. Calvin, *Institutes* 4.17.38.
48. Calvin, *Institutes* 4.17.4.
49. Calvin, *Institutes* 4.17.10.
50. Second Helvetic Confession, Cochrane, p. 278.

sacrament; they do not substitute for him, let alone replace him. Rather we must say he binds his divine action to our human action. Only in this way do we grasp what "remembrance" in the Reformed tradition means: *realization* of the presently active source, not merely historical (and therefore ineffective) "remembering." Seen in this way, Word and sacrament are in fact scarcely to be described as "means of grace" (certainly not in the "instrumental" sense of the Augsburg Confession, article V), but rather they belong within the realm of the "ethics" of witness.

If one thinks in terms of this tendency, then the dividing line between marks and attributes cannot be drawn as sharply as it usually is in the Protestant tradition. For the church is to testify visibly (and be recognized by means of this testimony) to precisely that which in its attributes it believes as its promise. All people "partaking . . . of the same spiritual food and drink," argues the Second Helvetic Confession, are in reality, as members of the "true" church, also members of one body. The attributes of unity and of catholicity are claimed unreservedly also for the *ecclesia militans,* which extends "through all parts of the world, and . . . unto all times," thus for the *visible communio sanctorum.*[51] The unity of the whole church dare not be understood as something merely invisible. Calvin himself, who always declared it to be a mandate,[52] proves thereby that it is to be visible, lest Christ be "torn into pieces." He was more prepared to overlook faults in doctrine and even in the administration of the sacraments than to permit them to alienate people from the communion of the one church.[53] This finally shows that it is the original Augustinian opposition between the true and false church — not the traditional later one between invisible and visible — which determines ecclesiology. The problem of the actual schism of the church, the separation from Rome, is "overcome" with the comment that detachment from the papal church was necessary "for Christ's sake."[54]

The Fourfold Office

Even if Calvin never wanted to give it the formal status of a *nota ecclesiae,* the weight which the question of the form and ordering of the church acquired is revealed by the sentence that neither the light and warmth of the sun, nor even food and drink, are nearly so necessary for the sustenance of temporal life "as

51. Cochrane, p. 262.
52. Cf. Calvin, *Institutes* 4.1.2; 4.12.11-13.
53. Calvin, *Institutes* 4.1.12; cf. Gassmann, pp. 124ff.
54. Calvin, *Institutes* 4.2.6.

the apostolic and pastoral office is necessary to preserve the church on earth."[55] The Second Helvetic Confession speaks directly of the "establishing" of the visible church by the "ministerium,"[56] and the French Confession devotes itself to this theme in no fewer than six of its total forty articles.[57] Why this unusual emphasis? It is because, in the face of the powers and forces which govern the world, the mere existence of the congregation is a foretaste and sign of God's eschatological victory. Here the work of God is pursued by those who recognize that God stands beside them "while the whole world oppose[s] and attack[s] them."[58] The "unique benefit" which God has bestowed on the church in order to demonstrate formally the promise of its permanent existence is manifested in the calling of teachers who as God's own tools carry out the "administration of the Spirit and of righteousness and of eternal life."[59] In particular he asserts that in the so-called Office of the Keys, which establishes church discipline, the "sum total of the gospel" itself is brought to fruition.[60]

The basic idea is simple: because "the ministry" is not born from a mandate of the congregation but brings the dominion of the risen Christ to direct representation, and because the gifts which constitute the congregation as the body of Christ are "taken up" in it in a given historical form, the ministry structure has such an overriding significance. To assert with R. Smend: "A community represents itself in its *offices*."[61] The offices belong to the essential features of its constitution. They are the necessary structuring element giving form to the congregation's growth. Here an appeal to the pure, contingent Word going forth is *not* adequate; it would shatter the links to the church's historical embodiment and its evolved structures, as well as to its invocation of a Spirit which "blows where it wills." To retreat into the free Word transcending all of history would mean methodologically to shut out that which we wish to assert over against the Roman understanding of ministry: the communal character of the church and its progressive growth. This may well also be the reason for the fact that Calvin emphatically does *not* relate the office of ministry to faith (as the Augsburg Confession does), but to the visible cohesion of the congregation on earth. But then it can exist only in the plural, as a multiple or, more precisely, fourfold-structured office. Its structure springs from the biblical-theological reflection on the irreplaceable functions of the "body of Christ."

55. Calvin, *Institutes* 4.3.2.
56. Cochrane, p. 268.
57. Cochrane, pp. 153-56.
58. Calvin, *Institutes* 4.11.1.
59. Calvin, *Institutes* 4.3.3.
60. Calvin, *Institutes* 4.11.1.
61. Cf. Dombois, *Recht der Gnade,* vol. 3 (1983), pp. 144-68.

Church Discipline

Finally, the emphasis with which the Reformed tradition handles church discipline can be understood only when one recalls that here as well we are dealing with the concrete form of a gift, with the "spiritual power" *(spiritualis potestas)* of the church, which is manifested in its doctrine, in its legislation, and in its jurisdiction.[62] Even if Calvin does not count church discipline among the *notae ecclesiae*, we are dealing here with an essential element of the *constitution* of the church, in this case that of jurisdiction, to which, under the title "The Order of the Community," Barth brought new distinction.[63] One may speak without exaggeration of the beginnings of a Protestant canon law being formulated here.

Part of the reason this third branch of the power of the church was later included in the catalogue of Reformed characteristics was surely due to practical considerations; primarily, however, it was included out of the theological recognition that the Word of promise, which goes forth in the sacrament as visible assurance of forgiveness, also takes visible form in a second, complementary way: it grounds the *law*, the "household regulations" of the congregation. To speak with the second Barmen thesis, it formulates "God's mighty claim upon our whole life."[64] Just as the preaching of the gospel absolves people and sets them free, it also binds them. These are inseparable: "if we do not wish to make void the promise of the keys, . . . we must give the church some jurisdiction."[65] Calvin well distinguished this from general doctrinal authority. For its foundation rests on the recognition that the gospel determines the relationship between Christ and his earthly congregation as well as what, according to the stipulations of this relationship, deserves to be called "justice" and "injustice." This is realized in the form of a "set and permanent order of the church."[66] Unfortunately, it is too often forgotten that Calvin called the administration of justice exercised in church discipline a "public reconciliation."[67]

Here as well, therefore, we find a basic idea that is simple: jurisdiction and church discipline are the necessary form in which the proclamation of the gospel brings to bear on the congregation its claim to be the guiding principle of the *oikodome*. "[A]s the saving doctrine of Christ is the soul of the church, so does discipline serve as its sinews, through which the members of the body hold together, each in its own place."[68] Judged formally, this is the same argu-

---

62. Calvin, *Institutes* 4.8.1.
63. Karl Barth, *Church Dogmatics* IV/2 (Edinburgh: T. & T. Clark, 1958), pp. 676-726.
64. Cochrane, p. 335.
65. Calvin, *Institutes* 4.11.1.
66. Calvin, *Institutes* 4.11.4.
67. Calvin, *Institutes* 4.1.22.
68. Calvin, *Institutes* 4.12.1.

ment which makes the sacraments marks of the church. The gift of God is received within the circumstances of our history where it is visibly represented in an earthly form — in this case, as the congregation's order.

The Church's Identity

The question of the *identity* of the church, however, is not answered simply by ascertaining its necessary marks. Rather, this question has accompanied Reformed congregations for as long as they have existed. For the original goal of the Reformation was by no means to call to life a sharply defined new Christian group, but was rather to renew the existing "one holy catholic and apostolic church" from the ground up. Of course, at the moment in which the newly established groups found themselves in fact a separate church, they were burdened with the demand to be precisely this renewed church. To the present day, this demand propels the question which is raised by the church naming itself Christian: To what are we called? Are we being true to our calling? Judged theologically, this and only this is the question of its identity. The question does not read, What have we become throughout the course of our history? Where do we stand today? By what are we distinguished within the choir of the various confessions and finally within a pluralistic society? These are also important questions. Yet they can be raised only with the self-critical intention to let them lead the church back to the living heart of the first question: What is our evangelical task? For what are we as a Reformed church responsible?

This question can obviously not be answered "phenomenologically," in reference to the phenotype of this church. For the church has always suffered from the discrepancy between doctrine and life, claim and reality, good theological concepts and their often unsuccessful realization. It also has no magisterium to decide this question in some so-called normative way. Further, it cannot simply turn to its own tradition, whether to Zwingli or to Calvin, nor to the subsequent two centuries of history broadly shared in Europe. For even if this tradition elicits, as we have seen, some helpful definitions which tell us what it does or could mean to be "Reformed," no appeal to the sixteenth century can establish with any certainty whether it is today in fact church.

So what shall we do? If churches take seriously the problem of their identity as an inquiry into their faith and lifestyle, as it was posed to the first generation of Reformed Christians, then they have the possibility themselves to take up the original Reformed impulse, i.e., to understand themselves as instruments for the process of today's church renewal. It is necessary to make a distinction here: there are European (and American) *problems*, such as the phenomenon of secularization, with its manifest consequences today — the silent erosion of the churches which results in increasing numbers of people leaving and, as a countermovement, the so-called new religiosity — but there are surely *no* conceivable European (and American) *solutions*. The troubled phenotype of the older churches can only change if it exposes its traditional marks to new ecumenical experiences and allows these to test them. For we are confronted today for the first time with the horizon of a universal Christian community, and in this situation our witness must prove itself in very different locations. To formulate this from a European perspective: we see ourselves over against a world, the so-called Third World, which, because of the freedom we have claimed for our own unrestrained craving for wealth, now suffers from hunger, economic dependency, and political incapacitation. We are witnesses to racial conflicts which have intensified and to some degree even triggered our own Reformed "doctrine."

In the face of these challenges it would be absurd to consider our identity as something given, which could be defined beforehand. Only the renunciation of all attempts to squeeze identity into formulas and dogmas can bring the churches closer to the truth of the gospel for which they seek to be responsible. For according to John 14:6, this truth takes the form of a way which one travels; it is a *process* to which we ourselves belong. The consequences are obvious: only a community of churches which understands itself as a traveling, *pilgrim* people of God has a chance to answer the question of its own identity. For its identity, understood in this way, can only be manifested in faithfulness to the "project" which arises from passion for the way of Jesus of Nazareth. Because this engages the history of the church's origins, which it shares with *all* the churches of the *oikumene*, it must again subject the landmarks and orientation points of this way to the question of *sola Scriptura*, of the meaning of the covenant, of the relation between law and gospel, and not least to the question of its visible form and the form of its praxis. At the outset I said that a church inquiring as to its identity must confess for itself the already familiar name; it is now clear that this cannot mean an anxious fixation on a past stage of its history. That which it has received from God, it should now give on to the world living today. To conclude, I will illustrate this with two points.

Contemporary Confession[69]

The word "confession" almost unconsciously connotes a *text* which contains a summary of the most important content of Christian faith. The fact that this

---

69. Cf. Lukas Vischer, "Confessio fidei in der ökumenischen Diskussion," in Lukas Vischer, *Gottes Bund gemeinsam bezeugen: Aufsätze zu Themen der ökumenischen Bewegung* (Göttingen: Vandenhoeck & Ruprecht, 1992), pp. 121-40, esp. pp. 132ff.

text intends to speak to a specific situation, that it has certain motives and purposes, that it thus has a *context* in which the church lives, tends to be overlooked. Yet this is the root of our difficulties relating to church tradition. "A confession which has arisen in a certain context cannot simply be transferred into a different situation."[70] A confession does record decisions made along the previously traveled way, as well as important experiences in relating to the Bible, but it does not do so in order to preserve them as a norm for all subsequent periods. It could better be compared to terrain in which one gropes one's way forward. It preserves the church from losing its sense of direction but cannot relieve it of the task of discerning its present situation and interpreting it from the gospel, thus of finding its *own* way in the face of the questions debated today (such as those of containing the streams of refugees or of the ecological crisis), to steer it through the most concrete decisions.

Such contextual confession oriented to the situation of a particular church is a conspicuous feature of the Reformed tradition. It has to the present day prevented a common Reformed confession from emerging, which may be one of the explanations for the ever-occurring divisions within the Reformed "family." Must the hope of speaking with *one voice* remain a pious wish? Whoever regards the various interlocking contexts to which liberation theology so compellingly points must today conclude differently: there is no challenge before which the church stands, no force it must resist, and therefore also no proclamation with which it responds to its own particular difficulties which do not have hidden implications for every other church and its situation.[71] Thus it is time to come to some agreement regarding those themes and contents which dare not be lacking from any contemporary confession. The goal is not a unified confession, but the communion of confessing churches.

Life in God's Covenant

Reformed churches today face the task of rediscovering the most important key theological concept of their tradition, that of covenant, in its encompassing breadth and its full specificity. The ecumenical emphasis on justice, peace, and the integrity of creation has made clear and concrete for many people where, beyond its traditional realms of activity, the responsibility lies for a

70. Vischer, p. 132.

71. Cf. *Have No Fear, Little Flock: Conference of the Minority Central and Eastern European Member Churches of the World Alliance of Reformed Churches on the Document, "Called to Witness to the Gospel Today,"* Kecskemet, October 8-10, 1986 (Budapest: General Synod of the Reformed Church in Hungary, 1987).

church which allows itself to be a steward of God's gifts. In a time of survival, it is to be a witness of *life;* in a time in which "love shall grow cold in many" (Matt. 24:12), it is to be a spring of mutual solidarity; in a time of resignation, it is to be a sign of resistance and hope. All this has become well known. Yet we must still think anew about the path toward making it in fact happen. For if it is true that in the covenant God has claimed the entire creation — plants, animals, human beings, *and* their habitats — then must not the marks by which God's congregation is recognized be conceived so broadly that they apply to the whole wealth of created gifts, and at the same time so precisely and concretely that these gifts remain identifiably God's gifts? And if it is true that the church's existence is the real sign of this covenant, then must quite a different weight not fall on its *visible* form, more than even Calvin himself brought to bear?

CHAPTER 17

The Church — Mother of the Believers

Lukas Vischer

"I believe in one holy . . . Church" — how do Reformed Christians explicate this article of faith? On the basis of their particular convictions, what do they have to say regarding the church?

The answer is not immediately obvious. At times the question itself is considered inappropriate. Some Reformed theologians like to assert that there is no "specifically" Reformed understanding of the church, nor can there be. Reformed theology, they state, is that which rejects as normative all historically given theological or spiritual principles, including its own; rather, in every generation it inquires solely and exclusively as to the Word of God:

> To be a member of a church in the Reformed tradition is not, first of all, to be a disciple of John Calvin or an advocate for the Presbyterian form of government. The prior commitment is the commitment to Jesus Christ. The first thing that must be said about who we are as participants in the Reformed tradition is that we are Christians: believers in Jesus Christ and members of the church, the people of God.[1]

Although such a statement rightly reminds us that the task of theology is not simply to explain and justify existing traditions, it also conceals a measure of self-deception. The attempt to reflect theologically about belief in the church does not take place in a vacuum. Rather, it is unavoidably *also* molded by the church tradition to which we belong. Even when we think we have left many

---

1. Wallace M. Alston, Jr., *The Church* (Atlanta: John Knox, 1984), p. 3.

Translated by Lisa Dahill.

aspects of the Reformed tradition behind, we are in fact much more profoundly shaped by its fundamental alternatives than we generally realize; and certain questions are so unavoidably presented by the tradition that they simply *must* be posed within any Reformed deliberation regarding the church. The assertion that there is no specifically Reformed understanding of the church thus rests upon an illusion; in fact, in many cases it effectively amounts to presenting as "the" Christian response a position which is in many respects actually highly Reformed. In such cases one realizes that supposedly postconfessional statements still subtly reflect clear confessional features.

And, is it not intrinsic to the topic itself that the question of the Reformed understanding of the church not only can but must be posed? The church is a historical entity. No matter how hidden its source and full scope may be, it is still a visible community whose radiance can be experienced and whose history can be described. Anyone who would reflect on belief about the church must speak of this visible community; it boils down to understanding better what this church in which we have been planted by baptism is all about. For Reformed theology, the community in which these reflections arise is most immediately the Reformed church. Theological questioning, of course, quickly leads beyond this one church's boundaries to more all-encompassing horizons and perspectives; one's attention will be drawn to what emerges from the Word of God for the whole church's future. The concrete place which serves as one's point of departure, however, must never slide from one's view. Thus, theological reflection will attempt to make clear how this Reformed church can become even more transparently a vessel through which the church of Jesus Christ may shine. Reformed theology has too often neglected this task. It has provided a broad sweep of information about how the church ought to look, without really bothering about the shape of the actual, experienced reality of the Reformed church. Yet what good does it do to wish away the concrete reality? It will catch up with us sooner or later. Only a theology which comes to terms with it is both theologically and ecumenically responsible.

What does it mean, then, as Reformed Christians, to inquire after the source, meaning, and goal of the church? Three points are important here.

Reform of the One Church versus the Reformed Church

Reformed inquiry into the nature of the church is shaped not only by the contents of the Reformation message, but also by the course of the Reformation from the sixteenth century to the present. The effect of the Reformation has necessarily forced such inquiry to take place within the tension between the church in its universality and the church of the Reformed confession. How do these two realms correspond to one another? The Reformation movement aimed at the reform of the whole church, which was supposed to find its way from its present corruption back to its roots, and thus to be renewed as the church of Jesus Christ. The establishment of a separate Reformed church was not the intention of the Reformers. Such a church resulted solely because the Reformation movement did not accomplish its actual goal. "In order to bring them together, when thus scattered," Calvin wrote in 1539, "I raised not a foreign standard, but that noble banner of thine whom we must follow, if we would be classed among thy people. . . . On this grievous tumults arose, and the contest blazed and issued in disruption. With whom the blame rests it is for Thee, O Lord, to decide."[2] The result was a breach in the church: there developed an opposition between the two churches, and in the course of time even more churches came into being. It is our task to interpret this history.

What happened? Did the Reformation reveal the true church of Jesus Christ in the form of the Reformed church? Has the task since that time simply been to defend this achievement and interpret it to the other churches? Did the papal faction's resistance to the Reformation cause Rome to become a nonchurch? Did the pope even function as the Antichrist from whom the true church must protect itself? Or was the split merely a passing matter? Was such resistance a sign that the Reformation was not yet complete, but required continuation and deepening? Did the Roman Church itself also retain traces of the true church, which would eventually come to be accepted? Was it thus the task of the Reformed church to pay attention to these traces of truth and seek continually the communion of the one church of Jesus Christ? What is the meaning in particular of the fact that the Reformation movement did not lead to a united church, but rather gave rise to many different traditions? Was the Reformed church forced then to distinguish itself as the true church also from all of them? Or was this variety the sign that the unity of the church from now on could be realized only in diversity?

Reformed theology has not been able to escape these questions in any generation since the time of the Reformation. And just as in previous centuries, responses to them today vary.

The tension is apparent. On the one hand it is clear that Reformed churches can never accept a smaller horizon than that of the one holy catholic and apostolic church. The people of God are to be made visible on this earth; Reformed churches will therefore never let go of the hope that the deepest intentions of the Reformation may be fulfilled within a communion of all churches. They will not be satisfied with mere withdrawal into themselves. In-

2. John Calvin, *Tracts and Treatises on the Reformation of the Church*, ed. T. F. Torrance, vol. 1 (Grand Rapids: Wm. B. Eerdmans Publishing Co., 1958), p. 59.

deed, they will resist any defensive hardening of the Reformed tradition. For the Reformed church would betray its own profoundest nature if it lost its ongoing readiness for new ventures. It would degenerate into a sect — and no one can deny that this temptation has closely shadowed the Reformed churches through the centuries. Reformed churches have the capacity to distinguish themselves through tremendous openness, but they can also at times succumb to a sectarian understanding of the church.

On the other hand it is equally clear that the Reformation was about the visible embodiment of the church of Jesus Christ and that Reformed churches are to maintain this emphasis; they may appeal to their origins only when they are possessed by this passion. Openness to the totality of God's people is not to mean the neglect of what is most important, namely, the actual realization of the church of Christ. Just as the Reformation was more than an abstract set of programmatic recommendations, so Reformed churches dare not be satisfied with merely preaching the idea of the true church in its generality. They must rather be prepared to be evaluated according to the historical reality they represent. This results in a dual struggle: to break through prematurely drawn boundaries and yet not lose touch with the reality of the Reformed church as it is manifest today; to remain open to new insights and yet devote everything to the preaching of the Word of God; to raise one's sights to encompass the whole of the church and yet, even in all imperfection and provisionality, be the church of Jesus Christ here and now. The path is narrow, and Reformed churches will inevitably err to one side or the other in fulfilling this mandate. Yet it belongs to the uniqueness of the Reformed tradition that this tension must be maintained.

What Is the Reformed Tradition?

Where do we begin when we as Reformed Christians seek to clarify our belief in the one church? With Calvin and the Reformers of the sixteenth century? With the confessions formulated in the sixteenth and seventeenth centuries by various Reformed churches? There can be no doubt that any response must orient itself in some way to these early witnesses. How could the Reformed church possibly interpret itself without reaching back to that period in which its separate existence originated?

And yet the story does not end with such an appeal to Calvin and the classical Reformed confessions. The Reformed tradition is richer than that; it cannot be encapsulated in these witnesses. Neither Calvin nor the confessions have so determined the Reformed understanding of the church that it could not subsequently be amplified, deepened, and in important aspects even altered through new insights. It would thus be an error to limit the response for today to that point in history.

From the beginning, Reformed churches have been distinguished by a certain diversity among themselves. Although the Reformation sprang from the same basic impetus everywhere, it took a different course in each place, according to local conditions and historical factors. Not only did the confessions being formulated accent differing points, but there also emerged varying models of the church: the order introduced in Zürich and Berne was not identical with the one Geneva is said to have received, and the order developed by the Reformed minority in France represents yet another original type. Each of these models builds on a different experience in relation to state and society. Each ought to have its own history.

The Reformers saw no danger in these various accents. As long as the gospel is preached and the sacraments administered according to the institution of Christ, "there, it is not to be doubted, a church of God exists," says Calvin. "[T]he church universal," he continues, "is a multitude gathered from all nations; it is divided and dispersed in separate places, but agrees on the one truth of divine doctrine, and is bound by the bond of the same religion."[3] Calvin is thus sustained by the trust that God calls the church in each place to life through the Word. Each church itself bears the responsibility for the building up of the whole church. As long as the "bond of religion" is preserved, differences of formulation and form can be of no consequence. The individual churches will seek unity, consult together, support and correct one another; they are not dependent on uniformity to embody the unity of the church of Christ. Overall, this stance has remained characteristic of Reformed churches. Of course, attempts at uniformity are continually being undertaken. Synopses were written to transcend the diversity of confessions.[4] Certain church structures have been declared binding. Yet none of these attempts has succeeded. The Reformed tradition has continued to be characterized by diversity; in fact, over the centuries this diversity has only increased.

Another factor is even more important, however. The Reformed tradition emerged in essence from the sixteenth century, yet in the following centuries it continued to develop. Since the Reformation, the Reformed churches have been led a long way, and in this time they have gained insights of far-

3. John Calvin, *Institutes of the Christian Religion*, ed. F. L. Battles and J. T. McNeill (Philadelphia: Westminster, 1960), 4.1.9.

4. An early attempt in this direction was the *Harmonia Confessionum fidei*, by the French pastor Salnar, which appeared in Geneva in 1581. In English: *The Harmony of Protestant Confessions*, trans. Peter Hall (London: J. F. Shaw, 1842); cf. August Ebrard, *Salnar's "Harmonia confessionum fidei"* (Barmen, 1887). The question was discussed at great length in the early years of the World Alliance of Reformed Churches. The hope of integrating the confessions into one common text was quickly abandoned, however.

reaching importance. The Reformers were aware that the richness of the Scriptures was far from exhausted by their message. Especially in the first decades, they declared themselves continually ready to accept any insight which "would lead closer to Christ and which is more conducive to common peace in the light of God's Word."[5] They were, however, not aware that the Reformed church, born of necessity, would have to continue to respond to new challenges in countless future generations, and thus would be led to new discoveries. In reality, the Reformation was the beginning of a living new tradition. All attempts to nail down the Reformed message for all time and wall it off from any change, such as at the time of Reformed orthodoxy, have failed to halt this process of development.[6] Insights which at the most were implicit in the Reformation message were formulated anew. Today these reformulations are part of the Reformed tradition, and when Reformed Christians interpret their belief in the church they must account for them no less than the Reformers' own statements about the church. A few examples will make this clear:

1. Today it is unanimously agreed in Reformed and even ecumenical circles that God calls the church *as a whole,* and in the same way entrusts it with the task of preaching and sends it into the world. "The Holy Spirit bestows on the community diverse and complementary gifts. . . . All members are called to discover, with the help of the community, the gifts which they have received and to use them for the building up of the Church and for the service of the world to which the Church is sent."[7] The Reformed church emphasizes the responsibility of the congregation as a whole. Each member participates in the fulfilling of the communal task; each member helps to lead the church.[8] "The various ministries in the church have the church's single and common ministry as their presupposition and basis."[9] As obvious as this emphasis may sound

5. Berner Synodus (1532), *Dokumente der Berner Reformation* (Berne: Haupt, 1978), p. 41.

6. The Helvetic Formula of Consensus of 1675 is an example of such an attempt. This is clear from the introduction: "In these lamentable and terrible times we must continually call to mind and hold fast to what the apostle of the people earnestly entrusted to his beloved son Timothy, namely that he should abide in what he had learned and believed and of which he was certain." Formula Consensus, "Vorwort," in E. F. Karl Müller, *Die Bekenntnisschriften der reformierten Kirchen* (Leipzig: A. Deichert, 1903), p. 861.

7. *Baptism, Eucharist and Ministry,* Faith and Order Paper no. 111 (Geneva: World Council of Churches, 1982), p. 20.

8. United Presbyterian Church in the USA, "Confession of 1967," pt. II, A, 2, in *Reformed Witness Today: A Collection of Confessional and Statements of Faith Issued by Reformed Churches,* ed. Lukas Vischer (Berne: Evangelische Arbeitsstelle Ökumene Schweiz, 1982), p. 212.

9. Jürgen Moltmann, *The Church in the Power of the Spirit: A Contribution to Messianic Ecclesiology,* trans. Margaret Kohl (Minneapolis: Fortress, 1993), p. 300.

today, it was not held from the beginning; only in later centuries did it gradually take hold. Instead, Calvin underlined much more the authority of the ministry over against the congregation. Although he was convinced that the congregation as a priestly community was not dependent on the mediation of priests for access to God, he never let himself be drawn to the conclusion that the responsibility for the fulfilling of its task lay with the congregation as a whole. Because he was convinced that the church lives from the preaching of the Word and the gift of the sacraments, he attached the greatest importance to the office of the ministry. "For neither the light and heat of the sun, nor food and drink, are so necessary to nourish and sustain the present life as the apostolic and pastoral office is necessary to preserve the church on earth."[10] And, in an exegesis of Ephesians 4:11-13, he writes, "We see that all are brought under the same regulation, that with a gentle and teachable spirit they may allow themselves to be governed by teachers appointed to this function."[11] The role of the congregation in the election of a pastor is limited to "consent and confirmation." When in the second half of the century the Frenchman Jean Morély upheld the thesis that the congregation was a brotherly community in which each member carried a shared responsibility for one another's salvation, and discipline was therefore to be carried out by the congregation as a whole, Théodore de Bèze contradicted him with great vigor. The congregational movement had to endure opposition and persecution for many years before it found widespread acceptance in Reformed circles.

2. "We testify that God is at work here and now when people obey Christ's commission to witness to him and make disciples of all nations."[12] Or: "As God sent Christ to us, so Christ sends us into the world. We are here to proclaim Christ in word and deed."[13] Statements of this type were not made in the Reformed tradition from the beginning. The *missionary sending* of the church was not a theme of the Reformers. Their concern was limited to giving the preaching of the Word a secure place in the life and structures of the church. God's Word was to be heard in the church. The idea that God's Word should be carried beyond the boundaries of the church into the world, even to the ends of the earth — in other words, the evangelistic and missionary task of the church — was rediscovered only much later. It is characteristic, for instance, that the Westminster Confession had to be expanded in 1902 with the following words: "Christ hath

10. Calvin, *Institutes* 4.3.2.

11. Calvin, *Institutes* 4.1.5.

12. Presbyterian Church in the United States, "A Declaration of Faith" (1976), chap. 8.2, in *Reformed Witness Today*, p. 257.

13. Presbyterian Church in Canada, *Living Faith: A Declaration of the Christian Faith* (Winfield, B.C.: Wood Lake Books, 1984), p. 26.

commissioned his church to go into all the world and make disciples of all nations. All believers are, therefore, under obligation to sustain the ordinances of the Christian religion where they are already established, and to contribute by their prayer, gifts, and personal efforts to the extension of the kingdom of Christ throughout the whole earth."[14] The understanding of the church was thereby placed within a fundamentally new perspective.

3. The emancipation of Jews, their persecution, and above all their destruction in the Third Reich (as well as the establishment of the state of Israel) have triggered in all churches, but especially in Reformed churches, a new conception of the relationship between the church and Israel — or better, between Israel and the church. It has become increasingly clear that Christians' earlier stance toward the Jews did not do justice to the biblical witness of God's promise to Israel. More and more people have become convinced that the church has been included within God's promises to Israel, that Israel was not rejected after Christ's coming but remained God's chosen people. Above all, it has become clear that the church must do everything possible in order not to give unintentional or unconscious religious grounding to anti-Semitism. Of course, the Reformed tradition has always distinguished itself through a particular attentiveness to the Jewish people. Calvin differentiated himself from the other Reformers by the self-imposed moderation of his criticism of the Jews.[15] Reformed theologians like Johannes Cocceius asserted that not all promises to Israel had reached fulfillment, so that the church waited with Israel for their fulfillment. From this perspective, the mission to the Jews received special prominence and was conducted in Reformed circles with particular energy. And yet the last few decades have witnessed a further step above and beyond these earlier attitudes. The dialogue with the Jewish people has become a fundamental part of the church's self-understanding; the Reformed tradition cannot be conceived apart from it any longer.

4. The fundamental equality between men and women has always been acknowledged in Reformed churches. Measured according to the ideas of his time, Calvin actually went relatively far in this direction. He praised marriage as the place given by God for community and mutuality. "Woman was not only created to populate the earth; . . . she was not only given to the man to sleep with him but to be his inseparable companion; for marriage encompasses all realms and needs of life."[16] Above all he emphasized that in sexual intercourse

---

14. "The Westminster Confession of Faith," chap. 10.4, in *The Confession of Faith of the Presbyterian Church in the United States* (Richmond: General Assembly of the Presbyterian Church in the United States, 1965), p. 68.

15. Cf. Jack Hughes Robinson, *John Calvin and the Jews* (New York: Peter Lang, 1992).

16. André Biéler, *L'homme et la femme dans la morale calviniste* (Geneva, 1963), p. 37.

there is neither domination nor subordination. "Paul demands here of the woman neither obedience nor submission."[17] However, Calvin shared the view that God has given man and woman different roles: "the woman is meant to be the helper of the man, the man should prove himself her leader and head."[18] It was only in the nineteenth and twentieth centuries that these perspectives began gradually to shift. Increasingly the consensus emerged that the fundamental equality of men and women must become visible in the life of both church and society. Being one in Christ ought to apply not only in principle but also in fact and truth. In particular, women ought to be able to be ordained to the offices of the church. Earlier generations had considered it obvious that the ordained offices were reserved for men. Since the beginning of the twentieth century, however, more and more Reformed churches have become convinced that this practice cannot stand up to the biblical witness.

5. It is true that Reformed churches have emphasized from the beginning the church's responsibility for social justice. Both Zwingli's and above all Calvin's social and political activities witness eloquently to this emphasis. The conviction that God's Word applies to all realms of human life is a constant Reformed theme through all the centuries. And yet the Reformed tradition has progressed decisively in the last few decades in this regard as well. The realization that the social reality is located within an ongoing process of change has sharpened the consciousness of the fact that the church is involved in this process, whether it wants to be or not. Thus it is not enough that each individual member of the church practice the "virtue of righteousness"; it is also not enough that the church call to mind the great principles of secular justice while leaving their application within social reality to individual members. Rather, the church must ask itself how it as a community can participate in and influence the process. How does the church relate to the powers which determine social processes? Over and over it has had to recognize bitterly that, through its complicity with certain social groups and events, it has shared in the guilt of oppression and injustice.

The question to what degree the church's witness necessitates participation in the struggles between forces in society has become increasingly urgent. The church has a critical function to fulfill in society, not only in words but also in deeds. The first priority, therefore, is analysis: the church must examine itself to determine the social forces with which it is linked. The Protestant Federation of France has undertaken this experiment in an exemplary way.[19] Above all, however, the church must manifest itself as a critical-liberating com-

---

17. Biéler, p. 46.
18. Biéler, p. 37.
19. "Eglise et Pouvoirs," *Bulletin du Centre Protestant d'Etudes de Genève* 165 (1971).

munity. The urgency of this task is mentioned in several newer confessions. In the confession of the Presbyterian Church of the USA, one reads that

> God's redeeming work in Jesus Christ embraces the whole of man's life: social and cultural, economic and political, scientific and technological, individual and corporate. It includes man's natural environment as exploited and despoiled by sin. It is the will of God that his purpose for human life shall be fulfilled under the rule of Christ and all evils be banished from his creation.[20]

Confronted with the system of apartheid, the Dutch Reformed Mission Church of South Africa declared (1982/86):

> We believe . . . that God by his life-giving Word and Spirit will enable his people to live in a new obedience which can open new possibilities of life for society and the world. . . . We believe that the Church as the possession of God must stand where he stands, namely against injustice and with the wronged; that in following Christ the Church must witness against all the powerful and privileged.[21]

6. The theme of the Holy Spirit was treated in the classical Reformed confessions with tremendous caution. In several, such as the Second Helvetic Confession and the Westminster Confession, the Spirit does not even merit an entire chapter. The Spirit is mentioned in sections about the Trinity, but the working of the Spirit is referred to only in reference to vocation and sanctification. For the most part attention is devoted to the appropriation of faith. The Heidelberg Catechism, for instance, limits its statements about the Holy Spirit to the lapidary response: "[I believe] first, that, with the Father and the Son, he is equally eternal God; second, that God's Spirit is also given to me, preparing me through a true faith to share in Christ and all his benefits, that he comforts me and will abide with me forever."[22] It is true that Calvin himself developed a rich doctrine of the Holy Spirit. He not only sees in the Spirit the power which produces faith, but unfolds his trinitarian understanding consistently to speak of the Spirit's efficacy in creation and redemption: "All divine work in its becoming-effective is the working of the Holy

20. United Presbyterian Church in the USA, "Confession of 1967," pt. III, in *Reformed Witness Today*, p. 217.

21. Dutch Reformed Mission Church, "The Confession 1982," in *A Moment of Truth: The Confession of the Dutch Reformed Mission Church, 1982*, ed. G. D. Cloete and D. J. Smit (Grand Rapids: Wm. B. Eerdmans Publishing Co., 1984), pp. 3-4.

22. Heidelberg Catechism, q. 53, in *The Heidelberg Catechism* (Philadelphia and Boston: United Church Press, 1962), p. 53.

Spirit."[23] Yet he also believed that the fullness of the gifts of God spoken of in the New Testament had been given to the church primarily in its early years. They were intended "to adorn the beginning of the Reign of God and earn prestige for the Gospel"; in later eras of the church, however, one can expect to encounter gifts of healing, prophecy, tongues, and exorcism only in exceptional cases.[24] This early caution — presumably caused by the struggle with the "enthusiasts" — conflicted too severely with the scriptural witness to be maintained for long. To the degree that Reformed churches became aware of the historical development of the church, they have also had to take up anew the topic of the Spirit. Above all, in the twentieth century the understanding of the church has unfolded more and more from this background. Recent confessions give the theme expansive treatment. The confession of the Presbyterian Church in the Republic of Korea, for example, states: "The Holy Spirit gives varieties of gifts for the common good of the community of believers . . . includ[ing] wisdom, love, gifts of healing, knowledge, the creative arts and service."[25] Numerous Reformed churches are according the theme of the Spirit more importance because they are being confronted by Pentecostal churches; this encounter is necessitating in more and more countries a new emphasis on the biblical message of the Holy Spirit.

These examples could easily be multiplied. The themes touched on here suffice, however, to show that an appropriate answer to the question of the essence of the church can only be given on the basis of the entire tradition. The insights won over the course of centuries and in the struggles of the present must all be included. As a living tradition, the Reformed tradition will never be sealed off forever. It is true that Reformed churches continually wrestle with the temptation to make definitive, as "the" Reformed answer, some particular stage of insight. But all attempts of this sort have proven short-lived. In each new situation it is the will to *be* church which has repeatedly liberated new impulses and opened the tradition to new points of departure.

Unity, Diversity, and Fragmentation

This history of the Reformed tradition has, however, not culminated in unity; rather, since the sixteenth century each era has brought its own new schisms.

23. Werner Krusche, *Das Wirken des Heiligen Geistes nach Calvin* (Göttingen: Vandenhoeck & Ruprecht, 1957), p. 339.

24. One finds statements in this regard primarily in Calvin's commentary on Acts, cited by Krusche, pp. 329-31.

25. Presbyterian Church in the Republic of Korea (PROK), "New Confession (1972)," V. 4, in *Reformed Witness Today*, p. 81.

Today Reformed churches are more divided, even fragmented, than those of nearly any other confessional tradition. The reason for this is that neither in their understanding of the church nor in their spirituality or the structures they have developed are Reformed churches equipped to locate their ongoing struggles over new insights *within* a broader unity. The unavoidable tension between fixed tradition and new initiatives has not been successfully kept in balance: new insights have almost always led to new churches. While the one side defended the original truths, the other side claimed to be continuing the Reformation. From the beginning, the journey has been characterized by the continuous formation of new churches. Some of these divisions have subsequently been overcome; most, however, have been maintained down to the present. Thus, new insights have not been available to the whole tradition but have been represented only by particular communities; genuinely Reformed perspectives were made into the banners of opposing camps. The result of this fragmentation has been that the tendency toward sectarianism which always seems to cling to Reformed churches has been further intensified.

All of this makes answering the question of the Reformed understanding of the church much more difficult. Encounter with the Reformed tradition cannot take place within an ecclesial community but rather consists of a complicated conversation with and between different communities, each of which emphasizes particular aspects of an understanding of the church. Both theological reflection and common witness in the ecumenical movement are crippled by this state of affairs. A true picture of the nature and mission of the church can only be given when the divided Reformed churches have come to some understanding among themselves. Thus, an attempt at a common answer to these questions presupposes a transition among Reformed churches.

The necessity of such a transition was strongly emphasized already in the nineteenth century by the American theologian John Williamson Nevin (1803-86), the true father of "Mercersburg Theology." He was convinced that the accelerating fragmentation he saw was the result of a superficial understanding of the church. The descendants of the Reformers had lost consciousness of the fact that the church is God's creation in history, preceding all human initiative. The Reformers themselves were clear that the church, the body of Christ, is the place in which God's salvation becomes present in history, and that for this reason no one comes to faith and Christian life except by belonging to this community which encompasses all of history. Calvin was able to refer to the church as "Mother": "let us learn even from the simple title 'mother' how useful, indeed how necessary, it is that we should know her. For there is no other way to enter into life unless this mother conceive us in her womb, give us birth, nourish us at her breast, and lastly, unless she keep us under her care and guidance until, putting off mortal flesh, we become like the angels [Matt. 22:30]."[26]

In the course of ongoing developments, however, this faith increasingly disintegrated. The forces released by the Reformation separated themselves further and further from their origins and led to a growing subjectivization and individualization of the church; in this way they laid the foundation for the establishment of continually new "sects." The forces of the church of Christ are nevertheless stronger than this movement. Precisely as the movement toward separation begins to accelerate, it testifies unintentionally to God's own presence. According to Nevin, the condition for speaking rightly of the church is the remembrance that the church

> is . . . a new supernatural creation, which has been introduced into the actual history of the world by the Incarnation of Jesus Christ; and which is destined to go on, causing "old things to pass away and all things to become new" [Rev. 21:4-5], till it shall triumph fully in the end over all sin and death, and the whole world shall appear transformed into its image and resplendent with its light.[27]

This divine creation unfolds within history; the church on earth is a process in which its own inner reality becomes ever newly visible. No matter how much it may change in the course of time, it is always the same one communion overarching all of history.

The church strives for unity. Jesus interceded in prayer for the unity of the church:

> Wonderful words, to be understood only by living in communion with the heart of Jesus himself. If such was the spirit of Christ, the spirit of the Church must necessarily be the same. The whole Church then must be regarded as inwardly groaning over her own divisions . . . as though Christ were made to feel himself divided, and could not rest till such unnatural violence should come to an end.[28]

The separation cannot be overcome by various programs and projects: the establishment of a new "antisect party" would, like the "Christ party" in Corinth, simply lead to the formation of further sects. The presupposition for the unity of the church is the overcoming of that spirit which negates the church, discarding it as a merely outward form and abandoning it to the fluctuations of

26. Calvin, *Institutes* 4.1.4.

27. James Hastings Nichols, ed., *The Mercersburg Theology* (New York: Oxford University Press, 1966), p. 58.

28. Nichols, p. 43.

personal judgment. "There can be no Church without Christ, but we may reverse the proposition also and say, no Church, no Christ."[29] The incarnation is robbed of its significance if this fact is not seen in its development in the world, that is, in the church.

Much within these statements is bound to the thinking of the nineteenth century. Examples include the differentiation between church as idea and as historical reality, the conception of the church as an idea unfolding within history, and above all the unbroken trust in a progress which leads rung by rung to a higher future. And yet the heart of Nevin's message remains relevant. Prior to every thought *about* the church must stand the recognition *of* the church; prior to every attempt to make the church and its message effective must take place a turning to that "true Church, the Mother with whom all the believers must live in communion." Only on this basis can there be any meaningful conversation about the Reformed understanding of the church.

What Is There to Ponder in This Conversation?

In order to move forward in this discussion and reach a common response, it is important to be aware of the internal tensions which characterize the Reformed tradition and in particular its understanding of the church. These tensions are not arbitrary but have their basis in opposing emphases which are inherent to the Reformed tradition from the outset, or which have developed within its history. Rather than bringing forth a fruitful and edifying relationship, these tensions have continually triggered separation. A Reformed answer to the question of the understanding of the church must find a way to represent both sides of the tension simultaneously, without allowing the polarity to harden into contradiction. Any response which neglects this imperative will inevitably enshrine existing tensions and perhaps even contribute to the formation of new churches. Each of the opposing emphases has its own dynamic and, taken alone, can lead to one-sided conclusions. The task of Reformed theology consists of holding them together in such a way that the temptations and dangers within them do not take root. This task needs attention not only on the level of theological reflection but also (and perhaps even more so) on the level of spirituality. This is so because perspectives that have been made theologically understandable are not thereby necessarily appropriated spiritually. Reformed spirituality has the tendency to think and act in polarities. The legacy of contradiction is anchored so deeply within the Reformed tradition that one-sidedness is spontaneously perceived as clarity. Even its language is satu-

29. Nichols, p. 66.

rated with this legacy. In order to develop a more all-encompassing image of the church, it is therefore necessary to develop a spirituality and a language which are able to resist the temptation inherent within simple oppositions.

Some of these contrasting emphases have been pointed out earlier. The following examples may serve to clarify the reflection further.

Community of the Chosen and the People of God

The theology and praxis of Reformed churches are characterized by the passion to give the glory in all things to God and God alone. The first commandment plays a central role in their life. No person and no thing should be positioned before God in such a way as to limit the glory and exclusive rule of God over church and world. God, the Father of Jesus Christ, is the only source of salvation; God is also the sole originator of the church. As little as God's grace lies within the grasp of human striving, so little is the church the result of human initiatives. The church arises and lives from the Word and Spirit of Jesus Christ. It is so utterly dependent on God's action that, strictly speaking, it can never become its own subject: it is church only by God's continually renewed devotion. The unlimited sovereignty of God in relation to humanity is expressed in the doctrine of election: God's choice, not our decision, brings about our calling. As the creation of God, therefore, in the end the church is not concretely discernible. Calvin states that "because a small and contemptible number are hidden in a huge multitude and a few grains of wheat are covered by a pile of chaff, we must leave to God alone the knowledge of his church, whose foundation is his secret election. . . . [H]ere we are not bidden to distinguish between reprobate and elect."[30]

The Reformed tradition, however, speaks with equal emphasis of the church as visible community. God places us into this community. "Just as we must believe . . . that the former church, invisible to us, is visible to the eyes of God alone, so we are commanded to revere and keep communion with the latter, which is called 'church' in respect to men."[31] Indeed, this visible community must take on a form. Like Israel in the Old Testament, it is the people of God on earth. It is called as a historical community to be a blessing for the nations. Thus the practice of discipline is essential. The building up and life of the church are similarly important. They are to correspond as completely as possible to the will of God. The church is the messianic people.

How can these two emphases stand alongside one another? They seem to

30. Calvin, *Institutes* 4.1.2 and 3.
31. Calvin, *Institutes* 4.1.7.

point in different, at times even opposite, directions. If the hiddenness of the true church is emphasized, the question immediately arises as to what degree the visible church can claim to be truly the church of Jesus Christ. The church in its visible form is relativized, a position one finds over and over among Reformed Christians. But the reverse is equally true. If the messianic mission of the church is emphasized, too much may be claimed for the visible church. The election of God may be identified too unreservedly with the church as a historical entity. The mystery of God's ways could disappear. The truly messianic could turn into the sectarian. The determination of the relationship between the invisible and visible church is therefore one of the indispensable tasks of Reformed ecclesiology. Both distortions can be avoided only by bringing the opposing emphases into balance.

Renewal and Continuity

According to the Reformed understanding, the church is a pilgrim people, gathered continuously anew by God's Word and Spirit. The experience of the Reformation shows that the church cannot rely on the external continuity of its historical existence. The church had come loose from its foundation and needed to be newly assembled. Could the same thing not recur in the Reformed church? Could it not also be so overwhelmed with sin, blindness, and error as to lose the way laid out for it? Indeed, is it not of the church's very essence that it must live in continuous renewal? It consists, after all, of human beings who now, as always, are marked by the power of sin. The church becomes visible as God's people wherever it clings to God's grace and gives space to God's freeing and healing Word. It ceases being the church of Jesus Christ whenever his Word is replaced with its own projects.

Yet, does this mean that the church of Jesus Christ at certain times ceases to exist in historical form, so that one cannot speak of unbroken continuity? From the beginning, Reformed theology has vehemently resisted this conclusion. The church has at all times existed as a historical entity. "For even though the whole human race has from the very beginning been corrupted and vitiated by Adam's sin, from this polluted mass, as it were, He ever sanctifies certain vessels unto honor [Rom. 9:23], that there may be no age that does not experience his mercy."[32] And the Heidelberg Catechism states with conscious emphasis: "I believe that, *from the beginning to the end of the world,* and from among the whole human race, the Son of God . . . gathers, protects, and preserves for himself . . . a congregation chosen for

---

32. Calvin, *Institutes* 4.1.17.

eternal life."[33] Although external continuity (in particular the apostolic succession) does not allow one to determine the continuity of the true church, nevertheless this true church is no less a historical reality. It rests on the promises of God, to which we cling in faith.

These two assertions stand in tension with one another. How can (on the one hand) the false security which accompanies a simplistic appeal to the tradition be overcome without (on the other hand) losing consciousness of God's faithfulness toward the church? How can freedom for the Word of God and for new initiatives in the life of the church be combined with respect for the church as it has preceded us? On the one hand, Reformed churches have a tendency to value the legacy of the past too lightly; to the extent that they appeal to the experience of the Reformation, they are relatively quick to latch onto innovations. On the other hand, they can also commit themselves decisively to traditions which in their eyes represent the true church but which are in fact anomalous traditions. Within the communion of Reformed churches one may find both the most "progressive" and the most "conservative" churches. A constructive use of the tension between renewal and continuity of the church is thus of decisive significance for Reformed churches.

Scripture, Spirit, and Church

Reformed churches emphasize the sole authority of Scripture. In their struggle against a church which opposed reform by calling on tradition and the authority of ecclesial office, the Reformers made their case on the basis of the biblical witness. For them the most important thing was not the principle of *sola Scriptura* in and of itself. Rather, the appeal to Scripture was much more the means to establish the sole lordship of Christ in the church. In the debate over what God's Word had to say to the church, Scripture was used as a referee. The early confessions speak first and foremost of the Word of God and mention Scripture as the foundation for proclamation and for debate, which was to be conducted *in* the church. Only in later confessions, initially in the First Helvetic Confession (1536) and then more completely in the Second Helvetic Confession (1566) and above all in the Westminster Confession (1647), was the reference to the authority of Scripture placed above all other statements. Scripture, inspired by the Holy Spirit (one now reads), is the authority which "alone deals with everything that serves the true knowledge, love and honor of God, as well as true piety and the making of a godly, hon-

---

33. Q. 54, in *The Heidelberg Catechism*, pp. 54-55.

est and blessed life."[34] As before, of course, the clear distinction between Word and Scripture is upheld. "The preaching of the Word of God is the Word of God," the Word which thus is proclaimed *within* the Church.[35] Yet, over time Scripture became an authority which stands like God's Word *over against* the church, containing the whole truth and pointing the way to life for the church as a whole and for all its members in all realms of life. The Scripture is its own interpreter. "The infallible rule of interpretation of Scripture," says the Westminster Confession, "is the Scripture itself; and therefore, when there is a question about the true and full sense of any scripture (which is not manifold, but one), it may be searched and known by other places that speak more clearly."[36]

If a comprehensive Reformed statement on the church is to be achieved, the question about the relationship of Scripture and church still needs clarification. How is the Spirit who blows through the Scripture related to the Spirit who in past and present times is at work in the church? To what extent is the Scripture the book of the church; that is, to what extent does it contribute to an understanding of the ecclesial community? The emphasis on the authority of Scripture as a voice independent of the church in every regard can easily turn into a fundamentalist understanding, and there can be no doubt that this is characteristic of Reformed churches, recurring constantly even to the present. Rather than Scripture being used as a witness, it is understood as an internally consistent system. One of the lines of separation between Reformed churches has this misunderstanding at its core.

In order to break free of this problem, it is not enough to point out the historical character of the biblical witness. As long as the historical-critical use of the text fails to bring about a new conception of the relation between Scripture and church, it, too, simply mirrors "fundamentalist" features: it still treats Scripture as if it were a self-contained document, though now a historical one. How then can the scriptural witness come to life in the church? How can it be taken up into the witness of the church? It is becoming increasingly clear that Reformed churches are inadequately equipped for this process. They do not possess structures which could steer the discussion about the scriptural witness into common paths and lead to common conclusions. Now, as always, the effort to interpret Scripture stands in unmediated tension with ecclesial praxis.

34. First Helvetic Confession (1536), cited in *Reformed Confessions of the Sixteenth Century,* ed. with historical introductions by Arthur C. Cochrane (Philadelphia: Westminster, 1966), p. 100.

35. Second Helvetic Confession (1566), in *Reformed Confessions of the Sixteenth Century,* p. 225.

36. "Westminster Confession," chap. 1.9, in *The Confession of Faith,* p. 30.

It is noteworthy that newer Reformed confessions are beginning to take account of this question. Nearly all newer texts distinguish emphatically between the Word of God and the scriptural witness, and they point to the role of the Spirit and the Spirit's working *within* the church to bring forth God's Word for the life and witness of the church. While earlier confessions saw the role of the Spirit in anchoring scriptural truth in believers' hearts, a few newer confessions even speak of the Holy Spirit and the church *before* coming to speak of Scripture. This indicates a new perspective. Even so, within the life of Reformed churches the debate still has a long way to go.

The Church on the Local, National, and Universal Levels

The Reformed tradition has always emphasized both sides: the church as the people of God in the place where God's Word is preached and heard, and the church as the universal community encompassing the entire world. The people of God are in all places. They encompass "the entire crowd of those who cling to God's truth and the teaching of his Word." The Heidelberg Catechism states that God gathers God's people "from among the whole human race." Reformed theology has however always directed its attention first and foremost to the church in its local manifestation. It is church in the full sense of the word. As important as is its belonging to the universal communion, it does not depend on this in order to be church. Wherever Jesus Christ is present through Word and sacrament, there *is* the church. "Under [this universal church] are thus included individual churches, disposed in towns and villages, according to human need, so that each rightly has the name and authority of the church."[37] The local church carries the responsibility for its own confession, worship, life, and witness. Of course, it also seeks communion with other churches. Local churches come together at synods in order to consult together, make decisions, and conduct their witness. In this way they appear in various geographical, national, or regional areas as a communion of local churches.

The strong emphasis on the church as located in a particular place raises numerous questions which have never been unanimously answered in Reformed churches. There is agreement that the source of all authority in the church is Jesus Christ himself, and that all decisions in the congregation or in gathered synods must be made on the basis of the scriptural witness. But how does the local church relate to the communion of local churches? To what extent is there such a thing as a level of church "above" that of local churches? To be sure, all Reformed churches assume that the corporate speech and action of

37. Calvin, *Institutes* 4.1.9.

churches must be conceived and carried out from below. They differ, however, in their understanding of the authority given to synods. To what extent can synods speak and make decisions for local churches? In what areas do they have decision-making jurisdiction? To what extent are local churches bound by common decisions? What is the significance of a group which is at best a minority within the larger body?

Although Reformed churches are generally capable of decisions on regional and national levels, they have remained much more cautious about extrapolation onto the global level. Granted, the idea of a general council is not absent from Reformed theology, and throughout history it has led to repeated attempts at international understanding. For the most part, however, these attempts have not got off the ground. The recognition of the catholicity and universality of the church is rarely found in praxis. It is probably characteristic of Reformed churches that, compared with other confessional world bodies, the World Alliance of Reformed Churches has been noticeably less well developed. This inhibition has cost Reformed churches dearly. It has resulted in national initiatives having every door opened for them, while any effective international coordination is thwarted from the outset. It is thus one of the decisive reasons why the missionary movement has resulted in a multiplicity of churches which in many countries to this day have very little mutual connection. Reformed churches have not known how to cultivate any larger sense of belonging.

In the face of the overwhelming challenges on the international level, every Reformed communication about the church must rethink this relationship between the local and universal church. Given the consequences thus far, how can we be satisfied with mere declamations about universality?

Witness, Conflict, and Reconciliation

Witness for God's justice in all realms of social life leads unavoidably to tensions and conflict. What is the will of God? To what extent can it be unambiguously determined in a given situation? To what extent can the church's witness in certain historical situations be declared binding for the whole church? Over and over in the church the question of the boundary between dialogical openness and unequivocal clarity reemerges. The church cannot withdraw from the consequences of the witness demanded of it. In situations where God's particular concern for the oppressed and suffering is at stake, the church must take a stand and enter the debate both among its own ranks and in the surrounding world. There can be no dubious compromises for the sake of peace and unity. Nevertheless, the church must also be concerned about the preservation of the community. It must devote all it has to ensure that the taking of sides associated with witness for divine justice never degenerates into permanent divisions. The church must make clear that its primary concern is to witness to God's love for all people, even those it opposes. In dealing with them, it must show that alongside all its decisiveness it is aware of the inadequacy of its witness.

Experience demonstrates how easily debates over social issues can lead, especially in Reformed churches, to divisions which extend far beyond the immediate occasion for the debate. This has to do with the fact that, on the one hand, confession and prophetic action are brought together more closely in Reformed churches than in other confessions, but also, on the other hand, that their awareness of the community given in Christ is not sufficient to resist the forces leading to division. How can the church be a place simultaneously of clarity and of reconciliation? How can it become clearer that God's ways are never completely identical with the paths emerging from human insight and choices? To what extent is the worshiping community of praise distinguishable from the community of confession and confessional action? Elucidation of these questions is one of the urgent desiderata of an appropriate Reformed ecclesiology.

CHAPTER 18

Presbytery and Leadership in the Church

Walter Herrenbrück

The following contribution has a limited and humble goal: it aims to link a traditional element of Reformed ecclesiology — namely, the assertion of a structured ministry (the clustering of various duties and functions in collegial congregational leadership), with particular attention to the office of elder — with the conceptions and intentions of a so-called missionary congregational structure as it was developed in an ecumenical study program in the 1960s. "The Church for others" was its motto; it spoke of "small congregations" and "discipleship groups" which transcend parish boundaries and help people to discover and, with others, celebrate shalom at the place where they live.[1] Jürgen Moltmann wrote that "[i]n the missionary church the widow who does charitable works belongs to the same mission as the bishop who leads the church, or the preacher of the gospel."[2] Such reflections assumed that the structures of the church had to change and that the usual congregational structures and church constitutions had proved to be outdated.

That may be true. In any case, ecumenical momentum for a structural reform of the church along the lines of the "missionary congregation" has not been very effective. It has remained at the level of preliminary documents, at least in the German churches that have a constitution. This has occurred despite the fact that its proponents voiced undeniably important ideas and in-

---

1. Cf. Wolfgang Ratzmann, *Missionarische Gemeinde: Ökumenische Impulse für Strukturreformen* (Berlin: Evangelische Verlagsanstalt, 1980), pp. 177ff.

2. Jürgen Moltmann, *The Church in the Power of the Spirit: A Contribution to Messianic Ecclesiology,* trans. Margaret Kohl (Minneapolis: Fortress, 1993), pp. 10-11.

Translated by Lisa Dahill.

sights, which were biblically and theologically well grounded and which responded to the current situation. Some of those included: the idea of mission as *missio Dei;* the idea that mission is a concern of the entire congregation; the idea that the "laity" are the real missionaries: witnesses who testify to and embody the gospel in the midst of the society in which they live; the idea of the missionary group as a community living as the sign of shalom within society and perceiving their responsibility for the world.

It remains to be asked whether in the 1960s people actually recognized correctly what was needed, yet in their thinking and planning somehow overlooked the lived reality of churches and congregations, so as merely to make further demands on them without any real change. Thus another question emerges: whether it would be more appropriate to examine given church structures which have evolved within the tradition as to their possible suitability for the congregation of Jesus Christ today, not in order to stabilize it as "state church" *(Volkskirche)* in the sense of a "civil religion of society" — here again, referring to the German situation — but to discover and develop it as a "missionary congregation" within the *Volkskirche.* Perhaps the "old growth" structures need not be clear-cut in order for ecumenical insights still to be transplanted into local congregations.

With these questions in mind, I plan to examine the office of elder, or presbyter, as an element of the leadership and building up of the congregation. I hope to show that (1) the "office of the laity" (which the documents call for), the service of volunteers in our congregations, and the service of staff members (which is indispensable for the building of the congregation) all have an example in the "office of elder," a good role model for Christian life devoted to the building up of the congregation; and that (2) elders and pastors as collegial congregational leadership could understand themselves in a position of service, playing a highly exemplary role for other groups in the congregation. After all, congregational leadership is finally nothing other than a certain form of congregational life itself.

The Office of Elder in the Church Order of Jülich-Berg (1671)

Using a document from the history of the church "reformed according to God's Word," we will first be reminded of how the office of elder was determined and developed practically in the Reformed tradition. It is not possible here to compile an exhaustive account examining all Reformed confessional writings and church orders; a look at *one* church order must suffice. We must keep clearly in mind here that, according to the Reformed understanding, church order belongs intrinsically to the doctrine of the church, and that Reformed church order understands itself "as an order of obedience heard in the preached Word."[3]

We shall examine a church order of the Lower-Rhine Reformed realm of the seventeenth century: it is entitled "The Church Order of the Christian-Reformed Congregations in the Provinces of Jülich and Berg," or Jülich-Berg Church Order of 1671 (abbreviated JBCO),[4] and is an order of the second or third Reformed generation. By this time the battles of the Reformation were already a part of the past, and many Reformed confessional writings existed; the first phase of Reformed confessional formation had come to an end. The JBCO clearly reveals the examples to which it is indebted, particularly the *Confession de Foy* and the *Discipline ecclesiastique* of 1559. I cannot here go into the volatile history of the JBCO's formation, nor the history of the Reformed Free Church of the Lower-Rhine — though it is remarkable in many ways — whose first general synod gathered in 1610. Still worth reading is the investigation by the legal scholar, historian, synod member, imperial and state parliamentary representative, and imperial minister of justice Johann Viktor Bredt, in which he outlines the "Constitution of the Reformed Church in Cleve-Jülich-Berg-Mark."[5] Bredt points out the general neglect of the fact "that the Lower Rhine was the only place in which a church was successfully established which did not rest on the principle '*Cuius regio eius religio*,' but rather on the will of the people. . . . In Cleve-Jülich-Berg-Mark the Reformed confession was pushed through under a Catholic nobility which, although overall rather tolerant, in no way favored the Reformed faith."[6] It is the case that the Lower Rhine congregations conceived of their shape and their constitution through communal listening to the Bible, through communal internalization of the Reformed tradition (whereby the Heidelberg Catechism played a decisive role), and through synodical decisions. And it was then the general synod which, following an intensive process of discussion, adopted the church order in 1671.

There is no reason to idealize the JBCO. It cannot be overlooked that the general synod mentioned above was overwhelmingly composed of pastors and

---

3. Hans-Helmut Esser, "Verwerfungen und Abgrenzungen innerhalb der Ämterlehre der Reformierten Bekenntnisschriften," in *Lehrverurteilungen, kirchentrennend?* ed. K. Lehmann and W. Pannenberg, vol. 3 (Freiburg im Breisgau: Herder; Göttingen: Vandenhoeck & Ruprecht, 1990), p. 239. Esser's essay provides both a short and well-informed summary of the essence of Reformed church order as well as the most important texts from the Reformed confessions on the doctrine of church offices.

4. Found in *Bekenntnisschriften und Kirchenordnungen der nach Gottes Wort Reformierten Kirche*, ed. Wilhelm Niesel (Munich: Chr. Kaiser, 1938), pp. 298-325.

5. Johann Viktor Bredt, *Die Verfassung der reformierten Kirche in Cleve-Jülich-Berg-Mark* (Neukirchen: Buchhandlung des Erziehungsvereins, 1938).

6. Bredt, p. 18.

that the concerns of pastors were taken more seriously and received more attention than those of elders. As is so often the case, praxis lagged behind correct insight; the pastors were thus in fact still the ministers determining the synod, and the elders became their assistants and underlings. Yet it was conceived and desired to be different — the JBCO demonstrates this. And as a document of such presbyterial-synodical intent, it is of interest here.

1. "Every church should have its consistory or church council, consisting of pastors, elders, and, as necessary, of deacons, who then . . . as need demands should meet together to promote the edification of the church, and to order what is good and abolish what is evil within it."

Thus does section 74 of the JBCO determine and describe the essence and task of the presbyterium. The presbyterium reflects how the constitution of the church is to be understood: the church is a "functional communion": "It comes about and exists so that certain functions will be fulfilled. . . . [These] functions require our attention because of the mission given to us, namely to preserve the doctrine of the holy Gospel in its purity, to support the Church, to guide the young, to care for the poor."[7] To attend to these functions means to do so communally. The JBCO underlines this in several ways. The manner in which the JBCO describes, for instance, the sequence of events in a meeting of the presbyterium bears in mind the idea of community: the meeting is opened with "prayer"; those "present and absent" are noted; "orders of business" are presented; "the positions voiced" on each matter are weighed; what is decided is incorporated into the "consistorial book"; the meeting is closed with prayer (§74). The fact that one is to "abstain from . . . unnecessary chatter in this meeting" is explicitly mentioned. It is also mentioned that "whatever cannot be settled should be brought to the Class" (§76). The meetings of the Class are

---

7. Jan Weerda, "Ordnung zur Lehre: Zur Theologie der Kirchenordnung bei Calvin," in *Calvin-Studien,* ed. J. Moltmann (Neukirchen: Neukirchener Verlag, 1960), pp. 162-63. The question of how the Reformed doctrine of ministry corresponds to Scripture cannot be explored here. The Reformed confessional writings "declare their ordering to be apostolic and therefore effective," states H.-H. Esser, referring to the Second Helvetic Confession 17 (Esser, p. 240). Calvin's *Institutes* derive the various ministries from Scripture, primarily from Eph. 4:11 (*Institutes of the Christian Religion,* ed. F. L. Battles and J. T. McNeill [Philadelphia: Westminster, 1960], 4.3.4ff.). Calvin speaks here of the "institution by Christ." If this is understood absolutely and literally, then such ordering would have to be taken as definitive. A church reformed according to God's Word, with ministries instituted by Jesus Christ, could then hardly be in communion with other churches which do without such ministries and thereby deny Christ's institution. But the "institution by Christ" is probably not meant to be understood so rigidly. And Weerda is likely correct when he writes, "A constitution for mission has the character of divine right through its relationship to God's salvific will, not simply through its establishing exactly four ministries" (p. 163).

attended by every congregation — generally each congregation is represented by a pastor and an elder (§80).

The presbyterium is an expression of the community which is essential for Reformed congregations. This does not mean that a community of human initiation grounds the church — the ground of the church is Jesus Christ himself and Jesus Christ alone. It simply means that this community brings to expression where and how a congregation gathers and how it becomes concrete. And when the church is referred to, the congregation is meant.[8] The congregation is not a part of the church, a "piece of Church"; rather it *is* the church. It is a congregation among and with other congregations. The JBCO explicitly asserts: "There shall also be no church above another, no pastor above another, having on account of his ministry some sort of primacy and power" (§33).

All of this is an expression of community as it is found in the New Testament images of "church": one body, many members. It corresponds to the fact that the Reformed congregations of the Lower Rhine originated not by decree of the rulers but by the faith decision of individual congregational members. This does not negate the fact that Jesus Christ is also the Lord of the church and that the congregation is more than the sum of pious individuals. Yet the formation of the congregation occurs "on a personal, not a territorial, basis."[9] This had a fourfold impact on congregational life.

a. The celebration of the Lord's Supper was a "communal celebration."[10] The Lord's Supper can only be celebrated in the community; it is therefore not proper to serve it to an individual at home. In celebrating the Supper the community of those who come to the table becomes the body of Christ, which has many members. For this reason the Lord's Supper should "not be readily offered to individuals," the JBCO states. It allows, however, explicitly for a "home communion" when, for instance, a believer, "because of bodily weakness," is "not [able to] attend the Holy Lord's Supper in the public congregation." In this case the Supper should — at the same time as the worship service of the gathered congregation — be celebrated in the home of the sick person "with two or three fellow believers" (§119). "Those who are so afflicted with dangerous, contagious diseases and plagues, or terrible infirmities," are not simply excluded from the Lord's Supper; rather there is to be found a form and place for celebration of the meal where these people too may "receive the Lord's Supper" (§125).

---

8. " 'Congregation' is actually the ever concrete form of the Church, and the Church is not somewhere above the locally gathered congregation, but rather 'in, with, and under' it." Otto Weber, *Versammelte Gemeinde*, 2nd ed. (Neukirchen-Vluyn: Neukirchener Verlag, 1975), p. 33.

9. Bredt, p. 51.

10. Bredt, p. 19.

b. In close connection with the celebration of the Lord's Supper is the "household visitation." Pastors and elders are to complete "annually at least one or two" such house visits "before the Communion." This visitation is intended to ascertain "whether the communicants are upright . . . in their faith"; they are asked about a "godly way of life" and whether they are living together "in peace and concord." Whatever could hinder people's coming to the Lord's Table is to be addressed (§128). The home visit has a double function: in the narrower sense to encourage the preparation for the Lord's Supper; in the broader sense to keep the community intact and to lead any wandering sheep back to the flock. Regular home visitation among the Reformed was and is therefore not merely pastoral care for individuals (to be conceived of from the individual's perspective); it was always also a contribution to the building up and preservation of the community (to be conceived of from the perspective of the congregation's edification).

c. The preservation of the community is the content and intention of church discipline. "All members of the Reformed churches should, without distinction or regard to persons or qualities, be submitted to the discipline of the church, and the pastors and elders should use the office of the keys against them when it is necessary, right, and according to the direction of the teaching of Christ our Lord" (§133). The congregation, as a communion of those who have voluntarily decided to belong to it, can only exist as a living community. "I believe that I am and forever will remain a living member of it eternally," affirms the Heidelberg Catechism (q. 54).

According to the JBCO, the congregation's life requires church discipline for preservation of the unity of faith, for education in faith, and for the building up of a *living* community, and also as an antidote for a congregation threatened by error. Such error can apply as much to doctrine as to life (§134). For the Reformed of the Lower Rhine the point was not the exercise of power and the rule of clergy over laity, but was rather the formation of a community of all those who were prepared to give God glory and to live what they believed.

An educational effect is thereby entrusted to the congregational community. Thus, following the occurrence of "an excommunication" the congregation is admonished to break off both table fellowship and everyday dealings with the excluded person, "so that he is thereby caused to be ashamed of himself and to come to knowledge of himself" (§139). There exists a clear and inseparable connection between the regulations of church discipline and questions of the Lord's Supper. Just as on the one hand the church order finds its *Sitz im Leben* in worship (to be sure, the JBCO does not directly state this, but it can be gleaned from many of its paragraphs — cf. chap. 1, "Von der Bedienung des Predigt-Amtes"), so on the other hand church discipline finds

288

its purpose in ensuring an orderly community of the Lord's Supper. The Supper is explicitly defined as "a communion together of believers with Christ" (§119).

Of course, it cannot be denied that the linking of church discipline and the Lord's Supper did not prove auspicious in practice, serving often more to obscure than to illumine the invitation to the table of the Lord; this can be seen in the widespread phenomenon of anxiety in approaching the Lord's Supper. Yet, it was the consciousness of being chosen and holding fast to one's election which gave church discipline much of its spiritual impetus. The fact that church discipline often managed to be so "unspiritual" lay less in the discipline itself (as a Christian penitential practice deriving from the gospel) than in the lack of faith and disregard of the Spirit on the part of the "discipliners." Although the praxis of church discipline has not always been successful for Reformed Christians, still the concern and will to shape the community as a congregation of brothers and sisters must be acknowledged.

d. The practice of church discipline — in the sense of preservation of the community — is the primary duty of elders. The JBCO describes the office of elder and the tasks of this office precisely and comprehensively. Elders are to "watch over the whole flock" (and to do so "alongside the pastor"). Elders are to "have diligent oversight of the doctrine, life, and conduct of both the pastors and listeners." Elders are to "visit the sick, poor, widows and orphans"; they are to "comfort the discouraged and afflicted"; they are to "punish those who lead a wicked life." Elders are to "provide for the living of church workers." Elders are to be prepared to lead singing; they are to "catechize" (which basically involved questioning catechumens on the Heidelberg Catechism and passages of Scripture); they are also charged "to pray in the absence of pastors."

In sum, the office of elder thus encompasses many duties (we spoke already of home visitation in addition to those listed here). From this enumeration it also becomes clear that the picture of the elder as a grim and controlling figure marking down transgressions, beating the bushes in the hunt to track down sinners, is false and inappropriate.

2. The JBCO emphasizes that the elder consider his or her ministry to be "alongside the pastor." The task of the elder is that of "special church discipline"; that of the pastor is the "general discipline of repentance" — and this occurs above all in the preaching of the gospel.

In chapter 1 of the JBCO one reads: "A true teacher should build the congregation not only with doctrines but also with his life, and to this end should himself with heart and mind confess the Evangelical-Reformed religion and also have such knowledge of the Christian religion and its languages that he may guide and teach others and rightly dedicate the Word of God to his listeners with comfort, admonishment, punishment, and warning for the strengthening of their faith and improvement of their lives . . ." (§3).

I would point out that both offices — that of the pastor and of the elder — exist, in their own ways, to promote the building up of the congregation (JBCO §3 and §58). And at times when "a member is completely excluded from the congregation, and is then taken back into the congregation," there "the pastors and elders" act "carefully and with mature judgment" (§138) — thus, always, in concert.

The leadership of the congregation occurs in the cooperation of the offices of pastor and elder. Elders and pastors together make up the presbyterium (church council). The pastor is a coelder, to whom the distinguished "service of the Word and sacraments is entrusted." In other words, the pastor as coelder attends to his or her task in the midst of the presbyterium and thereby also within the congregation, thus not as a representative of a spiritual estate which distinguishes itself from the so-called lay estate.

For this reason it was important in church buildings "that the steps to the pulpit lead up from the church [nave] itself, so that the pastor — as coelder — visibly climbs from within the congregation up to the pulpit and does not step out from a door located behind the pulpit, like a priest."[11] The pastor is not "more" than the congregation. In enacting the ministry of preaching, the pastor stands over against the congregation. But strictly speaking, the pastor does this not as an individual but rather as the holder of the office. The congregation cannot speak the gospel to itself; it must have it proclaimed to it. It can listen for the voice of the Good Shepherd — and the Good Shepherd is Jesus Christ, who makes use of the pastor.

Although the office of elder is to be distinguished from that of pastor, it shares with the latter office responsibility for the spiritual leadership of the congregation. Seen in this way, the office of elder is an episcopal office. We must note the particular ways in which the duties cross: the elder, who participates in the function of congregational leadership, submits to the "general discipline of repentance" as this is articulated by the preaching of the gospel, thus by the holder of the preaching office. At the same time the elder exercises a "special discipline of repentance" and attends to the life of the congregation as an overseer and watchperson. This includes careful monitoring of the preaching of the gospel. Elders and pastors are aware of the fact that fundamentally it is the congregation — as a community — which has the right to discipline. This means that elders and pastors must allow themselves to be questioned by the congregation as to how they are attending to their office.

It is important to observe that the elder does not exercise this office indi-

---

11. Bredt, p. 63.

vidually: there are always numerous elders (presbyters). The elder attends to his or her duties within the presbyterium: here, as well, the importance of "community" can be recognized. To be sure, the presbyter can occasionally perform duties in the congregation as an individual. Yet this is done only as a member of the ensemble known as the presbyterium. Thus the home visitation ought generally to be done by two or three elders together (Matt. 18). The presbyterium as a community corresponds to the image of the body of Christ and that of "the gathered congregation." It is therefore no accident that the JBCO explicitly specifies that all meetings, thus also those of the presbyterium, should begin with prayer and be ended with a "thanksgiving to God" (§64).

3. While the pastor is called for a lifetime, the JBCO intends a much shorter term for the office of elder. Elders should be in office two years, and half their number should turn over annually (§59). This noteworthy fluctuation has the advantage that the greatest number of congregational members — that is, of those who possess the appropriate gifts — can be involved in the spiritual leadership of the congregation. This fluctuation in the office of elder is balanced by continuity in the preaching office. The fact cannot be denied, however, that the praxis of Reformed congregations in later centuries looked much different; some elders functioned twenty or more years in the presbyterium (and thus earned for themselves the literal title of "elder").

Once a congregation was founded, a presbyterium had to be installed. This occurred through a congregational election. Bredt points out that in the Lower Rhine elections were "carried out by the whole congregation, with a universal right to vote."[12] If there was already a presbyterium in the congregation, then the elders' places were filled as they came open by the presbyterium. Those elected (called) were announced "from the pulpit" and then — assuming no significant hindrance emerged — were "publicly" confirmed "in their office according to the church form" (§56).

An elder is to be elected (or called) in an orderly way. As in the preaching office, the *vocatio externa* — the calling issued to the elders being elected — is of constitutive importance for the office. This external calling directs that the person called (or elected) will behave in a way appropriate to this calling and by his or her actions neither disavow Jesus Christ, the Lord of the church, nor disrupt and confuse the congregational community and its witness. The *vocatio externa* is to be distinguished from the *vocatio interna*, which is a gift of the Spirit of God corresponding to the external calling. The JBCO also describes a distinctive diaconal office. It refers to deacons as guardians of the poor or "alms-trustees" (§61). The deacon administered the gathered offerings

12. Bredt, p. 150.

and gifts. He visited "the poor in their homes" and came to their assistance "comfortingly in word and deed." The election and term of office for deacons are regulated similarly to those of elders.

It is worth noticing that, alongside the "classical" offices (of pastor, elder, and deacon) already mentioned, the JBCO describes other functions which can be discerned in the congregation. Thus it speaks of those who comforted the sick and infirm, and assisted the pastors, but had no right to administer the sacraments. There were "readers" in worship: "A reader should be a schoolteacher, elder, deacon, or some other godly person" (§93). Thus we may infer that Reformed church orders — for which the JBCO is a good example — had no interest in installing fixed offices, but rather thought more in terms of biblically grounded ministries allowing for a branching out of new functions. Even though it is not mentioned in the JBCO, there was even at that time the office of "churchmaster." Churchmasters were responsible for the entire external administration of the congregation; care for the church's property, especially its building; the receipt of income; the payment of expenses. They were the finance administrators of the congregations.[13] At the same time, they were a branching out from the office of elder: they were elders with a specific function.

When looking back at the development of the Reformed church and Reformed church orders, we must conclude that the office of deacon has merged with that of elder. Given the possibility of branching out (see above), this restriction to two basic offices seems appropriate. I would point out that there must be at least two offices if one is to speak of a "structured ministry" — or, in other words, of a dually structured office by which the congregation is to be led.

If we assume this dual form of (1) the office of pastor (to which the administration of the sacraments is also entrusted) and (2) the office of elder, which with the preaching office exercises churchly jurisdiction in the community and provides for the building up of the congregation (and which monitors both the scriptural relevance of the preaching of the Word and the proper administration of the sacraments), then it is remarkable that already in Reformed church history the possibility arises of differentiation within these two offices. "Pastor" can mean one who proclaims the gospel, catechizes, comforts the sick, gives pastoral care, and evangelizes; and "elder" can mean administrator, deacon, one who cares for the poor, and can also take over the tasks of comforting the sick and of pastoral care.

4. I will conclude these historical reflections regarding the office of elder — using an old church order from 1671 — with a few summary conclusions on

13. Bredt, p. 160.

the theological significance of the office within the Reformed church and its theology.

a. Of Calvin it can be said that his doctrine of the church is "the doctrine of the ministerium."[14] Calvin spoke less often of the community but a great deal about the "ministry" (note that he uses the expression *ministerium* only rarely in his writings, preferring in general the term *munus*). What is intended by this? Most likely the fact that the church is not a collection of pious, solo Christians and is not dependent on the subjective, emotional stirrings of the individual. Rather there are structural givens, institutions, duties, and functions which are authorized to communicate and spread the Word of God and to shape, order, and lead the community.

b. The ministry is not a mandate which the congregation discovers and determines and transfers to one of its members; the ministry is also not simply derived from the "priesthood of all believers." It is much more truly something given to the congregation and established by God. This means that the ministry is a given entity, willed by God and instituted by Christ and equipped with the promises of the power of the Holy Spirit, and is therefore a "special" ministry. But what makes it special is clearly not the holder of the office, i.e., the person of the one who is called into this ministry. The office points to the One who desires the service of the ministry for human well-being: Jesus Christ. "One is your Master, Christ," says Matthew's Gospel (23:8), "but you are all siblings." Congregational leadership is performed "in the midst of the congregation" and at the same time over against the congregation.

c. The ministry is ordered from within the congregation and in reference to it. Only the person whom the congregation calls can take on the office *(vocatio externa)*. This comes to expression through calling (election) and commissioning (ordination). To a particular office, a person is called who clearly and demonstrably has the gift (or gifts) of grace required for that office. Here the tension between charisma and office can be particularly felt; it is important to point out "that Paul in 1 Cor. 12 first speaks of the gifts of the Spirit and only then of ministries."[15] Yet, not every charisma can make a "ministry" for itself. So the office as a fundamental form precedes the charisma: and the charisma makes out of the office a living service.

d. The offices of pastor and elder together form the presbyterium and attend to the spiritual leadership of the congregation. Here it is to be underlined

14. Otto Weber, "Calvins Lehre von der Kirche," in *Die Treue Gottes in der Geschichte der Kirche*, Gesammelte Aufsätze, vol. 2 (Neukirchen-Vluyn: Neukirchener Verlag, 1968), p. 35.

15. Werner Krusche, *Das Wirken des Heiligen Geistes nach Calvin* (Göttingen: Vandenhoeck & Ruprecht, 1957), p. 322.

that the preaching of the Word, church discipline, and administration of the church's property are "spiritual leadership." The offices are to be understood functionally: they intend to promote the building up of the congregation and to make possible its leadership.

In sum: (1) The ministry is a structured ministry; within it the various duties are ordered. (2) Congregational leadership is, as spiritual leadership, collegial. There is no such thing as a clergyperson who is not a coelder. (3) The presbyterium is an ensemble of brothers and sisters who are responsible for the preaching of the Word, administration of the sacraments, and education; for the administration of the congregation and of its gifts and goods; and for the preservation of community ("church discipline," "discipline of repentance") within the congregation and the empowerment of the congregation for service to society. (4) Both the office of elder and that of pastor allow for differentiation (the placing of emphases). The standpoint of collegiality dare not be lost here.

The Office of Elder and Congregational Leadership

1. In May of 1949, the General Synod of the Dutch Reformed Church formulated its "foundations of and perspectives on confession." In Article 13, paragraph 6 it conclusively states: "The life and work of the Church is ordered and led by the service of the offices through which Christ exercises his prophetic, priestly, and royal ministry among the congregation. He commissions the office-holders for this service, yet without handing it over to them in the meantime. Only in submission and obedience to the witness of Christ does this service receive the authority and promise of the office." In paragraph 7 the document continues: "By means of the office Christ wishes to prepare his congregation for the prophetic, priestly, and royal service to which all its members are commissioned. The particular ministry does not replace the ministry of believers, but rather has the mission of strengthening and preparing the congregation more and more for the fulfilling of its call, that it may become what it is: a chosen race, a royal priesthood, a holy people, that it may proclaim the virtues of the One who has called it out of darkness to His own wondrous light."[16]

Here the text draws on the traditional doctrine of ministry: "the ministry [according to the 'commentary' section] makes Christ present with the congre-

---

16. *Lebendiges Bekenntnis: die "Grundlagen und Perspektiven des Bekennens" der Generalsynode der Niederländischen Reformierten Kirche von 1949,* German trans. Otto Weber (Neukirchen: Buchhandlung des Erziehungsvereins, 1951), p. 20.

gation (as against free-church views). The office-holder stands under the Scripture and must be judged according to it by the congregation (as against Catholic conceptions)."[17] It is to be underlined that the congregation is an acting subject: the topic is the "ministry of believers." The ministries of pastor and elder serve to support and encourage such a "ministry of believers." The "structured office" exists in order to prepare the congregation as a whole for the service of being a mission congregation.

The fact that congregations are essentially mission congregations and that raising this fact to consciousness and bringing it about in practical terms belong to the tasks of the ministry and congregational leadership is, in distinction from earlier confessional and church orders, a new accent. By the way they make space for the prophetic, priestly, royal work of the risen Christ, office-holders build up the congregation and are thus at the same time examples for the congregation itself. By the way they share the gifts of grace — without competition or rivalry, but supporting and complementing one another — they demonstrate what community under the royal dominion of Christ can be. By the way they lead the congregation, they demonstrate how the congregation can be a congregation of Jesus Christ. Congregational leadership is congregational life in its fullness.

2. If the idea of the structured office in which officeholders act only with others and only as an ensemble is taken seriously, then it must be asked what diversity this ministry allows for its structuring, or what possibilities of differentiation of the offices of pastor and elder there are. Which concrete congregational duties allow themselves to be developed within the scope of the two given foundational offices in response to current needs? The overarching question at this point is not, how can a traditional church office be fit to the prevailing times? The question must be more radical: What is the task of the congregation, and what shape can a congregation have in this social context, and how does congregational leadership bring about this change?

The differentiation of the offices, the shaping of tasks, and their mutual relationship are problems ever needing to be newly addressed. Karl Barth distinguishes foundational forms of the church's *speaking* and *acting*. The congregation's speaking includes: the praise of God in worship; the sermon; education; evangelism, i.e., spreading the good news in the vicinity of the congregation; mission; and theology (in which the congregation gives account of itself and others). The congregation's acting includes: prayer, as "a foundational element of the whole action of the congregation"; "pastoral care, as the bringing forth and existence of certain personal models of Christian being and

17. *Lebendiges Bekenntnis*, p. 38.

action"; diaconal work; prophetic action, i.e., "opening of the healing truth"; and community.[18]

Barth thus names two foundational forms. These encompass (a) the realm of doctrine (to which belong the speaking of faith, celebrating faith, inquiring into the truth of faith, relating the challenges of everyday life to one's everyday confession) and (b) the realm of life (which includes ordering the life of the congregation, providing for the preservation of the community, administering property, attending acutely to the proclamation of the Word and testing it with questions, motivating people for cooperative work, opening up space, creating freedom also for minorities, and even listening to radicals, since there could be a prophetic voice here).

The foundational forms mentioned are found also in the offices of pastor and elder. The preaching office stands in relation to the realm of doctrine, the office of elder in relation to the realm of life. Both offices are inseparable from one another (just as doctrine and life are inseparable; they interpenetrate one another), yet they are to be distinguished from each other (just as life and doctrine are to be distinguished: doctrine can for instance not be replaced by life, and vice versa).

3. We must yet inquire as to the relevant possibilities of the office of elder, and how the service of elders shapes the leadership of the congregation. This inquiry will demand integration of biblical-theological foundational statements on the church (keywords: "people of God," "body of Christ," "house of living stones"), insights of the Reformed tradition, and the requirements of the present day and the contemporaneity of the church.

a. First, an elder (whether male or female) is a member of the body of Christ, and this concretely in the congregation to which he belongs and which has called him into the office of elder. Whatever he does, he does with others. In other words, he is a part of the whole and dependent on others complementing him. He does not do what everyone else does; he does what others need from him and can expect from him. His charism becomes a charism of the congregation or its leadership. This is a point to consider when calling elders and putting together the presbyterium (a presbyterium should not be too small).

b. The elder (whether male or female) takes on responsibility; she acts and speaks responsibly. She can do this only if she listens to the sermon, and does so regularly. Strictly speaking, in fact, congregational leadership takes place in the Word of the sermon, in the message of the gospel. It proceeds from

18. Karl Barth, *Church Dogmatics* IV/3.2, trans. Geoffrey W. Bromiley (Edinburgh: T. & T. Clark, 1962), pp. 865ff.

there and is then taken up by the presbyterium. As one who listens to the sermon, the elder is in conversation with the pastor. To be sure, she cannot prescribe for the pastor what the pastor is to preach. But she can pay attention for agreement between the biblical text and the preached Word. At the same time, as one who listens to the sermon, she can push for understandability in the sermon: that it be understood by listeners, whose advocate she is, and that it correspond not only to theological principles but also to sound homiletical ones. A pastor who complains of a lack of response to his or her preaching can turn directly to the elder for help.

c. The elder bears responsibility not only for the sermon, but also for the worship of the gathered congregation. The elder does not thereby strip the congregation of its own reponsibility; he attends to it on behalf of the congregation, thereby continually reminding the congregation of its responsibility. This takes place through the careful cultivation of the community at the Lord's Table, through invitations to Sunday worship, through conversations about the shape of worship, through worship services in particular forms (in order both to underline the particularity of the gospel and to address various target groups), through an occasional "exodus" of the congregation from the church building to a hospital or park or school or barracks — the presbyter, above all, belonging consciously both to the Christian congregation and to the secular arena, knows where worship is occasionally needed, as well as where it generally is to take place.

d. The elder acts in a manner worthy of her office. And that includes acting as one who is materially and financially independent of the church. The church is not her employer. This uninhibited objectivity is part of the charisma of the elder.

e. The elder takes on responsibility in administering the congregation. An essential characteristic of church administration is the obtaining of money and the use of money. Whoever considers the former unimportant is an enthusiast; whoever neglects the latter is a miser. The elder ensures that neither extreme dominates.

The elder takes responsibility — together with the pastor — to see that administration and theology are never separated. There are hardly any actions in the presbyterium which demand more spiritual authority than that of setting up the budget. Very concrete questions must be addressed: Who receives what? With whom do we wish to share? What percent for the parsonage/manse? What percent for our partner church in Africa? Here administration becomes participation. And here the pastor (with reference to, e.g., Matt. 25:40) and the elder (with reference to, e.g., actual expenses and employee pay scales) can work together well. One must consider also how the present gifts of the congregation can be practically employed. That, too, belongs to administration: to consider whether, by using volunteer labor, some cemetery path could be laid or the church roof repaired, for free; and whether the money saved in this way could benefit someone who has "fallen among thieves." The diaconal perspective is often a good and concrete standard for church administration. Thus it can be helpful if a few of the elders in the presbyterium understand themselves in a particular way as diaconal-elders.

f. The presbyter is an example. This is meant in the sense that she does consciously and in the public eye what can be expected of every member of the congregation (and not more than that). She is an example in that she is a Christian (cf. Heidelberg Catechism, q. 32). To this belongs: speaking and acting in community; taking on challenges, clarifying positions, and making decisions; asking questions, giving voice to doubts, resisting evil; visibly standing in the discipleship of Jesus Christ.

Within the presbyterium there are majorities and minorities. The way the group deals with its minorities must also be "exemplary." The process of making decisions and the struggle for the truth take place in a collegial manner. The point is not that one person be right; it is that the group continually struggle for the truth. The courageous then speak their piece, as do those with prophetic gifts, and even those who may be off base. It is finally the Holy Spirit who leads us into all truth. And the Spirit desires to be not merely in one person, but *among* and *between* people. A presbyterium that takes such possibilities seriously will be correspondingly open.

It is sensible that meetings of the presbyterium generally not be public (this is for reasons of confidentiality). And yet a presbyterium should be always concerned about acting in a way that is publicly accessible, and involving as many people as possible in the processes of discussion and decision.

g. The elder is a "layperson." The term "layperson" is not used here in distinction from "clergy." This differentiation, which arose around the third century C.E., is unbiblical and was rightly put aside by the Reformers in referring instead to the priesthood of all believers. Rather, by the term "laity" is meant here a member of the "laos," the people of God. Laity are theologians whose theology was not acquired in the classroom. They are members of the congregation who are not ordained to the "service of Word and sacrament," yet without whom this service could not be performed.

Laypersons are representatives of the grass roots. A layperson is not a professional Christian, but is rather a Christian in his or her profession: she knows as a teacher, for instance, what being a Christian means in the school; he knows as a factory worker what being a Christian in industry means; she knows as a doctor what being a Christian means in the encounter with illness; etc. And if they do not know it, they can find out.

Some speak, not wrongly, of a "ministry of the laity." As the "office of the laity" within the congregation, this ministry becomes concrete in the office of elder. The elders enable the "laity" of the congregation to feel especially empowered. The pastor serves first and foremost the worship service on Sunday; the elder (as a layperson) serves first and foremost the worship service of daily life — and both together serve the "reasonable worship" of which Romans 12:1-2 speaks.

h. Congregational leadership always includes the congregation's willingness and preparedness to perceive the so-called challenges of the day and to open themselves to them. To be a congregation of Jesus Christ always means being a "congregation of one's time." And what the "time" brings with it, what it demands, how it circumscribes people (in mores, in the prevailing trends) — all of this can be gleaned from scientifically based analyses of the time. But such analyses are global and generalizing. The timeliness of church actions becomes concrete and rooted in the congregation through the elders, in that these consciously understand themselves as contemporary people. They detect the tensions between old and young; they are acquainted with the conversations in the pub or on the subway; they are advocates of the ordinary guy, the liberated woman — and they consciously bring that into the discussions of the congregational leadership. Woe to the pastor who has no ear for it! There are elders who establish a house circle in order to remain in conversation with people within and outside of the congregation. This is also an especially sound form of continuing education for elders.

i. The elder exercises his office without remuneration (outside of reimbursement for certain expenses). In this respect the elder is the example for all volunteer labor in the congregation. The volunteer worker (the elder) forms a conscious counterpart to the paid worker (the pastor) within the leadership of the congregation. In principle it is conceivable that a congregation or its leadership could manage without paid staff because of a lack of money, or of candidates. And it is equally conceivable that volunteers could serve even in the office of pastor. Why should a person who had studied theology not make a living as an administrative assistant or bus driver, and then in the evenings or on Sunday mornings be available for the preaching of the Word and administration of the sacraments? Here also it is important not to think only within a fixed image of a pastor, but to see congregational leadership as an ensemble which permits flexibility while maintaining the two fundamental forms spoken of earlier.

j. Congregational leadership must take place in such a way that through it — within the congregation, and as an inspiration to build up the congregation, and in the congregation's service to society — the three offices of Christ all take their turn: the prophetic office, the priestly office, and the royal office. Christ helps a Christian to be Christian: a Christian confesses; he presents himself as a thank offering; she shares (in free service to God's creatures) in the royal dominion of Christ. This occurs in the power of the Spirit. The Holy Spirit makes of the presbyterium a congregational *leadership*. And this leadership both practices Christian life and ignites congregational life. Here, as well, the elder receives an important task:

> The elder confesses what a Christian believes — and does so in creating conditions such that many can confess and live their Christianity in the congregation.
>
> The elder presents himself as someone who owes God thanks — he creates conditions such that there are spaces within the congregation where people can sing, pray, and act: spaces for groups for whom the praxis of loving their neighbor is an important fruit of their thanksgiving.
>
> The elder is a subject of the royal dominion of Christ — she creates conditions such that there are structures in the congregation which reflect this dominion of Christ. In such a congregation active peace groups, prayer fellowships, and international circles feel at home (and are not driven out of the church realm if they are uncomfortable or make a mess or cause a disturbance). The elder will cultivate a special relationship with these groups, which provide for movement and liveliness. She will test everything — and hold on to the good, as in 1 Thessalonians 5:21.

The present-day elder, as one who ignites a "missionary congregation," is (granted!) hardly to be compared to the presbyter of Geneva or Jülich of the past. But at the deepest level today's elder, as here described, is engaged in a properly developed form of congregational upbuilding and church discipline. The essence of building up the congregation consists of gathering members, supporting the discernment of and capacity for action, and glorifying God openly (and, after the removal of all images — second commandment! — presenting as a congregation a positive image). Church discipline consists of the preservation of the community: that the tendons and muscles and bones of the body of Christ do their duty well. To ensure this is, today as always, the task of the elder.

Finally: the elder is a witness, a "martyr." He can allow himself to be addressed in reference to his office of elder; he is dialogue partner for the congregation and for the public. He represents the church — and this often not by ready answers but by solidarity in seeking and questioning, yet always with the willingness to account for what the congregational leadership does and what matters in the church.

4. If the office of elder is taken seriously in this way and considered an important element of the leadership of the congregation, then three problems must be solved:

a. The congregation of Jesus Christ requires not only of those who hold the preaching office, but also of those in the office of elder, the sparking and encouragement of the gifts of grace and a solid preparation for taking on the office — not to mention an arrangement which will not lead to excessive demands on the elders. Alongside the guidance of the preached Word, elders need regular supervision and continuing education, to accompany them in their task, advise them, protect them against unjustified demands and accusations, and embolden them not to leave unchallenged the laziness and arrogance of pastors, should those ever arise.

b. Elders are to be commissioned for the service they are to exercise and installed in their office within the worship of the gathered congregation. The commissioning occurs *pro tempore* and *pro loco.* The installation in worship makes the commission of the elder public: she is presented to the congregation which called her. Together with the pastors, the elders exercise spiritual leadership; they are the bishops of their congregation. The commissioning and installation of elders must be accordingly solemn, analogous to the ordination and installation of pastors in their office, so that the equal weight of both offices is recognized.

c. The holders of the preaching office will have to learn to share the leadership of the congregation. They are coelders — no more than that. Whether this sharing will succeed and whether the marginalization of laity in the congregation can be reversed is, in any case — in the face of theologians (and their growing role) and a society which in principle wants clergy (servants of religion) more than coelders — an open question.

CHAPTER 19

Reformed Theology and Medical Ethics: Death, Vocation, and the Suspension of Life Support

Nancy Duff

On 14 December 1990 the parents of Nancy Cruzan arranged for a nurse to withdraw the feeding tube which had kept their daughter alive for seven years. An automobile accident in 1983 had left her in what doctors refer to as "a persistent vegetative state."[1] This condition indicates that no part of the brain is or ever can be operative except the brain stem, which controls only rudimentary bodily functions. For seven years Nancy Cruzan could not walk, talk, comprehend what went on about her, or respond to any outside stimuli except that which effects the most basic reflexive movements. From the time of her accident until the time of her death (twelve days after the feeding tube was removed), she had no awareness of what went on about her; furthermore, there was no chance that she would ever recover.[2]

Nancy Cruzan was not on a respirator or heart machine, nor was she receiving any treatment that could be deemed "heroic." She was simply provided the basic necessities of life, i.e., food and water. The Cruzans' request to withdraw the tube that gave their daughter the nutrition and hydration that kept her alive had to move through a Missouri probate court, the Missouri State Supreme Court, the United States Supreme Court, and back to the lower court

---

1. Often referred to as "PVS."
2. For a moving documentary regarding the Cruzan case, see "The Death of Nancy Cruzan," a Frontline PBS video.

before it was granted.[3] Right-to-life demonstrators stood outside the hospital (as they had earlier stood outside the Supreme Court) to protest the action. The chief hospital administrator as well as Nancy Cruzan's nurses disagreed with the decision to withdraw the tube. Family members of other PVS patients in the same hospital also voiced their disagreement with the Cruzans' decision.

Nancy Cruzan's case is only one of a growing number involving the question of whether withdrawing life-sustaining medical treatment is ever in order. Some cases push the issue even further, posing the question of whether one can ever actively take one's own or another's life when death is imminent and suffering is too intense to bear. There are always conflicting views about the appropriate course of action in these cases. There is no consensus regarding the morality of what has been referred to as "assisted death," "euthanasia," or "the right to die."

In searching for clarification regarding this complicated question of assisted death, some traditions find that only an ethic of absolute law adequately addresses the issue. Both the official Roman Catholic position and some Protestant groups oppose vehemently all forms of euthanasia, whether "passive" or "active."[4] Basing his stance on the affirmation of the "eminent dignity of the human person and, especially the person's right-to-life," Pope John Paul II, for instance, denounces any action which hastens the hour of death, claiming that such action "is a violation of divine law, an offense against the dignity of the human person, a crime against life and an attack on the human race."[5] While he acknowledges that once death is imminent one can reject medical treatments that "yield a precarious and painful prolongation of life," he maintains that "ordinary treatment that is due to the sick in such cases may not be interrupted."[6] According to this Roman Catholic position, withholding or with-

---

3. On 25 June 1987 the Cruzans wrote a letter, requesting the Missouri Rehabilitation Center to remove their daughter's feeding tube. The chief hospital administrator did not believe he had the right to grant such a request. A Missouri probate court granted the Cruzans' request to withdraw the feeding tube. The decision, however, was overturned by the Missouri State Supreme Court. On 25 June 1990, the United States Supreme Court upheld Missouri's right to refuse such a request if no adequate proof could be provided of the patient's stated wish not to be kept alive under such circumstances. On 2 November 1990 the first Missouri lower court heard further evidence from friends regarding Nancy Cruzan's previously articulated wish not to be kept alive in such a state. On 14 December 1990, almost four years after the original request, the Cruzans were granted permission to withdraw the tube.

4. See John Paul II, "Euthanasia: Declaration of the Sacred Congregation for the Doctrine of the Faith (May 5, 1980)," in *On Moral Medicine: Theological Perspectives in Medical Ethics,* ed. Stephen E. Lammers and Allen Verhey (Grand Rapids: William B. Eerdmans Publishing Co, 1987), pp. 440-44. Also found in *The Pope Speaks* 25 (winter 1980): 289-96.

5. John Paul II, p. 442.

6. John Paul II, p. 444.

drawing ordinary life-sustaining treatment such as that provided by a feeding tube is "always objectively wrong."[7]

In its favor such an absolute prohibition takes seriously the value of human life and our responsibility to vulnerable members of society. This position seeks to protect us from strictly pragmatic decisions that can lead to our devaluation of the lives of people who experience severe physical or mental disabilities. Nevertheless, this absolute prohibition can result in increased agony for those individuals who are kept alive against their wishes by simple or complex medical treatment. An ethic of absolute law tends to misread or overlook the particular and varied circumstances of each situation. This is witnessed in John Paul II's claim that "the pleas of the very seriously ill as they beg at times to be put to death are hardly to be understood as conveying a real desire for euthanasia." He insists that such pleas are instead "almost always anguished pleas for help and love."[8]

In direct opposition to the absolute prohibition against assisted death is a growing movement of support for "the right to die." Groups such as Concern for the Dying seek to repeal laws which prevent terminally ill patients or their families from refusing life-sustaining medical treatment. Some groups such as the Hemlock Society not only fight for a patient's right to refuse medical treatment, but also insist that people suffering from severe and permanently debilitating conditions such as Alzheimer's should have access to physician-assisted suicide. John Cobb shares this view:

> One should be able to seek guidance from those best qualified to know as to the appropriate time and as to how best to die with dignity and minimal pain. It should be socially acceptable for others to assist one in this termination. One could, therefore, assemble one's family and closest friends and bid them farewell before taking the poison or being injected with an appropriate drug.[9]

Those who defend assisted death often rely on the principles of utilitarianism to support their position.

The strength of the position favoring assisted death is found in its concern for the anguish of patients and their families who want relief from the

---

7. John Paul II, p. 442. Not all Roman Catholic moral theologians agree with this absolute prohibition. Lisa Sowle Cahill has written a provocative article disagreeing with the pope's position while remaining within a natural law argument. See "A 'Natural Law' Reconsideration of Euthanasia," in *On Moral Medicine*, pp. 445-54.

8. John Paul II, p. 442.

9. John Cobb, "The Right to Die," in *Matters of Life and Death* (Louisville: Westminster/John Knox, 1991), p. 45.

prolonged death sometimes created by medical treatment. When the healing art of medicine becomes a seemingly evil craft which prolongs the agony of death, these groups argue, it is time to stop medical treatment and perhaps even begin a process that will hasten a less painful death. While Pope John Paul II may believe that the dying person's plea for death is really a plea for compassion and understanding, many patients facing a prolonged and extremely painful death know that what they are pleading for is death.

The danger of this position lies in its potential for devaluing any life that is limited by physical or mental disabilities. If we allow people with severe disabilities access to assisted suicide, society might begin to wonder why *all* those with severe disabilities do not take advantage of the opportunity. Furthermore, one opens the door for allowing some people to argue that others no longer have the right to live. For instance, while John Cobb claims that he is referring only to the individual's freedom to choose death and not for the right to determine that others should die, he does admit that because of limited resources we may eventually have to choose to withhold treatment from someone in a vegetative state even if that person had earlier expressed wishes to be kept alive.[10] Cobb states clearly that he does not want the right to die to become the right to kill;[11] this is, however, always a potential danger of the right-to-die position.

Standing at the impasse between those who support the right to life and those who support the right to die, I hope in this essay to reflect on what Reformed theology as expressed by John Calvin and Karl Barth has to offer to this discussion. According to another Reformed theologian, Paul Lehmann, "the faith and thought of the Reformation provide insights into and ways of interpreting ethics which give creative meaning and direction to behavior."[12] That direction includes the rejection of the language of rights and focuses instead on the language of responsibility. It is my contention that the Reformed doctrine of vocation as well as Reformed theology's reflection on the place death holds in creation contribute to our definition of responsible action regarding the issue of assisted death.

---

10. Cobb, p. 66.

11. Cobb, p. 66.

12. Paul Lehmann, *Ethics in a Christian Context* (New York: Harper & Row, 1963), p. 14. For Lehmann's reflections on medical ethics, see "Responsibility for Life: Bioethics in Theological Perspective," in *Theology and Bioethics: Exploring the Foundations and Frontiers,* ed. Earl E. Shelp (Dordrecht: D. Reidel Publishing Co, 1985), pp. 283-302.

The Reformed Perspective on Death

According to Karl Barth, the gospel compels us both to admit that we are dying and yet never to fear death.[13] In admitting that we are dying, we are required to accept without qualification that when we are dead, we are *dead*. By the gospel account death involves no transmigration of the soul from one life to another, no simple transition from this state of life to that. With death all possibility of a second chance in this world is gone. What we did not accomplish in this world will not be accomplished. Nevertheless, at the same time that Christians admit honestly and without qualification the finality of death, Christians do not fear death because we put our faith in God, who is "for us where we can no longer in any sense be for ourselves."[14] According to Barth, our hope is not in the afterlife, although God promises everlasting life; our hope is not in the New Testament understanding of time. What makes us "fearless" is the One "to whom the New Testament with its understanding of time bears witness."[15] While Christians reject the Greek notion of the eternity of the soul, they affirm resurrection.

The starting point for all Christian reflection on death, therefore, is located within these two affirmations: we are going to die; we do not fear death. Reflection on the Christian perspective of death, however, will finally uncover two seemingly contradictory attitudes regarding the legitimate place death holds in creation according to the biblical and theological record.

Biblical Texts

On the one hand, the Bible teaches that death is a natural part of life and emphasizes the need for humanity to accept its finitude. Adam and Eve were never created to be immortal. In the story of the fall, we hear God say that Adam and Eve must be driven out of the garden lest they eat from the Tree of Life and become like the heavenly hosts, i.e., lest they become immortal (Gen. 3:22-23). That we are mortal, finite beings marks a difference between us and God. To rage against humanity's finitude is to deny our limitations as human beings. Such denial and rage is equivalent to those who built the Tower of Babel, seeking to be equal with God. The apostle Paul even seems to *prefer* death to life in his letter to the Philippians. Feeling hard-pressed to choose between life or death, his desire "is to depart and be with Christ, for that is far better" (Phil.

---

13. Karl Barth, *Church Dogmatics* III/4, ed. G. W. Bromiley and T. F. Torrance (Edinburgh: T. & T. Clark, 1961), p. 588.

14. Barth, *Church Dogmatics* III/4, p. 594.

15. Barth, *Church Dogmatics* III/4, p. 594.

1:21-23 NRSV). The Bible teaches us that to cling too tenaciously to life in this world, denying the reality of death or fearing death, is a form of idolatry.

Hence, it seems that one could appeal to the Bible to support claims for the right to die. Challenging those who would claim that human life has absolute value, this biblical perspective could encourage those who are near death or those whose quality of life is severely diminished to choose the appropriate time of death and willingly say farewell to this life.

On the other hand, the Bible teaches that death is the enemy. In this understanding death is not only viewed as the cessation of life, but stands for all the destructive powers of the world that cause pain and suffering by destroying life. Death stands among the "powers and principalities" and is, therefore, understood as something more than just an individual's loss of life. Paul tells us that death is a power that has dominion over the earth, and that death is an ally of sin. Death is for Paul the last enemy (1 Cor. 15:26).

This view seemingly challenges the first. We are not simply to view death as a natural part of life. Death for Christians is not a friend, not just a transition from one stage of life to another. Hence, as one poet said, we are not to "go gentle into that good night," but are to "rage, rage against the dying of the light." Jesus did not accept death, as Socrates did, willingly drinking from the poisonous cup; rather, Jesus prayed, "Let this cup pass from me" (Matt. 26:39 NRSV). Experiencing death as the enemy which separates us from God, Jesus cried from the cross, "My God, my God, why hast thou forsaken me?" (Matt. 27:46 RSV).

Here it seems that one could appeal to the Bible to support claims for the right to life. We are never to acquiesce in the destructive forces of death. Acknowledging that God has ultimate control over life as well as death, we should give people who want to die the compassion necessary to see them through their difficulties, but we should not take any direct or indirect action that would hasten their death. To do the latter is to join the forces of destruction and all that Christ stands against.

Hence the Bible makes two claims about death: we are to accept death as a natural part of life; we are to fight against death as the enemy. This contradiction (as some would call it) or dialectic (as others would see it) is reflected in the work of both John Calvin and Karl Barth.

John Calvin

Calvin does not tend to speak of death as a natural part of life or as the enemy so much as he speaks about whether Christians are to despise this life or are to celebrate life as God's good gift. Throughout his reflections on the future life, Calvin tends to echo Paul's preference for death expressed in Philippians, saying that "no one has made progress in the school of Christ who does not joyfully await the day of death and final resurrection."[16] He believes, in fact, that life itself is a kind of death, while death offers the ultimate freedom and happiness by giving us passage into the life to come:

> For, if heaven is our homeland, what else is the earth but our place of exile? If departure from the world is entry into life, what else is the world but a sepulcher? And what else is it for us to remain in life but to be immersed in death? If to be freed from the body is to be released into perfect freedom, what else is the body but a prison? If to enjoy the presence of God is the summit of happiness, is not to be without this, misery?[17]

Hence, Calvin seems to say that we are to despise this earthly life as we long for the life to come.

At the same time, however, Calvin claims that we are to hate life only to the extent that it keeps us subject to sin, and even then hatred of our sinful condition is not to lead us to be ungrateful for what God has provided us in life.[18] We are indeed to enjoy the life God has given us as a gift. Calvin was not a despiser of life or of beauty and joy. While he wants to put limits on excessive pleasure, he believes that we *should* enjoy the things God has created for us in our daily lives. Hence, we can enjoy food and clothing, trees and fruit, not just for the necessities of life they fulfill, but for the sheer pleasure they bring in taste and beauty, sight and smell.

Hence, Calvin holds that we are to despise life *and* to enjoy it. At the same time that he says we are "to accustom ourselves to contempt for the present life,"[19] he also claims that "if we recognize in it no divine benefit, we are already guilty of grave ingratitude toward God himself."[20] Calvin tends to emphasize our acceptance of death more than our resistance of it; nevertheless, he still recognizes the beauty of life which is not to be prematurely set aside.

> For he [Paul] acknowledges that he owes it to God to glorify his name whether through death or through life [Rom. 14:8]. But it is for God to determine what best conduces to his glory. Therefore, if it befits us to live and die to the Lord, *let us leave to his decision the hour of our death and life but in such a way that we may both burn with the zeal for death and be constant in meditation.*[21]

16. John Calvin, *Institutes of the Christian Religion,* ed. John T. McNeill and Ford Lewis Battles (Philadelphia: Westminster, 1960), 3.9.5.

17. Calvin, *Institutes* 3.9.4.

18. Calvin, *Institutes* 3.9.4.

19. Calvin, *Institutes* 3.9.1.

20. Calvin, *Institutes* 3.9.3.

21. Calvin, *Institutes* 3.9.4, emphasis mine.

Calvin clearly leans toward Paul's claim that "to depart and be with Christ" is "far better" than remaining in this life (Phil. 1:21-23). He does not, however, permit this preference for the life-to-come to result in either shirking our responsibilities or denying our pleasures in this world. Nor does he believe we can choose our own hour of death.

Karl Barth

Consistent with the biblical record, Barth's theology also affirms that death is both a natural part of life to be accepted by us and the enemy to be fought against.

First, one finds in Barth the admonition to accept death as a natural part of human life. Human finitude is "determined and ordered by God's good creation" and belongs to human nature as much as does birth.

> Death is man's step from existence into non-existence, as birth is his step from non-existence into existence. In itself, therefore, it is not unnatural but natural for human life to run its course to this *terminus ad quem*, to ebb and fade, and therefore to have this forward limit.[22]

It is within birth and death that each human being encounters his or her "unique opportunity." According to Barth, "We must seize this unique opportunity that is ours, not in spite of death, but in recognition that we are going to die."[23]

Barth is, however, equally emphatic in his understanding that death is the enemy. Death, which Christ overcame on the cross, is not simply a natural part of creation, but is "the condemnation and destruction of the creature, . . . the offender against God and the last enemy."[24] Barth believes that the understanding of death as "natural," "friendly," or "neutral" is alien to the New Testament. Instead, "death is the great mark of the unnatural state in which we exist," because it points to our present state of sin.[25]

Barth, therefore, claims both that death is a natural part of life *and* that it is not. Calvin holds that we must despise the world and long for the next *and* that we must not despise the world but enjoy the good fruits of creation until

---

22. Karl Barth, *Church Dogmatics* III/2, ed. G. W. Bromiley and T. F. Torrance (Edinburgh: T. & T. Clark, 1960), p. 632.

23. Barth, *Church Dogmatics* III/2, p. 632.

24. Karl Barth, *Church Dogmatics* III/3, ed. G. W. Bromiley and T. F. Torrance (Edinburgh: T. & T. Clark, 1960), p. 312.

25. Barth, *Church Dogmatics* III/2, p. 601.

God determines that our time to die has arrived. Some people will interpret these claims by Calvin and Barth as out-and-out contradictions. To the complex conversation regarding assisted death, it will seem to some that Reformed theology can only add double-talk and more confusion!

Karl Barth, however, understood that if one is concerned with truth, one cannot appeal to simplicity, because "in every direction human life is difficult and complicated."[26] Calvin and Barth affirm the seemingly contradictory claims that we are to both accept death willingly *and* resist death, because no simple formula regarding the proper attitude toward death will serve the truth. On the one hand, Reformed theology acknowledges that life is a divine gift, so that no matter what the cause of its cessation, we mourn its loss and look at death as life's defeat. On the other hand, Reformed thought is careful not to give absolute value to life nor to view the limits of humanity as evil in themselves. This "on the one hand" and "on the other" pattern of expression which so characterizes Barth's thought is necessary if one acknowledges the complexity of problems and issues brought on by the human experience of death.

The most significant point to make about this dialectical thinking regarding death is that it rejects the application of absolute moral law. Rather than saying we can never withhold life-sustaining medical treatment, it points to the need to ask in each situation whether if by continuing medical treatment we are denying our finitude or if by choosing to die we are denying the limitations of life within which God would have us live. Each case must be examined carefully to determine the responsible action appropriate to that specific situation.

In addition to rejecting the absolute prohibition of assisted death, this dual affirmation that includes the claim that death is the enemy also challenges the easy acceptance of death that is sometimes proposed by groups such as the Hemlock Society or by the pragmatic appeal of utilitarian arguments. Death is a natural part of life to be accepted readily in some situations; death is the enemy to be fought against in other situations.

In a similar fashion the Reformed doctrine of vocation challenges both the application of absolute law to each situation and the pragmatic, utilitarian idea that unproductive life is life not worth living.

The Reformed Doctrine of Vocation

In a conversation with the late Paul Lehmann, I expressed my sadness over the fact that my children are growing up so quickly. My twelve-month-old son, no

---

26. Karl Barth, *The Epistle to the Romans*, trans. from the 6th ed. by Edwyn C. Hoskyns (London: Oxford University Press, 1977), p. 5.

longer a newborn, is now walking about the house. My three-year-old toddler, no longer a baby, speaks in rather grown-up-sounding sentences. "It breaks my heart," I said, "to see my children grow up so fast." To my surprise Professor Lehmann did not respond with the sympathy of one who has experienced the same phenomenon. Instead he asked, "But you do appreciate where your children are right now, don't you?"

The intention behind Paul Lehmann's question coincides with the heart of the Reformed doctrine of vocation, which says to each of us individually, and to all of us collectively: "Your life matters; furthermore, your life matters where you are right now." To long for the "good old days" (no matter how truly good they were) or to postpone fulfilling our purpose to some time in the future is ruled out of bounds. Our lives have divinely ordained purpose where we are and who we are at any given moment.

The doctrine of vocation, of course, has usually been employed in Christian ethics to discuss moral issues in the workplace. Indeed, we cannot be true to the Reformed understanding of the doctrine of vocation unless it is concretely connected to work, for if we separate it from work, we say, in effect, that our spiritual lives have no relation to our daily secular lives. This separation is exactly what the Reformers argued against. The remarkable achievement of Reformed theology was to say that one can glorify God in the secular world of work as well as in the monastery. The doctrine of vocation affirms that *every* aspect of life is an avenue for fulfilling the purpose to which God calls us.

We cannot, however, allow the concept of "vocation" to become synonymous with "career." Our vocation cannot simply be equated with the work we do, for such an equation suggests that some people are not capable of having a vocation — e.g., retired people, people who have lost their jobs, people who cannot work because of physical or mental disabilities, people who are too young to work, etc. If our vocation (i.e., our divinely appointed purpose in life) and the work we do are identical, if we lose our job, or if we are never able to work, then our lives have no purpose.

Therefore, the doctrine of vocation refers to a much larger concept than that of human work. At the heart of the doctrine is the affirmation that we have been called into existence and called to be God's faithful people for a purpose. God created each of us with his or her own unique combination of gifts and limitations for a purpose. The doctrine of vocation, therefore, says to each of us individually and to all of us collectively, "Your life matters." It says that the life of each of us is significant in the kingdom of God.

John Calvin

The doctrine of vocation in this broadest sense cannot be separated from the Christian understanding of calling. Furthermore, it has fundamentally to do with the limitations surrounding each human life. Calvin believed that our vocation or calling is extended by God in part to put limits on human ambition and fickleness. Because human beings tend toward restlessness and the desire to "embrace various things at once," God has, according to Calvin, appointed each of us to a particular way of life with corresponding duties. "Therefore each individual has his own kind of living assigned to him by the Lord as a sort of sentry post so that he may not heedlessly wander about throughout life."[27]

Calvin believed that knowledge of these limits leads us to be at peace with who we are and where we are, "for no one, impelled by his own rashness, will attempt more than his calling will permit, because he will know that it is not lawful to exceed its bounds."

> A man of obscure station will lead a private life ungrudgingly so as not to leave the rank in which he has been placed by God. . . . The magistrate will discharge his functions more willingly; the head of the household will confine himself to his duty; each man will bear and swallow the discomforts, vexations, weariness, and anxieties in his way of life, when he has been persuaded that the burden was laid upon him by God.[28]

The weakness of Calvin's position, of course, is that it tends to counsel passivity in light of injustice. Knowing that we are not to exceed the lawful bounds of our calling can be interpreted to mean that we are not to push against the limits of injustice either. One can, however, reject any inclination Calvin has toward such passivity and still affirm his profoundly positive claim that those whom society deems worthless are not deemed worthless by God, and are, in fact, capable of glorifying the Almighty.

Furthermore, Calvin believes that even when we are required to perform a menial task, God does not consider us less worthy as a result, for "no task will be so sordid and base, provided you obey your calling in it, that it will not shine and be reckoned very precious in God's sight."[29] Calvin understood that one can glorify God no matter what lowly station or despairing situation one finds oneself in or however menial or unpleasant a task one is required to do. Again, he can unfortunately be interpreted to mean that however dire our situation in life, we should be content to glorify God and ignore human injustice.

27. Calvin, *Institutes* 3.10.6.
28. Calvin, *Institutes* 3.10.6.
29. Calvin, *Institutes* 3.10.6.

Rejection of this interpretation, however, does not cancel the more profound affirmation of the value of each human life regardless of society's evaluation of it. God has a purpose for our lives (a vocation to which we are called), no matter what stage or state of life we are in. The peasant is equally capable as the queen of glorifying God; the housekeeper is on par with the priest in praising God through her work. Or, more to the point here, the physically or mentally disabled person can glorify God equally as well as the athlete or seminary professor.

Karl Barth

Barth makes a similar connection between the idea of vocation and human limitations. According to Barth, prior to God's specific command to each of us, God placed certain limits on us. These limits constitute the concrete context in which God calls us each to a purpose. According to Barth, these specific limits, which define our vocation, are located in our age, our specific historical situation, our personal aptitudes, and our everyday sphere of operation.[30] Within these limits God has a purpose for each of us. Longing to be younger or older than we are, longing to live in a different point in history, longing to have talents that are not ours — in other words, longing to be someone other than who we are — is ruled out of bounds.[31] God has called us to be *this* particular person and not another.

For Barth, however, this does not mean that one is determined by these limitations so that one can never change from one situation to another. In fact, such movement and change can be made according to God's purposes. The situation in which we find ourselves is not, according to Barth, our grave, but our cradle.[32] We believe that we have been placed where we are for a purpose; part of our purpose, however, may very well be to challenge certain aspects of our situation or even finally to move on to another place.

Barth, therefore, like Calvin, affirms through the doctrine of vocation that no matter what age we are, no matter what our physical or mental condition, in light of limitations which define us positively and limitations which create suffering, our lives have purpose; we are called and enabled to glorify God. The doctrine of vocation, when understood as God's calling to each of us, sets limits which provide the freedom to be who God intends us to be.

As already pointed out, there are potential weaknesses as well as

30. Barth, *Church Dogmatics* III/4, pp. 607-47.
31. Barth, *Church Dogmatics* III/4, p. 624.
32. Barth, *Church Dogmatics* III/4, p. 622.

strengths involved in the Reformed understanding of vocation. A major weakness of the doctrine lies in its potential to be misused as a means to maintain the status quo in a situation of oppression or injustice. Unfortunately, Calvin believed that God uses calamities such as injuries or poverty to reduce one's overly enthusiastic love for this world. Hence, the doctrine of vocation can be (and has been) interpreted to mean that one should be content with one's allotted portion in life. One should, for instance, accept poverty as God's will. The doctrine of vocation can be misused to tell someone who is working for meager wages to work with industrious energy, patience, and fortitude — all to the glory of God — and not to protest unfair working conditions. In like manner it can be used to tell someone suffering from a severely debilitating illness to accept this limitation willingly and give glory to God without complaint.

Second, the doctrine of vocation has at times been distorted into the Protestant work ethic, supporting the view that productivity is a sign of our value as human beings. One's success at work, for instance, becomes a sign of how well one is glorifying God, while monetary gain is seen as a sign of divine blessing and favor. This emphasis on productivity results, of course, in the devaluation of persons who cannot make what is perceived by others to be a productive contribution to society. Hence, one could counsel medical neglect of an infant or adult based on the criterion of productivity.

The Reformed doctrine of vocation, however, is misused when placed in support of these two claims. If rightly interpreted, the Reformed doctrine of vocation as expressed by Calvin and Barth *challenges* these two errors. Regarding the first error, both Calvin and Barth acknowledge that one's vocation can actually require movement from one situation to another. Regarding the second, the positive affirmation given to human limits by the doctrine of vocation leads to the claim that one's rank or station in life or one's ability to be productive can*not* determine one's value and, therefore, one's so-called right to life.

The doctrine of vocation, therefore, initially provides us with a very cautious word as we approach the issue of whether life support can ever be suspended. Such a decision *cannot* be made strictly on the basis of severe disability or lack of productivity. "Quality of life" is not a concept wholly useful for Christians. We believe that God has a purpose for human beings whose quality of life we may deem nonexistent. The Christian understanding of vocation says that suffering itself does not destroy the purposes to which we are called. Therefore, limitations caused by mental disabilities, physical disabilities, and old age cannot be viewed automatically as cause to determine that one's life has no value. A brief look at these three human limitations will emphasize the affirmation of the Reformed doctrine of vocation that human limitations do not automatically negate human vocation.

Three Cases

1. *Developmental disabilities.* It is ruled out of bounds to consider the developmentally disabled as less than human or as not having the "right to live" or as having such a low quality of life that death is preferred. In cases of extreme disability we may or may not be able to discern God's purpose for calling some individuals into being, but that is not our question to ask. Recall Peter, who, after being told of his destiny, pointed to another disciple and asked, "But what about him?" Jesus essentially replied that that was none of Peter's business (John 21:21-22). We are required to ask what is *our* vocation (*our* purpose in life) in relation to this person who has been placed in our path. We cannot dismiss the value of any human being on the ground that he or she cannot make a contribution to society.

As Stanley Hauerwas says, retardation cannot be viewed as an unacceptable way of being human.[33] That we would consider the life of a child or an adult with a developmental disability to be a life not worth living reflects the values of a society that puts a premium on productivity and intelligence but not on compassion. It also represents a society which misunderstands developmental disabilities through its failure to recognize that the people who have them can be productive and wise as well as more compassionate than the people who would rather not have these people around. While developmental disabilities may limit a person's ability to perform some tasks, they do not limit the ability to fulfill God's appointed vocation.

2. *Physical disabilities.* The play and subsequent movie *Whose Life Is It, Anyway?* portrays an artist who, left paralyzed by an automobile accident, is connected to a lung machine and unable to work at his art anymore. Over the course of the movie he tells his girlfriend that he wants her to leave him and think of him as dead. Then he fights for and wins the right to be taken off the respirator so that he will indeed die. It is a compelling presentation; many viewers find themselves wanting to fight with Kim for the right to withdraw life support. Gloria Maxson, however, finds herself fighting for a different position.

> I take strong exception to the film *Whose Life Is It, Anyway?* for its underlying false premise: that the life of a disabled person could not be worth living, and should thus be "mercifully" terminated by suicide or euthanasia.

33. See Stanley Hauerwas, "Suffering the Retarded: Should We Prevent Retardation?" "The Moral Challenge of the Handicapped," "The Retarded, Society, and the Family: The Dilemma of Care," and "The Community and Diversity: The Tyranny of Normality," in *Suffering Presence: Theological Reflections on Medicine, the Mentally Handicapped, and the Church* (Notre Dame: University of Notre Dame Press, 1986), pp. 159-217.

As a chairbound victim of polio and arthritis, I strongly protest that the life I and my many disabled friends lead has genuine value in the sight of God — and humanity.[34]

She recalls all the times people have said to her, "If I were you I would kill my-self." It is, she points out, just a small step from that comment to the demand, "And why *don't* you?"[35]

A colleague of mine once commented that if he had found himself para-lyzed as a young man, he would have made the same decision as the character in the film. The thought of not being able to work or play in the ways he was accustomed would have made life unbearable to him at the time. Now, he says, as a middle-aged man, he would choose differently. "Even if I were severely dis-abled and attached to a machine to keep me alive," he said, "I would still want to watch my granddaughter grow up."[36] Similarly, and in a manner consistent with Calvin's claim that we are to enjoy the life God has given us, Gloria Maxson says, "No matter what the public feels, I will never willingly relinquish a life that contains my husband, family, friends, a home, lobster thermidor, music and P. G. Wodehouse!"[37] The Christian doctrine of vocation says that life has value and purpose even when lived in a disabled body.

3. *Old age.* According to Daniel Callahan, the formulators of public pol-icy have traditionally resisted using age as a criterion for determining when life support should be withheld. Against this position he proposes that "after a person has lived out a natural life span, medical care should no longer be ori-ented to resisting death."[38] He defines a "natural life span" as "one in which life's possibilities have on the whole been achieved and after which death may be understood as a sad, but nonetheless relatively acceptable event."[39] While claiming that "no precise chronological age can readily be set for determining when a natural life span has been achieved," he tends to point to the seventies or early eighties as the range within which life-extending medical treatment should stop. Medical treatment for those who live beyond this "natural life span" would, by Callahan's proposal, "be limited to the relief of suffering." In

34. Gloria Maxson, " 'Whose Life Is It, Anyway?' Ours, That's Whose!" in *On Moral Medicine,* pp. 470-72.

35. Maxson, p. 471.

36. This comment was made by Howard Stone, professor of pastoral theology at Brite Divinity School.

37. Maxson, p. 472.

38. Daniel Callahan, "Terminating Treatment: Age as a Standard," *Hastings Center Re-port,* October/November 1987, p. 25. See also Daniel Callahan, *Setting Limits: Medical Goals in an Aging Society* (New York: Simon & Schuster, 1987).

39. Callahan, *Setting Limits,* p. 66.

other words, medical treatment for the elderly should concentrate on care, not cure.[40]

On the one hand, Callahan rightly takes into consideration what has been discussed above regarding our acceptance of human finitude. Medicine must take into account — not deny or overlook — a person's age when considering which treatment is acceptable and when treatment should be withdrawn. Callahan's attitude toward the elderly is not intentionally callous. He is fighting against the abuse of technology which extends agony more than it extends life as most people want to live it. Nevertheless, however much he seeks to exhibit his respect for the elderly, his position is untenable. By failing to look at each individual case and seeking instead to formulate a policy for withholding life-sustaining medical care to all people who live beyond a certain age, he is, by intention or not, devaluing the lives of the very old by suggesting that their lives are not worth saving.

The doctrine of vocation prohibits us from assuming that a severely limited life in terms of developmental disability, physical disability, or age is a life not worth living. We cannot make a decision about assisted death based on a person's lack of productivity or contribution to society. The doctrine of vocation, therefore, rules a utilitarian ethic out of hand.

Karl Barth rejects the utilitarian argument when he directly addresses the issue of euthanasia. Barth asks whether "society as constituted and ordered in the state [has] a right to declare that certain sick people are unfit to live and therefore to resolve and execute their annihilation?" Having in mind here the "incurably infirm, for instance, imbeciles, the deformed, persons who by nature or accident or war are completely immobilized and crippled and therefore 'useless,'" Barth gives an unequivocal "No." Whereas ancient Sparta as well as the Third Reich adopted policies that would give the state the right to do away with the weak and infirm, Barth says such actions are never commanded by God.[41]

> A man who is not, or is no longer, capable of work, of earning, of enjoyment and even perhaps of communication, is not for this reason unfit to live, least of all because he cannot render to the existence of the state any notable or active contribution, but can only directly or indirectly become a burden to it. The value of this kind of life is God's secret. Those around and society as a whole may not find anything in it, but this does not mean that they have a right to reject and liquidate it.[42]

---

40. Callahan, "Terminating Treatment," p. 25.
41. Barth, *Church Dogmatics* III/4, p. 423.
42. Barth, *Church Dogmatics* III/4, pp. 423-24.

In agreement with Calvin, Barth seems to indicate that the time of death is to be determined solely by God. "How can participants in euthanasia really know, or, even if they agree, how can they be quite certain, that even the life afflicted with the severest suffering has ceased to be the blessing which God intends for this person?"[43]

Nevertheless, however clearly the Reformed doctrine of vocation leads us to reject the utilitarian response to assisted death, it also prohibits an absolute position against ever taking an action which would hasten death. The doctrine of vocation is *not a law*, but an *affirmation* that life is a gift to be cherished even in light of human suffering. It is, furthermore, an affirmation that falls short of giving absolute value to human life.[44] Coupled with the Christian understanding of death, here too we must reckon with human finitude. Therefore, Barth wonders if on occasion "the fulfillment of medical duty does not threaten to become fanaticism, reason folly, and the required assisting of human life a forbidden torturing of it."

> A case is at least conceivable in which a doctor might have to recoil from this prolongation of life not less than from its arbitrary shortening. . . . It may well be that in this special sphere we do have a kind of exceptional case. For it is not now a question of arbitrary euthanasia; it is a question of the respect which may be claimed by even the dying life as such.[45]

Neither an application of absolute law nor a utilitarian understanding of the value of human life will lead us to the most responsible action regarding assisted death.[46]

While both an ethic of law and a utilitarian ethic bring a certain clarity to the complicated issues and cases surrounding assisted death, they often do so

---

43. Barth, *Church Dogmatics* III/4, p. 425.

44. Barth, *Church Dogmatics* III/4, p. 324.

45. Barth, *Church Dogmatics* III/4, p. 427.

46. Thanks to laws passed regarding "advanced directives," terminally ill patients or patients with irreversible conditions in the United States can no longer legally be given life-sustaining treatment against their will. The problems, however, posed by assisted death are far from over. In some situations the removal of life-support treatment is often suggested far more readily if the patient is poor or black than if the patient is well-off and Caucasian. In some cases we spend thousands of dollars to keep a premature baby alive in spite of the pain caused by the treatment and the knowledge that the child may never completely recover from the premature birth, while we let an otherwise healthy baby with Down's syndrome die from lack of simple but life-saving surgery. Furthermore, doctors and nurses sometimes agonize over the decision of whether to stop treatment *not* from an unwillingness to accept human finitude or an inability to value disabled life, but because the situation makes it impossible to know with certainty which course of action is best.

in a moral vacuum. While an absolute prohibition against assisted death may be based on theological and moral affirmations, these affirmations can readily be set aside while the letter of the law rules. Utilitarian principles, on the other hand, can allow consideration of what is pragmatic to take precedence over what is moral and compassionate.

Christians need to enter the discussion about assisted death not with absolute rules nor with an eye solely to what is practical, but with a well-articulated vision regarding human life, human limitations, and human death.[47] For Christians from the Reformed tradition, such a vision acknowledges that life — even limited life — is a gift from God to be lived, appreciated, and celebrated. It also acknowledges that life does not hold for us absolute value.[48]

I am not proposing that these theological reflections are alone adequate for addressing the problems presented by assisted death or for writing public policy. Full reflection on the issue of assisted death requires that attention be given to the interwoven issues of justice and the allocation of medical care. Liberation theology, for instance, reminds us that the issue of withholding medical care is one born of privilege. While we contemplate whether or not life-sustaining equipment should be withheld, some countries (including our own) cannot (or in some cases will not) provide the most *basic* form of health care to some of their citizens. As we make decisions about what kind of care we want for ourselves and about how we would like the civil law to respond to this issue, we must not overlook those who have no medical care to withhold or withdraw to begin with. Furthermore, in order to formulate adequate public policy we need to listen to voices from medicine and from law, from sociology and from other religious traditions.

Nevertheless, the Reformed understanding of death and Christian vocation can help us come to terms with what we think about human limitations, when we believe that death should be fought against as the enemy, and when to accept that death is at hand. On the one hand, proper recognition of human limitations for the Christian means that we realize that no matter what strides have been made in medicine, medicine cannot cure us of our mortality.[49] We realize that for each of us, there comes a time to die. On the other hand, recognition of limits for the Christian means that we can fulfill God's purpose (we

---

47. The approach to Christian ethics being described here is consistent with what Paul Lehmann refers to as contextual ethics, and what Stanley Hauerwas proposes as an ethic of character.

48. To see how Karl Barth rejects the idea that human life has absolute value, see *Church Dogmatics* III/4, pp. 324ff.

49. See Stanley Hauerwas, "Salvation and Health: Why Medicine Needs the Church," in *Suffering Presence*, p. 68.

can have a purpose) in spite of and sometimes because of physical and mental limitations. We do not, in other words, choose death automatically because we find ourselves or someone we encounter faced with greater limitations than we want to live with.[50]

People who have to make decisions regarding assisted death as part of their vocational responsibilities or because of personal tragedy may say these theological reflections are not enough. Concrete principles outlining when assisted death is allowed and when it is prohibited may be demanded by them. Certainly a further step toward formulating a concrete policy is necessary. The theological reflections of the Reformers on death and vocation can nevertheless help lay a foundation for such policy making, in such a way that we are bound neither to legalism nor solely by what is practical. If the future of Reformed theology is wedded to the future complications of medical ethics, we can approach problems such as assisted death not in a theological and moral void that demands hard-and-fast rules while overlooking the complexities of situations and not bound solely to the dictates of practicality. We can approach such issues with a clearer vision of human life, of what makes life worth living, of when to hang on to life and when to acquiesce to the inevitability of death. While these issues will not be simple or without pain, Reformed theology can provide concrete foundations for making decisions about the way we live and the way we die.

50. Furthermore, one sees that there is a difference between withdrawing a feeding tube from a woman who has been in a persistent vegetative state for seven years and withholding life-sustaining treatment from an otherwise healthy newborn with Down's syndrome. One can see the difference between deciding to withdraw a feeding tube from a PVS patient in consultation with the patient's family and in light of the patient's previously stated wishes and making a pragmatic decision to withdraw systematically the feeding tube from every PVS patient regardless of the circumstances.

PART 3

TRADITIONS AND PRACTICES

CHAPTER 20

The Contemporary Relevance
of Calvin's Theology

Hans-Joachim Kraus

"Relevance" is a basic requirement of journalism; there it functions and commands high status. Theology must neither promote the demand for relevance nor be driven by it, for the presence and awareness of the spirit without which it cannot live is the work and working of the Holy Spirit. This we can learn from Calvin, whose theology is essentially pneumatology, the doctrine of the Holy Spirit. He was aware that the presence of the Spirit, not the doctrine of the Holy Spirit, decides the life and relevance of theology.

In our times, when theology threatens to deteriorate into a glass-bead game of intellectual formalism, into sociological functionalism and all kinds of confessional defensiveness, we will do well to allow ourselves to be taught some of the fundamental directives of theology's task by Calvin.

I see my assignment as having to ask what Calvin has to say to us today concerning difficult problems with which we are occupied, also precisely what he has to say in contrast to Luther and the Lutheran tradition that so often attempts to get far away from Luther. However, it must be maintained that Calvin understood himself during his life as a student of Luther, and that Reformed theology and the Reformed church followed him therein.

Today we are far removed from considering the quarrels of the sixteenth century about the Lord's Supper to be the essential distinctions between "Lutheran" and "Reformed." Nowadays decisive differences appear in arguments

---

Translated by Marietjie Odendaal.

about the falsely termed "doctrine of the two regiments." Since the engagement with this theme alone could take up one presentation or more, I want to limit myself. Within the framework of my introduction I want to point out at least the foci of the argument in this current controversy.

I start with the observation — opposed to other explanations — that Luther did not develop a doctrine of the two regiments. Rather, he made a distinction between the two regiments: the political regiment of this world and the spiritual regiment of Christ. Calvin followed Luther in this distinction. In the last edition of the *Institutes,* from 1559, he says: "Whoever knows how to distinguish between this present fleeting life and that future eternal life, will without difficulty know that Christ's spiritual Kingdom and this civil jurisdiction are things completely distinct."[1] Like Luther, Calvin also warned urgently against the confusion and combination of the two regiments. But the request to make a distinction was not Calvin's last word on this issue.

The persecution of the Huguenots and the distorted face of the Christian-Catholic state in France made him newly attentive. This is seen in his Daniel commentary of 1561. In Daniel 2, as is well known, the kingdom of God is compared to a stone which rolls down from above and destroys the statue, symbolizing kingdoms and states. Calvin identifies "kingdom of God" with Christ and explains "that by his advent Christ had taken away whatever was splendid and magnificent and wonderful in the world." Here the change in Calvin's opinion becomes visible: The kingdom of God that came down in Christ is crisis and judgment over all earthly kingdoms. Christ alone is Lord and King. And this is revealed in judgment and destruction? Calvin continues:

> If Christ is the eternal wisdom of God by whom kings reign, it does not seem at all congruous that by his advent he destroyed a political order, which we know God approved and indeed appointed and established by his power. I reply, that earthly empires are upheld and destroyed by Christ "accidentally," as they call it. For if kings perform their office well, it is certain that Christ's kingdom is not against their rule.[2]

The lordship of Christ, the kingship of Christ in the political realm, is the new theme that now shapes the nature of the relationship between the kingdom of God and the kingdom of this world. The lordship of Christ wants to be manifested in governments' execution of office, as *Institutes* 4.20 teaches: "In

---

1. John Calvin, *Institutes of the Christian Religion,* ed. Ford L. Battles and John T. McNeill (Philadelphia: Westminster, 1960), 4.20.1.

2. John Calvin, *Daniel I (Chapters 1–6),* trans. T. H. L. Parker, Calvin's Old Testament Commentaries, vol. 20 (Grand Rapids: Wm. B. Eerdmans Publishing Co., 1993), p. 88, translator's note.

peace *(pax)*, freedom *(libertas)*, and justice *(iustitia)*." Where the correct execution of office goes amiss or is turned completely into its opposite, there the corrupt state becomes subject to judgment. Calvin only starts to consider organized resistance to state violence in the last chapter of the *Institutes*. This is a step that his successor in Geneva, Théodore de Bèze, completed in the treatise *De iure magistratum* (Concerning the right of governments) with the establishment of democratic and liberal rights for state citizens. While a developed "two-regiments doctrine" that separates the realms was represented in Lutheran orthodoxy, and then under the influence of idealism, the Reformed tradition reached its zenith in the writing of Karl Barth, "The Christian Community and the Civil Community," not least out of the lesson from the German church struggle of 1933 to 1945.

This is all by way of introduction and tuning for this address that now wants to allow Calvin to speak to us through key words and themes.

Theology

Calvin's lifework rests on two pillars: the exposition of the Bible, the Old and New Testaments, in the comprehensive commentaries and the systematic, principal work *Institution christianae religionis* (Instruction in the Christian religion), accompanied by disputations and treatises on dogmatic and ethical themes. Calvin himself distinguished between the publications *in Scripturae expositione* (exegesis) and *in Dogmatibus* (doctrine). It is the relationship of the two works to each other that is exciting. It needs a twofold description: first, exegetical research and commentary continually revealed new aspects of biblical proclamation and continued to complete, form, organize, and correct the work on the *Institutes* (from 1536 to 1559, in the various new versions and editions); second, biblical theology shaped the dogmatic *Institutes* so profoundly that Calvin could call the systematic, principal work a "summary of gospel teaching."[3] In other places it means that the task of the *Institutes* consists in finding the sum total of that which God wanted to teach us in his Word. That which Karl Barth called the "biblical way of thinking" of dogmatics was executed with great clarity and consistency in the principal systematic work of the Reformation, the *Institutes*.

We have every reason to pay careful attention here and to learn from this dogmatics, which is rooted in biblical exegesis and theology, because today we have to declare ourselves again opposed to that which Calvin called the burglary by "that trifling philosophy" of the Christian theology and against "these empty

---

3. Calvin, *Institutes* 3.19.1.

speculators, indeed, to whom nothing is pleasing unless it be new."[4] But one would be quite mistaken if one deduced from these critical remarks that Calvin was the guardian of an old traditional speech and communication form of Christian teaching. On the contrary, the humanist Calvin, whose clear and modern Latin and French have been praised again and again, pursues in his systematic, principal work a responsible, contemporary, modern language. He explicitly attempts — for example, in the doctrine of the Trinity — to let *verborum novitas* (new concepts and words) determine his explanations. It can be neither the task of exegesis nor the goal of dogmatics to "patch together" theological sentences from biblical words.[5] This is a sharp objection against all biblicist repetition and declaration in theology, which use the supports of ancient biblical words from insecurity and dependency, while a contemporary language is not found. The root of such insecurity and dependency is ignorance. But Calvin writes in *Institutes* 3.2.2 that "faith rests upon knowledge, not upon pious ignorance."

Therewith we touch on a concept which is fundamental and essential to the *Institutes*, as it is to the catechism, and therefore also to the theology of the community: knowledge *(cognitio)*. It belongs to the "newness of concepts," or even to a modern language, when Calvin started his Geneva Catechism with a question that could be phrased today as it was formulated then.[6]

It goes like this: "What is the goal *(finis)* of human life?" This fundamental question about meaning is answered: "It is the purpose of human life to know God." The answer can be considered from two sides. From the one, the really formal anthropology of Aristotle is shattered. He saw the human being in the hierarchy of being separated from all other lower forms of being by its reason. But to what purpose do humans have reason? Calvin says it is to fulfill the purpose of their lives; namely, to know God. Otherwise they would sink below the animals. From the other side, one might have challenged Calvin with the fact that this knowledge of God, with which also the *Institutes* start, gives too much weight to the rational in theology. One would definitely make a mistake if one referred to the humanist interest or even the "rational French spirit" of Calvin. Calvin did not sever the concept "knowledge" from the biblical union of faith and acknowledgment.[7] That is also why the first

---

4. Calvin, *Institutes* 1.14.19.

5. Calvin, *Institutes* 1.13.3.

6. Otto Weber made a distinction between types of catechisms. The type called "synthetic catechism" offers a simple combination of the main articles of Christian doctrine, as, for example, Luther had undertaken in his *Small Catechism*. Differently, "analytic catechism" starts with a basic question and a combination of questions and answers that relate to one another and introduces the main pieces of Christian doctrine in that combination. Examples of analytic catechisms are the Geneva Catechism and the Heidelberg Catechism.

7. "We have come to believe and know" (John 6:69 NRSV).

answers and explanations pursue the question: Of what does true and correct knowledge of God consist? It consists of a knowledge in which God is honored, while the whole life accords with God's will. Then follows the question: How do we honor God rightly? The answer is: "When we put our trust in him; when we serve him so that we obey his will; when we call on him in all our predicaments and seek from him all our well-being and good; and when we acknowledge with heart and mouth that all good things come from him alone."

Knowledge of God is not a theory but a praxis: the praxis of trust and obedience, the praxis of life under God and his will. So it is essentially called in the *Institutes:* "all right knowledge of God is born of obedience."[8] And that means that only in listening to the Word of God in the witness of Holy Scripture can we rightly know God. But for theology that means that it is a gift, that theology is charisma. Nobody can understand the mysteries of God, only those to whom it is given. Just as the knowledge of God is praxis, so also is theology as charisma praxis, because, according to Calvin, it stands in a threefold definition: when it is executed correctly, it works *aedificatio* (the establishment of the community and the life of the Christian), bears *fructio* (fruit), and is characterized by *utilitas* (usefulness).

Israel

One has to regard it as one of the most terrible mistakes, and acts of reticence, in Christian theology that, since the beginnings of the church, the Jews have been considered the people disinherited and rejected by God and have been treated accordingly. This dogmatic appraisal of history was repeated constantly and never reconsidered or corrected. With one exception: It was Calvin who opposed the traditional and commonly accepted assumption of the rejection of Israel. What he had to say in this regard deserves the utmost attention and has wide-ranging significance for the Christian-Jewish dialogue, begun amongst us in recent decades. Calvin talks of the eternal, ongoing covenant of God with Israel and argues in the following way:

1. In the Old Testament the promise of election to Israel is linked to the promise of an eternal covenant.

> The mountains may depart
>   and the hills be removed,
> but my steadfast love shall not depart from you,

8. Calvin, *Institutes* 1.6.2.

and my covenant of peace shall not be removed,
says the LORD, who has compassion on you.

(Isa. 54:10 NRSV)

Also, the promise of the new covenant in Jeremiah 31:31-34 is explicitly directed toward Israel: "The days are surely coming, says the LORD, when I will make a new covenant with the house of Israel and the house of Judah" (v. 31 NRSV). Calvin thus uses biblical arguments for the eternal, ongoing covenant of God with Israel.

2. The promise of the new covenant for Israel is explicitly cited and confirmed in the New Testament, in Romans 11:26-27, and exactly in a context that deals with the final salvation and liberation of "all Israel." Calvin understands — as we now know, incorrectly — "all Israel" to be the people of God consisting of Jews and Gentiles. But what he adds to elucidate deserves maximum consideration. He writes in the Romans commentary on Romans 11:35: "When the Gentiles come in, the Jews will at the same time return from their defection to the obedience of faith. The salvation of the whole Israel of God, which must be drawn from both, will thus be completed, and yet in such a way that the Jews as the first born in the family of God may obtain the first place."[9] Calvin thus speaks of the unity of God's people, consisting of Jews and Gentiles, but he distances himself from the church's dogmatic tradition on two points: (a) The unity of God's people, consisting of Jews and Christians, is eschatological. It is achieved at the completion of God's kingdom. (b) For the present, the aspect of the *familia Dei*, the family of God, holds true in which the Jews are the firstborn, older brothers and sisters of the Gentile Christians. This primary election of the Jews, which is also emphasized strongly in the first chapters of the *Institutes*, persists into the eternal world of God. The precedence of the firstborn continues to exist in the consummation of God's kingdom. One still needs to add that Calvin puts the eschatological salvation of the Jewish people solely in the hands of God. The Gentiles, however, as it is put in Romans 11:26, must learn that Israel is the firstborn son of God and that the Savior, according to 11:25, will come "to those from Zion."

3. I now skip a whole series of further references in order to turn to the really important question: Why does Calvin insist so eagerly and untiringly on speaking of and teaching on the eternal, ongoing covenant of God with Israel? The answer is given in Romans 11:1: "Paul maintains the principle that since

---

9. John Calvin, *The Epistles of Paul the Apostle to the Romans and to the Thessalonians*, trans. Ross MacKenzie, Calvin's Commentaries, ed. David W. Torrance and Thomas F. Torrance (Edinburgh and London: Oliver & Boyd, 1961), p. 255, translator's note.

adoption is free and founded on God alone and not on men, it stands firm and inviolable however great may be the incredulity which conspires to overthrow it. This difficulty must be resolved, lest the truth and election of God should be believed to be dependent on human worthiness."[10] This is the decisive moment: God's truth and election do not depend on the effort and worthiness of human beings. God's covenant remains and is not ended.

All salvation depends on what happened to Israel. Solely God's covenant loyalty carries the people of God to completion and conquers every human disloyalty. In principle, if the primary election of Israel should be disowned, then the salvation of all of us would be doubtful. The unending covenant with Israel is the secure, constant foundation for the *iustificatio impii* (the justification of the sinner): "the gifts and the calling of God are irrevocable" (Rom. 11:29 NRSV).

Without any doubt, Calvin is Luther's student in the clear exposition of the "justification of sinners," but he proceeds differently in laying the foundations for this article. He ties the main article of the Reformation firmly to the Old Testament and to God's eternal covenant with Israel. Calvin speaks of the "disobedience" and "falling off" of Israel, but never of Israel ending in disinheritance and rejection. While Luther follows the comfortless tradition of the church and even sharpens the statements about the dismissal of Israel, Calvin breaks with the common church tradition and becomes a lonely voice, heard more clearly in the Dutch Reformed tradition than amongst us. Now the elaboration of this important breakthrough by Calvin is due in the Christian-Jewish dialogue.

Old Testament

The relationship of the Christian church to the Old Testament has always been heavily controverted. The issue was ever to hold on to the certainty that Jesus Christ was the promised Messiah of the Old Testament. One is reminded of similar statements by Augustine when Calvin states: "we must read Scripture with the intention of finding Christ therein. Whoever departs from this focus, could toil and study a whole life-time and never attain knowledge of the truth. Or could we be wise without the wisdom of God?"[11]

But then Calvin becomes aware of the historical Israel with its own existence and shape of life. Besides, he eagerly studied humanistic language

10. Calvin, *Epistles*, p. 238, translator's note.
11. *Ioannis Calvini opera quae supersunt omnia*, ed. W. Baum, E. Cunitz, and E. Reuss, 59 vols. (Brunswick: Schwetschke and Son, 1863-1900), 19:125.

research of Hebrew and applied it carefully in his Old Testament commentaries. The humanist Johannes Reuchlin published the *Rudimenta linguae Hebraicae* in 1506, a Hebrew grammar and cosmology. It was based on intensive engagement with the work of the important Jewish scholars of the early Middle Ages, David Kimchi, Abraham Ibn Ezra, and Solomon ben Isaac (called Rashi). For Hebrew studies, *ad fontes* (to the sources) must have meant reading and trying to understand the Hebrew Bible anew with the help of competent Jewish scholars.

However, it did not stop at linguistics. Christian theologians already recognized early on how important the Bible commentaries by Jewish scholars of the eleventh, twelfth, and thirteenth centuries were for the Christian exposition of the Old Testament. The Franciscan, Nicholas of Lyra, a teacher at the Sorbonne in Paris who died in 1340, compiled extracts from Jewish exegesis in his chief work, *Postillae perpetuae*. This compilation enjoyed wide popularity. Luther used it effectively as well. Of Calvin, on the other hand, we know now that he owned and studied the original comprehensive commentaries of Kimchi, Ibn Ezra, and Rashi, as did Oecolampadius in Basel and Wolfgang Musculus in Bern. Oecolampadius was of the opinion that Christian theology had to return to the *hebraica veritas* of the Old Testament. And Calvin concerned himself with the "Hebrew idiom," which only the Jews had preserved carefully after all. Such investigations led to penetrating insights.

One example: In his Genesis commentary Calvin occupies himself intensively with Genesis 3:15, a verse that is highlighted with bold print even in contemporary editions of the Luther Bible. This verse reads: "I will put enmity between you and the woman, and between your offspring and hers; They shall strike at your head, and you shall strike at their heel." In the church's exegetical tradition this verse was understood as *protevangelium*, that is, as "first Gospel" in the Bible of the Old Testament, specifically in the sense that the offspring of the first woman, namely, Jesus Christ, would smash the head of the devil's brood, symbolized in the snake. Calvin critically opposed this christological interpretation in his commentary. From the Jews he had learnt that *zerah*, in English "seed, offspring," must be understood collectively and does not point to an individual, specific offspring. He also indicated that it was wrong to interpret the snake as symbol for the devil. In the context of the primeval history there could be no such talk. Therefore, Genesis 3:15 deals with a conflict between human beings and snakes that spans all generations, a desperate conflict with no victor. Calvin reveals himself here in following the Jewish scholars as a harbinger and pioneer of lucid, relevant historical-critical research. He toppled the taboo of the so-called *protevangelium*. But unfortunately, the authors of the Heidelberg Catechism did not prove to be meticulous Calvin scholars. Rather, they revived the *protevangelium* in their formulation in question 19, "from the holy gospel which God himself revealed in the beginning in the Garden of Eden."[12]

Calvin's thought on this matter is revealed in his commentary on Psalm 72: "We must always beware that we give not the Jews occasion of making an outcry, as if we were purposed to draw to Christ by sophistry the things that agree not with him directly."[13] Calvin thinks that with such christological twists, which have no basis in the Hebrew text, we would have to be ashamed before the Jews. The witness to Christ in the Old Testament must be measured as to whether and how it is supported by the Hebrew text and defensible before the Jews. In any case, Calvin resists every attempt by Christians to monopolize the Old Testament text christologically and to take over the promises given to Israel.

Torah

Torah is the Hebrew word that is usually translated with the word "law." But this translation creates a false impression, which Martin Buber, specifically, criticized. Torah is the sum total of the God of Israel's expression of will and commandments, and is more accurately indicated with "instruction." No other Christian theologian appropriated the Old Testament–Jewish understanding of Torah as carefully and precisely as Calvin. During the Reformation period it became customary to demarcate a threefold function of the "law," the *lex:* firstly, the *usus elenchticus legis,* that is, the function of the law, working to uncover, accuse, and condemn sin; secondly, the *usus politicus legis,* that is, the significance of the law for political life, controlling misdeeds and criminal acts, encouraging behavior that promotes the political orders of life; thirdly, the *tertius usus legis,* the third use of the law as instruction for a Christian life in obedience to God's commandment and will.

While Luther held the first function of the "law" as decisive, especially in the context of the doctrine of justification, the third use of the "law," the *tertius usus legis,* was the really theologically important one in the context of sanctification for Calvin. He called it the *usus in renatis* (the use for those reborn). And exactly this "third use" is intricately connected to the Hebrew-Jewish understanding of Torah. This is seen clearly on two points:

1. Just as the Torah is always defined by the election grace and God's cov-

12. *The Heidelberg Catechism with Commentary,* trans. Allen O. Miller and M. Eugene Osterhaven (Philadelphia: United Church Press, 1962), p. 49.

13. John Calvin, *A Commentary on the Psalms of David,* vol. 2 (Oxford and London: Thomas Tegg, 1860), p. 255, translator's note.

enant with Israel in the Old Testament, so also for Christians the gospel and the act of salvation that took place in Christ are always prerequisites for their encounter with the "law." Calvin declared explicitly that the third use of the Torah "finds its place among believers in whose hearts the Spirit of God already lives and reigns."[14] One can therefore not reproach Calvin, as has often been done, that he creates a "legalistic ethic" in which people will win God's approval by observing the "law."

2. Just as in the Old Testament God's Torah brings joy, for example in Psalm 19 and 119, and as the day of the *simchat torah* (the day of Torah joy) is celebrated in the synagogue in the context of the festival of the booths to this day, so Calvin included such views in his Christian doctrine of Torah as: "The *Torah* of the Lord is perfect, renewing life; the precepts of the Lord are just, rejoicing the heart; the instruction of the Lord is lucid, making the eyes light up" (Ps. 19:8-9) or "Your word is a lamp to my feet and a light for my path" (Ps. 119:105).

> These do not contradict Paul's statements, which show not what use the law serves for the regenerate, but what it can of itself confer upon man. But here the prophet [the psalmist] proclaims the great usefulness of the *Torah:* the Lord instructs by their reading of it those whom he inwardly instills with a readiness to obey. He lays hold not only of the precepts, but of the accompanying promise of grace.[15]

Here great differences between Calvin and Luther appear. While Luther establishes a certain order, the law preceding the gospel (as the word that uplifts and saves people), Calvin places covenant and gospel before the law and so reflects the Old Testament–Jewish understanding of Torah. Never before in all of church history has Christian theology come so close to Judaism and met so openly with it on the basis of the Hebrew Bible as in the work of Calvin. This forces us now, in the new encounter with the Jews, to take careful note of this work.

Karl Barth takes up the perspective of Calvin, mediated by H. F. Kohlbrügge, in his theological ethic:

> Ruling grace is commanding grace. The Gospel itself has the form and fashion of the Law. The one Word of God is both Gospel and Law. It is not Law by itself and independent of the Gospel. But it is also not Gospel without Law. In its content it is Gospel; in its form and fashion it is Law. It is

---

14. Calvin, *Institutes* 2.7.12.
15. Calvin, *Institutes* 2.7.12.

first Gospel and then Law. It is the Gospel which contains and encloses the Law as the ark of the covenant the tables of Sinai.[16]

I still speak of "law," though, because this translation has become deep-seated in Christian theology, occasionally under stoic influence. It would have been appropriate to translate *Torah* consistently with "instruction."

In *Institutes* 2.8.15-59 Calvin presents an exegesis of the Decalogue, the Ten Commandments. Three comments are at present particularly significant.

1. In the first commandment we find the introduction, "and God spoke all these words: I am the Lord your God who brought you out of Egypt, out of slavery." Calvin emphasizes that the election and covenant promise, "I am the Lord your God," determines the intention of all the commandments. At the beginning is promise and address. Then Calvin points out that the God of Israel is portrayed as liberator, who redeems his people through his power and leads them into the reign of freedom. It becomes clear, not only in the important chapter of *Institutes* 2.19, *De christiana libertate* (Concerning the Christian freedom), how highly Calvin values freedom. He is also the one who introduced the important concepts *libertas conscientiae* (freedom of conscience) and *regnum libertatis* (reign of freedom) to Western culture. We, however, must now recognize that the commandments of God bear the signature of freedom. Karl Barth and Kornelis Heiko Miskotte interpret Calvin correctly when they understand the commandments as a detailed call: "Stay with your liberator!" God's commandments do not lead into "the realm of have to's," but into the realm of freedom. Obviously Calvin, following Luther's translation, refers to the formulation "the perfect law that gives freedom" in James 1:25.

2. Calvin's exposition of the second commandment, which disappeared in the Roman Catholic Church tradition and also with Luther, initiates the Reformed prominence of the prohibition of images in accordance with the synagogue. Whoever creates a material or a spiritual image of God confines God to certain traits originating from a heart that Calvin calls a *fabrica idolorum*, a factory of idols or a workplace of idols, in *Institutes* 1.11.8. God is free in his revelation or self-communication. The second commandment is a basic law of the realm of freedom.

3. God presented himself unmistakably and put himself within calling distance through his name. The third commandment, "You shall not misuse the name of the Lord your God," had the sense and purpose, according to Calvin, that "God wills that we hallow the majesty of his name!" Therefore all speech about God, even and especially in theology and in the church, is subject

---

16. Karl Barth, *Church Dogmatics* II/2, ed. Geoffrey W. Bromiley and Thomas F. Torrance (Edinburgh: T. & T. Clark, 1957), p. 567.

to this remark: "Whatever our mind conceives of God, whatever our tongue utters, should savor of his excellence, match the loftiness of his sacred name, and lastly, serve to glorify his greatness."[17]

Discipleship of the Cross

One of the first Protestants in France was Admiral de Coligny, who heard the call of the gospel in the discipleship of the cross, mediated by Reformed proclamation, and followed it. He joined the small, persecuted congregation in Paris and was killed in 1572 at the terrible Parisian massacre of Saint Bartholomew. On 16 January 1561 Calvin wrote a letter to Admiral de Coligny, from which I quote a few sentences:

> Monseigneur: We have indeed occasion to praise God for the singular courage which he has bestowed on us to serve his glory and the advancement of the kingdom of his Son. It were to be desired that you had many companions to aid you in your task, but though others are slow in acquitting themselves of their duty, nevertheless you ought to put in practice the saying of our Lord, that each should follow cheerfully without looking upon others. . . . Let every one go whither he shall be called, even if he should not have a single follower.[18]

Calvin, whose life and work was deeply bound to the fate of the persecuted Protestants in France, saw in the suffering of the Huguenots the way of discipleship of Christ, the discipleship of the cross that is demanded of all Christians and that has enduring significance for the church. It is a way along which every individual is called to free, independent, brave decision, and along which — when needs be, lonely — courage to stand up for one's belief alone has value and permanence. It is a way of *migratio* and *peregrinatio*, of wandering and being foreign, through a world that entices and bewitches with glitter and career promises, but also with religion and festive worship, a world in which the direction and the voice of the masses want to be decisive.

The church is also permeated by this worldly principle of power and majority. Then, as now, concern for the minority of disciples has been acute, the question concerning the small number of those who have heard the call of

---

17. Calvin, *Institutes* 2.8.22.

18. *Letters of John Calvin,* vol. 4, compiled from the original manuscripts and edited with historical notes by Jules Bonnet, trans. Marcus R. Gilchrist (New York: Burth Franklin, 1972), p. 165, translator's note.

Christ and have taken to the road without always looking back to "the others." It is a road that may lead to nonconformist political or social consequences.

There is a principle underlying Calvin's ethics, specifically in his doctrine of sanctification, which is developed in *Institutes* 3.7.1: *Nostri non sumus — Dei sumus* (We do not belong to ourselves — we belong to God). The Heidelberg Catechism says "that I belong not to myself, but to my faithful savior, Jesus Christ, who at the cost of his own blood has fully paid for all my sins and has completely freed me from the dominion of the devil."[19] True knowledge of God leads to the fundamental definition of my life: I do not belong to myself; I belong to Christ and, therefore, I live in discipleship to him. *Abnegatio nostri* (self-denial) is, therefore, no religious masochism, but finding my identity in belonging to and community with Christ, in freedom from myself through him who made me free and worthy to be a member of his kingdom, the kingdom of freedom. Whoever starts to live in this fashion, lives in the church, which Calvin calls (joining Augustine) the "mother of all believers."

Church Order and Discipline

Luther did not spend much energy on matters of church order. He entrusted the shaping of the church to the power of the gospel, and finally left the ordering of the church to rulers and political regents. Melanchthon criticized Luther's doctrine of the church. He reproached him for representing the invisible church *(ecclesia invisibilis)* as decisive and thereby changing the church into a *civitas platonica* (a platonic community). In contrast, Calvin emphasized the visible church *(ecclesia visibilis)* more and more in his ecclesiology. The church's outer appearance needed to be recognized for what it is: the people of God, the congregation of Jesus Christ, as "city upon the hill." That is why the questions about church order are not secondary problems but essential questions that are linked to the confession and doctrine of the church.

Therefore, the question about the order of the church also belongs to the confessions and catechisms of Calvin: the *ordonnances ecclésiastiques* in Geneva and the *discipline ecclésiastique* in the *Confession de Foy*, the confession of faith of the Huguenots. According to what he wrote in the introduction to the Geneva Church Order, Calvin deduced the "firm order and life-style" from the gospel of Jesus Christ. That implies that it is an evangelical church order, not influenced by any foreign laws or points of view. I would like to point out two principles that have become fundamental to the Reformed tradition:

1. In the presbyterial-synodal order (as we call it), the principle holds

19. *The Heidelberg Catechism,* p. 17.

that no church or congregation can claim preference or domination over others: no preacher over other preachers, no elder over the rest of the elders, no deacon over deacons. Each and every one must guard against even a hint of such a pretension and against every attempt to claim control. The congregation, as a result, has a way of life free of power *(herrschaftsfrei)*.

2. Should it happen that one or more congregations become impoverished, suffering a lack of money or other deprivation, then one congregation must help the others. Then mutual assistance must be the highest commandment. The way of life of congregations is therefore decided by mutual aid and selfless assistance. These are only two examples, and I do not need to point out their relevance.

Church discipline is also an element of church order. The concept "church discipline" might be off-putting. What is meant and intended with *disciplina ecclesiastica* must first become clear. It would be a denial of Calvin's own statements to judge too hastily that the church discipline in Geneva and in the Huguenot congregations was the work of a strict, legalistic, radical fanatic. To begin with, one should make a connection with what has been explained as discipleship of the cross. Church discipline is the ecclesiological shape of discipleship, touching the congregation as a whole. In it the gravity of discipleship of the cross is mirrored. Then one should take note of what Calvin discloses, in *Institutes* 4.12.5, as the meaning and purpose of church discipline. I want to quote the first sentences: "They who lead a filthy and infamous life may not be called Christians, to the dishonor of God, as if his holy church were a conspiracy of wicked and abandoned men. For . . . the church itself is the body of Christ." Church discipline therefore serves the holy church, the body of Christ, through which Christ wants to meet the world. One will have to take this approach, this statement about the meaning and purpose of church discipline, under careful consideration. The church is not an institution in which, to quote Dietrich Bonhoeffer, "cheap grace" can be used by everybody as cheap goods. Calvin, who is rather inconvenient in this matter, recalls the sanctification of the people of God, of the congregation as the body of Christ in the world. In discipleship of Christ the statement "you are the light of the world" holds true. Yes, Calvin is a zealot, a theologian who did not rest until everything he taught became praxis, who could not stand the bare speaking, declaiming, and constructing of Christian theories and church ideals.

Yet, what became of the church discipline in Geneva is something else: often a system of spying and denouncement, of moral supervision and making up other people's minds for them. So it is understandable that the prominent Calvin scholar who respects him very much, Karl Barth, could say: I would not want to live in that city of Geneva. But this comment is not a ground to dismiss the intentions of church discipline.

The Gift of Life

We have heard of discipleship of the cross, of suffering, and of persecution. But life is not only distress and suffering, although Calvin, a man marked by illness and heavy sadness, had to drink the cup of suffering to the lees. He had to bear his cross patiently. But from suffering his hope focused on the purpose of life. "*Meditatio futurae vitae* — Meditation on the Future Life" is the title of the ninth chapter of the third book of the *Institutes*. However, this meditation over the future does not imply a renunciation of the present, everyday life. Although Christians must always ponder that they are on the road and that their life is a journey, they should also open themselves wide to receive the gift of the present life. Calvin wrote against all ascetic tendencies and against contempt for all that has been given us in this life in the tenth chapter of the third book of the *Institutes*. In this chapter we learn how erroneous it is to make the Geneva Reformer into a strict, ascetic, life-hating zealot.

What he does say is that we should accept and enjoy the gifts which are given us in this life with gratitude. Certainly we should not forget that we are on a journey and that the enjoyment of all goods and gifts must be affected by this fact. Then, however, it means that "the use of God's gifts is not wrongly directed when it is referred to that end to which the Author himself created and destined them for us." And then it follows that

> now if we ponder to what end God created food, we shall find that he meant not only to provide for necessity but also for delight and good cheer! Thus the purpose of clothing, apart from necessity, was comeliness and decency. In grasses, trees, and fruits, apart from their various uses, there is beauty of appearance and pleasantness of odor. For if this were not true, the prophet [psalmist] would not have reckoned them among the benefits of God, that "wine cheers the human heart" and that "the face shines from oil" (Psalm 104:15). Scripture would not have reminded us repeatedly, in commending his kindness, that he gave all such things to men.[20]

Here Calvin encourages the gourmet, the fashion-conscious, the friend of wine and all that tastes good and smells pleasant. He calls it an "inhuman philosophy" to reduce all to the meager and the minimum. He beseeches urgently that the freedom of believers regarding these things should not be bound by specific formulas or subjected to some law. Only one thing is emphasized always again, that all gifts from God must be received in gratitude and also in recognition of God as creator. In the light of all these statements, one cannot turn Cal-

20. Calvin, *Institutes* 3.10.2.

vin into a narrow-minded, legalistic pietist, as has often happened. He is, much more, in light of the freedom of a Christian, a fighter for the *humanitas,* the humanity, of those who believe. At this point I refer once again to the letter from which this humanity, goodness, and friendliness radiates.

Unity of the Church

I have to conclude, and in the last sentences I would like to address a basic position of Calvin that one should not forget: his zeal for the unity of the church. The Geneva Reformer was an ecumenical teacher of the church. He suffered under every kind of division. And although he did not value the teaching of the Zürich Reformer, Zwingli, unity was reached in the Consensus Tigurinus (1549). In close collaboration with his friend Philipp Melanchthon, Calvin sought a union with Luther, which finally broke down with Melanchthon, however. Shortly before Luther died Calvin took a new initiative and asked Melanchthon to deliver a comprehensive letter to Luther. There was great consternation in Geneva when Melanchthon's reply arrived, including the remark that Calvin knew well enough that Luther was a stubborn, snorting ox, whom one could not approach with such a letter. Calvin rebuked Melanchthon in an answering writing: Luther is the highly honored father and beloved teacher of us all.

Calvin sought conversation and community of faith also with the Roman Catholic Church. He was of the opinion that the teaching of Augustine was the common basis. The Geneva Reformer urgently asked all his students to seek and strive for the unity of the church tirelessly.

CHAPTER 21

Calvin's Theological Realism and the Lasting Influence of His Theology

John Leith

John Calvin's *Institutes of the Christian Religion* is today a powerful and persuasive statement of Christian faith, although its last edition appeared 433 years ago. Calvin's intention in writing the *Institutes* was to make not a timeless statement of Christian faith, but a summary of faith for the particular situation in which he lived and to which his ministry extended in the middle of the sixteenth century. The *Institutes* is dated by the controversies of his time; by the scientific, historical, and literary knowledge available at the time; as well as by language. Yet even with this material, as a statement of Christian faith it remains certainly as persuasive, and in most instances more persuasive, than those that have appeared in the last half-century with the express purpose of speaking to the modern mind. In assessing the prospects of Calvinist theology for the future, the question must first be asked why Calvin's own theological writings, commentaries, letters, and tracts have maintained their persuasive power four and a half centuries after they were written.

The thesis of this paper is that Calvin's theological writings have a realistic quality that gave them power in Calvin's own time and makes them persuasive in new times and situations. Biblical scholars have noted the power of Jesus to cut through pretense, ostentation, the baroque and to distinguish what is real from what is illusion. He had the remarkable capacity to see things as they are and to speak about them clearly and concretely. This awareness for what is real gave power to the teachings of Jesus, and it also is a crucial factor in any Christian theology that is persuasive to people.

Robert Lowry Calhoun, as much as any theologian in this century, explicated Christian faith with clarity and precision and with an emphasis on the concrete revelation of God in Jesus Christ and on the simple realities of human life. His own comments about the sense of reality as an important factor in theology throw light upon the continuing influence of Calvin's theology:

> Two great moral principles that appear again and again in Jesus' teaching and practice, namely intelligence and integrity on the one hand and a life of faith and hope and love toward God on the other, are crucial for Christian faith and Christian theology. The first is a demand for intelligence and integrity: not simple shrewdness, nor technical competence nor rules-of-the-thumb honesty (though all these have their places) but a fundamental readiness in all situations to see and to acknowledge what is so. The temptation stories, the Sermon on the Mount, the sayings that deal with cup and platter, unwhitened graves, ceremonial cleanliness, the Sabbath day, all reflect, in one way or another, Jesus's insistence on truthfulness and realism in the presence of an objective order that men disregard at their peril. It should not be necessary at this late date to insist that the moral and religious teaching of Jesus is not that of a light-hearted visionary but one who insists at every step that reality should be squarely faced. Intellectual and moral integrity, clear eyes and candid minds, are required of all who seek to follow his lead.[1]

This capacity to see things as they are and to speak about them in clear and simple indicative sentences so that unsophisticated people can understand, distinguishes both the teaching of Jesus and Calvin's theology from much contemporary theology that is overly clever and overly sophisticated. E. L. Mascall once described certain modern theologies as both sophisticated and naive: sophisticated in that only a highly trained intellect could devise them, but naive in that no "ordinary person . . . could think Christianity was worth practicing if he thought this position to be true."[2] Calvin's theology is neither sophisticated nor naive but realistic and plainspoken about the world, about human existence, and about God's salvation of his people, the Christian gospel. A capacity to see things as they are and to speak about them in simple, concrete sentences is reflected in at least nine characteristics of Calvin's theology.

1. Calvin deliberately and intentionally rejected speculation in theologi-

---

1. Robert L. Calhoun, "The Gospel for This World," in *Making the Gospel Effective*, ed. William K. Anderson (Nashville: The Commission on Ministerial Training, the Methodist Church, 1941), pp. 33-34.

2. E. L. Mascall, *Jesus, Who He Is and How We Know Him* (London: Darton, Longman & Todd, 1985), p. 19.

cal works. He abided by the old principle of minimal theological development. He did not seek to create new doctrines if old doctrines would do, very much in the tradition of the theologians of Nicaea and Chalcedon. In his reply to Sadolet, Calvin wrote:

> You are just as little candid when you aver that we have seduced the people by thorny and subtle questions, and so entice them by that philosophy of which Paul bids Christians beware (Col. 2:8). What? Do you remember what kind of time it was when the Reformers appeared, and what kind of doctrine candidates for the ministry learned in the schools? You yourself know that it was mere sophistry and so twisted, involved, tortuous and puzzling, that scholastic theology might well be decided as a species of secret magic. The denser the darkness in which anyone shrouded a subject, and the more he puzzled himself and others with nagging riddles, the greater his fame for acumen and learning. And when those who had been formed in that workshop wished to carry the fruit of their learning to the people with what skill, I ask, did they edify the church?[3]

Calvin vigorously rejected theology that he perceived as fantasy contrived by human beings, even if this theology were very clever.

This emphasis upon a simple and concrete theology is pervasive in all of Calvin's writings. In his sermons on Timothy he declared: "When I expound on Holy Scripture I must always make this my rule: that those who hear me may receive profit from the teaching I put forward and be edified unto salvation. If I have not that affection and if I do not procure the edification of those who hear me, I am a sacrilege, profaning God's word." The congregation has a similar responsibility to distinguish the concrete and real from the fanciful and speculative: "and also those who read Holy Scripture or who come to the sermon to hear it, if they are looking for some silly speculations, if they are coming here as a pastime, they are guilty of profaning such a holy thing."[4]

In the *Institutes* Calvin explicitly ruled out the discussion of speculative questions. He would not attempt to answer what God was doing before he created the world[5] or whether the word of God would have become incarnate if human beings had not sinned.[6] These questions did not directly impinge upon

3. John Calvin, "Reply to Sadolet," in *Calvin's Theological Treatises*, Library of Christian Classics, vol. 22 (Philadelphia: Westminster, 1954), p. 233.

4. Calvin, sermon on 2 Tim. 3:16-17, in *Ioannis Calvini opera quae supersunt omnia* (hereafter cited as *CO*), ed. W. Baum, E. Cunitz, and E. Reuss (Brunswick and Berlin: Schwetschke and Son, 1893-1900), 59 vols., 54: 283-96.

5. John Calvin, *Institutes of the Christian Religion*, ed. F. L. Battles and J. T. McNeill (Philadelphia: Westminster, 1960), 1.14.1.

6. Calvin, *Institutes* 2.12.4.

human salvation and, moreover, Calvin knew of no way to answer them. Theology has as its purpose not answers for the conundrums of the human mind but restoration of human beings who have been broken by sin and unbelief.

Theology, for Calvin, is a modest enterprise and is dependent upon revelation. In rejecting the traditional scholastic theology, Calvin said in his sermon on Job 15:1-10:

> They want to inquire about that which God has never revealed, and even about those things which He wants to be hidden. Now we know when He has not spoken, He wants us to remain silent, nor does He want us to greet Him to ask what will be — but rather that we remain uninformed when He does not teach us. This is our real wisdom — that of not wanting to know more than that which God shows us in His instruction.

In the same sermon Calvin spoke of the scholastic theologians as "clever people because they are speculative, that is to say, they carry themselves in the air and have no steadiness."[7]

Ambition as well as curiosity and speculation lead to fantasy in theology:

> And furthermore, we should not give in to ambition to follow what pleases men as many do, who, seeing that they are applauded, always want to have some lively doctrine in which to take pleasure. On the contrary, let us look at what is useful to edify people in the fear of God. And also those who wish to profit from the word of God put away all curiosity. And when they come to a sermon, let it not be to have some doctrine which pleases them according to the flesh, but that they look to be taught to profit, that is, that they be incited to serve God better, to put their confidence in Him.[8]

2. Theology has as its purpose, as has been already indicated, to edify, not to satisfy idle curiosity. Theology is practical, not theoretical, intending the transformation of human life. It is an aid or help to the sermon and to the reading of Scripture. The sermon, not theology, has the primary place in Calvin's hierarchy of responsibilities. The secular notion of theology as an academic pursuit is unintelligible in a Calvinist context. Theology is not an end in itself but a means to an end; namely, a means to preaching, to teaching, and to the building up of a community of saints. A theology that is not preachable and teachable and that does not edify the local congregation is, by this very fact, declared defective. The final test of theological validity is always the testimony of the Holy Spirit to the truthfulness of that doctrine over a period of time in the life of the

---

7. Calvin, sermon on Job 15:1-10, in *CO* 33: 705-18.
8. Calvin, sermon on 1 Tim. 5:4-5, in *CO* 53: 453-66.

Christian community. "The theologian's task is not to divert the ears with chatter, but to strengthen consciences by teaching things true, sure and profitable."[9]

3. Calvin's work as an interpreter of Scripture also reflects a hard-nosed sense for what is real. From the beginning it was guided by two principles. The first was simplicity and brevity, which he enunciated with great clarity in his preface to his commentary on Paul's letter to the Romans, the first commentary he wrote. The second was an insistence that the interpreter is to explicate the "natural sense" of the passage. By natural sense Calvin did not mean so much the literal sense as the meaning which the writer expressed. The search for the natural sense made it not only possible but also necessary for Calvin to use his skills as a humanist in deciphering the historical and philological and linguistic meaning of the passage. Exegesis attempts to discover neither what the writer ought to have said nor what we wish he had said, but what the writer concretely did say. This emphasis upon the natural sense of Scripture has given Calvin's commentaries a permanence that is surprising to many contemporary exegetes. Students of Scripture today have far greater technical knowledge than Calvin did, but they seldom are as skilled in perceiving the actual meaning of the passage.

The realism of Calvin's exegesis unites the assumption that the exegete was seeking to understand what the author had written with the conviction that this text is the word of God. A contemporary critic may judge Calvin's presupposition that the Scriptures are the word of God as a theological error, but the interpreter of Calvin must note the concrete, simple realism of his conviction.

4. Calvin insisted that theology must deal with the concrete realities of human life in the language of ordinary human experience. This also reflects Calvin's distrust of speculation and sophistry. Theology is addressed to concrete human beings with quite specific human experiences. It does not live in a make-believe world but addresses the people to whom it speaks in their actual situation. Moreover, good theology, Calvin insisted, always uses the language of ordinary human discourse. For this reason Calvin discarded the sophisticated, abstract, and rationalistic language of scholastic theology. Critics can point to the imprecision of Calvin's definitions, to his use of words without clearly defining their meaning. This made necessary the theology of the schools which followed after Calvin's death. Nevertheless, the insistence upon the language of ordinary discourse, for all of its technical failures, contributes to the fact that ordinary Christians can read Calvin's *Institutes* today in the life of the church far more easily than they can read many twentieth-century university theologians.

9. Calvin, *Institutes* 1.14.4.

5. Simplicity is a remarkably apt description of Calvin's person as well as of his theology. He always preferred one word rather than two or three words and a simple word over against a sophisticated word. He opposed theatrical trifles in church ceremonies. He advocated moderation in life. He was, as a person and as a theologian, opposed to the pretentious, the pompous, the ostentatious, the baroque, the contrived, and the artificial. On the other hand, he stood for concrete, direct discourse. Simplicity for Calvin was very close to sincerity. The baroque, the ostentatious, the pretentious, and the sophisticated cover up reality. The simple uncovers reality for all to see.

The simple, clear language of ordinary discourse uncovers the theologian's actual faith as well as the meaning of theological assertions. William Hocking once declared that complicated and obtuse language always covered up confused thought. When a truth is understood, it can be expressed in simple, plain language. Simplicity lays bare the theologian's conviction and the content of theological ideas.

6. The realism of Calvin's theology also comes to expression in his willingness to face difficulties. Calvin was vividly aware of the evidences of damnation in the world, ranging from the inability of some mothers to nurse their babies to the unresponsiveness of people to sermons. When Calvin was optimistic he estimated that only 20 percent of the hearers of a sermon responded, and when he was pessimistic he reduced the number to 10 percent. What is the basis of these differences? Calvin was aware of the reality of damnation and deliberately refused to ignore it or to explain it away, as did some of his contemporaries. Critics of *Institutes* 3.21.24 rightly note that Calvin too simply attributes damnation to the will of God. The flaws in his answer to the question have long been pointed out. Critics, however, have too often forgotten to give Calvin credit for facing a concrete reality in human life and experience.

7. Calvin's theology also is realistic in its emphasis upon sanctification. Calvin's theology had as its purpose, as has already been indicated, the edification of human beings and of the church. This emphasis upon edification can be carried forward in Calvin's insistence upon the transformation of human life to correspond to the image of God. For Calvin the Christian life is not simply being, not simply believing, but also doing. Theology has as its purpose the transformation of human life so that persons who once lived in fear now live in confidence in God, so that persons who once lived aimlessly now understand their lives as a fulfillment of the purposes of God, so that people who once took what they could from society now seek to live in such a way that human life shall be enhanced to the glory of God. Calvin intended not only to express theology in concrete, simple sentences, but to embody it concretely in human life and community as well as in the structures of church and society.

8. Calvin's theology is realistic in that it authentically reflects the faith of

the writer. Calvin's theology is not the figment of his mind but the concrete statement of what God is actually doing in the world, in Calvin's own life, in Geneva, and in the church. Calvin's life was congruent with the theology he wrote.

Behind the *Institutes* and its power to persuade people is the reality of a theologian who actually believes that the Lord God reigns and that in Jesus Christ this God has brought salvation to the people. Calvin's *Institutes* is transparent to the faith of Calvin himself and, moreover, to the faith of the believer. All good theology ought to become like the sacraments under the power of the Holy Spirit, transparent to the very presence of God about which theology speaks.

9. Calvin was a theological realist. Theological doctrines correspond to reality. The doctrine of the Trinity is the way God is. Calvin never dreamt that you can have the conclusions or consequences of Christian faith without the foundations of that faith in the personal activity of the triune God. Christian doctrines, such as the Trinity, are not meaningful ways of relating to the world, or an understanding of existence, or the mutable grammar of faith. They have reference to what God has done in creation and human history and to the being of God himself. Calvin's theological realism was qualified by his doctrine of accommodation. God accommodates himself in his revelation to human sin and finiteness. Hence there is a brokenness and fragmentariness in our knowledge of God. Modesty and sobriety are marks of good theology. Yet doctrines, accommodated to human limitations, acknowledge God as he is. Calvin never used the language and rhetoric of theology to deceive people or to evade theological commitment.

Calvin's theological realism means that the substance of theology takes precedence over theological method and that the theological reality determines method and rhetoric. William Bouwsma has emphasized Calvin's anxiety and doubt.[10] Yet Calvin always willed and intended to believe. He never gives any evidence of thinking that one can have the fruits of faith without the faith. Compared to that of other human beings, Calvin's life exhibited a remarkable consistency of practice, of personhood and faith. It is this realism that makes his theology persuasive not only in the sixteenth century but also at the end of the twentieth century.

---

10. W. Bouwsma, *John Calvin: A Sixteenth-Century Portrait* (New York: Oxford University Press, 1988).

CHAPTER 22

Revelation and Experience
in Calvin's Theology

Willem Balke

The Subject Matter

To engage the topic of *experientia* means to stand squarely within what is real. Theology today must place itself in dialogue with the empirical disciplines.

In reflecting on the relationship between "revelation and experience," an important underlying question is that of certainty: scientific certainty, personal certainty, and the certainty of salvation. Certainty is a precious commodity on many levels, and it is won by means of experience. Economists would love to claim certainty regarding prices and interest rates, yet these remain matters which defy prediction. In the medical realm there can be no certainty regarding the course of a disease. In science one operates using principles, as-

Translated by Lisa Dahill.
Bibliography: H. Obendiek, "Die Erfahrung in ihrem Verhältnis zum Worte Gottes bei Calvin," in *Aus Theologie und Geschichte der Reformierten Kirche. Festgabe für E. F. K. Müller* (Neukirchen: Buchhandlung des Erziehungsvereins, 1933), pp. 180-214; W. Kolfhaus, *Christusgemeinschaft bei Johannes Calvin* (Neukirchen: s.n., 1939); W. van 't Spijker, "Experientia in reformatorisch licht," *Theologia Reformata* 19 (1976): 236-55; W. Balke, "Het Woord van God en de ervaring volgens Calvijn" and "Kan men bij Calvijn spreken van bevindlijke prediking," in *Omgang met de Reformatoren* (Kampen: J. H. Kok, 1992); W. van 't Spijker, " 'Extra nos' en 'in nobis' bij Calvijn in pneumatologisch licht," in *Geest, Woord en Kirk. Opstellen over de geschiedenis van het gereformeerd protestantisme* (Kampen: J. H. Kok, 1991).

sumptions, and models, yet no one can guarantee that these always and everywhere agree. Human experience, the only means by which we human beings can derive knowledge, is not sufficient.

Is there another way, such as revelation, a way by which God supplies knowledge? Through all ages the church has answered a resounding "Yes" to this question. Theology draws its life from revelation and derives its knowledge from the Holy Scriptures. This is the way of faith. Yet Christians — not only professional theologians but also ordinary believers — are constantly tempted to seek further support in experience and so to give experience a constitutive role.

The Danger of Using Inappropriate Methods in Theology

Theologians are often tempted to make uncritical use of current scientific methods in theology. The fact that this has enormous and ominous consequences for theology can be shown by the way the methodological principle of causality has led to the doctrine of predestination being transmuted into determinism. For Calvin the *Ordinatio* in creation does not have the character of the necessity of things and is not equivalent to natural law. In Calvin's view, it is a sign of the love of God for the creatures God has made. Calvin did not treat *Ordinatio* under the heading of *Praedestinatio* (which has to do with holiness), but rather under *Providentia*, which has to do with God's care for all things in this world. In his *Institutes* Calvin notes in the section on providence that God's fatherly hand can be seen in all that occurs; the stars can work no harm, every worry is groundless, because God rules. The *Ordinatio* comes from God, but the deviations from it, namely, extraordinary occurrences, also come from God. In this sense there is no significant difference between ordinary occurrences, such as the regular rhythm of day and night, and extraordinary occurrences such as earthquakes — or even amazing or unique occurrences such as " 'Sun, stand still at Gibeon'" (Josh. 10:12 NRSV).

For Calvin there is thus no sense that there could be supernatural acts and interventions. God's providence is obscured by those who connect this working of God only with special acts.[1] It is a serious misunderstanding to identify predestination more or less with determinism. In itself, the statement that Calvin believed in unchanging laws, and that this faith was strengthened by the doctrine of God's providence, appears to bear every mark of truth. Predestination and determinism do of course share the impli-

---

1. John Calvin, *Institutes of the Christian Religion,* ed. F. L. Battles and J. T. McNeill (Philadelphia: Westminster, 1960), 1.16.4.

cation that nothing can take place by accident. Yet predestination has to do with God's free will and desire and lays its entire weight on the Lord's governance in heaven, while determinism is a form of necessitarianism and is a matter of fate and exigency.

Calvin was more modern than the epicurean philosophers of his time, and history reveals to us that it was not determinism but voluntarism which opened new arenas for the development of science. At the same time we must note that the later Calvinist doctrinal system emphasized explicitly the orderliness of the universe; yet this emphasis has no connection with the doctrine of predestination in Calvin's view. Gradually the authentic doctrine of election was transmuted into determinism and Deism, because the natural sciences' methodological principle of causality was utilized within theology. And this had disastrous consequences: the separation of naturalism and supernaturalism.

The Uncertainty of Our Experience

In the previous century, the Dutch philosopher C. W. Opzoomer (1821-92), academic teacher in Utrecht, developed the philosophy of experience, so-called empiricism.[2] Allard Pierson (1831-96), born into an Enlightenment milieu (his parents were good friends of the poet Isaac da Costa),[3] was quite taken with this philosophy of experience. He spoke of "his passion for reality."[4] The result was the excision from revelation, from the Holy Scriptures, of everything which could not be verified as real by means of human experience. Only that which was measurable and tangible could hold up and was taken to be certain. Allard Pierson recognized honestly the implications of this and gave up his office in the church. Yet in his striving for truth he testified to his deep religiosity.

With these names we are situated in the nineteenth century. Furthermore, since the Enlightenment and romantic periods, experience has become a subjective occurrence. Above all, it has become a matter of sense and sensibility. Of course, this development had its roots earlier. Already in the eighteenth century a great deal of reflection went into the subject of the certainty of faith. On what basis is such certainty grounded? On revelation or on the experience

2. C. W. Opzoomer, *De wijsbegeerte de mens met zichzelf verzoenende* (Utrecht, 1849).

3. Isaac da Costa (1798-1860), Dutch poet, born into a Portuguese-Jewish family, became a Protestant and was baptized in Leiden in 1822.

4. Allard Pierson came from a family saturated with the spirit of the Enlightenment. He became a devotee of the modern theology, left the church, and gave up his ministry. He was an academic teacher in Heidelberg beginning in 1870 and in Amsterdam beginning in 1877.

of feeling? Or perhaps even on both? Yet, does experience play a constitutive role? In general one can say that two paths were followed toward this desired goal of certainty, two paths which we can characterize with the following antithesis: certainty of experience versus certainty that can be experienced. The first path, that of the certainty of experience, is the more often traveled. For many it is self-evident that we seek security by means of experience. And this opens the door to an enormous reduction. Can only data which permit verification be declared authentic? And is it clear that these data originate in the Holy Spirit, as if the Holy Scriptures were simply more words from any old source and were not the Word of the living God himself? Our verifications include much unsteadiness, so that whoever expects everything from them will be hopelessly disappointed. The path of experience leads nowhere but to absolute uncertainty.

The Certainty of Revelation

How different is the second path mentioned above, the path of certainty that can be experienced. This phrase implies that we can trust the Word of God, can trust confidently and serenely that it is true and reliable apart from our methods of verification. We gain access to this certainty from outside ourselves by way of *means,* that is, by way of Word and sacrament. This is the way of the prophetic Word which is quite solid. In the Word of the crucified and risen Christ the certainty which lies outside ourselves in him is proclaimed to us. This certainty is grounded securely in God's own faithfulness, God's own covenant, God's own oath. The way of means works through the justifying power of the Word in its actual use. In comparison with this "experienceable" certainty, even our most certain experiences are fragile as aspen leaves quaking in the wind. They are the certainty only of feelings which contradict one another, for no certainty can be securely anchored in feeling.

The path of *means* leads to the certainty of faith. The promises of God are not made to individuals but are directed to the church. Our faith yields to this — if, that is, we risk engaging only the naked Word of God, as H. F. Kohlbrügge (1803-75), the prominent Reformed preacher from Elberfeld, reminds us, reckoning as he did with all subjective experiences and feelings.

Calvin and Experience

Back to Calvin. We may ask: Does it make sense to query a man like Calvin, who sought to answer all problems decisively from the Holy Scriptures' witness to divine revelation, as to his position regarding experience? Yet everything which experience teaches us was extraordinarily important to Calvin. And thus it is that again and again there appears in him, next to the appeal to the revelation of God — that is, to the Holy Scriptures — also reference to experience. His commentaries and sermons teem with expressions like *Experientia docet, ostendit, clamat, confirmat, demonstrat, convincit, testatur;* also, *ipsa experientia satis docemur* or *usu ipso docemur.* From all this it is obvious that Calvin and his theology do not float detached from reality but constantly relate truth and reality to one another.

Of course, it is not appropriate to interrogate Calvin according to categories derived from our modern interests. Rather, we must be aware of the presuppositions from which he himself proceeded historically and theologically.[5] By posing this discussion in terms of the certainty of experience versus the certainty that can be experienced, we have moved very close to the Reformers, to Luther and Calvin. The Reformation began with the question of certainty. Luther found security in the promises of the gospel, outside us in Christ.[6] Here Calvin stands close to Luther. For Calvin this is no pietistic question: How do I know that the Word is bound for me with the Holy Spirit and that the Word is directed with certainty to me? Calvin's theology is not born from this sort of *Anfechtung,* but rather from the question of certainty. Calvin's theology comes not from his subjective experiences but from God, who bears witness to us of the divine salvation in the Word and in our experience. Calvin terms this witness of the Holy Spirit in our hearts the *testimonium spiritus sancti internum.*[7]

5. Regarding the etymology of the word *experientia,* we can say this: the Latin word is closely related to the verb *experiri.* This describes an active investigation and questioning. The stem found throughout is *per* (= through). Cf. also the Greek verb *peiro,* that is, to drill through, and *peiraomai,* that is, to try. Actually it means "to plumb," that is, "to stick a measuring rod into the water." This meaning is reached by two means: (a) Someone tests me and I make note of it as a test to which I am submitted; cf. the term *periculum* (= a danger to which I am exposed). (b) The result of the test is that I have now become experienced, thus *peritus* (an experienced person); cf. the Greek *pepeiramenos.* Thus, from the very origin of the term both the passive and the active meanings are interwoven. *Experientia* and *experimentum* were often used interchangeably. This is true also of Calvin. Only later were they differentiated. Thus, originally *experientia* meant an awareness which comes to us by means of perception. This is an objective occurrence. Later, however, the meaning became more subjective through the entire complex of subjective events and experiences. In this context it is important that Calvin in his French edition of the *Institutes* translates the Latin word *documentum* with "experience"; cf. *Institutes* 1.13.13; 2.7.11; 2.8.3; 3.20.15.

6. Cf. W. van 't Spijker, " 'Extra nos' en 'in nobis' bij Calvijn," pp. 166ff.; W. van 't Spijker, *Luther. Belofte en ervaring* (Goes: Oosterbaan & LeCointre, 1983), passim.

7. G. P. van Itterzon, "Het Testimonium Spiritus Sancti bij Calvijn," in *Belijnd Belijden* (Kampen: J. H. Kok, 1971), pp. 43-56.

Testimonium Spiritus Sancti

That which the Holy Spirit testifies in our hearts is invincible truth; not, Calvin writes, "as those miserable men, who habitually bind over their minds to the thralldom of superstition; but we feel that the undoubted power of his divine majesty lives and breathes there. By this power we are drawn and inflamed . . . to obey him, yet . . . more vitally and more effectively than by mere human willing and knowing."[8]

Calvin appeals to the experience of every believer and emphasizes that no verbal explanation of this *experientia* is ever fully adequate. Here the most rigorous science must respectfully stand back. This *experientia* consists of a conviction, a realization, and a feeling. He writes: "Such, then, is a conviction that requires no reasons; such, a knowledge with which the best reason agrees — in which the mind truly reposes more securely and constantly than in any reasons; such, finally, a feeling that can be born only of heavenly revelation."[9] The knowledge of God rests more truly on living experience than on lofty and vague speculation. Thus we believe, taught by our experience, that God is in fact just as he has revealed himself to be in his Word.[10]

Calvin and the Science of His Time

For Calvin, experience is tremendously important. He was a scientist, and he highly esteemed and promoted scientific research. The call to praise and honor God meant for Calvin that we are to explore the creation diligently and to praise God for all his works. We praise God with all our faculties, not only with our eyes but also with our reason. Calvin said those who neglect the exploration of the creation were as guilty as those who in their exploration allowed the Creator to fade into oblivion. He spoke sharply against the fanatics, the opponents of science, who said scientific research made people proud, and who did not recognize that such research was a very useful instrument in bringing us to true knowledge of God and to a way of life benefiting all people. Calvin concludes with the old proverb, "nothing is more arrogant than ignorance."[11] This way of framing the task of scientific research was not to be an oppressive law but was perceived as a task of joy and gratitude to God.

---

8. Calvin, *Institutes* 1.7.5.

9. Calvin, *Institutes* 1.7.5.

10. Calvin, *Institutes* 1.10.2.

11. *Ioannis Calvini opera quae supersunt omnia*, ed. W. Baum, E. Cunitz, and E. Reuss, 59 vols. (Brunswick and Berlin: Schwetschke and Son, 1863-1900), 49:429, hereafter cited as *CO*.

Calvin had a high regard for science, sympathizing not so much with "speculative" natural science but more with the dependable empirical sciences of his day. By means of these sciences, those who were zealous revealed the secrets of the macrocosm and the microcosm.[12] Those with the gifts and the time for this were not to withdraw themselves from such research.[13]

Although he was highly critical of pagan thinking, Calvin did not reject everything of heathen origin. His views regarding general grace preclude any total denial of the literary and scientific heritage of the Greeks. He was too realistic and too talented a humanist to think that the fall had resulted in a total corruption of humanity on the scientific level. In Calvin's view, the light of truth shone clear in heathen research, and if we say that the Spirit of God is the only source of truth, then we will never deny and look down on truth wherever this truth may be revealed, lest we insult the Spirit of God.[14]

We might expect that Calvin would follow the general practice of reading Greek cosmology into the Bible. To the contrary, however, he perceived more sharply than his contemporaries the discrepancy between the Aristotelian astronomy of his day and the worldview of Genesis. While Moses spoke of a single firmament, the astronomers distinguished several spheres. The source of this difference between Moses and the astronomers was that Moses wrote in a popular manner and style and conformed himself to that which everyone with normal understanding could follow, while the astronomers explored all that only the wisest aspects of human reason could grasp. Thus research is not reprehensible and science is not to be condemned, even though lunatics mindlessly denounce that which is foreign to them.[15]

Although he recognized the contradiction between the scientific system of his day and the biblical text, this freedom nevertheless made it possible for Calvin not to downgrade the results of scientific research. This openness of Calvin to the world also made it possible for him to confess that Copernicus's system was true even though there was no hint of it in the Bible. Prejudice has often led scholars astray on this point, in that Calvin has been made into a foe of Copernicanism, despite the fact that this view is very clearly not in agreement with Calvin's exegetical principles.

It is doubtless the case that Calvin's view of accommodation exercised a significant influence in Protestant countries through Copernican scientists.

---

12. Calvin, *Institutes* 1.5.2 and 3.
13. *CO* 23:22 (commentary on Gen. 1:16).
14. Calvin, *Institutes* 2.2.15.
15. *CO* 23:22.

Calvin's Exegesis

Calvin's exegetical methods were grounded in the Reformation insight that the religious message of the Holy Scriptures is accessible to everyone. Moses compiled his work for everyone to use. Whoever desires to delve into astronomy and other profound science would have to look elsewhere.[16]

The freedom of scientific research, which can only hunt after the truth of God in the creation, does not impede Calvin in his understanding that the Bible is the Word of God, in the fullest sense of the term,[17] yet is a word in which the Holy Spirit voluntarily obscured the divine glory by means of the veil of humanity. The limitations of Pauline logic are by no means a restriction of heavenly wisdom; but rather, thanks to the special providence of God, we are instructed regarding the greatest mysteries of God by means of the contemptible lowliness of these words. Our trust rests not on human articulation but only on the effectivity of the Holy Spirit.[18] It is clear that in Calvin's view there exists a parallel between the lowliness of the Word which became flesh and the Word which became Holy Scripture.

In his commentary on 1 Corinthians, Calvin comes to speak of *humaniora* and *rhetorica;* he says these are excellent gifts of the Holy Spirit and should not be condemned as if they were in opposition to piety.[19] Nevertheless, if Paul had preached the cross with philosophical acuity and rhetorical flourishes, the sermon would have lost its power and appeal.[20] It must be accepted without any amelioration of its scandal.

Despite being the Word of God, the letters of Paul are at the same time words of Paul. Calvin claims for himself the freedom to criticize their style and language and even to point out the dependency of Paul's commands on his particular time. Calvin reduces the warning against long hair to the Greeks' view of this as effeminate. Paul considers the old practice to be natural, even though at Paul's time in Germany and France it would have been considered unthinkable to cut one's hair.[21] Calvin also admitted the possibility of a factual error in the original text. Facts and numbers in Stephen's speech do not correspond with Old Testament texts. Calvin says this is demonstrably a mistake that must be corrected but admonishes us to attend to the central message of the text rather than anxiously torturing ourselves with single words.[22]

16. *CO* 23:18 (commentary on Gen. 1:6).
17. *CO* 52:382f. (commentary on 2 Tim. 3:16).
18. *CO* 49:98 (commentary on Rom. 5:15).
19. *CO* 49:321 (commentary on 1 Cor. 1:17).
20. *CO* 49:320 (commentary on 1 Cor. 1:17).
21. *CO* 49:478 (commentary on 1 Cor. 11:14).
22. *CO* 48:137f. (commentary on Acts 7:14-16).

Experience as Hermeneutical Key

Calvin thus understands the Scriptures not as objective truth or scholastic doctrine, but as a living message rooted in life and connected to reality. It is for this reason that experience plays such a great role in his exegesis. Experience can function as a hermeneutical key in the service of exegesis. The Bible places us in the middle of the battle of faith *coram Deo,* and therefore in the foreword to his Psalms commentary Calvin can testify that he has himself experienced that which the Scripture testifies. His experiences in the church in the battle over its reformation qualify him as an interpreter of Holy Scripture; they serve him as a key to open the Scriptures. Granted, he relates this primarily to the Psalms because within the Bible these represent something particular: they are able to describe more of human suffering and other experiences than other parts of Scripture, which tend simply to pass on what God has commissioned their writers to convey to us.[23] But Calvin's *Institutes* and commentaries taken as a whole demonstrate that in no biblical book does he find exclusively an explication of doctrine. Throughout, the Bible reveals the faith struggles of its writers. It is simply that in the Psalms this emerges so centrally in the forefront that they especially open up this dimension of Scripture for thematic treatment. We might also note that it was not in his first interpretation of Romans, written when he was in his thirties, that Calvin placed experience as a motto overarching the whole, but rather he speaks of it only toward the end of his journey — this derives from the nature of experience itself.[24]

Calvin is not a theologian of experience in the sense of placing his own mystical experiences at the forefront. Yet he is also no scholastic presenting only systematic truths. For him the Scriptures are not a collection of dogma, but he sees them embedded in the life of faith of the community and the individual, in the fabric of sustaining faith within Christian and ecclesial existence. Thus it is proof of proper use of the Bible when in Chrysostom's exegesis there is so much presented of the life of the church in which he lived. And thus Jerome can also be faulted because his exegesis reveals nothing of his Christian and ecclesial existence and is of no help in the "practice in Christianity" (to use Kierkegaard's terms).

---

23. *CO* 31:20 ("Iehan Calvin aux fideles et debonnaires lecteurs, Salut. Comm. Pseaumes").

24. D. Schellong, *Calvins Auslegung der synoptischen Evangelien,* Forschungen zur Geschichte und Lehre des Protestantismus, 10/XXXVIII (Munich: Chr. Kaiser, 1969), p. 18.

The Word of God and Our Experience

God instructs us by two means: through his Word and through his actions which we experience.[25] In both cases we are dealing with the same God. Our experience shows us the same God as does the Word; experience teaches us that God is just as he reveals himself to be in his Word.[26]

There are two forms of perception: The first is the *scientia fidei,* which we derive from the Word, although the content itself is not yet visible. The other is the *scientia experientiae* or *experimentalis,* in which God permits the fulfillment to follow immediately and thereby proves that he has not spoken in vain.[27] There is thus a knowledge of faith which is awakened solely through faith, and conversely, an experiential knowledge arising from the working of the Word.[28] Calvin concedes to the Word of God the absolute priority. Experience is never a priori but always a posteriori. It is effected through the Word, and it confirms, after the fact, the reliability of the Word. The perception and certainty of the grace of God can be sought and found only in the Word. From this then proceeds experience as confirmation.[29] Such experience does not have to do with moods and feelings but rather with the saving acts of God. Nothing can strengthen faith more than the remembrance of the acts by which God has given us extraordinary proof of his grace, truth, and power.[30] These experiences are signs with which God proclaims the steadfastness and power of his promises.[31]

In his reading of Psalm 27, Calvin speaks beautifully of the correlation between faith and experience. He understands the face of God in reference to the perceptible working of the grace and favor of God. "Help, Lord, that I may truly experience that you have been near to me." Faith longs for the tangible working of the grace and goodness of God. At the same time, however, the primacy of the Word remains unchallenged. We must pay attention to the connection between the Word of God and the experiential perception of grace. For, if God is to demonstrate his presence to us by means of actions, then one must have previously sought him in his Word.[32] The same God stands behind both Word and experience, providing an inner agreement between the Word and the experience. Experience is not direct speech from God; *experientia nuda*

---

25. *CO* 31:660 (commentary on Ps. 71:17).
26. Calvin, *Institutes* 1.10.2.
27. *CO* 44:162 (commentary on Zech. 2:9).
28. *CO* 42:596 (commentary on Joel 3:17).
29. *CO* 31:435 (commentary on Ps. 43:2-5); *CO* 31:463 (commentary on Ps. 46:7).
30. *CO* 31:276 (commentary on Ps. 27:2).
31. *CO* 31:576f. (commentary on Ps. 60:8).
32. *CO* 31:276 (commentary on Ps. 27:9).

does not serve us. It requires the Word[33] and enlightenment. Experience appears in close proximity to the Word. It has to do with truth and reality. Truth tends always toward reality. The Scripture is true; we will experience it. This gives the faith perspective an eschatological power. The *scientia Dei* transcends the world; it reaches higher than the heavens, to bring knowledge of hidden things, for our holiness is invisible. We are not hoping for things we can see. Believers are granted to know that Christ was sent to us from the Father, and to know this in the reality of our experience.[34] Calvin's concern is to make clear that both realms, that of the Word and that of experience, of truth and of reality, are governed by the reign of the one Holy Spirit.

The Contradiction of Experiences

Calvin is a theologian and not an anthropologist or an empiricist. He does not wish to divert our devotion from the Holy Scripture and onto our own experience. He knows only too well how inadequate and imperfect our experience is. There is no real access to God from those deepest depths of our hearts which so fascinate all true mystics. Like Luther, Calvin places the method of experience, so to speak, in juxtaposition to that of faith. There is only one way of coming to God, namely, the way of faith in the Word of God. We cannot recognize and grasp the favor of God from our *experientia nuda,* our naked experience, but rather only from the witness of the Holy Scriptures.[35] If our faith experience does not rest on this foundation, it is hanging in the air and can quite easily be exposed to the aberrations of our feelings. Faith transcends experience, and transcends it greatly. The presence of God cannot be measured by our experiences; they never entirely correspond to one another. For if we were to measure God's help on the basis of our feeling, our faith would soon waver and we would lose our courage and every last flicker of hope.[36]

Thus it is that Calvin arrives at the point of placing the *salvifica Dei notitia* in opposition to the *experimentalis notitia* which does not penetrate to our hearts. This *notitia evalida* is devoid of roots and life.[37] It is the perception of God on the part of the godless, who nevertheless must recognize that the Lord is God. And in this way Calvin can say, in the words of a quite well known

33. *CO* 31:424 (commentary on Ps. 41:12).
34. *CO* 44:162 (commentary on Zech. 2:9).
35. *CO* 31:424 (commentary on Ps. 51:12).
36. *CO* 31:103 (commentary on Ps. 9:13).
37. *CO* 31:778 (commentary on Ps. 78:19).

proverb of his day, "experience is the master of fools."[38] How dumb must one indeed be if the lessons of experience do not make one wise!

Calvin's concern is that our awareness and the experience of faith might come together. He considers this very important for a teacher in the church.[39] Experience is authenticated from the outset by the testimony of the Scriptures. In itself, however, it is unreliable.

Experientia contra Experientiam

To the unreliability of experience in itself is connected the fact that experiences can be quite contradictory. Calvin knows of the paradox of experience; for instance, God hides the granting of his favor and withdraws it from our perception. For this reason it is an incomprehensible paradox that God is near to us even as our heart is being consumed with sadness.[40] Calvin knows that the believer can experience such contradictory things every day. According to human perception, one may often seem to have been abandoned by God. Here only the recourse to the Word of promise can help. Things that are incomprehensible to the mind, and that seem to be mutually contradictory, represent real temptations to experience and are overcome solely through faith which listens obediently to the Word. These contradictory experiences with which faith must wrestle, such as the mutually contradictory experiences of fear and hope, emerge in one and the same human heart. Experience teaches that even where hope reigns in the heart, fear can rear up alongside. When it seems poised to get the better of us, we can be helped only by flinging ourselves on the naked Word of promise.[41] The promises of the gospel give us the power to press on, right in the midst of temptations toward unbelief, in praise and hope in the Lord. And that, says Calvin, underwrites the fact that God is nevertheless trustworthy, even in those places where we may not perceive his goodness and power, yet where we do not give up ascribing to his Word its sure glory.[42] Our experiences are often inadequate and contradictory. To our limited minds, experience often does not correspond to the promise of God.[43]

38. *CO* 31:486 (commentary on Ps. 59:11).
39. *CO* 32:2 (commentary on Ps. 91:1-4).
40. *CO* 31:344 (commentary on Ps. 34:19).
41. *CO* 31:548f. (commentary on Ps. 56:45).
42. *CO* 31:525f. (commentary on Ps. 52:3).
43. *CO* 31:703 (commentary on Ps. 75:7).

Interpretation of Psalm 116

It is clear from his interpretation of Psalm 116 that Calvin has a double understanding of experience. On the one side is the engagement with the Word which leads to the certainty of faith and salvation; on the other, the various experiences taking place in times of despair and temptation, experiences into which the believer is drawn over and over again through the same Word which had awakened his or her faith. According to Psalm 116, David had actually experienced help from great danger, for which help he is thanking God. Here his soul is addressing itself: "Be now content again, for the Lord has done good for you." But Calvin wonders here whether the actual experience alone of God's gracious help can heal the fear and trembling in our soul. He answers that, on the contrary, this can occur only through faith in the promises which remain in force even when God is hiding the signs of his graciousness and help.[44]

In such negative experiences the only thing that helps is an uninterrupted attentiveness to the Word. For the peace of God is higher than all reason (Phil. 4:7). This is what enables believers to remain calmly rooted in their lives even when the whole world is beginning to totter.[45] Within the paradox of these experiences the believer holds on to the Holy Scriptures as the decisive means of help in grappling with temptations. The true knowledge of our experience remains hidden from us if the Word does not enlighten us.[46]

Faith and Experience

Faith is a "full and decisive" certainty, "as is usual in regard to matters ascertained and clear."[47] The reason for this lies in the Holy Scriptures. Faith grants to the Scriptures the *Plerophoria* in which God's goodness is placed before our eyes, free of all doubt. And this must occur so that we feel its loveliness in truth and experience it within ourselves.[48] Here as well experience confirms faith. Both in fact and in experience God demonstrates his grace.[49] We are allowed to perceive the very being of God by means of the various experiences we have of him. In this way we become certain that God is gracious to us. For if the grace

---

44. *CO* 32:194 (commentary on Ps. 116:7).
45. *CO* 32:194 (commentary on Ps. 116:7).
46. *CO* 31:577 (commentary on Ps. 60:8).
47. Calvin, *Institutes* 3.2.15.
48. Calvin, *Institutes* 3.2.15.
49. *CO* 32:829 (commentary on Ps. 89:47-49).

of God were not made known to us through the experiences we have every day, how should we ever come to joyful confidence in it?[50] Now, God is probably also patient toward the godless, but they are not receptive to any grace. But the faithful receive God's goodness with the living affect of faith.[51]

What does Calvin mean by this *experientia fidei* or *sensus fidei?* The miracle of the Holy Spirit is a total, spirit- and heart-transforming occurrence. The effectivity of the Spirit of God as *interior magister* is a double one: illumination and sealing. Faith has both a noetic and an affective side. The decisive accent, however, lies on the affective moment; faith is primarily a matter of the heart. The illumination of the mind by the Holy Spirit goes hand in hand with the Spirit's working in the heart. The seal of the Spirit makes the authority of the divine Word certain and opens the door to trust in the promise of divine mercy. For this is not an affair "of the tongue but of life. It is not apprehended by the understanding and memory alone, as other disciplines are, but it is received only when it possesses the whole soul, and finds a seat and resting place in the inmost affection of the heart."[52] *Experientia* is not an independent spiritual property of the human being, but is the working of the new-creating Spirit. It participates in objective reality. The Spirit testifies in both the Word and the heart. The believer hears this and experiences it. In the appeal to the heart, one's affect and the will to action as the obedience of faith are included. Piety is not a life of feelings but a practice of piety. The bare Word does not by itself create new life. The Holy Spirit must plant the gospel deep in our hearts.[53] But the goal is a life of sanctification to the glory of God. Thus for Calvin the question of experience never revolves around events or feelings as such, but around the witness of the Holy Spirit which is proven true in our hearts. This has its christological foundation in that the Holy Spirit is the Spirit of the Son continually drawing us to Christ and thus simultaneously to the Father. The center of the faith experience is communion with Christ. This experience receives an especially personal accent in our implanting into Christ. Yet the Holy Spirit never works individually but always communally. Implanting into Christ always also means our incorporation into his community. Thus Calvin cuts off all religious individualism at its root, and there can also be no spiritualizing talk.[54] This is what distinguishes Calvin from all mystics, even among subsequent Reformed Christians. Christ has reconciled us to God the

---

50. *CO* 32:274 (commentary on Ps. 119:132).
51. *CO* 32:415 (commentary on Ps. 145:8).
52. Calvin, *Institutes* 3.6.4.
53. Calvin, *Institutes* 3.6.4.
54. W. van 't Spijker, "Experientia in reformatorisch licht," p. 251.

Father and gathered us from dispersion into the community of his body, so that we may grow together though his Word into one soul and one body.

Election and Experience

Paul Wernle writes, "One cannot emphasize enough that the belief in predestination is the final consequence of faith in grace and Christ in the face of the puzzling facts of experience."[55] The doctrine of election is intended to provide an answer to the *magnae* and *arduae quaestiones* arising from the fact that the proclamation of the Word does not reach all human beings and is accepted only by a few of those it reaches.[56] Calvin teaches the mystery of election as a student of Scripture, but he explains it also from experience and perception. Experience shows the stupidity of those who foolishly proclaim that grace has reached all without any distinctions.[57] The proof from experience, besides the testimony of Scripture, helps to assert the reality of election. The questions about God's election are unavoidable. Thus one must tell the believers what to think about it. Every grace is received through God's mercy, and only in this way is God's honor upheld. When Paul witnesses God's election, he speaks about something we know from experience.[58]

Calvin also knows of an inner experience of election. He points to the effects of election. Election is based upon God's benevolence, but the latter is recognized from its effect on us.[59] This effect is the spirit of sanctification. The expressions of the new life in purity and holiness become signs and specimen.[60] Our blessedness comes from God's unmerited grace. At the same time, it must be applied by us through the experience of faith in a way that God thereby sanctifies us, that is, makes us into his property through the Holy Spirit.[61] Although Calvin summons us powerfully not to seek the certainty of our election within ourselves but rather to become certain of it in Christ as the mirror of our election, this does not detract from the fact that he also speaks of signs of election, namely, the Spirit's sanctification and enlightenment. Werner Krusche has provided compelling observations on this point.[62] Thus we do

---

55. P. Wernle, *Der evangelische Glaube nach den Hauptschriften der Reformatoren*, vol. 3, *Calvin* (Tübingen: J. C. B. Mohr, 1919), p. 403.

56. *CO* 55:209 (commentary on 1 Pet. 1:1).

57. *CO* 31:605 (commentary on Ps. 65:5).

58. *CO* 51:261 (sermon on Eph. 1:3-4).

59. *CO* 55:208 (commentary on 1 Pet. 1:1).

60. *CO* 55:311 (commentary on 1 John 2:3).

61. *CO* 55:209 (commentary on 1 Pet. 1:1).

62. W. Krusche, *Das Wirken des Heiligen Geistes nach Calvin* (Göttingen: Vandenhoeck & Ruprecht, 1957), pp. 252ff.

find within ourselves a legitimate confirmation of our election.[63] The Reformer also calls us to a certain self-examination as to whether the inner marks are in us; namely, the roots of the fear of God and of faith.[64]

Although Calvin does not use the syllogisms, we must nevertheless observe that one finds some hints to them, to both the *syllogismus practicus* and the *syllogismus mysticus*. That being said, however, the Reformer is not primarily concerned with experience in and of itself but with that to which the Holy Spirit attests in our hearts. In all this he does not require us to imprison ourselves within our inner experience. We are elected in Christ and thereby *extra nos*.[65] And Calvin also does not demand that we examine ourselves as to whether our trust seems to be strong enough to be considered real faith, but he rather encourages us to let our trust in the Word be strong enough. Thus while he does provoke an interest in reflecting on one's own trust in faith, at the same time he calls us away from that, toward a believing trust in the salvific promise of the Word of God which alone grounds our faith. Where, however, this thread of self-reflection makes itself autonomous — and this actually occurred in later Calvinism — it becomes a deadly threat to the assurance of salvation which Calvin always taught so freshly and joyfully along with Martin Luther. The fact that a path leads from here to an introverted pietism cannot be denied. But Calvin himself did not follow this path. Rather, he invites us to an unshakable self-surrender into rest in God's promises.[66] That is necessarily the end of all reflection. Moreover, Calvin names perseverance in faith as one of the unmistakable signs of election. Thus he grounds the certainty of election by means of something which is completely withdrawn from human experience and reflection.[67]

The Connection of Word and Spirit

Calvin warned explicitly against separating Word and Spirit. In opposition to enthusiasts and spiritualists — and among these he numbers not only the sectarian spiritualists but also the pope — Calvin passionately held up the holy bond *(sacer nexus)* between Word and Spirit. Calvin says frankly that these

---

63. *CO* 52:206 (commentary on 1 Thess. 2:13).

64. *CO* 40:281 (*praelectiones in Ezekiel* 13:9).

65. *CO* 51:147 (commentary on Eph. 1:4).

66. Calvin, *Institutes* 3.24.7.

67. H. Otten, *Prädestination in Calvins theologischer Lehre*, 2nd ed. (Neukirchen-Vluyn: Neukirchener Verlag, 1968), p. 63.

groups are dealing not with the Spirit of God but with the spirit of the devil in separating the Spirit of God from the Word of God.[68]

God's Spirit does not lead away from the Word nor transcend the Word, but leads us into the Word. Calvin can describe the intimacy of this *sacer nexus,* this holy bond of Word and Spirit, with very strong expressions such as: God never separates his hand from his mouth; he never comes with only the bare sermon, but his hand is somehow included *(quodammodo inclusa)* in his Word. God desires that the power of his Spirit be somehow included in the proclamation of the gospel. With this characteristic phrase both the close bond between Word and Spirit and the eternal freedom of God are brought to expression.[69]

Therefore, says Calvin, we should not anxiously question our brothers' and sisters' election but, on the contrary, respect them on the grounds of our own vocation so that we acknowledge as chosen all those who by faith are part of the community.[70] And that means that by means of this preaching of election, faith blossoms into full certainty and trust when the believer experiences that salvation is grounded in God's eternally electing love. We can never be certain of our election if we are dependent on signs perceptible within ourselves — namely, the strength of our faith, our possession of the Spirit, or the trustworthiness of our sanctification.

The certainty of faith is not to be achieved by means of introspection, of reflection on the state of our own faith, but only by means of our gaze on Christ, the mirror of our election.[71] Our gaze on him in whom we are elected makes us certain of our salvation.[72] Here it is not a matter of human steadfastness but of God's own faithfulness and the steadfastness of his covenant. The gift of perseverance is not a condition of faith but is an eschatological gift of the God who in freedom is the Faithful One, who does not take back his election but perfects it. This certainty of the promise of perseverance is not a certainty grounded in our experience (although it is experienced in faith) such that we could create our security from our own experiences. It is the certainty of faith which is ever given anew, by means of which we move into experience and overcome our doubts.

---

68. *CO* 47:355 (commentary on John 14:26).
69. *CO* 41:112 (*praelectiones in Daniel* 8:17).
70. *CO* 55:207 (commentary on 1 Pet. 1:1).
71. *CO* 54:54 (sermon on 2 Tim. 1:9-10).
72. *CO* 51:281 (sermon on Eph. 1:4-6).

The Wisdom of the World and the Wisdom of the Holy Spirit

In his interpretation of 1 Corinthians 1, Calvin, with Paul, contrasts the wisdom of this world and the wisdom of the Holy Spirit.[73] The wisdom of the world is all that human beings can comprehend with the natural powers of their reason, making use of perception, learning, and science. Calvin appreciates this knowledge and science very highly as gifts of the Holy Spirit. He calls science the greatest gift of God in this world. Knowledge and science are part of the nobility of humanity by which human beings are raised above all other creatures. The sciences are to be held in highest honor; they serve civilization; they are a contribution to the *vere humanum,* the true humanity.

Yet Calvin says God makes this entire wisdom into foolishness, thus condemns it to folly. For the knowledge of all sciences is merely smoke if it is not connected to the heavenly wisdom given to us through Jesus Christ. Human beings with all their sharp wits are nevertheless as helpless to understand the hidden things of God as a donkey trying to understand a musical concert.[74] Or, to use another image, with all our wisdom we are color-blind when it comes to distinguishing the wisdom of God. And it is foolishness when, trusting our own reason, with the help of our knowledge, we try to flee to heaven, to pass judgment on the deep mysteries of the reign of God, and to break through to its knowledge, for this is all hidden to human reason. We can be highly educated and still not perceive God. Yet it has pleased God to reveal his true wisdom to his children.

Conclusion

Calvin is not interested in human religious experience in and of itself, but much more in that which is experienced in faith, that to which God attests in his Word and which he confirms in our experience. Calvin never says, with Bernard of Clairvaux, "Credo, ut experiar." This represents the clear boundary between all mystics and the true, biblical Christian community, which for Calvin was so extraordinarily important. Thus for Calvin, experience was at root an objective occurrence. Even in *experientia* his concern is that to which God testifies — in the heart, and in the history of the church and the world. Therefore Calvin erects a strong bulwark against the wave of anthropocentric subjectivism and individualism already surging in the Renaissance. As a leader of the second generation of the Reformation, Calvin saw this more clearly than did

73. *CO* 49:324 (commentary on 1 Cor. 1:20).
74. *CO* 49:324 (commentary on 1 Cor. 1:20).

Luther, thanks to the more intensive debate with the enthusiasts shortly after Luther, in which the onslaught of modern humanism and rationalism announced itself. Luther and Calvin both become theologians of the Holy Spirit by means of the existential challenge of the Word of God which led them to living faith in Christ and salvation. This is especially true of Calvin. Luther considered *experientia* primarily a factor of the *Anfechtung* he experienced so very excruciatingly and profoundly, by means of which he was driven to the heart of the gospel, namely, the free grace of Jesus Christ, which made him utterly certain of his salvation by the divine Word of comfort. His *Anfechtungen* taught him to attend to the Word. Calvin, of course, knows also the resulting paradox of the *simul iustus ac peccator,* but his faith experience was primarily an encounter with the sovereignty of divine grace. This grace happens for him, just as for Luther, in the crucified and risen Christ, who through his Spirit creates new life through the discernible transformation of our existence, which in its totality must be submitted to the rule of God in Jesus Christ according to his will. This works itself out primarily thanks to the community of Christ which the Holy Spirit creates through Word and sacrament, by means of a conscious incorporation into the body of Christ, i.e., the *communio sanctorum.* For this reason church and congregation mean more to Calvin than to Luther. In a certain sense that is even true of his doctrine of ministry — or, better, ministries. He sees all the biblically grounded ministries in the church as establishments by the Lord, who gave his Spirit that we might serve him in the Spirit. It is for this reason that faith given by Word and sacrament is the presupposition of all legitimate service in ministry in the congregation. Thus the question of the minister's own faith experience, including theological doctrine, is not inappropriate. But his teaching and practice of church discipline show that Calvin considers confession of faith and proof of Christian transformation to be sufficient.

Pietism's challenge to Reformation theology, regarding the personal religiosity of the Christian, the preacher, and the teacher, has a certain justification in light of the *vocatio interna* by which the Holy Spirit calls people to the service of Christ and his Word. In Calvin's view, however, such a challenge is to be dismissed when it makes certain experiences and events into criteria of faith (though, of course, he would grant that such faith is never without an experiential aspect). The church with its life and service stands in the world; today's church, reduced to (and blessed with) unpretentiousness, stands in this world which is more and more a de-Christianized world. Its proclamation and pastoral care are therefore strongly mission-oriented, and must thus take up the justifiable question of contemporary humanity, struggling with so much uncertainty, as to the possibility of experiencing God and the divine reality. It must do this not by trying to deliver new proofs for the existence of God. But it is a matter of inviting the people of our day, with Luther and Calvin, to seek certainty not in the authenticity of their own experiences but in the reliable Word of the gospel.

And with this we may conclude: whoever seeks security in human experience will never find it. True security lies outside us in Christ, whom God reveals to us. And that is a knowledge which surpasses all reason.

CHAPTER 23

The Contemporary Relevance
of Calvin's Social Ethics

Hans-Helmut Esser

Introductory Remarks

This subject is not new. But it emerges whenever in global or local crisis situations the sixteenth-century solutions (especially those of Geneva) are consulted as paradigms for modernity. Thus, e.g., a quarter-century ago the most knowledgeable scholar of Calvin's economic and social ethics, André Biéler, announced the present and future significance of Calvin's relevant teachings under the provocative title "God's Commandment and the Hunger of the World: Calvin, Prophet of the Industrial Age. Foundations and Methods in Calvin's Social Ethics."[1] We may avert the misunderstanding of "prophet" as eccentric visionary by recognizing that *"propheteuein"* in the New Testament sense is best translated in the sixteenth century as well as today by "relevant preaching." Biéler himself guards his study against the dangers of anachronism and against the assertion "that Calvin's economic and social ethics could be applied unaltered to modern industrial society." Nevertheless, he risks "summarizing the degree to which Calvin was an innovator in the field of social ethics, one who recognized the harbin-

---

1. A. Biéler, *Gottes Gebot und der Hunger der Welt — Calvin, Prophet des industriellen Zeitalters. Grundlage und Methode der Sozialethik Calvins,* trans. from the French by A. Döbli (Zurich: EVZ Verlag, 1966). Original edition: *Calvin, prophète de l'ère industrielle* (Geneva: Editions Labor et Fides S.A., 1961).

Translated by Lisa Dahill.

gers of the West's economic development, and the extent to which therefore his methods of interpreting Holy Scripture and of doing social ethics take into account the new conditions of the modern industrial world."[2] Calvin's groundbreaking innovations in the field of social ethics depend on "the two-fold basis of a strict knowledge of biblical revelation, on the one hand, and of a clear analysis of social and economic reality, on the other." Biéler attempts "to carve out a method for thought and action which could be an example for theology and Christian ethics of all times . . . , in tune both with the dynamic character of biblical theology and with the particular movement of social forms, and thus capable of constructing an effective connection between theology and the world."[3] In this process he draws from a variety of times and places.

Twenty years following the aforementioned study, Ludi Schulze treated the problem of Calvin's "social ethics" in a more qualified manner.[4] He places less emphasis on structural change resulting from the social ethics of Geneva. Rather, he highlights the Reformer's uncovering of an ethic of personal responsibility in the social realm, made possible under the forgiveness of sin as life lived in thanksgiving within the *tertius usus legis*.[5] Yet within the scope of a very thorough, systematic treatment of the theme, even Schulze, in the epilogue, risks pointing to its contemporary relevance: "[Calvin's] thought is . . . still relevant today . . . ; by highlighting the 'everlasting gospel' (Rev. 14:6) and the fundamental attitude of man towards God and his fellowmen he was confronting his own times, even as ours, with the basic relations in which man lives, no matter how much times are changing. Therefore it would be apt to draw up a balance here as regards Calvin's relevance for our time."[6] And Schulze concludes the "balancing act" with this perspective:

> From the viewpoint of the human responsibilities a vast panorama unfolds itself in which the life of thanksgiving can bear its fruits — from international help and development to "bind all men in mutual service," to the most "personal" and simple relation of two people serving and helping each other according to their particular situation. Human responsibility,

2. Biéler, *Gottes Gebot und der Hunger der Welt*, p. 5.

3. Biéler, *Gottes Gebot und der Hunger der Welt*, p. 6.

4. L. Schulze, *Calvin and "Social Ethics": His Views on Property, Interest, and Usury* (Pretoria: Kital, 1985).

5. Citing from the prologue to Schulze's book, thesis 6: "Yet Calvin expounded some biblical truths which still hold true in our modern world and give some provocative answers to many of our modern economic ills." Thesis 7: "Social ethics, being a call to exchange compassion for a merciless crusade against 'structures' (whatever they may mean) has lost sight of the most important thing in economic life: man himself."

6. Schulze, p. 84.

though frail, implies freedom — the freedom of the children of God — and must never be submerged or replaced by a political, economic, or social system or a model as the norm for the whole world.[7]

Historical, Theological, and Ecclesial Presuppositions of Calvin's Social Ethics

John Calvin (1509-64) proposed no formal or closed system of social ethics, yet in both phases of his Geneva activity (1536-38 and 1541-64) he contributed decisively to the social ordering and Reformation structuring of the city-state, both as the most significant theologian of the Western Reformation and as a humanistic jurist of the highest order (a contributor to the Geneva Constitution of 1542-43); here he made use also of his experience within the Strassburg city-state (1538-41).

Calvin's main social-ethical ideas are found in the church orders he produced, in the *Institutes* (parts 3.10 and 4.20), and also in numerous passages of his biblical commentaries, sermons, and letters.[8] His social-ethical approach is characterized by four features: (1) It is anchored solidly in theology and is completely dependent on the center of evangelical faith, on the person and work of Christ; it is thus *christocentric-pneumatological*. (2) The accurate knowledge of *biblical revelation* emerging within it is interpreted in dynamic relation to a society's historical changes. (3) It contains a *scientific* method for analyzing social and economic data. (4) It achieves exceptional historical effectiveness because it demands action that, by means of a *dialectical* method, is attuned to circumstances and inexhaustibly renewed by contact with reality.

"The great break with medieval social ethics is finally completed in Calvin . . . [as an] act of honesty and intellectual uprightness corresponding to the desire to bring doctrine and life, words and works into harmony."[9] In no way does Calvin understand the helping function in a legal sense, but it is bound to Christology and to the work of the Holy Spirit.[10] The key concept of the evangelical relationship between the law and those who are born again is *aequitas* as joyful serenity, which leads for Calvin into a concrete, Christian philosophy of

---

7. Schulze, p. 104.

8. Cf. the index in André Biéler, *La pensée économique et sociale de Calvin* (Geneva: Librairie de l'université, 1959).

9. Herbert Lüthy, "Nochmals: Calvinismus und Kapitalismus — Über die Irrwege einer sozialhistorischen Diskussion," *Schweizerische Zeitschrift für Geschichte* 11 (1961): 131, 133.

10. J. Calvin, *Institutes of the Christian Religion*, ed. F. L. Battles and J. T. McNeill (Philadelphia: Westminster, 1960), 2.7 and 8; 3.6ff.

law.[11] Righteousness "is taught in vain by the commandments until Christ confers it by free imputation and by the Spirit of regeneration."[12]

The *church* as the congregation of the elect is the primary "external means" used by the Holy Spirit to bring people into connection with Christ. The proclamation of the gospel entrusted to it, and its doctrine, aim toward awakening faith and ensuring the communal sanctification of the members of the congregation. Both gifts produce among the faithful unanimity of faith and of order. The sacraments nourish and strengthen faith and sanctification.[13] The congregational leadership — organized into the four realms of service of pastors, doctors, elders, and deacons — exercises spiritual authority within the church. Its authority, even in the tasks of leading people (elders) and caring for the poor and sick (deacons), is that of the Word of God through which Christ himself leads the congregation and gives the ministers, in cooperation with the people, effectiveness by the power of his Spirit.[14] After Word and sacraments, discipline is the third mark of the church. Thus church discipline can only be exercised by means of spiritual authority. It rests on the voluntary insight of faith. It plays a doxological, ethical, and pedagogical role in the congregation and is a part of pastoral care.[15] While not a *societas perfecta*, the congregation of Christ takes responsibility in a special way for the universal public honesty and humanity of the entire society. True piety, however, does not rest on keeping the church's laws.[16]

The Relevance of Calvin's Basic Approach to Social Ethics

The continuing importance of the fundamental presuppositions sketched here emerges above all when they are understood not as program but as promise, set in motion and sustained by those who practice their social ethos of service through the avenues described by the "marks" above. Even in secularist conditions which do not correspond to the microcosmic character of a *corpus christianum* like Geneva, the basic impulses of Calvinistic social ethics remain valid, as do its projected goals. The great social-ethical initiatives of our century, marked by the Barmen Theological Declaration of 1934 (whose keynote was the "royal lordship of Christ in all realms of life") and also by the increas-

---

11. Cf. Dieter Schellong, *Das evangelische Gesetz in der Auslegung Calvins* (Munich: Chr. Kaiser, 1968), p. 69.

12. Calvin, *Institutes* 2.7.2.

13. Calvin, *Institutes* 4.1.1.

14. Calvin, *Institutes* 4.3.2 and 4.8.2.

15. Calvin, *Institutes* 4.12.5.

16. Calvin, *Institutes* 4.10.27.

ing emphasis on the threefold office of Christ in Roman Catholic social ethics after the Second Vatican Council, with all its consequences of becoming a "church for others," move within the fundamental approach uncovered by Calvin in the sixteenth century.[17]

The Relevance of Some Aspects of Calvinist Social Ethics

1. The *work* of Christians is one of the most important aspects of their faithfulness, no matter how little that work can be an end in itself, personally or socially, let alone a justification of one's existence.[18] It gains its worth from God's commission and providence. Just as the various gifts of grace originate in the one Spirit of God, so the various aptitudes, even among the unchurched, come from God's favor.[19] The following "equations" parallel one another:

> original human condition = joyful work
> human sinfulness = curse and alienation
> sacrifice of Christ = liberation from the torment of work.[20]

By the grace of Christ, even arduous labor always gains something of joy as a sign of this grace.[21] Lazy idleness is inconsistent with human destiny.

The conception of work as endurance in faith, on the one hand, and as the responsible ordering of the world derived from that faith, on the other, is paradigmatically illustrated in their inseparable double relationship by the "Prayer before Work" which was added to the Geneva Catechism of 1562:

> Above all, Lord, you will to remain with us through your Holy Spirit, that we may faithfully carry on our profession and calling without deceit and disappointment, so that we may pay more attention to following your ordinances than to satisfying the hunger for riches. Yet if it should please you to permit our work to flourish, give us also the courage to help those who

17. Cf. H.-H. Esser, "Calvinistische Sozialethik," in *Wörterbuch des Christentums*, ed. V. Drehsen and M. Baumotte (Gütersloh: Gerd Mohn, 1989), pp. 189-91. On the Roman Catholic appreciation of Calvin's social ethics, cf. Alexandre Ganoczy, *Ecclesia ministrans. Dienende Kirche und kirchlicher Dienst bei Calvin*, trans. into German by Hans Sayer (Freiburg: Herder, 1968), pp. 45-56.

18. Cf. Calvin, commentary on Luke 17:7-10, in *Ioannis Calvini opera quae supersunt omnia*, ed. W. Baum, E. Cunitz, and E. Reuss, 59 vols. (Brunswick and Berlin: Schwetschke and Son, 1863-1900), 45: 413-15, hereafter cited as *CO*.

19. Cf. Calvin, commentary on Exod. 31:2, in *CO* 25: 58-59.

20. Cf. Calvin, commentary on Gen. 2:15 and 3:17-19, in *CO* 23: 44, 72-77.

21. Cf. Calvin, commentary on Ps. 128:2, in *CO* 32: 327.

live in poverty, according to the authority which you will give us. Keep us in all humility, so that we may not elevate ourselves above those who have not experienced such generosity from you. And if you lay upon us greater poverty and deprivation than our weakness could desire for itself, may you give us the grace to direct our faith wholly toward your promises.[22]

"Work" is placed here into a salvation-historical context, understood as "worship in the daily life of the world," in steadfast overcoming of all obstacles and temptations. This is the origin of the Protestant consciousness of duty, which appears to be considerably beleaguered at present under the pressure of superficial or ideologically determined definitions of work. Some understandings of work find themselves corrected here, such as that which is exclusively focused on the workers' *becoming* human through work (through means of production ostensibly or actually in workers' possession), which wears out the producers of goods as if they were themselves goods. Present-day society would be spared many ritualized worker and class battles if its tariff partners would bring ethical criteria to bear, instead of narrowly selfish and overwhelmingly profit-oriented ones. In the same way, an apotheosis of work, in and of itself, is combated. The constitutions of highly technological nations would find among the overarching premises mentioned above the freedom to acknowledge dialectically both the duty and the right to work, as an expression of ethical social responsibility. So-called solidarity pacts for the defusing of crises might more easily find a basis for common core values.

This contemporizing excursus has introduced the Reformation foundation of the fundamental *freedom to choose one's vocation.* For his own time, Calvin addresses the charismatic restriction of this freedom: in choosing a vocation, a person should respond to God's calling,[23] yet the will of God aims more toward a vocation of service than toward one of striving after profits.[24] Parents are good advisers of their children when they guide this choice of profession by encouraging love of neighbor and the common good.[25] An undesired form of work can be taken on patiently, until God alone opens the desired vocational door.[26] In opposition to the prejudices against so-called unproductive work, Calvin asserts the equal value of all work whose sweat serves human society, whether raising children within the family, teaching, public or private administrative duties, etc.[27] Because God intends to bless

---

22. Cf. Calvin, commentary on Matt. 20:1, in *CO* 45: 547-48.
23. Calvin, commentary on Matt. 20:1, in *CO* 45: 547-48.
24. Cf. Calvin, sermon on Eph. 4:26, in *CO* 51: 627-31.
25. Calvin, sermon on Eph. 4:26, in *CO* 51: 627-31.
26. Cf. Calvin, commentary on Exod. 31:2, in *CO* 25: 58-59.
27. Cf. Calvin, commentary on 2 Thess. 3:10, in *CO* 52: 313.

honest work, there is a right to work and to the nonwithdrawal of the means of work.[28]

In light of the high percentage of present and future output that is being displaced from production into service sectors in highly technological societies, and the temporary unemployment and necessity for retraining which this causes — and especially in the need for increasing ecological service — this entire emerging arena makes Calvin's social-ethical guidelines sound downright visionary.

2. "All human community is a reflection of that holy covenant in which two people become one heart and soul."[29] Within the divine natural order of *monogamy*, which is determined as the first step of human community moving toward perfect harmony, God gives man and woman their best help for living. This station and vocation is also permeated with many shortcomings because of human sin, yet even all human sin has not been able fully to extinguish the divine blessing, once spoken.[30] Personal attraction and spouses' joy in one another are to strengthen marital fidelity, according to God's will. The purpose of marriage is double: to produce offspring and to channel free-floating urges.[31] Everything which endangers marriage, e.g., fornication, lasciviousness, and libertinism, is to be punished by the community and not tolerated in public.

A constitution upheld (and therefore taken seriously) by Christians enacts protection for marriage and the family, and this unites this social-ethical Reformation approach to the general Christian one. It is astonishingly modern in describing the inherent value of marriage as an end in itself, prior to the question of its social purpose. The realism with which shortcomings and threats to marriage are seen would be good for modernism, especially following the so-called sexual revolution of the sixties. The fact that the "bringing forth of offspring" is not merely some medieval relic has been discovered only recently and secondarily by liberal democratic society; here it can be seen in claims to a generational accountability which finds expression in measures for the protection and strengthening of unborn and young human life. The protection of marriage and family publicly — and by public, legal (and thus budgetary) means — from the dangerous influence of the mass communication media seems imperative if in fact *minima moralia* do not apply anymore in public. The wariness toward commitment in so-called marriagelike relations in the modern day — as also in the pre-Reformation

28. Cf. Calvin, commentary and sermon on Deut. 24:1-6, in *CO* 24: 657-58; 28: 149-63.
29. Calvin, commentary on Gen. 2:18, in *CO* 23: 46.
30. Calvin, commentary on Gen. 2:18, in *CO* 23: 46-48.
31. Cf. Calvin, commentary on Gen. 1:28, *CO* 23: 28-29.

Renaissance[32] — must be questioned as to whether it does not shortsightedly forfeit both the marital- and the social-ethical promises offered by the biblical Reformation understanding of marriage.

3. Calvin's *political theories*, which in Geneva could be implemented only in part, brought about powerful historical repercussions and have occupied political and social scientists to the present day.[33]

a. Calvin understands the state as an organic community analogous to the patriarchally ordered family or the head-body relationship. The emphasis here is not primarily on power relations but on citizens' mutual accountability to one another, serving to fulfill both the individual being and the communal responsibilities of human persons. The organismic idea in political theory[34] is grounded transcendentally, beyond its social and biological analogies, in human creatureliness generally and in the rule of Christ specifically, under which Christians know themselves to live.

Even though the analogy to patriarchal ordering is today, for theological and sociological reasons, being replaced by one grounded in the *imago Dei* of man and woman in community,[35] and the transcendent origin of the state is understood as anchored in a thoroughly biblical way in the Trinity,[36] still the assumed binding power of the state as a "gracious ordering of God"[37] continues. In gratitude to God it is then possible secondarily, even within a generally secular understanding of the state, to be reminded of the organismic idea; this

32. Cf. also Gottfried Wilhelm Locher, *Die Zwinglische Reformation im Rahmen der europäischen Kirchengeschichte* (Göttingen: Vandenhoeck & Ruprecht, 1979), pp. 154f. and passim, on the marriage courts of Zürich.

33. Among others, Max Weber, *The Protestant Ethic and the Spirit of Capitalism,* trans. Talcott Parsons (New York: Charles Scribner's Sons, 1930); Ernst Troeltsch, *The Social Teachings of the Christian Churches,* trans. Olive Wyon, 2 vols. (Louisville: Westminster/John Knox, 1992); Biéler, *La pensée économique;* Jürgen Baur, *Gott, Recht und weltliches Regiment im Werk Calvins,* Schriften zur Rechtslehre und Politik 44 (Bonn: H. Bouvier, 1965); cf. the summary of the latter work in H.-H. Esser, "Die Staatsauffassung Calvins und Caspar Olevians," *Monatshefte für Evangelische Kirchengeschichte des Rheinlandes* 37/38 (1988/89): 247-65. This summary contains numerous references to sources in Calvin.

34. Cf. Josef Bohatec, *Calvins Lehre von Staat und Kirche* (1937), and Erik Wolf, *Theologie und Sozialordnung bei Calvin* (1952).

35. Cf. H.-H. Esser, "Der Mensch — Bild Gottes. Eine Grundformel jüdisch-christlicher Anthropologie," in *Kirchlicher Dienst und theologische Ausbildung,* Festschrift für H. Reiss, ed. H. Begemann and C. H. Ratschow (Bielefeld: Luther-Verlag, 1985), pp. 78-90.

36. Cf. Barmen Theological Declaration (1934), Thesis 5, in connection with Theses 1 and 2.

37. Barmen Theological Declaration, Thesis 5.

is especially important when divergent special interests of an egoistical nature compete for dominance.[38]

b. The state is determined in its essence by the *decreed order of the laws.* On the one hand this protects the members of the state, and on the other it is an instrument of power of the government. The positivization and promulgation of laws continue to be indispensable. The ordering of the state serves the protection of peace at home and abroad.

The idea of the rule of law, based on declarations of fundamental and human rights, is not explicitly known to Calvin; yet historically it develops as a moral claim on the representatives of higher and lower power for the purpose of *legitimacy* to protect the people, materially including also the principle of judicial power that characterizes modern Western democracies, in which the forum of last appeal in open questions of law lies with a supreme court. The idea of the necessity of the same law for all thereby attains the same rank as the obligation of authority for those governing. The positive law and the appeal to written law have repeatedly served to bring out specific contradictions inherent within the ideologically usurped administration of justice, and have thereby prepared the final collapse of dictatorial powers.

c. Calvin's depiction of the relative *position, rights, and duties of governors and governed* can be related immediately to the question of relevance. As we have seen, Calvin grounds his ethical position on this subject in a charismatic understanding of vocation. Despite a thorough, secular understanding of the state today, vestiges of this understanding are still found in the oath of office taken by governmental officials, as well as in the critical judgment, on the part of the governed, of those officials who have demonstrated their incompetence. This latter, negative outcome demonstrates Calvin's maxim that the vocational boundaries set by the divine call may not be crossed; this is a healthy reminder for those who work together in government in any age, and its observance (including, among other things, the requirement of confidentiality regarding current proceedings and integrity in the face of temptations to corruption) would noticeably reduce the popular disdain for political matters. Even Calvin's old-fashioned and seemingly undemocratic rule (to which he himself scarcely adhered), that a private citizen should not meddle in governmental affairs, has a certain significance if understood properly. Resisting any attempt to set up a permanent direct democracy, it functions to strengthen representative democracy, which is threatened by continual reliance on opinion polls. A compromise solution would entail regular and lively dialogue between representatives and the people they represent, as the constitution itself intends. In respect for the boundaries of their office, those who govern shall pursue their official du-

38. Cf. Baur, p. 272.

ties willingly. The divine call also gives the holder of an office his or her legitimation. Thus far Calvin.

This encouragement by the Reformer also appears tailor-made for governments lacking in drive, delaying decisions, or engaging in filibuster tactics. Once again we encounter the anchoring of social-ethical perspectives in the divine law. The Reformer's argumentation moves under the assumption of the given and perceptible *providentia Dei*. It is in precisely this arena that his controversial position, i.e., that the external cause by which an official comes to be in office is uninteresting because God's providence is demonstrated in his or her rank and position, has a relative historical justification. In any case, this position, based on a functional understanding of Romans 13, has made possible for Christians the temporary, patient acceptance of hated governments in the dictatorships of our century.

Churchwide synodical decisions have also suggested a similar acceptance which is neither deterministic nor to be understood as uncritical. According to Calvin, a structured system of ranks guarantees, besides the privileges and honor of those who govern, also their obligations. This hierarchical order, which Calvin taught on the basis of historical wisdom and which he consistently extended to include such obligations, also has its own enduring significance. Not only in traditional hierarchical states does it promote the honor of the upper classes and their necessary admonishment by those below. But in fact it has never been refuted, even by flimsy ideal-communistic mass-leveling measures such as the so-called Chinese "Cultural Revolution."[39] Because the government stands in the realm between God and humanity, it is obligated to both. Those governed are, according to Calvin, to carry the yoke laid upon them and give glory to God in the person of those who govern them.

This proposition could be misunderstood as an entree into a stifling subservient existence, except that it takes seriously the fact that in every age being governed involves being burdened. Stated absolutely, this would not be acceptable if in his political theory Calvin had not also advocated the *ultima ratio* of a right and duty of resistance.[40] In fact, Calvin's overall political theory signifies a mutual submission of governors and governed for the sake of the system of government. The ethical standard of this relationship is love.

Calvin assigns the tasks of those who govern to both tables of the Decalogue. The realm of religious duties (first table) stands as of first importance before the realm of political-moral duties (second table). The first priority is concern for the worship of God, without which creation itself loses its

---

39. Cf., as an antiutopian example, George Orwell's *Animal Farm* (New York: Brace, 1946).

40. Cf. the concluding remarks in Calvin, *Institutes* 4.20.

purpose. From this follows the protection of true religion. People who believe differently are to be won for evangelical doctrine through the working of the government. According to Calvin, stubborn perseverance in false religion deserves to be suppressed by the sword. Like most of his contemporaries in the battle for the pure gospel, Calvin lies quite a distance removed from the idea of religious neutrality. As much as Calvin in Geneva worked toward the separation of realms of jurisdiction between church and state, he remains — in allowing for repressive state protective functions — still ensnared in medieval *corpus christianum* thinking, to the detriment of the freedom of the gospel. Calvin also entrusts the promotion of schools and their preservation in purity to the government's realm of religious duty.

In the secular circumstances of a post-Enlightenment world, Calvin's postulate appears, as noted above, to have no relevant significance. Yet the fundamental right of the *general freedom* of religious expression remains for all modern constitutions an indispensable desideratum which is to be positively established not solely in regard to majority Christian governments but equally in regard to non-Christian or atheistic governments. The history of twentieth-century dictatorships makes clear how seldom dictatorial governments can very long withstand the appeal to the realm of their religious duty before (even finally for opportunistic reasons) granting the elemental human right of religious freedom at least some limited space.

In the arena of international law, the religious tolerance practiced by a given government within a close-knit world community, as well as the religious freedom guaranteed by its constitution, are of importance for its legal action regarding partner states which wall themselves off in fundamentalistic ways and oppress religious minorities.[41] After many failed contemporary attempts at merely educational programs, the entrusting of the school system's promotion and preservation in purity to the government's religious duty appears highly relevant: a school education without models of formation and without appropriate religious socialization leads demonstrably to a society without orientation or common ethical core values.

In the realm of *political-moral duty,* according to Calvin, the government is responsible for peace and for public integrity. From it is demanded zeal for law and fairness. Also to it, as to a shepherd, is entrusted the protection of the poor and needy, along with the building of hospitals and hostels, the support of students, and the salaries of teachers. It is prohibited from cruelty, theft, violence.

To these principal outlines of the sixteenth century there is fundamentally nothing to add for the twentieth and twenty-first centuries, although

---

41. Cf. the WCC study "Dialogue with Foreign Faiths and Ideologies" (1980).

these points must be variously differentiated on both sides of the global North-South boundary and in the relation of highly technological nations to the countries of the so-called Third World, as well as with consideration as to ecological consequences. The short catalogue of vices mentioned above could be supplemented by addressing the deep roots of great evil: the planned deviousness of governmental measures, corruption, and participation in covert economic criminality. Public integrity would be positively promoted above all by means of legislative, executive, and judicial power, which when possible would require its formal concretization in particular parliamentary codes of honor, without degenerating into moralistic casuistry.

Calvin emphasizes that for the securing of external peace the government requires strength, courage, and military force. The primary goal of every military defense is the reestablishment of peace. This brief foundational concept encompasses military ethical premises which continue to be effective to the present day: the exclusive use by a state of a strength of force appropriate to the potential necessity and possibility of defense, which under today's technological circumstances means the reduction of all arms buildups and excessive armaments; suspicion of all offensive wars and wars of conquest; and reestablishment of the status quo even following unavoidable preventive wars of defense against clear aggression.

Even within a socially ordered state under the rule of law, Calvin gives preference to the greatest possible decontrol of local congregational social ministry by structured church organizations. Up into the present, this diaconal right and privilege has proved itself manifoldly against a selective governmental welfare system, which again and again allows neglected or excluded groups of needy people to fall through its cracks (disabled, refugees, homeless, those suffering racial discrimination, etc.). The fact that the Christian congregation hereby takes over something more than filling gaps — namely, the realization of the well-organized, imaginative service of love universally commissioned to it, dynamically corresponding to all situations of need — can be traced back to the Geneva model, among other places.

Working together with the church's discipline, the government for its part is to ensure the repudiation of wasteful luxury in favor of modesty and moderation in lifestyle, i.e., an "inner asceticism." The lifestyle of inner asceticism, of "having as if one had not," which not only ensured the survival of the center of the Western Reformation at that time but became paradigmatic for Reformed Christianity throughout its historical course, has lost nothing of its model character for modern technological nations outdoing one another in selfish bickering, doctrines of growth, and the throwaway mentality. It will help to maintain the dynamic difference between rich and poor in the face of an overpopulated earth, vanishing natural resources, and encroaching ecological catastrophe. It cannot rest on a socialistically or communistically pre-scribed empty egalitarianism. Rather it has its roots in free ethical agreement which is finally grounded in hearing the Word of God.[42]

d. In *critiquing various types of state*, Calvin gives preference to a charis-matic *aristocracy* based on democratic election. He sees the benefit of this type of state in the distribution of the state's authority and in the related duty of mu-tual solidarity and accountability of those who govern, whose succession in of-fice is not bound to a family. Under the influence of early absolutism, Calvin de-velops an increasing aversion to the monarchy, especially the universal monarchy which (in view of the papacy and empire of his day) necessarily seemed to him to tend toward universal dictatorship. Calvin equally rejects pure democracy as direct democracy, based on his intensive knowledge of the history of antiquity. He feared in it the danger of distortion into an irresponsible anar-chistic ochlocracy. Overall, Calvin's judgment demonstrates the historical relativizing of all types of state. The inner measure of a positive evaluation for him appears to be the achievement of the highest possible level of public good. The correspondence of the charismatic-democratic aristocracy model to the principle of the structured congregational leadership should not be overlooked.

Since today's Western democracies can essentially be traced back genea-logically to the Geneva city-state model, the question of this model's relevance is to be posed primarily in regard to the quality of its realization, not in refer-ence to the facticity of representative-democratic states. The difficulty of dis-covering, calling, and encouraging the actual *"aristoi"* from within the prevail-ing party systems of Western democracies — in distinction from those who with a grip on their own bootstraps decide "to become a politician" — appears to be considerable. In a living representative democracy there needs therefore to be a *"diakrisis pneumaton"* from below, from those who are to be governed. In this process an increasing importance adheres to the effect and above all the responsibility of modern media editing, because above all else it guides and in-fluences the flow of representation between those governing and those gov-erned. It is to be hoped that the European and worldwide leadership bodies to-day will act in antidictatorial and representative-democratic ways — in the sense of Calvin's warning. Today, as always, ochlocracies manifest anarchic, de-structive tendencies. They become and must in historical experience remain enthusiastic-rigoristically short-lived.[43] The achievement of "the highest pos-

42. Cf. the papers "Grundwerte und Gottes Gebot" (1979) and "Verantwortung für die Schöpfung" (1985), both published by the Council of the "Evangelische Kirche Deutschlands" and the German Conference of Bishops.

43. Cf. J. Staedtke and H.-H. Esser, "Staat B. Reformiert," in *Evangelisches Staatslexikon*, 3rd ed., ed. H. Kunst, S. Grundmann (Stuttgart: Krenz Verlag, 1987), vol. 2, cols. 3360-67.

sible level of public good" by means of the best type of state in the transition to the twenty-first century cannot be understood anymore in short-sighted national (let alone nationalistic) steering of interests, but only in worldwide responsibility.

4. Calvin's doctrine of the *relation between church and state* considers both the differentiation or separation of the powers as well as their cooperation. In the tradition of Augustine and Luther, Calvin also represents a two-kingdoms doctrine, but with his own original modifications. The differentiation between the spiritual and the civil regiment extends according to Calvin both to the inner person as well as to historical power relationships, yet without full correspondence between inner and outer. Accordingly Calvin also teaches the irreconcilability of worldly and spiritual office. Similarly, spiritual and worldly jurisdiction are to be sharply separated from one another. Worldly power dare not disregard the judgment of churchly power, and may in no case overturn an existing church order. The church is accorded unlimited freedom to teach. It alone determines the content of the faith to be taught.[44] Calvin strongly rejected the right of governmental censorship of theological literature, though he was unsuccessful in opposing the Geneva magistrate on this. The aforementioned blurring of the boundary in cooperation between church and state can be expressed in the following formula: When the good of the whole church is in question, congregation and authorities must support one another by mutual admonition and must strengthen each other with their power. In questions of the ecclesial property and goods which had previously belonged to the Roman Church, as in questions of church wealth, Calvin even conceded to the government the supervision of ecclesial administration. The theological foundation for this cooperation, which bears theocratic features, is the understanding of church and state as expressions of the divine will. Of course, Calvin assumes that the authorities are hearing God's will spoken here and now through the preaching of the gospel.

It is doubtless the case that the Calvinistic dialectic of the separation and cooperation of the powers is based on the attempt to correspond to the Chalcedonian understanding of the two natures of the Christ-reality as "unmixed and undivided." Overlooking the "unmixed" could lead to the politicization of Protestantism, as in the Huguenot Wars.[45] The alternative to this was the "way of the congregations under the cross," which, even after the collapse of the first way, remained open. Both ways, with the consistent em-

---

44. Cf. the Geneva Church Order, Articles 16 and 19.

45. Cf. Richard Nürnberger, *Die Politisierung des französischen Protestantismus. Calvin und die Anfänge des protestantischen Radikalismus* (Tübingen: J. C. B. Mohr, 1948).

phasis on the second, the way of suffering, are found in Calvin's conception: only the one who is prepared to take the second way may choose the first.

The premises which Calvin developed for determining the relationship between church and state still reverberate in a number of Western democracies and have succeeded in shaping the relationship of the two bodies in the direction of free partnership. In the twentieth century the instruments regulating this relationship in the corporate legal sense are primarily contracts of state-church law, which determine the various realms of jurisdiction. Both partners seek dialogue in questions of ethical and social-political relevance which cut across these lines (such as the protection of life, issues of social justice, alternatives to military service, development aid, education in theology and social work, etc.). In Germany the churches have the status of a public corporation and are therefore publicly and legally privileged over against pressure groups and governmental lobbies. The authorized representatives of the major church bodies have a seat at the governmental table. Governmental representatives are enlisted occasionally as elected synod members. The history of the suffering and failure of the churches in the century now ending proves that legal enactments of the relationship do not necessarily protect from encroachment on the part of the government, and equally little from ecclesial conformist apostasy. Within the church, Calvin's determination of the relationship between church and state could be of significance also for the evaluation and reappraisal of *this* history, following now the end of the rule of "real existing socialism." This is especially the case when the necessary reappraisal by those seeking and granting forgiveness stands under the sign of the "joy of repentance."[46]

5. Calvin's differentiated position on the *right of resistance* makes the admissibility of resistance against unlawful force dependent on the social position of those who resist. He distinguishes between the private citizen, the "lower authority" *("inferiores"* or *"populares magistratus"),* and the "public avenger" *("vindex publicus").* According to Calvin, the private citizen, that is, one holding no political office, has only the right to passive resistance, and then only when the *clausula Petri* (Acts 5:29) applies in reference to authorities who do not any longer fear God. This passive disobedience is directed, however, not against the office itself, but against the person holding the office. In hopeless cases, Calvin advises escaping from a godless government's sphere of influence by flight. Because of their special vocation, however, pastors are obliged to remain with their congregations. The "lower authorities" are responsible for ameliorating the monarchs' despotism. They are not to tolerate usurpers or ty-

---

46. Julius Schniewind, *Die Freude der Buße* (Göttingen: Vandenhoeck & Ruprecht, 1956).

rants, although they have no right to revolt. Calvin concedes this right exclusively to the highest estate, which is itself capable of taking power. The goal is a "reformatory resistance"[47] which avoids a general bloodshed. Like Luther,[48] Calvin emphasizes God's free capacity to awaken "public avengers" (Gideon and Samson in the Old Testament) by direct vocation. By means of the *"legitima Dei vocatio,"* these have the *duty* of active resistance, the commission of bringing the regime tainted with evil to justice and freeing the oppressed people from its wretched torment. The presupposition of such action is the firm certainty of such a calling. The freedom of God cannot be usurped. It is important that Calvin grounds the right of resistance in faith and not, like his successors, in natural law. In every case of commanded resistance, the divine law has priority; other sovereignties remain excluded as its rationale. Resistance serves the maintenance and reestablishment of the state under the rule of law, which for its own part is also anchored in the system of laws determined by the divine will. The overall tenor of this teaching can be formulated as the divine legitimation of the right and duty to resistance, and the simultaneous restriction of this right and duty to the circle of those who are called to them.[49]

By the nineteenth and early twentieth centuries, the Christian right and duty to resistance had so slid into oblivion that even those who prepared themselves to resist the Hitler dictatorship first had to be reminded of the Reformation roots of this right. The participants in this resistance effort actualized both the Reformation foundations of this right as well as those of the Jesuit *Monarchomachen* of the sixteenth century. In processing the events around the shattering of the resistance on 20 July 1944, the Reformation insights played an important role.[50] Since that time, above all under the impulses of Dietrich Bonhoeffer's theology, ethical reflection on the right to resistance has continued within the ecumenical movement as a whole, provoked situationally by tyrannical dictatorships arising violently in nearly all parts of the globe. In its constitution (Article 20, paragraph 4), West Germany has recorded the historical experience of the German resistance and thus paid clear tribute to it a posteriori: "Against any who would attempt to do away with this ordering [mean-

47. Cf. Ger van Roon's 1964 book *Neuordnung im Widerstand,* published in English as *German Resistance to Hitler: Count von Moltke and the Kreisau Circle,* trans. Peter Ludlow (London and New York: Van Nostrand Reinhold Co., 1971), regarding the Kreisau Circle's resistance to Hitler (20 July 1944).

48. Cf. the appendix to the work by the Norwegian resistance bishop Eivind Berggrav, *Man and State* (Philadelphia: Muhlenberg Press, 1951), "When the coachman is drunk. . . ."

49. Cf. Baur; and Eßer, "Die Staatsauffassung Calvins."

50. Cf. H. J. Iwand and E. Wolf, "Entwurf eines Gutachtens zur Frage des Widerstandsrechts nach evangelischer Lehre," in H. Kraus, *Die im Braunschweiger Remerprozess . . . erstatteten Gutachten* (1953), pp. 9-18.

ing the establishment of West Germany as a "democratic and social federal state," according to paragraph 1 of Article 20], all Germans have the right to resist if no other remedy is possible."[51] The ecumenical discussion regarding an ethically legitimate "theology of revolution" continues for the reasons mentioned above.[52] Even after the end of the Cold War, there appears to be no consensus within the church as a whole. The disputed realm encompasses the following: those responsible versus mass movements; destructive results versus limitation of harm in highly technological systems; protection or not of the ruling class which is to be deposed; avoidance of catastrophic worldwide results; and the question of the use of passive or violent, even escalating, resistance with the most modern means of destruction.

In all this, Calvin's differentiated model of action is even now capable of teaching us to keep complementary solutions in mind in light of the *"finis pax."* The total surveillance of a society's life in totalitarian states raises a special problematic for all those who plan ethically grounded resistance: Is one to retain the ethically commanded progression from public dissent into active resistance, or does this consign potential resisters prematurely to persecution? Must the core group of active resistance not work a priori with the greatest secrecy, with espionage techniques like those of a secret service, even with its own secret code? Must it not in fact risk the "long path through the hostile institutions" in order to disrupt them from within on Day X?[53]

6. Calvin's "economic ethics"[54] can be characterized as a flexible, situationally determined ethics of responsibility. Under the pressure of economic and social relations in Geneva, it risks a new and both favorable and critical position toward the monetary economy: the charging of interest is permitted and at the

---

51. The commentary asserts on this point: "17. The right to resistance concedes an emergency law in favor of the state for the case in which considerable dangers from the citizenry or from the authority of the state threaten the democratic state of law. One form of the right to resistance is the political strike. 18. The right to resistance is subsidiary. It is merely the means of last resort and thus presupposes that the state is no longer itself in a position effectively to combat the threat at hand." R. Stober, *Das Grundgesetz der Bundesrepublik Deutschland und Nebengesetze. Textausgabe mit Anmerkungen und Verweisungen* (1978), p. 39.

52. The WCC Assembly "Church and Society" (Geneva, 1966) recorded an interim high point in its collection, *Die Kirche als Faktor einer kommenden Weltgesellschaft* (Stuttgart: Kreuz Verlag, 1966).

53. Cf. W. von Trott zu Solz, *Widerstand heute oder das Abenteuer der Freiheit* (1958); H. Franz and K. Gerstein, *Außenseiter des Widerstandes gegen Hitler,* Polis, vol. 18 (1962).

54. Cf. Biéler, *La pensée économique,* and H. H. Esser, "Calvins Sozialethik und der Kapitalismus," in *Hervormde Teologiese Studies* 3/4, 48 (1992), Festschrift für A. D. Pont, p. 783 (English abstract).

same time the rate of interest is limited (5.0–6.6 percent). The following ethical directives apply:

a. Money lending for interest should not be made into a profession unto itself.
b. No interest may be charged to the poor or economically distressed.
c. Interest-bearing capital investments may be carried out only when they do not restrict the capacity to help the needy.
d. Interest agreements may be finalized only according to natural fairness and the Golden Rule of Christ (Matt. 7:12).
e. The capital debtor must be able to make a greater profit from the money lent to him or her than the one receiving interest could.
f. The standard for the setting of the interest rate must not simply be common law, but must be the Word of God.
g. Interest transactions may not be carried out only according to private considerations, but their effects on common economic life must be taken into account.
h. Existing legal regulations must always be applied according to the fundamental law of equity (thus they may not serve to justify interest transactions which are forbidden for other reasons).

Socio-ethically and organizationally, Calvin fights for the protection of the trades, even those newly established; for their right to associate; and for the incorporation of refugees and the unemployed into new relationships of production. The proletariat of beggars arising in that period of drastic change is guided into workplaces by an organized social welfare system. Regarding individual ethics, Calvin warns as strongly against a self-chosen revolutionary liberation from poverty as against the luxurious, loveless misuse of wealth. He institutes a dynamic range from "rich" to "poor," according to needs and situation, rather than trying to force everyone into a flat equality.

Calvin's ethical directives regarding the interest economy, which for his own time represented a liberating innovation, appear still today ideally applicable for all societies in crisis in which — because of the high-interest politics of an ensconced banking establishment (which the Geneva pastors discouraged during Calvin's lifetime) — private lending and production-stimulating credit are blocked over the long term. It is of course questionable whether, under today's basic presuppositions, private lending or credit allocation has any role beyond its corrective function, and whether the Christian congregation in the social welfare sphere can ever muster the powers of organization and leverage in its own location which would enable it to perform the guidance into new workplaces mentioned above. If so, then there would emerge within today's East-West and North-South barriers, and according to the guidelines outlined earlier, far and away more investments for so-called joint ventures than have been pursued to date. Meanwhile, for the past four decades ecumenically and globally, all campaigns of Church World Service, Catholic World Relief, etc., have consciously or unconsciously operated according to the pattern invented 450 years ago in Geneva. The possibilities among individual Christians and congregations for partnership according to the eight Geneva theses named above are only initially being explored. Instead of the usual security and fortress mentality, such initiatives would provide a living dynamism and imaginative riches even transcending centralist barriers.

The so-called *Max Weber thesis*,[55] and its continuation by Ernst Troeltsch,[56] attempts, among other things, to trace Western capitalism back in a causally demonstrable way to a pattern of Calvinistic provenance and its integration of early capitalism. Yet Weber's theoretical bridges between Calvin, Calvinism, Puritanism, and the neo-capitalism of the nineteenth century are not historical-critically convincing; he himself even questioned some of the places where data was forced into his system.[57] Nevertheless, the fact remains that the impressive solution of social problems in a city both of the Reformation and of simultaneous radical social change clearly became accepted over several centuries in the Western world, presumably not so much on the basis of the reproducing of social teachings as on the basis of a social behavior continually being shaped by preaching, the congregation, and the reality of faith. In this regard it is worth considering that the preaching indicated was to a large extent a *teaching* sermon in which the use of the law in sanctification *(tertius usus legis)*, sanctification as ethical preservation in gratitude, and the realm of inner asceticism (meaning inner freedom from worldly possessions) played a large role.

If the root grounding of Calvinistic, Reformed social ethics in this sense is maintained, then a positive prognosis for its relevance here and now can be asserted with Biéler, Schulze, and others. This would mean a continuing struggle both to free Reformed social ethics from the ongoing temptation of the secularism of limitless self-realization and to lead it back to a rooted, living, secularization standing in *unio cum Christo* and thereby led by the Spirit.[58]

---

55. Cf. Weber, pp. 155-63.

56. Cf. Troeltsch, 2:642ff.

57. Weber, p. 195; cf. Esser, "Calvins Sozialethik und der Kapitalismus."

58. On the relationship between secularism and secularization, cf. Friedrich Gogarten, *Despair and Hope for Our Time,* trans. Thomas Wisser (Philadelphia: Pilgrim Press, 1953).

Conclusion

Fundamental elements of the content of the Calvinistic teaching sermon — and of its corresponding historical continuation — were and are: the invitation to an active shaping of the world in the sense of the *dominium terrae,* shaped by an ecological ethic of self-limitation, *and* the understanding of earthly life as a grace-filled time of preservation granted to the elect congregation for cultivating the praise of God within the worship of daily life. Two relevant concluding thoughts: "Calvin's theocentric thinking is not to be grasped as a detriment, for it is only in this way that the worldly order first receives the true inner binding power which makes it independent of external pressures."[59] In Calvin we recognize an example only to the extent that he unforgettably showed the church of his time the way of obedience, obedience of thinking and action, social and political obedience. A true student of Calvin can follow in only one way: "to obey not Calvin, but the *One* who was Calvin's master."[60]

59. Baur, p. 272.
60. Karl Barth, in *Calvin,* textes choisis par C. Gaguebin (Paris, 1948), p. 11.

CHAPTER 24

The Incarnation and the Sacramental Word: Calvin's and Schleiermacher's Sermons on Luke 2

Dawn DeVries

As often as Christ calls us to the hope of salvation by the preaching of the Gospel, he is present with us. For not without reason is the preaching of the Gospel called Christ's descent to us.

CALVIN, COMMENTARY ON JOHN 7:33

I am sure you will gladly testify, dear friends, that from the time you received the milk of the gospel in your first instruction in Christianity, right up until the present day, every such encounter with scripture was like a new, joyous, and powerful appearance of the Lord himself.

SCHLEIERMACHER, SERMON ON LUKE 24:30-32

No one did more to disturb the confidence of nineteenth-century theologians in their historical claims and assumptions than David Friedrich Strauss (1808-74). The publication of his *Life of Jesus* in 1835 marks a watershed in the history of Christian thought. Although others (including the English Deists) had already raised some of the same questions about the historical reliability of the Gospel narratives, no one had at that time carried out the thoroughgoing decomposition and reinterpretation of the Gospel stories from beginning to end that Strauss attempted. And Strauss's questions have endured as persistent, nagging problems for theology ever since.[1]

Strauss himself was well aware of the disturbing results of historical criticism not only for the academic theologian, but also for the preacher. Could a minister any longer preach in good conscience on a Gospel narrative that very likely did not relate an actual event? Strauss saw four theoretical alternatives for preachers faced with this predicament, and only the last one was a real option. First, preachers could try to raise their congregations to their own consciousness so that their hearers would no longer be disturbed by the possibility that the Gospels were fiction. But this would be impracticable since not everyone in the church is theologically sophisticated. Second, preachers could try to come down to the church's consciousness and preach as if all the stories were true. But then they would be hypocrites. Third, they could leave the ministry, which is clearly a desperate course and a last resort. The only reasonable course for preachers to take, then, is a fourth option — to reconcile their own consciousness and the consciousness of the church. Strauss describes the method of a preacher pursuing this option succinctly:

> In his discourses to the church, he will indeed adhere to the forms of the popular conception, but on every opportunity he will exhibit their spiritual significance, which to him constitutes their sole truth, and thus prepare — though such a result is only to be thought of as an unending progress — the resolution of those forms into their original ideas in the consciousness of the church also. Thus . . . at the festival of Easter, he will indeed set out from the sensible fact of the resurrection of Christ, but he will dwell chiefly on the being buried and rising again with Christ, which the Apostle himself has strenuously inculcated. This very course every preacher, even the most orthodox, strictly takes, as often as he draws a moral from the evangelical text on which he preaches: for this is nothing else than the transition from the externally historical to the inward and spiritual. It is true, we must not overlook the distinction, that the orthodox preacher builds his moral on the text in such a way, that the latter remains as an historical foundation; whereas with the speculative preacher, the transition from the biblical history or the church doctrine, to the truth

---

1. Karl Barth notes, "He and no other man has the merit of having put this question, the historical one, that is, to theology, with such a grasp of the basic issue. Since then theology has talked round it in many and various ways. . . . Many people have not been able to overcome Strauss to this day; they have simply by-passed him, and to this very day are continually saying things which, if Strauss cannot be overcome, should no longer be said" (*From Rousseau to Ritschl*, trans. Brian Cozens [London: SCM Press, 1959], p. 388).

which he thence derives, has the negative effect of annihilating the former. Viewed more closely, however, the transition of the orthodox preacher from the evangelical text to the moral application, is not free from this negative tendency; in proceeding from the history to the doctrine he implies at least this much: the history is not enough, it is not the whole truth, it must be transmuted from a past fact into a present one, from an event external to you, it must become your own intimate experience.[2]

Strauss's contention that precritical preaching and postcritical preaching do virtually the same thing provides an interesting point of entry into the question of the relationship between classical and liberal Protestantism. How much difference did historical criticism actually make to the way Christ was preached in the church? Were liberal preachers only beating a hasty retreat from the advances of criticism when they moved from the "external" to the "internal" miracle? Or were they also following a path already opened up by their predecessors? In the following essay, I want to explore this question by comparing the preaching of John Calvin and the preaching of Friedrich Schleiermacher on the Christmas narrative of Luke 2.

I will argue that in fact at least some of the questions raised by historical criticism make little difference to the way Schleiermacher preaches on this text because for him, as for Calvin, what is of central importance is the real presence of Christ in the church's proclamation. This sacramental understanding of preaching is, I believe, a characteristic feature of the Reformed tradition, and it may prove useful not only in contemporary christological discussions (as I will suggest in section 4) but also in ecumenical dialogue.[3]

It must be admitted, of course, that there are significant differences between Calvin and Schleiermacher, not least concerning what they regard as the historical facts essential for faith. Nonetheless, Schleiermacher's understanding of preaching as, in effect, an incarnational event that re-presents the person and work of the Jesus of history may be seen as a genuine development of Calvin's notion of the sacramental word, a development that made possible a relative indifference to doubts about the historical details of the life of Jesus. The

---

2. Strauss, *The Life of Jesus Critically Examined,* ed. Peter C. Hodgson, trans. George Eliot, 4th ed. (Philadelphia: Fortress, 1972), pp. 783-84.

3. The sacramental word is not a doctrine peculiar to the Reformed tradition. It has a long and rich history in Christian thought. See Richard H. Grützmacher, *Wort und Geist: Eine historische und dogmatische Untersuchung zum Gnadenmittel des Wortes* (Leipzig: A. Deichert'sche Verlagsbuchhandlung [Georg Böhme], 1902). And because it is a doctrine common to several major branches of the Christian church, it may have an especially useful function in ecumenical dialogue. There is particular promise in dialogue on this theme with post–Vatican II Catholics. See, for example, Karl Rahner, "The Word and the Eucharist," in *Theological Investigations,* trans. Kevin Smyth, vol. 4 (New York: Crossroad, 1982).

assaults of historical criticism in the eighteenth and nineteenth centuries on the Gospel narratives did not force Schleiermacher to retreat from the claims of precritical theology about the redemptive power of Jesus Christ, but rather encouraged him to apply Reformation principles more radically and consistently. After a brief discussion of their respective theologies of preaching (section 1), I will compare two of Calvin's sermons (section 2) with two sermons of Schleiermacher (section 3); finally (section 4), I will draw some conclusions about the way in which Calvin and Schleiermacher each integrates his understanding of preaching into his larger theological program.

1. Calvin's and Schleiermacher's Theology of Preaching

Calvin, like Luther before him, borrowed from Augustine the notion that sacraments were "visible words." While this meant that the Reformers tended to verbalize the sacraments, it also led them to "sacramentalize" the Word.[4] But what do we mean when we say Calvin had a doctrine of the sacramental word? We mean, in short, that the Word can be understood to operate in the same way a sacrament does and can be said to convey the same gift a sacrament does, namely, Jesus Christ and all his benefits.[5]

Calvin's favorite descriptive term for the word that conveys Christ is "the

---

4. T. H. L. Parker described this feature of Calvin's doctrine of preaching in his *The Oracles of God: An Introduction to the Preaching of John Calvin* (London: Lutterworth, 1947), pp. 53-56. Ernst Bizer notes the same characteristic in Luther's theology in his important study *Fides ex auditu: Eine Untersuchung über die Entdeckung der Gerechtigkeit Gottes durch Martin Luther* (Neukirchen: Verlag der Buchhandlung des Erziehungsvereins, 1958), p. 160. Others have referred to the sacramental word in Calvin's theology. See B. A. Gerrish, "The Reformers' Theology of Worship," *McCormick Quarterly* 14 (May 1961): 29; Richard Stauffer, "Le Discours à la première personne dans les sermons de Calvin," in *Regards contemporains sur Jean Calvin* (Paris, 1965); Georges Bavaud, "Les Rapports entre la prédication et les sacrements dans le contexte du dialogue oecuménique," in *Communion et communication: Structures d'unité et modèles de communication de l'évangile. Troisième Cycle romand en théologie practique (1976-77)* (Geneva: Labor et Fides, 1978), pp. 69-73; B. A. Gerrish, *The Old Protestantism and the New: Essays on the Reformation Heritage* (Chicago: University of Chicago Press, 1982), pp. 106-17; John H. Leith, "Calvin's Doctrine of the Proclamation of the Word and Its Significance for Today," in *John Calvin and the Church: A Prism of Reform*, ed. Timothy George (Louisville: Westminster/John Knox, 1990), pp. 211-12, 219; B. A. Gerrish, *Grace and Gratitude: The Eucharistic Theology of John Calvin* (Minneapolis: Augsburg/Fortress, 1992), chap. 3.

5. John Calvin, *Institutes of the Christian Religion*, ed. Ford Lewis Battles and John T. McNeill (Philadelphia: Westminster, 1960), 4.14.17. It is impossible within the limits of this essay to consider the massive literature on Calvin's sacramental theology. See Gerrish, *Grace and Gratitude*.

Gospel."[6] It is the gospel that communicates Christ or presents Christ to us.[7] The gospel unites us to God and Christ.[8] In fact, it is the gospel that brings salvation.[9] The content of the gospel, for Calvin, is the fatherly goodwill of God.[10] But Calvin is explicit in asserting that it is the gospel *preached* that is sacramental.[11] The private reading of Scripture would not achieve the same result.

What does the preached word do? Calvin often speaks of preaching as a mirror in which we can behold the face of Christ and of God.[12] The word in this sense reveals the gracious character of God and the love of the Savior. Yet Calvin is not satisfied with an understanding of the Word that could be merely educational and would appeal only to the cognitive faculties of human beings. As in his discussion of sacraments, Calvin explicitly denies that the word is a *bare* sign — that is, a sign devoid of the reality it represents. The Word itself is efficacious, it brings what it presents.[13] The gift of the Word is the presence of Christ with all the benefits that he has secured for the elect — specifically the twofold grace of justification and sanctification.[14] And the preaching of the Word is itself the true exercise of the keys of the kingdom: it has the power both to save and to damn.[15] Calvin even speaks of preaching as "ratifying" the salvation secured in Christ's death.[16]

---

6. This is the term used in the text from Calvin that I chose for an epigraph to this essay (*Commentary* on John 7:33, *Ioannis Calvini opera quae supersunt omnia*, ed. W. Baum, E. Cunitz, and E. Reuss, 59 vols. [Brunswick and Berlin: Schwetschke and Son, 1863-1900], 47:178). Further references to Calvin's commentaries will be abbreviated *Comm.*, and their location in the *Calvini opera* (hereafter cited as *CO*) will be given with the volume number followed by a colon and the page number(s).

7. Calvin, *Comm. Gal.* 1:7 (*CO* 50:173); *Comm. 1 Pet.* 1:13 (*CO* 55:221); *Comm. Titus* 1:3 (*CO* 52:407).

8. Calvin, *Comm. 1 John* 1:3 (*CO* 55:302).

9. Calvin, *Comm. Acts* 5:20 (*CO* 48:106-7); *Comm. Eph.* 3:7 (*CO* 51:180).

10. Calvin, *Comm. Eph.* 2:17 (*CO* 51:173).

11. See Calvin, *Comm. Rom.* 1:16; 16:21 (*CO* 49:19, 290); *Comm. Titus* 1:3 (*CO* 52:407).

12. See Calvin's sermon 31 on the harmony of the Gospels (*CO* 46:378); see also *Comm. Matt.* 4:1 (*CO* 45:128); *Comm. Luke* 2:30 (*CO* 45:90); *Comm. John* 3:14; 8:19 (*CO* 47:62-63, 195); *Comm. 1 Pet.* 1:13 (*CO* 55:221).

13. Calvin, *Institutes* 4.17.5, 10; *Comm. John* 1:12; 6:51 (*CO* 47:12, 153); *Comm. Heb.* 4:2, 12 (*CO* 55:45-46, 49-52); *Comm. 1 Pet.* 1:23, 25 (*CO* 55:228-31); *Comm. 1 John* 1:1-2 (*CO* 55:301-2).

14. See Calvin's *Short Treatise on the Lord's Supper* (*Calvin: Theological Treatises,* trans. J. K. S. Reid, Library of Christian Classics [Philadelphia: Westminster, 1954], p. 143); see also *Comm. John* 15:3; 17:17 (*CO* 47:340, 385); *Comm. Acts* 5:20; 10:36 (*CO* 48:106-7, 244).

15. Calvin, *Institutes* 4.1.22; cf. *Comm. Matt.* 3:12 (*CO* 45:123); *Comm. 1 Tim.* 4:16 (*CO* 52:303-4).

16. Calvin, *Comm. Acts* 26:18 (*CO* 48:542); cf. *Comm. John* 20:23 (*CO* 47:441).

Calvin understands the function of the preached Word analogously to the function of sacraments: the Word is an instrument.[17] God uses the Word in such a way that its power and efficacy remain God's. Calvin is careful to avoid what he takes to be the mechanistic implications of the Roman Catholic view that sacraments function *ex opere operato*.[18] Only when the Word is effectively sealed by the Holy Spirit can it be said to offer and present Christ to us. And Calvin reserves the possibility that God can work faith in the hearts of the elect quite apart from any outward signs. In other words, God is not bound to communicate grace only through the Word.[19] Having said that, however, Calvin is quick to add that preaching, like the sacraments, is the regular and ordinary means by which God chooses to communicate the benefits of Christ's work.[20] Like the sacraments, preaching works, according to Calvin, in appealing to the entire person (not just the intellect) through an attractive picture. Preachers present Christ so forcefully that their hearers can "see" and "hear" Christ themselves as if he were confronting them directly.[21]

Perhaps the nagging question for the modern reader of Calvin's theology is, Why does God use human instruments to speak God's Word? Why are preachers needed to represent Christ? Such a theology could feed the worst kind of pretensions to divine authority in clergy who are only too fallible. Calvin offers several explanations. Preaching, he says, is another form of divine accommodation, the way in which God brings himself down to our level. God addresses us in human fashion so as not to "thunder at us and drive us away."[22] The human mediation is an exercise in humility. If God were to speak to us directly from heaven, everyone would hear and believe, because everyone would be terrified at the majesty of God's glory. "But when a puny man risen up from the dust speaks in God's name, at this point we best evidence our piety and obedience toward God if we show ourselves teachable toward his minister, although he excels us in nothing."[23] Further, the ministry provides "the chief sinew by which believers are held together in one body."[24] If individuals were allowed to interpret Scripture for themselves in isolation, each would despise

---

17. Calvin, *Institutes* 2.5.5; 4.14.12; *Comm. Acts* 10:5, 44 (*CO* 48:228, 250-51); *Comm. Rom.* 11:14 (*CO* 49:219); *Comm. Eph.* 3:7; 4:12 (*CO* 51:180, 199); *Comm. 1 Thess.* 2:13 (*CO* 52:151); *Comm. 1 Pet.* 1:23, 25 (*CO* 55:228-31).

18. Calvin, *Institutes* 4.14.14; cf. *Comm. Acts* 7:35 (*CO* 48:149).

19. Calvin, *Institutes* 1.7; 1.8.3; 4.14.14, 17; *Comm. Acts* 16:14 (*CO* 48:378); *Comm. Eph.* 5:26 (*CO* 51:223-24).

20. Calvin, *Comm. Rom.* 10:14; 11:14 (*CO* 49:205, 219).

21. Calvin, *Comm. Isa.* 11:4 (*CO* 36:240); *Comm. Gal.* 3:1 (*CO* 50:202-3).

22. Calvin, *Institutes* 4.1.5.

23. Calvin, *Institutes* 4.2.1.

24. Calvin, *Institutes* 4.3.2.

the other, and there would be as many churches as there are individuals. Ultimately, however, the use of human mediation for the word is, like the incarnation itself, part of the mystery of divine grace in salvation. Christ's own office of proclaiming the name of God and of filling all things is fulfilled through the ministry.[25] Thus the preached Word not only conveys Christ, but continues Christ's living presence in the world.

Schleiermacher must have been well aware of Calvin's doctrine of the sacramental word, and his own reflections on preaching may be seen as a development of it. Like Calvin, Schleiermacher thinks the sermon does much more than convey information about Christ.[26] In fact, he describes the desired effect of preaching in the same terms in which he describes the effect of Christ's redemptive activity. The Redeemer's "assumption" of believers into the power of his own God-consciousness and unclouded blessedness constitutes the heart of his redemptive work.[27] This activity is "best thought of as a kind of invasive activity that is nevertheless embraced by those it works upon as an activity that draws them to itself — just as we ascribe a power of attraction to anyone to whose formative influence on our minds we surrender ourselves willingly."[28] For present-day Christians, this powerful influence of the Redeemer is no longer exerted by his corporeal presence, but by the "picture" of him that is present within the church. And the sermon is the primary location of that picture. Carrying on the prophetic and priestly work of the Redeemer, preachers, in giving testimony about their own experience of Christ, "assume" their hearers into the power of their God-consciousness and exert a powerful influence over them, just as Christ influenced the disciples. The preacher embodies the word of Scripture and enlivens it so that, instead of a dead letter, the hearer is confronted by the living Word.[29] And since any success preachers have in affecting their hearers is due to the presence of the Holy Spirit in their proclamation, it is certain that their congregations are meeting the Redeemer

25. Calvin, *Institutes* 4.3.2; *Comm. Heb.* 2:11 (*CO* 55:29).

26. For a fuller discussion of Schleiermacher's understanding of preaching, see *Servant of the Word: Selected Sermons of Friedrich Schleiermacher*, trans. and ed. Dawn DeVries (Philadelphia: Fortress, 1987), pp. 1-23.

27. Friedrich Schleiermacher, *Der christliche Glaube nach den Grundsätzen der evangelischen Kirche im Zusammenhange dargestellt*, ed. Martin Redeker, 7th ed., based on the 2nd ed., 2 vols. (Berlin: Walter de Gruyter, 1960), §§100-101, cited hereafter as *Gl.* All translations, unless otherwise noted, are from the standard English translation, *The Christian Faith*, ed. H. R. Mackintosh and J. S. Stewart, trans. of the 2nd German ed. (1928; reprint, Philadelphia: Fortress, 1976).

28. Schleiermacher, *Gl.* §100.2; translation by B. A. Gerrish.

29. For more on Schleiermacher's notion of preaching as an "embodiment" of the Word, see Dawn DeVries, "Schleiermacher's Christmas Eve Dialogue: Bourgeois Ideology or Feminist Theology?" *Journal of Religion* 69 (1989): 169-83.

himself in the sermon.[30] Thus, for Schleiermacher, the sermon is the transparent medium through which we encounter the Redeemer.

The preached word works, for Schleiermacher, in much the same way that Calvin understood its operation. By translating the language of the biblical texts into the parameters of present experience, preachers re-present Christ in a vivid picture so that for their hearers Christ is, as it were, immediately present. Human communication "embodies" Christ's word — gives it a human face and the concreteness of an individual character. Preaching, then, may be described as an "incarnational event" in which Christ becomes present through the one proclaiming the Word.[31]

Schleiermacher, no less than Calvin, however, recognized that there must be norms by which to judge human testimony about the divine. Not all human communication about God can become an "incarnational event." Perhaps the most important norm for Schleiermacher is that of the ecclesial context for preaching. In his discussion of the work of Christ, Schleiermacher distinguishes between three ways of understanding Christ's influence on the believer — magical, empirical, and mystical — and argues that only the last one is an adequate descriptive term. The magical conception assumes that Christ works immediately in the lives of individuals apart from a community of faith. The empirical conception asserts that Christ's influence is purely educational: he provides believers with teaching and an example. The mystical conception insists both on the mediation of Christ's work through the community of faith and on its source in the person of Christ.[32] Preaching, therefore, as the locus of Christ's continuing work, must take place within the historic community that is connected to Christ's person, and in which dwells the Holy Spirit. Only there can the elect expect to encounter the living Christ.

Schleiermacher's reasons for insisting on the human mediation of the Word are somewhat different from Calvin's. He insists that Christ's work in us happens in natural, not supernatural, ways.[33] He believed he found this doctrine in Scripture. In fact, he argues, the meaning of resurrection faith is that

---

30. Schleiermacher, *Gl.* §100.1.

31. See Schleiermacher, *Gl.* §108.5. This, I take it, is what is being expressed in the passage from one of Schleiermacher's sermons that I chose as an epigraph to this essay (*Friedrich Schleiermachers Sämmtliche Werke* [Berlin: Georg Reimer, 1834-1864], II/2:190, hereafter cited as *SW*). For more on the re-presentational character of preaching in Schleiermacher's theory of religious communication, see Wilhelm Gräb, "Predigt als kommunikativer Akt: Einige Bemerkungen zu Schleiermachers Theorie religiöser Mitteilung," in *Internationaler Schleiermacher-Kongress Berlin 1984*, ed. Kurt-Victor Selge, 2 vols., Schleiermacher Archiv I (Berlin: Walter de Gruyter, 1984), pp. 643-59.

32. Schleiermacher, *Gl.* §100.3; cf. *Gl.* §108.5.

33. Schleiermacher, *Gl.* §§13, 88.4.

the living Christ is working in the church's proclamation.[34] Moreover, this view, Schleiermacher notes, "has behind it the whole apostolic usage and the express witness of Scripture."[35]

The parallels between Calvin's and Schleiermacher's theologies of preaching should by now be clear. Both thought preachers must do more than simply *educate* their hearers about Scripture or doctrine. Rather, they must apply Christian doctrine to life and interpret Scripture in the language of their own experience. Moreover, both Calvin and Schleiermacher describe the event of preaching and its effects in christological, and more specifically *sacramental* or *incarnational*, terms. Preaching is the means by which Christ, through the power of the Holy Spirit, makes himself present in the church. The sacramental concept of preaching, common to both Calvin and Schleiermacher, controls not only the form but also the content of the sermon. In order to demonstrate this more clearly, we must now analyze and compare Calvin's sermons on the Christmas narrative of Luke 2 with Schleiermacher's sermons on the same text. Only after such a comparison will we be able to draw out the similarities in the way each of them *uses* this narrative.

2. Two Sermons of Calvin

The four sermons chosen for comparison here are all based upon the first twenty verses of Luke 2.[36] This text provides a perfect test case for our question because it contains (1) what purports to be information on the facts of Jesus' birth and (2) an account of the angelic appearance to the shepherds — two parts of the Jesus tradition that were disputed already in Schleiermacher's day.[37] Further, since Schleiermacher had already published his own critical commentary on Luke in 1817, there can be no doubt that he was aware of the historical questions about Luke's birth narrative when he preached in 1831. Finally, since we are considering sermons preached late in the respective careers of Calvin and Schleiermacher, we can reasonably assume that the interpretations of the texts which they present express the mature standpoint of their authors.

34. See his sermon on Acts 3:13-15, in *Servant of the Word*, pp. 73-84.

35. Schleiermacher, *Gl.* §108.5.

36. We have fifteen sermons of Calvin and six sermons of Schleiermacher on Luke 2. Only four of Calvin's sermons are on the birth narrative of the first twenty verses, and only the two sermons of Schleiermacher that I chose to discuss treat these same verses.

37. See Friedrich Schleiermacher, *Über die Schriften des Lukas, ein kritischer Versuch*, in *SW* I/2:v-220; ET, *A Critical Essay on the Gospel of St. Luke*, trans. Connop Thirlwall (London: John Taylor, 1825).

Calvin begins the first of his sermons that we are considering by stating a principle that controls all his preaching: "We have already declared that it will not profit us much that the Son of God was born into the world unless we know why he was sent to us and what blessing he has brought to us."[38] The benefit of Christ's incarnation only becomes efficacious when it is appropriated by the believer through faith. The objective, historical events are not enough in themselves; they "will not profit us except we be touched with such a fear and reverence as those shepherds felt."[39]

The angel's message to the shepherds, however, reminds us that our fear of God should be tempered, since he speaks not in judgment but in love and "takes the part of a good and loving Father" who holds his children in his arms.[40] Although we rightly feel dismay at our sins and at the majesty of God's Word, joy abounds when we recognize that God reconciles us to himself in Jesus Christ. This is the joy the angel speaks of — a joy which shall be to all people. And this is especially significant for us, Calvin adds, since we are all Gentiles who were included in God's promise only after the Jews. Here already one sees Calvin moving the reference of the Gospel story from the past tense to the present. Although the historical facts of the angel's message are, for Calvin, beyond question, the *mere* facts are not enough: they must be appropriated in the believer's own life history.

The Christian's joy in Christ's birth is the same in all times. It cannot be a joy in the pleasures and delights of the world, which "intoxicate" us and draw us away from God. No, it must be like the joy the shepherds experienced after they went away from the manger and returned to their flocks. They did not get any special worldly gain from their knowledge. And neither will *our* wealth or honor be increased by the gospel. But we can never cease to be caught up in a "spiritual joy" since we have peace with God through Christ. Indeed, our joy must be so great that we can rejoice in our afflictions, knowing that God works them for good.[41] The joy brought to us by the gospel has its foundation in Jesus Christ, for in Christ God was reconciling the world to himself, "and today he still continues this work when the Gospel is preached to us."[42] Note that in the last sentence Calvin equates the reconciling work of Christ in the past with the preaching of the gospel in the present. The work of Christ is not merely an external exchange between the Father and the Son in the past, which the be-

---

38. *CO* 46:285. This sermon is the twenty-fourth in his series on the harmony of the Gospels, and it addresses Luke 2:9-14.

39. *CO* 46:286.

40. *CO* 46:286.

41. *CO* 46:289-90.

42. *CO* 46:291.

liever now appropriates intellectually. Rather, the work of Christ somehow takes place in preaching.

Calvin notes with special care that the angel said the Savior is "born to *us*." God planned in advance to answer the doubt of those who say that although the Redeemer is indeed born, it makes no difference for us. The angel proclaims: He is born to you! And if we have Christ, what do we lack in the perfection of wisdom, justice, life, and glory?[43] The angel, Calvin continues, also identified the Savior: he is Christ the Lord, the Anointed One, the receiver of gifts from God's Spirit. Christ received these gifts not for his own use, but so that we might be "participators" in them.[44] We participate when we draw from Christ's fullness, "and it is not necessary for us to make long journeys to come to him, for by the Gospel he declares that he is still ours today."[45] Once again, Calvin's overriding concern seems to be the move from the past tense to the present. It is particularly interesting that he denies the need for "long journeys" to come to Christ. The "Gospel history" does not create an unbridgeable gap between the story and the hearer. Rather, Gospel as a genre works in the same way in both the past and the present. The Gospel confronts the hearer with the *presence* of the Son of God.[46]

Calvin has made at least three important moves in this sermon. First, he has insisted that the hearers of a sermon must enter into the Gospel history and participate in the events it records. Second, he has identified preaching as the present locus of the redemptive work of Christ. Third, he has suggested that interpretation of Scripture ought to be more concerned with the present than with the past. Now we must see if the same themes are carried through in the second sermon.

Calvin begins on a striking note: "We know that it is our good, our joy, and rest to be united with the Son of God."[47] That is why we must contemplate Christ's birth, for none of us could have reached so high as to approach him. He had to come to us and make himself our Brother. Although for Calvin the historical core of the narratives is beyond question, the *point* of the "history"

---

43. *CO* 46:292.

44. This closely parallels Calvin's discussion of the three offices of Christ in the *Institutes*, where Christ is said to have received the gifts peculiar to each office not only for himself, but also to share with believers in the church (*Institutes* 2.15).

45. *CO* 46:293.

46. In his commentary on the harmony of the Gospels, Calvin defines a Gospel as "an Embassy, by which the reconciliation of the world with God, once for all accomplished in the death of Christ, is daily conveyed to men" (*A Harmony of the Gospels: Matthew, Mark, and Luke*, ed. David W. Torrance and Thomas F. Torrance, trans. A. W. Morrison, vol. 1 [Grand Rapids: Wm. B. Eerdmans Publishing Co., 1972], p. xi).

47. *CO* 46:955. The sermon is on Luke 2:1-14.

of Christ's birth, he tells us, is not to inform us of past events. Rather, in the Gospel history we see "that the Son of God, even our Mediator, has united himself to us in such a way that we must never doubt that we are sharers both of his life and of all his riches," and "we must learn from those who are here ordained as teachers and leaders how we must come to our Lord Jesus Christ."[48] The "teachers" here mentioned are poor shepherds. Not the wise or presumptuous, but the simple of this world show us the way to come to Christ. From them we must learn that he who would be reputed Christian must be a fool in this world. In particular, we must look at their faith. They were not astonished or repelled by the scandal of the Redeemer's birthplace. They humbly accepted God's Word without questioning what seemed contrary to reason in its presentation.[49] And so it still remains in Christ's church. The Word appears in the words of a mere man, in a "drop of water" in baptism, and in the "piece of bread and drop of wine" of the Eucharist. It seems to us "that such ceremonies which have no great pomp can have no value. So then, we see still better how what is here mentioned about the Shepherds pertains to us and how we should profit by it today."[50]

Calvin stresses the similarity of Christian experience within the Gospel history and after it. It was no easier for the shepherds to believe that the babe in the manger was the Son of God than it is for us to believe that the words of a mere man can be God's Word. The decision with which faith presents the hearer of the Word is the same in all time, and only two responses to it are possible: belief or unbelief.

Curiously, after this eloquent argument for the wisdom of God which is a stumbling block to the Jews and folly to the Greeks, Calvin returns to the theme of "proofs" of the Redeemer's identity. "For if the shepherds had had no other sign than the stable and the manger, we could say, 'Look at the poor idiots who make themselves believe foolishly and without reason that he was the Redeemer of the world.' That would be altogether too easy for us. We could, then, be in doubt. But the Shepherds were confirmed by other means to be certain that he was the Son of God."[51] They had the testimony of angels and the fulfillment of prophecy. God did not send the angels, however, just for the sake of the shepherds, but so that "we might be able to come to our Lord Jesus Christ with a ready courage and that we might no longer be held back by dispute or scruple . . . [from him] by whom God willed to communicate himself to us."[52] The host of

---

48. *CO* 46:958.
49. *CO* 46:958-59.
50. *CO* 46:960.
51. *CO* 46:961.
52. *CO* 46:962.

angels, the fulfillment of prophecy — all were given more for *us* than for the shepherds, and "that is how we must apply to our use and instruction the things here discussed. For it is not the intention of St. Luke . . . simply to write us a history."[53]

Calvin concludes the sermon with the same theme with which he began — union with Christ. The message proclaimed by the angels is "that it is now God in us, as much as God with us. Our God with us is declared when he willed to dwell in our human nature as in his temple. But now it is God in us, that is, we feel him joined to us in greater power than when he showed and declared himself mortal man."[54] Calvin seems to be arguing here that, in fact, the believer's communion with Christ is *more,* not less, intimate after his physical departure from the world, and that *we* can know Christ in us as much as, or more than, his earthly companions did. And so it is quite appropriate that the final note of this sermon is a eucharistic one. In the Holy Supper we may not doubt that "although we perceive only bread and wine . . . [Christ] really dwells in us, and that we are so joined to him there is nothing of himself that he is not willing to communicate to us."[55]

In sum, one is struck by the fact that for Calvin the point of the story in Luke 2 lies wholly in what it discloses to us about the presence of Christ today, in our own lives. He had no reason to doubt that the narrative was factual, a report of actual events. But would it, one wonders, have totally undermined his message if someone (some sixteenth-century Strauss) had persuaded him that things very likely did not happen quite the way they are recorded?

3. Two Sermons of Schleiermacher

Schleiermacher titles his sermon for Christmas Day 1831, based on Luke 2:15-20, "The Diverse Ways in Which the Proclamation of the Redeemer Is Received."[56] It is divided into two main sections. In the first, Schleiermacher considers these diversities of reception of the gospel in themselves, while in the second he considers their relationship to the current form of Christian fellowship. There are only very few Christians who receive the gospel as did the Virgin Mary and "ponder all these things in their heart." More are like the shepherds, who did not deny the testimony of the angels but went out of their way to see whether what they had been told was true. Without a doubt, most peo-

---

53. *CO* 46:963.
54. *CO* 46:966.
55. *CO* 46:966.
56. *SW* II/2:329-42.

ple are like those who wondered at what the shepherds told them.[57] We might think that the reason for these various reactions is the extraordinary event of Christ's birth itself. But Schleiermacher begins by showing that in ordinary human affairs, whenever something new is announced, the same types of reactions occur.

Having established the homogeneity of Christian experience in the Gospel narratives and in the world as we know it now, Schleiermacher returns to the story of the text. We ought not to be quick to judge either the "wonderers" or the "shepherds" for their weakness of faith. Those who wondered had every right to be suspicious, given all the messianic pretenders that were current at the time. And their wondering in itself shows that they at least had an open mind. The Redeemer might have said of such people what he said of another on a different occasion: "He who is not against us is for us."[58] Similarly, although we do not know whether the shepherds ever became Christ's disciples, we must not be too quick to judge them. They perhaps never had the opportunity to see Jesus again, or else, if they did, perhaps they did not connect him with the one for whom they praised God on the night of his birth. We cannot blame them if they did not come into a closer relationship with the Redeemer, for in their own way they were bearers of the Word.[59]

There are many among us in the church today, Schleiermacher argues, who are "wonderers." They see that the Christian religion has sprung from a very unlikely source and has grown to influence many nations, yet it does not really change the lives of those who profess it as one would expect it to. And there is some truth in such skepticism, for "much greater things ought to have happened in the human race through the fellowship [of believers], had only the relation of Christians to Christ been stronger and closer."[60] We can answer the skepticism of these wondering brothers and sisters by telling them that it is only human weakness and confusion that has prevented the powerful working of the church within the human race.

The "shepherds" in our church are those who "diligently investigate the stories to which Christian faith attaches itself, and make divine revelation the object of their reflection."[61] Schleiermacher notes that these in their own way receive the gospel, test it, confirm it through their investigation, and then spread the Word to others. Yet what we often hear about them is that they are lacking the most important part of piety — the silent pondering that one ob-

---

57. *SW* II/2:330-31.
58. *SW* II/2:334.
59. *SW* II/2:335.
60. *SW* II/2:337.
61. *SW* II/2:337-38.

serves in a Mary. But just such "shepherd" types are responsible for maintaining the purity of the Christian witness; through their inquiry, the Holy Spirit reforms the church.

When he finally turns to Mary, Schleiermacher highlights the ambiguity of her position. It was in no way remarkable that she, who had already had a personal visit from an angel, should ponder all these things in her heart! But was her faith true and blessed faith already then? Was not Mary slow to believe the divine message of her Son? With Mary and all the "Marian types," it is important to remember that their faith also contains the seed of unbelief; that their confirmation in faith is also a work carried out gradually over a period of time; and that in them, too, the Word must be ever anew enlivened to movement and growth.[62]

The conclusion is that we must all work together, each receiving and communicating the Word in the way that he or she best can. Only in this way will it become clear that the Savior who was born is not the Savior of a handful of individuals alone, but of the entire world. Clearly, in this sermon Schleiermacher is making the same general move that we saw Calvin making in his sermons on Luke 2. He draws his hearers into the Gospel history by asserting the homogeneity of Christian experience in the past and in the present. As an interpreter of the text, Schleiermacher's concern, too, is much more with the present meaning of Scripture than with the proper construction of its meaning in the past. The sermon in some sense renders the story present.

Schleiermacher begins his sermon on Luke 2:10-11, entitled "The Redeemer's First Appearance: A Proclamation of Joy That Awaits All People," by emphasizing the already–not yet character of the angel's announcement; although the promised joy which *shall* be to all people is clearly in the future tense, the event upon which it is founded has already happened.[63] When we examine the scene of Christ's first appearance, however, we strive in vain to see *there* the signs of a joy of world-historical proportions. But our faith as Christians presupposes that already at his first appearance Christ was the Son of God, the Word made flesh. The angel's announcement gives us a clue about how we should celebrate Christmas. That is, we should move from what has already happened to what is yet to come, from the past to the future. Thus, the sermon will be divided into two main parts. In the first, the proclamation of Christ's appearance will be considered as the archetype of a joy that we can have in the future; in the second, we will see now that the faith that grasps this future joy is our only assurance in the face of all the anxieties we have about our future.[64]

62. *SW* II/2:339-40.
63. *SW* II/3:132-42.
64. *SW* II/3:134.

The angel's announcement to the shepherds reminded them of the Old Testament prophecies about the Messiah. But if they had fixed their attention solely on that reference to the past, it is not likely that they would have grasped the gospel in faith. So much of what they expected on the basis of these prophecies would be missing from the scene that encountered them.[65] All prophecies about the future — whether Old Testament, New Testament, or even our own images of the future — are only uncertain representations. Just as the shepherds did not know *how* the babe in the manger would fulfill his mission as the Christ, so we do not know how the church will consummate its mission in the world.[66]

Someone might argue that if our joy in the future can only attach to such uncertain images, it completely loses its worth for us. But, Schleiermacher maintains, everything we can know about the future has only one truth for us, and belongs to the blessings of our life only if it agrees with our innermost longing and brings us peace. We do not know what happened to the shepherds after they returned to their flocks. Perhaps they forgot all about what had happened to them. But shortly after our text, we are told of Simeon, whose whole life had been spent in longing for the Redeemer. Although he was not permitted any clear picture of the future, his joy was complete because his longing was fulfilled. And the same is true of us. We can only have joy in the future if we are longing for something the Lord can develop within us in that future. We must be seeking and striving for his salvation, for peace between God and humanity.[67]

Our comfort and joy in the future, however, are entirely a matter of faith, just as our understanding of what happened in the past comes to us through faith.[68] The angel gave the shepherds a sign to demonstrate the truth of his proclamation. But what a dubious sign! Unless they had already believed that such a Savior was to be born, that sign would have never convinced them. And that is always the way it is: "Faith alone can hold on to joy in the form of the Redeemer, a joy that shall be not only to all the people, but also to the entire human race."[69] When the Redeemer himself taught on earth and went around doing miracles, only faith received his wonderful works as proofs; those who did not believe persistently misinterpreted his words and deeds. That is why the apostle Paul said the preaching of the gospel was a stumbling block to the

---

65. *SW* II/3:135.
66. *SW* II/3:136.
67. *SW* II/3:138.
68. *SW* II/3:139.
69. *SW* II/3:139.

Jews and folly to the Greeks; they were both lacking the faith by which they could grasp the future in the present.

When we have anxiety about our future, when we see that good is not triumphing over evil or that much of what we are trying to achieve seems to be failing, the source of these worries is always unbelief. But if we truly believe that the Savior is born *to us,* then we cannot be led astray about the future. We will remember that everything for which we thank and praise God can be summed up in what we have done in the name of the Lord — those deeds in which he became *present* to us. This experience, Schleiermacher tells us, "repeats itself in every significant [human] relationship," and it is "the key for everything that has happened in the period from when the Redeemer first appeared on earth to the present day."[70] That is, our joy in the future, like the shepherds' joy, is based on a faith that has "seen" the Redeemer — "seen" him wherever he has become present for us. And this is assurance enough that the heavenly light streaming out from this divine child will indeed one day totally penetrate the darkness of this world.[71]

4. Theological Conclusions

There are, of course, many points of difference in the ways in which Calvin and Schleiermacher interpret specific parts of this text. Perhaps most amusing are their nearly opposite constructions of the shepherds — for Calvin the simple, unlearned teachers, while for Schleiermacher the historical scholars; for Calvin the models of true faith in Christ, while for Schleiermacher examples of a "second-class" faith. But regardless of the material differences in their sermons, there are significant formal parallels between their respective homiletic methods. At the risk of oversimplifying, I will single out only two of these methodological principles they share, two that are intimately related to each other. First, both Calvin and Schleiermacher constantly shift from the past tense to the present. "The shepherds *did,* so *do* we." In none of the four sermons just examined is a purely historical point of view sustained for more than a paragraph. In fact, many of the interesting details of the narratives are simply overlooked. But this shift from past to present is not like the similar move that an Enlightenment preacher might make in urging Jesus as our moral example, nor is it patterned according to the medieval *imitatio Christi* model. (That is, "the shepherds did, so *should* we.") Rather, both Calvin and Schleiermacher repeatedly stress the homogeneity of Christ's appearing in the Gospel narratives

70. *SW* II/3:141.
71. *SW* II/3:142.

and in our own world. What the shepherds saw and heard and did is not really any different from what we see, hear, and do.

Second, in all of the sermons there is a strong emphasis on the necessity of union with Christ. Only through such union does he communicate to us the benefits of his incarnation. Only when Christ is "present" for us do we grasp our future joy in the present. The theme of union with Christ is not readily deducible from this narrative, as it would be from John 1, for example. Yet Calvin and Schleiermacher both manage to find a place for it in their sermons. Why is that? Because it, too, functions as a formative principle in their preaching. The Christ who is of concern to us is the Christ who saves us — the Redeemer. He saves us when he unites with us and so communicates his life to us. Thus, the only Christ the preacher can preach is the Christ with whom the believer is made one, the *Christus praesens,* the Christ here-and-now in the Word. But how does this sermonic theme present itself in the respective dogmatic systems of Calvin and Schleiermacher?

The reader of Calvin's *Institutes* is struck by the apparent disjunction between books 2 and 3 (or perhaps more precisely, between Christology and soteriology).[72] After developing what seems to be mainly an objective, vicarious doctrine of atonement in the former, Calvin opens the latter with something that sounds very different: "As long as Christ remains outside of us, and we are separated from him, all that he has suffered and done for the salvation of the human race remains useless and of no value for us."[73] In fact, Calvin's entire soteriology is based upon the notion of union with Christ — a union effected through the Word, which is grasped by faith through the work of the Holy Spirit. Although Calvin is clear in insisting that this union is necessary for salvation, he is unclear how it relates to the objective, and presumably self-sufficient, "work" of Christ that he set out under the rubric of Christology.

---

72. That is, does the substitutionary atonement of Christ that Calvin seems to favor in book 2 actually accomplish salvation, or does it merely open up the possibility of a salvation to be accomplished later, when the believer unites with Christ? Calvin's own comments at the opening of book 3 seem to suggest the latter answer: "As long as Christ remains outside of us, and we are separated from him, all that he has suffered and done for the salvation of the human race remains useless" (*Institutes* 3.1.1). On this tension in Calvin's system, cf. Paul van Buren, *Christ in Our Place: The Substitutionary Character of Calvin's Doctrine of Reconciliation* (Edinburgh: Oliver & Boyd, 1957); B. A. Gerrish, "Atonement and 'Saving Faith,'" *Theology Today* 17 (July 1960): 184. It must be said, further, that there is no scholarly consensus about Calvin's doctrine of the work of Christ. For a helpful overview of this matter, see Robert A. Peterson, *Calvin's Doctrine of the Atonement* (Phillipsburg, N.J.: Presbyterian and Reformed Publishing Co., 1983). In his discussion of the threefold office of Christ (*Institutes* 2.15), Calvin clearly understands Christ's work to be a work in which Christians participate.

73. Calvin, *Institutes* 3.1.1.

Schleiermacher, on the contrary, defines the work of the Redeemer from beginning to end in terms of a necessary union of Christ and the believer. The work of Christ is redefined in such a way that it does not refer to an act of appeasing God's wrath in the past, but rather to an "influence" *(Wirkung)* — an operation or effect — on the believer in the present.[74] If Schleiermacher achieves a significant improvement over Calvin by demonstrating the correlation between Christology and soteriology, he also explains somewhat more clearly how the union with Christ is effected. Like Calvin, he insists upon a conjunction of Word, faith, and Spirit. But more than Calvin, he is able to explain the Holy Spirit's "inner testimony" or "illumination" (Calvin's terms!) as a hermeneutic event that entails a human act of interpretation. The influence of Christ, he says,

> consists solely in the human communication of the Word, in so far as that communication embodies Christ's word and continues the indwelling divine power of Christ himself. This is in perfect accord with the truth that, in the consciousness of a person in the grip of conversion, every sense of human intermediation vanishes, and Christ is realized as immediately present in all his redeeming and atoning activity, prophetic, priestly, and kingly.[75]

The sermon confronts the hearer with the same Word with which the apostles were confronted. The whole procedure of redemption, Schleiermacher tells us, is the same for all races and for all ages. Our faith must have not only the same content, but also the same source, as the faith of Jesus' first disciples. And that source is a confrontation with the sacramental Word — the Word powerful enough to effect what it promises.[76]

If we return now to the question with which we began, that is, what difference historical criticism makes to the way Schleiermacher preaches Christ, it should be clear that both his theory of preaching and his soteriology render him *relatively* immune to the attacks of historical skepticism. Calvin simply reiterates the Chalcedonian doctrine of the person of Christ and a more or less Anselmian doctrine of the atonement. Thus Calvin's Christology presupposes the historicity of the total biblical story of Christ, from his virgin birth to his bodily ascension into heaven. Schleiermacher, following the rationalist lives of Jesus, rigorously limits the historical core necessary for his Christology. The virgin birth, resurrection, and ascension of Christ, for instance, are no longer properly constituent parts of the doctrine of his person.[77] But more impor-

74. Schleiermacher, *Gl.* §§100-101.
75. Schleiermacher, *Gl.* §108.5.
76. Schleiermacher, *Gl.* §108.5.
77. Schleiermacher, *Gl.* §§97.2, 99.

tantly, Schleiermacher succeeds in redefining the work of Christ in such a way that historical criticism cannot disturb him, insofar as Christ's work is no longer regarded as a transaction between the Father and the Son that happened in the past, but rather as a reconciling influence of the *Christus praesens* in the church. Schleiermacher's reformulation of Christology does not, however, do away with the need for *some* historical facts about the life of Jesus. And the historical claim upon which Schleiermacher's whole Christology is built — that "the ideal must have become completely historical in Him [Christ]" — is no less problematic, as D. F. Strauss's critique made clear, than is Calvin's need for a supernatural God-man who rose from the dead on the third day.[78]

In the course of our analysis of the preaching of Calvin and Schleiermacher on the Christmas narrative of Luke 2, we have uncovered an important line of continuity between the classical and liberal Reformed tradition. For both Calvin and Schleiermacher regard preaching as a sacrament. Preachers do not merely educate and inform their hearers; rather, in proclaiming the word, they re-present Christ to the congregation. The past events recounted by the Gospel narratives become present experience — the Word, once again, becomes flesh. It was in following Calvin's view of preaching as an incarnational event that Schleiermacher was able to redefine the redemptive work of Christ as a *present* rather than a *past* act of the Redeemer. Schleiermacher simply applies Calvin's principles more radically and consistently than did Calvin himself. The question, however, still remains: What is the relationship between the *Christus praesens* and the historical Jesus? And to what extent is the efficacy of the church's proclamation dependent upon a minimum of assured information about the historical figure who gave rise to the church's preaching? Neither Calvin nor Schleiermacher was able to sever all connections with the Jesus of history, yet both of them maintained that it is the *Christus praesens* of the proclaimed word which the believer must grasp in faith, and not the Christ of the distant historical past.

78. Strauss, pp. 768-73.

CHAPTER 25

Radical and Reformed: The Ecumenical Contribution of the Czech Reformation

Jan Milič Lochman

The Evangelical Church of the Czech Brethren has an exceptional place among the member churches of the World Alliance of Reformed Churches (WARC). The spiritual roots of this church do not primarily relate to the Reformed tradition of the sixteenth century, but to the reform movement of the fourteenth and fifteenth centuries in Bohemia and Moravia. The question may be asked: Is the membership of such a church within the Reformed Alliance legitimate? Most of the Czech Protestant theologians do not hesitate to answer this question affirmatively. They recall that a strong majority of the members of this church were Reformed at the moment of its reconstitution in 1918. They had become so by conscious choice. In 1781, after 150 years of severe Hapsburg counterreformation, a limited tolerance was granted to the remnants of the persecuted crypto-Protestants, and the only choice allowed them was between Lutheran and Reformed confessions. Under these circumstances most of them opted for the Reformed church.

There was a confessional "logic" behind that choice. There is indeed a deep spiritual and theological affinity between the Czech and the Swiss reformations. When contacts between the two had become possible in the sixteenth and seventeenth centuries, the inclination particularly of the Unity of the Czech Brethren was toward the Reformed churches in Switzerland and Germany. The Calvinist universities at Basel, Geneva, Strasburg, and also at Heidelberg and Herborn became the favorite schools to which their students were sent. Thus, with good reason the Evangelical Church of the Czech Brethren found its place within the Reformed family.

There is another side to this ecumenical relation. The presence of the Czech Protestants in the Alliance is helpful and inspiring not only for them as a minority church that finds its moral and occasionally economic support from the worldwide Reformed community (a classical and faithfully practiced concern of the Alliance); this presence has inspiring and challenging implications for the WARC as well. The specific contribution of the Czech theological heritage (like that of the Waldensians) helps the Alliance to keep the ecumenical horizon of its Reformed identity open for voices that share its fundamental confessional insights, but not in a narrow confessionalist sense. Such openness is of essential importance for our confessional bodies in their relation to the broader ecumenical movement. It is with this conviction that I dare to present a contribution on the Czech Reformation in a volume devoted to Reformed theology today.

Reformers and Martyrs

The Czech Reformation was a multifaceted, dynamic reform movement which began already in the fourteenth century and culminated in the fifteenth century. Generally we speak of "Hussitism" with reference to the key figure of the Czech Reformation, the Prague scholar, preacher, and martyr Jan Hus. But the movement was broader than this. There was the Unity of the Czech Brethren after Hus, and there was a remarkable reform movement in the fourteenth century before Hus. One name particularly should be recalled in this connection, that of Jan Milič from Kromě íž (1325-75). He has been called the "Father of the Czech Reformation," and for good reason: he already embodied in his life and work the basic emphases of the movement.

Jan Milič was a church dignitary of high rank and a royal bureaucrat at the time when the Kingdom of Bohemia, with its capital, Prague, was unquestionably one of the most important centers of Christian civilization. Prague was the seat of Emperor Charles IV and home of the oldest university north of the Alps. Naturally Milič acquired deep insights into the power and glory — but also the manifold corruption — of the church and the state. At the same time he was a biblically committed Christian. The confrontation of the biblical vision with the actual conditions of church and society led to a personal crisis with far-reaching consequences. Milič gave up his lofty position to become a servant of reform.

Three particular emphases characterized the work of Jan Milič, and they remained the constitutive elements for the whole of the Czech Reformation:

1. There was a strong *eschatological motivation* and orientation. The vision of the kingdom of God, and still more concretely, of the coming city of

God, was of paramount importance not only as a source of private consolation but also as a challenge to the established ecclesiastical and social order. The biblical book of Revelation aroused and drew special theological and ethical attention, both in its message of apocalyptic judgment (the motif of the Antichrist was an exciting influence) and in its ultimate promise of the "new heaven and new earth" — of the coming "new Jerusalem." The Hussite hope for the renewal of church and society was present already in Milič.

2. The instrument for renewal was the *preaching of the Word of God*. Milič became a passionate preacher. The eschatological vision was no amorphous enthusiasm; it had to be clearly articulated and guided by the original word of Jesus, and it had to be based on the prophetic and apostolic witness. Milič did not preach to the educated only, in Latin, or to the upper classes of Prague society in German. He addressed himself expectantly to the people of Prague in general, using the Czech language. The eschatological hope and task was by no means to be entrusted to the privileged ones, in either the social or spiritual senses. Through the Word of Christ, the whole people of God enters into the heritage of the children of God. Milič and his disciples ("the young eagles," as he called them) tried to awaken the consciousness and the conscience of Prague.

3. There was a strong emphasis on the *practical ethical consequences* of the eschatological witness. The preacher cannot remain in the pulpit. He has to ask for practical results. This implies an act of personal conversion. But not only that; Milič also raised the prophetic question about new conditions for those who were converted. It is not enough to proclaim the gospel of the new life and then let people go back into the old social conditions. New structures were needed for the new life. So Milič began a revolutionary experiment. In the center of Prague he established a foundation for the most despised people in medieval society — the prostitutes — in order to provide an effective new start for them after their conversion. He called that house the New Jerusalem. The prostitutes and the New Jerusalem — what a contrast! An outrage? Indeed, and Milič was promptly accused by the establishment powers and called before the pope. Yet he defended his preaching and actions as legitimate and biblical: a clear witness that the "city of God" has something to do with the concrete conditions of our secular cities. The eschatological promise mobilizes Christians to practical response, with social consequences.

"The Father of the Czech Reformation" died while defending his cause in Avignon. He left many "children" in Bohemia, the most important of which was Jan Hus (1372-1415). He reminds one in many respects of Milič. Hus also started a most promising career — an academic one — and became one of the best-known professors, and even rectors, of Prague University. Yet career status was not his ultimate concern. His heart belonged primarily to the truth of

Christ. He underwent no spectacular conversion; rather, he engaged in a long spiritual struggle connected with his theological and philosophical work. Hus participated in passionate disputes at Prague University between the realists and nominalists. Are "universals" (general concepts) names or realities? Hus was a realist even when, from the point of view of academic debates, this already seemed to be an obsolete position. But he remained a realist not primarily for speculative reasons, but rather for ethical ones. For him the question of truth was at stake. What is the truth? This was the key issue for Hus and for the Czech Reformation.

In answering this question, Hus rediscovered the *biblical concept of truth.* To him truth *(pravda)* was not only intellectual insight into the structure of being (as the Greek *aletheia*), but even more the supporting, challenging, and binding reality of the living God and his righteousness (the Hebrew *emeth*). To know truth necessarily implies doing it, responding to its vision in obedient action. For, ultimately, truth is Jesus Christ. And Jesus Christ is the incarnate Word, who calls for the "incarnation" of his words in the life of his church and the world. Theological theory has to relate to reality both in its personal and social aspects. Thus a philosophically realistic view of truth sets the established order in motion in order to transform it according to the revealed will of Christ.

As a consequence of this understanding and teaching, reforming and even revolutionary unrest broke out within the university and the city of Prague. For, measured by its apostolic origins, established Christendom appeared in many respects as apostasy; some of its orders flatly contradicted the will of Christ. Hus contrasted particularly the commitment of Jesus, the poor "King of the Poor," with the self-centered power and glory of the pope and his church.

As long as the scholar remained within the confines of the university, there were tensions but not an open crisis. But Hus could not limit himself to academic teaching. He became a powerful preacher, whose Czech sermons in the Bethlehem Chapel (not far from Milič's New Jerusalem) soon reached the broad masses of Prague. The authorities, and eventually the pope himself, intervened. A ban was declared against Hus, and an interdict against the city of Prague was enforced.

Hus left the city, but he refused to give up his preaching and teaching. He appealed to Christ — no earthly authority had the right to silence God's truth — and continued his activities outside Prague, where he was joined by the masses of Bohemia. This alarmed not only the pope (or popes, for there was a schism in Christendom) but also the council which was to meet in Constance. Hus was offered a hearing at the council, and he accepted.

The Council of Constance was supposed to be an instrument of church reform. But the Czech reformer was too radical for the reformers of Constance, including people like Pierre d'Ailly and John Gerson. They were not willing to listen to his arguments. Against all the assurances of the emperor, Hus was imprisoned and urged to recant. He refused. Hus was not stubborn; he was ready to listen to the arguments of the council fathers, but only on the condition that they corresponded to the truth of Christ. This truth could not be compromised, even if it might cost physical existence for the believer. The council put Hus to the ultimate test. He was sentenced as a heretic and burned at the stake on 6 July 1415.

Semen ecclesiae est sanguinis martyrum (the blood of the martyrs is the seed of the church) — not often has this ancient saying been so manifestly confirmed as in the case of Hus. The whole Kingdom of Bohemia rose up in his defense. The political representatives protested, and the masses of the Hussites defended the reformation against a whole series of crusades launched against the Bohemians. In 1432 the Hussites came to Basel to defend their case again before the council, but now as partners, not as the accused. The council had to acknowledge their reformation. This was still the Middle Ages, yet in the midst of Western Christendom an alternative church was constituted.

At its beginnings the Hussite movement was very dynamic both spiritually (the Hussites were well versed in biblical knowledge) and socially. But certainly, after years of warlike and spiritual wrestling with powers of the counterreformation (and its crusaders, whom the Hussites effectively defied), Hussitism weakened inside and out. The Hussites turned to so-called Utraquism, a reformed church of a strongly conservative character, but still one in which a serious impulse toward biblical Christianity was never abandoned.

The true evangelical inspirations, nevertheless, were represented especially by the *Unitas Fratrum* (the Unity of Brethren), which arose around 1457 out of a handful of determined Christians. They gathered in the small village of Kunvald in east Bohemia in order to build there a real Christian community, fashioned after the apostolic model. The *Unitas Fratrum* expanded in Bohemia and Moravia, but it always remained a small minority in the population. Furthermore, throughout almost all its history it was persecuted or suffered great duress. Nevertheless, the Unity of Brethren presented, in its profound spiritual resources as well as through its particular cultural achievements, the clearest phenomenon of Czech religious life in the sixteenth and seventeenth centuries. Here one thinks of its eminent theologians and thinkers, such as Lukas of Prague, Jan Blahoslav, and especially Jan Amos Comenius (1592-1670).

This promising development of Czech Protestantism applied not only to the Unity of Brethren but also to the Utraquist church (to which 90 percent of the people belonged). Considerably enriched by its contact with the German and Swiss reformations, it became more evangelical. However, this promising development was tragically destroyed in 1620. The Protestant army and its king, Friedrich von der Pfalz, were defeated in the battle of the White Mountain, near Prague, by the fanatically Catholic Hapsburgs. A ruthless counterreformation, certainly one of the most thorough in all Europe, was waged in Bohemia and Moravia. The leaders of the evangelical aristocracy were put to death; the evangelical faith was labeled a crime against the state; free citizens were driven to either become Catholic or to flee; and the subjects bound to the soil were simply impressed into the Catholic religion without any choice. Protestant life in Bohemia and Moravia was crippled during the long decades of the counterreformation. For many good reasons, this time was called "the era of darkness."

Finally, after 150 years (in 1781), the Edict of Toleration was issued by Austrian emperor Joseph II, who realized the political and spiritual dangers both of oppression and of open resistance from the underground evangelical groups, especially in Moravia. This edict assured the remainder of the evangelical churches a limited toleration. In spite of the radical operations of the counterreformation, over seventy thousand of the "quiet ones in the land" now opted for the evangelical faith. They wanted to hold on to the legacy of the Czech Reformation bequeathed by the Hussites and the Brethren. But that was not permitted, as they could choose only to become Lutheran or Reformed. Thus there grew up in our country a Lutheran and a Reformed church. Both met hard times. During the Catholic rule of the Hapsburgs, both were merely tolerated and for decades not given equal rights. Only in 1861, and, in a real sense, only after the fall of the Hapsburg monarchy in 1918, did they secure equal rights. In 1918 the old wish was finally granted, as both Czech evangelical churches united on the basis of the Czech Reformation. They were now called the Evangelical Church of the Czech Brethren. A new era of Czech Protestantism had begun.

The Magna Charta of the Czech Reformation

What was the theological shape — the program — of the Hussite Reformation? It is not easy to give a concise answer to this question. The movement had developed a whole spectrum of different trends and factions: the radical Taborites, the more cautious Prague party, and later the Czech Brethren. Yet there was a distinct common denominator in this multifaceted movement. All of the main groups among the Hussites subscribed to a common manifesto, the Magna Charta of Hussitism: the Four Articles of Prague (1491). They mark the basic theological outline of the Czech Reformation.

1. *The Word of God is to be preached freely.* First things first. With its first principle, the Czech Reformation pointed to its origins, both historical and spiritual. These origins were identical with those of the church itself, and consisted of the prophetic and apostolic message of the Word of God. In the course of history the apostolic foundation had been covered by the dust and splendor of ecclesiastical tradition. In many respects the immediate contact with the biblical message had been interrupted. The free preaching of the Word of God was the instrument of its renewal. Both parts of the formulation have to be emphasized. *Preaching* of the Word was to be encouraged, not just interpretation and translation of the biblical texts. To be sure, translation is important, and the Hussites worked on a Czech Bible. Yet the real renewal of faith arises out of a living encounter with the living Word, in dialogue between a preacher and a congregation. Both Milič and Hus were masters of such dialogue.

This preaching has to be *free.* This applies first to the Word of Christ; it has to be set free from its traditional strictures. It would be wrong to say that the medieval church had forgotten the biblical message. Yet, under the authority of its traditional magisterium, this message had been narrowed down. There had been a tendency to monopolize the exposition of the Bible, while the walls of dogmatic tradition were built up around it. The Hussites opposed these developments. The Word, Christ himself, will defend its truth. Its spiritual presence in the church cannot be bound to institutionalized conditions. Consequently the freedom of preachers had to be enlarged. There could be, strictly speaking, no monopoly of preaching. It is a universal gift entrusted to the whole people of God. The Taborites went so far as to question the institutionalized office of preachers. Everyone, men and women, may be called to witness. Everyone should have immediate access to the Word. Therefore free preaching is the first principle of Hussitism.

2. *The sacrament of the body and blood of Christ is to be served in the form of both* (sub utraque) *bread and wine to all faithful Christians.* For the Hussites, this second article had been of central importance. In celebrating the Last Supper, they returned the cup into the hands of all communicants. The cup became the symbol of the Czech Reformation. Is this to be understood as a liturgical novelty? Some church historians have tended toward this conclusion: "You do not reform the church and the world by a reform of ceremony" (A. Hauck). Yet this is a deep misunderstanding. For the Hussites (and, I would claim, not only for them!), the Lord's Supper was much more than a mere ceremony. In this sacrament the main lines of their faith and theology converged. Three points seem to me particularly important here:

a. The infamy of the established church was blatantly apparent. In withdrawing the cup, church authorities dared to manipulate even the sacramental memory of the death and resurrection of Jesus Christ himself. The realization of the contradiction between the articulate "last will" of Christ and the practice within the church was a real shock to the Hussites. Their leader after Hus, Jacobellus, said: "All priests are actually the thieves of the blood of Christ." They had reserved that blood for their exclusive use.

b. The *social implications* of the Last Supper became relevant. The blood of Christ is the bond of salvation for all the people of God, and must not be made into a privilege of church officials. In the presence of the Lord, all distinctions dissolve; all the children of God join in their common heritage. All are the priests — all are subjects and not just objects of the celebration. The experience of the Christian brotherhood, so strongly felt and grounded in the sacramental community, radiates into all spheres of life. From this center, the ecclesiological and social initiatives of the Hussites, particularly the Taborites, are to be understood. Therefore the *sub utraque* was more than a ceremonial reform. The cup is in fact the symbol of the eschatological brotherhood and sisterhood of women and men.

c. The *eschatological* aspect of the Lord's Supper was particularly strong with the Hussites. They celebrated Communion as an anticipation and representation of the coming kingdom of God. It is the sacrament of the new age, empowering believers to stand and to overcome the temptations and struggles of the old age. Frequently the sacrament was celebrated on mountaintops (the eschatological symbolism is apparent). In this understanding, the Hussites went a different (and possibly more biblical) way than the Reformers of the sixteenth century. Much of the spiritual energy of the latter reformation was devoted to the ontological aspects of Christ's presence in the sacrament; the question of the "elements" and their metaphysical status preoccupied their minds and debates. The Hussite emphasis on Christ's eschatological presence in the brotherhood of believers might actually be closer to the original meaning of the sacrament than the sixteenth-century discussions.

3. *Priests are to relinquish earthly position and possessions, and all are to begin an obedient life based on the apostolic model.* This article indicates the ecclesiological consequences of the Hussite program. What are the *notae verae ecclesiae* (signs of the true church)? "Word and sacrament" is their reply in the first and second articles, as if anticipating the classical position of the Lutheran Reformation. But the Hussites continued and added a very practical concern: an obedient life based on the apostolic model is also a sign of the true church. This was an attack on the lifestyle and structure of the Constantinian church. It struck at the privileged position of the priests, because in their case the contradiction between apostolic and Constantinian Christianity was especially sharp. Yet more was at stake — all of the church was to be confronted with the apostolic way. The apostles were the disciples of Christ; they followed his way

not only in teaching but also in living. The "apostolic model" is the way of service in solidarity, particularly with those who are poor and underprivileged. Likewise, a renewal that must produce practical and concrete social discipleship was the goal of the Hussite movement.

4. *All public sins are to be punished, and public sinners in all positions are to be restrained.* With its last article, the Hussite Reformation demanded moral discipline in all realms of life. This article may sound like legalistic moralism. No doubt there were legalistic tendencies among the Hussites, but at their best, their emphasis on law and discipline surpassed legalism. Like the later Calvinists, the Hussites recognized that a real reform of the church and society has to develop structural aspects. The moral and legal orders are not indifferent. Among Christians, they should reflect the "law of Christ." This implies discipline. Precisely in this article, the Hussite Reformation showed its revolutionary "teeth." It spoke of sinners "in all positions." There is only one order of justice in light of the kingdom of God. His law refers to all classes and all people; no positions can claim special privileges. The Lord is to be obeyed more than the lords, and the lords are to be judged under the supreme authority of the Lord. Not only the church but also the society is to be shaped in conformity with the royal authority of Jesus Christ. *Ecclesia et societas semper reformanda.*

The Ecumenical Contribution

Our cursory attempt at charting the spiritual and theological territory of the Czech Reformation raises the issue of its theological significance and possible actual relevance. Is there a legitimate *ecumenical contribution* of this reform movement? Many theologians and church historians seem to have doubts about this. If one looks at traditional textbooks of church history, vivid illustrations of these hesitations will be found. From the perspective of mainstream Roman Catholic historiography, the Hussites — like the Waldensians before them — were typical medieval heretics, although since Vatican II this view has been corrected by some researchers, particularly in relation to Jan Hus himself. For most church historians of the great Protestant churches, the Czech reformers are the "little brothers," attractive and sympathetic in the initiatives they took, but from a truly Reformation stance definitely "underdeveloped"; that is, they were mere precursors and heralds of the classical Reformation of the sixteenth century.

I would like to challenge this evaluation. What follows is a plea for more attention to, and appreciation of, the distinctive contribution of the Czech Reformation to ecumenical and particularly to Reformed Christianity. Behind this plea is the personal experience of the theological relevance of this heritage. Let me try to give the rationale for this judgment. I will do so in three steps, dealing with the issues of (1) the "Two Reformations," (2) the specific theological challenge, and (3) the contemporary significance of the Czech Reformation.

Against a Narrow Concept of Reformation

In the traditional understanding, the term "reformation" is generally reserved for the movements of the sixteenth century and is used in association with names like Luther, Calvin, Zwingli, and Knox. There are two criteria for measuring what is truly reformational: the "formal principle" in the doctrine of the sovereign authority of Scripture, *sola Scriptura,* and the "material principle" in the emphasis upon justification by faith alone *(sola fide).* Developments in church history are viewed from this perspective, and according to the degree of their agreement with these criteria, they are classified as "reformation" or "prereformation."

There are some persuasive arguments for this concentration upon the classic movements of the Lutheran and Reformed type. To be sure, the comprehensive development of both principles was not achieved until the Reformation of the sixteenth century. This should be acknowledged and under no circumstances relativized. For Reformed theology, it would be a threat to its identity to neglect or ignore the insights gained at that time.

However, a certain relativization of the traditional usage of the term "reformation" could be justified in that we draw attention to the fact that the reformation of the church is a many-sided and comprehensive movement. This is something the Reformers of the sixteenth century were well aware of. Their churches consciously promoted the principle of *semper reformanda,* the program of permanent reformation. For this very reason, reformation can never be identified solely with one historical form of reformation, even with the most classical forms. Every restriction of the term should be viewed with caution. It limits and impoverishes our understanding of reform. Every "cult" of a single reformation or even of the one or other reformer — and often have such "cults" been encouraged in the history of Protestantism — is really destroying the way to genuine, that is, permanent, multisided, comprehensive, reformation. Such an approach limits the reformation to its historical or even biographical context. This then stabilizes the movement. What were once vital and historically appropriate fronts are now transplanted into another set of circumstances, which results easily in the overlooking of the pertinent but altered reformation needs of the new historical situation. Of all people, it is often reformation-idolizing confessionalists who miss the urgent reformational requirements of their contemporary context.

In view of this danger, the encounter with the Czech Reformation could help ecumenical and, above all, Reformed theology to overcome such limitations of the reformation concept. Such an encounter, however, presupposes the willingness to respect and take seriously the particular significance of this movement; that is, not to force it into the role of a "precursor" on the basis of predetermined criteria. Reformation was already happening with the Hussites (and the Waldensians). Several Czech theologians have been trying for years to do justice to this fact by speaking of "Two Reformations," based upon a suggestion of the Prague dogmatic historian Amedeo Molnar. By the "first reformation" they mean the Waldensians, Hussites, and the Czech Brethren. The "second" is the reformational movements of the sixteenth century, primarily the Lutheran and the Calvinistic.

This terminology should not be misunderstood. It is not intended as an evaluation nor as a listing of rank or priority, and certainly not as a distancing from the "second reformation." This would be nothing more than another, no-less-problematic stylization, limitation, and legalistic abuse of the concept of reformation. The goal of this terminology is oriented elsewhere; it places the "legalistic abuse" of the concept in question, is a reference to the dynamic character of biblically understood reformational thinking, and above all, is an appeal for dialogue between both (and other!) reformations. The monotony of every fixed definition of "what is reformation" should be replaced by the ecumenical polyphony of biblically oriented renewal movements.

Toward Radical Renewal

Consideration of the "first reformation" is also significant today in the material sense, particularly in view of the content of its specific challenge. The Czech Reformation understood itself as a part of the broad reform movement within ecumenical Christianity. It did not intend to break the unity of the church; rather, it intended to renew and strengthen it on its apostolic foundation. When Jan Amos Comenius looked back at its history, he underlined the solidarity of the reformers with their reform programs — and he included among the former also some popes and councils of the Middle Ages. Particularly, the close affinity to the Reformation of the sixteenth century was highlighted. In spite of this broad solidarity, however, the Czech reformers had their own and distinct theological accents. One could perhaps characterize their intention with the term "radical renewal."

The word "radical" has two meanings here. It refers to the two aspects which seem to me to be typical for the Czech Reformation. On the one hand, in their confrontation with the established church, which was in such need of reform, the Czech reformers referred back to the origins — to the *radix*, the "roots" — of the church, that is, to its apostolic origins. Particularly, the praxis of the primitive church played a normative role for them; it constantly occurs in their theological declarations, together with references to the sovereign authority of Scripture, as an appeal to binding discipleship. In this *memoria apostolorum*, they hoped for, and sought to promote, the restructuring and renewal of the contemporary church.

In returning to the church's origins — a step which had parallels in the Reformation of the sixteenth century — the Czech theologians developed the second accent of their radicality, which lends them their specific image and importance. By referring to the apostolic origins, they emphasized the *practice* of the early church in its exemplary purport and placed these practical aspects in the foreground. Such an *orthopraxy* is no less important for the reform of the church than an *orthodoxy;* neither side should be played off against the other, nor should they be separated from one another. To know and to teach the truth means to *do* it.

In this connection, the Czech reformers' constant appeal to the *example of Jesus,* to his law and his actions, played an orienting role. The Czech Reformation turned directly to the Bible, placed it in the hands of believers, and translated it, but, above all, the Czech Reformation prized the vitally preached Word as a challenge to discipleship. In so doing, it set unmistakable accents in the selection of its texts. It was the Gospels, primarily the Sermon on the Mount, which received the greatest amount of attention. Without desiring to set up false alternatives, the following distinction could be made: where the later reformation concentrated its theology on the Pauline message of justification, the Czech focused on the evangelical commandment of Jesus.

This orientation reached its concrete expression with an emphasis which opened the Hussites to the Waldensians: the call to evangelical and apostolic poverty. As is well known, this was the basic motive in the conversion of Peter Waldo: the voluntary poverty of the wealthy merchant for the sake of discipleship and of credible proclamation. But for Jan Milič and Jan Hus, too, the reference to Jesus as the "King of the Poor" played an important role in the critique of church and society. The true church of Christ is apostolic in the sense that it understands itself as the *"church of the poor."*

There is a double significance in this: The church first devotes itself to the poor and takes a stand for them. This was practiced with revolutionary consequences by the Hussites in particular. And then the church should live in the spirit of poverty: worldly domination jeopardizes and contradicts the inner constitution of the church, destroying the credibility of its word and mission. Therefore the Czech reformers challenged the established church in its institutionalized lifestyle; they revealed the church in its wealth and power interests — e.g., the sale of indulgences — as a church in contradiction with itself. In this regard there was a strong polemic accent in this reformation. But the Hussites and the Czech Brethren did not merely polemicize; rather they put their message into practice, lived out an *alternative,* and took the person and Word of their Lord seriously. The Hussites, particularly the Taborites, attacked the unjust social structures of "Constantinian Christendom" and experimented with "classless models" of a Christian society. The Czech Brethren concentrated on forming the committed fellowship of resolute disciples of Jesus outside the mainstream of society at first, yet radiating the spirit of Christ into the surrounding culture indirectly and effectively. Common to all was the deep conviction that both the personal and social life of Christian people is to be creatively related to the promise and challenge of the coming kingdom of God. As the revolutionary Prague preacher Jan of Želiv put it: *"Status mundi renovabitur"* (The state of the world will be renewed).

Some aspects of this type of thinking and acting may seem, from the perspective of several centuries later, to have been too enthusiastic, sectarian, and alien to the world's realities. There are elements of apocalypticism and legalism. Some presuppositions and consequences had to be clarified and examined theologically. This the Reformation of the sixteenth century would do, and its corrections would not be unheard by the churches of the Czech Reformation.

It would, however, be foolish in this process of correction to overlook the permanent contribution and challenge of this reformation: the emphatic insistence that a true and serious reform of the church — a radical reformation — must have its social-ethical and *social-critical dimensions.* Or, to put it another way, the *semper reformanda* must never be applied only to the realm of doctrine and ecclesiastical theory, but also to the lifestyle and practical engagement of the church, i.e., to both the personal life of the Christian as well as the institutional life of church and society. A biblically radical reform movement has its integral ethical, even political, dimension. Lacking this dimension, the implications of Christian renewal are not fully developed, and reformation is not understood radically enough.

Contemporary Significance

In its emphasis on faith's radical relationship to reality, I see the charisma of the Czech Reformation and its relative "plus" in comparison with other reform movements, including that of the sixteenth century. Was it not a danger of the great Reformers of the sixteenth century that their passionate commitment to renewal was related too one-sidedly to doctrine and to the inner realm of the church? Certainly this is not exclusively so. Particularly, the Calvinist churches were not so one-sided. But looking at the Reformation as a whole, their efforts and initiatives did have this tendency.

One cannot overlook the ecumenical significance and achievements, for example, of Lutheran theology and church life. However, one should not ignore the shadows which accompanied them. I am thinking of a certain inadequacy in the area of the practical and social consequences of the Reformation. Luther's one-sided and gruff "no" to the peasants' revolt demanding more justice and freedom is symptomatic. I do not wish to underestimate the complexity and difficulty of decision in the given historical moment (1525) and exercise cheap criticism from the safety of temporal distance. But Protestant church history has been profoundly burdened by fear or theological hesitations in regard to the practical and social demands of reformational freedom; in part, with explicit reference to Luther's attitude. The failure of the established evangelical churches in the social area is at least in part explained by this. The relative absence of the other voices, like those of the Czech Reformation, and the notorious underestimation they are given in the perspective of established Protestant orthodoxy, has had negative consequences for church and society.

Today, a more positive revaluation of the contribution of the Czech Reformation for ecumenical Christianity might be in our common interest. Within ecumenical Christianity today we are experiencing a veritable explosion of social-ethical engagement, both in Protestant and Roman Catholic churches (the manifold "liberation theologies" are examples of this). At the same time, a growing anxiety is being felt in some ecclesiastical and political circles as reaction to this engagement. There is a dangerous process of polarization in our churches. The crisis is further deepened by shattered structures and membership losses in many traditionally Reformed areas, e.g., in Switzerland.

More than ever, concentrated theological reflection on these burning issues is essential. While social involvement by Christians is an urgent challenge today in view of the global distress of humankind, it is persuasive and effective only when it is not the overreaction of unreflective activism compensating for lack of spiritual discipline and concentration, but rather issues from thoughtful and dynamic faith. Here is where theology has an important task. But theology will hardly be able to fulfill its charge unless it looks at its own "house" and searches out sources and models for a new beginning. Some of those traditionally neglected ones might prove particularly helpful. To my thinking (and frequent ecumenical experience), the "radical and reformed" voice of the Czech Reformation is such a source and model.[1]

1. For further study of the theological and social profile of the Czech Reformation (in English), the following works can be recommended: Peter Brock, *The Political and Social Doctrines of the Unity of Czech Brethren* ('s Gravenhage: Mouton & Co., 1957); Howard Kaminski, *A History of the Hussite Revolution* (Berkeley and Los Angeles: University of California Press, 1967); Matthew Spinka, *John Hus: A Biography* (Princeton: Princeton University Press, 1968); Jarold K. Zeman, *The Hussite Movement and the Reformation in Bohemia, Moravia, and Slovakia (1350-1650): A Bibliographical Study Guide* (Ann Arbor: Michigan Slavic Publications, University of Michigan, 1977); Jarold K. Zeman, *Renewal of Church and Society in the Hussite Reformation* (Bethlehem, Pa.: Moravian Theological Seminary, 1984).

CHAPTER 26

Some Distinctive Contributions of the Dutch-American Reformed Tradition

John Hesselink

Introduction

Ethnicity is a multifaceted concept. Earlier in American history it was frowned upon, because the ideal was that of the melting pot. In recent years that notion has been challenged. Now, it is maintained, ethnic values and distinctives should not be despised and wiped out but valued and enhanced.[1] The image of the melting pot has been replaced by that of the salad bowl. Diversity is now approved of as long as it contributes to the common good. All of this relates to the concept of ethos, which is defined as "the characteristic and distinguishing attitudes, habits, beliefs, etc. of a racial, political, or other group";[2] or, more briefly, as "the characteristic spirit and beliefs of a community."[3]

Both terms are important for understanding the thesis of this essay. For there is within the Reformed family in North America a rather clearly definable group of Reformed Christians whose ethnic background is Dutch. Most of them belong to either the Reformed Church in America (RCA) or the Chris-

---

1. Despite the more positive evaluation of ethnicity, the noun "ethnic" does not always connote something positive but suggests rather a minority person, often of color, who is not a part of the mainstream.
2. *Webster's New World Dictionary of the American Language. College Edition* (Cleveland and New York: Collins and World Publishing Co., 1974).
3. *Oxford American Dictionary* (New York: Oxford University Press, 1980).

tian Reformed Church of North America (CRC),[4] although many Christians of Dutch origin are found in other denominations, particularly in the Presbyterian Church (U.S.A.).

The RCA and the CRC are both small denominations, each with approximately 200,000 active communicant members. Yet their theological vitality and influence have been disproportionately great, particularly in the last quarter-century. Much of this vitality and theological activity finds its center and focus in a very circumscribed area in western Michigan. The centers of this theological tradition are Grand Rapids, Michigan, where Calvin College and Calvin Theological Seminary (CRC) are located,[5] and Holland, Michigan, the site of Hope College and Western Seminary (RCA). Nearby are several little towns bearing the names of the provinces and towns in the Netherlands from which their first settlers came: Zeeland, Vriesland, Overisel, and Drenthe.

In contrast to the first Dutch Reformed churches which were organized in New York City (the first congregation was organized in New Amsterdam in 1628), the Hudson Valley, and New Jersey, the ethos of the Reformed churches in the Midwest and western Michigan in particular is the outgrowth of a second wave of immigrants from the Netherlands in the mid–nineteenth century.[6] The leader of the group that settled in Holland (Michigan) in 1847, Albertus C. Van Raalte, came from a secessionist group in the Netherlands. There, in 1834, a group of Reformed dissenters began to form a new church in reaction to the moribund state church which had become extremely liberal and oppressive. The secessionists were persecuted, and many of them fled to the United States. One group settled in western Michigan, and another group, led by Hendrik Scholte, founded a colony in Pella, Iowa. From these two centers immigrants then moved out to the Chicago area, Wisconsin, Iowa, and other midwestern states. Not only were these Reformed immigrants very orthodox and fiercely independent, but many of them had also been influenced by a renewal movement in the Netherlands called the "awakening." Thus these

---

4. There are a number of very small Reformed churches in North America whose roots are in the Netherlands, such as the Protestant Reformed Church, a splinter group from the CRC; the Netherlands Reformed Church; the Canadian Reformed Church (to be distinguished from the CRC or RCA in Canada); and the American Reformed Church.

5. The Reformed Bible College is also located in Grand Rapids, but its emphasis is on training lay Christian workers and missionaries. However, one of its historians, Professor Lyle Bierma, is an able Reformation scholar whose writings are known and respected by sixteenth-century scholars.

6. For the history of the RCA, particularly its Eastern origins, see Howard G. Hageman, *Lily among the Thorns* (New York: Reformed Church in America, 1953; 4th printing [revised] 1975).

midwestern Dutch Reformed Christians were influenced by both a concern for doctrinal purity and a peculiar Dutch piety.

By 1848 the *classis* (presbytery) of Holland was formed, and by 1850 it had decided to cast its lot with the Reformed Church in the East. It was not long, however, before troubles began within the Holland *classis*. Some of the more recent immigrants were very critical of certain practices in the Reformed Church in America, such as the introduction of singing hymns (versus only psalms), open communion, and the failure to preach sermons based on the Heidelberg Catechism at all services. This led to the withdrawal of several congregations from the Holland *classis* in 1857. Thus, the Christian Reformed Church was founded. Another group of churches broke away in 1882 because of a controversy over Freemasonry. Most of the immigrants from this time on joined the Christian Reformed Church, so that by 1900 it had 144 congregations, mostly in the Midwest.[7]

The RCA and the CRC: Unity in Diversity

What is important for our purposes is not so much the origins of this separation as those issues which continue to keep these two denominations apart today. Their relations are no longer characterized by bitter rivalries and nasty charges and countercharges. But there are at least four areas where the two denominations continue to have their differences.

1. *The interpretation of Scripture.* In general the CRC is more conservative in its hermeneutic. One result is the differing positions in regard to women serving in church offices. The RCA has ordained women to the gospel ministry

---

7. For the history of the midwestern Reformed church, see Arie R. Brouwer, *Reformed Church Roots* (New York: Reformed Church Press, 1977). For a history of the Christian Reformed Church, see Henry Zwaanstra, *Reformed Thought and Experience in a New World: A Study of the Christian Reformed Church and Its American Environment, 1890-1918* (Kampen: J. H. Kok, 1973). For more specialized studies of the background and causes of the secession and formation of the CRC, see Gerrit J. ten Zythoff, *Sources of Secession: The Netherlands Hervormde Kerk on the Eve of the Dutch Immigration to the Midwest* (Grand Rapids: Wm. B. Eerdmans Publishing Co., 1987); Elton J. Bruins, "Immigration," in *Piety and Patriotism: Bicentennial Studies of the Reformed Churches in America, 1776-1976*, ed. James W. Van Hoeven (Grand Rapids: Wm. B. Eerdmans Publishing Co., 1976); Elton M. Eenigenburg, "Reformed Theology and the Second Dutch Immigration," and M. Eugene Osterhaven, "Saints and Sinners: Secession and the Christian Reformed Church," both in *Word and World*, ed. James W. Van Hoeven (Grand Rapids: Wm. B. Eerdmans Publishing Co., 1986); Elton J. Bruins, "The Masonic Controversy in Holland, Michigan, 1879-1882," in *Perspectives on the Christian Reformed Church: Studies in Its History, Theology, and Ecumenicity*, ed. Peter De Klerk and Richard De Ridder (Grand Rapids: Baker, 1983).

since 1978. The CRC came close to adopting this position in 1990 but then voted down the proposal at its General Synod in 1992.

2. *Confessionalism.* The CRC generally upholds its confessions (which are the same as those of the RCA: the Belgic Confession, the Heidelberg Catechism, the Canons of Dort) more strictly than the RCA. This is reflected also in the colleges of the denomination. Tenured professors at Calvin College must become members of the CRC. At Hope College one must only believe in "the historic Christian faith," which allows for Roman Catholics and non-Reformed Christians to be on the faculty.

3. *Kuyperianism.* Theologically, the greatest difference between the RCA and the CRC is the dominating influence of the theology of Abraham Kuyper in the latter. There are various strains in this thought, some of which may be in tension, but the notion of antithesis has been adopted by portions of the CRC with the result of an over-againstness in regard to certain aspects of American culture in contrast to the transformationist model. The result, in any case, has been a denominational support of Christian schools at every level. The RCA, at least in principle, has supported public schools. Other principles by Kuyper, such as common grace and the necessity of a *Weltanschauung* (world and life view), have found some acceptance in the RCA.

A more recent development, however, is the impact of the philosophy of Herman Dooyeweerd of the Free University of Amsterdam on the CRC. This is a form of neo-Kuyperianism in which there is a "tripartite notion of revelation: besides (and perhaps through and before) the Inscripturated (Bible) and Incarnate (Christ) Word stood God's creation ordinances (the Law Word) by which the Christians' redemptive witness to all areas of society and culture could proceed."[8]

This approach has not been universally accepted in the CRC, and has in fact been a source of tension in its colleges. It has its representatives at Calvin College, however, in the person of emeritus professor H. Evan Runner and his disciples, and has found a home in the Institute for Christian Studies in Toronto.

4. *Ecumenism.* Whereas the RCA has consistently allied itself, albeit not without tensions, with major conciliar groups such as the National Council of Churches (NCC) and the World Council of Churches (WCC), the CRC has only affiliated with more conservative fellowships such as the National Association of Evangelicals. That relationship has not always been a comfortable one, however, so for the most part, the CRC has only aligned itself with other conservative Reformed or Presbyterian denominations within a fellowship for-

---

8. See James D. Bratt, "The Dutch Schools," in David F. Wells, *Dutch Reformed Theology* (Grand Rapids: Baker, 1989), p. 26.

merly called the Reformed Ecumenical Synod (now renamed the Reformed Ecumenical Council). The RCA, on the other hand, has been a longtime member of the World Alliance of Reformed Churches, to which the CRC has only sent an observer in recent years.[9] The practical consequences of this differing outlook can be seen in the denominations' respective overseas mission policies. The RCA has usually cooperated with the indigenous national Presbyterian church in a given country — if there is one — or with a United church in the country, such as it does in Japan and South India. The CRC, on the other hand, has usually cooperated overseas with smaller, conservative Reformed or Presbyterian denominations. A consequence in this country is that the CRC and its institutions have been generally accepted in evangelical circles, whereas the RCA has either been overlooked or regarded with suspicion because of its "entangling alliances" and its sometimes ambiguous position in regard to evangelical causes. Fortunately, some of these stereotypes are breaking down. One illustration of this is the recently published *Encyclopedia of the Reformed Faith*, edited by Donald McKim (Louisville: Westminster/John Knox, 1992), in which the CRC and RCA each have ten or more contributors.

All these differences notwithstanding, there is a solid core of belief which unites these denominations more than it separates them. This theological outlook, in turn, cannot be separated from the distinctive milieu and ethos in western Michigan which influences and colors the lively theological activity which flourishes in the colleges and seminaries of the CRC and RCA. This is further facilitated by the three major publishing houses in Grand Rapids, all of whose owners are Christian Reformed, viz., Eerdmans, Baker, and Zondervan. Moreover, the denominational magazines of both denominations, *The Banner* (CRC) and *Church Herald* (RCA), are published in Grand Rapids, as well as the influential *Reformed Journal* (now defunct) of CRC background and *Perspectives* (originally an RCA publication but now combined with the *Reformed Journal*). All this, as well as the fact that the headquarters of the CRC and a regional office of the RCA are in the Grand Rapids area, adds up to an impressive and formidable concentration of educational, ecclesiastical, and theological power and influence in a very limited area.

Out of this unique ethos has emerged a distinctive Dutch-American Reformed theology. Some people from within the tradition think it would be more accurate to speak of a plurality of theologies. Moreover, it would generally be conceded that there is considerable diversity not only between CRC and

---

9. For the RCA situation see Herman Harmelink III, *Ecumenism and the Reformed Church* (Grand Rapids: Wm. B. Eerdmans Publishing Co., 1968). For the CRC see John H. Kromminga, *All One Body We: The Doctrine of the Church in Ecumenical Perspective* (Grand Rapids: Wm. B. Eerdmans Publishing Co., 1970).

RCA theologians but also within their own denominational circles. Within each denomination, as in any denomination, there are progressives and conservatives, but there is still a surprising degree of commonality within and among those communities. Even when they argue with each other, these Reformed theologians often betray their common ethno-theological roots. This is particularly true in the case of the Christian Reformed. Some of their fiercest theological battles within the last half-century, e.g., over common grace and the scope of the atonement, were waged from within a common framework.[10]

All these intramural tensions and denominational squabbles notwithstanding, I maintain that there is still a discernible, distinctive theology, or at least a theological approach, which distinguishes this variety of Reformed theology from Hungarian and German Reformed versions of the tradition in the United States or the American Presbyterian tradition.

Two Specific Illustrations

Before giving a brief historical background and proceeding to the five subtheses which illustrate this thesis, it may be helpful to compare two Dutch-American Reformed works with similar efforts by Presbyterian theologians.

First, let us consider M. Eugene Osterhaven's *The Spirit of the Reformed Tradition* (Grand Rapids: Wm. B. Eerdmans Publishing Co., 1971) and John H. Leith's *Introduction to the Reformed Tradition* (Atlanta: John Knox, 1977).

---

10. Concerning these controversies see James D. Bratt, *Dutch Calvinism in Modern America: A History of a Conservative Subculture* (Grand Rapids: Wm. B. Eerdmans Publishing Co., 1984), chap. 8 and pp. 207ff. For a more succinct treatment of these controversies, see Bratt's essay, "The Dutch Schools," in *Reformed Theology in America: A History of Its Modern Development*, ed. David F. Wells (Grand Rapids: Wm. B. Eerdmans Publishing Co., 1985), pp. 145ff. Another essay in this volume is also relevant to the theme of this essay, viz., George Marsden's "Reformed and American." Both essays appear unaltered in a subsequent, smaller volume, also edited by David F. Wells: *Dutch Reformed Theology*. Bratt's book is a brilliant tour de force, and the essays by Bratt and Marsden in the two symposia are very perceptive and helpful, but they both suffer from the same one-sidedness, i.e., both focus largely on the CRC situation. This is understandable, given the fact that both authors are Christian Reformed and teach or have taught at Calvin College (Marsden is now at the University of Notre Dame). Even so, in view of the fact that Bratt knows the RCA situation quite well, it is misleading and unfortunate to dismiss the RCA contributions to Dutch-American Reformed theology to one paragraph and a couple comments in his conclusion. Granted, RCA theology generally has not been as self-consciously confessional as CRC theology, but this does not mean that it has not been Reformed or productive in recent years. I have documented the virility of this scholarship in an essay, "Prose and Poetry: Reformed Scholarship and Confessional Renewal," in *Word and World*, pp. 93ff.

Both volumes are of similar size, have the same purpose, and appeared within the same decade. Both are by highly respected, longtime professors in seminaries of their respective denominations. Osterhaven taught systematic theology for thirty-five years at Western Seminary in Holland, Michigan (RCA); Leith taught historical theology and, later, systematic theology at Union Seminary in Richmond, Virginia, for approximately thirty years and represents the Southern Presbyterian tradition (technically, the Presbyterian Church in the U.S., prior to the union with the United Presbyterian Church). Both wrote their doctoral dissertations on John Calvin — Osterhaven's at Princeton Seminary, Leith's at Yale Divinity School. Both are staunchly Reformed and are appreciative of and indebted to the confessions of their respective churches. Both are also influenced by so-called neoorthodox theology. Both would be in almost complete agreement on the nature of the gospel and the mission of the church. Moreover, both theologians have a similar understanding of what it means to be Reformed.

And yet, when these books are read one after another, one senses a different background, outlook, and spirit reflecting the respective subcultures of the authors. The differences are not substantial, only nuanced, but they provide a clue as to what makes the Dutch-American Reformed tradition distinct. In the case of these two books it is basically one of different confessional backgrounds. Osterhaven was raised on the Heidelberg Catechism and is steeped in the Belgic Confession and Canons of Dort; Leith, on the Westminster Confession and Catechism.[11] The differences become more apparent in observing their respective mentors. Leith cites the Niebuhrs, both Reinhold and Richard, frequently; Osterhaven cites them not at all. Leith is also indebted to a leading Southern Presbyterian theologian, James Henley Thornwell, whom, together with Charles Hodge, he regards as "the most influential American Presbyterian theologian of the nineteenth century."[12] But Osterhaven refers to Hodge only once and Thornwell not at all. Osterhaven, however, is indebted to several Dutch theologians, particularly A. A. van Ruler. What is equally significant is his omission of any reference to Abraham Kuyper, something unimaginable for a Christian Reformed theologian.

What is the net result of these differences? Nothing substantial, only nuances and accents. Osterhaven places more emphasis on piety, a life lived in the

---

11. Osterhaven is the author of a popular commentary on the Belgic Confession, *Our Confession of Faith* (Grand Rapids: Baker, 1964); Leith wrote on the history of the Westminster Confession in *Assembly at Westminster: Reformed Theology in the Making* (Richmond: John Knox, 1973).

12. John H. Leith, *Introduction to the Reformed Tradition* (Atlanta: John Knox, 1977), p. 147.

presence of God, and the nature of the church; Leith more on preaching, tradition, and ecumenism. But these are only differences of emphasis; the fundamental agreement far outweighs the minor differences.

Secondly, we consider Gordon J. Spykman's *Reformational Theology: A New Paradigm for Doing Dogmatics* (Grand Rapids: Wm. B. Eerdmans Publishing Co., 1992) and Daniel L. Migliore's *Faith Seeking Understanding: An Introduction to Christian Theology* (Grand Rapids: Wm. B. Eerdmans Publishing Co., 1991).

Written within a year of each other, these two systematic theologies demonstrate more clearly the differences between a middle-of-the-road Presbyterian approach to theology and a neo-Kuyperian understanding of theology. Spykman, like Migliore, was born and reared in the United States, but had his college and seminary training at Calvin and did his doctoral work at the Free University in the Netherlands. Migliore's training was more "American," i.e., Westminster College, Princeton Seminary, and his doctorate from Princeton University.

They have much in common; however, each can rightly lay claim to being a Reformed theologian. Both have a high view of Scripture, the Trinity, justification by grace through faith, church and sacraments, and the witness of the church in the world. Both handle these themes and others with typical Reformed accents. Moreover, both appreciate Calvin and cite him often (as well as Augustine, Luther, and others), and both reflect their respective confessional confessions, albeit with some curious omissions. Spykman cites the Belgic Confession and Heidelberg Catechism frequently but almost totally ignores the Canons of Dort. Migliore rarely refers to the classical Westminster Confession and Westminster Catechism but obviously likes the new Presbyterian Brief Statement of Faith.

There, however, the similarities cease. Both quote Karl Barth frequently and often with approval, while Spykman is put off by Barth's alleged "strictly second-article theology."[13] What is at stake here is more than a different evaluation of Karl Barth. Spykman wants to give the first article of the creed — the doctrine of creation — its due, which he feels gets short shrift in Barth and much contemporary theology. Migliore is quite content with a more christocentric approach.

Also quite different are their evaluations of Jürgen Moltmann. Spykman refers to him once and very negatively, whereas Migliore is clearly very appreciative of and indebted to the Tübingen theologian. The real divide comes, however, in their respective responses to liberation theology. Spykman *appears*

---

13. Gordon J. Spykman, *Reformational Theology: A New Paradigm for Doing Dogmatics* (Grand Rapids: Wm. B. Eerdmans Publishing Co., 1992), p. 175.

to be oblivious of it; Migliore is enamored with it.[14] As a result, Spykman's theology has a conservative cast to it while Migliore's is moderately avant-garde. Yet each in his own way is self-consciously Reformed, and both are in fundamental agreement concerning the nature of the Christian faith.

Even more than was the case with Osterhaven and Leith, the determinative factors are backgrounds, milieu, and audience. The one reflects his Dutch-American ethos and a career of teaching at Calvin College, the other his Eastern environment and a career at Princeton Seminary. It is not that Spykman is an obscurantist; one of his favorite non-Dutch authors is Otto Weber, one of the finest Reformed theologians in Germany of the last half of this century. Migliore is also fond of Weber, and both authors engage in dialogue with other contemporary German theologians: Pannenberg, Jüngel, Rahner, Küng, et al. The key difference is the host of Dutch and Dutch-American authors whom Spykman cites constantly — and almost always with approval — names like Bavinck, L. and H. Berkhof, Berkouwer, Dooyeweerd, Hoekema, Hoeksema, Kuyper, Ridderbos, and Schilder.

Above all, what distinguishes Spykman's theology not only from Migliore's but also from that of other Reformed theologians in the Dutch-American tradition is his *reformational* perspective. This is a specific variety of Reformed theology which goes beyond Calvin and traditional Calvinism. It is often described as neo-Kuyperian, for it is heavily indebted to the great Dutch theologian, educator, and politician Abraham Kuyper. Spykman is not altogether satisfied with Kuyper, however, and finds the inspiration and basis for his theological approach in two Dutch philosophers, D. H. T. Vollenhoven (d. 1978) and Herman Dooyeweerd (d. 1977). Together they promulgated "the philosophy of law-idea," otherwise designated as a "cosmonomic philosophy." It is interesting to note that this philosophy has made a negligible impact on theologians in the Netherlands, even at the Free University where these two philosophers taught. This is another illustration of how Dutch theology gets transposed into another key in its North American setting.

This philosophy provides the basis and rationale for Spykman's reformational theology. Here prolegomena is all-important. "Seeking to do theology without a self-conscious philosophical orientation is an 'impossible possibility,'" avers Spykman.[15] Accordingly, he devotes 136 pages of his 560

---

14. I italicize the word "appears," for Spykman participated in a yearlong study of the situation in Central America, visited several countries there with his study group, and later edited a sensitive study of the situation there: *Let My People Live: Faith and Struggle in Central America*. Migliore may be drawing on an earlier study of his, *Called to Freedom: Liberation Theology and the Future of Christian Doctrine*.

15. Spykman, *Reformational Theology*, p. 7.

pages of theology to prolegomena. Migliore, on the other hand, in a more Barthian fashion, does not attempt to provide a philosophical substructure for his theology, but begins — as does Barth — with Anselm's approach, viz., "faith seeking understanding" *(fides quaerens intellectum)*. Migliore deals briefly with the task of theology and various methodological questions, but he provides no philosophical underpinnings for his theology. He simply begins with the meaning of revelation and the authority of Scripture.

Such tensions within the Reformed family are not new, even within an orthodox framework. Nearly a century ago Abraham Kuyper accused the Princeton theologians, Charles Hodge and B. B. Warfield, of wanting to establish a rational apologetic as the basis for a prolegomena in theology. The Amsterdam theologians, in turn, were called fideists. Spykman claims that his approach is in the Kuyperian mode, but I submit that the shoe is now on the other foot. That is, Spykman gives the impression of being more rationalistic, whereas Migliore is the one who begins more strictly with revelational, faith presuppositions. Spykman would argue, however, that prolegomena must be as faith-based as the theology which follows it.

Moreover, such tensions exist also within the Dutch-American Reformed tradition. Spykman does not speak for all of the Christian Reformed theological community and certainly not for most of the Reformed (RCA) theologians. Even so, an examination of the CRC and RCA theologians in the last quarter-century reveals a surprising degree of commonality which to some extent reflects the special Grand Rapids–Holland, Michigan, axis, i.e., the western Michigan ethos.

Five Theses

These similarities can be stated in terms of five theses, some of which have already been indicated in various ways. They are not all of equal importance. Some speak more to the past, others to the future; some are more descriptive, others more prescriptive.

The theses are the following:

1. There is a distinctive Dutch/American Reformed theology which has its roots in western Michigan.
2. There always has been and will continue to be a theological pluralism within this Calvinistic context.
3. The shape of this theology will continue to be nourished and influenced by its Dutch Reformed theological roots and heritage, but it will increasingly address itself to ecumenical and American issues and concerns.

4. The character of this distinctive Reformed theology will be more classical and evangelical and less parochial and polemic than in the past.
5. If a distinctive Dutch/American theology is to flourish and be influential in the coming decades, there must be increasing dialogue and interchange between CRC and RCA scholars and institutions.

Thesis 1: There is a distinctive Dutch/American Reformed theology which has its roots in western Michigan.

At the outset, it may be necessary to recall that "western Michigan" here refers primarily to the Reformed academic institutions located in Holland and Grand Rapids: Hope College and Western Theological Seminary in Holland, Calvin College and Calvin Theological Seminary in Grand Rapids.[16] Much theologizing, of course, in both the RCA and CRC takes place outside these institutions, so this thesis does not intend to suggest that this distinctive theology can be limited to a specific locale. Hence, it might be better to call this a "neo–Dutch/American theology," since it transcends geographical boundaries.

This thesis would be challenged by some people who maintain that theologically our diversity is greater than our unity and that it is unrealistic to speak of a common theological approach. There is indeed great diversity, which has already been noted; this will be dealt with in the next thesis. Nevertheless, I think a strong case can be made for not only a common basic theology which these two traditions share but also a certain *Weltanschauung* which we have in common. This should not be too surprising in view of certain "givens" which are incontrovertible. The first of these is our common historical and theological heritage. We both trace our roots to the Reformed churches in the Netherlands. The plural — "churches" — is important because many people in both denominations — to the extent that they are aware of their ties with the Netherlands — assume that the RCA has its origins in and principal ties with the Nederlands Hervormde Kerk, often considered the liberal state church, whereas the CRC exclusively relates to the Gereformeerde Kerken in Nederland (GKN), its great theologians Herman Bavinck and Abraham

---

16. There are also two other RCA colleges, Central College in Pella, Iowa, and Northwestern College in Orange City, Iowa, the former being almost as old as Hope. Thus, RCA influence has been more fragmented than that of the CRC, which until fairly recently had only one college and one seminary, both of which are operated by one board of trustees. Dordt College, Sioux Center, Iowa, was founded in 1955; Trinity Christian College, Palos Heights, Illinois, in 1958; King's College, Edmonton, Alberta, in 1979; and Redeemer College, Hamilton, Ontario, in 1982, thereby diverting a portion of CRC students who in years past would in most cases have gone to Calvin College. It should be kept in mind that Western Seminary's impact on the RCA does not quite correspond to that of Calvin Seminary's in the CRC because, again, there is more decentralization.

Kuyper, and its theological schools in Kampen and the Free University at Amsterdam.

What is often overlooked is that the immigrants who settled in Holland, Michigan (and Pella, Iowa), were in many cases also the children of the schism in the Netherlands.[17] Although the CRC came to tie its fortunes more and more exclusively with the Gereformeerde Kerken[18] and the Free University, both have contributed in various ways to the life and thought of the RCA, particularly in the Midwest. The GKN also regards the RCA as a sister church, and the Free University has official ties with Western Seminary.[19]

More important, from the beginning until the present we have shared the same three confessional standards: the Belgic Confession, the Heidelberg Catechism, and the Canons of Dort. Although the forms of subscription vary slightly, in both churches those seeking ordination must affirm their adherence and loyalty to these three standards of unity. Notwithstanding the differences in emphasis and accent in the first half of our century, today the graduates of both our institutions share a similar training in the same confessions.

We are also inheritors of a common piety, both in its Dutch origins and in its contemporary Americanized modified form. Those early immigrants who settled in western Michigan, in Iowa (especially the Pella area), and later in Illinois (the Chicago area), Wisconsin, and farther west represented various strains of Dutch church life and thought, but many of them were pietists,[20] and some of this distinctive Dutch piety continues to influence our theology today despite the inroads of American evangelical piety. Here is a piety which is quiet and subdued, usually hesitant and restrained in speaking of one's faith, but at the same time warm, confident, and caring. This is combined with a profound reverence for God, a delight in worship, a love of the Scriptures and of good theology. At its worst, it degenerates into a virtual fatalism and legalism, but at its best it produces a fidelity and solidity often admired by others.

17. See Brouwer, *Reformed Church Roots,* pp. 110-18.

18. With the formation of the Reformed Ecumenical Synod in 1946, certain official ties were established, apart from direct church-to-church relationships. The RCA and the Nederlands Hervormde Kerk, on the other hand, were linked together through their membership in the World Alliance of Reformed Churches.

19. This is not to deny that until very recently the ties between Calvin Seminary and the theological faculty of the Free University have not been much closer. Whereas the RCA has had only three of its theologians receive their doctorates from the Free University (Winfield Burggraaff in 1928, William Goulooze in 1950, and Charles Van Engen in 1981), many graduates of Calvin Seminary have done graduate work at the Free University, but none in recent years.

20. Cf. Eugene P. Heideman, "The Descendants of Van Raalte," *Reformed Review* 12 (March 1959): 33-42; and M. Eugene Osterhaven, "The Experiential Theology of Early Dutch Calvinism," *Reformed Review* 27 (1973/74): 180-89.

A new type of evangelical piety, secularism (some would say American-ization!), a dispersion of once fairly solid ethnic enclaves, and the acids of modernity (e.g., Sunday afternoon professional football games) have made inroads, but something of the Old Dutch/American Calvinistic piety perseveres, and this colors our theologizing more than we may realize.

Thus far few people would deny a common heritage and outlook, but I submit that there is much more that the RCA and CRC have in common. Because of space limitations I shall simply list twelve such characteristics (in addition to the Calvinistic Dutch heritage and three confessional standards held in common):

1. A deep piety without the usual trappings of pietism.
2. A theological approach to life and an appreciation of doctrine, the life of the mind, and education.
3. A growing appreciation for our liturgical roots.
4. A reverence for the Lord's Day and a loyalty to the church (despite increasing difficulties with the evening service).
5. A high view of preaching and a love of solid doctrinal preaching, although popular evangelical piety is taking its toll here.
6. A strong sense of God's sovereignty and providential care (with an increasing questioning of decretal theology and double predestination).
7. A high regard for the law — especially its third use, as a norm and guide for the Christian — with a diminishing legalism.
8. An evangelical commitment and concern which extends to the cause of Christ around the world.
9. A concern not only for the church but also for the wider causes of the kingdom, including social justice.
10. A continuing appreciation for the confessions without an attendant confessionalism.
11. A hermeneutical approach to the Scriptures which hinges on the key of the one covenant of grace.
12. A due regard for the Reformation principle of *sola Scriptura* along with a concern for *tota Scriptura*.[21] (Thanks to its hermeneutical approach, the unity of Scripture and the significance of the Old Testament are esteemed as in few other traditions.)

---

21. See Fred H. Klooster, "The Uniqueness of Reformed Theology, a Preliminary Attempt at Description," *Calvin Theological Journal* 14 (1979): 32-54. "[T]he question of *sola scriptura* calls for attention to *tota scriptura* at the same time; not only 'Scripture alone' but also 'the whole of Scripture,' the entire canon, is at stake" (p. 39).

It is the combination of these characteristics, together with many intangibles, which makes this theology and *Weltanschauung* unique and differentiates it from the American Presbyterian approach, whether or not that of the Presbyterian denominations.

Thesis 2: There always has been and will continue to be a theological pluralism within this Calvinistic context.

When I speak of a theological pluralism, I am referring not only to separate strains and distinctive emphases which divide our two communions, but also to those varieties and types within the CRC and RCA.

In my book *On Being Reformed* (published originally at Ann Arbor by Servant Books, 1983; 2nd ed., New York: Reformed Church Press, 1988), in which I deal with this theme by considering twelve misunderstandings of what it means to be Reformed, I point out in passing that even within the RCA it is not at all easy to decide what it means to be Reformed today. I then point out that I perceive approximately ten different types within the Reformed Church, all of whom would claim the title "Reformed." Examples of these types are: traditional orthodox, i.e., scholastic Reformed; neo-Calvinist, i.e., those who are particularly influenced by Abraham Kuyper; "classical" Reformed, i.e., those who go back to the confessions and skip for the most part the developments of later Presbyterian orthodoxy or Dutch neo-Calvinism, i.e., those who find their inspiration primarily in Calvin rather than in the confessions; neoorthodox, i.e., those who interpret the Reformed confessions through the eyes of Karl Barth and other more recent so-called neoorthodox theologians; the van Ruler school; the Latitudinarians, i.e., those who are not confessionally minded but still appreciate Reformed polity and the Reformed tradition broadly interpreted; and finally, political social activists, i.e., those whose concerns are not so much doctrinal as ethical and practical. This does not exhaust the list because the RCA has within it its own special American brand of Calvinism in the person and approach of Robert H. Schuller, minister of the Crystal Cathedral in Garden Grove, California.[22]

The CRC, like the RCA, also has its impatient young Turks (and some not so young!) as well as the traditionalist diehards and those who are convinced that the foundations have been irreparably shaken, if not destroyed. Overall, there are countless shades and varieties of Calvinism and understandings of what it means to be Reformed, but there is still a fairly solid, discernible, and distinctive core of Reformed understanding and belief which is common to both traditions.

---

22. Cf. his book *Self Esteem: The New Reformation* (Waco: Word, 1982).

Thesis 3: The shape of this theology will continue to be nourished and influenced by its Dutch Reformed theological roots and heritage, but it will increasingly address itself to ecumenical and American issues and concerns.

If this theology is to continue, flourish, and make a real impact upon the American scene, it must not cut itself off from its distinctive Dutch heritage. That means, in the first place, continuing to plumb the riches — though not uncritically — of the Dutch confessions, viz., the Heidelberg Catechism, the Belgic Confession, and the Canons of Dort. Too often they have been used as apologetic battering rams against foes, imagined or real, both within and without. If we truly believe that our confessions must always be subservient to Scripture, then we will continue to raise questions about certain expressions, even certain points of doctrine, that are found in our confessions.

Above all, we should maximize the use of that "jewel of the Reformation" which is also a part of our heritage, namely, the Heidelberg Catechism. Although this confessional classic is German, not Dutch, it is utilized and appreciated more in Dutch Reformed circles than anywhere else, although it received considerable attention in Germany on the occasion of its 400th anniversary in 1963 and is also included in the *Presbyterian Book of Confessions.*

In the RCA, a special commemorative commentary was commissioned and published by the denominational headquarters: *Guilt, Grace, and Gratitude,* edited by Donald J. Bruggink.[23] The nine contributors were all RCA ministers and professors, six of whom eventually taught at Western Seminary. The efforts of the CRC were rather modest.[24] The most significant contributions were a collection of sermons on the Heidelberg Catechism written by a number of Canadian CRC ministers and a new translation of that catechism by a synodically appointed committee which was approved by the CRC Synod of 1975.[25]

In recent years, however, the CRC has made up for any previous lack in this regard by publishing several studies and guides to the Reformed confessions. One is a splendid study of the Reformed creeds and confessions designed for

---

23. Donald J. Bruggink, ed., *Guilt, Grace, and Gratitude: A Commentary on the Heidelberg Catechism Commemorating Its 400th Anniversary* (New York: The Half Moon Press, 1963).

24. See Thea B. Van Halsema, *Three Men Came to Heidelberg* (Grand Rapids: Christian Reformed Publishing House, 1963); Edward J. Masselink, *The Heidelberg Story* (Grand Rapids: Baker, 1964). These are both brief, popular accounts.

25. *Sermons on the Heidelberg Catechism* (Grand Rapids: Board of Publications of the Christian Reformed Church, 1970); "The Heidelberg Catechism," in *Ecumenical Creeds and Reformed Confessions* (Grand Rapids: Board of Publications of the Christian Reformed Church, 1979), pp. 7-63.

laypeople, namely, *A Place to Stand,* by Cornelius Plantinga, Jr.[26] Here, for the first time, all three of our standards are considered together and in a way which is both understandable and relevant to lay Christians. This is also a model of relating our specific Dutch Reformed heritage to American issues and concerns. Plantinga's book has found almost as much response in RCA churches as in the CRC. The CRC is also in the forefront in regard to studies of the Heidelberg Catechism, upon which it published two fine commentaries in recent years. The one, *Comfort and Joy* (Grand Rapids: CRC Publications, 1988), is by Andrew Kuyvenhoven, a Dutch-Canadian pastor in the CRC who served as editor of their weekly magazine, *The Banner,* for several years. The other, *A Mighty Comfort* (Grand Rapids: CRC Publications, 1990), is by Fred Klooster, emeritus professor of theology at Calvin Seminary. Earlier, Allen Verhey, a Christian Reformed professor at Hope College, had published a study of the Heidelberg from an ethical perspective: *Living the Heidelberg: The Heidelberg Catechism and the Moral Life* (Grand Rapids: CRC Publications, 1986).

When I speak of Reformed theological roots, I am thinking not only of the three confessional standards shared by the CRC but also of the great theological tradition that is part and parcel of the theological makeup of the Dutch-American Reformed churches in the United States. There were two theologians who dominated the theological landscape in the Netherlands in the late nineteenth and early twentieth centuries, viz., Herman Bavinck and Abraham Kuyper. Kuyper's name and fame have been duly recognized, particularly in the CRC, whereas Bavinck has still not come into his own.

One of the major theological distinctives of the RCA and CRC churches might be that the former reflects more the theology and spirit of Bavinck, the latter more that of Kuyper. Originally the influence of Kuyper in the RCA was direct and considerable. He had personal contacts and corresponded with Albertus C. Van Raalte, the founder of Holland, Michigan, and an influential pioneer RCA minister, as well as with many of Van Raalte's followers. Kuyper's works, such as the Princeton Stone Lectures, *Lectures on Calvinism,*[27] and *The*

---

26. Cornelius Plantinga, Jr., *A Place to Stand: A Reformed Study of Creeds and Confessions* (Grand Rapids: Board of Publications of the Christian Reformed Church, 1979). This volume is a part of the Bible Way series. A helpful sequel to this volume was published in the same series, also by Cornelius Plantinga, Jr., *Beyond Doubt: A Devotional Response to Questions of Faith* (Grand Rapids: Board of Publications of the Christian Reformed Church, 1980). Here Scripture and confession are joined together in the context, and personal issues are dealt with in a devotional manner. Another contribution to this cause by CRC Publications has been a fresh translation of all three standards. The RCA Theological Commission has also recently produced new translations of the three standards of unity.

27. *Lectures on Calvinism: Six Lectures Delivered at Princeton University* (1898), under the auspices of the L. P. Stone Foundation (Grand Rapids: Wm. B. Eerdmans Publishing Co., 1953).

Work of the Holy Spirit,[28] were also read widely in RCA circles. Yet neither Van Raalte himself nor his descendants in the RCA could be considered Kuyperian.[29] Moreover, there was never an attempt in the RCA to try to apply Kuyper's views of sphere sovereignty in the United States (and later in Canada), as there was in the CRC, albeit unsuccessfully.[30]

Bavinck, however, though not cited so frequently in RCA circles or periodicals as in the CRC, was the subject of two studies by RCA ministers,[31] and has been indirectly influential in the RCA through two of its leading theologians, M. Eugene Osterhaven and his pupil and former colleague, Eugene P. Heideman. Moreover, it is only recently that Bavinck's helpful view of the authority and inspiration of Scripture has been properly recognized in North America, by a scholar who is of neither CRC nor RCA background. I am referring to the works of Jack Rogers, particularly the monumental study, *The Authority and Interpretation of the Bible*, by Rogers and Donald K. McKim.[32] In this response to Harold Lindsell's *Battle for the Bible*,[33] Rogers and McKim submit that there is a middle way between liberalism and the Reformed scholastic approach typified by the old Princeton school of which Charles Hodge and Benjamin B. Warfield were the principal figures. That middle way, they propose, is found in Dutch Calvinism as represented by Kuyper and Bavinck, particularly the latter.

The riches of our Dutch heritage, however, have not been exhausted by any means in the persons of Kuyper and Bavinck. There are other worthies of our own time, some of whom have received little attention and who could greatly enrich our Dutch/American theology, such as Kornelis H. Miskotte, Theodorus L. Haitjema, Gerrit C. van Niftrik, and Oepke Noordmans, to name

---

28. *The Work of the Holy Spirit* (New York: Funk & Wagnalls, 1900, reprinted many times by Wm. B. Eerdmans Publishing Co. after World War II).

29. See Elton J. Bruins, "From Calvin to Van Raalte: The Rise and Development of the Reformed Tradition in the Netherlands, 1560-1900," in *Servant Gladly: Essays in Honor of John W. Beardslee*, ed. Jack D. Klunder (Grand Rapids: Wm. B. Eerdmans Publishing Co., 1989), pp. 89-103. Bruins contends against Gordon Spykman, *Pioneer Preacher: Albertus Christian Van Raalte, A Study of His Sermon Notes*, Heritage Hall Publications 2 (Grand Rapids: Calvin College and Seminary Library, 1976), that Van Raalte was a Kuyperian.

30. Zwaanstra, pp. 306-7.

31. Bastian Kruithof, "The Relation of Christianity and Culture in the Teaching of Herman Bavinck" (Ph.D. diss., University of Edinburgh, 1955); Jerome B. DeJong, "The Ordo Salutis as Developed by the Dutch Theologian Herman Bavinck" (Th.M. thesis, Union Theological Seminary, New York, 1947).

32. *The Authority and Interpretation of the Bible: An Historical Approach* (New York: Harper & Row, 1979). See esp. pp. 329-30 and 388-93. Cf. an earlier work, Jack B. Rogers, ed., *Biblical Authority* (Waco: Word, 1977), pp. 41-44.

33. Harold Lindsell, *The Battle for the Bible* (Grand Rapids: Zondervan, 1976).

only four of the leading Nederlands Hervormde Kerk theologians of a past generation.[34] At the same time, we must not repeat the failures of the past and simply adopt Dutch theological thought for North American consumption. Their culture, milieu, and issues are not ours, and hence this evolving theology must be more *American* than Dutch, even though it is continually nourished and renewed by sources from across the Atlantic.

Thesis 4: The character of this distinctive Reformed theology will be more classical and evangelical and less parochial and polemic than in the past.

By "classical" I mean two things: first, that this theology, though not neglecting its Dutch roots and heritage, will get back to its even deeper roots in the Reformation; secondly, that it will not limit itself to Dutch-American or denominational concerns but will also seek to address the larger critical issues of each age and thereby make an impact beyond its boundaries. In regard to both aspects I am encouraged by recent developments, but the successes are limited and partial.

Whereas our fathers and forefathers knew the Heidelberg Catechism and were steeped in Kuyper, Bavinck, Hodge, Augustus H. Strong, and later, Louis Berkhof, they knew little of Calvin and the Reformers. My father and father-in-law, both pastors who graduated from Western Seminary over half a century ago, have told me this was the case when they were students at Western, and I suspect the situation at Calvin Seminary was not much different. Calvin's *Institutes* played only a minor role at best in their theological education, and his commentaries were not recommended and hence not purchased. Subsequently, several RCA scholars did doctoral dissertations on Calvin, and with the advent of Osterhaven as professor of systematic theology at Western Seminary in 1952 that situation soon changed. The same has been true at Hope College since World War II, where courses on Calvin's theology are taught regularly.

This is also true at Calvin College where John H. Bratt has been a leader in Calvin studies. In addition to courses and numerous published articles about Calvin, he also promoted and edited the Heritage Hall Lectures, 1960-1970.[35] Moreover, a remarkable Festschrift of essays on Calvin was published in his honor on the occasion of his retirement in 1976.[36] I say "remarkable" be-

34. Cf. my essay, "Contemporary Protestant Dutch Theology," *Reformed Review* 26 (1972/73): 67-89. The focus of this essay, however, is on what I have dubbed "the big three" of Dutch theology, viz., Berkouwer, van Ruler, and Hendrikus Berkhof.

35. *The Heritage of John Calvin: Heritage Hall Lectures, 1960-1970,* ed. John H. Bratt (Grand Rapids: Wm. B. Eerdmans Publishing Co., 1973).

36. *Exploring the Heritage of John Calvin: Essays in Honor of John H. Bratt,* ed. David E. Holwerda (Grand Rapids: Baker, 1976).

cause all nine essays are substantial, scholarly studies of various aspects of Calvin's thought.

In recent decades there have also been doctoral dissertations on Calvin by CRC scholars,[37] although not so many as by their counterparts in the RCA. In four ways, however, Calvin College and Calvin Seminary have made a signal contribution to Calvin studies in recent years: (1) by being the prime movers in organizing and hosting the colloquia of the Calvin Studies Society; (2) by bringing the distinguished Calvin scholar Ford Lewis Battles to the campus in 1978 (unfortunately, his death the following year cut short a very fruitful and promising relationship);[38] (3) by initiating and continuing the most comprehensive Calvin bibliography ever attempted, edited by Peter De Klerk;[39] and (4) by the establishment of the Calvin and Calvinism Collection in the Calvin Library, enlarged in 1982 to become the H. Henry Meeter Center for Calvin Studies. Here is housed the finest contemporary collection of Calvin studies in the world, in addition to an excellent collection of original and early publications of Calvin's works. In addition, the theological journals of Calvin and Western Seminaries — the *Calvin Theological Journal* and the *Reformed Review* — continue to publish solid and helpful essays on Calvin.

All this notwithstanding, until quite recently we were far better known for our neo-Calvinism than for our Calvin studies. In the CRC, for example, there were the fierce debates over common grace, and both denominations in recent years have had to concentrate their exegetical and theological efforts on internal struggles about women in ecclesiastical office and the interpretation of the first three chapters of Genesis.

Thus, despite our contributions to Calvin scholarship, the Reformed scholarship which emanates from Grand Rapids and Holland has tended to be ingrown, parochial, and generally irrelevant to the American theological scene as a whole. There are, to be sure, some exceptions: Louis Berkhof's *Systematic Theology* is still known and used in conservative circles; and contemporaries like Hoekema, Osterhaven, Boer, Klooster, Henry Stob, C. Plantinga, Heide-

---

37. Quirinus Breen, *John Calvin: A Study in French Humanism* (Grand Rapids: Wm. B. Eerdmans Publishing Co., 1931); Lester R. DeKoster, "Living Themes in the Thought of John Calvin: A Bibliographical Study" (Ph.D. diss., University of Michigan, 1964); and Marvin P. Hoogland, *Calvin's Perspective on the Exaltation of Christ in Comparison with the Post-Reformation Doctrine of the Two States* (Kampen: Kok, 1966).

38. See John H. Kromminga, "Calvin Seminary's Encounter with Ford Lewis Battles," *Calvin Theological Journal* 15 (1980): 158-59; James O'Brien, "Ford Lewis Battles; 1915-1979, Calvin Scholar and Church Historian Extraordinary," *Calvin Theological Journal* 15 (1980): 166-89.

39. This has, with one exception, since 1972 appeared annually in the November issues of the *Calvin Theological Journal*.

man, and Hesselink are known and recognized in limited evangelical or Reformed or Presbyterian circles, but most of these names would not be recognized in the average Protestant denominational seminary today, let alone Roman Catholic schools. The same would be true of our biblical and mission scholars who have recently published major studies or commentaries: James I. Cook, Lester J. Kuyper, Marten H. Woudstra, John H. Piet, and Richard R. DeRidder. The best-known biblical scholar from our circles among conservatives would be the CRC scholar William Hendriksen, largely because of his New Testament commentaries. In the area of Calvin studies Calvin Seminary's Richard Gamble, who is also the director of the Meeter Center for Calvin Studies, and John Hesselink[40] of Western Seminary are known both in the United States and abroad for their publications about Calvin and their leadership in the Calvin Studies Society.

The best-known Dutch/American Reformed scholars, however, do not teach at Calvin or Western Seminaries but at Fuller Theological Seminary in California, viz., Richard J. Mouw[41] and Lewis B. Smedes,[42] both Christian Reformed, and Charles Van Engen, a Reformed Church missiologist who taught briefly at Western Seminary, who is in the School of Missions at Fuller Seminary.[43] Another former Calvin College professor who is nationally recognized, the historian George Marsden,[44] went to Duke University and is now at Notre

40. Hesselink has published many essays on Calvin's theology in the United States, Europe, Australia, and especially Japan, where he served as a missionary for many years. His studies of Calvin have also appeared in Festschriften for Oscar Cullmann, Ford Lewis Battles, and Gottfried Locher. His major work is *Calvin's Concept of the Law* (Allison Park, Pa.: Pickwick, 1992).

41. Cf. his *Political Evangelism* (Grand Rapids: Wm. B. Eerdmans Publishing Co., 1973); *Politics and the Biblical Drama* (Grand Rapids: Wm. B. Eerdmans Publishing Co., 1976); *Called to Holy Worldliness* (Philadelphia: Fortress, 1980); *Distorted Truth: What Every Christian Needs to Know about the Battle for the Mind* (San Francisco: Harper & Row, 1980); *The God Who Commands* (South Bend: University of Notre Dame Press, 1991).

42. See *All Things Made New: A Theology of Man's Union with Christ* (Grand Rapids: Wm. B. Eerdmans Publishing Co., 1970); *Love within Limits: A Realist's View of 1 Corinthians 13* (Grand Rapids: Wm. B. Eerdmans Publishing Co., 1978); *Sex for Christians: The Limits and Liberties of Sexual Living* (Grand Rapids: Wm. B. Eerdmans Publishing Co., 1976); *Mere Morality* (Grand Rapids: Wm. B. Eerdmans Publishing Co., 1983); *Forgive and Forget* (San Francisco: Harper & Row, 1984); *Choices* (San Francisco: Harper & Row, 1986); *Caring and Commitment* (San Francisco: Harper & Row, 1988); and *A Pretty Good Person* (San Francisco: Harper & Row, 1990). *Forgive and Forget* was on the *New York Times* nonfiction bestseller list for several weeks.

43. See his *God's Missionary People: Rethinking the Purpose of the Local Church* (Grand Rapids: Baker, 1991).

44. See his highly acclaimed historical studies: *The Evangelical Mind and the New School Presbyterian Experience: A Case Study of Thought and Theology in Nineteenth-Century*

Dame. Hope College and Western Seminary professors have been fairly pro-lific in recent years, but most of them are known only in limited academic cir-cles outside of the RCA-CRC orbit. Actually, the fame of Calvin College rests particularly with its philosophers such as Alvin Plantinga, now at Notre Dame University, and Nicholas P. Wolterstorff, now at the Yale Divinity School, and a host of other distinguished former students of the late W. Harry Jellema. Probably the best-known RCA theologian (and preacher) is Howard G. Hageman, an Easterner, who is the product of a quite different milieu, viz., New York State University, Harvard University, and New Brunswick Theolog-ical Seminary.[45]

It might be argued that a distinctive Reformed theological approach will never have a general appeal on most university or seminary campuses; nor will it ever be welcomed widely by American pastors, who tend to be practical and pragmatic. A realistic aspiration, however, is that our efforts and impact would be felt in the larger Reformed world both here and abroad. If so, our inspira-tion and resources must come not only from Reformed theologians of Dutch background, whether Dutch or American, but also from other great Reformed theologians of our time, such as Karl Barth — however one may feel about cer-tain aspects of his theology — Thomas F. Torrance, and Otto Weber.

Thesis 5: If a distinctive Dutch/American theology is to flourish and be influ-ential in the coming decades, there must be increasing dialogue and inter-change between CRC and RCA scholars and institutions.

Here, too, this is already being accomplished in a minimal way, but the meager efforts leave much to be desired. The annual Calvin-Western faculty gatherings are pleasant but do not contribute to serious scholarship. The same is true of the annual meetings of the Hope and Calvin College religion facul-ties. Granted, it is difficult even to get scholars within our campuses to collabo-

---

America (New Haven: Yale University Press, 1970); *Fundamentalism and American Culture: The Shaping of Twentieth Century Evangelicalism, 1870-1925* (New York: Oxford University Press, 1980); *Reforming Fundamentalism: Fuller Seminary and the New Evangelicalism* (Grand Rapids: Wm. B. Eerdmans Publishing Co., 1987).

45. His best-known book is *Pulpit and Tablet: Some Chapters in the History of Worship in the Reformed Churches* (Richmond: John Knox, 1962), the Princeton Seminary Stone Lec-tures concerning worship in the Reformed tradition. While Hageman is recognized as one of the foremost U.S. scholars of Reformed liturgics, Donald J. Bruggink, church historian at Western Seminary, takes pride of place as the foremost authority in the country in the area of Reformed architecture. See Donald J. Bruggink and Carl H. Droppers, *Christ and Archi-tecture: Building Presbyterian/Reformed Churches* (Grand Rapids: Wm. B. Eerdmans Pub-lishing Co., 1965), and Donald J. Bruggink and Carl H. Droppers, *When Faith Takes Form: Contemporary Churches of Architectural Integrity in America* (Grand Rapids: Wm. B. Eerdmans Publishing Co., 1971).

rate on projects, but in an age of increasing specialization some sharing or dialogue at a preliminary level could be highly beneficial.

In conclusion, I want to speak to the danger of a "Reformed elitism," an issue raised by Marlin Van Elderen (CRC), now with the WCC in Geneva, in an essay in the *Reformed Journal* dealing with the theme "On Being Reformed."[46] He addresses a broader problem, viz., the ethnic and denominational temptation to move from "parochialism to elitism, even arrogance." This arrogance takes various forms, one of which is theological. So Van Elderen warns, "In the Reformed community, the price of taking our faith seriously is too often taking ourselves — our community and its institutions and its theology — even more seriously."[47]

This is indeed a danger for any group that takes its confessional stance or some nonconfessional position (such as Southern Baptists) very seriously. The CRC, being more zealous in this regard than the RCA, has been particularly prone to a superiority attitude not only against liberalism but also against Arminians and fundamentalists. This is amply documented in the fascinating Yale dissertation by a son of the CRC, James D. Bratt: *Dutch Calvinism in Modern America: A History of a Conservative Subculture* (Grand Rapids: Wm. B. Eerdmans Publishing Co., 1984). Fundamentalism in the early decades of this century was viewed as "the opponent of the right"; modernism "the enemy on the left."[48] In general, there was the feeling of the superiority of the Calvinistic view to "American religiosity."[49]

In the RCA of that era, these feelings were not quite so pronounced, except in certain Midwestern pockets where the prevailing attitudes did not differ perceptibly from their sister denomination. Due to greater Americanization in the RCA, there was generally less self-consciousness about their distinctive heritage and theology. However, John E. Kuizenga, a Western Seminary professor who closed out his career at Princeton Theological Seminary, wrote a series of articles in the *Intelligence-Leader* (predecessor of the *Church Herald*) in the 1920s in response to the modernist-fundamentalist controversy of that time in which he portrayed the Reformed confessions as an orthodox middle way.[50]

While such attitudes are less prevalent or at least muted today, and Pharisaic attitudes are never appropriate, it must be conceded that one characteristic of the Reformed position is its mediating role between the extremes of funda-

---

46. Marlin J. Van Elderen, "A Chosen Race," *Reformed Journal* 32 (March 1982): 12-13, 16-18.

47. Van Elderen, p. 13.

48. Bratt, *Dutch Calvinism in Modern America*, chap. 9; cf. the reference to "Arminian odors" on p. 132.

49. Bratt, *Dutch Calvinism in Modern America*, pp. 272-73.

50. Cited in Bratt, *Dutch Calvinism in Modern America*, p. 134.

mentalism and liberalism. Yet we have much in common with conservative evangelicals and can carry on fruitful dialogue with chastened liberals or so-called neoorthodox types. On social issues, for example, several of our people — Merold Westphal, former professor of philosophy at Hope College; Richard Mouw, formerly of Calvin College; and Paul Henry, former professor at Calvin College, then congressman from Grand Rapids until his death — have been involved with evangelical social activists sympathetic to the stance of *Sojourners* and *The Other Side;* and Arie Brouwer, former general secretary of the RCA, deputy general secretary of the WCC, and general secretary of the NCC,[51] and Harvey Hoekstra,[52] longtime missionary and former president of the RCA, have in various ways made an impact on the World Council of Churches.

I have little fear of overconfidence or arrogance as our friends, colleagues, and those who succeed them continue to pursue theology in this Dutch/American Reformed milieu. For the most part, I believe our sins of this sort are largely a thing of the past: the petty legalisms; denominational pride and exclusiveness; a defensive, negative mentality; and a scholastic, doctrinaire approach to theology. What I fear, rather, is a timidity and a desire to be so respected in the larger academic community that we lose or water down these distinctives which are our contribution to the cause of theology: a comprehensive *Weltanschauung,* God-centered piety and disciplined Christian life, a covenant- and kingdom-focused hermeneutic, a sense of God's sovereignty and providential leading, an appreciation for the third use of the law, and a strong ecclesiastical loyalty.

If these distinctive characteristics of our heritage and theological perspective can be preserved, deepened, and enlarged, there is indeed a future for a distinctive Dutch/American theology — in the service of the whole church of Jesus Christ and to the glory of God.

51. See his *Ecumenical Testimony* (Grand Rapids: Wm. B. Eerdmans Publishing Co., 1991).

52. See his critique, *The World Council of Churches and the Demise of Evangelism* (Wheaton, Ill.: Tyndale House, 1979).

CHAPTER 27

Jonathan Edwards's Dispositional Conception of the Trinity: A Resource for Contemporary Reformed Theology

Sang Hyun Lee

The Reformed tradition has always emphasized God's active involvement in the created realm. The doctrine of God's sovereign and providential rule over history and nature has been a hallmark of Reformed theology. But precisely this divine involvement in the temporal world has become a controversial issue in the contemporary reevaluation of the Christian theological tradition. The question, simply put, is this: How can God, who is perfect and changeless, as the traditional Christian theology has it, be conceived of as being really involved in temporality?

Recent Reformed theologians have made serious and innovative attempts to deal with this question. Barth, for example, conceived of God's inner being as essentially dynamic so that it could be in harmony with God's activity outside of himself in history. God's act of self-revelation in Jesus Christ, Barth maintained, is not strange to God's own being. God's being, in other words, is inherently a dynamic reality. According to Barth, God, who is himself in the event of Jesus Christ, can only be an eternal event in his own being. What God does in Jesus Christ, in other words, is grounded in God's primordial being-in-act in the inner-trinitarian relationships of the Father, the Son, and the Holy Spirit. God's being-in-act in Jesus Christ is then a "reiteration" in time of God's being-in-act in the immanent Trinity. In the way God is within God's own being, God is already an openness to being related to the world. God's being himself in Jesus Christ, therefore, is nothing strange to God.[1]

There has been a significant discussion about Barth's attempt to introduce an element of "becoming" into God's being without compromising God's perfection or self-sufficiency. What has hardly been noticed, however, is that a Reformed theologian on this side of the Atlantic, Jonathan Edwards, set forth over two hundred years ago a dynamic reconception of the divine being which is still an instructive resource for today's theological reconstruction.[2]

The ways in which Edwards and Barth handle the issue at hand contain intriguingly similar concerns as well as some profoundly different ideas. While Barth dealt with the issue of being and becoming in the divine being by seeing God as the being that is inherently "in act" or "in relation," Edwards conceived of the dynamic nature of God in terms of God's being as inherently disposed to more being. Both Barth and Edwards use the concept of self-repetition or self-reiteration to conceive of God's involvement in time — an involvement that shows not God's deficiency but God's self-sufficiency. Barth and Edwards are different, however, in their views on where in time God reiterates himself. For Barth, Jesus Christ is the event of God's temporal reiteration, while for Edwards the entire creation was created to be God's self-repetition *ad extra*.

The aim of the present essay, however, is not to offer a systematic comparison of Barth and Edwards and the interesting implications of their differences as well as of their similarities. This essay rather prepares for such a full comparison. We shall in this essay simply present an interpretation of Edwards's dispositional reconception of God — more specifically, of the immanent Trinity.

Recent Edwards scholarship has not been totally unaware of the close relationship Edwards sees between the immanent Trinity and the trinitarian character of God's activity in history. It has been noted that Edwards broke away from the traditional Western theology's tendency to see the immanent Trinity as untouched by temporality and began to see God's inner being as strictly correlated with God's activities in time. Scholars, most recently Robert W. Jenson, for example, have pointed out that for Edwards what God does in history and what God is in his be-

---

1. See, for example, Karl Barth, *Church Dogmatics* II/1 (Edinburgh: T. & T. Clark, 1975), pp. 257-321, 608-77.

2. An exception is a brief but thoughtful discussion by George S. Hendry of Edwards's attempt to reconceive the changelessness of God. See George S. Hendry, "The Glory of God and the Future of Man," *Reformed World* 34 (1977): 147-57. For the discussions of Barth on the same theme, see, for example, Hendry, and also Eberhard Jüngel, *The Doctrine of the Trinity: God's Being Is in Becoming* (Grand Rapids: Wm. B. Eerdmans Publishing Co., 1976), and Colin E. Gunton, *Becoming and Being: The Doctrine of God in Charles Hartshorne and Karl Barth* (New York: Oxford University Press, 1978).

ing are absolutely consistent.[3] The immanent Trinity, for Edwards, is not a speculative theory far removed from the story of God's salvation here on earth, but rather the very ground and pattern for that story. Amy Plantinga Pauw, in her splendid thesis on Edwards, has also shown that Edwards's idea of the divine disposition to communicate himself functions as the bridge between the immanent and economic trinities. The divine disposition that is in God's inner being is what is expressed in the trinitarian activity of God *ad extra,* thereby bringing the immanent and economic trinities in harmony. In this way, Pauw has helpfully pointed to the notion of the divine disposition as the "bridge" between the immanent and economic trinities, although she has not discussed Edwards's articulation of the inner-trinitarian relations in terms of the exercises of the divine disposition.[4]

It is quite clear that for Edwards the inner being of God is trinitarian and dynamic. What, then, is the exact nature of the dynamic character of the inner Trinity? Edwards's dispositional reconception of the divine being, I believe, is the clue to this question. It is our thesis that Edwards's dispositional conception of God's being enables him to introduce an element of becoming or potentiality in God's being without compromising God's actuality as God. An exposition of Edwards's doctrine of the Trinity in all of its aspects cannot be attempted in this essay. I shall directly focus upon the dispositional conception of the immanent Trinity and upon the particular sort of dynamism Edwards is thereby enabled to see in the divine being.

Dispositional Ontology

What undergirds Edwards's rethinking about God and the world is his dispositional ontology. Disposition (which is also referred to as habit, tendency, inclination, temper, and law), for Edwards, is an ontologically real, active principle that has a mode of reality apart from its manifestations in actions and events. "All habits [are] a law that God has fixed, that such actions upon such occasions *should* be exerted," Edwards writes.[5]

---

3. Robert W. Jenson, *America's Theologian: A Recommendation of Jonathan Edwards* (New York: Oxford University Press, 1988); Bruce M. Stephens, "The Doctrine of the Trinity from Jonathan Edwards to Horace Bushnell" (Ph.D. diss., Drew University, 1970), pp. 14-45; Herbert W. Richardson, "The Glory of God in the Theology of Jonathan Edwards: A Study in the Doctrine of the Trinity" (Ph.D. diss., Harvard University, 1962).

4. Amy Plantinga Pauw, "The Supreme Harmony of All: Jonathan Edwards and the Trinity" (Ph.D. diss., Yale University, 1990).

5. "Miscellanies," No. 241, in *Works of Jonathan Edwards,* gen. ed. John E. Smith, vol. 13, *The "Miscellanies,"* ed. Thomas A. Schafer (New Haven: Yale University Press, 1994), p. 358, hereafter referred to as *"Miscellanies."*

Having defined dispositions as active and ontologically real, Edwards lets them play the role that substances and forms used to play in traditional Western thought. Dispositions abide even when there are no exercises of them in actions or events. So, like substances, dispositions function as the principles of permanence. Things, for Edwards, are not substances but rather dispositions and habits. Defining dispositions also as causal laws that govern the pattern of actions and events, Edwards tells us that "it is laws that constitute all permanent being in created things, both corporeal and spiritual." Hence, "[the soul's] essence consists in powers and habits."[6]

One of the important consequences of such a dispositional reconception of reality is that being is inherently disposed for further and further activities and relationships. If dispositions are not merely dispositions to action but also dispositions to being, then the exercises of dispositional essences of entities will increase being. Therefore, operational increase means ontological increase. Being is essentially disposed to increases or repetitions. This point, as we shall see below, will have important consequences in Edwards's reconception of the divine being.

Thus, reality for Edwards is essentially a network of dispositional forces rather than a system of particular substances. Being, therefore, is essentially disposed to further activities and thus to further increases of being. The world is essentially tending to further increases in being.[7]

God as Disposition and Actuality

Edwards uses his dispositional reconception of being in his articulation of the divine being. "It is [God's] essence to incline to communicate Himself," writes Edwards. This "disposition to communicate Himself" is what "we must conceive of as being originally in God as a perfection of his nature." Edwards then resolves this communicative disposition of God into God's "disposition effectually to exert Himself."[8] In other words, God's disposition to operate as God *is*

---

6. "Subjects to Be Handled in the Treatise on the Mind," No. 36, in *The Philosophy of Jonathan Edwards*, ed. Harvey G. Townsend (Eugene: University of Oregon Press, 1955), p. 72, hereafter referred to as Townsend; "Miscellanies," No. 241, Yale MSS.

7. For a fuller discussion of Edwards's concept of habit and his dispositional ontology, see my *The Philosophical Theology of Jonathan Edwards* (Princeton: Princeton University Press, 1988), esp. pp. 34-114.

8. "Miscellanies," No. 107[6], in *"Miscellanies,"* pp. 277-78. "Concerning the End for Which God Created the World," in *Works of Jonathan Edwards*, gen. ed. John E. Smith, vol. 8, *Ethical Writings*, ed. Paul Ramsey (New Haven: Yale University Press, 1989), pp. 433-34, hereafter referred to as "End of Creation"; "Miscellanies," No. 1218, in Townsend, p. 152.

the essence of the divine being. God's being is dispositional. Since God, for Edwards, is also true beauty and a knowing and loving being, God's being is essentially the disposition to know and love the true beauty.

If God is essentially a disposition, God, for Edwards, is also a perfect actuality. "God is infinitely, eternally, unchangeably, and independently glorious and happy."[9] So God's dispositional essence is also completely exercised within God's being. Therefore, in conceiving of God as essentially a disposition, Edwards was not ready to compromise God's actuality. Now an important question arises: Can the divine being be both disposition and its infinitely complete exercise?

If actuality is going to be truly a mark of the divine perfection, then disposition and actuality could not be juxtaposed within God's being in such way that disposition is even logically (certainly not temporally) prior to actuality. This is so because if disposition had any sort of priority within God's being, there would be a principle of potentiality prior to the actuality of God. The full reality of God as the final ground of all reality would then be weakened.

But then disposition and actuality could not be thought of as coexisting in God alongside each other, either. If this were so, the true actuality of God as God would again be compromised. Finally, actuality could not be considered as prior to disposition, either. This is not acceptable because Edwards wants to see the very essence of God as dispositional. God's disposition to communicate himself, for Edwards, is conceived of "as being originally in God as a perfection of his nature."[10]

Edwards's intention is clear. He wants to see God as essentially a disposition, but he does not want to compromise the prior actuality of God as the ultimate principle of all reality. The only way to state the matter may be to say quite paradoxically that the essence of God's being, for Edwards, is at once actuality and disposition. For God *qua* deity, disposition and actuality *coincide*.[11] No further explanation is possible. Edwards says as much when he tells us that "there is no distinction to be made in God between power or habit and act," although "the divine perfection will not infer (i.e., imply) that his understanding is not by idea and that there is no indeed such a thing as inclination & love in God."[12]

9. "End of Creation," p. 420.

10. "End of Creation," pp. 433-34.

11. This represents a change of interpretation from my book, where the coincidence of disposition and actuality was attributed to the Father and not the other two persons of the Trinity.

12. "An Essay on the Trinity," in *Jonathan Edwards: Representative Selections*, ed. Clarence H. Faust and Thomas H. Johnson (New York: Hill and Wang, 1962), pp. 375-76, hereafter referred to as Faust and Johnson.

What this means further for the doctrine of the Trinity is that if God's being as God is at once disposition and actuality, then each of the three persons of the Trinity will have to be thought of as at once actuality and disposition. The primordial coincidence of actuality and disposition would be true for each of the three subsistences of the one essence of God.

Being and Becoming in the Immanent Trinity

We saw above that Edwards introduces the category of disposition into the very essence of the divine being. But no real distinction of any sort is allowed between actuality and disposition as far as the inner being of God *as God* is concerned. A distinction between actuality and disposition is allowed, however, for the self-communication of God. For the internal exercises of the divine dispositional essence, there is at least a logical distinction between disposition and actuality, and this distinction constitutes the distinction among the persons of the Trinity. The inner divine being, for Edwards, is not only differentiated in terms of trinitarian relationships but also contains a movement (though eternal in nature) from disposition to actuality through the way the trinitarian relationships are formulated.

Edwards articulates the doctrine of the Trinity using both the logic of dispositional ontology and also John Locke's psychology of the self — namely, the self, the self-reflexive idea of the self, and the self's love of the reflexive idea. The three distinctions in God, says Edwards, are "God, the idea of God, and delight in God."[13] The first subsistence of the divine being, or the Father, is then God in his first true actuality. Edwards writes:

> The F. is the Deity subsisting in the Prime, unoriginated & most absolute manner, or the deity in its direct existence. The Son is the deity generated by God's understanding, or having an Idea of himself & subsisting in that Idea. The Holy Gh. is the Deity subsisting in act, or the divine essence flowing out and Breathed forth in God's Infinite love to & delight in himself.[14]

The description of the Father as God's "direct existence" is explained further by Edwards:

> That knowledge or understanding in God which we must conceive of as first is His Knowledge of every Thing possible. That love which must be

---

13. "Miscellanies," No. 94, in Townsend, p. 257.
14. "An Essay on the Trinity," in Faust and Johnson, p. 379.

this knowledge is what we must conceive of as belonging to the essence of the Godhead in its first subsistence.[15]

God in his first subsistence knows and loves "every Thing possible," and thus is truly actual. But the Father, in Edwards's view, would have to be disposition as well as actuality since the Father is the first subsistence of the essence of the divine being. Discussing the Son as the complete communication of the Father's being, Edwards writes:

> The Father's begetting of the Son is a complete communication of all his happiness, and so an eternal adequate and infinite exercise of perfect goodness that is completely equal to such an inclination in perfection.[16]

The Father, then, is disposition and actuality, just as the other two subsistences of the divine being are. How, then, is the Father distinguished from the other two persons? Here Edwards is quite traditional. What distinguishes the Father as the Father is that he is "unoriginated" or "unbegotten." In terms of the dispositional logic, one could say that the Father is not a result of the self-communication of God, while the other two persons are. But, then, all three persons are equally God — the one essence of God which is at once disposition and actuality.

The Father, then, is a disposition to communicate himself, just as he is an eternally perfect actuality. Therefore, God as the Father is disposed to further exercise, and this exercise can only bring about a repetition of what God already is and not any kind of self-realization of God as God. This is so because God is primordially actual. Using the Lockean image of the human self as well as the logic of dispositional ontology, Edwards writes:

> And I do suppose the deity to be truly & Properly Repeated by God's thus having an Idea of himself & that this Idea of God is truly God, to all Intents and Purposes, & that by this means the Godhead is Really Generated and Repeated.[17]

And, as we saw, the Son is "a complete communication of all his [the Father's] happiness." When the Father's disposition is exercised beyond the complete actuality of the Father's being, a perfect repetition of the Father, namely, the Son, results. And this "generation" of the Son by the Father is eternal, the reflexive

---

15. "An Essay on the Trinity," in *Treatise on Grace and Other Posthumously Published Writings*, ed. Paul Helm (Greenwood, S.C.: Attic Press, 1971), p. 130.

16. "Miscellanies," No. 104, in *Exercises Commemorating the Two-Hundredth Anniversary of the Birth of Jonathan Edwards* (Andover, Mass.: Andover Press, 1904), app. I, p. 37.

17. "An Essay on the Trinity," in Faust and Johnson, pp. 376-77.

idea of God being "eternally begotten by him." There is no succession in God. There was never a time when the Son was not actually generated.[18]

So there is no temporal distinction between the Father's disposition and its full exercise. However, there is a logical distinction; the Father's disposition is not its full reflexive exercise. The Father's disposition/actuality is not the reflexive repetition of that disposition/actuality in the Son. And the eternal exercise constitutes the eternal begetting of the Son by the Father. The distinction between disposition/actuality *and* its repetition also constitutes the distinction between the Father and the Son. So the Father is unoriginated while the Son is the intellectual self-repetition of the Father.

After the intellectual exercise of the Father's disposition which results in the Son, only one other kind of exercise of the Father's disposition remains — namely, the affectional or volitional exercise. "The Father loveth the Son as a communication of himself as begotten in pursuance of his eternal inclination to communicate himself," explains Edwards. So "the Holy Gh. is the Deity subsisting in act, or the divine essence flowing out and Breathed forth in God's Infinite love & delight in himself."[19] Here again the psychological analogy and the logic of disposition are combined. The Holy Spirit is God's love of God's own idea of himself as well as the self-communication or self-repetition of God in an affectional exercise of the divine disposition.

Edwards speaks of the Holy Spirit as both the Father's love of the Son and also the love between the Father and the Son. Edwards's meaning seems to be that the Father's love of the Son naturally involves the Son, just as the self's love of its own idea of itself involves that reflexive idea. The Father's love of his own idea of himself is the exercise of the Father's divine disposition, but this exercise does not happen without the idea which is loved. So, in the Father's love of the Son "the deity becomes all act."[20] The Holy Spirit is God in God's third subsistence, and the Holy Spirit's distinction from the other two persons is that it is proceeded or breathed forth from them. This "procession" is the eternal movement of the affectional exercise of the divine disposition.

What we have here is a profound change from the traditional Western theology's doctrine of God. God is essentially a disposition and not just actuality. Further, a movement (though eternal) from potentiality to actuality is introduced into the inner-trinitarian life of God. Both of these factors lay the ground within God for God's activity in the world. God's activity in relation to the world is not an accident but a result of God's inner nature.

---

18. "Miscellanies," No. 104, in *Two-Hundredth Anniversary*, p. 37.

19. "Miscellanies," No. 104, in *Two-Hundredth Anniversary*, p. 38.

20. "An Essay on the Trinity," in Faust and Johnson, p. 377; "Miscellanies," No. 133, in *Two-Hundredth Anniversary*, p. 18.

Recent discussions have brought out the necessity of the doctrine of the Trinity as the only appropriate way to conceive of God in view of God's redemptive activity in the world. If God himself is present in God's self-revelation in Jesus Christ, it has been noted, God's own inner being can only be thought of as inherently relational or as going out of oneself to the other. Hence the need to conceive of God's immanent being as triune. Paraphrasing Karl Barth, Eberhard Jüngel has written:

> This means that God can enter into relationship *(ad extra)* with another being . . . , because God's being *(ad intra)* is a being *related to itself.* The doctrine of the Trinity is an attempt to think out the self-relatedness of the being of God as Father, Son, and Spirit.[21]

In Edwards also, the doctrine of the Trinity functions as an appropriate explanation for God's capacity to be related with the world. Edwards, however, has gone one step further. He has made disposition the dynamic force in the intra-trinitarian relatedness and formulated the intra-trinitarian relations as the eternal exercises of the divine disposition which in turn constitute the eternal movements of God's self-repetition *ad intra.* The net effect of what Edwards has done is that the dynamic nature of the intra-trinitarian relations is given an explicit articulation. And this is done without compromising the prior actuality of God as God, and thus without making God dependent upon the world for God's self-realization as God. Patricia Wilson-Kastner has criticized Edwards for making creation "necessary" for God for God's self-realization. This is in contrast, according to Wilson-Kastner, to the dynamically trinitarian view of God in Gregory of Nyssa, who is able to see God as creative and yet not dependent upon what he creates. What Wilson-Kastner says about Gregory, however, is thoroughly applicable to Edwards. Wilson-Kastner writes:

> I find particular value in Gregory's view that neither God nor creation are static. God's infinity is a perfect act of communion between Father, Son, and Spirit, and creation is a finite image of God's infinity in its unending progress of the partaking of his life. Such a scheme can speak of a God who is active without being in search of himself.[22]

---

21. Jüngel, p. 99.

22. Patricia Wilson-Kastner, "God's Infinity and His Relationship to Creation in the Theologies of Gregory of Nyssa and Jonathan Edwards," *Foundations* 21 (1978): 305-21, here p. 319. In her criticism of Edwards's making creation "necessary" for God, Wilson-Kastner assumes that for Edwards creation is "necessary" for God's self-realization as God. She writes: "It is hard to understand how the necessity for creation is not an internal limiting of God, because he does, in fact, *need* a reality in some sense distinct from himself in or-

The Creation of the World and the Reality of Temporality

God's creative activity *ad extra* has its ontological foundation within God's inner being — that is, in God's disposition to communicate himself and in the eternal movement of God's self-repetition *ad intra*. God's disposition to communicate himself is exercised completely *ad intra*. The intra-trinitarian self-repetition of God is "completely equal" to the divine disposition. But the divine disposition is naturally disposed to be exercised "in all kinds of its exercise." So God's disposition to communicate himself now exercises itself externally in creating the world. So "God made the world that He might communicate, and the creatures receive, His glory."[23]

This temporal exercise of God's disposition is of course the temporal re-iteration of the eternal movement of God's self-repetition *ad intra*. Thus, God's creation of the world is to be conceived of as a repetition of a prior actuality — "an increase, repetition, or multiplication" in time of God's internal "fullness."[24]

The movement of self-repetition *ad intra* is an eternal movement, transcending temporal succession, while the movement of self-repetition *ad extra* is spread out in the temporal span and will take an everlasting duration. This is so because "the sum total of the glory God is to receive is infinite." Such an infinite aim must take an unending amount of time. In fact, "there never will come the moment, when it can be said, that now this infinitely valuable good has been actually bestowed." God's self-repetition in time will even continue to increase endlessly in heaven.[25]

A central implication of Edwards's dispositional conception of the im-

---

der to complete his own being" (p. 312). What has to be pointed out, however, is that God for Edwards is inherently disposed to create a world, *not* to complete himself as God (which is completely actual *ad intra*), but rather to repeat the prior actuality. The notion of repetition has to be remembered.

23. "Miscellanies," No. 448, in *Two-Hundredth Anniversary*, p. 47.

24. "End of Creation," p. 433.

25. "Miscellanies," No. 1099, quoted in Yale MSS, p. 712; "End of Creation," p. 536; see Lee, pp. 236-41. An interesting question is, if the world is the result of the exercise of the original disposition of God, the world then is meant to be the fourth subsistence of the divine being! Edwards in fact holds the remarkable view that God's aim in creation can be said to have the church (as united with Christ) "admitted into the society of the blessed Trinity" ("The Excellencies of Christ," a sermon quoted in *Ethical Writings*, p. 736). It is only logical that God, who aims at the highest good, could only aim, in creating the world, that the world become an infinitely perfect repetition of God and thus achieve "the most perfect union with God." But Edwards emphatically denies that this would ever become actualized. By denying the eventuality of such a moment, Edwards preserves the crucial distinction between God and the world ("End of Creation," pp. 534-36).

manent Trinity is that God in God's own being is a readiness for activity *ad extra*. In this light, the full meaning of what Edwards says in the following quotation becomes clear. After pointing out that if God had not created the world such attributes as power, wisdom, goodness, and mercy "never would have had any exercise," Edwards continues:

> It is true that there was from eternity that act in God, *within himself*, and *toward himself*, that was the exercise of the same perfection of his nature. But it was not the same kind of exercise; it virtually contained it, but there was not explicitly the same exercise of his perfection. God, who delights in the exercise of his own perfection, delights in all the kinds of its exercise. The eternal act or energy, of the divine nature *within him* whereby he infinitely loves and delights in himself, I suppose imply, fundamentally, goodness and grace towards creatures, if there be that occasion, which infinite wisdom sees fit. But God, who delights in his own perfection, delights in seeing those exercises of his own perfection explicitly in being, that are fundamentally implied.[26]

So God creates a new reality outside of himself not only because God is inherently disposed to communicate himself in all the ways possible but also because doing so is "fundamentally implied" in what God already does in his own being. Within God, there is not only the essential disposition to exert himself but also "that eternal act" or the eternal exercise of the essential disposition. When God creates the world, therefore, God is doing something that is natural for God to do. Paraphrasing a similar point in Barth, Jüngel writes:

> This "Yes" of God to himself constitutes his being as God the Father, God the Son and God the Holy Spirit. And at the same time, from the beginning, this constitutes the historicality of God's being, in which all history has its basis.[27]

Through the eternal act within God's own being, God for Edwards, to borrow Jüngel's expression again, "*makes space* within himself for *time*."[28]

If the world results from the tendency of God's own being, then what happens in the world does matter to God. God does not need the world for him to be God. God *already* is, and the world only repeats this. But the world matters to God as God's repetition or enlargement of his own internal fullness. Edwards writes:

---

26. "Miscellanies," No. 533, in *Two-Hundredth Anniversary*, pp. 48-49.
27. Jüngel, p. 96.
28. Jüngel, p. 96.

Though it be true that God's glory and happiness are in and of himself, are infinite and can't be added to . . . ; yet it don't hence follow, nor is it true, that God has no real and proper delight, pleasure or happiness, in any of his acts or communications relative to the creature . . . ; in some sense it can be truly said that God has the more delight and pleasure for the holiness and happiness of his creatures.[29]

From this Edwards draws the practical conclusion that "we are to seek the glory of God as that which is a thing really pleasing to Him."[30]

If our interpretation of Edwards's doctrine of the immanent Trinity is correct at all, this has implications for the interpretation of his theology as a whole. In his theology, God's self-sufficiency and sovereignty are preserved. But, in his theology, God is going to be really involved in time, and history is going to be taken seriously.

Perhaps there is a connecting thread among many recent studies of Edwards that have all pointed to the theological significance of temporality in Edwards's way of thinking. The astonishing integration of humanity and divinity in Edwards's conception of the person of Jesus Christ has been noted.[31] Edwards's strong emphasis upon the indwelling of the Holy Spirit as a new habit of mind in the sanctified person has also been well documented.[32] Edwards's well-known postmillennialism has also highlighted the actual contribution that the events of history can make to the realization of God's will in this world.[33] The never-ending significance of temporality in Edwards's conception of the increasing nature of happiness in heaven has also been duly noted.[34]

My discussion in this essay at least suggests that all these emphases in Edwards's theology upon the ultimate importance of time and history are not an accident but rather are undergirded by a dynamic conception of God and of his relation to the world. And this certainly is one of the reasons why Edwards remains an important resource for contemporary Reformed theology.

29. "End of Creation," pp. 445-46.

30. "Miscellanies," No. 208, in Townsend, p. 129.

31. Jenson, pp. 91-122.

32. See, for example, Lee, pp. 231-36; Thomas A. Schafer, "Jonathan Edwards and Justification by Faith," *Church History* 20 (1951): 55-67.

33. See, for example, C. C. Goen, "Jonathan Edwards: A New Departure in Eschatology," *Church History* 28 (1959): 25-40; John F. Wilson, "History, Redemption, and the Millennium," in *Jonathan Edwards and the American Experience*, ed. Nathan O. Hatch and Harry S. Stout (New York: Oxford University Press, 1988), pp. 131-41.

34. See, for example, Lee, pp. 236-41; Pauw, pp. 285-333; Ramsey, app. III: "Heaven Is a Progressive State," in *Ethical Writings*, pp. 706-38.

CHAPTER 28

The Future of Reformed Theology: Some Lessons from Jonathan Edwards

Amy Plantinga Pauw

I t may seem odd to appeal to the figure of Jonathan Edwards in search of directions for Reformed theology at the end of the twentieth century. Outside of Reformed circles, this "American Augustine"[1] has been a resounding failure as a theological influence within his own country. The onset and aftermath of the American Revolution dealt his theological standing a blow from which it has never recovered. In the succeeding centuries, the main currents of American religious culture have blithely passed him by. And even among Reformed Christians, current sensitivities to issues of globalization, feminism, and ecology make this eighteenth-century Massachusetts pastor seem more parochial than ever.

Despite this, in the more than two centuries of American religious history since his death, there have been persistent theological appeals to Jonathan Edwards. To simplify a complicated picture, Edwards has found champions among two very different sorts of Reformed Christians — those who emphasize correct doctrine, and those whose focal point is what Edwards called the religious affections. Twentieth-century appeals mirror in an interesting way those of the previous century, and have expanded Edwards's influence beyond the evangelical camp. After a necessarily sketchy look at these contemporary claims to the Edwardsian legacy, we shall turn our attention to a third major twentieth-century Reformed group that for the most part has not claimed Edwards —

---

1. The phrase is from H. Richard Niebuhr, *The Kingdom of God in America* (New York: Harper Torchbooks, 1959), p. xvi.

those who find the focus of the Christian life in local and international efforts at social transformation.[2] What resources does Edwards's thought offer those who hold this prominent perspective in Reformed theology today?

Nineteenth-century Old School Presbyterians, centered at Princeton Seminary, appealed to Edwards in defense of creedal orthodoxy. Edwards's views on the bondage of the human will, divine election, and Christ's substitutionary atonement, which were already an offense to the emerging theological sensibilities of his day, were upheld as the identifying marks of genuine Reformed theology. At the same time the Princeton theologians firmly rejected Edwards's theory of the religious affections, in particular its implications for faith and ethics, as a regrettable idiosyncrasy. Having purged Edwards's theology of everything that conflicted with their more intellectualist approach, the Princeton theologians claimed Edwards's theological mantle in their attempts to preserve an "unvarnished classical Calvinism."[3]

Some contemporary conservatives, like their nineteenth-century Princeton School forebears, continue to make doctrinalist appeals to Jonathan Edwards. While these appeals are often joined with a greater enthusiasm for the evangelistic triumphs of the Great Awakening than Charles Hodge could muster, the emphasis on doctrinal orthodoxy remains central.[4] Contemporary doctrinalists point out that the strength of Edwards's convictions about the divinity of Christ, God's special grace to the elect, and the depravity of fallen humanity never wavered; indeed, the warmth with which he expounded these doctrines provided much ammunition for later theological detractors. Edwards is a doctrinalist hero because his mature thought reveals no trace of apology for — in fact, even a delight in — what have been called the "angularities" of Calvinism. There is no foreshadowing in his theology of the twin nineteenth-century temptations: washing over the objectionable doctrines with the pastel tones of a "consistent Calvinism," or letting an emphasis on religious affections eclipse doctrinal concerns altogether.

And yet, Edwards's approach to doctrine, if not always his doctrinal stances themselves, shows a much freer spirit toward the Reformed tradition.

2. I am adapting George Marsden's helpful distinctions between culturalist, doctrinalist, and pietist streams in American Reformed theology. See "Reformed and American," in *The Princeton Theology,* ed. David F. Wells (Grand Rapids: Baker, 1989), pp. 1-12.

3. Mark A. Noll, "The Contested Legacy of Jonathan Edwards in Antebellum Calvinism: Theological Conflict and the Evolution of Thought in America," *Canadian Review of American Studies* 19 (1988): 149-64, here p. 155. I am indebted to Noll's account of the conflicting nineteenth-century appeals to Edwards.

4. See, for example, John H. Gerstner, *Jonathan Edwards: A Mini-Theology* (Wheaton, Ill.: Tyndale House, 1987); *Steps to Salvation: The Evangelistic Message of Jonathan Edwards* (Philadelphia: Westminster, 1960).

Hopkins's testimony that Edwards "called no man 'Father,'" alongside its *prima facie* appeal to feminists, highlights Edwards's rather irreverent attitude toward such venerable Reformed figures as Calvin himself. Though accepting the label Calvinist "for distinction's sake," Edwards emphatically declared his theological independence: "I utterly disclaim a dependence on Calvin, or believing the doctrines which I hold, because he believed and taught them; and cannot justly be charged with believing in everything just as he taught."[5]

For Edwards, genuine Reformed theology need not look only backwards for its authority, and authentic new expressions of it need not always coincide with previous attempts. In the preface to Bellamy's *True Religion Delineated*, Edwards declared that attempts to bring "any addition of light" to true religion

> ought not to be despised and discouraged, under a notion that it is but vanity and arrogance in such as are lately sprung up in an obscure part of the world, to pretend to add anything to this subject, to the informations we have long since received from their fathers, who have lived in former times, in *New England*, and more noted countries.[6]

The inexorable progress of redemption history promises ever greater knowledge of God. As human faith and love of God increase, the revelation of God's beauty continually overflows the earlier bounds of doctrinal definition and propels the faithful understanding in new efforts at theological articulation.

In contrast to his later doctrinalist champions, Edwards lacked, on one hand, any pretensions to metaphysical purity and, on the other, any illusions about a permanent alliance between Christian faith and a particular philosophical tradition. This meant that every age held the possibility of fruitful new interfaces between traditional doctrines and contemporary intellectual currents. On the Edwardsian model, an ad hoc correlation between Christian belief and contemporary culture, including strands that are in their essence neutral or even antagonistic to the Christian faith, is central to the theological task. This is done not out of a yen for theological trendiness, but out of a conviction of, and gratitude for, God's continuing presence with the church.

Edwards pursued his theological reflections in the midst of what we now call a paradigm shift. In his private notebooks, the *Miscellanies*, one finds extended doctrinal experiments, in which various philosophical frameworks are

5. *The Works of Jonathan Edwards*, gen. ed. Perry Miller, vol. 1, *Freedom of the Will*, ed. Paul Ramsey (New Haven: Yale University Press, 1957), p. 131.

6. Joseph Bellamy, *True Religion Delineated* (Morristown, N.J.: Henry P. Russell, 1804), p. iv. The view of doctrine assumed here clashes with Hodge's infamous boast that "a new idea never originated at Princeton Seminary." A. A. Hodge, *Life of Charles Hodge* (New York, 1881), p. 521.

tested for theological fruitfulness. Even in his published writings, Edwards showed a bold eclecticism, drawing on Lockean psychology, Cambridge Platonism, and, of course, Berkeleyan idealism. The aim — and the result — is not so much perfect theological consistency as a vigorous and imaginative recasting of the Christian faith. What makes Edwards still rewarding to read today is his willingness, even without the conditions of what Thomas Kuhn has called "normal science," to venture into the deep waters of real theology, not to hang back in the shallows of theological methodology.

With no consensus regarding a new theological paradigm in sight, contemporary followers of Edwards would do well to follow him into the depths. Obviously, they need not "believe in everything just as he taught." Indeed, contemporary Reformed Christians will want to declare their own theological independence from Jonathan Edwards at points. He was, after all, a slave owner with a decidedly patriarchal bent. His philosophical idealism plagued his theology with irremediable problems, as did his enthusiastic double predestinarianism. But Edwards's spirit of theological adventure is one Reformed Christians would do well to imitate. Following Edwards's example, it would be entirely appropriate for contemporary Reformed theologians to recast doctrines with the aid of a variety of intellectual approaches current in their own day, such as analytic philosophy, feminist thought, or narrative approaches to Scripture. In so doing they may genuinely hope for "addition of light."

In critiquing modern doctrinalist appropriation of Edwards, I am echoing in part observations made by a nineteenth-century professor of moral philosophy, Noah Porter. Edwards's genius, in Porter's view, lay in his impatience with "servilely copying the compromising philosophy" of his Reformed fathers, and in his eagerness to explore innovative alliances between contemporary philosophies and the Christian faith.[7] As an exponent of New England theology, Porter represents the other main contender for Edwards's theological mantle in the previous century. Centered at Andover and later at Yale, the New Englanders countered Princeton's doctrinal focus by emphasizing Edwards's convictions about the role of the affections in Christian piety. It was as "evident" to them as it had been to Edwards "that religion consists so much in affection, as that without holy affection there is no true religion: and no light in the understanding is good, which don't produce holy affection in the heart."[8]

---

7. Noah Porter, "The Princeton Review on Dr. Taylor and the Edwardean Theology," *New Englander* 18 (1860): 736ff. See Noll, p. 157. I depart from Porter's confidence, however, in human "moral intuitions" as the philosophical basis for Christian theology.

8. *The Works of Jonathan Edwards,* gen. ed. Perry Miller, vol. 2, *Religious Affections,* ed. John Smith (New Haven: Yale University Press, 1959), p. 119. All subsequent references to *Religious Affections* will be to this edition.

While departing from Edwards's doctrinal views on human will and divine atonement, they found in Edwards's numerous writings on the revivals, as well as in his magisterial work *The Nature of True Virtue*, a welcome emphasis on human religious subjectivity.

Among twentieth-century theologians, H. Richard and Richard R. Niebuhr[9] have retained a self-consciously Edwardsian emphasis on the religious affections and have achieved, in my view, the most fruitful modern engagement with Jonathan Edwards. This success is perhaps as much evident in their departures from New England theology as in their debts to it. Like the New Englanders, they have argued that Christian belief is inextricably linked with the human emotions of trust, humility, and gratitude. But, in the words of H. Richard Niebuhr, they have also shown an intense "interest in maintaining the independent reality of the religious object, from that which is purely immanent in religious experience to that which is also transcendent."[10] This emphasis on divine transcendence has enabled Niebuhrian theology to rise above the plateaus of nineteenth-century "consistent Calvinism."

Eschewing nineteenth-century confidence in the deliverance of a universal moral sense, the Niebuhrs have dared to sound the Edwardsian theme of divine judgment over human moral striving. And their skepticism about the capacities of human reason has also led to a recovery of Edwards's insistence on divine grace, by which the saints are given a *new* capacity to perceive the "glory and beauty of God's nature."[11] As Richard R. Niebuhr has written, "Faith is the vessel that carries the mind from its first glimpse of wonder to the far country where its eye is opened wide and drenched by visions of glory."[12]

Even in their departures from Edwards's accounts of original sin and the bondage of the human will, the Niebuhrs have retained Edwardsian insights that were obscured by the optimistic individualism of the nineteenth century. In rejecting the New Englanders' assertion of "the untrammelled will of man,"[13] they have preserved the Edwardsian insight on the priority of the heart over the will in grounding human moral identity. Their portrayal of individual sin as a matter of fundamental disloyalty more than of discrete acts resonates well with Edwards's dispositionalism. And they have shown much greater sensitivity than the New England theologians to the social and structural reality of

---

9. The term "Niebuhrian" extends as well to the host of younger scholars whom they have inspired.

10. H. Richard Niebuhr, "Religious Realism in the Twentieth Century," in *Religious Realism*, ed. D. C. Macintosh (New York, 1931), pp. 416, 419.

11. *Religious Affections*, p. 248.

12. Richard R. Niebuhr, *Streams of Grace: Studies of Jonathan Edwards, Samuel Taylor Coleridge, and William James* (Kyoto: Doshisha University Press, 1983), p. 12.

13. Edward A. Park, "New England Theology," *Bibliotheca Sacra* 9 (1852): 212.

sin. In all these ways the Niebuhrs have shown the aptness of Edwards's affectional theology for contemporary Reformed Christians.

What is missing in the Niebuhrian appropriation of Edwards is his marriage of subjective affections with objective doctrines. Edwards insisted that authentic religious affections are always attended by a conviction "of the reality and certainty of divine things." Truly gracious affections shore up the doctrinal convictions of believers, so that "the great, spiritual, mysterious, and invisible things of the gospel . . . have the weight and power of real things in their hearts."[14] Reciprocally, for Edwards, even arcane doctrines like the Trinity "are glorious inlets into the knowledge and view of the spiritual world, and the contemplation of supreme things; the knowledge of which, I have experienced how much it contributes to the betterment of the heart."[15] Contemplation of true doctrine serves to shore up religious affections, and thus can be of great benefit "towards the advancing of holiness." By contrast, in Niebuhrian theology a Kantian skepticism about the human capacity to perceive "divine things" tends to quell doctrinal certitude. While it is clear that human religious affections point beyond themselves to a transcendent reality, genuine "knowledge and view of the spiritual world" seem elusive. The Niebuhrian appropriation of Edwards excels in charting the ambiguities of the believing heart more than in instilling a "certainty of divine things."

H. Richard Niebuhr suggested one more contemporary avenue of approach to Edwards by including him in his well-known chapter on Christ as transformer of culture: "Jonathan Edwards, with his sensitive and profound views of creation, sin, and justification, with his understanding of the way of conversion and his millennial hopes, became in America the founder of a movement of thought about Christ as the regenerator of man in his culture."[16] This regeneration has taken different historical forms. In the nineteenth century, as revivalism returned to center stage of American religious life, Edwards's writings on conversion enjoyed a renewed popularity that transcended deep differences between enthusiastic followers of Finney's "new measures" and sober Old Side Presbyterians. Edwards's *Personal Narrative* and youthful *Resolutions* became paradigms of individual Christian piety, while his mature work *Religious Affections* became the standard for discerning and implementing mass revivals. Beyond concerns with personal and regional conversions, the antebellum period was also suffused with hope for a larger national regenera-

---

14. *Religious Affections*, pp. 291-92.

15. Miscellanies, #181, Beinecke Rare Book and Manuscript Library, Yale University, New Haven, Connecticut. Used with permission.

16. H. Richard Niebuhr, *Christ and Culture* (New York: Harper & Row, 1951), pp. 219-20.

tion. And here evangelicals linked Edwards's name with America's political Founding Fathers, as a key to the transformation of the new nation into a righteous Christian republic.[17]

This revivalistic stream of the nineteenth-century American appeal to Edwards has largely dried up in mainstream Reformed churches.[18] More than a century later, a different kind of transformation occupies center stage on the ecclesiastical agenda. The concern is not primarily the inner transformation of individuals, much less the creation of a righteous American empire. Rather, the focus is on the outward transformation of social structures around the world. The proceedings of the most recent General Council of the World Alliance of Reformed Churches (WARC), which was attended by thirty-five delegates from North American Reformed churches, will serve as a broad example of this new culturalist emphasis. Despite the assembly's stated theme — Jesus' question to his disciples, "Who do you say that I am?" — its theological emphasis was not on christological doctrine nor on personal trust in Jesus Christ. Rather, the assembly focused on the question of the church's identity as it pursues social justice, world peace, and the integrity of creation. General Secretary elect Milan Opocensky justified his choice of Mark 10:35-45 for the text of his closing sermon on the conviction "that the common denominator of all our efforts, deliberations, programmes and projects is service. The Son of Man has come to serve us, and in his footsteps we are sent out to serve. Jesus of Nazareth is an example and paradigm of what true service means."[19] The pronounced tendency, revealed in both the assembly's structured agenda and its individual speeches, was to seek the identity of the Reformed churches in shared service to the world.

If it is not continuous with nineteenth-century evangelical concerns for doctrine, personal conversion, or mass revival, neither is the contemporary Reformed emphasis on social transformation simply a replaying of past liberalism. Much less sanguine about the possibility of coming to agreement based on common reason or moral intuition, contemporary Reformed culturalists more freely acknowledge Christian particularity. They tend to locate the orientation for their mission not in some kind of universal moral sensibility, but in the prophetic tradition of the Hebrew Bible and its recapitulation in the Synoptic Gospels. Christian service to the world means sharing God's bias toward

17. See Joseph Conforti, "Antebellum Evangelicals and the Cultural Revival of Jonathan Edwards," *American Presbyterians: Journal of Presbyterian History* 66 (winter 1988): 227-58.

18. Though it remains vigorous in certain evangelical circles, through the work of John Gerstner, Richard Lovelace, John Piper, and others.

19. *Notes from Proceedings of the Twenty-second General Council of the WARC*, ed. Edmond Perret (Geneva: WCC, 1990), p. 290, henceforth cited as *WARC Proceedings*.

the stranger, repenting of sins against neighbors far and near, and finding in Christ the possibility of true reconciliation with them.

This acknowledgment of the formative influence of religious tradition and community greatly mutes the nineteenth-century liberal emphasis on individual moral self-determination. Given the communal nature of religious and moral formation, individual Christian identity must be predicated on participation in the fellowship of the church. And participation in the community of Christians is what fuels identification with and saving action in the larger human society and the natural world. Contemporary Reformed churches see themselves not simply as mobilization centers for pious individuals, but as an international, transdenominational community whose social vision emerges out of a faith that is formed and nurtured by joint worship.[20]

Yet the doctrinal and affectional center of contemporary Reformed faith and worship is remarkably hard to locate. Though outgoing secretary Allan Boesak proclaimed in his opening sermon that "believing in Jesus Christ as Saviour is at the heart of our struggles for justice and peace, liberation, and the integrity of creation,"[21] it is difficult to discern what this common belief comes to, or what its relation to these continuing struggles is. Nor is there explicit agreement about the energizing force behind these struggles for peace and justice. Given the culturalist appreciation of the structural character of sin both within and without the church, the answer cannot simply be human initiative.[22] Collective human effort in the church is bound to be as futile as individual human effort. Yet theological analysis of the religious affections grounding communal Christian social action is hard to find.

Certainly Christian service to the world feeds a common faith, as well as receiving nourishment from it. Without public exercise, private religious affections wither and die. The historical divisiveness among Reformed Christians stemming from unyielding demands for uniformity in doctrine has squelched opportunities for common service to the world, and impoverished their own faith in the process. Articulation of a common faith within the larger Reformed community requires a tolerance, even an appreciation, for diversity in doctrine and affectional expressions. In pleading for Christian unity, WARC speaker Lukas Vischer noted that "when we speak of unity, we should not think of uniformity but of fellowship and exchange. Unity is the opposite not

---

20. The Twenty-second WARC General Council declared that "our common testimony of faith is rooted and grounded in our worship." *WARC Proceedings*, p. 26.

21. *WARC Proceedings*, p. 59.

22. H. R. Niebuhr's indictment of "that part of the social gospel which expected to change prodigal mankind by improving the quality of the husks served in the pigsty" (*Christ and Culture*, p. 220) would seem to apply.

of diversity but of rupture or non-existence of communication."[23] But amidst the host of diverse voices, contemporary culturalists still need to sense Edwards's conviction of "the reality and certainty of divine things." The notion of boundaries is intrinsic to the definition of any community, if rupture and lack of communication are to be avoided.[24] Without any theological boundaries for the present diversity within the Reformed churches, a communally discerned and enacted mission is unlikely to emerge.

Implicit in the contemporary Reformed commitment to service is the conviction of the communal nature of all reality. What the present mainstream Reformed churches need is a theology of community that can accommodate both their conviction that living out the Christian faith in community somehow reflects the purpose and reality of God, and that being a Christian in today's world implies a fundamental interrelatedness with the entirety of God's creation.[25] Ironically, Jonathan Edwards, to whom previous centuries looked for the standard morphology of individual conversion, can provide both. Edwards's theological prescriptions, couched in traditional language and conceptualities, may seem like strong medicine to most contemporary Reformed culturalists. But his theology offers largely untapped resources for understanding the complex issues of Christian practice and communal life. The remainder of this essay will sketch Edwards's reflections on community, particularly as found in his mature treatises *Religious Affections* and *The Nature of True Virtue*.

Religious Affections builds on a foundation established early on in Edwards's theological reflections: the intrinsically social nature of both divine and human reality. Regarding human sociality, Edwards wrote, "God has so made and constituted the world of mankind, that he has made it natural and necessary, that they should be concerned one with another, and their inclination to society."[26] Had he stopped here, Edwards's theology of community would have been entirely uncontroversial. But Edwards insisted that human delight in society and fellowship with others is not a mere creaturely limitation. Rather, human society is a created reflection — an "image and shadow" of divine reality:[27] "The

23. "Living in and under God's Covenant," *WARC Proceedings*, p. 120.

24. See Mary Douglas, *Purity and Danger: An Analysis of the Concepts of Pollution and Taboo* (London: Routledge and Kegan Paul, 1978).

25. Regarding the "integrity of creation," the Twenty-second WARC General Council affirms that "The God of whom the Bible speaks seems clearly to want a world in which all the parts, though different from one another, exist in harmony." *WARC Proceedings*, p. 199.

26. Miscellanies, #864, Beinecke Rare Book and Manuscript Library, Yale University, New Haven, Connecticut. Used with permission.

27. While the Niebuhrs have excelled in articulating the intrinsically social nature of humanity, they have characteristically fallen short of affirming this as a reflection of divine reality.

eternal infinite happiness of the divine being seems to be social, consisting in the infinitely blessed union and felicity of the person[s] of the trinity so that they are happy in one another; God the Father, God the Son are represented as rejoicing from eternity one in another."[28] The paradigm for human community is the Godhead, daringly described by Edwards as that "society or family of three." All Christian attempts at forging a social unity amidst human diversity must look first to the unity "among the persons of the trinity, the supreme Harmony of all."[29]

Because created reality is irreducibly social, it is fitting that the final goal of God's magnificent and elaborate work of redemption be relational: bringing sinners into a harmonious union with God and neighbor. The church as a benevolent community of praise and acts of love provides an earthly glimpse of this harmony. In the fullness of redemption in heaven, the saints "shall all be one society, they shall be united together without any schism, and there shall be a sweet harmony, and a perfect union."[30] Because divine reality is also primordially social, this heavenly harmony must find its center in the Godhead: "Christ has brought it to pass that those that the Father has given him should be brought into the household of God, that he and his Father and they should be as it were one society, one family, that his people should be in a sort admitted into that society of the three persons in the Godhead."[31] The saints' union with Christ permits not only a repetition, but a gracious expansion of the intra-trinitarian fellowship.

In *Religious Affections*, Edwards focused on the communal nature of the earthly church. It is in some ways one of Edwards's most socially conservative writings, written in the wake of the emotional excesses of the Great Awakening, and reasserting the need for due submission to local clerical authority. Yet, in it, Edwards presents a theology that undercuts the individualistic and introspective tendencies of revivalism and provides a robust vision of communal Christian practice. While the zeal among contemporary Reformed Christians for distinguishing the saved from the unsaved has waned, debates over the connections between private piety and public practice have not.

If the essence of Christian life lies in private spiritual experience, then the Christian community plays a distinctly secondary role as a disengaged observ-

28. Unpublished sermon on Acts 20:28, Beinecke Rare Book and Manuscript Library, Yale University, New Haven, Connecticut. Used with permission.

29. Miscellanies, #182, Beinecke Rare Book and Manuscript Library, Yale University, New Haven, Connecticut. Used with permission.

30. *The Works of President Edwards with a Memoir of His Life*, ed. Sereno E. Dwight, vol. 8 (New York: S. Converse, 1829-30), p. 258.

31. Miscellanies, #571, Beinecke Rare Book and Manuscript Library, Yale University, New Haven, Connecticut. Used with permission.

er with no unmediated access to the experience of the individual. The role of the community is then limited to making external judgment on accounts of personal religious experiences. As, in Edwards's opinion at least, the vigorous piety of the revivals degenerated into self-affirming emotionalism, he gradually developed a "hermeneutic of suspicion" regarding accounts of individual conversions. There is more than a tinge of sarcasm in Edwards's rejection of accounts of private religious experiences as a measure of a true Christian:

> Christ nowhere says, Ye shall know the tree by its leaves or flowers, or ye shall know men by their talk, or ye shall know them by the good story they tell of their experiences, or ye shall know them by the manner and air of their speaking, and emphasis and pathos of expression, or by their speaking feelingly, or by making a very great show by abundance of talk, or by many tears and affectionate expressions.[32]

The richness of life together in Christ depended on more than the community's discernment that an individual "talked like one that felt what he said."[33] But the intrinsically private nature of these experiences rendered them immune to effective evaluation by the Christian community.

Edwards's discouragement with the course of the revivals and the failure of his Northampton ministry drove him to reaffirm the Puritan appeal to sanctification as externally visible Christian practice. It is the Christian community as a whole that discerns the "sincerity of a professing Christian." The preeminence of love in a Christian's life must be visible "to the eye of his neighbours and brethren."[34] This conclusion had two important ramifications. First, it denied the privileged access of the individual to her own spiritual states. Secondly, it denied the primacy of individual conversion experience over "holy practice" within the community.

"Christian practice is the sign of signs, in this sense that it is the great evidence which confirms and crowns all other signs of godliness."[35] In *Religious Affections,* Edwards denied the antinomian dichotomy between experience and practice: "To speak of Christian experience and practice as if they were two things, properly and entirely distinct, is to make a distinction without consideration or reason." Religious experience is not an intrinsically private and internal affair. Holy love visibly exercised in the Christian community is also a form of religious experience. In fact, Edwards affirmed that holy practice is not only "one kind of part of Christian experience" — "both reason and Scripture

---

32. *Religious Affections,* p. 407.
33. *Religious Affections,* pp. 408-9.
34. *Religious Affections,* p. 407.
35. *Religious Affections,* p. 444.

represent it as the chief and most important and most distinguishing part of it."[36] Religious experience of this practical kind was an intrinsically social affair: it involved the outward expression of divine love among the members for each other.

It might be objected that the kind of Christian practice Edwards described in *Religious Affections* is not of the sort which accommodates well the contemporary culturalists' insistence on cooperation with non-Christian efforts toward peace and justice in the world.[37] Edwards, after all, insisted that natural dispositions toward virtuous action are "entirely diverse" from true virtue as absolute benevolence to God. If this distinction between natural and supernatural virtue was "the Achilles heel" in Edwards's ethical reflections for his would-be followers at Princeton,[38] is it not even more of a weakness from the twentieth-century Reformed perspective, which so strongly repudiates any hint of Christian imperialism?

The resonance of Edwards's account of distinctively Christian practice with contemporary Reformed concerns for service in the world depends at least in part on the harmony between his general moral philosophy and his theological ethics. If they are inseparable, as Paul Ramsey has urged, then Edwards's *Nature of True Virtue* can be read as his ethics of creation. In it, Edwards described a common morality, planted in human nature from its creation and held in place by God's continuous action, which bears an indelible "resemblance" to true virtue, both in nature and effects.

This "natural morality" is, in Ramsey's phrase, "a rather splendid thing."[39] First, there is a natural sense of beauty, which extends to immaterial reality as well as material objects. For Edwards, the harmonious workings of society are beautiful. The reciprocity of kindnesses among friends is beautiful. The demand for human justice and peaceful coexistence among nations is beautiful. Secondly, there is a natural self-love which is not opposed to true

36. *Religious Affections*, pp. 450-51.

37. The new Presbyterian *Directory of Worship*, for example, exhorts Christians to "acts of advocacy and compassion . . . through cooperation with agencies and organizations committed to these ends." *The Constitution of the Presbyterian Church (U.S.A.): Book of Order, Part II* (Louisville: Office of the General Assembly, 1990), W-7.3003. Likewise the Twenty-second WARC General Council, in an "Open Letter to the Children and Young People of the Planet," urges that "God calls us to become partners in the creation, re-creation and redemption of the world." *WARC Proceedings*, p. 193.

38. The phrase is Mark Noll's, in Noll, p. 156.

39. *The Works of Jonathan Edwards*, gen. ed. John Smith, vol. 8, *Ethical Writings*, ed. Paul Ramsey (New Haven: Yale University Press, 1989), pp. 33-34. All subsequent references to *The Nature of True Virtue* and *Charity and Its Fruits* will be to this edition. The interpretation which follows is indebted to Ramsey's account of Edwards's ethics.

virtue, but indeed makes possible a great extension of love to others. As Ramsey notes, "God's moral constitution sustains and bends purely private personal self-love to extension into larger communities of common interest."[40] Natural self-love can also instill a love of the various social virtues, even when the self discerns no direct advantage.

Thirdly, natural human conscience is an internal form of this self-love which urges human persons toward moral consistency and integrity. This harmony with self is a shadow of both the divine consent within the Godhead and truly virtuous human consent. And finally, Edwards posits instinctual affections which account for natural feelings of love within families and communities and of pity toward those who suffer. These instincts are a source of earthly stability, joy, and comfort for all God's creatures.

Edwards's insistence on the divine nature of true virtue denies neither the existence of deep and abiding natural morality among human persons nor the possibility of interfaith collaboration toward common moral goals. But as splendid as this natural morality is, Edwards judged it "fundamentally and essentially defective," because it lacks a "supreme regard to God."[41] If God is part of the universal "system of beings," God must be "the chief part . . . in comparison of whom and without whom all the rest are nothing, either as to beauty or existence. And therefore certainly, unless we will be atheists, we must allow that true virtue does primarily and most essentially consist in a supreme love to God; and that where this is wanting, there can be no true virtue."[42] Putting love to God at the center of Christian ethics, however, does not diminish the importance of Christian love of neighbor. In Edwards's view, all natural love is private and narrow, confined by the orbit of self-interest. Only when others "are loved not because of their relation to self, but because of their relation to God,"[43] is truly virtuous love possible. The divine nature of this neighbor love is shown by its scope: Christian love is not confined to "the children of God," but embraces all who share the "natural image of God," including those who are "unthankful and evil."[44] Only in relation to God, the Being of beings, is the soul "related to everything it stands connected with" and able to discern the fullness of human life in community.

Thus, for Edwards, all truly virtuous love among created beings "is dependent on, and derived from love to God."[45] This will not stop Christians

---

40. Ramsey, in *The Nature of True Virtue*, p. 38.

41. *The Nature of True Virtue*, p. 560.

42. *The Nature of True Virtue*, p. 554.

43. *Charity and Its Fruits*, p. 264.

44. *Charity and Its Fruits*, p. 264. While Edwards's idealism and historical context rendered current ecological themes irrelevant, Reformed concerns for the "integrity of creation" would undoubtedly fall under the same purview as love of neighbor.

45. *The Nature of True Virtue*, p. 557.

from joining forces with others who yearn for the day in which peace and justice embrace. Indeed, their confessional commitment to living out the story of God's reconciling acts with humanity requires these transformative efforts. But it will also keep them from placing their ultimate trust and hope in these efforts. The love and gratitude that empowers their social mission also points them beyond it, to a confidence not in human powers, but in Christ's triumph over the forces of death and sin.

While contemporary Reformed culturalists are quick to insist that faith in God must result in a thirst for love and justice on earth, they have been slower to acknowledge that a full-orbed earthly ethic can only originate from a thirst for God. Edwards provides a needed but perhaps troublesome reminder that Christian love to fellow creatures must always be consonant with faith's vision of "the reality and certainty of divine things." Christians will rejoice with others in new forms of human fellowship, in the crumbling of old hostilities and prejudices among persons of different cultures, races, genders, and religions. But their delight in human harmonies will always be rooted in a delight in God's beauty and therefore a yearning for earthly society to resemble heavenly society.

If contemporary Reformed culturalists are to claim Edwards's vision of the rich interplay of doctrine, religious affection, and Christian practice, they must abandon a bland religiosity that seeks above all not to appear foolish or give offense. In so doing they will rediscover that gentleness and reverence are not incompatible with a forthright accounting of the hope that is within them. Following Edwards, they will seek their neighbor's good at the source of their own happiness. And in that source they will find divine power for their continuing efforts toward "justice, peace, liberation, and the integrity of creation."

CHAPTER 29

The Sum of the Gospel: The Doctrine of Election in the Theologies of Alexander Schweizer and Karl Barth

Bruce McCormack

Introduction

The jury is still out with regard to the question of whether theology has now entered into a "postmodern" period. Certainly the voices telling us that the modern period in theology is over are many and varied, but as yet the outcome is uncertain. Perhaps the time has come, however, when we can more calmly consider the relative merits of the two most impressive constructive theologies produced in the modern period — those of Friedrich Schleiermacher and Karl Barth — than could a previous generation still caught up in the heat of battle. There are signs that some would like to seek a way "beyond the impasse" between Schleiermacher and Barth. Unfortunately, efforts at seeking points of contact between them have concentrated far too much on questions of method (where little rapprochement may be expected), to the neglect of material questions in dogmatics.[1]

In this essay, I will examine the doctrine of election and the understanding of its place and importance for constructive theology as a whole in the thought of Alexander Schweizer and Karl Barth. I choose Schweizer — who was arguably Schleiermacher's most gifted student — rather than the master

---

1. See the essays contained in James O. Duke and Robert F. Streetman, eds., *Barth and Schleiermacher: Beyond the Impasse?* (Philadelphia: Fortress, 1988).

himself because of the Züricher's vast knowledge of the Reformed tradition and because of his lifelong preoccupation with the doctrine of election. What we will find is that, although disagreement will remain between Barth and Schweizer, there is a tremendous convergence of interest which lies back of their respective formulations of the doctrine. Impulses which gave rise to Schweizer's reflections on the doctrine of election are not simply ignored by Barth but taken up afresh and handled in a different way. What this suggests is that Barth's theology did not constitute a simple repudiation of his "neo-Protestant" forebear, but rather a fulfillment of many of his deepest concerns in a new framework. And so if the differences in starting point and method will not go away, perhaps the realization of shared concerns between Barthians and Schleiermacherians will at least have the effect of teaching both of their need for one another in a vital Reformed theology of the future.

Predestination: "Central Dogma" of the Reformed Churches?

Until the Barthian revolution so dramatically altered the theological landscape in the 1920s, it was widely assumed that the distinguishing feature of Reformed theology in all of its classical forms was the prominence given to the doctrine of predestination. The decisive impetus to this view was given in 1844 by Alexander Schweizer in the first volume of his *Die Glaubenslehre der evangelisch-reformierten Kirche.*[2] The *Glaubenslehre* was a *Lehrbuch* — a textbook of Reformed doctrines, systematically arranged and composed largely of lengthy citations from sixteenth- and seventeenth-century texts, set forth to illustrate Reformed teaching on the various doctrinal loci of Christian theology. Schweizer's motivation in writing such a work was not purely antiquarian; he had a constructive theological aim throughout. He was a devoted follower of Friedrich Schleiermacher, and his constructive goal was to demonstrate that Schleiermacher's theology represented a revival of the Reformed tradition (albeit in thoroughly modern dress) after it had suffered virtual eclipse in the eighteenth century.

In Schweizer's view, what distinguished the theology of the Reformed churches from Lutheran theology was, initially at least, a differing *Grund-*

2. Alexander Schweizer, *Die Glaubenslehre der evangelisch-reformierten Kirche, Dargestellt und aus den Quellen belegt*, 2 vols. (Zürich: Orell, Füssli und Comp., 1844-47). For a fascinating study of Schweizer and the problems which shall occupy us in this section, see Brian Gerrish, *Tradition and the Modern World: Reformed Theology in the Nineteenth Century* (Chicago: University of Chicago Press, 1978), pp. 99-150. Those familiar with Gerrish's work will immediately recognize the great debt which I owe to him in the interpretation of Schweizer which follows.

richtung. Lutheran theology concerned itself above all with overcoming and eliminating from the church every last vestige of "Judaizing" — the teaching that justification occurs through works. Reformed theology, by contrast, was centrally concerned with the "paganization" of the church through the divinization of the creature (e.g., the fundamentally polytheistic worship of Mary and the saints, the sacralization of nature in the Eucharist by means of the doctrine of transubstantiation, etc.).[3]

Out of this initial difference in *Grundrichtung,* Schweizer argued, there then arose a further difference in "material principle."[4] According to Schweizer, the "material principle" of Lutheran theology was the doctrine of justification by faith alone, whereas for the Reformed churches it was the sense of "absolute dependence upon God alone" (which was articulated dogmatically in the doctrine of predestination). Again, this difference in "material principle" signals a difference in orientation; the two principles in question are directed to two different basic questions which determine the shape of each theology taken as a whole. The Lutheran question was: What is it in humankind that makes blessed? and the answer given was faith, not works. The Reformed question looked in a very different direction. It asked: Who makes

---

3. Schweizer, *Die Glaubenslehre der evangelisch-reformierten Kirche,* 1:38-43.

4. The origins of the distinction between the "formal" and "material" principles of Protestantism (or alternatively, of Lutheran dogmatics) was carefully researched and presented by Albrecht Ritschl in an essay written in 1876. It was above all August Twesten (one of Schleiermacher's earliest students as well as his successor in Berlin in 1835) whom Ritschl held responsible for coining the formula in the form in which it became a commonplace from the mid-nineteenth century on. In his "Vorlesungen über die Dogmatik der evangelisch-lutherischen Kirche" (1826), Twesten spoke of the authority of Holy Scripture as the "formal principle" of "Protestantism," and of the doctrine of justification by faith as the "material principle" of Lutheran dogmatics. From the beginning, the use of this conceptual pair was plagued by imprecision — a fact which influenced Ritschl to argue for its abandonment. Of the greatest interest for us here are the problems surrounding the notion of a "material principle." Is it to be understood in the bold sense of a *source* from which all other doctrines proceed (in which case, it is not easily reconciled with the notion that Scripture is the sole authoritative source of dogmatics); or is it to be understood in a more modest way as the one dogma which, more than any other, determines the shape and meaning of the rest? The answer to such a question is not at all self-evident, which means that close attention must be paid to individual usage if an injustice is not to be done to a particular theologian. Schweizer, as we shall see, would have answered in terms of the "softer" sense. See Ritschl, "Über die beiden Principien des Protestantismus; Antwort auf eine 25 Jahre alte Frage," in Ritschl, *Gesammelte Aufsätze,* vol. 1 (Freiburg: J. C. B. Mohr, 1893), pp. 234-47. Cf. Albrecht Ritschl, *Die christliche Lehre von der Rechtfertigung und Versöhnung,* vol. 1 (Bonn: Adolph Marcus, 1870), pp. 157-73; ET, *A Critical History of the Christian Doctrine of Justification and Reconciliation,* trans. John S. Black (Edinburgh: Edmonston and Douglas, 1872), pp. 152-67.

blessed or damns, the creature or God alone? and the answer was, of course, God alone. Therefore, Schweizer concluded, the "material principle" of the Lutheran church was *anthropological* in character; the "material principle" of the Reformed churches was *theological* in the strictest sense.[5]

Before taking leave of Schweizer's *Glaubenslehre,* we must look more closely at his understanding of the "material principle" of Reformed theology, for it is precisely at this point that twentieth-century criticism of his historical work has been focused. The Reformed "material principle," Schweizer said, differs from its Lutheran counterpart in that it is far less receptive to being cast in the "form of a *Principialsatz.*" The feeling of absolute dependence on God is "not one dogma alongside of others . . . it is much rather the most heightened religious feeling and consciousness itself and as a result, it will be everywhere present and will work in the whole of dogmatics as its all-permeating soul. . . ."[6] Thus, in its original and pure form, the "material principle" which Schweizer ascribed to Reformed theology is not a doctrine at all. Dogmatics will inevitably seek to articulate the contents of this apprehension in the form of a doctrine (and did so classically in the locus entitled "the decrees of God"), but that occurs at a second step, removed from the original apprehension. The significance of this (thoroughly Schleiermacherian) distinction between the contents of religious consciousness and its doctrinal articulation — as applied to the notion of a "material principle" — is that, for Schweizer, the value of an articulated "material principle" was only relative. However central it may be for dogmatics as a whole, a "material principle" stands under the same reservation to which all doctrine is subjected in a Schleiermacherian framework: it is a thoroughly fallible attempt to articulate the contents of the original apprehension and, as such, stands in constant need of correction. Given all of this, it would have been very surprising indeed had Schweizer envisioned a *system* of

---

5. Schweizer, *Die Glaubenslehre der evangelisch-reformierten Kirche,* 1:42. It is hard not to hear in such statements the later judgment of Karl Barth, that the principal difference between the Lutheran and the Reformed views of justification lay in the fact that, whereas the Lutherans were interested primarily in the faith which justifies, the Reformed were interested in the God who justifies through faith. "[T]he Reformed faith differs from the Lutheran in that the essence of it is not *fiducia,* though that is part of it: the essence of it is that it is *God's gift* . . . ; here all Christianity, including faith, is a human totality pointing to a Creator and Redeemer; here the final interest is in God and only in God." Karl Barth, "Reformierte Lehre, ihr Wesen und ihre Aufgabe," in Barth, *Das Wort Gottes und die Theologie* (Munich: Chr. Kaiser Verlag, 1924), p. 207; ET, "The Doctrinal Task of the Reformed Churches," in *The Word of God and the Word of Man* (Gloucester, Mass.: Peter Smith, 1978), p. 263. There can be little question that Barth's interpretation of the Reformed tradition — especially in the formative decade of the 1920s — owed a good deal to the historical work of Alexander Schweizer, though Barth scarcely ever acknowledged the debt.

6. Schweizer, *Die Glaubenslehre der evangelisch-reformierten Kirche,* 1:43.

doctrine derived more or less deductively from a single material norm. The critical distance which he maintained from all doctrinal explications of the religious consciousness would never have allowed such a move. And the truth is that he did not take that step. What Schweizer did say was that the "material principle" — once articulated — will condition the contents of the other doctrines.[7] But that is not to make of theology a deductive system; it is simply to lay stress on the interconnectedness of all dogmatic thinking.[8]

Schweizer's thesis that predestination constituted the doctrinal articulation of the "material principle" of Reformed theology was further elaborated and defended ten years later in a genetic-historical study entitled *Die protestantischen Centraldogmen,* and to this day it remains one of the most impressive attempts to trace the evolution of Reformed theology.[9] Certainly, it did much to shape the historiography of classical Reformed theology throughout the remainder of the nineteenth century. In this work Schweizer declared the doctrine of predestination to be the "center" of a constellation of "central doctrines" (shared with Lutheranism) and made this center the focal point of his genetic study. To that extent, we are justified in attributing to Schweizer the view that there was a single "central doctrine" of Reformed theology and that that doctrine was predestination.[10]

With the historical work behind him, Schweizer proceeded in the 1860s to produce his own constructive theology. Already the title is quite significant, for it testifies to Schweizer's deepest-lying ecclesial concerns: *Die christliche*

---

7. Schweizer, *Die Glaubenslehre der evangelisch-reformierten Kirche,* 1:44.

8. The critical distinction between the unthematized contents of the religious consciousness and their subsequent doctrinal articulation had the same significance for Schleiermacher and Schweizer that the critical distinction between the Word and the human words (employed to bear witness to the Word) had for Karl Barth; viz., both distinctions had the effect of relativizing all doctrinal formulations — a move which gave to both approaches to dogmatics a quite definite *un*dogmatic character.

9. Alexander Schweizer, *Die protestantischen Centraldogmen in ihrer Entwicklung innerhalb der reformierten Kirche,* 2 vols. (Zürich: Orell, Füssli und Comp., 1854-56).

10. Brian Gerrish has made much of the fact that Schweizer spoke of "central doctrines" (plural) and not of a single "central doctrine." His goal in doing so is to set aside the mistaken idea that Schweizer believed that there existed a "central dogma" from which "the rest could be derived or developed." Gerrish, p. 147. Gerrish is absolutely right in insisting that Schweizer did not hold to a "central dogma" in the sense described. But this does not exclude the possibility that Schweizer held that there was a single "central doctrine" of Reformed theology in a different sense. The fact is, as Gerrish also readily acknowledges, that Schweizer did believe that the doctrine of predestination was the *Mittelpunkt* around which other "central doctrines" were clustered and that, as such, it "determined" their shape and content. See Schweizer, *Die protestantischen Centraldogmen,* 1:16. But if the so-called central doctrines are clustered around one of their number as the center, then surely that doctrine must be "central" in a way that the others are not.

Glaubenslehre nach protestantischen Grundsätzen.[11] What Schweizer was offering was a *Glaubenslehre* for a united church (Reformed and Lutheran) such as had existed in Germany since the Prussian Union of 1817.[12] Drawing upon what he regarded as the best elements of both theological traditions, Schweizer skillfully synthesized them into a coherent whole. As in his previous works, so too here the contribution the Reformed tradition could make to a union church lay close to his heart. But it was also clear to him that modifications of that tradition would have to occur if its most basic concerns were to be united with those of the Lutheran tradition. And so it happened that Schweizer now set forth as the "material principle" of the *Evangelical Protestant* Church in terms of the *Grundsatz* that "only in faith in divine grace in Christ is justification to be attained."[13] Historically, this *"oberste Materialprinzip"* which was basic to both traditions was modified by each (according to their differing orientations) and given a slightly different form (which, as before, Schweizer defined as anthropological on the one side and theological on the other).[14] But such modifications were seen by Schweizer to be the result of historical conditions which no longer pertained and which were, consequently, dispensable. The goal of a contemporary *Glaubenslehre* must be to recast the idea in a purer form. Not surprisingly, this conviction gave to Schweizer a tremendous freedom in his handling of the "central doctrine" of the Reformed churches. In his hands, the doctrine in its traditional form was subjected to a fairly radical recasting. No longer was it a doctrine of decrees (an idea Schweizer found insuperably problematic), but a doctrine of "applicative grace"; i.e., it provided an answer to the question as to how human beings appropriate the redemption actualized in Christ (thereby also answering the question of why some people believe and others do not).[15]

Unfortunately for Schweizer, the timing of the publication of his dogmatics was not propitious. Albrecht Ritschl's more historically oriented approach to dogmatics was the wave of the future (at least for the last third of the nineteenth century), and that meant that a strict *Bewußtseinstheologie* like Schweizer's would not attain a great following. And with the onset of the Barthian revolution, the historiography created by Schweizer was also swept aside.

11. Alexander Schweizer, *Die christliche Glaubenslehre nach protestantischen Grundsätzen,* 2nd ed., 2 vols. (Leipzig: S. Hirzel, 1877). It should be noted that the first volume made its first appearance in 1863; the second in 1872.

12. See especially Schweizer, *Die christliche Glaubenslehre,* 1:4-36.

13. Schweizer, *Die christliche Glaubenslehre,* 1:193.

14. Schweizer, *Die christliche Glaubenslehre,* 1:193.

15. We will return to a closer examination of Schweizer's doctrine of "applicative grace" in the next section.

It was Barth himself who laid the theological foundations for what became the standard criticism of Schweizer's historical work. In his first lectures on dogmatics, given in Göttingen in 1924, Barth emphatically rejected the notion of a "material principle" in dogmatics. "Strictly speaking, there is *no* material principle, *no Fundamentalsatz.*"[16] What Barth was rejecting under this heading, however, was the thought of a material dogmatic norm, given *in advance* of the encounter with revelation through Scripture (through, let us say, the *experience* of justification) and requiring only to be validated by means of a *subsequent* appeal to Scripture as the so-called "formal" norm.

> For the *Lutheran* dogmatician, it is self-evident that dogmatics is constituted through the combination of the formal principle . . . with a so-called *material principle.* . . . On the basis of this content, which in the prolegomena to Lutheran dogmatics is at once stated and established as a so-called basic principle [*Fundamentalsatz*], dogmatics proper will then be analytically developed with the help of the formal principle, usually in the form of a so-called *system.* The system is nothing other than the logical unfolding of the basic principle and its individual parts.[17]

Against such a procedure, Barth said it is the task of dogmatics to critically test *all* pious words which give expression to the contents of the religious consciousness (and that includes any supposed fundamental doctrine) by the *one* norm of doctrine in the church: the Word of God himself as witnessed to by the canonical Scriptures. He and he alone is the fullness of content, the "formal" principle and the "material" principle in one. The source of doctrine in the church is Scripture alone, for it is only in and through Scripture that the Word makes himself available in the church. Given the pluriformity of the

---

16. Karl Barth, *"Unterricht in der christlichen Religion": Erster Band, Prolegomena, 1924,* ed. Hannelotte Reiffen (Zürich: TVZ, 1985), p. 365.

17. Barth, *"Unterricht in der christlichen Religion": Erster Band,* p. 362. Whether Barth was being altogether fair to Lutheran dogmaticians of his time in attributing to them such a bold conception of a "material principle" (i.e., in the sense of a material norm distinct from Scripture which is rightfully employed as a source for the remaining contents of dogmatics) is a question which will have to be left open here. Suffice it to say that there was precedent for the kind of understanding which Barth here describes. C. E. Luthardt, for example, having defined the doctrine of justification by faith as the material principle of "Lutheran Protestantism," went on to say: "The material principle . . . forms the genetic principle of development for dogmatics; the holy Scripture as the documentary report of the saving revelation forms the normative means of proof [*Beweismittel*] for the individual statements of dogmatics." See Luthardt, *Kompendium der Dogmatik,* 3rd ed. (Leipzig: Dörffling und Franke, 1868), p. 23. It should be noted that Luthardt's "Compendium" was among the works cited by Barth in support of his reading of Lutheran dogmatics.

scriptural witness, it follows quite naturally that a "system" of doctrine will be extremely unlikely and — on Barth's view — is something not to be sought.[18] For these reasons, he opted to organize the contents of dogmatics loosely, along the lines of *loci communes*.[19] Barth was quite confident that in taking this stance, he had the Reformed tradition on his side.

> The Reformed confessions distinguished themselves from the Augustana . . . by placing themselves in a measured distance from the *one object* of all doctrine, not staking everything on *one doctrine* but rather . . . satisfying themselves with relating all doctrine to the one object; leaving it to God to be *the* truth — not their *thoughts* about God but God *Himself,* God *alone* in His *Word. . . .*[20]

In the decade that followed, Barth's position on these questions moderated to some extent. In large measure this was due to the fact that with the development of his concept of analogy, he was able to place a much higher valuation on doctrine. In his *Church Dogmatics,* the emphasis would fall not so much on the distance which separates all doctrine from the object to which it testifies, but rather on the analogical *relation* of the two. And so, it could come about that in *Church Dogmatics* II/2 he could calmly say, "It is a well-known historical fact that more than any other doctrine the doctrine of predestination stamped itself upon the face of the Reformed Church, or rather of 16th and 17th century Reformed theology, thus distinguishing it from others."[21] Such a position did not signal a retreat from his early objections to the notion of a "material principle"; and he still denied that the doctrine of predestination had served as such a principle in classical Reformed theology.[22] But he had arrived at a more balanced assessment of the importance of the doctrine, not only for the old Reformed but for his own theology as well; an importance

18. Barth, *"Unterricht in der christlichen Religion": Erster Band,* p. 368.

19. Karl Barth, *"Unterricht in der christlichen Religion"; Zweiter Band: Die Lehre von Gott/Die Lehre vom Menschen, 1924/25,* ed. Hinrich Stoevesandt (Zürich: TVZ, 1990), p. 8.

20. Barth, "Reformierte Lehre, ihr Wesen und ihre Aufgabe," p. 189.

21. Karl Barth, *Church Dogmatics* II/2 (Edinburgh: T. & T. Clark, 1957), p. 36.

22. Barth, *Church Dogmatics* II/2, pp. 77-78: "[T]here can be no historical justification for taking the concept 'central dogma' to mean that the doctrine of predestination was for the older Reformed theologians a kind of speculative key — a basic tenet from which they could deduce all other dogmas. Not even the famous schema of T. Beza was intended in such a sense. Its aim was rather . . . to show the systematic interconnexion of all other dogmas with that of predestination in the then popular graphic fashion. There was no question of making the latter doctrine a derivative principle for the rest. And even in the *Westminster Confession* . . . it was not a matter of deducing all dogmatics from the doctrine of predestination."

which he expressed not in the language of a "material principle" but in the language of "the sum of the gospel."[23]

In the third section of this paper, we will be looking more closely at what Barth meant in speaking of the doctrine of election as "the sum of the gospel." The point to be made here, in advance of that discussion, is that in coming to this position Barth had moved much closer to the view of the importance of the doctrine which had actually been intended by Alexander Schweizer; i.e., what Schweizer intended by the language "material principle" and "central doctrine" is quite close to what Barth meant by "sum of the gospel." And this is a fact which has been largely lost on those influenced by Barth's earliest comments on the problem.

Historians today are by and large united in rejecting the validity of Schweizer's assessment of the importance of the doctrine of predestination for classical Reformed theology — especially as it touches upon Calvin. Many there are today who would argue that Calvin's theology had no center at all. Among those who think there was at least some kind of existential center, the leading candidate is his eucharistic theology and the Christology which underlay it, *not* his doctrine of predestination. It was Wilhelm Niesel, a student of Barth's during his Göttingen period, who first succeeded in marginalizing Calvin's doctrine of predestination vis-à-vis his theology as a whole. In his great work on Calvin's theology in 1938, Niesel noted the then still widespread view that predestination was Calvin's central dogma and observed:

> If this be the case, then all that we have so far said is false. Then Calvin's doctrines are not like so many signposts pointing through the far-ranging and complex fields of the Bible to the one incarnate God. It would rather be true to say that Calvin's theology is a system of thoughts about God and humankind proceeding from the one thought of the utter dependence of humanity upon God.[24]

Niesel's tendency to minimize the importance of Calvin's doctrine of election was given added impetus by Francois Wendel in 1952. Wendel's argument was based largely on external considerations of arrangement (the doctrine of predestination only appears at the end of book 3 of the 1559 *Institutes* and receives scant mention elsewhere).[25] While there is no doubt a great mea-

---

23. Barth, *Church Dogmatics* II/2, p. 1.

24. Wilhelm Niesel, *The Theology of Calvin*, trans. Harold Knight (Grand Rapids: Baker, 1980), pp. 159-60.

25. Francois Wendel, *Calvin: Origins and Development of His Religious Thought* (Durham, N.C.: Labyrinth Press, 1987), pp. 263f. Wendel singles out Schweizer as the source of the — in his view — mistaken notion that predestination was the "central doctrine" in Cal-

sure of truth in the current consensus on Calvin (it being readily granted that there is no *systematic* center to Calvin's theology), it is a truth whose significance is easily overstated. There is grave danger today that the oft-repeated judgment that predestination was of marginal importance for Calvin might easily lead to the conclusion that it ought to be of marginal importance for Reformed Christians in the present as well. And that would be a great pity, for not only would the errant notion of a double predestination be affected but, along with it, the utterly central truth of the unconditionality of divine grace.

Alexander Schweizer and Karl Barth were at one in the belief that, whatever critical corrections may be necessary with regard to the form which the doctrine of predestination was given in the sixteenth and seventeenth centuries, the theological intention which lay behind it was essentially correct. For both, the heart of that intention lay in the emphasis on the unconditionality of grace, while the form (the dualism between elect and reprobate) was a secondary question (and in their view, easily amended). And they were united in the belief that the doctrine of predestination, rightly interpreted, is of central importance for Christian theology as a whole and, as such, cannot be minimized without doing serious damage to the Reformed witness to the truth revealed in Jesus Christ. In the exposition which follows, it should become clear that if there is a genuine heir of the most basic theological concerns which lay behind Alexander Schweizer's appropriation of the Reformed tradition, that heir would have to be Karl Barth.[26]

---

vin's theology. But as Brian Gerrish rightly points out, Wendel never bothered to ask what Schweizer meant by a "central doctrine." See Gerrish, p. 147.

26. I must leave to one side at this point the intriguing question as to the accuracy of Schweizer's historical judgment with respect to the Reformed tradition in order to concentrate on the systematic question of the proper place and significance of the doctrine of election in Christian dogmatics. With regard to Schweizer's reading of the tradition, I will only say that I think the question of the importance of the doctrine for Calvin's theology as a whole (or for Zwingli's theology, for that matter) has yet to be treated with the care it deserves. When it is, we may well find that the nineteenth-century historians knew far more than they are usually given credit for and that — in the words of Brian Gerrish — "Schweizer may well offer the most serious alternative — at least in kind — to Barthian historiography of the period . . ." (p. 146). The only point to be added is that the most penetrating critic of "Barthian historiography" in the twentieth century is Karl Barth himself! Consider for example the following passage in which Barth, having granted the validity of the protest raised by his Calvin-scholar brother Peter and his student Niesel against the thought that predestination constituted for Calvin "a basic tenet from which all other doctrines may be deduced," raises a caveat against the new "Barthian historiography." "But we must still ask whether in combatting this traditional error some recent writers have not underestimated the function of the doctrine in Calvin's theology." Is not that which Calvin says with regard to this doctrine "far too important and far too prominent for us to be able to say that this

The Doctrine of God and Applicative Grace: Alexander Schweizer

In his own constructive theology, Alexander Schweizer's reflections on election (or "applicative grace") were everywhere controlled by decisions already made in his doctrine of God. Our task in this section will be to show the extent to which Schweizer's revised doctrine of election was built on a foundation laid in his doctrine of God.

Schweizer built up his doctrine of God in three stages which reflect his most basic decision that the doctrines taught in the Christian churches should be *Glaubenslehre* — deliverances of the religious consciousness. The most general sphere in which the awareness of absolute dependence on God is discerned by the pious is the world of nature. In this sphere the religious consciousness discerns the world's absolute dependence on God for its existence. In accordance with this awareness, religion posits God as the Creator and Sustainer of the world and accordingly ascribes to God the corresponding attributes of omnipotence *(Allmacht)* and omniscience *(Allwissenheit)*. Because, however, the "all" contained in these terms is too indefinite, "pious interest" cannot rest content with them but must press on (through the *via negativa*) to heighten these attributes to the level of the infinite. When this is done, the result is that these two basic attributes are seen to have been at work always and everywhere; i.e., "the basic attributes of omnipotence and omniscience are *eternal* and *omnipresent* in their efficacy."[27] The second sphere in which the pious subject discerns her absolute dependence upon God is that of ethical life. Here God is seen as the One who calls ethical life into existence and rules over it. The attributes which modify the divine causality in the ethical world are goodness and holiness, wisdom and righteousness. Here again, these attributes are eternal and omnipresent in their efficacy, which tells us that God is truthfulness and faithfulness in itself (i.e., "eternity" and "omnipresence" carry with them the thought of a "timeless" consistency in God's operations — a faith-

---

doctrine should not be used, and that Calvin did not mean it to be used, to shed decisive light on all that precedes and follows? Undoubtedly Calvin did not understand or handle the doctrine as a basic tenet. But this does not mean that he placed it on the same level as all the rest. Between these two views there is a third. What Calvin did appear to find in the doctrine of election was this: a final word (and thereby also a first word) concerning the entire reality of the Christian life, a word which tells that the Christian life has its existence, its continuance and its future utterly and wholly on the basis of the free grace of God. But all Christian doctrine, even that of God at the beginning and that of the Church at the end, deals substantially with this reality of the Christian life, with the life of the person whom God has claimed for Himself in Jesus Christ. And if this be the case, then how can we help thinking of the doctrine of election as the last or first word of the whole of Christian doctrine?" Barth, *Church Dogmatics* II/2, p. 86.

27. Schweizer, *Die christliche Glaubenslehre*, 1:241.

fulness of God to himself in all times and places). The third and highest sphere in which the pious discerns her absolute dependence on God is that of the religious life. Here God is seen to be the sole author of our salvation, and the corresponding attributes which the pious person ascribes to God are love, fatherly wisdom, and forbearing mercy. It should be noted that Schweizer has here moved throughout from the general to the particular (from the lowest or most general level of pious awareness to its most fully developed, redemptive form). Thus, the second stage builds upon the knowledge given in the first, and the third stage builds upon the knowledge given in the first two stages.

The conception of God which emerges from all of this corresponds in most of its details with the God of classical theism. Schweizer wanted nothing to do with pantheism or even with what is widely referred to today as "panentheism" (i.e., process theological conceptions).

> That it [the world] is related to Him [God] . . . as the body is to the soul (God thereby being seen as the world-soul) appears to be an insufficient illustration, for so far as we know the body is not absolutely dependent upon the soul. Rather, the body interacts with the soul. Therefore, the soul is also dependent upon the body, whereas God is in no way dependent upon the world. The opinion according to which God first comes to consciousness in the course of time by means of the world and perfects Himself through the world successively ennobled by Him contradicts the religious idea of God, even though one adds by way of explanation that the Self-perfecting of God precedes by an immeasurable distance the perfecting of the world. For a God who in this way or any other must first perfect Himself, a becoming God, is not the God of the religious consciousness.[28]

For Schweizer, God is the sovereign Creator and Ruler of the world who is in no way conditioned by the world.[29] He also rejected every version of

---

28. Schweizer, *Die christliche Glaubenslehre,* 1:269-70; cf. p. 253.

29. In its *original* usage, the term "panentheism" would not have been inappropriately applied to Schweizer — or to Schleiermacher for that matter. The term was the invention of one Karl Friedrich Christian Krause, a contemporary of Schleiermacher, who used it to describe a view in accordance with which (1) God is understood to transcend the world as the source of its existence (God and the world are not identical); and (2) the "world" is understood to be "in" God, not "outside" of God. See Rudolf Eisler, *Wörterbuch der philosophischen Begriffe,* vol. 2 (Berlin: Mittler und Sohn, 1910), p. 970. Thus defined, Schweizer (and Schleiermacher) would qualify as panentheists, but to avoid confusion with process theology it is necessary today to add a modifier. Schweizer and his great mentor might well be styled "*absolute* panentheists" in order to lay stress on their shared conviction that there is no reciprocity in the God-world relation; i.e., what happens in the world does not condition God. God — we might accurately say — is the Absolute, the Unconditioned.

emanationism,[30] as well as the notion that God created the world as a builder does, out of materials found ready to hand. For him, everything that is (including the so-called "chaos" of Genesis 1)[31] owes its existence absolutely to the power of God.

But Schweizer also departed from classical theism in two notable ways. He held, first, that the world has no beginning and no end. Did that make the world eternal and therefore undermine the Creator/creature distinction that he was concerned everywhere else to maintain? No. The fundamental distinction between God and the world for Schweizer is that God alone is "eternal" (in the sense of completely transcending time); the world, however, is structured by time. The word Schweizer chooses to describe the existence of the world is *Sempiternität*[32] ("always existing" — from the Latin *sempiternitas*); a word which suggests something of temporal structure (in the root word *semper* — "always").[33] Schweizer was moved to this conception above all by the belief that if the all-powerful God is eternally and omnipresently effective (as the religious consciousness in the natural sphere says he is), then he must always have created the world. It was unthinkable for Schweizer that an all-powerful God could ever have lacked an object upon which to exercise his omnipotence; or that a living God could be conceived of as ever having been completely at rest and only moving into action at a point in time. He buttressed this line of argumentation (which was based on deliverances of the religious consciousness) with the further argument that the idea of a beginning to the world is self-contradictory. If the world had a beginning in time, then there must have been something "before" time. But since one cannot speak of this "before" without projecting the notion of time — which belongs properly to creation — back into a premundane world, then the conception of a beginning of the world leads to irresolvable contradiction. The net effect of these rather Origenistic considerations was that God's creative action must be conceived of as an eternal one, not a temporal one. And that also means that creation was not completed in a moment of time. Creation is a continuous divine activity,

---

30. Schweizer, *Die christliche Glaubenslehre*, 1:245.

31. Schweizer, *Die christliche Glaubenslehre*, 1:243.

32. Schweizer, *Die christliche Glaubenslehre*, 1:266.

33. This distinction between "eternity" (as an attribute of God) and *Sempiternität* (as an attribute of the world) is not simply a linguistic trick; it rests on a real distinction between the kind of being God has and the kind of being the world has. "[A] world without a beginning is still a world, i.e. something existing in time and space and therefore, structured and divided into parts, at every point conditioned and conditioning, changeable, in all of its particulars transient or mutable, limited or finite through and through. God, however, is the very opposite of all that." Schweizer, *Die christliche Glaubenslehre*, 1:266.

according to Schweizer, and cannot finally be separated from God's providential upholding of the world.[34]

Schweizer's other deviation from classical theism lay in his conviction that creation was in a sense necessary for God. It should be noted that he was not altogether happy with the language. Freedom and necessity, he said, are antithetically related only for humans, not for God. Properly formulated, the question should read: Are the works of God accidentally or necessarily related to the being of God? Schweizer noted that even the old Reformed dogmaticians had understood the world planned for by God (in the doctrine of the decrees) to be the best of all possible worlds and, as such, a perfect reflection on the creaturely level of the divine being — i.e., not accidentally but necessarily related to the divine being. The only remaining question then is whether God could have chosen not to create at all. Schweizer's answer to this question is already contained in the previous paragraph. God must always have created if he is the eternally omnipotent, all-knowing God. And since the world he created was the expression of his being, creation was a necessity for God.[35] Schweizer is quick to point out, however, that this "necessity" has its ground in the divine being, not in anything external to him. "One cannot say that God would have had to create the world even if He had not wanted to; as little as one can say that He desired it out of need, to remedy some lack in Himself."[36]

How is all of this then related to Schweizer's doctrine of election? Schweizer's criticism of the classical doctrine of the decrees, so far as it touches upon election, was already prepared for by his criticism of the same in relation to the doctrine of creation. In both cases the idea of decrees is rejected on the grounds that it is too anthropomorphic. It envisions God as a wise man who carefully considers all the options open before him before selecting the best among them and acting. God, said Schweizer, does not have to reflect first on the problem of which of all possible worlds is the best; he knows the best option (the one most in accordance with his own being) by means of his perfect and immediate self-knowledge and does it automatically, by an eternal action. Therefore, there can be no temporal or quasi-temporal gap between thought and action, between a so-called world plan (contained in the doctrine of decrees) and the act of creation. Similarly, in the case of election, God does not have to first reflect on the problem of how best to illustrate his glory — for the simple reason that the problem does not exist for him. He necessarily and immediately does that which is consistent with his being as love. When con-

34. Schweizer, *Die christliche Glaubenslehre*, 1:244.

35. Schweizer, *Die christliche Glaubenslehre*, 1:260-63.

36. Schweizer, *Die christliche Glaubenslehre*, 1:268.

fronted by sin, he responds graciously. Thus, creation and election stand in a relationship of the most perfect analogy. Both refer to an eternal action, consistent in all times and places.

It should be noted, however, that creation and election have this relation only because they are determined for it in advance by Schweizer's doctrine of God. The foundation for the whole of Schweizer's theology of creation and redemption is laid in the doctrine of the eternally active, omnipotent, and omniscient God (which is to say, in the doctrine of the divine attributes). It is only because God is what he is that creation and election are *necessarily* what they are. But then, it must also be noted in turn that Schweizer has built his doctrine of God on a foundation laid by a process of abstraction (i.e., through the *via eminentiae* and the *via negativa*) from alleged deliverances of the religious consciousness in the sphere of nature. Thus, every attribute ascribed to God as the absolute cause of the world at the first stage controls and determines in advance what may be said of God at the second and third stages, thereby controlling the doctrine of redemption as well.

The stage is now set for Schweizer's revision of the doctrine of election. The eternal ground of grace is located by Schweizer in the being of God himself, rather than in divine "decrees" — it being a fixed principle for him that "what God does in time must be grounded in His eternal being."[37] "Grace" is the divine attribute of love insofar as that love is confronted by sinful human beings. Thus, the word refers to a modification in the divine relating to human beings which occurs as a result of sin. Grace, being a modification of the eternally and omnipresently active divine attribute of love, cannot be contingent upon the presence or absence of faith in men and women. If the love of God is eternally and omnipresently active, then it will (by definition) be universal in its scope. Therefore grace, too, is universal in its scope.[38]

But then the question arises: If grace is universal, why is it that some believe and others do not? The answer lies in the nature of "applicative grace." Applicative grace, for Schweizer, is not an irresistible, compulsive force.[39] It does not overwhelm the individual but must be willingly received. It works more or less naturally, through the orders of life which have been ordained by God. So, whether a person responds to grace offered depends on the conditions of life in which that person is found. Some are predisposed to respond in faith; others are not. That this difference among men and women arises at all is not accidental; it is itself a function of God's providential ruling of the world.

Thus, "in its eternal nature grace is *universal,* but in its historical effects it

37. Schweizer, *Die christliche Glaubenslehre*, 2:307.
38. Schweizer, *Die christliche Glaubenslehre*, 1:394-400, 406-22.
39. Schweizer, *Die christliche Glaubenslehre*, 2:313-21.

is *particular*"[40] — and both the universality and the particularity are expressions of the will of God. Is then God's will to be gracious toward all frustrated when some do not believe? Schweizer's answer is no; God's grace must ultimately triumph over all human resistance (though this may happen in many cases only in an afterlife). There are, of course, problems with this solution. Schweizer has really succeeded only in relocating the irresistibility of the divine willing in the doctrine of providence, not in eliminating it, as he clearly wanted to do. If the free decisions of men and women are conditioned by the circumstances of their lives and those circumstances are themselves a function of God's providential rule, then God's will still remains irresistible in the only meaningful sense of the word. Schweizer has simply made election to be a subcategory of providence; the determinism present in his doctrine of providence is the silent presence which presides over his revised doctrine of election.

More serious, however, are the problems which arise as a result of Schweizer's method. What Schweizer did was to generate first a doctrine of God (on the basis of deliverances of the religious consciousness operating in the sphere of nature) and then make the doctrine of election (or applicative grace) to be a function of it. There are at least two problems with this procedure. The first is that it produces an absolute God which can only with great difficulty be reconciled with the God of the Bible. It is this concept of God which then controls all that follows. Second, on an even more basic level, Schweizer's starting point in the religious consciousness does not allow him to accomplish what he wanted to accomplish in his revision of the classical doctrine of the decrees. Schweizer wanted to show that what God does in time is grounded in God's eternal being. But his method will not finally yield such a statement. Employed with strict consistency, a theology of religious consciousness will not finally be able to tell us anything about what God is in himself; it will only tell us something about how God relates to human beings. Schweizer tells us as much in the context of his rejection of the doctrine of an ontological Trinity.[41] The so-called attributes of God are then not so much attributes of *God* as they are attributes of the relation between an unknown God and human beings.[42] Schweizer has made a herculean effort to narrow the gap between the being of God "in himself" and the being of God "for us" through his repeated insistence that the being of God is pure actuosity; there is no final distinction, he says, between the "attributes" of God (omnipotence and omni-

---

40. Gerrish, p. 141.

41. Schweizer, *Die christliche Glaubenslehre*, 1:404.

42. Schweizer, *Die christliche Glaubenslehre*, 1:408: "Because all divine attributes are built up as determinations of the divine causality . . . therefore, they should correspond to the *works* of God" (emphasis mine).

science) and the "functions" of God (creation and providence).[43] So, in a real sense, God is what God does. The problem is that Schweizer's method will not really allow him to say this. In order to be in the position to say that God *is* what God does, Schweizer would have to know something of what God is in himself. But Schweizer preferred at the decisive point to remain consistent with his method and disdained all claims to knowledge of God in himself. The effect of these methodological difficulties is that they thoroughly undermine Schweizer's central conviction in the doctrine of applicative grace: that what God does in time is grounded in the eternal being of God. If we follow Schweizer's method to the end, we can never be sure that God really is the gracious God he *appears* to be in his works. In truth, what Schweizer hoped to accomplish with his revision of the doctrine of predestination can only be fully realized with a quite different theological method.

In spite of Schweizer's radical reinterpretation of the doctrine, his belief that something essential to Christian religious consciousness lay behind it was clearly a constant in all of his life's work. The doctrine of predestination, as Brian Gerrish has put it, "answers to quite essential devout feelings, which a purer manner of doctrine must not curtail. The heart of these feelings lies in the humility that ascribes the entire life of salvation wholly to the grace of God as its eternal foundation."[44] The only remaining question then is whether Schweizer understood his revised doctrine of election as something like the "central doctrine" of his *Glaubenslehre*. There can be little question but that that was his intention. He did, after all, make grace (and justification) to be the "material principle" of his "Protestant" theology. And he understood a "material principle" to be "a governing doctrine, on which other doctrines are dependent." Hence, he could maintain, "the methodological division must . . . lift them [the twin doctrines of grace and justification] up as of decisive impor-

---

43. Schweizer, *Die christliche Glaubenslehre*, 1:235-36.

44. Gerrish, p. 138. Gerrish is perhaps guilty of overstatement when he writes, "[I]f the earlier, historical studies had already led us to anticipate, not a recital, but a recasting of the old dogmas which would carry him beyond historical analysis, we are scarcely prepared for the radicalness of the final, constructive work. We expect a recasting of the dogma of predestination: what we find is more like a discarding of it" (p. 136). If our expectations based on Schweizer's earlier works are confounded, that might easily be taken to imply that Schweizer had changed his mind with regard to his original conviction that the doctrine of predestination had in it an idea which was essential to Christian faith. And that, I think, would be a mistaken reading. It is quite true, of course, that Schweizer abandoned the classical *form* of the doctrine of predestination (i.e., the doctrine of the decrees). But he could not abandon the essential idea which lay behind it, for he continued to regard that idea (viz., that redemption is wholly dependent on divine grace alone) as the (wholly salutary) Reformed contribution to a synthetically conceived "material principle" of the Protestant churches. See Schweizer, *Die christliche Glaubenslehre*, 1:8-12, 190-208.

tance which would not be the case if the governing doctrines appear merely as individuals in a series of others. . . . Much rather, the chief division of the material will already make clear its determination by those governing doctrines as *Prinzipien*."[45] Thus, Schweizer's intention is clear. But it has to be admitted that Schweizer was unable to adequately fulfill this intention. His doctrine of God was almost entirely fleshed out without reference to grace and justification. And when grace is finally introduced as a modification in an essential attribute of God, its content is controlled by that doctrine of God. Thus, if Schweizer's intentions were to be fulfilled, a different framework of thought would be required.

Election and the Doctrine of God: Karl Barth

That election is "the sum of the gospel" was grounded by Karl Barth in the fundamental claim that the primary object of election is not humankind, but God himself. In Barth's view, the primal decision of God (the "decree" if you will) is to never be God apart from humankind. Alternately expressed, God chooses himself for us; he decides himself for grace. In this wholly gracious, wholly free, unconditioned primal decision of God for grace is contained *in nuce* all else that follows in time:[46] the election of the eternal Son for incarnation, suffering, and death on a cross; the election in him of the whole of humanity for communion with God; the outpouring of the Spirit, the creation and upbuilding of a community of believers who represent the whole of humanity. It is at this point that Barth's most original contribution to the historical development of the doctrine of election must be seen to lie. In making God not only the subject of election but also its primary object, Barth was making election the key to his doctrine of God. Barth would have been in formal agreement with the Schweizerian dictum ". . . what God does in time must be grounded in the eternal being of God"; indeed, it was one of his most cherished convictions. But the material connections in which such a claim stands

---

45. Schweizer, *Die christliche Glaubenslehre*, 1:90.

46. Barth, *Church Dogmatics* II/2, pp. 13-14: "[T]he election of grace is the whole of the Gospel, the Gospel *in nuce*. It is the very essence of good news. . . . God is God in His being as the One who loves in freedom. This is revealed as a benefit conferred upon us in the fact which *corresponds to the truth of God's being*, the fact that God elects in His grace, that He moves towards humanity in His dealings within this covenant with the one man Jesus and the people represented by Him. All the joy and benefit of His whole work as Creator, Reconciler and Redeemer . . . all these are grounded and determined in the fact that that God is the God of the eternal election of His grace. In the light of this election the whole of the Gospel is light" (emphasis mine).

in Barth's theology as a whole give to it a very different meaning than it had for Alexander Schweizer.

Barth took as the starting point for all of his dogmatic reflections the self-revelation of God in the history of Jesus Christ; i.e., the incarnation, life, death, resurrection, and ascension of the God-man. To put it this way is already to suggest that the starting point is not simply the man Jesus as he appeared on the surface of history. The starting point is the God-man as witnessed to in Scripture, and the history of this God-man begins in the way taken by God in taking to himself a fully human life as his very own (in all of its limitations, up to and including death). It is that history which Barth has in mind.

On the basis of this self-revelation, he then asked, what must God be like if he can do what he has in fact done? What is the condition of the possibility in eternity for the incarnation, death, and resurrection of the Son of God in time? In taking this approach, Barth was taking a principled stance against the more traditional procedure (followed in large measure by Schweizer) of beginning with an "abstract" concept of God (which is to say, one that has been completely fleshed out without reference to God's self-revelation in Christ), and only then turning to that revelation to find in it confirmation of what was already attributed to God without it. Such a procedure, as we have already seen in relation to Schweizer, determines in advance what revelation in Christ will be allowed to say. Against this procedure employed by theism in all of its forms (classical and neo-Protestant), Barth proposed to work in an a posteriori fashion, beginning not with a general concept of God or a general concept of human being but with a most highly concrete reality, Jesus Christ.[47] And so, if God has in fact done something, it will not do to say that he cannot do it. Theologically responsible reflection will only be able to ask, what is the eternal ground for God's acts in time?

The effect of this procedure on the doctrine of election is as follows. The foundation of the doctrine of election is located by Barth in the single point in which God makes himself to be what he is — i.e., in Jesus Christ. When we concentrate our attention on this point, we find that "under this name God Himself realized in time, and therefore as an object of human perception, the Self-giving of Himself as the covenant partner of the people determined by Him from and to all eternity." We find that in what took place in Jesus Christ, "God Himself possesses this people: swearing to it the same fidelity He exercises towards Himself; directing to it a love no less than that with which, in the

---

47. Cf. Walter Kreck, *Grundentscheidungen in Karl Barths Dogmatik* (Neukirchen-Vluyn: Neukirchener Verlag, 1978), pp. 188f.; George Hunsinger, *How to Read Karl Barth: The Shape of His Theology* (New York: Oxford University Press, 1991), pp. 32-35.

person of the Son, He loves Himself; fulfilling His will upon earth as it is already fulfilled in heaven, in the eternal decree which precedes everything temporal."[48] We find, in other words, that the reconciliation accomplished in Christ is a wholly gracious event; i.e., it is based in a wholly unmerited, free divine decision.

The question now becomes, how can what God has done in Christ be seen to be the self-revelation of God, how can Jesus Christ be God in this movement, *unless* what God has done in time has its ground in the eternal being of God? And the answer is that the gracious work of God in time is indeed grounded in the divine being.

For Barth, the being of God is self-determined being; it is a being which God gives to himself in the primal decision in which he determines himself for this gracious relation to humankind. "We cannot go back on this decision if we would know God and speak accurately of God. If we did, we should be betrayed into a false abstraction which sought to speak only of God, not recognizing that when we speak of God, then in consideration of His freedom and of His free decision, we must also speak of this relationship."[49] God is God *only* in this gracious relation to humankind — by his own act of self-determination or "Self-ordination."[50] This decision — in which God ordains himself to have his being only in the gracious movement which reaches its climax in the cross and resurrection — is election. God elects himself for us in Jesus Christ. Such a conception of the wholly gracious being of God in relation to the world does not exclude, of course, the element of judgment or reprobation. But it does make comprehensible how and why this element must be the wholly subordinate servant of the purposes of grace. The divine No in which opposition to human sinfulness is expressed is the servant of the divine Yes of grace because grace is the beginning and end of all the ways of God in which God has his being.[51]

Election is the *primal* decision (in German "*Urentscheidung*") of God.[52] The word "primal" is meant to exclude every hint of temporality. The word has logical force, describing the "logical origin" behind which it is not possible to inquire further and, as such, takes the place of the category *Ursprung* which had been widely used in Barth's two commentaries on Romans. That there is nothing behind this decision means first of all that there are no heights or depths in the being of God which lie back of this decision (in which God might

---

48. Barth, *Church Dogmatics* II/2, p. 53.
49. Barth, *Church Dogmatics* II/2, p. 6.
50. Barth, *Church Dogmatics* II/2, p. 89.
51. Barth, *Church Dogmatics* II/2, pp. 12-13.
52. Barth, *Church Dogmatics* II/2, p. 50; cf. *Die kirchliche Dogmatik* II/2, pp. 53f.

somehow be other than the God of this gracious history). It means, second, that there is nothing outside of him which could condition this decision; it is the decision from which all the works of God flow (creation, reconciliation, and redemption). "There is no *extra* except that which has its basis and meaning as such in the divine election of grace."[53] Therefore, it is a completely free decision.

It should occasion no surprise that Barth's understanding of the primal character of divine election has enormous implications for his doctrine of God. Where for Schweizer the doctrine of God determined and shaped his doctrine of election, just the opposite is the case for Barth. It is his doctrine of election which controls the content of his doctrine of God.

> [T]he true God is the One whose freedom and love have nothing to do with abstract absoluteness or naked sovereignty, but who in His love and freedom has determined and limited Himself to be God in particular and not in general, and only as such to be omnipotent and sovereign and the possessor of all other perfections.[54]

God's perfections are what they are in the service of the divine decision for grace. And so the power of God, for example, is not to be defined in abstraction from the reconciling activity of God (and the eternal decision in which it is grounded). To ascribe "All-power" to God in the light of the divine election of grace is to say that God possesses all the power necessary to carry out his covenantal purposes with humankind. If this be true, it will not do to say, as Schweizer did, that the omnipotence of God must have a "sempiternal" world as an object upon which it can be exercised. Such a claim rests upon an abstract definition of "omnipotence." Rather, the meaning and significance of power in God are defined by God's eternal decision. Therefore, whatever use is made of power by God (in eternity as well as in time) will be in accordance with its meaning and significance as grounded in the eternal being of God, since whatever God does will be in accordance with the decision which determines the being of God. Schweizer's other thesis — that God cannot be conceived of as ever having been idle since (as pure actuosity) God cannot move from rest to action — falls to the ground for the same reason. Pure actuosity was defined by Schweizer in such a way as to allow for no real movement or change in the divine action. But such a definition is a mere abstraction; it bears no relation to the *history* of God's covenantal dealings with humankind as witnessed to in Scripture.

It is not hard to guess what Schweizer's objection to Barth's doctrine of

---

53. Barth, *Church Dogmatics* II/2, p. 95.
54. Barth, *Church Dogmatics* II/2, p. 49.

God would be. He would say that Barth's emphasis on decision, on the *freedom* of God in deciding to create, reconcile, and redeem, would make God arbitrary. Barth's answer would be sympathetic up to a point. Schweizer is absolutely correct in asserting that the works of God are not accidentally related to the divine being. But if the decision to create and redeem is already contained in the primal decision in which God's being is itself determined, then the decision to create and redeem is — by definition — fully consonant with the divine being. In fact, it is the expression of that being. Does the freedom of God as expressed in the primal decision mean that God could have decided *not* to create and redeem? Absolutely. God could have decided to be sufficient in himself, to possess in himself (in his triune being) the perfectly sufficient object of his love.

The promise contained in the Schweizerian principle, that what God does in time must be grounded in the eternal divine being, could not be realized by Schweizer himself because he was unable to secure it against doubts that God might not be in himself what he appears to us to be through his works. That promise is realized, however, by Karl Barth. For here, it finally becomes clear how the works of God are grounded in the eternal divine being as it really is in and for itself. We can have complete confidence that God will never turn out to be anything other than the God of electing grace.

The Sum of the Gospel: The Place of the Doctrine of Election in Barth's Theology

That the doctrine of election is the sum of the gospel means ultimately for Barth that it is a doctrine which shapes both the form and the content of all other doctrines.

> There can be no Christian truth which does not from the very first contain within itself as its basis the fact that from and to all eternity God is the electing God. There can be no tenet of Christian truth which, if it is to be a Christian tenet, does not necessarily reflect both in form and content this divine electing. . . . Because this is the case, the doctrine of election occupies a place at the head of all other Christian dogmas.[55]

In order to testify to the importance of the doctrine of election, Barth placed it within the doctrine of God, at the head of all other doctrines which speak of the works of God *ad extra* (creation, reconciliation, and redemption). In doing

---

55. Barth, *Church Dogmatics* II/2, p. 77.

so, he was quite aware that he was taking a step that was unprecedented in the history of Christian theology. But he felt that the step was justified. The doctrine of election is not only the first, last, and central word in the whole of the doctrine of reconciliation; it tells us "who and what God is in His dealings with His creation. . . ."[56] In truth, Barth's doctrine of election (in *Church Dogmatics* II/2) really ought to have come before his doctrine of the "perfections of God" (in II/1), for it is election which determines the meaning and significance of the divine perfections.[57] Be that as it may, it is clear that Barth's understanding of the doctrine of election as "the sum of the gospel" satisfies all the basic criteria of what Schweizer intended by the language of "central doctrine": it is a doctrine which determines the form and content of all other doctrines. Certainly, it is not a "material principle" in the analytic sense. But it is a doctrine which has a great deal of impact on the others.[58]

Is the doctrine of election, then, *the* central doctrine of Barth's theology? Is it the one doctrine which, more than any other, is the determinative center of Barth's theology? Our answer must be a cautious one. Barth's doctrine of election was, after all, christologically grounded — which means that the doctrine of election and Christology reciprocally condition each other at every point in a rather complex, dialectical way. It would be more accurate to say that

---

56. Barth, *Church Dogmatics* II/2, p. 88.

57. That Barth did not take this step was probably due to the circumstances of his theological development. In a recent work on the development of Barth's theology, I have argued that Barth's doctrine of election experienced significant material modification after he heard a lecture on the subject by Pierre Maury in 1936. See Bruce L. McCormack, *Karl Barth's Critically Realistic Dialectical Theology: Its Genesis and Development, 1909-1936* (Oxford: Clarendon Press, 1995), pp. 455f. The effects of that material decision on the doctrine of election were already felt in Barth's doctrine of the divine perfections (written in 1938-39), and therefore did impact his doctrine of God in the way we have described in this essay. But if the full methodological consequences of this material decision ever dawned on Barth, it could only have happened as he was at work on *Church Dogmatics* II/2, as he was at work on the problem of the place of the doctrine — by which time it was too late to alter the order of treatment.

58. If space permitted, it would be possible to demonstrate this in Barth's doctrines of creation, providence, and Christology. The internal basis of creation, Barth would later say, is the covenant — which makes God's gracious election to be the purpose expressed in all of God's creative activities (*Church Dogmatics* III/1). Likewise, the hidden ground and meaning of God's providential sustaining, accompanying, and governing of creation is once again the covenant made with humankind in Jesus Christ (III/3). Election even influences the material unfolding of Barth's Christology to the extent that the actualistic ontology entailed in the notion that God's being is self-determined being determines Barth's reinterpretation of the Chalcedonian formula — according to which the meaning of the two "natures" is defined by what God actually does and not through abstract concepts of "natures" (IV/1).

492

if Barth's theology had a "center" on the level of doctrinal expression, that center was an ellipse with two foci: election and Christology.

Conclusion

We have seen that Schweizer's intention of making the doctrine of election to be (at least a part of) the "central doctrine" of Christian theology and to ground everything he says in that doctrine in the eternal being of God could not be realized within the framework provided by his starting point and method. It was, however, realized within the framework provided by Barth's quite different starting point and method. The lesson to be drawn from these observations is this: while it remains true that Barth and Schweizer cannot be reconciled on the level of method, and that those of us who are confronted by their disagreement in method will inevitably take sides (as I have done here), it nonetheless remains true that they participated in a community of shared theological concerns. At the very least, they were chewing on two ends of the same bone. And that, I think, should have tremendous ramifications for Reformed theology in the present. Reformed theology in the present needs above all to have representatives of these two most vital and profound streams within the Reformed tradition of the modern period in constant dialogue with one another, seeking to identify their common concerns and searching for doctrinal formulations which will do even greater justice to them than Schweizer and Barth were able to attain. If the representatives of these two great streams continue to ignore one another or continue to engage in the kind of polemic which rests content with questioning one another's character and motives, the Reformed churches of the present will be the losers.

CHAPTER 30

Reforming the Theology and Practice of Baptism: The Challenge of Karl Barth

Daniel Migliore

K arl Barth challenged the church, and especially the Reformed church, to a fundamental rethinking of its theology and practice of baptism. Although the controversy prompted by his challenge has abated, many issues that he raised remain unresolved. Whether in agreement or disagreement, Reformed theology in the future will likely continue to wrestle with his criticisms of traditional understandings and practices of baptism.

In his theology of baptism, as in his other christocentric reconstructions of Christian doctrine, Barth refused to allow tradition to have the final word. He held that while theology must be respectful of tradition, it must always remain open to the call to reform based on the Word of God. Only a theology liberated again and again from captivities in its own patterns of thought and practice will be able to contribute to the liberating and renewing mission of the church in the world.[1]

The Development of Barth's Theology of Baptism

Barth's theology of baptism underwent important, and even dramatic, changes from the first edition of his commentary on Romans to the final fragment of the *Church Dogmatics* published shortly before his death. While we cannot

---

1. See John W. de Gruchy, *Liberating Reformed Theology: A South African Contribution to an Ecumenical Debate* (Grand Rapids: Wm. B. Eerdmans Publishing Co., 1991).

provide a detailed survey of this development in this essay, it is possible to note three major phases of his thinking about baptism.[2]

A. The first phase runs roughly from 1919 to the late 1930s and early 1940s. In the first (1919) and second (1922) editions of his commentary on Romans, Barth speaks of baptism as a sacrament, as a form of the Word of God, as a sign and seal of God's gracious action for us in Jesus Christ, and as a means of grace. While the truth and power of baptism can neither be enclosed in an ecclesiastical ritual nor identified with a religious experience, nevertheless in baptism we are drawn into God's new creation in the death and resurrection of Christ.[3] Barth's understanding of baptism is expanded in his first lectures in dogmatics in Göttingen (1924-25) — now being published for the first time.[4] To underscore the importance of baptism and the Lord's Supper, he locates them respectively at the beginning and end of the doctrine of the Christian life, linking baptism with Christian vocation and the Lord's Supper with the perseverance of the saints. While continuing to speak of baptism and the Lord's Supper as sacraments, Barth cautions against subsuming them under some general category of "sacrament" or "symbol." Instead, they are to be understood as particular and unique signs of God's once-for-all work of reconciliation in Jesus Christ. A sacrament is not just "one sign among many others any more than God is God next to many other gods."[5] Baptism bears concrete and powerful witness to God's grace and of our inclusion in the event of reconciliation of which "God and only God is subject."[6]

According to Barth, a distinguishing feature of the Calvinistic doctrine of the sacraments is its unrelenting reference to the sovereignty and freedom of God in explaining the relationship between the creaturely signs and the divine reality that they attest. The sign and the reality signified must neither be identified (as Barth thinks the Roman Catholic doctrine of baptism tends to do), nor must the sign be reduced to an empty cipher or mere illustration (as happens in Zwinglian teaching). While taking creaturely form, the grace of God always remains free and beyond our control. Hence, from the Reformed perspec-

---

2. Cf. Richard Schlüter, *Karl Barths Tauflehre* (Paderborn: Verlag Bonifacius, 1973), pp. 33-56; John Thompson, *The Holy Spirit in the Theology of Karl Barth* (Allison Park, Pa.: Pickwick, 1991), pp. 114-31.

3. See *Der Römerbrief,* 1st ed. 1919 (Zurich: EVZ Verlag, 1963); 2nd ed. (Munich: Kaiser Verlag, 1922).

4. Karl Barth, "Unterricht in der christlichen Religion," vol. 3 (unpublished typescript), pp. 187-254. See my introduction to the English translation of these lectures: *The Göttingen Dogmatics,* vol. 1 (Grand Rapids: Wm. B. Eerdmans Publishing Co., 1991), pp. xv-lxii.

5. Karl Barth, "Unterricht in der christlichen Religion," p. 202.

6. Karl Barth, "Unterricht in der christlichen Religion," p. 191.

tive, one cannot speak of an absolute necessity of baptism for salvation; one can only say that Christ has called us to make use of this sign.

In this early period of his development, Barth staunchly supports infant baptism. He agrees that it is indeed scandalous that we are baptized as crying children "entirely without our agreement and consent," when we are "more helpless than every young cat of the same age."[7] But he asks: "Does it make any sense to be ashamed of infant baptism on the grounds that human reason and experience are absent in this act? As if they are not *always* lacking with respect to what this act means. As if even the baptism of the most mature, most pious, and most rational adult could be in principle anything other than 'infant' baptism. . . ."[8] In these early writings Barth speaks of the "monergism of grace" and the "absolute one-sidedness" of the relationship between God and the children of God.[9] As a scandalous and contingent event that happens once at the beginning of Christian life, baptism corresponds to the scandalous, contingent, and once-for-all event of God's reconciliation of the world in Jesus Christt.

Substantially the same view of baptism can be found in Barth's *Christliche Dogmatik* of 1927[10] and in his lengthy essay on "The Doctrine of the Sacraments" published in 1929.[11] As signs of God's grace, the sacraments point to an event that cannot be controlled by the church. God does not cease to be God in condescending to meet us as we are and accommodating to our condition as fallen creatures. In baptism we are assured that God's grace has found us and claims our faith and obedience. Barth thus rejects both the so-called objective view of the sacraments, according to which there is a miraculous mediation of grace with which faith has nothing to do, and the so-called subjective view, according to which the real power at work in the sacraments is none other than the power of our faith. Following Calvin, Barth lifts up "the majesty of God and the freedom of his grace."[12] God is really present in the sacramental action by the power of God's Word and Spirit. Passages on the sacraments in the initial volumes of the *Church Dogmatics* add nothing fundamentally new to these emphases of Barth's earlier writings.[13]

7. Karl Barth, "Unterricht in der christlichen Religion," p. 203.
8. Karl Barth, "Unterricht in der christlichen Religion," p. 204.
9. Karl Barth, "Unterricht in der christlichen Religion," pp. 204-5.
10. Karl Barth, *Die christliche Dogmatik im Entwurf*. 1. Die Lehre vom Worte Gottes. Prolegomena zur christlichen Dogmatik, 1927 (Zurich: Theologischer Verlag, 1982), pp. 392-96.
11. Karl Barth, "Die Lehre von den Sakramenten," *Zwischen den Zeiten* 7 (1929): 427-60.
12. Karl Barth, "Die Lehre von den Sakramenten," p. 458.
13. In *Church Dogmatics* I/1, 2nd ed. (Edinburgh: T. & T. Clark, 1975), for example,

B. The second phase of the development of Barth's theology of baptism began in the late 1930s and found fullest expression in his essay "The Teaching of the Church regarding Baptism," published in 1947.[14] While there are many strands of continuity between this essay and his earlier writings on baptism, Barth now speaks of baptism as the witness not only to all that God has accomplished in the death and resurrection of Jesus Christ but also to "the praise of God which breaks from the lips of the forgiven sinner and is accepted by grace."[15] In other words, the event of baptism attests not only that God has graciously acted on our behalf but also that we are responsible partners in the covenant of grace. "Baptism then is a picture in which man, it is true, is not the most important figure but is certainly the second most important."[16]

In this widely read essay of 1947, Barth defines the *essence* of baptism as "the representation of a person's renewal through participation by means of the power of the Holy Spirit in the death and resurrection of Jesus Christ, and therewith the representation of a person's association with Christ, with the covenant of grace which is concluded and realized in him, and with the fellowship of His church."[17] Barth also speaks in this essay about the *power* of baptism (the self-attestation of Jesus Christ); the *intention* of baptism (the glorifying of God in the upbuilding of the church through the promise of grace and the call to service); the *order* of baptism (the practical administration of baptism in the church which, if inadequate, can obscure its essence, power, and meaning but cannot fundamentally invalidate it); and the *efficacy* of baptism (the baptized person is placed under the sign of the death and resurrection of Jesus Christ, and thus, under the sign of hope).

In the section dealing with the order of baptism, Barth takes issue with the practice of infant baptism because, he now argues, it obscures the freedom and responsibility of the person baptized. He contends that this practice amounts to treating the baptizand as a mere passive object rather than an ac-

---

Barth quotes question 66 of the Heidelberg Catechism with approval: "What are the sacraments? — They are visible, sacred signs and seals appointed by God, so that through the use of the same He may the better give us to understand the promise of the Gospel and seal the same, namely, that for the sake of the one sacrifice of Christ accomplished on the cross He graciously grants us remission of sins and eternal life" (p. 56).

14. Karl Barth, *The Teaching of the Church regarding Baptism* (London: SCM Press, 1948). As early as 1938, Barth writes in a letter to A. Koechlin that he had come to "completely negative conclusions over Calvin's argument for infant baptism." See Eberhard Busch, *Karl Barth: His Life from Letters and Autobiographical Texts* (Philadelphia: Fortress, 1976), p. 286.

15. Karl Barth, *Teaching of the Church*, p. 13.

16. Karl Barth, *Teaching of the Church*, p. 14.

17. Karl Barth, *Teaching of the Church*, p. 9.

tive partner in the covenant of grace. The practice of baptism in this form becomes "arbitrary and despotic."[18] While the baptized is not the chief actor in the event proclaimed by baptism, he or she is certainly the second actor.[19] To ignore this is to make baptism "an act of violence."[20] Barth further contends that the traditional New Testament proofs for infant baptism are weak at best, declares Calvin's linking of infant baptism and circumcision unconvincing, and doubts that infant baptism can be adequately defended on the grounds that it offers an impressive demonstration of the free antecedent grace of God. By the same argument one could also try to justify mass and even forced baptisms.

Barth conjectures that the most likely reason the church has refused to give up the highly problematic practice of infant baptism is that it does not want to relinquish its privileged position within the *corpus christianum* which has existed since the time of Constantine. In brief, the church is unwilling to give up its power and status within the existing cultural and political arrangements.

No doubt Barth's critique of infant baptism as the anchor of the church's easy accommodation to state and culture was heightened by the German church struggle under Nazism. But other important factors contributed to the revision of his doctrine of baptism: his intensive study of the biblical witness, the ever increasing christological concentration of his theological work, and in particular his reconstruction of the doctrine of election in *Church Dogmatics* II/2 (1940), which underscored the fact that God's electing grace is rooted solely in the being and decision of God rather than in any familial, national, or racial bond.

C. A third and final phase of the development of Barth's theology of baptism is evident in passages on baptism in the doctrine of reconciliation (*Church Dogmatics* IV/1-3) and takes fullest form in the fragment of *Church Dogmatics* IV/4, published in 1967.[21] In this, his "last word on the subject,"[22] Barth radicalizes the position he adopted in the 1940s. Acknowledging the influence of the study of baptism by his son Markus,[23] Barth now emphatically rejects the description of baptism as a sacrament, speaks of baptism primarily as an act of witness, sharply distinguishes between Spirit baptism and water

18. Karl Barth, *Teaching of the Church*, p. 41.

19. Karl Barth, *Teaching of the Church*, p. 42.

20. Karl Barth, *Teaching of the Church*, p. 47.

21. Karl Barth, *Church Dogmatics* IV/4 [fragment] (Edinburgh: T. & T. Clark, 1969), hereafter cited as *CD* IV/4.

22. Karl Barth, *CD* IV/4, p. ix.

23. Markus Barth, *Die Taufe — ein Sakrament?: Ein exegetischer Beitrag zum Gespräch über die kirchliche Taufe* (Zollikon-Zurich: Evangelischer Verlag, 1951).

baptism, and argues that water baptism is properly interpreted not as a divine but as a strictly human act. The doctrine of baptism is presented as a part of the ethics of reconciliation; it marks the beginning of the life of free human partnership in the covenant of grace. Writing that he is now concerned primarily with "the mature Christian and mature Christianity," Barth seeks to clarify and strengthen his opposition to "the custom, or abuse, of infant baptism."[24]

Thus the direction of Barth's development in his theology of baptism is from exclusive emphasis on the activity of God to an emphasis on water baptism as free human response to the grace of God. This development corresponds to the movement from his early emphasis on the deity of God to the later emphasis on the humanity of God.[25] The activity of the God of free grace does not exclude but includes humanity as covenant partner.

The Context of Barth's Theology of Baptism in *CD* IV/4

A doctrine of baptism cannot be isolated from its larger theological context. Luther's interpretation of baptism is inseparably connected with his doctrine of justification by grace through faith, and Calvin's teaching is closely related to his doctrine of the covenant. Similarly, Barth's doctrine of baptism is embedded in his entire theology and lights up its central themes. What Barth says about baptism in *CD* IV/4 is a key to the intention of the whole of the *Church Dogmatics:* to affirm the sovereign grace of God in Jesus Christ as the basis and goal of true human freedom in partnership with God.

CD IV/4 contains Barth's final revision of his theology of baptism. It is a fragment of the unfinished volume on the ethics of reconciliation. In this volume Barth planned to deal with baptism as the commencement of the Christian life; with the Lord's Prayer as a guide to concrete Christian practice; and with the Lord's Supper as the act in which Christian life is continually renewed in thanksgiving, memory, and hope.

The overall structure of *CD* IV was thus planned to be: *first,* the description of God's gift of reconciliation in the history of Jesus Christ in its three aspects — the Lord as Servant (IV/1), the Servant as Lord (IV/2), and the True Witness (IV/3); and *second,* an account of the free human response to God's gracious work in Jesus Christ which has its public beginning in the act of bap-

---

24. Karl Barth, *CD* IV/4, p. x.
25. For Barth's own description of this shift of emphasis, see *The Humanity of God* (Richmond: John Knox, 1960), pp. 37-65.

tism, continues in the life of prayerful discipleship, and is strengthened and renewed in the celebration of the Lord's Supper (IV/4).

Recognition of this wider context of Barth's treatise on baptism helps to clarify his intent to follow the portrayal of God's astonishing freedom for the world in the history of Jesus Christ (IV/1-3) with the depiction of Christian life as a free, mature, and glad human response to God's free grace. The concern to honor, in due order, both divine and human freedom is present everywhere in the *Church Dogmatics*. It is also — or more precisely, especially — evident in the final volume on baptism. The two chapters of *CD* IV/4, entitled "Baptism with the Holy Spirit" and "Baptism with Water," deal respectively with the divine and human aspects of baptism. Barth's aim is to express the differentiated unity of divine and human action in baptism.

A. By "baptism with the Holy Spirit," Barth means the free act of the Spirit of God whereby human beings are personally liberated and enabled to participate in the divine work and word of reconciliation in the ministry, death, and resurrection of Jesus Christ. By the work of the Spirit, the history of Jesus Christ is actualized not only *extra nos* and *pro nobis,* but also *in nobis.* The Holy Spirit is active among human beings, empowering them to become "responsible subjects"[26] of the new human history inaugurated in Jesus Christ. According to Barth, the Holy Spirit is the power of God moving human beings to say a free and glad Yes to God's Yes to them in the history of Jesus Christ, to give this history a central place in their own lives, and to allow themselves to be newly identified by it. Barth allows that his description of the renewing work of the Holy Spirit *in nobis* as "baptism with the Holy Spirit" (cf. Mark 1:8 par.; 1 Cor. 12:13; John 1:33; Acts 1:5; 11:16) involves "a certain exegetical liberty."[27]

Barth insists that baptism with the Holy Spirit calls for baptism with water, and that in turn baptism with water presupposes and points to baptism with the Holy Spirit. Yet the two are not identical. "Water baptism and the Spirit's baptism . . . though they stand in strict correlation, are two very different things as man's free work on the one side and God's free work on the other."[28] Thus, under the theme of baptism with the Holy Spirit, Barth asserts the freedom and initiative of the gracious God and rejects any restriction of the divine activity to the sphere of the institutional church and its ministries. For Barth "baptism with the Holy Spirit" is a metaphor which describes the antecedent activity of the Holy Spirit as the source of Christian life and is not

26. Karl Barth, *CD* IV/4, p. 26.
27. Karl Barth, *CD* IV/4, p. 30. While the expression "baptize with (or by) the Holy Spirit" appears several times in the New Testament, the phrase "baptism with the Holy Spirit" is never used. See *The Work of the Holy Spirit* (UPCUSA, 1970).
28. Karl Barth, *CD* IV/4, p. 88.

to be understood in the Pentecostal sense of a "second blessing" or fuller work of the Holy Spirit after one has become a Christian.

B. If, for Barth, "baptism with the Holy Spirit" designates God's act of free grace whereby human beings are turned to Jesus Christ and liberated to appropriate personally what he has objectively accomplished for their salvation, "baptism with water" names the free human action of response to God's gracious initiative. This act does not bring about any sort of sacramental "divinization" of human life. Water baptism is a free act of witness, freely requested by the person to be baptized, and freely performed by the community of Jesus Christ. In it the baptizand publicly declares the lordship of Jesus Christ, and thus gives appropriate answer to the deed and word of God in him. Water baptism represents the first step that a Christian takes in response to the prior decision and activity of God. Barth unfolds his understanding of water baptism under the following three headings.

1. The *basis* of baptism is to be found not in the "brute fact" that the church has always practiced it, nor even in the command of the risen Jesus in Matthew 28:19 taken in isolation. Instead, its basis is in the whole history of Jesus Christ as epitomized in his own willingness to be baptized in the Jordan by John. While the necessity of baptism is properly a *necessitas praecepti* rather than a *necessitas medii*, the call to be baptized is not an arbitrary command. It is grounded in Jesus' own life-act of free obedience to God which commences with his own baptism. In this act at the beginning of his ministry, Jesus subordinated himself to the purpose of God, placed himself in solidarity with sinful humanity, and in free obedience entered the service of the reign of God. The basis of Christian baptism is thus the grace and command which go forth from the whole life-act of Jesus which had its beginning in the baptism in the Jordan and its completion in the baptism of the cross.

2. The *goal* of water baptism lies beyond itself in the promised coming of Jesus Christ by the Holy Spirit. We must not attempt to find the goal of baptism in either the faith of the candidate or the faith of the baptizing church. The goal is God's own act of judgment and grace in Jesus Christ, which is both an accomplished and a promised and coming reality. Hence "baptism is prayer."[29] Together with the church the baptizand prays: Come, Lord Jesus! and *Veni Creator Spiritus!*

3. The *meaning* of water baptism is that it is a free human act which attests and corresponds to the liberating, forgiving, reconciling, promising grace of God in the ministry, death, and resurrection of Jesus Christ. Water baptism does not duplicate, supplement, or complete the work of God in Jesus Christ with our own work. It is simply the free human response — a "wholly free,

---

29. Karl Barth, *CD* IV/4, p. 210.

conscious, and voluntary decision"[30] — to God's free act of grace. Water baptism is "the first step of a human life which is shaped and stamped by looking to Jesus Christ."[31] In water baptism one freely affirms the determination of one's life by the death and resurrection of Jesus Christ and the promise which issues from him for oneself and for the world. While not an autonomous decision, it is a "free and responsible human act," which consists simply in following — corresponding to — the death and resurrection, "the justification and sanctification, the cleansing and renewal of sinful humanity which God has accomplished and revealed in Jesus Christ."[32] Grounded in God's own renunciation of human sin and God's own pledge of new life in the cross and resurrection of Jesus Christ, water baptism marks our own corresponding renunciation of sin and pledge to live in new life and service of God.

It is on the basis of this interpretation of water baptism as a free human response to God's judgment and grace in the history of Jesus Christ that Barth finds himself compelled to reject the practice of infant baptism. His chief objection is that this practice is incompatible with the New Testament meaning of baptism as the beginning of a new life in free obedience to and hope in the free grace of God. He contends that in his discussion of baptism "there has been no place at which there could even be any question of thinking that the candidate to whom we have constantly referred as a partner of the community in baptism might be an infant, an unconscious child, who is qualified for the position by his Christian parents." Only human beings "who are capable of thought and action . . . may be summoned as such to conversion."[33]

Barth repeats the charge made in his essay of 1947 that infant baptism grew out of and perpetuates the idea of a *corpus christianum*, undercuts the importance of the freedom and responsibility of Christian discipleship, and thus seriously weakens the church. Instead of calling for mature Christian discipleship, the church of infant baptism baptizes people in their sleep or without regard to their free, responsible decision. While not flatly rejecting infant baptism as invalid, or advocating rebaptism,[34] Barth calls it a "profoundly ir-

---

30. Karl Barth, *CD* IV/4, p. 163.
31. Karl Barth, *CD* IV/4, p. 149.
32. Karl Barth, *CD* IV/4, p. 159.
33. Karl Barth, *CD* IV/4, pp. 165-66.
34. It should be noted that Barth never called for the rebaptism of those baptized as infants, nor did he ever seek to be rebaptized himself. ". . . I regard it as more correct and important to take my one baptism very seriously. Part of this requires calling on the church to remedy the disorder [of infant baptism] in the future." See Karl Barth, *Letters, 1961-1968*, ed. J. Fangmeier and H. Stoevesandt (Grand Rapids: Wm. B. Eerdmans Publishing Co., 1981), p. 189.

regular" practice, an "ancient ecclesiastical error," a "wound from which the church suffers" and which will continue to harm it in the future.[35]

Even this brief summary is sufficient to show that a central concern of Barth in his doctrine of baptism is a proper construal of the relationship of the activity of God and human freedom. While emphasizing the sovereignty and prevenience of the grace of the triune God in creation, reconciliation, and redemption, he underscores the fact that the activity of this God does not destroy but establishes human freedom. Precisely because baptism with the Holy Spirit is the work not of a tyrannical God but of the God of covenantal grace made known in Jesus Christ, it enables and calls for a free human response. "The point is that here, as elsewhere, the omnicausality *(Allwirklichkeit)* of God must not be construed as His sole causality *(Alleinwirklichkeit)*. The divine change in whose accomplishment a man becomes a Christian is an event of true intercourse between God and man. If it undoubtedly has its origin in God's initiative, no less indisputably man is not ignored or passed over in it. He is taken seriously as an independent creature of God. He is not run down and overpowered, but set on his feet. He is not put under tutelage, but addressed and treated as an adult."[36]

Barth makes this same point in numerous passages. God's power is not preemptive or coercive. The free God wills partnership with free and mature human beings who obey God gladly and from the heart.[37] Thus for Barth, in the covenant of grace realized once-for-all in Jesus Christ, human beings are called to freedom and become active subjects and genuine partners of God. While they can only follow the activity and word of God, they are liberated and summoned to follow with their own heart, and mind, and will. "Matters are not decided over their heads. They are not just objects who are discussed, moved, and pushed around. Precisely in the covenant of grace, the house of the Father, the kingdom of Jesus Christ and the Holy Spirit, there can be no talk of divine omnicausality."[38]

These passages — and there are many more like them — articulate the central theme of Barth's theology of baptism: that the free grace of God establishes and calls forth human freedom and responsibility; that God's exercise of freedom and genuinely free human action are not incompatible, nor competitive; that God wants to be God not in solitude but in relationship, that God lives in community both *ad intra* and *ad extra;* that God wills to have covenant partners who for all their dependence on God are nevertheless enabled and

35. Karl Barth, *CD* IV/4, p. 194.
36. Karl Barth, *CD* IV/4, pp. 22-23.
37. See Karl Barth, *CD* IV/4, p. 35.
38. Karl Barth, *CD* IV/4, p. 163.

called to decide in responsible freedom and act as mature disciples. The gracious action of God aims at human beings who stand on their own feet, live as persons come of age, and act as free subjects before God.

There can be no mistaking the fact that with his doctrine of covenantal partnership Barth honors the summons to freedom and maturity expressed by Kant, Nietzsche, and other philosophers of the modern period, even if Barth sets these great themes of modernity in a vastly different frame of reference. Barth's theology affirms human freedom and responsibility on a new basis. The idea of "God everything, humanity nothing," which remains a popular caricature of Barth's theology, is for him not only sheer nonsense but an attack on the gospel of "the humanity of God." The theme of God's humanity, of God's will to have communion and establish partnership with humanity, grows steadily in the *Church Dogmatics* and bears what for many readers must be a surprising fruit in the fragment of IV/4. Yet this final fragment can be seen as a consistent development of the trinitarian and christocentric theology of previous volumes. Eberhard Jüngel rightly observes that the final version of Barth's doctrine of baptism should be viewed not as a curious appendix but as a kind of "test case" as to whether one has appropriately understood what Barth has been up to all along in the *Church Dogmatics*.[39]

Barth's model of the interaction of the free God and the free human being is Jesus Christ. In Jesus Christ the initiative of God's free grace on the one hand and free human obedience on the other is perfectly united. In Jesus Christ free divine action and free human action are conjoined rather than competitive. The increase of one does not require a decrease in the other. Barth intends that his doctrine of baptism display the same "Chalcedonian pattern" of thought present everywhere in his theology:[40] God's self-determination for us is the basis and goal of human self-determination. True human freedom takes the form of free and glad obedience, uncoerced following of the gracious determination of human life by God. As a free human response to the grace of God, Christian faith and discipleship become a correspondence, analogy, or likeness of the communion and partnership of God and humanity in Jesus Christ. In requesting baptism with water, the Christian acts in correspondence with Jesus' own baptism in obedience to God's will, in solidarity with sinners, and in hope of God's coming reign. The life of the Christian, from beginning to end, is characterized by this participation in and analogy to the way of Jesus Christ.

---

39. Eberhard Jüngel, *Barth-Studien* (Zurich: Benziger Verlag, 1982), p. 287.

40. On the "Chalcedonian pattern" of Barth's thought, see George Hunsinger, *How to Read Karl Barth: The Shape of His Theology* (New York: Oxford University Press, 1991), pp. 185ff.

If the way of participation in and correspondence to the history of Jesus Christ is to govern Christian life in general and baptism in particular, infant baptism is in Barth's judgment simply a theological muddle, a "deeply disorderly" practice that damages the proclamation of the gospel and the vitality of the church. Barth thus calls for a "demythologizing" of Christian baptism.[41]

Barth's criticism of infant baptism clearly has nothing to do with synergistic presuppositions that are sometimes at work in the critique of this practice. Perhaps especially in the North American context, Barth's questioning of infant baptism is apt to be misunderstood as a softening of the *sola gratia* of the Reformation and an elevation of religious experience and personal decision to the center of baptismal theology. This is certainly not his intent. His aim is in no way to qualify the freedom and priority of grace but instead to interpret that grace as transforming power that liberates and enables a corresponding human freedom in the service of God.

Open Questions in Barth's Theology of Baptism

Up to this point I have attempted to sketch the development of Barth's doctrine of baptism and to identify its wider context in the *Church Dogmatics*. In particular, I have shown that Barth's chief concern is to present God's grace in Jesus Christ as claiming and empowering free and responsible human life in partnership with God. Now I wish to consider a few basic questions about Barth's theology of baptism.

A. Is baptism a "sacrament"? In the final phase of his thinking about baptism, Barth unequivocally declares that "baptism is not a sacrament," that its meaning is to be sought instead in its character as "a true and genuine human action which responds to the divine act and word."[42]

But just what does Barth mean in denying that baptism is a sacrament? He is, first of all, denying that baptism is in the same category with the unique sacrament which is God's work of salvation in Jesus Christ. He is also rejecting the idea that baptism is a necessary means of grace. "Baptism cannot be — as though this were necessary — a repetition, extension, representation, or actualization of the saving event. It is a basic Yes to God's grace and revelation, but not a 'sacrament,' not a means of grace and revelation."[43]

---

41. Karl Barth, *CD* IV/4, p. 105.

42. Karl Barth, *CD* IV/4, p. 128. See also Barth's posthumously published lecture fragments of *CD* IV/4, *The Christian Life* (Grand Rapids: Wm. B. Eerdmans Publishing Co., 1991), p. 46.

43. Karl Barth, *CD* IV/4, p. 118.

Early and late, Barth stands with the classical Reformed understanding of baptism in refusing to see it as absolutely necessary for salvation. Just as the preaching of the Word by the church serves the Word of God and is efficacious only by the power of the Spirit, so the renewing action of the Holy Spirit cannot be confined to water baptism. The free grace of God is not held hostage within the walls of the church or imprisoned within its rites and practices.

Even if one agrees, however, that baptism is not a *necessary* means of grace in the sense rejected by Barth, one must ask why baptism, like the witness of Scripture and the preaching of the church, may not *become* a means of grace in the sense of a special mediation of God's promise to us in Jesus Christ. If the witness of Scripture and church proclamation are said to be human words in and through which, by free grace, God's Word may be spoken from time to time, why may not something comparable be said of baptism and the Lord's Supper? Why should we not understand water baptism as *both* a unique declaration and confirmation of God's gracious promise in Jesus Christ *and* a human action in response to grace?[44]

When Barth says Spirit baptism (God's action) and water baptism (human action in response to God's) are two aspects of the same event, he implies that their relationship is to be understood after the analogy of the differentiated unity of divinity and humanity in the one history of Jesus Christ — a unity without confusion or mixture on the one hand and without division or separation on the other. Yet Barth seems far more concerned to guard distinctiveness than to affirm union when he speaks of the relationship of Spirit baptism and water baptism. But does this do justice to the New Testament description of baptism as a single concrete event in which God's forgiveness and promise on the one hand and human repentance and hope on the other are united?

That baptism is first a gift and promise of God to be received, as well as being also a human response to this divine initiative, is underscored in New Testament baptismal passages that speak of something that happens to us and not only of something that we do. In baptism we die and are buried with Christ (Rom. 6:3ff.); we are incorporated into Christ (Gal. 3:27); we are washed, justified, and sanctified (1 Cor. 6:11); we receive forgiveness of sins (Acts 2:38). Both E. Jüngel and T. F. Torrance note that Barth's way of differentiating Spirit baptism and water baptism tends toward a dualism rather than a dynamic unity.[45]

---

44. See Walter Kreck, "Karl Barths Tauflehre," in *Zu Karl Barths Lehre von der Taufe*, ed. Fritz Viering (Gütersloh: Gerd Mohn, 1971), pp. 22-23.

45. Jüngel, pp. 263ff.; T. F. Torrance, *Theology in Reconciliation* (London: Geoffrey Chapman, 1975), p. 99, quoted by Thompson, p. 115.

Barth's dismissal of baptism and the Lord's Supper as sacramental "means of grace" is also flawed because it fails to attend sufficiently to the participation of the natural order in the purposes of God. Surely it is a serious mistake, in an era so desperately in need of a new awareness of the place of the natural order in the divine economy, to disregard the significance of baptism and the Lord's Supper as acts in which use is made of the nonhuman creation to assist in communicating the message of grace and the call to responsible exercise of freedom. Being washed with water and sharing bread and wine become concrete witnesses to God's promise of new creation in Jesus Christ. As Barth emphasized in his earlier writings, sacraments have their place alongside the proclaimed Word in their address to the *whole* person.[46] We are embodied creatures, and God's gracious Word of promise comes to us enfleshed, not in disembodied, denaturalized form. God's redemptive aim embraces the whole person and the whole cosmos.

The point of these comments is not that the term "sacrament" as traditionally defined should continue to govern our interpretation of baptism and the Lord's Supper. The word is heavily burdened by its history. Baptism and the Lord's Supper must be understood in their own terms rather than as instances of a definition of sacrament that we dream up in advance. As many Protestant and Catholic theologians would now agree, the meaning of the sacraments must be redefined in terms of the activity of God in Jesus Christ, who is the fundamental sacrament. A proper christocentric understanding of the sacrament of baptism would protect both the freedom of God and human freedom, and would give expression to the genuinely incarnational character of God's presence and activity in the world.

B. How are baptism and personal faith related? For Barth, this is "the one great dogmatic problem of the doctrine of infant baptism."[47] He admits that for several decades he himself invoked what he calls the strongest of the arguments for infant baptism; viz., that it is "so remarkably vivid a depiction of the free and omnipotent grace of God which is independent of all human thought and will, faith and unbelief."[48] But he abandoned this argument because it views the baptized person as a passive object rather than as an active subject and partner of God.

Barth's concern to present the grace of God as liberating rather than coercive is of great importance. His recovery of the ethical dimension of baptism and the Lord's Supper is one of his lasting contributions to any future theology of the sacraments. We would ask, however, whether Barth in turn would not

46. Karl Barth, "The Doctrine of the Sacraments," p. 435.
47. Karl Barth, *CD* IV/4, p. 185.
48. Karl Barth, *CD* IV/4, p. 189.

agree that human freedom is always freedom within certain contexts and conditions. True human freedom presupposes time for development and growth. It presupposes a nurturing matrix and the loving patience of caregivers. An absolutized individual freedom that supposedly has no history and no indebtedness to others is an illusion of the ahistorical self of the Enlightenment. Given Barth's own critique of absolutized human freedom and his own view of freedom as freedom in relationship, the temporal and communal matrices of personal freedom must not be ignored in the doctrine of baptism.

Hence, while Barth is surely right in taking with utmost seriousness the essential bond between baptism and the response of personal faith, he fails to demonstrate that the two must necessarily be simultaneous. As Barth would surely agree, one dimension of God's grace is the patience of God. God gives human creatures, who are temporal to the core, time to respond. Whether the baptized person is adult or infant, the promise of God expressed in baptism cannot be appropriated completely in a single moment. It must be responded to and prayed for throughout one's life. That the obedience that corresponds to grace is not completed in an instant but extends over a lifetime is no less true of a baptized adult than of a baptized child.

As for the idea of "vicarious faith," which Barth strongly rejects, it is true that no one — not parents, sponsors, or community — can act as substitutes for the person baptized. Authentic faith and free decision are inseparable. But when children are baptized, the parents or guardians do not substitute their faith for that of the child. Instead, they promise to surround the children with Christian love and to encourage their growth in Christian faith until they can make their own free personal response to the Yes of God addressed to them in baptism. Thus infant baptism need not be construed, as Barth contends, as a violation of human freedom by an imperialistic act of grace, any more than the loving words and deeds of a parent for a child are necessarily acts of violence simply because they precede, perhaps for years, the intentional response of the child.

C. How are baptism and the covenantal, community-making purposes of God related? This is undoubtedly the crucial question in a Reformed theology and practice of baptism. The New Testament unfolds the meaning of baptism in many rich images: dying and rising with Christ, washing of a sin-stained life, rebirth by the Holy Spirit. But the New Testament theme that is especially lifted up by the Reformed understanding of baptism is incorporation. "In the one Spirit we were all baptized into one body — Jews or Greeks, slaves or free" (1 Cor. 12:13 NRSV). In baptism we are marked by the name of the triune God, whose life is in shared love and open community. Whether as infants or adults, we are welcomed at baptism into the community of Christ. We do not have to understand fully the promise that is confirmed to us in this event before we begin to be shaped by it. Indeed, we can never claim to comprehend fully the mystery of God's free grace.

Baptism is an event of solidarity: the triune God's gracious solidarity with us in Jesus Christ by the power of the Holy Spirit, and our solidarity in Jesus Christ and the Spirit with others and with the whole groaning creation. As I have attempted to argue elsewhere, baptism is the sacrament of solidarity and the Eucharist is the sacrament of sharing.[49] Both have to do essentially with the coming into being and sustaining of a new and inclusive community of justice and love through God's activity and promise in Jesus Christ by the power of the Holy Spirit.

The very title of the *Church Dogmatics* shows that Barth opposed all forms of individualism and subjectivism in his theology. From the first to the last volume of this work he underscored the objective history of reconciliation in Jesus Christ and the relative priority of the faith and life of the church to that of the individual Christian. While critical of individualism, Barth was also rightly suspicious of collectivistic notions of becoming Christian. He had good reason for refusing to follow Calvin's effort to justify infant baptism on the analogy with circumcision. The people of God brought into being by the new covenant in Jesus Christ is not like a nation constituted by biological, linguistic, or cultural ties.

Baptism cannot be properly understood within either an individualistic or a collectivistic framework of thought. It is the sign of our inclusion in the promised new creation of God, who has come to us in the ministry, death, and resurrection of Jesus Christ and who arouses us to new life and hope by the power of the Holy Spirit. In our baptism we begin to take part in God's victory of life over death in Jesus Christ that promises an end to all the destructive divisions, oppressive hierarchies, and abusive power structures of our world estranged from God. In baptism we are given a new identity as a people marked by God's own life of mutuality, communion, and shared love. If our attention is focused on this personal and social meaning of baptism as the beginning of our participation in God's new community of justice and love, the debate about infant or adult baptism is no longer of central importance.

While infant baptism should not be considered the only or even the standard form of Christian baptism, it *may* be practiced if it is understood to be a visible confirmation of God's grace that builds inclusive community and claims us as partners in this labor. Infant baptism is abused, however, whenever it is thought that membership in the covenant community is a matter of family connection or social convention.

49. Daniel L. Migliore, *Faith Seeking Understanding* (Grand Rapids: Wm. B. Eerdmans Publishing Co., 1991), pp. 211-26.

Barth's criticism of infant baptism was developed in a context of its centuries-long use as the basis and legitimation of the official religion of an empire or nation. In the United States today the problem is more accurately defined as the misuse of infant baptism as a religious rite of the bourgeois family.[50] In many Protestant churches in America, the Victorian family ideal is a real threat to a proper understanding of new community in Christ. This new community into which we enter at baptism is one that transcends all divisions of race, class, and gender. "There is no longer Jew or Greek, there is no longer slave or free, there is no longer male and female; for all of you are one in Christ Jesus" (Gal. 3:28 NRSV).

A Reformed theology of baptism developed in our own time will do well to retain the classical Reformed emphases. It will emphasize the priority of God's grace, as did Barth's early theology of baptism, and it will also present God's gracious activity as a power that sets human beings free to become partners with God in the ministry of reconciliation, as did Barth's final theology of baptism. But a Reformed theology of baptism today will have a new focus. It will emphasize solidarity in Christ as a new form of human community that transcends the many destructive patterns of segregation and domination in both church and society. Although Barth has provided important resources for a new theology of baptism centered on the themes of solidarity and praxis, the new life in Christ into which we are baptized must be described in far more concrete ways than Barth himself did.

Our solidarity in Christ, attested in our common baptism, breaks down the walls of separation of people on the basis of race, class, gender, or any other demarcation. As John de Gruchy writes: "A true understanding of baptism not only undermines apartheid in the church; it should also undermine apartheid in society, and all other forms of oppression as Paul indicates in Galatians 3:27-28. For baptism is a sign of human solidarity redeemed in Christ."[51]

But if the promise of God in Jesus Christ aims at new and inclusive community in which the solidarity of all creatures in suffering and hope is recognized and celebrated, then the baptism of children is *in principle* theologically legitimate, even though it is always a daring and dangerous practice that can be easily misunderstood and misused. Fear of misuse, however, cannot be a reason to disallow every practice of infant baptism. For danger attends every teaching and practice of the church in the sense of their being vulnerable to misuse and misinterpretation.

Whenever the church dares to practice infant baptism, it declares God's

---

50. See Janet Fishburn, *Confronting the Idolatry of the Family: A New Vision for the Household of God* (Nashville: Abingdon, 1991).

51. De Gruchy, p. 216.

love for this vulnerable, helpless, needy, dependent, powerless human being. Members of the community are called to recognize their responsibility in Christ to provide support and friendship for the newly baptized, even as they are invited to remember their own baptism and their own poverty and continual need of God's grace. But we must go further and say that the very mission of the Christian community is epitomized in the act of baptism. The practice of infant baptism in particular should serve to remind the community of Jesus Christ of its special calling to minister to the vulnerable and the marginalized, the poor and the powerless, whatever their race, gender, class, nation, or age. In his baptism, Christ entered into utmost solidarity with all broken and suffering humanity. He blessed the poor, ate with the outcast, befriended women, and ministered to children, explicitly instructing his disciples to allow the little children to come to him.

While acknowledging diversity, our postmodern culture is woefully deficient in affirming and cultivating the solidarity of all people, and indeed of all creatures, in suffering and hope. The responsible practice of baptism, infant and adult, should bear a countercultural witness to the new world of friendship, community, and service promised to us and to the world in Jesus Christ.

A Reformed theology of baptism for our time will thus reclaim an understanding of God's grace as a liberating power that works for new human community and for new solidarity with the whole groaning creation. All the ways of God — the triune God — begin, continue, and end in community, shared love, and mutual self-giving. Our practice of baptism, infant or adult, will cohere with the gospel of the triune God when it bears witness to God's purpose in Jesus Christ by the power of the Holy Spirit to rescue us from our deadly divisions for life in inclusive community.

CHAPTER 31

The Closeness of the Distant: Reformed Confessions after 1945

Eberhard Busch

W here do "we Reformed" stand today? Or, if we would rather be moving than standing: *Quo vadis, ecclesia reformata?* Or again, if we question ourselves critically using the title of a 1735 treatise by the Lutheran theologian V. E. Löscher: *Quo ruitis?* (Where are you falling?). What are we required today to say and to confess, to pray and to accomplish? What unites the worldwide Reformed family, which is so diverse and at the same time so fragmented? Even if we wish to be full of ecumenical spirit, we may still ask: What makes us Reformed? What is hidden behind the term "Reformed" which our ecumenical conversation partners can consult when necessary? What gives us the right to claim as our title "a Church reformed according to the Word of God"?[1]

These are a few essential questions which a responsible representation of Reformed churches must address. They are questions to which I anticipate a response when I open Lukas Vischer's 1982 anthology *Reformed Witness Today.*[2] For this book was published in order apparently to give at least some in-

1. Cf. also the anthology, *Bekenntnisschriften und Kirchenordnungen der nach Gottes Wort reformierten Kirchen,* ed. Wilhelm Niesel (Zollikon-Zurich: Evangelischer Verlag, 1938).

2. *Reformed Witness Today: A Collection of Confessions and Statements of Faith Issued by Reformed Churches,* ed. Lukas Vischer (Bern: Evangelische Arbeitsstelle Ökumene Schweiz, 1982). The numbers cited parenthetically within the text refer to the pages of this book. (Translator's note: The German version, *Reformiertes Zeugnis heute: Eine Sammlung*

Translated by Lisa Dahill.

formation regarding such questions. It contains more than thirty "newer confessional texts" from Reformed churches on every continent. Even if the collection is probably not exhaustive, one can assume that the texts were chosen to be relatively representative of the "spirit" of the present global Reformed family. The book is suitable not only to respond to questions such as those above; it also provokes a response to them from us.

To be clear at the outset: in the following pages I examine the texts as a Reformed theologian who has been engaged many years in the Swiss church and now works in Germany. No particular claims follow from this statement. As will become clear, the very texts gathered in this book deny me any such claims. I mean merely to indicate the place in which I stand and from which I notice and reflect on what (according to the book) is going on in the global Reformed family, and the official ecclesial statements it has produced in the past decades. Thus I write the following as someone who desires primarily to listen, though I do so as a participant, that is, as a member with others of the Reformed church.

New Confessional Eagerness

Lukas Vischer establishes in the book's preface that among Reformed churches there has been "no time in which . . . so many confessions have been compiled as in the last three decades" (*RZ*, p. v). In some ways that is not as surprising as it may at first sound, because, in distinction from the Lutheran view, the Reformed understanding of confession considers it quite possible and legitimate to inaugurate new confessions for new situations. Within the Lutheran camp the voice of T. Harnack was that of a dissenting minority when he, speaking of the Reformation confession, understood as an antiheretical summation, said it was "not immediately and encompassingly sufficient in the face of new tensions."[3] The majority Lutheran opinion considered confessions to be a clearly

---

neuerer Bekenntnistexte aus der reformierten Tradition [Neukirchen-Vluyn: Neukirchener Verlag, 1988], is more than simply a translation of the 1982 English original edition. It has omitted four of the confessional statements contained in the English; has substituted newer texts written in the 1980s for two of the older confessions in the English edition; and has added six completely new confessions, also written or adopted subsequent to the 1982 text. When references cite confessions not contained in the English version, the page reference to the German text [or, if possible, to the published texts of those confessions in English elsewhere] will be provided. The German text will henceforth be indicated by the abbreviation *RZ*, followed by the indicated page number[s].)

3. Cited by E. Wolf, "Die Bindung an das Bekenntnis: Bemerkungen zu Wesen und Funktion des formulierten Bekenntnisses," in *Wort und Welt* (East Berlin, 1968), p. 327.

defined and closed collection of texts which are valid for all Lutheran churches of all times and places, regardless of their particular contexts.

Within the Reformed churches, in contrast, a double motif has been characteristic since the period of the Reformation itself. On the one hand many more confessions were formulated here in the various regions than within Lutheranism. On the other hand, there has been a conspicuous absence both of any confession binding on all Reformed churches and of an official church collection of the various confessional texts.[4] Is this the result of a Reformed relativism, possibly even grounded in the supposedly Reformed principle *Finitum non capax infiniti?* Such is not the case. Where there is relativism, there can be no confession. On the contrary, Reformed churches *have* made resolute confession, and they continue to do so anew to this day! Furthermore, of course, Reformed Christians have nowhere confessed the above principle. It is more "typically" Reformed to play with the sentence, so that one may oppose the (equally unfortunate) formulation *Finitum capax infiniti* by reversing it completely, insisting that *Infinitus capax finiti.* If all this is true, then one can only conclude that there are decisively *theological* reasons for the typically fluid relationship between the Reformed church and confession.[5]

Its basis is found first of all in the emphasis on the enduring priority of the Holy Scripture over confession. This is of course true for every church confession. With this priority, Reformed Christians point out that the question of a confession's correspondence with Scripture is not necessarily answered by the confession itself. This means that a confession is binding for a community not *because* but *insofar* as it corresponds to Scripture. For this reason a mature community can, indeed should, continually raise the question of correspondence to Scripture.[6] For

---

4. For reflection on the principles underlying this, cf. Karl Barth, "The Desirability and Possibility of a Universal Reformed Creed," in *Theology and Church: Shorter Writings, 1920-1928,* trans. Louise Pettibone Smith (London: SCM Press, 1962), pp. 112-35. The most complete collection of Reformed confessions in German is still that of E. F. Karl Müller, *Die Bekenntnisschriften der reformierten Kirche* (Leipzig: A. Deichert, 1903).

5. Karl Barth brings this out in the previously cited essay. The extent to which he made these theological reasons his own, despite all necessary nuancing, can be seen in his treatment of the concept of confession in *Church Dogmatics* I/2 (Edinburgh: T. & T. Clark, 1956), pp. 620-60, which clearly follows the pattern of the essay.

6. The fact that the Heidelberg Catechism provides Bible passages for each of its questions is, of course, an exception, but it bespeaks in any case the text's intention not only to stand in correspondence with Holy Scripture but also to be examined for such correspondence by mature Christians. In this the catechism is simply taking seriously the general Reformed recognition articulated, for instance, by the Basel Confession of 1534: "Finally we desire to submit this our confession to the judgment of the divine Biblical Scriptures. And should we be informed from the same Holy Scriptures of a better one, we have thereby expressed our readiness to be willing at any time to obey God and His holy Word with great

this reason also, a confession can at times be corrected or even dropped, or be supplemented or replaced by a new one.

A further reason for the specific relationship of the Reformed to church confessions is connected to this. It has to do with the church's understanding of the concrete "gathered congregation,"[7] which is not dependent on a church located above it, but rather *is* the one holy church in its place. Thus, regarding the Reformed world as it actually exists, Karl Barth gave an accurate exaggeration: "Reformed folk do not walk in leading strings, controlled from above."[8] Whatever is "above" the "gathered congregations" must first be delegated by them as *synodus;* that is, it can only exist as "gathered congregations." This means that a church confession in the Reformed tradition is in each case a word spoken within a relatively comprehensible realm, by an assembly with concrete responsibility for it. Their confession can often gain acceptance in other geographically specific church districts. But it is not accidental that there is no global Reformed confession for this reason.

The fluid relationship to confession within the Reformed world is further connected with the fact that it takes seriously the liveliness of the Holy Spirit. Of course, a church that takes the Spirit seriously does not continually have to formulate new confessions, but can live a long time with an "old" one. Yet in the Spirit's own time it can also establish a new one. Taking the Spirit seriously does not necessarily mean formulating a confession only when new errors must be repudiated, but it can also serve the building up of the congregation (and will thereby, of course, also be excluding some things, if only tacitly). Yet taking the Spirit seriously also means that every time and place may not find the same point to be at stake in the denial or confession of Jesus Christ. It need not be an accident, therefore, that the new Reformed confessions at times lack assertions of that which was considered "Calvinist" in the sixteenth century. Trust in the guidance of the Spirit keeps Reformed Christians from needing always to define themselves only by the sixteenth century. They wish to remain open for whatever the Spirit of God may show them anew, at whichever point today the "church stands or falls."

If confession is understood along these lines, it is not in itself necessarily surprising that in our time Reformed churches have formulated new confes-

---

thanksgiving," cited in *Reformed Confessions of the Sixteenth Century,* ed. and with historical introductions by Arthur C. Cochrane (Philadelphia: Westminster, 1966), p. 96. The Berne Synod, the Scottish Confession, and Ursinus on the Heidelberg Catechism are similar. Cf. Jan Rohls, *Theologie reformierter Bekenntnisschriften* (Göttingen: Vandenhoeck & Ruprecht, 1987), pp. 317f.

7. Cf. Otto Weber, *Versammelte Gemeinde* (Neukirchen-Vluyn: Neukirchener Verlag, 1949).

8. Barth, "Desirability," p. 117.

sions, even "in great numbers." Yet in a certain sense this development is frankly astonishing. This is so because for long stretches of the history of the Reformed church its actual experience of confession unfolded in ways only marginally, if at all, related to what is described here. In fact, for a long time in the course of this history the fluid relationship to confession was replaced by a stance in which there was no relationship at all to church confession, in which this fluidity consisted merely of movement away from it. In place of the freedom at times to confess and at other times to enact one's confession, there emerged a freedom to do nothing, a freedom *from* confession.

This was the reaction to the attempts undertaken particularly in the seventeenth century to administer the Reformed confessions as if they were laws, requiring acceptance by church members and even by servants of the church.[9] At the root of this lay a problematic conception of God, in which God's freedom was thought of as a despotic regime which did not tolerate human freedom. Some of the damage this caused can be seen in A. Schweizer of Zürich, who sighed: "Our fathers confessed their belief, and we endeavor to believe their confession."[10] In the liberation from confessional coercion — the reaction against this legalistic execution of confession — there likely moved a breath of the original Reformed freedom within which the Reformers themselves confessed. Yet that freedom was now found not merely in mitigating the effort to believe the confession of the "fathers," but even further in not needing "to confess the faith" at all with them. And behind this stood a conception of humanity whose freedom, wrenched from coercion, had deteriorated into capriciousness in relation to God.

Since the beginning of the eighteenth century — with few exceptions, which too often only prove the rule[11] — new confessing has thus not occurred much at all in Reformed churches. In later years a segment of these churches went so far as to abolish formally the Reformation confessions.[12] And this oc-

---

9. A both symptomatic and revealing scene took place at the beginning of the eighteenth century when the Lausanne professors, who were all being forced by the Berne authorities to sign the Consensus Formula of 1675, at first refused to sign but finally did so — after being assured that their signatures were merely "to enhance the prestige of the authorities," while the scholars could think what they wished for themselves. Cf. *Realenzyklopädie für Protestantische Theologie und Kirche*, 3rd ed., ed. A. Hauck (Leipzig: J. C. Hinrichs, 1886-1913), vol. 7, pp. 652f. Cf. also A. Werdmüller, *Der Glaubenszwang der zürcherischen Kirche im XVII. Jahrhundert* (Zurich, 1945).

10. Cited by Hermann Dörries, *Das Bekenntnis in der Geschichte der Kirche* (Göttingen, 1946), pp. 6-7.

11. Müller, pp. 870ff., does provide eleven confessions or confession-like texts from the nineteenth century.

12. Thus, for instance, around the turn of the nineteenth century the confessions and/or their binding nature were discarded in all Swiss canton churches, in part by the authorities, in part by the churches themselves. Cf. the historical appendix provided by Walter

curred not in order now to confess anew and differently, but because the church had simply become weary of confessing. Naturally, when people think that instead of confessing their belief they must "believe" a confession, perhaps even one from the past, they soon perceive this as coercive and think they can create breathing room by doing away with it. Yet such a church will call into question its very origin and mission along with its "confession," and be at a loss as to why it deserves to be called a church of Jesus Christ. Then faith inevitably becomes a "private affair," recoiling assiduously from other people's "private affairs," and getting along by wholesale conformity with a world now become overwhelmingly secular.

Alternatively, one could avoid abolishing the confessions by just putting them in a museum. And in this museum one could retain and even refresh the legacy of the Reformation confessions as honored mementos worthy of preservation, memorials of a fine era of the past. Against the claim that one must attempt to believe in the confession of the "fathers," one could respond with the counterclaim that such effort is instructive or even "admirable" — but all without ever oneself actually confessing the faith with the "fathers"! Probably this was the logic and the problem of the "new Reformed movement," which from the end of the nineteenth century into the 1930s set the tone for Reformed churches. In any case, this was what its slogan of a necessary "preservation of Reformed interests" meant, a cause which the movement took up.[13] With the best intentions of reviving the old confessions, this slogan introduced into their understanding an accent which was originally foreign to them. These old confessions had confessed not in order to assert outwardly the particular apologetic claims of one church, nor to impress insiders with their beauty, but rather in order to declare: The church which articulates this insight is the representative in its place of the one holy catholic and apostolic church.

It is on precisely this point that the confessions which in the last three decades have been written "in such numbers," and which Vischer has placed before us, differ from the "new Reformed" efforts. They do not turn back to the sixteenth century and its confessions (although those often echo within them). Rather, they confess — like them and with them — *anew*. They confess not because they hold to a special Calvinistic tradition, nor because they wish to define what "Reformed" actually means. They confess because they (alone as Re-

---

Hildebrandt and Rudolf Zimmermann in Heinrich Bullinger, *Das zweite Helvetische Bekenntnis* (Zurich: Zwingli Verlag, 1966), pp. 156-61. R. Probst describes the process within a single canton-church in *Der aargauische Protestantismus in der Restaurationszeit: Beiträge zum Verhältnis Staat-Kirche* (Zurich, 1968), esp. pp. 110ff.

13. Cf. Herwart Vorländer, *Aufbruch und Krise: Ein Beitrag zur Geschichte der deutschen Reformierten vor dem Kirchenkampf* (Neukirchen-Vluyn: Neukirchener Verlag, 1974), esp. pp. 11ff.

formed, or with other denominations in the frequently occurring case of a merger of churches) find themselves called to confess their identity as the church of God and of Jesus Christ. Thus one text states: "Within the one, holy, catholic, apostolic Church the United Reformed Church [in the United Kingdom] acknowledges" the following . . . (p. 459). Or in the 1981 confession of the Indonesian Toraja Church: Here "we [confess our faith] together with all the saints of all ages and all places" (p. 48). Or the United Church of Zambia (1965): "The United Church holds the faith which the Church has ever held in Jesus Christ, the Redeemer of the World . . . in accordance with the revelation of God which he made, being himself God incarnate, it worships one God, Father, Son and Holy Spirit" (p. 292). Indeed, in a true confession of faith a church does not confess itself, its tradition, or its particular concerns and existence, but rather it confesses God in Jesus Christ according to the Holy Scripture, and itself as the representative of the one church.

What is new is that these "newer confessional texts" speak in this way. Regardless of the details of their content, this makes them confessions. And, however they may variously relate to the Reformed confessions of the sixteenth century, this places them in actuality on the same level as those confessions. This is then certainly an astounding fact, that "in the last three decades" — after epochs of pronounced "confessional weakness"[14] and reluctance, barely influenced by the ambition to restore the old confessions at the beginning of the century — a multitude of members of the world Reformed family have clearly come at last to an unmistakable, living, new *confessional eagerness!* This is a fact which no one could have predicted from the preceding centuries. It is a fact which calls for recognition. Apparently a number of Reformed churches have actually taken seriously the working of the Holy Spirit in their intention to formulate anew the correspondence of their words and actions with Holy Scripture, and thereby to appeal to the mature community. I have characterized this phenomenon with the phrase "the closeness of the distant," and it has here in part a temporal meaning; namely, that that which occurred in the distant past, in the confessional development of the sixteenth century, has now come vividly near, so that something analogous has taken place anew in our immediate presence. The phrase also has a somewhat geographical meaning, however, as we shall see.

14. This is Karl Barth's formulation, in particular reference to the situation of the Swiss churches since their dismantling of a binding confession: *Das Bekenntnis der Reformation und unser Bekennen*, Theologische Existenz heute 29 (Munich: Christian Kaiser Verlag, 1935), pp. 24-25.

New Closeness

An even greater surprise than the fact *of* such a renewed upsurge of readiness for confession in the past few years comes about when one ascertains *where and by whom* this confession is taking place. Although one might consider Vischer's collection one-sided and incomplete,[15] one notices first, *negatively,* that it contains no confessions from the Reformation's countries of origin, Switzerland and Germany, and also none from other "classically" Reformed countries such as France, Scotland, Holland, or Hungary. Is this a sign that in these countries people are still living with and renewing the old confessions from the Reformation period? Or does it, rather, indicate that the churches of these countries are characterized by something like a "confessional weakness"? In any case, it is clear that they of all churches are not leading participants in this new confessional eagerness. We can apparently no longer speak of a "Germania resp. Helvetia docet" in matters regarding Reformed confession today.

On the other hand, one notices *positively* that nearly two-thirds of the texts come from churches in Africa, Asia, Latin America, and Australia, and that of the remaining third those which are unquestionably the most important derive from the churches of North America. One may remember that only a hundred years ago the missions expert Gustav Warneck, while not attributing to the German-speaking churches any superiority in the abstract, did grant their paternal right of oversight and nurture toward those literally understood as "young churches."[16] And one may further remember at this point how only fifty years ago Dietrich Bonhoeffer certified that North American Christendom had no "fixed credal formulation" because it had never, "and today less than ever," confessed nor desired "a struggle for the truth in preaching and

---

15. One could make the case that the "new confessional eagerness" first showed itself in the Theological Declarations of Barmen in January (Free Reformed Synod) and May of 1934. According to the criteria by which Vischer has assembled his collection, one could also have included two Dutch confessional texts, i.e., the 1941 Doorn Theses and the 1949 "Foundations and Perspectives of Confessing." Similarly, the 1973 Leuenberg Concordat could also have been included.

16. Gustav Warneck, *Outlines of a History of Protestant Missions from the Reformation to the Present Time: A Contribution to Modern Church History,* authorized trans. from the 7th German ed. by George Robson (New York: Fleming H. Revell, 1901), pp. 348-49. To be fair, Warneck articulated the goal as one of "the founding of independent national churches, self-supporting, self-governing, self-propagating." And he did explain these churches' need for European "superintendence" precisely "as a bulwark" against the "civilised Western world, which is ever more and more overflowing, dominating, and decomposing" them. Nevertheless, it is not certain whether he envisioned these churches ever coming "to full independence of the old missionary Christendom."

doctrine."[17] If one examines Vischer's "collection of confessions and statements of faith" with such assertions echoing in one's memory, one cannot miss discovering a new and profoundly transformed situation. That sphere in which the churches of the Reformation's origins have for so long been the foremost, definitive leaders seems now to have become equally the arena of others. The formulation of indigenous confessions — precisely in those parts of the world which were distant in this way from the Reformed churches of central Europe — has moved the Christians of those countries close to their European partners; at the very least, they can claim a place in the conversation and speak their piece in that vital "struggle for the truth of preaching and teaching."

Reformed Christians of central Europe cannot interpret this development as a credit to ourselves, as the good fruit of the work of guidance which Warneck entrusted to us. It is not merely a fitting exercise in humility to recognize soberly that we have likely done more to hinder the emergence of such original church confessions outside our own sphere than we have to encourage them or make them possible. Indeed, from our perspective the credit can only go to God for bringing about such confession. From our perspective we cannot merely say that the churches in other regions are now conversing and confessing as we do, but rather this assertion must contain a more reflective note emphasizing that these others are doing today, in their places, what our forebears once did; that something is apparently alive and well there which was once alive here. And it is alive in those places in such a way that "confession" does not necessarily separate into "confessions," but rather unites divided churches: not from any weakness of confession but rather in the power of a newly given and newly risked confession.[18] Reformed Christians of the Reformation countries cannot contemplate the new initiatives of confessional eagerness outside our own territory without thinking here of Luke 13:19-20,[19] and thus asking ourselves whether that which is alive there is also analogously alive here.

Yet this is precisely what can foster the connectedness of the churches within and outside the classically Reformed countries. Such connectedness was of course recommended and extended even before the promulgation of these

17. Dietrich Bonhoeffer, "Protestantism without Reformation," in *No Rusty Swords: Letters, Lectures, and Notes, 1928-36*, ed. and introduction by Edwin H. Robertson, trans. Edwin H. Robertson and John Bowden (London: Collins, 1965), p. 96.

18. Thus the second part of Vischer's collection (pp. 267-468) is filled with confessions formulated for the union of Reformed churches with those of other denominations.

19. Karl Barth does so in *Church Dogmatics* IV/1 (Edinburgh: T. & T. Clark, 1956), pp. 706-7, where he compares the confessional formulation within the constitution of the Reformed church of his hometown of Basel with the corresponding constitution of the Sumatran Betak Church in 1951, formulated "without any Western participation."

new autonomous confessions. Nevertheless, the establishment of confessions in these regions of the world kindles a deepened intensity of relationship and communion within the global Reformed family. By their confessions, Reformed Christians of the broader ecumenical community have in a new way moved close to us Reformed Christians of central Europe. We can clearly not avoid recognizing any longer the full, unqualified extent of our communion with them. Yet, if these confessions allow us truly to recognize the connectedness and kinship of the worldwide family of Reformed churches, there still arises the question of what unites this family — and even more, what unites it in such a way that it distinguishes itself as *reformed*. This question goes beyond the fundamental point made in the first section; namely, the centrality for Reformed churches of the fact that they do not understand or regard themselves as a special brand of church, but rather as representative of the one holy universal Christian church. At the same time, it would result in a denial or violation of the problem of ecumenism among all Christian churches to imply by such mention of this centrality that the question of what exactly distinguishes the Reformed churches as reformed within this ecumenism were already settled.

The difficulty in answering this question in the case of Reformed churches in particular is, as has been demonstrated in the first section, above all the characteristic fluidity of the Reformed concept of confession. On the basis of this fluidity it is possible to find within these churches manifold diverse confessions existing alongside one another, not to mention their being corrected, removed, or replaced with new ones. At the same time, because of this fluidity, there has never developed a generally binding Reformed confession. In particular, the "newer confessional texts of the Reformed tradition" differ considerably not only among themselves, but even more from the confessions of the "Reformed tradition" of the sixteenth century itself. Must we therefore give up trying to respond to the question of whether or how that which unites Reformed Christians and characterizes them as Reformed can be recognized in the face of these new confessions? On the contrary, the new texts actually permit an attempt at a positive answer to that question. Without trivializing the difficulties already mentioned, without flattening the particularities of the various texts, yet also without playing down their freedom in regard to the older tradition, still there can be detected in the texts in question certain common outlines. These common lines permit one to speak of a thoroughgoing *Reformed profile* which unites at least the majority of the new confessional texts with one another, as well as with a majority of the classical texts of the Reformation period.[20] This distinctively Reformed profile can be

---

20. For different reasons, I consider, for example, in the sixteenth century, the Berne Synod of 1532 (because of its sharp separation between the Old and New Testaments and its

grasped particularly in two fundamental structures of thought which have in fact been characteristic for Reformed theology since its beginning and which, as far as I can see, also stand out conspicuously in a great many of the newer texts.

On the one hand, the Reformed profile emerges first in the polarity of its fundamental theological assertions, as is characteristic already of Calvin's theology. This is not to be confused with the old bipolar Roman way of thinking, which, precisely at the point where the Reformers emphasized their *solus* (alone), spoke its often elaborate "both-and": nature *and* grace, reason *and* revelation, Mary *and* Christ, etc. Calvin's bipolar thinking stands clearly on the firm ground of Reformation decisiveness and states no less resolutely than Luther: Scripture *alone*, Christ *alone*, grace *alone*, through faith *alone*. Yet on this firm ground he believed that that which the one Word of God has communicated to us by pure grace in the one mediator, Christ, we cannot say in one word, but always rather in *two*:[21] God's majesty *and* God's abasement, the glory of God *and* the salvation of humanity, Christ as truly divine *and* truly human, Word *and* Spirit, gospel *and* law, eternal life *and* ordering of temporal existence, justification *and* sanctification, faith *and* obedience. With their bipolar thinking, the Reformed pioneers stood more in the Antiochene than in the Alexandrian tradition of the ancient church. And they made use in certain ways here of the Chalcedonian conceptual formula, "unmixed and undivided."

The newer Reformed witnesses are also shaped by a corresponding polarity of theological thinking. In a parallel way we note here as well: the one Scripture in Old *and* New Testaments is witness of the "norm" of faith *and* of life (pp. 16, 350; *RZ*, p. 141). It testifies to God in both love *and* justice, in grace *and* in power (pp. 90, 108, 126; *RZ*, pp. 8, 134), and to Jesus Christ as the crucified Reconciler *and* as the victorious Lord and Judge over all powers (pp. 34-35, 79, 205-6; *RZ*, p. 138). Thus, justification occurs by grace alone, excluding all self-redemption, and it is nevertheless inseparable from human sanctification, renewal, and discipleship (pp. 52-53, 256ff., 293, 350; *RZ*, pp. 16, 67, 136, 148). Thus, in regard to the church, we hear that it must be determined both by gathering *and* by sending, by preservation of its identity *and* by engaged openness to the world around it (pp. 210ff.; *RZ*, pp. 143ff. and throughout), by the calling of all Christians to service *and* through the ministerial office in the con-

---

antinomistic tendency) and, in the modern period, the confession of faith of the Presbyterian Church of Cuba (Vischer, pp. 165ff., primarily because of its identification of the will of God with human efforts to establish a very particular sociopolitical order, the "new community") to be atypical cases within the Reformed tradition.

21. Cf. Karl Barth, "The Doctrinal Task of the Reformed Churches," in *The Word of God and the Word of Man*, trans. with a new foreword by Douglas Horton (New York: Harper & Row, 1957), p. 256.

gregation (pp. 298ff.; *RZ*, p. 71). Thus, in the sacraments both God's grace *and* human response are manifested (pp. 216-17, 251-52, 294ff.; *RZ*, p. 146). And thus, regarding the relationship to state and society, both loyal cooperation *and* the command warning of obedience to God more than humans (pp. 254-55; *RZ*, pp. 15, 17, and throughout) are affirmed. Again and again we run up against the characteristic doubling of assertions, in which throughout both are united yet remain unmixed; and both are differentiated yet remain undivided, let alone made into opposites. One might say that the Reformed profile reveals itself in this duality.

On the other hand, not only the form but the content of this distinctive pattern is revealed if we further note that the new documents are also shaped by the characteristic battlefield in which the Reformers were thinking already at the beginning of the Reformation. It is a battlefield which does not exclude that in which the Lutheran Reformation saw itself, but instead presents a somewhat different line of vision. With his 1863 formula, A. Schweizer already envisaged the central issue; viz., that "we see the shape of Lutheran [Protestantism] as primarily anti-Judaistic, Reformed as anti-pagan."[22] What this means is that the Lutheran tradition dissociates itself especially from "Judaism," i.e., from works righteousness, whereas the Reformed tradition dissociates itself also or even more so from paganism, and in particular from the paganism which threatens Christendom from within itself to make peace with false gods. This formula clarifies why the classical Reformed theologians remained so vigilant against any form of "creature idolatry": neither in a depiction of God, nor in the understanding of Jesus Christ (no ubiquity of Christ's human nature), nor in the conception of the spiritual office, nor in the sacraments. The formula also illumines why these modern texts call for watchfulness against the "gods" seen in the ruling power of race, class, and gender — as well as superstitions and magic — and viewed as the root of sin and misfortune (pp. 90ff., 121, 126-27, 182-83, 246; *RZ*, p. 11). In addition, the formula clarifies what is also and even more true of the new texts; namely, that because of the caution regarding any paganism, a much more open and intimate relationship is made possible with the Old Testament and God's people Israel than in the Lutheran tradition (cf. pp. 232-33, 237ff.; *RZ*, pp. 67-68, 132, 136-37). On the basis of this characteristic battlefield, one understands also the especially distinctive way in which the old and new texts do not consider the problem of doing good works to be settled with the negative judgment of "works righteousness." They reflect the positive concern to also take seriously, alongside the recognition of the sin-forgiving justification of the sinner by God, the

22. Alexander Schweizer, *Die christliche Glaubenslehre nach protestantischen Grundsätzen*, vol. 1 (Leipzig, 1863), p. 8.

sanctification of life by God's good command. The law of God does reveal to us sinners our inability to redeem ourselves, but at the same time it shows those freed by Christ "concretely the shape of our freedom" (pp. 260, 77; *RZ,* pp. 135-36, 207). Because of this connection of justification and sanctification, of God's gospel and command, that which is Christian cannot remain stuck in an individual inner world while the outer world goes by untouched. Rather, God's imperious goodness forces one outward into a form of life corresponding to this goodness.

And this results first in a form of life for the *church!* Where God's grace becomes so much a part of people that it claims them also for itself, then the majority of the congregation is not understood as mere receivers of official ministerial activities, but the entire congregation must be understood and organized as a mature community. The newer texts reach back to assertions of Calvin, and put to shame our middle-European conceptions of church, when they show how self-evidently for them belonging to the church means explicit confession of Jesus Christ in word and lifestyle, in active participation (pp. 296-97, 348-49, 413).[23] But the claim of God's command aims also at the shape of *public life.* In line with the classical Reformed confessions, yet going much further than they do, the new confessions almost all refer to action reflecting obedience to God's will in the concrete challenges of the present time: for peace (pp. 170, 186-87, 259; *RZ,* pp. 8, 151-52), for freedom (pp. 85, 91ff., 158; *RZ,* pp. 10-11, 15, 208), for human rights and democracy (pp. 85, 91-92, 106-7; *RZ,* p. 151), for social justice (pp. 92, 105, 254-55; *RZ,* pp. 72, 151), and for an ecological ethos (pp. 58, 73ff., 233ff.; *RZ,* pp. 72, 206-7). Thus the conviction that Christians *as* Christians may enter these conversations is grounded in the faith that the head of the church is also the "Lord of history" (pp. 48, 84-85, 90, 106, 130; *RZ,* pp. 11, 138). To articulate even more pointedly what has been said: the common lines which despite all differences can be traced between the old and the new confessional texts, and between the latter among themselves, make it possible for the dispersed Reformed family to recognize concretely that its members, regardless of all their particular characteristics, stand on the common ground of their *Reformed kinship.*

23. This is the reason why these texts manifest a much greater openness for the practice of believers' baptism than is the case among central European Reformed Christians. Cf. pp. 55, 216-17, 251, 294-95, 352ff.; *RZ,* pp. 146-47, 215. It is also the basis for the texts' decisive advocacy for the equal status of genders and races: pp. 22, 82, 199, 225; *RZ,* p. 8 and passim.

New Distances

But let us look also at the differences between the old and new texts and among the new texts themselves. These differences include not only matters which may be thought or said in different ways at various places within the Reformed family, but also those which are *disputed*, which can be interpreted as neither merely the expression of living richness nor the result of differing contexts. Regardless of the mutual connectedness of the members and their common ground, these are points which are discussed theologically and urgently within the family and so must first be clarified. The divergences must be acknowledged and opened for debate *because* we belong to one another in this family and desire to preserve this mutual belonging.

As noted above, the newer texts generally draw more strongly than the older ones the connection between confession of the great acts of God on behalf of God's people and God's demand for certain actions from us. The action envisaged is overall perhaps more likely here than in the earlier texts to be considered not merely an individual's action within the given structures, but also the imperative of improving or changing those very structures. This movement takes a further step when, especially in churches which suffer under massively unjust structures, the confession of divinely mandated resistance action is grounded in the confession of faith in God's own action, which consists fundamentally in God's solidarity with the oppressed: God is "the God of the suffering" and "stands therefore on the side of those who are victims of injustice" (pp. 22, 78-79, 85, 88; *RZ*, pp. 8, 12, 48, etc.).

It is clear that this same confession is a sore point for the churches in those countries which are responsible for the emergence of such widespread suffering. We who are members of those churches must realize that ecumenical communion itself is at stake in the question of whether we will evade the issue or not, whether we comprehend how far from us those who are suffering see themselves — and how far from us they see God, the One they confess as the "God with us." Nevertheless, one must make clear that although the newer texts do go decisively further than the older ones in this direction, they still do so in ways familiar with them. Already in the Scots Confession of 1560, for instance, numbered among the good works commanded by God is "to save the lives of the innocent, to repress tyranny, to defend the oppressed."[24] Already there one also finds this command of God in correspondence with God's own promise, intended — inequitably — for those "who from the beginning have suffered violence, injury, and wrong, for righteousness' sake," while the "cruel persecutors" are those at whom God's wrathful

24. Cochrane, p. 173.

displeasure is aimed.[25] Of course, not all Reformation confessions, not even all the newer ones, speak with such sharp certainty. These are differences which are nonetheless possible within the bounds of the "Reformed tradition" and which permit, under certain circumstances, such radicalization.

Another disagreement, however, threatens the very heart of our identity. It is found not only between the older and newer texts, but also among the newer texts themselves. Here one cannot assert, at least not using Vischer's collection, that the division between one side and the other coincides with the boundary between the so-called First and Third Worlds. In fact, one could say that the problem which shows up in this disagreement is not even specifically Reformed, but runs like a fault line through all denominations today. The problem has to do with the confession of God's action and God's claim on our action. In itself, the problem is not one of interest in the necessary relationship between these two; interest in it can clearly be found on both sides of the disagreement. The problem is rather around the question of how each relates more closely to the other, how therefore the relationship between them both may be exactly ascertained. Within this question is a disagreement so deep that one can speak not merely of tension but actually of a split in the church and between churches of the Reformed world.

In relation to this question, some of the newer texts reflect the view that God's salvific action and the action of human beings, in particular that of Christians, go together hand in hand to such an extent that they cannot be distinguished and, in fact, merge together. Not only God but also the church is able "in this world" truly "to establish [God's] justice" (p. 22; *RZ*, p. 8) and/or "to make it real in the world" (*RZ*, p. 151). The church "builds God's Reign," and it does so by taking up the endeavor "to change man and to save society" (p. 83). The "confession of faith" of the Presbyterian-Reformed Church of Cuba contains a material variant of this idea, stating that the "Socialist State" is able to bring this reign about and thus that the church can be said to "live" in the degree to which each of its members "works for the . . . reconstruction of the human being" (p. 182) in this state, and the church as a whole participates in "realizing fully the new humanity on the earth" (p. 168). Again, we hear a liberal version of this same thinking in the "Declaration of Faith" of the English Congregationalists: We Christians are to join in a community built on freedom and tolerance so that "the long struggle for the right in which mankind shares will have its satisfying fulfilment in the final Kingdom of God" (p. 148; *RZ*, p. 99).

It is remarkable in these texts how surprisingly negligible the contribution provided by God appears to this well-intentioned human action toward

25. Cochrane, p. 171.

the well-being of society and humanity. God's contribution here consists not in *doing* anything, let alone having first done anything, but rather in "wishing" for that which humanity undertakes to establish and to realize (*RZ*, p. 8). God's role in all this is the statement of the divine "intention," namely, that which "we" are to fulfill in the establishment of justice and a new humanity, and which certain people are already actually fulfilling (pp. 183-84). Continuing in this direction, the cross and resurrection are not interpreted anymore as God's action toward us, but rather as a symbol for inherent laws which apply to our good works: the cross of Jesus is "exposing the evils and the death of humanity and showing love, reconciliation, and faith in God" (p. 90). Are we mistaken in our assumption that, according to these and similar statements, the contribution of God to human salvation boils down to a mere *idea,* which people can and should make real — that God provides only an idea to ground our action toward the social well-being of humanity? If this is the case, then one must question whether at this point the heart of the gospel has been made into a law.

In any case, we must perceive that the sort of thinking revealed in such confessional statements represents more than merely a slight deviation from the Reformation confessional writings, and from other new texts in the collection. In fact, it makes a profound and serious difference whether the ecclesial and Christian mandate is seen (with the original Reformed thinkers) as the testimony to the graciously salvific and sanctifying work of God in Jesus Christ toward and for us, or whether it consists (according to these new formulations) in the realization of the salvation willed by God — a salvation which therefore has no reality without our action to realize it, but is in fact only of an ideal nature. If the latter is true, one may pose a double question. First: Is this not asking too much of humanity? Indeed, does not this way of thinking inevitably replace humanity's absolution by the liberating action of God for and toward people with the expectation of now having to satisfy a new demand laid upon them? And second: Is this not also entrusting too much to humanity? This has the result that people will eventually think: it's obvious that we aren't supposed to rely so completely on the action of God for us; no, God's action is more of a demonstration of ideas for us to follow, and naturally we can also find these ideas more or less easily in places other than the history testified to in the Bible.[26]

---

26. It is therefore no coincidence that these texts take for granted that alongside the "special" revelation of God one must reckon with a "general" revelation (pp. 56, 75, 116ff.; *RZ*, p. 15). One may well question whether the openness to a "natural knowledge of God" in many texts does not consistently follow from the train of thought outlined above. Where so much is expected of and considered possible for people, they become uncertain whether

Once again, I note that among the newer confessional texts are those which do not speak in this way, which instead actually contradict them.[27] One of these confessions is perhaps shoring itself up on this side when it declares, "We must not distort the gospel by weakening its promises or demands . . . by pointing to ourselves instead of Christ" (p. 257). According to these other confessions, there can be no such confusion and Christians can therefore not go about claiming to be saviors of society, because even and especially they cannot exempt themselves from the power of sin.

> Because *we* are sinful, the society in which we live is also sinful. There are no exceptions. Every system is implicated. We are part of the evil of the world, its violence, negligence, and injustice [*RZ*, p. 136]. . . . [Indeed,] virtuous men through the ages have sought the highest good in devotion to freedom, justice, peace, truth, and beauty. Yet all human virtue, when seen in the light of God's love in Jesus Christ, is found to be infected by self-interest and hostility. All men, good and bad alike, are in the wrong before God and helpless without his forgiveness. Thus all men fall under God's judgment. No one is more subject to that judgment than the man who assumes that he is guiltless before God or morally superior to others. (pp. 206-7)

Such sentences in these texts are not abstract doctrinal statements about human depravity, but are rather the flip side of their confession of Christ. Thus one must affirm that they differ from the others above all in their understanding of Jesus Christ. Jesus functions here not merely as the bearer of an impetus — even a quite powerful impetus — to our realization of just relationships; and his death and resurrection here are more and other than examples for how it can and will go for us in our efforts toward this goal. Instead, in his sending, death, and resurrection, redemption occurred from a need in which all are caught and from which none can free themselves. "In giving himself freely for them he took upon himself the judgment under which all men stand convicted," and thus won "the victory over sin and death for all men" (pp. 205f., cf. p. 242; *RZ*, p. 138). This bespeaks a salvific reality toward whose efficacy Chris-

---

they are truly so dependent on what God has prepared for them in the biblically attested events; and in this uncertainty they convince themselves that they can just as well find greener grass elsewhere. The statement of faith of the English Congregationalists states this generally: "The revelation of God takes place where, confronted with realities in which he is at work, human conscience is awakened and instructed by his love and his judgement" (117). On this basis the statement speaks of deriving a "knowledge of God . . . from other than Christian grounds" (p. 118)!

27. I am thinking here principally of the texts which derive from churches in the United States and Canada (pp. 191-265).

s do not need to contribute anything, but which instead frees and chal-
es Christian people to their own particular contributions, and does not
i first to be brought into "reality."

> The whole work of man's salvation is effected by the sovereign grace of
> God alone. . . . To God in Christ men are called to respond in faith. To this
> end God has sent forth His Spirit. . . . [As part of this response, human ac-
> tion does not build the reign of God, but is] pledge and foretaste of that
> coming reconciliation and renewal which is the end in view for the whole
> creation. (pp. 409f.)

It is noteworthy that the new confessions examined so far which are
?ed in this way are not somehow less decisive in emphasizing the divine
ımand of Christian engagement in the social needs and problems of the
ent; they are also no less open to encounter with non-Christian peoples of
ʟoday, with atheists or followers of non-Christian religions. One could rather,
in this regard, consider it virtually a consensus among the newer confessions
(1) that deployment for social justice and human rights, for peace, and for ecological renewal belongs among the most immediate Christian tasks and that,
therefore, these things have a legitimate place in the confession of the church;
(2) that today in particular an opening for an unprejudiced encounter with
representatives of "other religions" is appropriate; and (3) that the church is to
understand and structure itself as a mature community in such a way as to correspond to its message and to the message's orientation toward its surroundings, so that both women and men can flourish equally.

It is an astounding fact that, despite their various starting points and
premises, the newer confessions agree in all this. Yet this is also a problem.
Could one not logically say that the theological foundation is immaterial as
long as it produces this or that which is useful? One would need to test each
confession individually to see whether the various foundations actually result
in the consequences which unite them, following the principle *Duo cum
faciunt idem, non est idem.* One could show that the position in which human
action is understood as a witness to and not a realization of the reign of God is
better protected from the illusion that the best social condition humanly attainable would be more than human. This does not keep one from standing up
and fighting for the necessary improvement and change of present conditions;
it does not keep one from believing in the quickening power of the coming
reign of God; it does, however, keep one from being or becoming uncritical
about one's own desires and achievement.

But even more important than the question of the results of the various
theological foundations in their practical consequences is the insight that what

seems at first obvious, namely, the conclusion that theological foundations are relatively unimportant compared with what really counts (i.e., practical results), is in fact fatal. It is fatal because it would then appear, and be difficult to root out, that theological foundations are fundamentally merely a sort of detour which one can spare oneself with no inconvenience, or a sort of ballast which must be accepted, or thrown off, or replaced by some other, depending on whether it helps one support intentions and views formulated elsewhere. Would this not allow the God called upon here to appear to be an arbitrarily malleable, and thus eventually unnecessary, entity? And this right in the heart of a Christian confession of faith! Would this idea not in any case undermine the endeavor of such a confession of faith in the God of the Bible, in regard to whom it is supposedly enough for Reformed Christianity to unite in up-to-date work programs? The issue here is more than and different from questions about a correct standard doctrine. The issue is one of clarifying the fact that, in the work we are commanded today to do, we are standing at the service of the living God who is witnessed to us in the Holy Scripture, and are not therefore in servitude to various opinions or wishes that have moved into God's own place.

All of this means, however, that the communion of Reformed churches may not be content today with being more or less united around what Christians have to *do* in the face of the great needs and challenges of our time. They urgently require *theological* discussion — not to distract them from necessary action, nor to trivialize it as unnecessary. According to all of the new confessional texts, Reformed Christianity is united in that we are to do "something brave" (Zwingli) for God's sake. And nevertheless — and even so — we urgently also need theological discussion, because of the apparent and obviously considerable difference in understandings of the *divine* action for humanity and of the relationship of this divine action to that which is mandated for us to do. We need theological discussion in order to move from this rift to some clarity, and ideally to unity. We need this discussion so that it may not happen that, in the very process of going about our necessary action, we saw off the branch on which we are standing.

And should it not be possible to come to clarity, if the witness of the Holy Scripture, interpreted by the Reformation confessions, is diligently and newly heard? The Reformed communion appears not to be united, yet should be able to come to unity, around the fact that the biblical God is the living God, who is in fact in solidarity with people in the suffering and challenges of our time, and yet whose divine action is such that we cannot identify ourselves and our action with it. For it is only where the believed and promised reality of God's reign remains *beyond* us, where we hope for it as something which *God* creates and brings in and not something we also do, that this reality becomes for us the critical and soaring power which preserves us from pride and lethargy, from high-flying illusions and crushing pragmatism, from arbitrariness and resignation. There we are called to be *witnesses* of this reality, to be neither more nor less than this: continually failing, even in our best intentions, and yet continually raised up again, drawn forward and brought along the way, "useless servants" who nevertheless do what we ought to do (Luke 17:10).

Contributors

WILLEM BALKE, Professor of Reformation History, University of Amsterdam, Netherlands

EBERHARD BUSCH, Professor of Reformed Theology, University of Göttingen, Germany

JOHN DE GRUCHY, Professor of Christian Studies, University of Cape Town, South Africa

DAWN DEVRIES, Professor of Theology, Union Theological Seminary in Virginia, U.S.A.

NANCY DUFF, Professor of Theological Ethics, Princeton Theological Seminary, U.S.A.

HANS-HELMUT ESSER, Prof. em. of Reformed Theology, University of Münster, Germany

BRIAN GERRISH, Professor of Theology, Union Theological Seminary in Virginia, U.S.A.

WALTER HERRENBRÜCK, Superintendent (ret.), Reformed Council of Churches, Germany

JOHN HESSELINK, Professor em. of Systematic Theology, Western Theological Seminary, U.S.A.

HANS-JOACHIM KRAUS, Professor em. of Reformed Theology, University of Göttingen, Germany

SANG HYUN LEE, Professor of Systematic Theology, Princeton Theological Seminary, U.S.A.

Contributors

JOHN LEITH, Professor em. of Theology, Union Theological Seminary in Virginia, U.S.A.

CHRISTIAN LINK, Professor of Theology of the Christian Faith (Dogmatics), University of Bochum, Germany

JAN MILIČ LOCHMAN, Professor em. of Systematic Theology, University of Basel, Switzerland

BRUCE McCORMACK, Professor of Systematic Theology, Princeton Theological Seminary, U.S.A.

ALEXANDER McKELWAY, Professor em. of Religion, Davidson College, U.S.A.

BEATRIZ MELANO, Professor of Theology, United Theological Seminary Buenos Aires, Argentina

DANIEL MIGLIORE, Professor of Systematic Theology, Princeton Theological Seminary, U.S.A.

JÜRGEN MOLTMANN, Professor em. of Systematic Theology, University of Tübingen, Germany

JANOS PASZTOR, Professor of Theology, Reformed Theological Academy, Budapest, Hungary

AMY PLANTINGA PAUW, Professor of Doctrinal Theology, Louisville Presbyterian Theological Seminary, U.S.A.

WILLIAM PLACHER, Professor of Philosophy and Religion, Wabash College, U.S.A.

CHOAN-SENG SONG, Professor of Theology and Asian Cultures, Pacific School of Religion, Berkeley, U.S.A.

THOMAS TORRANCE, Professor em. of Christian Dogmatics, University of Edinburgh and New College, Edinburgh, Scotland

LEANNE VAN DYK, Professor of Systematic Theology, Western Theological Seminary, U.S.A.

LUKAS VISCHER, Professor em. of Ecumenical Theology, University of Bern, Switzerland

WAFIQ WAHBA, Professor of Theology, Evangelical Theological Seminary in Cairo, Egypt

NOBUO WATANABE, Calvin Research Institute, Tokyo, Japan

MICHAEL WELKER, Professor of Systematic Theology (Dogmatics), University of Heidelberg, Germany

DAVID WILLIS, Professor of Systematic Theology, Princeton Theological Seminary, U.S.A.

EDMUND ZA BIK, Professor of Theology and Mission, Myanmar Institute of Theology, Insein, Myanmar